AMERICAN CREDO

American Credo

The Place of Ideas in US Politics

MICHAEL FOLEY

OXFORD
UNIVERSITY PRESS

OXFORD

UNIVERSITY PRESS

Great Clarendon Street, Oxford OX2 6DP

Oxford University Press is a department of the University of Oxford.
It furthers the University's objective of excellence in research, scholarship,
and education by publishing worldwide in

Oxford New York

Auckland Cape Town Dar es Salaam Hong Kong Karachi
Kuala Lumpur Madrid Melbourne Mexico City Nairobi
New Delhi Shanghai Taipei Toronto

With offices in

Argentina Austria Brazil Chile Czech Republic France Greece
Guatemala Hungary Italy Japan Poland Portugal Singapore
South Korea Switzerland Thailand Turkey Ukraine Vietnam

Oxford is a registered trade mark of Oxford University Press
in the UK and in certain other countries

Published in the United States
by Oxford University Press Inc., New York

© Michael Foley 2007

The moral rights of the author have been asserted
Database right Oxford University Press (maker)

First published 2007

British Library Cataloguing in Publication Data

Data available

Library of Congress Cataloging in Publication Data

Data available

Typeset by SPI Publisher Services, Pondicherry, India
Printed in Great Britain
on acid-free paper by
Biddles Ltd., King's Lynn, Norfolk

ISBN 978–0–19–923267–3

1 3 5 7 9 10 8 6 4 2

For Adele, Nick, and Dylan

Acknowledgements

This study is the result of a long period of observation and reflection during which I have drawn upon the comments and insights of a rich variety of fellow watchers. It would be unfair to single out any specific individuals because they have all played their different parts in contributing to a project whose period of gestation has stretched over many years. A collective thanks is owed to their separate strands of keen judgement and guiding light.

I would also like to express my gratitude to the editorial and production staff at Oxford University Press. I am particularly thankful to Dominic Byatt, Elizabeth Suffling, Aimee Wright, Kate Hind, Natasha Forrest, and Charles Lauder. I would also like to thank Daniel Hucker for his invaluable assistance in producing the index.

No acknowledgements would be complete without giving due recognition and sincere thanks to the extraordinary contribution made by two anonymous referees. Their close reading of the text generated a host of analytical insights and strategic refinements which were of inestimable value in making the study's purpose and design cohere more effectively with the historical and social foundations of the subject area. Their depth of interest and scholarship provided a treasury of learned and apposite suggestions for which I can only express my appreciation for the work involved and for the positive spirit in which their comments were conveyed.

In addition to the thanks I owe to my family for their patience and forbearance, special recognition must also be given to my colleagues in the Department of International Politics at the University of Wales, Aberystwyth. This study has benefited enormously from the intellectual stimulus of the department's research culture and in particular its graduate school. Together they have afforded a continuous and positive challenge to the formation of this analysis. On a more personal note, I am particularly indebted to Professor Andrew Linklater and Professor Michael C. Williams for their encouragement in the extended endeavour required for a study of this scope.

Many have helped with the load but the final responsibility for its composition and direction lies quite properly with the author. Errors, misjudgements, and omissions are mine alone.

Aberystwyth 2007

Contents

Part I
Approaches

Introduction

The place of political ideas in the United States has a mixed reputation. The society is commonly characterized as one rooted in eighteenth-century strictures on natural rights, personal freedoms, and the ethos of limited government. Constitutional precepts pertaining to the legitimate sphere of the state in society, combined with a historical development in which the condition of liberty has been a constant theme, have fostered a cultivated usage of concepts in the normal conduct of political exchange. Yet, running concurrently alongside this social ease towards complex conceptual themes is an equally well-founded reputation for a poorly developed repertoire of political thought and for a public sphere characterized more by a dearth of political ideas than by an exuberance of conceptual invention. American identity has become closely associated with a settlement of principle that has allowed the United States to establish a self-image of exceptionalism. While other societies and cultures have been afflicted with deep ideological conflict, it can be claimed that America's historical and social unity has displaced the need for advanced critical thought. In effect, American politics can be said to have followed a template of social formation in which the range of ideas has arguably narrowed to the point of conceptual collapse.

NO IDEAS NEED APPLY

At first sight, a preponderance of evidence would appear to coincide with the latter perspective. The apparent needlessness of conceptual innovation and critical evaluation remains a popular virtue in a society that has a strong conviction in its spontaneous emanation from the natural conditions of the New World. Its atypical status as a society apart from the rest has encouraged a view of itself that is centred upon the existence of a single and integrated set of core values (e.g. freedom, individualism, democracy, egalitarianism, rights, and the rule of law). Such a professed consensus, or creed of genetically indivisible ideas, can be used explicitly, or implicitly, to explain the absence of those European ideologies that are derived from intractable positions on both the right and the left. Louis Hartz's dictum on living within a monolith of ideas underlines the connection between the volume of American political activity and its narrowness of range. The settlement of deep moral questions on the basis of a 'submerged and absolute liberal faith'[1] marks the end of speculation upon them: 'It is only when you take ethics for granted that all problems emerge as problems of technique'.[2] Far from diminishing politics, the existence of an intuitive agreement on fundamentals gives licence to an expansive sphere of political position taking and, with it, a capacious potential for negotiated settlement. In this framework, the imposition of ideas giving rise to radical alternatives and polarizing attitudes are deemed to be egregious, dysfunctional, and more likely than not, un-American in character.

This restricted outlook upon the role of ideas in American society was particularly salient during the cold war when the primary imperative was to maximize national integration while at the same time minimizing the potential for class-based divisions to align upon ideological alternatives. In competing with the Soviet Union and its allies, American leaders and opinion formers worked assiduously to develop a national consciousness based upon the thematic unity of American ideas and upon the open assimilation of diverse groups into American society through the agency of a universal doctrine of rights and freedoms. In this guise, American political ideas came to represent not only the prospective sphere of western liberation but also the social substance of America's classless pluralism.

It was during this era that some American scholars pronounced 'the end of ideology'. The post-war social consensus in the United States seemed final proof that America was the model of a successful society because it appeared to have palpably overcome the need for ideologies. In the light of this perspective, the problems of industrialization and modernization had been effectively resolved. The only disputes that remained were those that could be negotiated to a satisfactory solution through the use of technical adjustments. The discipline and solidarity produced by the cold war helped to intensify the consensus still further. In doing so, it also helped to establish the idea of a society with neither the capacity nor the need for critical and analytical thought. During these years, the United States believed itself to be the 'good society' incarnate. This view was shared, either enthusiastically or reluctantly, in many other areas of the world. The United States gave the impression of a new kind of progress that had superseded and moved beyond those ideologies that had originated in the nineteenth and early twentieth centuries. It saw itself as the vanguard of western societies, showing how, under the right conditions, clashing political ideologies of the left and right could wither away to a residue of democratic competition between endlessly compatible interests.[3]

The close relationship between a high level of social cohesion and a controlling paradigm of dominant ideas was just as evident after the cold war. With the disintegration of the eastern bloc and the subsequent abandonment of communism as a viable alternative to liberal capitalism, the United States was left in the position

---

[1] Louis Hartz, *The Liberal Tradition in America* (New York: Harcourt Brace, 1955), p. 10.

[2] Ibid.

[3] See Seymour M. Lipset, *Political Man* (London: Heinemann, 1960), pp. 403–17; Daniel Bell, *The End of Ideology: On the Exhaustion of Political Ideas in the Fifties* (Cambridge, MA: Harvard University Press, 2000), ch. 13; Arthur M. Schlesinger, Jr., *The Vital Center: The Politics of Freedom* (Cambridge, MA: Riverside, 1961).

of being not only the sole remaining superpower but also the emblematic culmination of a pre-eminent ideology. When in 1992 Francis Fukuyama pronounced the 'end of history',[4] there was little doubt that his affirmation of universal liberal democracy and technologically driven capitalism had been inspired by the United States. Fukuyama's exposition carried such conviction in the 1990s because it resonated with a policy shift towards neoliberal priorities (e.g. privatization of public services, deregulation of industry, budget deficit reduction, labour markets flexibility, and trade liberalization) and because it rationalized the increasing scale of globalizing conformity by reference to a 'Washington consensus' upon the axiomatic requirements of progress.[5] In these conditions, Fukuyama was able to popularize the notion that ideological evolution had reached an end point. He postulated that western liberal democracy had emerged as the final form of human government. As such, it could be concluded that all the major questions of contemporary political order had in essence reached a state of final and conclusive settlement.

To those who believe that American society is distinguished by an aversion to ideological engagement, the post-cold war era bears a close relationship to the cold war period. Both epochs can be deployed as material support in advancing the proposition that the historical and social experience of the United States has produced an extraordinary capacity either to transcend ideological dispute or to reduce different ideologies to an uncontested values system. The same predisposition towards non-ideological unanimity appeared to mark the reaction of the United States to the terrorist attacks on New York and Washington in September 2001. The impulse to rally defensively around the flag was extended to more offensive responses with an ease of transition that suggested an underlying exclusion of ideas. Joan Didion, for example, complained during this period that the country had come to tolerate many 'fixed opinions, or national pieties, each with its own baffles of invective and counterinvective, of euphemism and downright misstatement, its own screen that slides into place whenever actual discussion threatens to surface'.[6] At a time of national emergency, it appeared that the collective endorsement of American ideals and purpose was to be embodied in a generic avoidance of ideational complexities.

This apparent aversion to, or dismissal of, ideological politics can be conveyed in various forms. It is suggested by the widely cited significance of an absent socialist tradition and a failure to challenge the dominion of concentrated property with alternative constructions of historical progress, democratic action, and the public interest. The asserted dearth of political ideas in American politics is also attached to the notion of a dominant paradigm of social formation, historical tradition, ethical attachment, and national distinction. The avowed openness of an assimilative and legally non-hierarchical polity set in a predominantly

---

[4] Francis Fukuyama, *The End of History and the Last Man* (London: Penguin, 1992).

[5] See John Williamson, 'What Washington Means by Policy Reform', in John Williamson (ed.), *Latin American Adjustment: How Much Has Happened?* (Washington, DC: Institute for International Economics, 1990).

[6] Joan Didion, *Fixed Ideas: America since 9.11* (New York: New York Review of Books, 2003), p. 24.

rights-based culture accounts for another rationale supporting a lack of ideational consciousness within the society as a whole.

What is common to all these interpretive alignments is the operational premise that the United States is not merely bound by a unifying corpus of ideas but is defined by these ideas, by the presumption in their internal coherence, and by their popular currency as points of cultural allegiance. As a consequence, it is commonplace for the United States to be referred to as a moral community based upon a unanimity of belief. In the twenty-first century, the United States retains its distinctive identity as a society bound together not by race or descent but by its interior conformity to a civil religion and to the sense of national purpose generated by a catechism of public beliefs. During the cold war, Richard Hofstadter made the following celebrated observation: 'It has been our fate as a nation not to have ideologies, but to be one'.[7] This spirit of cohesion based upon a common foundation of principle continues to be invoked in the present era and has lain as the subtext to a profusion of speeches given by President George W. Bush in his call to arms, and minds, in the 'war on terror'. In his second inaugural address, for example, the President stressed the significance of a unity of national purpose formed from the social cohesion of shared values:

When the Declaration of Independence was first read in public and the Liberty Bell was sounded in celebration, a witness said, 'It rang as if it meant something.' In our time it means something still. America, in this young century, proclaims liberty throughout all the world, and to all the inhabitants thereof. Renewed in our strength—tested, but not weary— we are ready for the greatest achievements in the history of freedom.[8]

The implication of these maxims, and the conventions of usage that surround them, can be interpreted as tantamount to a restriction of perspective and to the presence of an intuitive conformity to a fixed repertoire of values. In essence, it can be claimed that in possessing only one set of values, American society denies to itself the basis for a fully developed form of ideational politics.

CREEDAL PASSIONS

While this attenuated conceptual landscape has been given widespread credence, it provides neither a wholly accurate picture of the status and leverage of ideas in the public domain of the United States, nor a sense in which these key ideas are fused together with traditions, values, and interests in the synergy of American political discourse. On the contrary, it can be claimed that it gives a distorted perspective of the dynamics between political ideas and public action in the United States. Far from constituting a homogenized concomitant of a durable and self-sustaining

[7] Quoted in Seymour M. Lipset, *American Exceptionalism: A Double-Edged Sword?* (New York: Norton, 1996), p. 18.

[8] President George W. Bush, 'Inaugural Address', 20 January 2005, http://www.whitehouse.gov/ news/releases/2005/01/20050120-1.html.

consensus, the clash of competing principles, contested categories, and normative claims represent an equally enduring feature of American political behaviour. Political themes are routinely invested with the rhetoric of high principles and fundamental values. In like manner, political positions are habitually dismantled to reveal their inner composition in relation to the deep-set values of the United States.

The capacity for principled division can even be said to be rooted in the very traditions of the United States and in its processes of political development. Rogers M. Smith, for example, has been highly influential in using immigration policies, naturalization regulations, and citizenship laws to substantiate the assertion that the United States has had throughout its history a conspicuously illiberal tradition of inegalitarianism alongside the more established orthodoxies of liberalism and republicanism. In Smith's view, the United States cannot adequately be accounted for by reference to one overarching tradition. He refers instead to a condition of 'multiple traditions' and to a historiography that cannot be reduced to Hartz's consensus ideology, relying as it does upon the cultural premise of Lockian liberalism conjoined to an indigenous equality. Instead, Smith and many other analysts of civic identity and political development point to the presence of 'ascriptive' processes relating to an entrenched behavioural and normative inegalitarianism that has not only condoned but actively promoted discriminatory practices based upon race, gender, ethnicity, religion, heredity, and country of origin.[9] These popular and legal constructions of citizenship are cited as having had far-reaching consequences for American society—particularly in the projection and understanding of political differences and the way they have been habitually expressed in terms of competing conceptions of fundamental ideas. To Smith, the various infringements and restrictions in relation to citizenship were 'blatant, not "latent"' and revealed that 'America was not born equal but instead has had extensive hierarchies justified by illiberal, undemocratic traditions of ascriptive Americanism'.[10]

The extent to which the notion of 'multiple traditions' can be said to be responsible for the nature of political debate is an issue that is open to interpretation. What is not in question is that the United States possesses a marked facility for expansive debate. The language of political advocacy and critique in the United States is conspicuously impregnated with references to cultural norms, moral strictures, republican values, and national narratives because it is through this medium that the competition for legitimacy is conducted. As a consequence, American politics is distinguished by an evident facility for organizing political engagement by reference to a set of unresolved tensions between, and within, a series of core ideas. It is not merely that value-based terms are habitually deployed in political debate, but that those who deploy them do so with a willingness and an intention to inject fundamental precepts and non-negotiable distinctions into

[9] Rogers M. Smith, 'Beyond Tocqueville, Myrdal, and Hartz: The Multiple Traditions in America', *The American Political Science Review*, vol. 87, no. 3. (Sept. 1993), pp. 549–66; Rogers M. Smith, *Civic Ideals: Conflicting Visions of Citizenship in U.S. History* (New Haven, CT: Yale University Press, 1997).

[10] Smith, *Civic Ideals*, pp. 15, 36.

the political discourse. It is for this reason that American politics has a reputation for inflammatory rhetoric and principled intransigence. As a consequence, it is commonly observed that because in the United States 'political debate revolves around values to a much greater extent than in Europe ... even technical matters become moral questions'.[11]

The incidence of value-laden political argument is sufficient to pose serious questions about the sustainability of such principled conflict within a stable political order. A common response is to claim that for the most part ideational dissonance is sublimated into a form of viable coexistence which is periodically punctuated by eruptions of ideologically charged political insurgency. For example, the languid consensus politics of the 1950s was followed by the disjointed radicalism and social disorder of the 1960s. The tumult induced by war and civil dissent, drugs and crime, urban riots and political assassination, pornography and violence provided the background to a widespread questioning of the social and economic order of the United States. The drive for revelation, realism, and critical evaluation produced a sceptical revision of the 1950s. Americans became far more sensitized to the existence of structures of political thought. They became more aware of the linkages between political belief and social conditions. As a result, the 'end of ideology' became recognized for what it had always been: an ideology in its own right.

In raising the ideological stakes and subjecting the customary parameters of the core ideas of the United States to critical review, the political energy of the 1960s not only polarized political attitudes but also created a sense of disjunction between the apparent tranquillity of the ideologically suppressed 1950s and the fervent attachment to ideational speculation in the social dislocation and moral agitation of the succeeding decade. This era of ferment became increasingly identified with disorder, instability, violence, and governmental failure. Subsequently, the period's propensity for critical and innovative ideas became widely discredited as divisive, counterproductive, and even degenerate. As a consequence, the turbulence quickly subsided in the 1970s, which came to acquire a reputation for retrenchment and consolidation. During this period, American politics became preoccupied with the contemporary challenges of the industrial order (e.g. 'stagflation', unemployment, energy shortfalls, pollution, and budget and trade deficits). These problems were generally interpreted to be technical in nature.

The spasmodic character of the 1960s gives material support to those analysts who hold to the theory that the course of American history discloses a rhythmic pattern of ideational intensity and political activism. In this light, the currency and impact of conflicting ideas are confined to a recurrent cycle in which episodes of heightened sensitivity to the emancipatory potential of core principles and traditional norms are followed by periods of reconstructed equilibrium. For example, in *American Politics: The Promise of Disharmony* (1981),[12] Samuel Huntington

---

[11] 'Living with a Superpower', *The Economist*, 4 January 2003.

[12] Samuel P. Huntington, *American Politics: The Promise of Disharmony* (Cambridge, MA: Belknap, 1981).

specifically portrays American history and social movement in recurrent terms. He posits the existence of a cycle of political and ideational activity in respect to the republic's creed of liberty, equality, individualism, democracy, and the rule of law. According to Huntington, this cycle has produced four such outbursts of supercharged devotion to the political creed of the United States (i.e. 'creedal passion'): the American Revolution, the Jacksonian era, the Progressive age, and the angst of the 1960s and early 1970s.[13] They were all motivated by the desire to resolve the dichotomy between promise and practice in American politics.[14]

The principal problem relating to the formulation of such cycles is the underlying premise that the periods of stated normality are in some way ideologically neutral or ideationally quiescent. One corollary to this premise is that American social stability is dependent upon an absence, or near absence, of conscious social thought. Another corollary is that the operation of ideas can only generally be equated with explicit division and conflict. These assumptions, however, overlook the steady-state capacity for individual values, and even different civic traditions, to conflict with one another on a day-to-day basis within the remit of American politics. The 1990s, for example, was widely characterized as an era of conservative ascendancy which was distinguished by an ostensible consensus on market-driven growth, deregulation, and deficit reduction. Yet, during this period, conservative forces were as attentive as ever to the need to consolidate and advance the conservative leverage on the formation of issues, agendas, and coalitions. So much so in fact that it is estimated that in the 1990s, conservative think tanks, research institutes, and advocacy organizations spent over $1 billion on framing the terms of political debate in the United States.[15]

To confine the system's capacity for ideological disputation to aberrant and unsustainable episodes of value consciousness is to dismiss the preponderant condition of coexisting values held in varying degrees of tension. The strains between values with equal credentials to American authenticity are very much part of the normal state of political existence in the public sphere of the United States. Far from being an unusual or egregious feature of social development, the clash of values can be seen as thoroughly conventional.

Contrary to popular reputation, it is therefore quite possible to be ideologically contentious in the United States and still remain genuinely American. It is wholly legitimate to challenge political ideas and principles with other political ideas and principles without being regarded as subversively ideological or irredeemably divisive. In fact, it is the general norm. An ideological challenge can be particularly effective when it is based upon a set of principles integral to the indigenous experiences and traditional ideals of the United States. Many campaigns in support of principled changes to an established mix of value and policy priorities have

---

[13] Huntington, *American Politics: The Promise of Disharmony*, ch. 5.

[14] For a different formulation and timescale of American historical cycles, see Arthur M. Schlesinger, Jr., 'The Cycles of American Politics', in Arthur M. Schlesinger, Jr. (ed.), *The Cycles of American History* (Harmondsworth, UK: Penguin, 1989), pp. 23–48.

[15] David Callahan, *$1 Billion for Ideas: Conservative Think Tanks in the 1990s* (Washington, DC: National Committee for Responsive Philanthropy, 1999).

been successful not by denying the indigenous capacity for ideational challenge and experimentation of the United States, but by exploiting its potential for interpretive latitude.

The American facility for engaging in conflict based upon, and expressed through, divergent ideas should not be underestimated. Even those who claim the existence of a cultural singularity of values concede that the strains and divisions occasioned by the interpretive variability of such core principles can be no less intense than those conflicts based upon explicit ideological dichotomies. As Huntington makes it clear, a general agreement on values can actually promote conflict. Other commentators, who are sceptical of the Hartzian perspective of American society, point out that even if a liberal consensus is assumed to exist, 'a liberal mold does not end the opportunities for political disagreement'.[16] On the contrary, 'interesting and plausible though theories such as Hartz's are, they are not necessarily correct in asserting that the American political agenda will be tightly constricted'.[17]

Far from being synonymous with a calming equanimity, the presence of core values can be seen as a licence for dispute. The object of concord becomes a medium in which complaints are advanced in relation to how shared principles can and should be applied, as well as to how they have been reconfigured, subverted, or even ignored. In spite of the claims that the United States possesses a unitary foundation of liberal ideals, American politics is animated by a furious competitive urge to align positions with core principles. It is conceivable that it is precisely because the United States has such a strong attachment to a set of guiding dogmas that it promotes an extraordinary array of inventive strategies to secure for different positions the imprimatur of American authenticity.

The continual struggle over the priorities given to different variants, derivatives, and constructions of American values and the language of ideational engagement that accompanies it is symbolized by what is loosely termed the 'culture wars' of the United States.[18] A series of issues (e.g. abortion, pornography, sex education, drug abuse, gun control, gay rights, 'family values', the place of religion in public life) have allegedly underlined the existence of deep-seated public differences not just over the definition and application of core values, but also over the composition and ownership of American identity. Notwithstanding the general assumption that American values possess a unitary and interdependent quality, advocates on both sides of these controversial issues argue their cases on the grounds of high principle and absolute moral conviction. Whether these adversarial groupings

---

[16] Graham K. Wilson, *Only in America: The Politics of the United States in Comparative Perspective* (Chatham, NJ: Chatham House, 1998), p. 26.

[17] Ibid.

[18] See John K. White, *The Values Divide: American Politics and Culture in Transition* (New York: Chatham House), 2003, p. 18. See also William J. Bennett, *The Broken Hearth: Reversing the Moral Collapse of the American Family* (New York: Doubleday, 2001); John Sperling, Suzanne Helburn, Samuel George, John Morris, and Carl Hunt, *The Great Divide: Retro vs. Metro America* (Sausalito, CA: PoliPoint Press, 2004); Sidney Blumenthal, *The Clinton Wars* (New York: Viking, 2003), chs. 2, 3, 5, 11, 12.

are termed traditionalists and progressives, or religious dogmatists and secular humanists, the polarizing properties of their respective outlooks underlines the way that American values such as equity, freedom, democracy, choice, and legal protection can be used to support diametrically opposed positions.

While there may continue to be a consensus on what American values are in the abstract, there remain sharp disagreements over what they mean in an operational sense. The resultant debate is 'a struggle not just for political supremacy...but over the idea of just what values the nation stands for, and how they should be translated into public policy'.[19] Far from being atypical of American politics, it can be claimed that the mindset and language of the 'cultural wars' are thoroughly representative of the style that gives the conduct of political exchange in the United States its particular character. The paradox of divisions forming over a supposed unity of fixed principles is a controlling theme of American political discourse. It is one that requires exceptional agility in the formulation of arguments, and imaginative subtlety in the competitive displacement of opponents seeking to give the same points of reference a different coloration.

This kind of conflict can be depicted in many different ways. For example, it can be characterized as a dispute between different liberalisms, between the respective claims of liberty and democracy, or between the distinctive implications of freedom and equality. It can be said to assume the form of a divergence between a generalized presumption of equality and the sustained social presence of different categories of inegalitarianism. Alternatively, conflict may be depicted as an episode in which a 'liberal establishment' is pitted against a movement of conservative insurgency. On the other hand, it may constitute evidence that the 'political system has no genuine Left but does have a genuine Right'.[20] Another perspective presents an established liberal order having been ideologically outmanoeuvred by radical conservatives who have assumed an ascendant position as a 'new governing elite'.[21] Its compulsive appeals to American ideas have enabled this emergent elite to shape the 'frames of reference that are used repeatedly in policy debates'.[22] In effect, it is not only the legitimacy of the participants' respective positions that are disputed amongst themselves, but also the interpretations that are given to their conflicts by observers which remain continually open to question.

Some argue that the central value of the American tradition is liberty; others, equality; still others, communal solidarity. These schools of thought are all partially correct, but ultimately wrong. The perennial American tradition cannot be defined in terms of any single value. Rather it consists of a complex of values—values that are complementary, not contradictory.[23]

---

[19] White, *The Values Divide*, p. 18.

[20] Walter D. Burnham, 'The Turnout Problem', in A. James Reichley (ed.), *Elections American Style* (Washington, DC: Brookings, 1987), p. 127.

[21] Robert Reich, 'Dismal Democrats', *Prospect*, May 2004.   [22] Ibid.

[23] Ted Halstead and Michael Lind, *The Radical Center: The Future of American Politics* (New York: Anchor, 2001), p. 33.

Even Halstead and Lind's measured conclusion is open to dispute because in many respects the severity of much of the political argument in the United States is fuelled by the intrinsic contradictions of the society's purportedly complementary values.

A COMPOUND REPUBLIC

The controlling premise of this study is that the United States possesses a little-understood ability to engage in deep conflicts over political ideas, while at the same time reducing adversarial positions to legitimate derivatives of American history and development. Americans may be hostile to the thought of ideologies. They may ostensibly regard social theory to be an uncomfortable and unnecessary diversion. The United States may simply not have the background or temperament for the totality of European-style ideologies. Nevertheless, what remains noteworthy is that the normal processes of American politics are distinguished by having both the means and the motivation to engage in profound disputes over political ideas but without succumbing to the intractability and entirety of European ideological conflicts.

In many respects, America's historical experience can be translated into a history of its experience with the role of ideas in politics. This has produced an enriched idiom of ideational engagement in which American political discourse can draw upon a set of political currents set within its own historical and social development. These currents are intensely varied in content and application. They provide American politics with the raw material for its conduct, in that this repository of ideas, along with the values and traditions enfolded into them, serves to inform the language of political discourse and to provide the currency with which issues are identified and argued out in American society. Such a common core of indigenous principles can be used in varying permutations and with different degrees of emphasis to produce a startling diversity of political rationales.

The fundamental aim of this study is to examine the traditions and usages of American political ideas within the arena of practical politics. By locating them in their respective contexts, it will be possible to assess both their changing meanings and their shifting relationships to one another. In surveying the core ideas of the United States both in isolation and in combination, it will enable the study to reach an informed awareness of their political and cultural leverage as forms of persuasion and sources of legitimacy. The intention is to root the examination of American political ideas in the milieu of social drives, political movements, and contemporary issues within which the ideas themselves are embedded. This will not only allow the study to investigate the interior properties and traditional priorities of the key values of the United States but also permit the conceptual implications and practical consequences of these ideas to be traced and evaluated. In effect, the inquiry accepts the complex usage of ideas on its own multidimensional terms.

In embarking upon this survey, it is important to underline the self-imposed limitations of the project. Because the emphasis is laid firmly upon the employment of ideas in political activity, the objective is neither to provide a genealogy of American ideas within their different social and development contexts, nor to offer a philosophical inquiry into the meaning, logic, and implications of different ideas elicited from within an American framework. The study recognizes 'the inter-dependence of political theory and practical controversy'[24] but it gives primary consideration to the effect of this symbiosis on the latter rather than upon the analytical or philosophical developments of the former. The prospectus, therefore, is not one of using the United States as an instrument of explication and analysis on behalf of a series of individual ideas; and it is not one of fashioning a history of ideas through the lens of the American experience. While some elements of these approaches and perspectives will be discernible, they remain secondary to the main objective of examining the ways in which the origins, properties, and usages of a set of seminal ideas give the nature of American politics its special resonance.

Other caveats need to be underlined. The purpose of the exercise is not to use analytical political theory in order to arrive at an integrated account of belief systems, or at an overarching project of conceptual organization. It is equally the case that the study is not motivated by an intention to provide a survey of ideas and contextual interpretation for the purpose of eliciting generalizations over the dynamics between categories such as history, language, meaning, identity, legitimacy, socialization, consciousness, culture, and political action. An extensive and sophisticated literature already exists that explores the theoretical, conceptual, and empirical complexities involved in formulating any clear and uncontested rules of engagement in the construction of symmetries within such a multidimensional area.[25] While many rich insights may be accrued from this literature, the study is not guided by an ambition to add to it in any concerted way. The animating theme is more modest but arguably no less challenging in the scale of its remit: to examine the way in which a set of ideas has informed, and continues to structure, both the framework of American political discourse and the character of American national identity.

The book's organization reflects both the nature of the subject matter and the strategy of inquiry suggested by it. The analysis is organized into two main parts. Part II provides a set of individual surveys in which each of nine elemental ideas are closely inspected, and Chapters 1–9 examine the abstract characteristics and principled components of each idea. In addition, they review the historical and social circumstances that transformed these ideas into political traditions that

---

[24] Ronald Dworkin, *Sovereign Virtue: The Theory and Practice of Equality* (Cambridge, MA: Harvard University Press, 2002), p. 4.

[25] For example, see Quentin Skinner, 'Meaning and Understanding in the History of Ideas', *History and Theory*, vol. 8, no. 1 (1969), pp. 3–53; J. G. A. Pocock, *Politics, Language and Time: Essays on Political Thought and History* (London: Methuen, 1972); Terence Ball, James Farr, and Russell L. Hanson (eds), *Political Innovation and Conceptual Change* (Cambridge: Cambridge University Press, 1989); Michael Freeden, *Ideologies and Political Theory: A Conceptual Approach* (Oxford: Clarendon Press, 1996); Gerald F. Gaus, *Political Concepts and Political Theories* (Boulder, CO: Westview Press, 2000).

continue to animate the content and style of political argument in the United States. Again it is important to note the imposed limitations of these chapters. They are not intended to provide a comprehensive survey of each idea or a system- atic analysis of their historical lineage and patterns of indigenous development. The aim is not to establish a prospectus that offers a detailed account of how each particular idea came to possess its contextual currency. Likewise, the rationale of the study is not to identify the complex patterns of historical evolution, or to establish clear reasons for the variability in both their meanings and their relationships to one other. To this extent, the book is not centred upon the *history of ideas* as such. It is rather more concerned with acknowledging the significance of history in examining the usages and continuities of these ideas in contemporary American politics. The standpoint, therefore, is not that of working from the past and tracing the course of ideas to the present, but of using the past to illustrate the social significance, the cultural depth, the political leverage, and the civic legacies that continue to be invested in each idea.

With this in mind, the individual surveys given in Chapters 1–9 are intended to convey the sweep and scale of each idea within the substance of American politics. In order to achieve this effect, it is necessary to refer to historical illustrations and to discernible traditions within American experience. Almost inevitably the presented evidence will be selective. This is not only because of the constraints of space but also because of the nature of the analytical agenda itself which is focused upon producing a concise but accurate representation of the richness, range, and depth of the ideas that inform and animate American political exchange.

The social currency and ubiquitous usage of these basic ideas allow for a profusion of common linkages and substantive connections to be made between them. In fact, their adhesive qualities in the American context give rise to an array of important coalescences and aggregates amongst them, which dominate the architecture of political argument in the United States. Six of the most durable and influential of these corporate entities are surveyed in Chapters 10–15 (i.e. Part III). The selection of these conceptual composites may well provoke some dispute because of the exclusion of other well-qualified illustrations. In response, it is contended that the choice was made in order both to demonstrate the usable variability of the foundational ideas and to convey the inventiveness and adaptability with which these core themes can be conjoined for political effect. Even though composites like communitarianism and feminism are not allotted chapter-length space, they are taken into account, either implicitly or explicitly, in the course of the analysis. This will not resolve the disputes over the choice of compounds for extended inquiry, but it will underline the contestable nature of what best epitomizes the dynamics within these amalgamations.

Part III is central to the purposive rationale of the entire study. It illustrates the phenomenon of political argument being rooted in collective aggregates of core ideas. In doing so, it makes manifest the political effects of what in the United States is a conventional inclination, and even a compulsive drive, to incorporate the full set of these ideas into political positions in the competition for cultural legitimacy. While these clusters of ideas may have radically different interpretive profiles and policy implications, they share a common connection to a historically and socially embedded foundation. The emphasis in the analysis is therefore placed upon revealing the presence of what is arguably an extraordinary agility in organizing ideas for principled conflict, while at the same time giving recognition to the conditioning and constraining effects of the shared source base of those ideas. Accordingly, the focus is primarily directed to this ideational matrix, and to the compounds that are reducible to it, rather than to an agenda seeking to determine the precise relational aspects of different ideas in respect to philosophical categories or to changing historical periods. While the latter fields of inquiry will often be germane to the study, the book is not designed to offer a concerted or systematic engagement with these alternative approaches.

In Part IV, Chapter 16 offers an overview of the ecology of ideas in American politics. It discusses the various means by which political participants engage with a multiple constituency of core values in the competitive struggle for advantage and legitimacy. It also reviews how analysts have sought to come to terms with the dual existence of a fixed set of central principles within society, and the fluid and innovative style by which these core values are articulated and aggregated for political effect. Finally, Chapter 17 discusses the contemporary challenges confronting the established conventions and dynamics associated with America's ideational arrangements.

The ensuing survey proceeds on the understanding that ideas are a basic part of associational life in the United States. They are not merely an incidental feature of political exchange. Ideas have an instrumental role and a substantive status in the way that issues are defined and contested. Just as the foundations of American society are universally expressed in the language of ideas, so is political conflict articulated in terms of different value claims, or more particularly by reference to divided interpretations of commonly recognized values. As a consequence, American discourse is suffused with grand statements relating to big questions and sweeping principles. But the net effect of this form of politics is not a monochrome world of mutual disengagement. It is a densely packed space in which complex cross-currents of ideas are selected and formulated into hosts of nuanced hybrids in order to maximize their political appeal. James Madison's reference to the segmented yet interdependent structure of American government as a 'compound republic'[26] finds its equivalent in the aggregative dimension of the republic's core principles. In the United States, ideas are nothing if not promiscuous. Their advocates are equally eclectic in the manner in which they fashion ideas into evermore adaptable mutations. It is the virtuosity of these ideas and their usages to which this book is dedicated.

---

[26] James Madison, 'Federalist Paper No. 51', in Alexander Hamilton, James Madison, and John Jay, *The Federalist Papers*, introduced by Clinton Rossiter (New York: Mentor, 1961), p. 323.

Part II

Elements

1

Freedom

INTRODUCTION

The most abiding and durable self-characterization of the United States is that of freedom. The concept of freedom lies at the heart of American identity. It is at one and the same time a foundational ethic, a cultural reference point, a defining ideal, a controlling precept, a depiction of social reality, a medium of political exchange, a mobilizing source of aspiration, and a device of historical and political explanation. The idea of liberty is integral to the American republic. It permeates not only the origins and development of the United States, but also the nation's sense of what it embodies as a social entity. As a consequence, American consciousness remains firmly attached to the principles and demands of liberty. The success of the United States as a national and cultural entity is habitually equated with its success in being free and in embodying a universal idea of liberty. Just as problems are habitually defined in terms of freedom, so are solutions presented and rationalized by reference to their ability to restore or refine or enlarge human freedoms. Given the cultural centrality of citizenship rights such as the freedom of religion, freedom of assembly, freedom of speech, and freedom of conscience, and given that liberty has been the dominant theme in the narratives of success in the United States, it is widely acknowledged that freedom is the 'most resonant, deeply held American value'.[1]

Freedom is seen to be not merely an attribute but a vast organizing theme giving shape and continuity to the history and composition of the American experience. Essentially, freedom occupies a central position in the national narratives that give form to the identity of the United States. In the United States, the concept and social meaning of freedom remains fused with a sense of time and place. The origins of American freedom and the inception of the United States are regarded as being simultaneous and interconnected developments. The claim that America commenced with a state of freedom, and subsequently remained inextricably rooted within that condition, quickly acquired the status of a self-evident truth.

This axiomatic equation of the United States with liberty was founded upon a compound of political principle and social situation. The original eighteenth-century appeal of natural rights, social contract, constitutional liberties, and

[1] Robert Bellah, Richard Madsen, William M. Sullivan, Ann Swidler, and Steven M. Tipton, *Habits of the Heart: Americans in Search of Themselves* (New York: Harper & Row, 1985), p. 23.

republican self-government was conjoined to a set of conditions that made colonial Americans not only highly susceptible to the substance of these principles but in many respects also gave them the appearance of providing the natural contexts and immediate expressions of these principles. The transition to the United States, therefore, was widely accepted as marking a reaffirmation of the social attachment to the ideals of freedom. Since then, Americans have been raised with the conviction that their society first rose to national consciousness during the revolutionary era when the 'sons of liberty' defied the imperial superpower in order to defend their liberties. They then resorted to a declaration of independence, to a rebellion, and to a long war of emancipation from the British Crown (1775–83) in an effort to secure those liberties for themselves and to make America free from outside control.

The nation is therefore celebrated for having been 'conceived in liberty' and dedicated to the proposition that freedom is a natural right which conditions and constrains all succeeding social arrangements. Patrick Henry's admonition to 'give me liberty or give me death' was the rallying call of the War of Independence, but it also became the battle cry of all subsequent American wars. The pre-eminence of liberty in the formative processes of America is still visible in the symbols and mottoes of those states, which declared their independence in 1776. While the flag of Virginia portrays the destruction of tyranny, New York's flag is dedicated to the figures of liberty and justice. The flag of New Jersey also features the cap of liberty and has the motto, 'Liberty and Prosperity'. Pennsylvania promotes 'Virtue, Liberty, and Independence' and Massachusetts declares that 'With the sword she seeks peace, order, and liberty'. Such signs and symbols help to sustain the belief that America originated in a condition of freedom and that American liberty was accordingly 'a matter of birthright and not of conquest'.[2] In Thomas Jefferson's words, 'the God who gave us life, gave us liberty at the same time',[3] by which he meant that the acquisition of independence was not simply a historical event, but a recognition that liberty was a condition natural to America and integral to its independent existence. Even when it was necessary for the Founding Fathers to form a stronger union and a necessarily more centralized framework of government, the effort was still successfully couched in terms of 'securing the blessings of freedom'.[4] The circumstances of America's emergence as a separate entity had made 'liberty an American speciality'[5] and set America on a course that would forever combine it with the prospects and promises of liberty and, thereupon, render America an exceptional society of universal and prophetic significance.

---

[2] Arthur M. Schlesinger, Jr., *The Politics of Hope* (London: Eyre & Spottiswoode, 1964), p. 63.

[3] Thomas Jefferson, 'A Summary View of the Rights of British America', in Merrill D. Peterson (ed.), *The Portable Thomas Jefferson* (Harmondsworth, UK: Penguin, 1977), p. 21.

[4] Taken from the Preamble to the Constitution of the United States.

[5] Peter Gay, *The Enlightenment: An Interpretation*, vol. II—*The Science of Freedom* (London: Weidenfeld & Nicolson, 1970), p. 557.

FREEDOM AND AMERICAN IDENTITY

The relationship between the United States and the concept of liberty, therefore, is not generally seen as merely a loose conjunction of history and principle. On the contrary, these component elements are normally interpreted as constituting a symbiosis in which liberty becomes indistinguishable from the formative processes and subsequent evolution of the United States. With freedom taken to be both a fixed essence and a conditional republican reflex, the political culture is one that is permeated with the meanings and values of liberty. American society continues to be bound up with the ideals and intoxication of liberty. 'No idea is more fundamental to Americans' sense of themselves and as a nation than freedom. The central term in our political vocabulary, "freedom" ... is deeply embedded in the record of our history and the language of everyday life'.[6] The country possesses a formidable array of symbols, legends, and insignia, which ensure that America's equation with freedom remains a constant theme and an irrepressible object of commendation. As a result, outside 'observers have frequently been struck by the depth of Americans' devotion of freedom, as well as our conviction, as James Bryce put it, that we are the "only people" truly to enjoy it'.[7] Because of this attachment both to the virtues of freedom and to the conviction in its existence in the New World, the 'idea does seem to occupy a more prominent place in public and private discourse in the United States than elsewhere'.[8] Ultimately, liberty can be said to be 'more deeply embedded in the nation's system of values than any of the others'.[9] As a consequence, '[n]o value in the American ethos is more revered'.[10]

Whenever the United States is mobilized into an enhanced state of historical consciousness, it is almost invariably done so by recourse to the need to protect or extend freedom. In 1941, President Franklin D. Roosevelt sought to energize the American nation in the preparation for war by portraying a future world order drawn from the American experience of liberty. President Roosevelt was persuasive because he 'presented a vision in which the American ideals of individual liberties were extended throughout the world'.[11] In articulating 'the ideological aims of the conflict ... he appealed to Americans' most profound beliefs about freedom'. The necessity for war was based upon what Roosevelt termed the 'four freedoms'[12]:

---

[6] Eric Foner, 'American Freedom in a Global Age', *The American Historical Review*, vol. 106, no. 1 (February 2001), p. 7.

[7] Eric Foner, 'The Meaning of Freedom in the Age of Emancipation', *The Journal of American History*, vol. 81, no. 2 (September 1994), p. 436.

[8] Foner, 'American Freedom in a Global Age', p. 5.

[9] Herbert McCloskey and John Zaller, *The American Ethos: Public Attitudes towards Capitalism and Democracy* (Cambridge, MA: Harvard University Press, 1984), p. 18.

[10] Ibid.

[11] National Archives, 'Powers of Persuasion', http://www.archives.gov/exhibit_hall/powers_of_persuasion/four_freedoms/four_freedoms.html.

[12] Ibid.

The first is freedom of speech and expression—everywhere in the world. . . . The second is freedom of every person to worship God in his [*sic*] own way—everywhere in the world. . . . The third is freedom from want, which, translated into world terms, means economic understandings which will secure to every nation a healthy peacetime life for its inhabitants—everywhere in the world. . . . The fourth is freedom from fear, which, translated into world terms, means a worldwide reduction of armaments to such a point and in such a thorough fashion that no nation will be in a position to commit an act of physical aggression against any neighbor—anywhere in the world.[13]

During the cold war, President John F. Kennedy committed the United States to 'pay any price, bear any burden, meet any hardship, support any friend, oppose any foe to assure the survival and the success of liberty'.[14] At the time, this was not regarded as an excessive declaration so much as a simple statement of compulsive intent driven by the country's generic association with liberty. America's entry into the First World War had been marked by a similar avowal of national purpose, i.e. 'for the rights and liberties of small nations, for a universal dominion of right by such a concert of free peoples as shall bring peace and safety to all nations and make the world itself at last free'.[15] In similar vein, the United States' engagement in the Second World War was defined by the choice between 'human slavery and human freedom'.[16] As the 'perpetual home of freedom', there was no choice for, as President Roosevelt stated, 'our freedom would never survive surrender'.[17]

An American crisis, therefore, is always defined as both a crisis *of* liberty and a crisis *for* liberty. When the United States was subjected to a series of coordinated terrorist attacks on 11 September 2001, President George W. Bush did not hesitate in identifying the perpetrators as simply the 'enemies of freedom'. As a result, the 'country [had been] awakened to danger and called to defend freedom'.[18] No other rationale or mission would have been as effective in eliciting the emergency response. The President explicitly equated the safety of the nation with its self-image as the bastion of liberty. In a succession of speeches, he repeatedly used the theme of freedom to define both the nature of the crisis and the form of the response. In his address to a joint session of Congress in September 2001, he declared that freedom and the United States were in jeopardy: 'Freedom and fear are at war. . . . I will not relent in waging this struggle for freedom and security for the American people'.[19] On other occasions, he underlined America's historical commitment to spreading freedom to beleaguered parts of the world that had

[13] President Franklin D. Roosevelt, 'Message to Congress', 6 January 1941, http://www.libertynet.org/~edcivic/fdr.html.

[14] President John F. Kennedy, 'Inaugural Address', 20 January 1961, http://odur.let.rug.nl/~usa/P/jk35/speeches/jfk.htm.

[15] President Woodrow Wilson, 'War Message to a Joint Session of Congress', 2 April 1917, http://www.geocities.com/presidentialspeeches/warwilson.htm.

[16] President Roosevelt, Radio Address Announcing the Proclamation of an Unlimited National Emergency, 'We Choose Human Freedom', 27 May 1941, http://www.usmm.org/fdr/emergency.html.

[17] Ibid.

[18] President George W. Bush, 'Address to a Joint Session of Congress and the American People', 20 September 2001, http://www.whitehouse.gov/news/releases/2001/09/20010920-8.html.

[19] Ibid.

been denied liberty and which, as a result, had become centres of oppression and even terrorism.

Our commitment to liberty is America's tradition.... The advance of freedom is the surest strategy to undermine the appeal of terror in the world. Where freedom takes hold, hatred gives way to hope. When freedom takes hold, men and women turn to the peaceful pursuit of a better life. American values and American interests lead in the same direction: We stand for human liberty.[20]

President Bush applied pressure in precisely the way that previous presidents had done in the past. He connected events to the touchstone of American identity and, thereby, maximized the potential for social cohesion and national purpose.

In the view of Michael Novak, the 'interpretive key' of President Bush's speeches has been the 'concentration of liberty as the scarlet thread of human affairs', and a sense that the nation's history can effectively be encapsulated by the driving imperative of freedom.[21] This was exemplified in the President's Second Inaugural Address (2005) which was in essence an elegy to 'America's ideal of freedom' and to 'the great liberating tradition of this nation'.[22] In rededicating the nation to the epic battle for 'freedom's cause', President Bush made it clear that the United States would work to enhance the moral sphere of freedom at the direct expense of tyranny: 'There is only one force of history that can break the reign of hatred and resentment, and expose the pretensions of tyrants, and reward the hopes of the decent and tolerant, and that is the force of human freedom'.[23] Such a blanket affirmation of freedom as the centrepiece of a national strategy to combat global terrorism prompted one discerning commentator to remark that 'such a speech could only have been delivered in the United States'. The spread of freedom was 'advanced by a government not just as part of a non-military strategy but as *the* entire strategy and even as a way of avoiding ... other things'.[24]

FREEDOM AS A CONTESTED CATEGORY

In spite of the reputation of the United States as a reification of freedom, the exact nature of this reciprocal identity has been highly problematic. For example, even

[20] President Bush, 'Announces that Major Combat Operations in Iraq Have Ended', Remarks by the President from the USS *Abraham Lincoln*, 1 May 2003, http://www.whitehouse.gov/news/releases/2003/05/iraq/20030501-15.html.

[21] Michael Novak, 'W., Underestimated: The Surprisingly Good Speeches of President Bush', *National Review Online*, 2 December 2003, http://www.nationalreview.com/novak/novak-200312020910.asp.

[22] President Bush, 'Inaugural Address', 20 January 2005, http://www.whitehouse.gov/inaugural/.

[23] Ibid.

[24] Anatol Lieven, 'Bush's Choice: Messianism or Pragmatism?', *Open Democracy*, 22 February 2005, http://www.opendemocracy.net/democracy-americanpower/article_2348.jsp.

if the proposition of an original state of freedom is accepted as the foundational condition of the republic, it raises the question of how that freedom has been, or can ever be, reconciled to the needs of a social organization. An amorphous and even abstract freedom may be a benign ideal and one that is capable of assimilating a range of different constructions and emphases. Nevertheless, such liberty is only viable up to the point where it becomes necessary to determine its priorities, to apply it to material conditions, and to define how it relates to other values.

Another dimension to this problem relates to the difference between a liberating experience and acquiring the experience of freedom. Liberation may be a precondition of freedom but, as Hannah Arendt has explained, this is not the same as a sustainable condition of liberty. This is a far more elusive property and one that is dependent upon social arrangements.[25] In the American context, the anarchic freedom of being liberated from European forms and structures needed to be transformed and organized into a set of material practicalities. Thereupon, each immigrant would have had to come to the realization that liberty needed to be placed in a social context of reciprocal obligations and restraints before it could acquire meaning and actual content. But in being accommodated to social arrangements, the pure water of idealized liberty would necessarily be muddied with qualifications, provisos, and ambiguities.

Another problem is posed by the attributed relationship between American history and the presence of freedom. The difficulties posed by attempting to translate a protean concept into a single thematic construction of a complex and contested history are not so much surmounted as habitually dismissed or transcended. At root is a circular process of mutual definition. Just as liberty is categorized as a historical condition, so is history used both to reaffirm the validity of the specified point of origin and to legitimize any succeeding development in terms of a necessary continuity from that base. This dynamic generates a loop in which freedom becomes a static and generalized presumption, while history compounds the obfuscation by becoming a prolonged adjunct to an underlying state of presumptive freedom. The net effect is that American freedom becomes evermore opaque and rooted in an increasingly formalized and arguably indeterminate past.

A further difficulty raised by the close association of freedom with the United States relates to the way that each tends to become the litmus test for the other. This can allow alternative interpretations to be overlooked. More significantly, it can lead to the United States being assessed and appraised not so much in terms of itself but as an abstract exemplar of liberal society per se. By being used as the society that typifies the principles and norms of mainstream liberal order, the United States becomes the object of generalized evaluations based upon undifferentiated attitudes towards liberalism in a wider global context. The lack of discrimination often leads either to unqualified praise or, alternatively, to complete condemnation on the grounds of what the United States *represents* rather than how American society functions in practice.

---

[25] Hannah Arendt, *On Revolution* (New York: Viking, 1963).

Severe though these problems may be, it can be argued that they are not as contentious or as disruptive as another source of difficulty surrounding the principle and practice of freedom in the United States. This relates to the profusion and depth of tensions that pervade the pursuit of freedom in a social organization. Far from being reconciled within a liberal society, these tensions constitute an integral and continuing part of it. The divisions and disjunctions drawn from the divergent claims of liberal priorities characterize American society and dominate the conduct of American politics. In fact it can be claimed that no other society attaches greater significance or devotes more resources to the analysis and evaluation of these competing claims of liberal legitimacy. Enumerated below are some of the most cited points of interpretative contention to have characterized the political arguments surrounding freedom in the United States. These contested perceptions and constructions of freedom have both shaped the interplay of political positions in the United States and defined the properties and strategies of American political engagement.

- Freedom conceived as an a priori general condition within society; as a consequence, freedoms are seen as reducible to, and motivated by, a core conception of a generic and unified freedom ... *set against* ... Freedom which can only be explained and valued through the existence of defined freedoms that may or may not necessarily be derivatives of a single notion of freedom.

- Freedoms translated into absolute rights that are treated as non-negotiable claims ... *set against* ... Freedoms as individual claims contingent both upon negotiated accommodations with other freedoms and upon social requirements and responsibilities.

- Freedom in which the emphasis is on emancipation from the restraining structures of society and government ... *set against* ... Freedom that takes account of the extent to which individuals are in a position to exercise their freedoms, and which allows government to take remedial action to secure a minimal level of economic opportunity and freedom of choice.

- Freedom as a continuously mutating and open-ended process of adaptation, interpretation, and refinement ... *set against* ... Freedom as a closed and completed product in which positions can be argued out in fundamentalist terms by reference to a fixed, static, and historically sanctioned finality.

- Freedom as a distant source of general and varied inspiration ... *set against* ... Freedom as a specific source of detailed instruction and designated output.

- Freedom as primarily an economic value ... *set against* ... Freedom as primarily a social value.

- Freedom as the origin and expression of a single, capacious, and binding culture ... *set against* ... Freedom as the licence to permit a diversity of multiple coexisting cultures.

- Freedom viewed and used as a motivating cause and a protest ideal used to precipitate social change and reform ... *set against* ... Freedom viewed as a current de facto condition and used defensively as a device by which to challenge, oppose, obstruct, resist, and retard the onset of change.

- Freedom associated with the provision of civil rights secured and guaranteed by government ... *set against* ... Freedom in the form of civil liberties in which government is prevented from intervening in the private and public spheres of the individual.

- Freedom conceived as a primary value and as an end in its own right ... *set against* ... Freedom conceived as a secondary principle with only an instrumental or functional value related to the utility of those outcomes secured through its operation.

- Freedom accepted as a basis for social order ... *set against* ... Freedom characterized in terms of an emancipatory and libertarian impulse against the constraints of order.

- Freedom centred upon, and expressed through, the individual as the foundational core and primary condition of a free existence ... *set against* ... Freedom as an aggregate expression of a group or communal identity privileging a collective claim to substantive liberty.

The issues arising from these disjunctions are a testament to the way that the meanings, usages, traditions, and logics of this iconic principle have not only been generic to American political history and development but have also sustained an enduring level of intensive cultural engagement. If the United States can be said to have a prevailing public philosophy and a defining discourse, then it is one that pivots upon the meaning of freedom and its leverage as a political resource. The value of freedom either as a presumptive condition or as an aspirational objective has been an integral feature of Americanization and an epic reference point in the emergence of national narratives on the theme of a collective identity. Just as the society developed an extensive capacity for assimilation, so the theme of American freedom underwent a comparable process of accommodation. As a cultural point of reference, it has remained unsurpassed and has allowed American society to be successively reconfigured under the aegis of a unifying ideal.

In the nineteenth century, for example, the United States rapidly developed into an increasingly industrialized society. American traditions and understanding of freedom evolved in line with this social transformation. Accordingly liberty was recast in terms of personal acquisition, technological efficiency, material prosperity, and social progress. As wealth was no longer reducible to land, freedom was no longer synonymous with land ownership. This was a world in which the old rural frontier was being replaced by new 'frontiers' in the form of scientific invention, social mobility, profit maximization, industrial production, and concentration of ownership. As liberty in this new abundance was emancipating the inner resources of the continent, the new wealth was vindicated in terms of what it could provide to ever-larger numbers of people.

A similarly radical recasting of liberty occurred during the great wave of immigration in the late nineteenth and early twentieth centuries. Under these conditions, the freedoms associated with Thomas Jefferson's ideal of yeoman farmers facilitating a graduated maturation of republican virtue were displaced by a more mass-produced notion of an instantly acquired freedom secured by the passage to Ellis Island.[26] Freedom became a commodity to be acquired through movement and relocation. As a consequence, it was increasingly seen to be a matter of consumer choice and a concomitant of mass migration. The commonplace conviction at the time was that because America was a place of freedom, it made people free and kept them free by force of location. As a result, freedom became a narrative of re-enactment for every immigrant and has continued to be so up to the present day.

These kinds of reconfiguration did not resolve the tensions and disputes engendered by a culture formally dedicated to freedom. On the contrary, they underlined the continuing salience surrounding the meaning of liberty and its significance as a medium of exchange and leverage within American society. In a 'nation obsessed with liberty',[27] the currency of political dispute has remained dominated by this competition for authenticity, i.e. the legitimation of an interpretation or construction of freedom by reference to its relationship to past conditions or foundational intentions. It is precisely because the idea of liberty is so central to American culture that there continues to be so much interest in its origins. The status of American liberty as idiosyncratic, and therefore authentic, has always been strongly influenced by its own historical roots. America's conception of itself as liberated enough to be uniquely free from the rest of the world is necessarily linked to the conception of its formative processes. In this way, the forward march of American liberty has been led by a continual and compulsive retrospection in pursuit of historical verification. It is for this reason that the origins of American freedom have continued to play such a vital role in the architecture of political debate in the United States.

THE ROOTS OF AMERICAN LIBERTY

The controversy which best illustrates the nature and influence of this search for validity, and which remains a source of so many claims and counterclaims over the rightful conception of American freedom, is the central dispute over genealogy. The debate pivots upon whether liberty in the New World was primarily a product

[26] See Maldwyn A. Jones, *American Immigration*, 2nd edn (Chicago, IL: University of Chicago Press, 1992), chs. 7, 8; Alan M. Kraut, *The Huddled Masses: The Immigrant in American society, 1880–1921*, 2nd edn (Wheeling, IL: Harlan Davidson, 2001), ch. 4.

[27] Clinton Rossiter, *Conservatism in America: The Thankless Persuasion*, 2nd edn, rev. (New York: Vintage, 1962), p. 72.

either of experience or of ideas. Those who base the conception of American freedom within the dimension of received experience give primary consideration to the ingredients and processes of a particular social chemistry that is alleged to have produced an unprecedented and spontaneous form of sustained liberation. According to this perspective, the engine of emancipation was based upon the unmediated experience of American conditions and upon the social dynamics generated by them. Individuals were thrown into entirely novel circumstances from which communities arose that were free from the dynastic, class, and feudal divisions of the Old World. The sheer abundance of land and other resources provoked allusions to a state of nature and to a unique historical opportunity to engage in a continuous process of individual and collective liberation. It was not simply that America was seen as having relatively more freedom within its borders than that of other contemporary societies. It was the conviction that America could be nothing other than an agency of emancipation from prior structures and patterns of social organization. In this respect, the state of American nature conferred upon liberty the conditions not only of its own existence but also of its fullest maximization.[28] As a consequence, American freedom was, and continues to be, depicted as the summation of its extraordinary experience. Thus, America was free; it made people free and kept them free by force of its own spontaneous dynamics.

It is liberty in this visceral and immediate sense which has remained a defining characteristic of the United States. Liberty in such a guise has a seductive power in offering the simple prospect of experiencing freedom by experiencing America. The correlate of this guiding premise is that the United States is free from the Old World of Europe. It has been common feature of the American outlook to assert with pride that 'America was new in nature, new in people, new in experience, new in history. Nothing had prepared the old world for what now confronted it, fearfully, alluringly, implacably'.[29] Many in the Old World were only too willing to concur with this vision of America and to add their weight to the notion of America being the embodiment of liberty. Goethe, for example, praised the fact that the Americans were not riven by useless memories and that there were no crumbling castles in America to keep alive the dissensions of feudalism. Hegel also celebrated America. He saw it as 'the land of the future...and of desire for all those who are weary of the historical lumber-room of Old Europe'.[30] In this respect, America appears to be a wholly exceptional society in that by freeing itself from the Old World, it emancipated itself from all preconceived structures and impositions; so much so that America is often reputed to be the first entirely new

[28] See Perry Miller, *Nature's Nation* (Cambridge, MA: Harvard University Press/Belknap Press, 1967).
[29] Henry S. Commager, *The Empire of Reason: How Europe Imagined and America Realized the Enlightenment* (London: Weidenfeld & Nicolson, 1978), p. 64.
[30] Quoted in Hugh Honour, *The New Golden Land: European Images of America from the Discoveries to the Present Time* (London: Allen Lane, 1976), p. 248.

nation, free from the past, free from historical processes, and, therefore, free from the intractable restrictions upon liberty found elsewhere.[31]

It can be claimed that the United States was not, and is not, an unqualified haven of civil liberties, constitutional rights, and political freedoms. Nevertheless, this is overlooking the central point of such an experience-centred perspective. In this respect, the American order was extraordinarily liberal both in the circumstances of its inception and in its subsequent development. In effect, the society is interpreted as the embodiment of a 'bottom-up' arrangement of social processes released through the special circumstances of the New World. The notion of a self-generated national character drawn from an accelerated mix of history and people in combination with a generalized attachment to libertarian doctrines continues to be a compulsively attractive proposition. The nature and appeal of this idiosyncrasy is perhaps best represented in the work of Daniel J. Boorstin. In *The Genius of American Politics*, for example, Boorstin responds to the American desire to be as free of external influences as it is of theoretical accoutrements by referring to the notion of 'givenness' in the manner of America's inception and durability.[32] Givenness relates both to the belief in American values having been 'preformed' within the peculiarities of the American experience and to the idea that American history has an inherent conformity so that 'our past merges indistinguishably into our present'.[33] The conviction in a 'perfectly preformed theory'[34] that is believed to have been 'born with the nation itself'[35] has created a 'naturalistic approach to values'[36] which to Boorstin means that the 'quest for the meaning of our political life has been carried on through historical rather than philosophical channels'.[37] The principle of givenness makes Americans the rightful beneficiaries of a natural inheritance and in the process precludes the need for them to 'invent a political theory'.[38] It was axiomatic to Boorstin that America had no need for theoretical abstractions because it already possessed a core theory through the processes of its history:

The limitations of our history have perhaps confined our philosophical imagination; but they have at the same time confirmed our sense of the continuity of our past and made the definitions of philosophers seem less urgent.[39]

Set against this background of historical spontaneity, the challenge of understanding American freedom could simply be reduced to apprehending the experience of the New World.

An alternative way of explaining the origins and, thereby, the nature of American liberty is through the influence of ideas. This approach to American freedom

[31] Miller, *Nature's Nation*.
[32] Daniel J. Boorstin, *The Genius of American Politics* (Chicago, IL: University of Chicago Press, 1953).
[33] Ibid., p. 9.   [34] Ibid., p. 13.   [35] Ibid., p. 14.   [36] Ibid., p. 25.
[37] Ibid., p. 19.   [38] Ibid., p. 23.   [39] Ibid., p. 33.

throws into doubt not just its claim to social autonomy, but also its claim to be the cradle of liberty. For example, it can be argued that the early American affection for the classics led to a cultural dependence on the principles and virtues of antiquity. These interpretations plot the influence of Greek and Roman authors like Plato, Aristotle, Sophocles, Thucydides, Plutarch, Cicero, Tacitus, Seneca, Ovid, Cato, Justinian, Lucretius, and Polybius upon the development of colonial ideas on law, forms of government, political stability, republicanism, tyranny, and liberty. It is claimed that these ideas became so ingrained in colonial political life that they were a major source of the Americans' ideology of dissent against Britain, and later became the inspiration behind the new constitutions of the independent republics in the 1780s.[40]

Another interpretation gives emphasis to the more immediate contemporary context of the British constitution, within which the initial American struggle took place, and in reference to which much of the subsequent American speculation concerning the roots of government and the meaning of liberty has been made. Since the 'colonists of every political shade were dedicated wholeheartedly to the English constitutional tradition...and could count no greater blessing...than their inheritance of the English form of government',[41] it could be said that the newly independent Americans could not help but be moulded by hallowed English precedents. It is claimed that the Americans were guided by the desire to reinstate the ideal of the English balanced state through the strength of their own Whig allegiances and their zeal for the liberties of England's Glorious Revolution of 1688.[42]

An important variation of this perspective holds that while American conceptions of liberty were strongly influenced by Britain's political culture, that influence was drawn far more from what was called the republican or 'Commonwealthman' tradition. This term refers to those early eighteenth-century dissenters and radicals who sought to revive the spirit of an ancient English liberty which had been so effectively exploited by the republican apologists of the Commonwealth in the seventeenth century (e.g. James Harrington, John Milton, and Andrew Marvel). These writers identified authentic English liberty as existing in the freehold tenure of Saxon times before the imposition of the Norman 'yoke'.[43] Over the centuries, this original state of indigenous freedom had been progressively

---

[40] Richard M. Gummere, 'The Classical Ancestry of the United States Constitution', *The American Quarterly*, vol. 14 (Spring 1962), pp. 3–18; Gilbert Chinard, 'Polybius and the American Constitution', *Journal of History of Ideas*, vol. 1, no. 1 (January 1940), pp. 38–58.

[41] Clinton Rossiter, *Seedtime of the Republic: The Origin of the American Tradition of Political Liberty* (New York: Harcourt Brace, 1953), p. 143.

[42] See Michael Lienesch, 'In Defense of the Anti-Federalists', *History of Political Thought*, vol. 4, no. 1 (Spring 1983), pp. 65–88; Herbert J. Storing, *What the Anti-Federalists Were for: The Political Thought of the Opponents of the Constitution* (Chicago, IL: University of Chicago Press, 1981).

[43] See Caroline Robbins, *The Eighteenth-Century Commonwealthman: Studies in the Transmission, Development and Circumstance of English Liberal Thought from the Restoration of Charles II until the War with the Thirteen Colonies* (Cambridge, MA: Harvard University Press, 1959).

reinstated, but the process had not been completed. The struggle continued. The Glorious Revolution (1688) of the Whigs was not the culmination of the process. On the contrary, the Commonwealthmen concluded that liberty was as fragile as ever and constantly in danger of being eroded away. It was this Commonwealthman tradition which, it is claimed, appealed to the non-conformist American dissenters and which permeated their conception of liberty and republicanism. Instead of the founding of America being dominated by the constitutional arrangements, legal rights, and property consciousness of the Whig tradition, it has been argued that it was much more the product of an English-cum-classical republican ethos which stressed civic virtue, moral fervour, self-sacrifice, and the ideal of community.[44]

The historiography of the civic republican tradition in America has itself been the subject of some dispute.[45] As noted above, some have located the republican strand in the principles and controversies surrounding the Commonwealthman discourse. But others see the lineage stretching back not only to the world of Renaissance republicanism and of Florentine thought in particular, but even to the classical period of Aristotle.[46] In the process, they have sought to underline the existence of a continuity of civic republicanism that can and does embrace the American republic. Another point of controversy that has been particularly pertinent in the United States is the nature of the relationship between commerce, property, and money on the one hand, and the virtues and logic of republicanism on the other. Again, opinions have varied between those historians of civic republicanism who claim that private property was an inherently corrupting force in a republic, and those who believe that there was no inconsistency and that republicanism was properly attentive to the protection and support of property ownership.[47] These republican debates have been highly significant in the United States not just also because of the cultural importance attached to

---

[44] See Bernard Bailyn, *The Ideological Origins of the American Revolution* (Cambridge, MA: Belknap Press, 1967); Gordon S. Wood, *The Creation of the American Republic, 1776–1787* (Chapel Hill, NC: University of North Carolina Press, 1969); Robert E. Shalhope, 'Toward a Republican Synthesis: The Emergence of an Understanding of Republicanism in American Historiography', *William and Mary Quarterly*, vol. 29, no. 1 (January 1972), pp. 49–80.

[45] For example, see Robert E. Shalhope, 'Republicanism and Early American Historiography', *William and Mary Quarterly*, vol. 39, no. 2 (April 1982), pp. 334–56; Daniel T. Rogers, 'Republicanism: The Career of a Concept', *Journal of American History*, vol. 79, no. 1 (June 1992), pp. 11–38; Joyce Appleby, *Liberalism and Republicanism in the Historical Imagination* (Cambridge, MA: Harvard University Press, 1992); Anthony Molho, 'Italian Renaissance, Made in the USA', in Anthony Molho and Gordon S. Wood (eds.), *Imagined Histories: American Historians Interpret the Past* (Princeton, NJ: Princeton University Press, 1998), pp. 263–94.

[46] For example, see J. G. A. Pocock, *The Machiavellian Moment: Florentine Political Thought and the Atlantic Republican Tradition* (Princeton, NJ: Princeton University Press, 1975); J. G. A. Pocock, 'The Machiavellian Moment Revisited', *Journal of Modern History*, vol. 53, no. 1 (March 1981), pp. 49–72; J. G. A. Pocock, 'Civic Humanism and its Role in Anglo-American Thought', in J. G. A. Pocock, *Politics, Language, and Time: Essays on Political Thought and History* (Chicago, IL: University of Chicago Press, 1989), pp. 80–103.

[47] William J. Connell, 'The Republican Idea', in James Hankins (ed.), *Renaissance Civic Humanism: Reappraisals and Reflections* (Cambridge: Cambridge University Press, 2000), pp. 14–29.

America's republican identity but because of the substance and meaning that has been imputed to republicanism as a prior historical and ethical standard against which contemporary society can be judged and resistance justified. In essence, republicanism and its historically rooted conception of an instinctive communal liberty can be cited as an authentic American tradition and one that can be differentiated from the more conventional liberal construction of American development.[48]

Notwithstanding the attachments to a republican ethos, the genealogy of American liberty has customarily given emphasis to the liberal ferment of the eighteenth-century Enlightenment which coincided with America's rise to independence. This era witnessed the rise of the modern concept of nature being a single entity directed by its own permanent and objective principles of operation. The belief that the rational order of nature's laws was accessible to human intelligence became the inspiration behind the Enlightenment's emancipation of reason. Building upon John Locke's arguments in the seventeenth century for natural rights as representing the central condition behind the original formation of any civil government, the Enlightenment thinkers proceeded on the assumption that nature was no longer simply a philosophical device to reason into the source and meaning of social arrangements, but a material force to be elicited and channelled into positive use. Since humanity was part of the natural order, it was believed that the mechanics of social nature could be discovered, and political organizations could be constructed that would provide the best fit for mankind's inner properties. Many American scholars have been particularly susceptible to the idea that clinical reasoning and a conscious synthesis of empirically derived knowledge on government and politics explain the origins of America's constitutional freedom. Accordingly, America can be seen as having been 'conceived by a mental act, in the spirit of liberty'[49] by which emancipated reason became the handmaiden of colonial liberation.

Gertrude Himmelfarb points out that the American Enlightenment bore a close resemblance to the latitudinarian instincts and social virtues (e.g. compassion, benevolence, sympathy) of the British Enlightenment, in contrast to the violent certitude of rationality associated with the French Enlightenment. Notwithstanding this shared element of reasonableness, Himmelfarb concludes that America was the only Enlightenment culture in which political liberty became the central motivating force for change.[50] Within such a milieu, the pursuit and organization of freedom in America became a practical science.[51] It is within such a context that the creation of the American polity could be depicted as 'history's first

---

[48] For example, see Rogers M. Smith, *Civic Ideals: Conflicting Visions of Citizenship in U.S. History* (New Haven, CT: Yale University Press, 1999).

[49] Garry Wills, *Inventing America: Jefferson's Declaration of Independence* (Garden City, NY: Doubleday, 1978), p. xv.

[50] Gertrude Himmelfarb, *The Roads to Modernity: The British, French, and American Enlightenment* (New York: Knopf, 2004).

[51] Gay, *The Enlightenment: An Interpretation*, pp. 555–67.

great political experiment and massive effort at political engineering'.[52] From this standpoint, it is possible to construe American liberty as being so direct a derivative of Enlightenment principles that it might justifiably warrant the depiction of America as the talisman of the Enlightenment's emancipatory spirit.

It should be acknowledged at this point that the Enlightenment amounts to a generic term that includes a variety of philosophical and social agendas which are resistant to any coherent or exclusive set of meanings. Robert Ferguson is particularly adept at dissecting the different strands of the American Enlightenment and in underlining the way that it was deeply connected to a 'Bible culture of extraordinary vitality'.[53] Distinctions between the secular and the religious were not as clearly drawn as the reputation of the Enlightenment would imply.

The American Enlightenment does not quarrel with religious orthodoxies as its French counterpart does; it rests, instead, in the common or shared rhythms and patterns that the Enlightenment has taken from Christianity. The parallels in intellectual reference— salvation and progress, the health of the soul and the corresponding gauge of public interest, the regenerate Christian and the virtuous citizen, exultation of the divine and celebration of design—are homologies in American thought rather than substitutes, one for the other, as in European philosophy.[54]

In this view of the American Enlightenment, the emancipatory potential of reason can be interpreted as being correlated with the dissenting social energies of vigorous Protestantism.

Notwithstanding the different nuances and cultural stimuli even within the American Enlightenment, the realm of organized reason and principled logic does amount to a noteworthy alternative construction of American freedom compared to the explanations drawn exclusively from the themes of historical continuity, cultural autonomy, and traditional habits.[55] Instead of viewing liberty simply as a pre-existing condition or primordial inheritance, those who give emphasis to the history of ideas point to a level of cultural dependence and cosmopolitan intrusion which the advocates of a unique historical experience tend to dismiss as either marginal in effect or a gross distortion of the past. Whether these allegedly seminal ideas are perceived as inherently European in origin, or whether they are seen as being transmuted into essentially American principles of foundation, the net effect is one in which the priority is given and value is afforded to the presence of fundamental principles. These revered ideals constitute an external framework

---

[52] Austin Ranney, ' "The Divine Science": Political Engineering in American Culture', *American Political Science Review*, vol. 70, no. 1 (March 1976), p. 140.

[53] Robert A. Ferguson, *The American Enlightenment, 1750–1820* (Cambridge, MA: Harvard University Press, 1997), p. 77.

[54] Ibid., pp. 42–3.

[55] For a highly sophisticated synthesis of the influence of eighteenth-century republican ideology, and the idiosyncratic nature of New World conditions whereby Americans could not be said to have been born free but came to be so as a result of the long-term repercussions of the American Revolution, see Gordon S. Wood, *The Radicalism of the American Revolution* (New York: Vintage, 1993).

of fixed norms that offer a continuing standard of political legitimacy in relation to the everyday interplay of political interests and social experience. Of these central ideas which shape, condition, and structure political debate, none has as much cultural significance or operational leverage as that of freedom.

FREEDOM AS A MEDIATING DEVICE

The exact genealogy of American freedom has always been an open question and it remains an area of constant inquiry and heated reference. In reality, the currents of political thought are interwoven into social experience. The appeal of certain ideas is governed by what they offer in terms of cultural integrity, political mobilization, or master narrative. In the United States, freedom has a generic priority because of the way it can account for, and give expression to, an identity rich in axiomatic principle and experiential narratives.

The duality inherent in the concept and usage of freedom continues to shape political argument. In some circumstances, ideas can seem to lag behind experience. For example, it can be claimed that eighteenth-century concepts of liberty have had to be transformed in order to accommodate more modern notions of franchise extension, racial equality, and women's rights. In other circumstances, it would appear that on the evidence of experience many aspects of American society have failed to fulfil the normative standards espoused in the founding documents of the republic. In these circumstances, a fundamentalist approach to eighteenth-century principles can provide a compelling point of critique and prescription. An eighteenth-century perspective can serve to highlight the contrast between historical ideals and current realities. Such principles can be enjoined to point up the occurrences of illiberal behaviour, to underline the repressive disjunctions and anomalies within an otherwise liberal society, and to act as the mobilizing points for arguments and pressure in support of remedial action.[56]

The relationship between ideas and experience—between norms and conduct—continues to animate American politics and to account for much of its energy and ingenuity of argument. This is because the prize is so valuable: the mantle of authentic American freedom. But this is a prize which is never secured for the benefit of any one position for any length of time. The state of American freedom and the authenticity of claims to American freedom are continuously contested. In *The Myth of American Individualism*, for example, Barry Shain challenges the explanatory value of both the liberal and republican traditions in accounting for the origins and development of American freedom.[57] To Shain, the secularism of the liberal and republican conceptions of social order have

---

[56] See Rogers M. Smith, 'Beyond Tocqueville, Myrdal, and Hartz: The Multiple Traditions in America', *The American Political Science Review*, vol. 87, no. 3 (September 1993), pp. 549–66; *idem*, *Civic Ideals: Conflicting Visions of Citizenship in U.S. History*.

[57] Barry A. Shain, *The Myth of American Individualism: The Protestant Origins of American Political Thought* (Princeton, NJ: Princeton University Press, 1994).

overlooked the religious basis of American community life during the formative
period of the United States. Because individual well-being and spiritual salvation
were intrinsically tied to a communally directed ethos, freedom in Protestant
settlements was seen more as an instrumental rather than an intrinsic value. Shain
concludes that early American society was approvingly oriented towards the conformity of the faithful and coercive will of communal oversight. Another strand
of critical review focuses on the issue of American immigration and assimilation.
The record of controls and regulations are replete with instances of discrimination
against minorities in the face of traditional structures of power and the customs
of established social orders.[58] The history of immigration and naturalization has
prompted Gary Gerstle to echo Shain's reference to a conflation of liberty and
compulsion. Freedom on the margins of society could thus be characterized as
being a 'mixture of opportunity and coercion',[59]—both of them being 'intrinsic to
our history and the process of becoming American'.[60]

A more recent encounter with the disputatious properties of American freedom
has centred upon foreign policy. Earlier in the chapter, attention was drawn
to the enriched references made by President Bush in mobilizing support for
the campaign to counter terrorism. But even in the circumstances of a national
emergency, he was not able to monopolize the usage of freedom as a political
instrument. Others were able to call upon the principles of liberty in order to
underline the areas of 'unfreedom' present in American society and, in particular,
to allege that American foreign policy had illiberal properties. Critics deployed
a different usage of freedom to challenge the systemic continuities of policy and
to open up the space for dissent in support of an emancipatory campaign for a
substantive freedom from conditions such as exploitative trading practices, global
inequality, environmental degradation, disease, and starvation.[61]

Instead of freedom to consume U.S. products and lifestyles, a definition of freedom focusing upon human rights is needed. Bush's political freedom, in part, has stemmed from
wrapping himself in the vagueness of freedom and its centrality to the mainstream of
American ideology ... the real work of freedom lies not in the waging of war, the unchecked
depletion of resources, or the feeding of the treadmill's voracious appetite, but rather in
combating these practices.[62]

This form of indictment follows a well-worn path of using freedom as a point
of reference with which to subject a dominant or conventional construction of
freedom to critique. The use of freedom in this setting becomes a way of throwing
the internal tensions of a purportedly liberal society into high relief. As Eric Foner

[58] For example, see Desmond King, *Making Americans: Immigration, Race, and the Origins of the
Diverse Democracy* (Cambridge, MA: Harvard University Press, 2000).

[59] Gary Gerstle, 'Liberty, Coercion and the Making of Americas', *Journal of American History*, vol.
84, no. 2 (September 1997), p. 557.

[60] Ibid., p. 558.

[61] Noam Chomsky, *Profit Over People: Neoliberalism and Global Order* (New York: Seven Stories
Press, 1999).

[62] Andrew D. Van Alstyne, 'Freedom', in *Collateral Language: A User's Guide to America's New War*
(New York: New York University Press, 2002), p. 91

points out, from the very beginning of American history 'freedom has been a central value for countless Americans and a cruel mockery for others'.[63]

Because freedom is raised to such elevated levels of national veneration, it allows dissidents of every persuasion to frame their positions in terms of the anomalies and contradictions implicit in the established configurations of liberty. Critics of American society defer to the foundational ideas of republican liberty in order to press for the emancipation of American citizens, and even global citizens, from the allegedly illiberal conduct of the United States. From this perspective, it is customary to declare that in contemporary America 'freedom exists in theory more than it gets exercised in practice'.[64] The corollary is one of confronting a notional freedom with substantive freedom: 'Our nation was born in revolution. It was dedicated to freedom and fairness. ... That was a radical idea in 1776 and it remains a radical idea today—and one worth fighting for'.[65] In the same way as the United States becomes a Rorschach test of interpretive perception for the meaning and presence of freedom, the theme of liberty comes to represent a Rorschach test for the condition of American society.

The matrix of American political argument, therefore, is characterized by a diversity of competing claims to represent the real essence of American freedom. What further compounds the complexity is the salience of other political values that are not explicitly or conclusively reducible to the principles of freedom. The shaping of issues and policy in the United States is strongly influenced by the interplay between the central status of freedom in American culture on the one hand and those values and conditions that have a distinctive meaning and an alternative significance in the realm of political ideas on the other hand. It is now necessary to give consideration to these other elements and to their interpretive dynamics that can not only dispute the definition of freedom in the American context, but can also challenge its primacy as an organizing theme of American purpose.

---

[63] Foner, 'The Meaning of Freedom in the Age of Emancipation', p. 437.

[64] Mark Hertsgaard, *The Eagle's Shadow: Why America Fascinates and Infuriates the World* (London: Bloomsbury, 2003), p. 87.

[65] Ibid., p. 205.

2

The Individual

INTRODUCTION

American freedom has a protean and mercurial quality but that elusiveness is diminished when the scale shifts from the general to the particular. Freedom acquires a greater solidity as a claim upon society when the focus is tightened to include specific liberties and precise entities in possession of such liberties. Individual citizens satisfy both these requirements. They provide a point of convergence at which the subject and object of liberty seem to reach an optimum point.

American liberty is traditionally a property that acquires its meaning through the agency of individuals, rather than that of classes, social orders, or nationality. In American eyes, it is a matter of simple logic that a society dedicated to liberty should have as its hallmark the freedom of the most fundamental constituent unit of that society (i.e. the individual citizen). America is believed by its inhabitants to be free because of the way that American experience offers scope to the reach of human possibilities. The realization and maximization of individual potential is the currency of the American ethos. In American society, individuals are given 'the opportunity and encouraged to develop and to use their powers, to live their own lives and to participate in the renewal and development of the culture and in the development, reform and functioning of the social structure'.[1] It is accepted that in the tradition of the 'small republic' the principle of self-government is conditioned by the notion of communal liberty. The early state constitutions, for example, were structured upon the republican linkage of individual freedoms to a community of governance. This was the primary rationale of the inclusion of a bill of rights in these constitutions. Notwithstanding this element of republican traditionalism, it has to be conceded that the development of American political culture has generally given priority to the direct attribution of freedom to the individual.

In American conditions, the individual and liberty are invariably seen as being synonymous with one another. While freedom is only really comprehensible in terms of the actions and thoughts of self-governing individuals, individuality is seen as meaningless without the attribute of freedom by which a person can be emancipated into the fullness of his or her potential. The substance, imagery, and

---

[1] E. M. Adams, 'Introduction: the Idea of America', in E. M. Adams (ed.), *The Idea of America: A Reassessment of the American Experiment* (Cambridge, MA: Ballinger, 1977), p. 5.

symbolism of freedom in the United States carry a presumption of the individual as both the main source and the primary beneficiary of such a condition. The individual is accepted as the basic unit of resource and measurement—as the irreducible core of human freedom to which the American republic is formally dedicated.

This linkage between liberty and individualism has a long and complex set of origins. It includes the autonomous and voluntarist impulses of an immigrant culture; the individualized nature of divine contact and salvation in the Protestant tradition; the geographical dispersal of settlement over remote areas; and the decentralizing forces associated with the oceanic distance between America and centres of European hierarchy and imperial outreach. It can be argued that these and other strands, which stimulated and supported an individualistic outlook, receive their strongest expression in America's signature attachment to natural rights and, in particular, to the political logic of John Locke's theory of the state.

THE LOCKIAN BEQUEST

The philosophy of John Locke remains embedded not only in the foundations of the republic and by extension in America's present-day conception of liberty. The resonance of Locke in the New World was first established in the eighteenth century. The American colonists valued the utility of Locke's thought in giving a different and altogether more pliable alternative dimension to the complex legalities that were entailed in the protracted constitutional dispute with Britain. The appeal of Lockian liberalism was further enhanced by its particular pertinence to the social milieu and political predicament of the emergent elites in Northern America. Locke's philosophy had been employed in practical politics a century earlier when his exposition of Whig principles had made a major contribution to the debates surrounding the Glorious Revolution in 1688. Now the self-appointed heirs of this past Whig ascendancy used Locke in their own campaign against the executive power of the British crown. Locke's appeal was immediate and far-reaching because it allowed the colonists to transcend the technical strictures of a constitutional dispute by reconfiguring the conflict into a complaint based upon a radical inquiry into the nature of government and the basis of political obligation.[2]

Significantly, Locke's point of departure lay not with the state but with the individual. According to Locke, each person was an individual creation of God's universe and, therefore, a unit of intrinsic moral worth. Locke reasoned that God-given natural rights were an organic part of each person's individuality. Individuals, therefore, exercised their own liberties through their own being and on their

---

[2] See Morton White, *The Philosophy of the American Revolution* (Oxford: Oxford University Press, 1981), pp. 23–35, 42–8, 64–78; Garry Wills, *Inventing America: Jefferson's Declaration of Independence* (Garden City, NY: Doubleday, 1978), pp. 169–75, 181–5, 208–15, 240–5.

own authority—not on behalf of others or through an intermediary agency.[3] It was this central proposition of the individual ownership of rights which led, ultimately, to the modern ethos of individualism in which any individual is seen literally as being their own person.

In Locke's philosophy, the composite natural rights of life, liberty, and property were not objectives to be fulfilled, so much as a birthright from a pre-existing natural condition and one that invoked inviolable limits on the operation of any subsequent state. Locke's position was that while men and women were born free in a stateless condition, there was sufficient unpredictability and enough inconvenience for them to form civil societies, and thereupon states, to promote peace, safety, and the public good. In doing so, individuals would inevitably suffer some restriction in the operation of their personal discretion but they would not, and could not, relinquish their basic natural rights. To Locke, any assertion that they had done so would be both implausible and irrational. This is because the entire objective of governing arrangements was always to protect and preserve natural liberties of individuals. Far from being an end in itself or a device to ensure order and peace at any price, Locke's state was formed by the express consent and contract of free individuals in order to serve their interests and to promote their welfare. If a state were to fail in the obligations entrusted to it, then the citizenry would have a right of revolution to reformulate the structure of government, in order to make it a better medium for the exercise and enjoyment of individual liberties.

Locke's philosophy established the individual as the seat of moral worth. Individuals and their liberties were claimed to be in existence prior to the formation of the state and, as a consequence, they remained ethically superior to any subsequent civil organization. Accordingly, the authority and legitimacy of a state were made dependent upon the protection it afforded to individual liberties. The influence of Locke's fundamental theory of the state and of the citizen's relationship to it was clearly evident in the Declaration of Independence (1776).

We hold these truths to be self-evident, that all men are created equal, that they are endowed by their Creator with certain unalienable Rights, that among these are Life, Liberty and the pursuit of Happiness. That to secure these rights, Governments are instituted among Men, deriving their just powers from the consent of the governed. That whenever any Form of Government becomes destructive of these ends, it is the Right of the People to alter or to abolish it, and to institute new Government, laying its foundation on such principles and organizing its powers in such form, as to them shall seem most likely to effect their Safety and Happiness.[4]

The animating ideas of radical individual liberty, natural rights, and a contractually based government bore the hallmarks of Locke. These features also reflected the extent to which these kinds of ideas had become a prevailing creed that conformed so closely to general attitudes in society.

---

[3] John Locke, *Two Treatises of Government*, introduced by Peter J. Laslett (Cambridge: Cambridge University Press, 1967), p. 305.

[4] Declaration of Independence (1776).

During this pivotal period of inception, America was soaked in the pungent ideals and vocabulary of natural rights and personal freedoms. During the eighteenth century, the 'great common denominator of American social thinking was the ideal of social freedom—freedom to rise, that is—individualism, and social fluidity'.[5] America's attachment to the principle of individual liberty culminated in the Declaration of Independence.

> There could be no clearer statement of the right of revolution or of the principle that government is the servant, not the master, of the people and that it serves at their pleasure. Fully as clear is the emphasis upon the individual human being as the basic unit of society and government, and the assumption that the foremost consideration is the basic right of each human being to live in freedom.[6]

These sentiments became America's guiding ideals and are as prevalent today as they were in the eighteenth century. The significance of the American Revolution, therefore, might be said to lie 'less in battles and martial triumphs than in the creative effort ... of building constitutions and declaring systems of rights'.[7]

The emphasis upon natural individual rights was later reaffirmed both in the preamble to the US Constitution[8] and in the subsequent attachment of the Bill of Rights which stands today as the chief monument to American individualism. The Bill of Rights includes the personal rights of free speech, free assembly, the free exercise of religion, and the free access to a fair trial. This inventory of rights represents the clearest statement of the American belief that freedom preserved *by* the state must always be qualified by guarantees of freedom *from* the state. The act of inaugurating a central state, therefore, coincided with the equally significant act of ring-fencing it with prohibitions and constraints defined through individual freedoms. It was the currency of natural rights that would provide the anchorage of absolutism to keep the new government within its constitutional framework.

THE SOCIAL FORMATION

The social currency of Lockian principles relating to individual rights is integrally connected to the impulses and promises of American life. In the same way that Locke himself speculated on the Americas' approximation to a state of nature, so immigrants to the New World have traditionally associated their journey with one of personal liberation. This has often taken the form of a movement motivated by individual dissent and opportunity. Whether the early settlers were motivated

---

[5] Max Savelle, *Seeds of American Liberty: The Genesis of the American Mind* (Seattle, WA: University of Washington Press, 1948), p. 280.

[6] Max J. Skidmore, *American Political Thought* (New York: St Martin's Press, 1978), p. 46.

[7] Ernest Barker, 'Natural Law and the American Revolution', in Ernest Barker, *Traditions of Civility: Eight Essays* (Cambridge: Cambridge University Press, 1948), p. 328.

[8] The preamble to the US Constitution asserts that 'we the people of the United States, in order to form a more perfect union ... and secure the blessings of liberty to ourselves and our posterity, do ordain and establish this Constitution'.

by the desire for religious toleration, or by the need to escape political persecution, or by the drive for economic security, their objectives were reducible to
the prospect of liberation. This represented a form of freedom that could be
sensed by the individual conscience and expressed through personal independence
from previous states of social existence. The formation of communities reflected
both the rapidity of accelerated settlement, and the fluidity of social conditions
that accompanied the advancing aggregates of individuals in search of their own
conceptions and enclaves of progress.

The low density of population and the easy availability of land permitted the
widespread ownership of property. When these conditions were combined with
the radicalism of the various dissenter traditions, the result was a developed
enmity towards external forms of hierarchy that assigned individuals to fixed
class positions on the basis of blood and rank. Most Americans reacted strongly
against the notion of a static order within society. The hostility was based not only
upon an objection to what was seen as an artificial imposition but also upon a
conviction that such an order would stifle liberty and, in particular, the freedom
of individuals to find their own level within society.

An open-textured society implied a social mobility that afforded individuals the
opportunity of self-improvement and self-determination.

Americans never picked up the European concept of social station—which meant that
you were born into your position in the world. For most Europeans of the 18th and
19th centuries, success meant maintaining your place in the fixed order.... In France, a
shoemaker's son could become a shoemaker and inherit not only his father's business but
his father's standing in the community. In the United States, the indentured immigrant
who worked his way up to a prosperous shoemaking shop had met the standard of success.
But to meet the same standard his son had to push on to something, or somewhere else.[9]

American society quickly became noted for its premise of social fluidity and for
its absence of any established scheme of social stratification. At the end of the
eighteenth century, 80 per cent of white men were self-employed as entrepreneurs,
professionals, farmers, merchants, and craftsmen. This demographic profile was
reflected in Hector St John de Crevecoeur's celebrated answer to the question:
'What is an American?' De Crevecoeur referred to the remarkable fact that in
America there were 'no aristocratic families, no courts, no kings, no bishops,
no ecclesiastical dominion, no invisible power giving to a few a very visible one'.
Instead, there were simply individuals occupying open spaces and creating open-
ended forms of human existence: 'We are a people of cultivators, scattered over an
immense territory ... united by the silken bands of mild government, all respecting
the laws, without dreading their power, because they are equitable. We are all
animated with the spirit of an industry which is unfettered and unrestrained,
because each person works for himself'.[10]

---

[9] Quoted in J. W. Anderson, 'The Idea of Success', *Washington Post* supplement published in the
Guardian Weekly, 29 August 1976.

[10] Quoted in Henry N. Smith, *Virgin Land: The American West as Symbol and Myth* (New York:
Vintage, 1950), pp. 143–4.

America became distinguished for its viability in the face of an apparently unstructured set of social arrangements in which 'there was no established system of feudal ranks, no historical memory of an aristocratic order of society which could provide a model for a new social hierarchy'.[11] Some Americans may have been concerned about a society that lacked the harmony of established social orders. But in the main, the emphasis upon the individualist nature of the emergent society became accepted as an ideal in its own right. Gordon Wood describes this shift in social relationships as the defining and radical outcome of the American Revolution. The impulse against deference and paternalism altered the way that people related to one another. It generated an erosion of class distinctions and traditional bonds, and produced a highly mobile society based upon personal independence. Wood describes the emergence of an equality of attitudes that conferred legitimacy upon the individual, and upon an open market of individual advance, as part of a generic order devoid of preordained or presumptive hierarchies.[12] Selfishness in this respect was ennobled by reference to its place in a flattening process of radical emancipation. As a consequence, social harmony could be conceived or constructed as an aggregate equilibrium of individual self-interest. Individualism, therefore, was not merely a residual property in a society devoid of an established hierarchy of social authority. It could be seen as the epitome of a free society in which the only hierarchy would be that of a de facto natural aristocracy drawn from those whose skills and talents had exploited the available opportunities for individual advancement to the full.

In this sense, America can be portrayed as the forerunner of a development that came to dominate the Western world: the usage of individuality as the basis for an entire social order. Kenneth Minogue comments upon the general contribution of individualism to modern Western civilization but his observations have a particular resonance where the United States is concerned. Individualism is described as 'a unique civilizational creation' which has 'now spread remarkably' throughout the West.[13] It has been 'a daring episode in human evolution' because it is marked by 'a situation in which individuals have the discretion to make their own judgements'.[14] Minogue develops the point further:

This was how the modern Western world rejected castes, social hierarchies and even automatic respect for elders. It was a remarkable adventure, requiring a great deal of nerve, and conducted amid the wailing of those who believed that, unless we conformed to some ideal pattern of a good society, we should inevitably come to grief.[15]

Seen through this perspective, America's virgin lands evoked a virgin society of displaced individuals whose emancipation from European estates and hierarchies

---

[11] Tom B. Bottomore, *Classes in Modern Society* (London: George Allen & Unwin, 1965), p. 41. See also Louis Hartz, *The Liberal Tradition in America: An Interpretation of American Political Thought Since the Revolution* (New York: Harcourt Brace, 1955), ch. 1.

[12] Gordon S. Wood, *The Radicalism of the American Revolution* (New York: Vintage, 1993).

[13] Kenneth Minogue, 'The Ego and the Other', *Times Literary Supplement*, 8 January 1999.

[14] Ibid.   [15] Ibid.

revealed an inner potential not just for innovative vitality but also for imaginative joint action and the effective organization of a whole society.

THE GRAND NARRATIVE

The political culture has also been permeated by a profusion of references to the central significance of the individual as an agency of social dynamism and explanation. For example, just as the republic was established by a small number of founding fathers, so the course of the United States is characteristically depicted as having been segmented into presidential administrations in which the actions or inactions of individual presidents are deemed to be historically pivotal. In the same vein, American heroes have almost invariably been seen as heroic individuals engaged in individualized projects. Social developments and movements have been regularly reduced either to the motivational energy of individual actors, or to the aggregate effect of multiple agents acting independently from one another. In addition, America quickly achieved the reputation of offering opportunities to individuals who wished to establish model communities to reflect a particular personal vision of a divine or just social order. On a more spontaneous and unpremeditated level, the 'anarchic individualism'[16] of America's frontier people has been widely cited in American historiography as being responsible for the formation of democratic society. The westward pattern of settlement and the consequent mobility of the frontier are thought to have generated a highly mutable and open-ended form of development, one that reflected the shifting matrices of individual interactions both with one another and with the natural environment.

For a society with a strongly developed historical consciousness and a distinct sense of the past affording legitimacy to the present, the early history of the United States is distinguished by a sudden expansion of individual ambitions and enterprises leading to a sense of flux in the social order. Just as the scale of individual opportunity was seen to be symptomatic of a free society, so liberty was increasingly recast in terms solely related to individual advance. It was during this early ferment of individualism in the 1830s that Alexis de Tocqueville visited the United States and provided a classic social commentary of a democratic society in formation. His analysis became established not only as an integral part of American history in its own right, but as a mixture of observation and evaluation that has maintained its relevance to issues confronting modern America. One of his most trenchantly argued assessments centred upon the scale of American individualism that he witnessed and upon the dangers posed by this phenomenon.

De Tocqueville's sociological overview of the early United States affirmed what to him was an extraordinary feature of democratic life. It was he who coined the term 'individualism'. He did so specifically with reference to the conditions he found in America: 'Individualism is a recent expression arising from a new

---

[16] Smith, *Virgin Land*, p. 36.

idea'.[17] De Tocqueville used it to convey the 'reflective and peaceful sentiment that disposes each citizen to isolate himself from the mass of those like him and to withdraw to one side with his family and his friends, so that after having thus created a little society for his own use, he willingly abandons society at large to itself'.[18] He noted that Americans possessed an enthusiastic attachment to this outlook: '[O]ne finds a great number of individuals who ... owe nothing to anyone, they expect so to speak nothing from anyone; they are in the habit of always considering themselves in isolation, and they willingly fancy that their whole destiny is in their hands.'[19]

This was not exactly egotism but to de Tocqueville it was not far removed from it. The term individualism was devised in order to denote a more moderate version of egotism. Nevertheless, the drive within individualism could lead to social isolation and, thereby, to the dislocation of the social order. Under these conditions, 'not only does democracy make each man forget his ancestors, but it ... separates him from his contemporaries; it constantly leads him back toward himself alone and threatens finally to confine him wholly in the solitude of his own heart'.[20] This represented an ominous feature of American society. Under the guise of individual liberty, a new despotism might emerge that could engulf the multitude of isolated and mutually antagonistic entities. Their limited resources would be insufficient to resist a central power. Social mobility and individual self-determination might be commendable properties in isolation, but they would be no match for any concerted force.

In spite of the deep-set nature of what he deemed to be a form of behavioural dysfunction, de Tocqueville could offer the comfort of another discernible feature of American society. It represented a redeeming corrective that prevented social dissolution. What made it so significant was that it was in de Tocqueville's view the only available antidote to the burgeoning individualism of American society. The partial remedy he alluded to was the high incidence of group formation and civil association that coexisted alongside the high value placed upon individual priorities. The immediacy and cohesion of local organizations set within a social environment of rural and small-town communities promoted not only a culture of participation and collective activity but also a consciousness of common identity and shared predicaments:

Local freedoms, which make many citizens put value on the affection of their neighbors and those close to them, therefore constantly bring men closer to one another, despite the instincts that separate them, and force them to aid each other. ... Although private interest directs most human actions. ... it does not rule all. I must say that I often saw Americans make great and genuine sacrifices for the public, and I remarked a hundred times that, when needed, they almost never fail to lend faithful support to one another.[21]

---

[17] Alexis de Tocqueville, *Democracy in America*, translated, edited, and introduced by Harvey C. Mansfield and Delba Winthrop (Chicago, IL: Chicago University Press, 2000), p. 482.
[18] Ibid., p. 482.   [19] Ibid., pp. 483–4.   [20] Ibid., p. 484.   [21] Ibid., pp. 487, 488.

According to de Tocqueville, it was this ethos of communal responsibility that both moderated the effects of individualism and created the intermediary organizations that would resist the formation and intrusion of any large-scale organized force. The relationship between the insecurity and isolation of individualism, and the ethos of community was a functioning balance, but as de Tocqueville warned it was also a very fragile balance.

A NORMATIVE REACTION

De Tocqueville's concerns over individualism revived the central question of the purposes served by personal freedom. In the Protestant tradition, freedom of conscience was accepted as a means to the end of serving God undistracted and unrestricted by clerical or hierarchical intrusion. In the republican tradition, individual liberties and government by consent were envisaged as the guarantors of civic integrity and virtuous citizenship. With the onset of population growth, manufacturing activity, and economic prosperity, personal freedom was increasingly being cited as an agency of wealth creation through the interplay of competitive individualism. The reconfiguration of individualism into an engine devoid of any clear moral direction constituted a source of genuine anxiety. The ideals and virtues of individual liberty had the appearance of being co-opted by an all-enveloping philosophy of acquisition that defined objectives solely in terms of its own criteria of human motivation and social benefit. It is noteworthy that the first philosophical movement to object to the imperatives of encroaching industrialization in the first half of the nineteenth century was centred solely upon the individual.

The Transcendentalists sought to escape the present by retreating not only into the past through recourse to an uncorrupted nature, but also into the interior of the self through solitude. Through spiritual intuition and personal conscience, the individual could break free from the accoutrements of a material society and elicit essential truths. Writers like Ralph Waldo Emerson, Nathaniel Hawthorne, and Henry David Thoreau proceeded on the premise that the individual was the ultimate medium of the deepest reality. They immersed themselves in their own self-consciousness confident in the belief that 'a single man contains within himself, through his intuition, the whole of experience'.[22] It was possible for the individual human mind or soul to establish a direct and harmonious relationship with the immensity of the universe.

Because the self could elicit and accommodate the cosmos, it was necessary for an individual to assign paramount meaning and value to the medium of the self. Allegiance to the principles of self-reliance and self-trust afforded the space that would allow the individual to heal itself not through a form of alienation, but from

---

[22] F. O. Matthiessen, *American Renaissance: Art and Expression in the Age of Emerson and Whitman* (London: Oxford University Press, 1941), p. 7.

an enhanced reconnection with nature. If Emerson advocated a submersion of the individual into nature as a way of apprehending the divine, Thoreau epitomized the usage of individualism as a channel to a pre-industrial haven of simplicity. In his journal of solitude written at Walden Pond, he complained that humanity 'live[d] meanly, like ants' with life 'frittered away by detail',[23] speed, and complexity: 'We do not ride on the railroad; it rides upon us'.[24] The Transcendentalists pursued a rejectionist stance against the imposition of a changing society. Their expressive and emotional individualism was a reaction against the dominant individualism drawn from the calculating pursuit of material interests.

De Tocqueville was also alarmed over the seismic implications of a mass society for American democracy. It is not clear whether his emphasis upon the existence of communal groups and local partnerships represented an integral and alleviating feature of possessive individualism, or whether instances of individuals adopting ad hoc devices of mutual security were reactive antidotes to social change. Notwithstanding the interpretive differences, the individual remained in jeopardy as far as de Tocqueville was concerned. The individual would be weakened either by isolation, or by the orthodoxies of a mass society. The defences of intermediary organizations would find it difficult to resist both the centrifugal forces of personal acquisitiveness and the centripetal demands of organizations with ever-increasing economies of scale. Not even de Tocqueville, however, could have foreseen the actual magnitude of the assault upon the individual that was occasioned by the exponential development of the United States over the next century.

A SINGULAR ECLIPSE

The American individual has been under assault for much of the twentieth century. The rise of mass production, automated processes, integrated industrial organization, and corporate monopolies combined with the closure of the frontier, high immigration, the rise of conurbations, and continental transportation systems have all contributed to an environment in which the individual is increasingly marginalized. The self-employed person constituted the original heartland of the republic. But over the course of the nineteenth and twentieth centuries, this sector has been progressively replaced by wage and salary earners. In the main, they work in large and highly stratified organizations whose primary purpose is the maximization of efficiency in pursuit of profit. As self-interest has been merged into collective corporate interest, the individual has been eclipsed by an organizational culture that provides order and security at the expense of personal autonomy. Social mobility in the form of 'rags to riches' elevation has become in reality a remote opportunity presented as a mythic birthright by a limited number

---

[23] Henry David Thoreau, *Walden or, Life in the Woods and On the Duty of Civil Disobedience* (New York: New American Library, 1960), p. 66.

[24] Ibid., p. 67.

of super-rich 'winners'. The norm for most Americans is one of social fixture and valued stability. Instead of rugged self-reliance and the adventure of the self-made man, the general experience is one of company commitment in which 'small increments in wages and security take over independence in aspiration'.[25]

It is possible to assign a positive construction to the development of mass production by underlining the benefits of mass consumption and, with it, the emergence of what can be seen as a substantial compression of social hierarchies. The scale of a continent-wide industrial economy, together with the development of a burgeoning middle class facilitated a consensus on the relationship between national wealth, personal security, and individual freedom. The process could be said to have fostered an exceptional dynamic of consumerism, classlessness, and social stability.[26] But in the main the exponential growth in the economies of scale and mass consumption have brought in their wake severe concerns over the debits rather than credits of advance. More often than not, these doubts have identified the meaning and status of the individual as the primary casualty in a society in which class has apparently been deradicalized and replaced with open-textured variations of minor and negotiable differences. The major category of concern in corporate America has been that of personal autonomy within a system of social conformity.

The new middle classes of the post-Second World War era, for example, were particularly conscious of the need to imitate the assumed models of previous middle class behaviour and style. But as Olivier Zunz points out, the marked inflation in the middle classes at this time became a vindicating monument not merely to the industrial and commercial advances of the American economy, but also to the dominant matrix of institutions that succeeded in propagating a pervasive vision of a middle-class community of consumption with affluence as the defining centrepiece of American democracy. The reconstruction of America as an entity driven and governed by a middle-class norm of mass acquisition was seen as being instrumental in weakening class identities and undermining the radical potential of class hierarchies.[27] The burgeoning middle class with its implications of social mobility also eroded the traditional ethos of the individual as collective organizations and economies of scale in science, production, and technology increasingly marginalized the significance of the lone inventor or the small producer. The average American now came to be located in the uniformity of burgeoning suburbs and in a redefinition of success in line with occupational security, graduated promotion, and pension provision.

Several contemporary studies reflected the scale and significance of the transition to this new order of affluent anonymity, depersonalized advance, and apparent classlessness. C. Wright Mills' study of white-collar workers during this period revealed a pattern of self-depreciation coexisting with a rationalization of their

[25] William Issell, *Social Change in the United States 1945–1983* (Basingstoke: Macmillan, 1985), p. 67.
[26] Olivier Zunz, *Why the American Century?* (Chicago, IL: University of Chicago Press, 2000), chs. 3–5.
[27] Ibid.

position based upon rising levels of affluence and material acquisition. While Vance Packard documented the social preoccupation with status distinction and lifestyle aspirations,[28] William Whyte charted the rise of the 'organization man' who not only worked for the company but belonged to it as well in return for a stable career structure and middle class benefits. White believed that vast hierarchies of corporate management produced high levels of technical specialization but at the expense of a moral myopia.[29] The organization man 'may agree that industrialism has destroyed the moral fabric of society' and that 'business needs to be broken up unto a series of smaller organizations.... But he will go his way with his own dilemmas left untouched'.[30]

These studies enjoyed considerable popular success because they reflected contemporary mores back upon the American public. But they were all eclipsed by a particularly trenchant exposition of the ecology of individualism within a mass society during the middle of the twentieth century. It was a measure of the resonance that the study possessed in American society that it was still being cited as a salient account of attitude structures at the end of the century. In his study of an emergent consumer society, David Riesman demonstrated how it was possible to combine a culture of conformity with the collective effect of isolation and alienation. In *The Lonely Crowd*, Riesman posited the existence of different types of social character that distinguished separate periods of historical development.[31] The onset of affluent mass suburbia marked the rise and domination of the 'other-oriented' character whose behaviour was guided not by tradition or by an internalized ideal, but by a desire and need to be exceptionally sensitive to the actions and requirements of others. According to Riesman, the 'other-directed' person does not seek to control other individuals so much as to relate to them. This character type needs to know that they were emotionally synchronized with those around them. The depiction of the individual's predicament within a corporate culture and mass society was representative of an age of deepening conformity. The sense of self was being conditioned by an increasingly complex and interconnected society. Within such an environment, Riesman drew attention to the individual's amorphous sense of self and, with it, a dread of loneliness because it was only through the agency of other people that individuals might be said to possess a reference point for their own existence. As the demands of the corporate career intensified, the 'lonely crowd' offered security and solidarity as well as social approval and moral guidance; but all at the alleged cost of individual autonomy.

By the end of the century, various initiatives were being taken in an effort to reduce the position of work as the prime indicator of individual success and self-fulfillment (e.g. family leave, leisure time). Nevertheless, the driving dynamic of even high-status professionals remains one of working for ever-larger organizations in accordance with rules and procedures laid down by others. The

---

[28] Vance Packard, *The Status Seekers* (Harmondsworth, UK: Penguin, 1961).

[29] William H. Whyte, *The Organization Man* (Harmondsworth, UK: Penguin, 1960).

[30] Ibid., p. 16.

[31] David Riesman, *The Lonely Crowd: A Study of the Changing American Character*, rev. edn (New Haven, CT: Yale University Press, 1970).

overall effect of these developments has been widely depicted as representing a shift towards a more uniform conception of life chances subsumed under a dominant mainstream of standardized consumer products, stereotypical living space, and an impulse towards social and political conformity. In essence, an increasingly mass society was seen as necessarily analogous to the submergence of individual distinction. As a consequence, an individualistic culture could be depicted as being subverted by growing evidence of its antithesis in the form of impersonal forces and of structures far removed from a human scale.

This apparent decline in American individualism has often been correlated with an alleged contraction in the social capital of the United States. The community consciousness, which de Tocqueville identified as a derivative and also an antidote to the excesses of American individualism, is reputed to have dramatically diminished over the past twenty-five years. Robert Putnam's pioneering study in this field revealed a set of social trends, which by accumulation suggested that Americans had increasingly withdrawn not only from the public sphere, but also from one another. Rising divorce rates, declining church attendance, reduced trade union membership, diminished political participation, and dwindling involvements in a range of social activities (e.g. school associations, youth groups, local political parties, and even bowling leagues) are cited as evidence that American's civil society is being progressively undermined.[32] Given that group norms, social networks, and reciprocal trust help to integrate society with a basic sense of citizenship and collective purpose, then any erosion of this substratum represents a serious indictment of American's social cohesion.

Many factors are cited as causal agents in the alleged increase in civic disengagement: the channelling of political power to distant state capitals and Washington, DC; the deteriorating condition of neighbourhood infrastructures; the increased incidence of divorce and family breakdown; the migration of women from the household to the workplace; more competitive employment practices; and the growth of television viewing as a leisure activity. Such influences raise disturbing questions over the stability of America's social order and over the need for institutional and moral frameworks to be reconstituted in order to prevent any further deterioration to the fabric of society. The level of concern over the state of liberal society and even the prospect of societal dissolution has provoked an entire genre of communitarian critiques addressing what are seen to be emergent conditions that threaten the viability of liberal society. The communitarian reaction can take the form of an abstract exposition into the meaning of community as a social concept and into the contemporary challenges facing it.[33] More generally,

---

[32] See Robert D. Putnam, 'Tuning In, Tuning Out: The Strange Disappearance of Social Capital in America', *PS: Political Science and Politics*, vol. 28, no. 4 (December 1995), pp. 664–83; Robert D. Putnam, *Bowling Alone: The Collapse and Revival of American Community* (New York: Simon & Schuster, 2001).

[33] For example, see Charles Taylor, *Sources of the Self: The Making of Modern Identity* (Cambridge, MA: Harvard University Press, 1992); Michael Sandel, *Liberalism and the Limits of Justice*, 2nd edn (Cambridge: Cambridge University Press, 1998); Francis Fukuyama, *The Great Disruption: Human Nature and the Reconstitution of Social Order* (New York: Touchstone, 2000).

communitarians are better known for their more practical proposals for reversing the trends of civic disengagement. The main technique is one of attempting to regenerate communities through citizen action programmes designed to integrate individuals back into associational life.[34]

But these disintegrative processes pose equally difficult questions concerning the state of America's individual capital. All these attributed factors indicate the presence of processes that result in personal isolation, distance, and alienation. Recent research has shown that children, for example, not only spend significantly less time with their parents than they used to, but are alone for an average of three and half hours a day which is longer than they are with their family and friends. The conclusion is that child loneliness, as well as the strategies to mitigate its effects (e.g. day care, prescription drugs), succeed only in raising the levels of alienation, resentment, aggression, obesity, and even feral behaviour within society.[35] Whether or not the conclusions drawn from this kind of research are wholly valid, they are symptomatic of a deep concern over the perceived malaise in society and over the viability of an open informed and active citizenry.

Far from revealing an independence and inventiveness of spirit, the research on social capital in many respects points to a logical culmination of the mass society: a population of passive, distracted, and self-absorbed individuals trapped in reluctant satisfaction and devoid of any triumph over external pressures and forces. De Tocqueville had warned that 'individualism at first dries up only the source of public virtues; but in the long term it attacks and destroys all the others and will finally be absorbed in selfishness'.[36] Without the restraining counter-weight of social capital, it was a commonly held view at the end of the twentieth century that American individualism had become the victim not merely of the sheer scale of contemporary organizations, but also of the citizenry's immoderate preoccupations with the privacy of economic security, lifestyle distinctions, and personal agendas.

AMERICAN INDIVIDUALISM REVISITED

While many of these assertions and interpretations carry significant weight, they fail to take account of contrary indicators and traditions which reveal a much more ambiguous picture. Far from disclosing an unqualified decline in individualism, considerable evidence exists to show that the evaluative and explanatory emphasis placed upon the individual remains a persistent and highly potent theme in

[34] For example, see Amitai Etzioni, *The Spirit of Community: The Reinvention of American Society* (New York: Touchstone, 1994); Amitai Etzioni, *The New Golden Rule: Community and Morality in a Democratic Society* (New York: Basic Books, 1996); Robert D. Putnam and Lewis Feldstein with Donald J. Cohen, *Better Together: Restoring the American Community* (New York: Simon & Schuster, 2003).

[35] Mary Eberstadt, *Home-Alone America: The Hidden Toll of Day Care, Wonder Drugs, and Other Parent Substitutes* (New York: Penguin/Sentinel, 2004).

[36] De Tocqueville, *Democracy in America*, p. 483.

American society. For example, even though most Americans work for and benefit from large organizations, they continue to assess each other's social position and material standard of living on the basis of individually generated achievement. Moreover, they are likely to view their own success or failure in highly personalized terms. Income levels remain closely tied to assessments of individual worth and self-esteem. Responsibility for individual status is almost invariably assigned to the person rather than to the structures or conditions.

The high prestige that is still assigned to individuals who move into the conspicuous ranks of the super-rich remains consistent with this ethos of social mobility through individual effort. The instinctive presumption continues to be that of merit prevailing over impersonal forces and static structures. In a self-proclaimed market society, personal success suggests legitimacy on the grounds that it is derived from an intense process of competition. Whether they are show business celebrities (e.g. Tom Cruise), or entrepreneurs (e.g. Bill Gates, Jeff Bezos), their spectacular rise to prominence provides public reassurance of social mobility and also an apparent reaffirmation of a free society's 'natural aristocracy' of individual talents and skills. The same faith in the inherent capacity of the individual to have a disproportionate effect upon organizational existence is evident in the popular appeal of leadership courses and guidebooks that purport to show how individuals can maximize their leadership potential for the benefit of themselves and the organizations for whom they work. The exhortations to the individual to make the critical difference are explicitly conveyed in the titles of such publishing blockbusters as Wess Roberts's *Leadership Secrets of Attila the Hun*[37]; Anthony Robbins's *Awaken the Giant Within: How to Take Immediate Control of Your Mental, Emotional, Physical and Financial Life*[38]; and Stephen R. Covey's *The 7 Habits of Highly Effective People: Powerful Lessons in Personal Change.*[39]

The contemporary mystique surrounding the pivotal individual in the strategic position is also evident in the political preoccupation with the presidency and with the personal constituents of leadership in the White House. The same regard for individual leadership is evident in the economic significance that is assigned to the identity of companies' chief executive officers (CEOs). Their high status and huge remuneration packages reflect the presumption that personal qualities can permeate institutional structures. Because of this conviction, share values can be highly susceptible to the transfer market in high-profile CEO personnel.

This faith in individual leadership is also evident in the contemporary appeal of individuals attempting to take charge of themselves and to reconfigure their own lives through self-help or will-power. Whether this is seen as social mobility or a form of psychological displacement, the search for inner conversion and spiritual release has become a growth industry in its own right. It takes various forms

[37] Wess Roberts, *Leadership Secrets of Attila the Hun* (New York: Time Warner Electronic Publishing, 1995).

[38] Anthony Robbins, *Awaken the Giant Within: How to Take Immediate Control of Your Mental, Emotional, Physical and Financial Destiny* (New York: Free Press, 2003).

[39] Stephen R. Covey, *The 7 Habits of Highly Effective People: Powerful Lessons in Personal Change* (New York: Free Press, 2004).

ranging from psychic counselling and holistic self-discovery to exercise and dietary regimes; and from transcendental meditation and New Age inner harmonies to self-assertion courses and the quest for personal transformation under the guidance of gurus with best-selling handbooks typified by Deepak Chopra's *Way of the Wizard: 20 Spiritual Lessons for Creating the Life You Want*.[40] All elements of this industry bear witness to the enduring meaning of the individual in America's mass society and to the way that problems and solutions tend to be defined in terms of personal attributes.

Another widely cited indicator of sustained individualism in the United States is the high incidence of voluntary activity in society. Notwithstanding the evidence and conclusions produced by Putnam, it is possible to produce alternative indicators of associational activity that place individual contributions to the community in an entirely different context.[41] For example, an estimated 110 million Americans engage in some form of voluntary work every week.[42] This huge resource was given further acknowledgement in 2002 when both President Bush and the US Senate proposed bills designed to expand the ranks of full-time volunteers and to offer incentives to give additional encouragement to short-term voluntary work in charitable organizations. Local groups and civic clubs also retain a high profile in American society. National non-governmental organizations (NGOs) operating in such issue areas as environmental protection, anti-globalization, and citizens' rights have experienced dramatic surges in size over the past ten years. According to the WorldWatch Institute, 70 per cent of the 2 million NGOs in the United States were created in the past thirty years.[43] Organizations like the American Association of Retired Persons and the Sierra Club have witnessed huge increases in membership.[44] While it can be claimed that 'members of such groups have ties to a common agenda [and] not to one another'[45] their activities nevertheless represent a heightened level of consciousness over the need for individuals to assert their economic concerns and also their moral anxieties over large and complex issues.

Another feature of this need to undertake individual action in support of community welfare is the strong social tradition of philanthropy. Although federal and state governments have increasingly assumed responsibility for social security, housing, health care, and welfare, the flow of charitable donations from individuals has remained unsurpassed by other nations. Corporations and

---

[40] Deepak Chopra, *Way of the Wizard: 20 Spiritual Lessons for Creating the Life You Want* (New York: Harmony, 1995); see also Phillip C. McGraw, *The Self Matters Companion: Helping to Create Your Life from the Inside Out* (New York: Simon & Schuster, 2003).

[41] For example, see Everett C. Ladd, 'The Data Just Don't Show Erosion of America's Social Capital', *The Public Perspective*, June/July 1996; Everett C. Ladd, *The Ladd Report* (New York: Free Press, 1999).

[42] See 'A Nation of Volunteers', *The Economist*, 23 February 2002.

[43] Nancy Dunne and Peronet Despeignes, 'Americans Take Fresh Pride in a Do-It-Yourself Public Service', *Financial Times*, 7 September 2001.

[44] For example, the AARP had 400,000 members in 1960. In 2004 the membership had increased to 35 million.

[45] George F. Will, 'A Nation of Solo Bowlers Is Sliding into the Gutter', *International Herald Tribune*, 5 January 1995.

foundations engage in extensive form of charitable giving but the proportion of donations coming from individuals continues to account for well over 80 per cent of the charitable sector-with over 70 per cent of American households making regular contributions.[46] In comparisons with other large countries, the United States is ranked top in the per capita level of donations with 1.85 per cent of GDP accounted for in philanthropic donations.[47] Individual conscience, combined with a sense of personal autonomy and collective responsibility, generate a substantial resource for private organizations, and especially religious organizations, in the United States.[48] Bill Gates's donations of $26 billion to the Bill and Melinda Gates Foundation and Warren Buffet's estimated transfer of $31 billion to the same organization are the best known recent examples of the impact made by individuals upon charitable works.[49]

Of the numerous systemic effects attributed to personal autonomy in the profile of American attitudes, perhaps the key reference point for the contemporary salience of American individualism relates to the cultural value placed upon personal rights. The United States has a distinctive rights-based outlook that is reflected in the language and organization of its politics. The process of democratization was in the past driven by demands that rights be respected as universal attributes of citizenship. Restrictions and discrimination, therefore, were progressively minimized, in order to allow individuals to become active participants in the democratic process. Arguments and debate continue to be structured according to different rights claims and the need to reach adjustments between them. Minorities and marginal groups still press their respective cases for redress of grievances by resorting to the currency of individual rights to act as leverage in the pursuit of social campaigns and group demands. This is because the ultimate point of legitimacy remains that of the individual—so much so that it has led to numerous complaints that individual rights now constitute an American fundamentalism:

The recent academic view of the U.S. constitution in general and the Bill of Rights in particular has stressed the defense of *individual* rights to the exclusion of everything else, as if the U.S. Bill of Rights embodies something like the moral theory of Immanuel Kant and as if its political purpose is to ensure that governments treat individuals as 'ends in themselves'.[50]

---

[46] Figures from Giving USA Foundation, http://www.aafrc.org/gusa/.

[47] See 'The Business of Giving: A Survey of Wealth and Philanthropy', *The Economist*, 25 February 2006.

[48] The total amount of private philanthropy funds recorded in 2003 was $241 billion. See US Census Bureau, *Statistical Abstract of the United States 2006*, 'Table 570. Private Philanthropy Funds by Source and Allocation: 1990 to 2003', http://www.census.gov/compendia/statab/social_insurance_human_services/philanthropy_nonprofit_organizations_volunteering/.

[49] See Carol J. Loomis, 'Warren Buffet Gives It Away', *Fortune*, 10 July 2006. Note should also be made of Gordon Moore, the co-founder of Intel, who over a five-year period (2001–5) gave more to charity than Bill Gates.

[50] Alan Ryan, 'The British, the Americans, and Rights', in Michael J. Lacey and Knud Haakonssen (eds.), *A Culture of Rights: The Bill of Rights in Philosophy, Politics and Law, 1791–1991* (Cambridge: Cambridge University Press, 1991), p. 377.

The critique is that rights are so pervasive and absolute in character, they have become increasingly privatized with the effect that the social and democratic dimensions related to rights tend to be overlooked. Political demands are almost invariably transmuted into claims that rights be recognized and honoured irrespective of social context. As a consequence, notions of citizenship are heavily skewed to the idea that individuals are clients of the government whose sole task it is to service their rights. The problem is that different rights constantly impact upon one another, thereby, leading to prolonged and ultimately fruitless searches for agreeable compromises. This in turn leads to assertions that the deepest crisis in American politics comes from the vibrant but extreme nature of individualism in the United States: 'Rights talk...impedes identifying the public interest because of our propensity to formulate nearly all political conflicts in terms of conflicting rights.... Because individualistic Americans tend to think about public policy issues in terms of individual rights, no public policy issue is immune to a rights claim'.[51] Moreover, it can be alleged that the 'American dialect of rights talk disserves public deliberation not only through affirmatively promoting an image of the rights-bearer as a radically autonomous individual, but through its corresponding neglect of the social dimensions of human personhood'.[52]

The systemic effects attributed to individualism are rooted in the profile of American attitudes relating to personal autonomy and culpability. Social surveys reveal a predominant attachment to a configuration of individual rights and personal responsibilities.

CONCLUSION

Very few would contest the validity of William Whyte's assertion that of 'all peoples it is we who have led in the public worship of individualism'.[53] Many more, however, would dispute the nature, meaning, and significance of America's attachment to the principle of individualism. In the United States, individualism comes in many different, and at times exotic, forms. It can be denoted as a utilitarian value that promotes or facilitates the preservation or extension of aggregate outcomes that are considered to be beneficial. It can also refer to an emancipatory experience in which the emphasis is upon personal expression and self-fulfillment.

The tumult of the 1960s, for example, is often characterized as a period when these two conceptions of individualism came into open conflict. The materialistic categories of possessive individualism and a stable social order ran up against a challenging youth culture motivated by the imperatives of personalized autonomy, experimentation, and iconoclasm. It was left to Christopher Lasch to formulate a

---

[51] William E. Hudson, *American Democracy in Peril: Seven Challenges to America's Future* (Chatham, NJ: Chatham House, 1995), pp. 96, 94.

[52] Mary A. Glendon, *Rights Talk: The Impoverishment of Political Discourse* (New York: Free Press, 1991), p. 109.

[53] Whyte, *The Organization Man*, p. 9.

collective indictment of both forms of individualism for being engrossed in a kind of narcissism that produced a narrowing of horizons and a myopic perspective of the limits of individualism in meeting its very own objectives. Accordingly, he condemned the contemporary state of American individualism on its very own terms. Citizens had become self-absorbed consumers who were oblivious both to the past and to the future, and who lived in a permanent state of spiritual desolation because of the cultivated need to satisfy a perpetual stream of fabricated desires. Because the original reasons for individual autonomy and dissent had now passed from memory, individualism itself had become a self-justifying and self-sustaining vacuity.[54] Lasch's jeremiad has remained a salient commentary on the culture of American anxiety. The original indictment has simply been extended to incorporate the contemporary concerns not only over the social effects of personal computers, i-Pod downloads, online games, and virtual networks, but over the myopia of what is termed the 'MySpace Generation' that is centred upon constant choice, personal therapy, transferred liability, and the primacy of individual well-being.

But other dimensions and interpretations of individualism are also evident in American society. For example, individualism can be associated with personal autonomy and civic voluntarism, but it can also proffer a dark side in allowing isolation and insecurity to facilitate the rise of ascriptive ideologies and institutions whose repressive and discriminatory measures offer the prospect of a more settled social and national identity.[55] From another perspective, individualism can on some occasions be seen as an integral component of an outward- and forward-looking social perspective. While at other times, it is linked to an inward nostalgic past with a moral certainty drawn from homestead farms and small-town communities. In this context, individualism often provides the lynchpin in the confrontation between the old and the new; between the known in decline and the emergent in formation. In the view of Robert Bellah et al., it is this 'inability of the old moral order effectively to encompass the new social developments [which] sets the terms of a cultural debate in which we as a nation are still engaged'.[56]

The cultural emphasis upon the individual has persisted throughout the vast social transformations that the United States has experienced over the past 200 years. The individual remains as the formal centrepiece and immutable figurehead of the American story. American heroes continue to be embodiments of individual autonomy: the person who takes on anonymous structures and breaks the rules in order to achieve moral objectives guided by the conscience of personal agency. The role models of the past used to be the self-reliant cowboy, the principled outlaw, or the embattled small-town businessman. Now the heroic mantle is more convincingly portrayed by the crusading lawyer, the investigative

[54] Christopher Lasch, *The Culture of Narcissism: American Life in an Age of Diminishing Expectations* (New York: W. W. Norton, 1991)

[55] See Rogers M. Smith, *Civic Ideals: Conflicting Visions of Citizenship in U.S. History* (New Haven, CT: Yale University Press, 1997).

[56] Robert Bellah, Richard Madsen, William M. Sullivan, Ann Swidler, and Steven M. Tipton, *Habits of the Heart: Americans in Search of Themselves* (New York: Harper & Row, 1985), p. 43.

journalist, the corporate whistle-blower, or the solo crime buster. The contexts may have altered but the mythic characteristics of self-reliance and individual action have not diminished in America's popular imagination. These cultural archetypes share a hybrid status of isolates operating within a public sphere. In doing so, they offer the appealing paradox of being located *within* society but not compositionally *of* it. Despite the scale of America's culture, it nevertheless maintains an individualistic outlook that can offer refuge and repose to those who value the privacy of anonymity, and who wish to be alone but not apart from humanity.[57] Such a milieu can also offer the space within which individuals can exercise their freedom of conscience in order to engage critically with current orthodoxies and injustices.[58] This kind of context gives rise to a positive construction in which the individual is seen to fulfil the promises of American society by constituting both the agency and beneficiary of a progressive and increasingly emancipated society.

On the other hand, individualism can also legitimize a critical and negative perspective of American society in which the individual stands as a symbol of what is being lost, or unfulfilled, or corrupted. The nobility and heroism of the self-possessed individual pitted against a hostile landscape of nature or modernity can be portrayed as a reference point for that which is claimed to be no longer present. This kind of individualism is fuelled by anxiety and suspicion, resentment, and at times by active dissent. Individualism in this context is a form of sanctuary and defiance. It is closely associated with an acute distrust of contemporary conditions and relies upon an idealized conception of an individualistic past to act as a standard by which to condemn the present. Later in this study, it will be shown how both the positive and the negative variants of individualism can be particularly powerful agents of political mobilization. But before proceeding to review these and other effects of the fusion of liberty and the individual, it is necessary first to examine the relationship between personal freedom and the wealth of the New World.

---

[57] See Jonathan Franzen, *How To Be Alone: Essays* (New York: Picador, 2003).

[58] For an incisive commentary on the relationship between individualism and dissent, see Edward Hoagland, 'The American Dissident: Individualism as a Matter of Conscience', *Harper's Magazine*, August 2003.

3

Wealth

INTRODUCTION

American society is not noted for its poverty of action and achievement. On the contrary, enrichment is a signature trait of American culture and one that is characteristically associated with the pursuit and security of private property. Material wealth has not only been integrally linked to the founding ideals and narrative themes of the republic, but has also been central to the principles, methods, and objectives of government. The right to acquire and to own property has been privileged in America as a fundamental feature of citizenship and this has led to profound consequences for the nature of civil society and the remit of public policy. The theme of wealth being appropriated and protected by the natural rights attributed to individuals has served to shape conceptions of personal liberty and also to define the values, identity, and internal dynamics of an expansionist social order. Wealth and the organization of social life through property draw upon, and are informed by, many other American values. By the same token, the principle of property rights contributes to, and cultivates those values. It can even be plausibly asserted that the rights of property acquisition and security have a dominant position over other sources of principle and legitimacy.

ORIGINS

The inception of the United States was marked by an act of liberation from the British Empire. This process of political independence coincided with, and was to a significant extent driven by, a form of economic liberation impelled by the drive to remove the crown's feudal claims to the chief source of wealth in the New World. The colonial disputes had been at the heart of the Americans' conflict with Britain. Property rights gave focus and expression to the philosophical and constitutional currents of thought that shaped the rationale of independence.

These property-based motivations were reflected not only in the foundational texts of the new states and the federal republic, but also in the authoritative interpretations of the new governing arrangements. For example, the Pennsylvania Constitution of 1776 stated that all men were 'born equally free and independent' and that their inherent rights included 'possessing and protecting property'. Furthermore, 'no part of a man's property [could] be justly taken from him, or applied to public uses, without his own consent, or that of his legal representatives'.[1] Political tensions and governmental problems were assumed to be mainly derived from property relationships. The premises guiding James Madison's constitutional design were that property rights originated from the 'diversity in the faculties of men', and that the 'protection of these faculties [was] the first object of government'.[2] To Madison, the 'most common and durable source of factions' lay in the 'unequal distribution of property'.[3] The key to good government was to acknowledge that there would always be a variety of propertied and unpropertied interests with 'different sentiments and views'.[4] The coexistence and 'regulation of these various and interfering interests' represented the 'principal task of modern legislation'.[5]

The emphasis upon property and its conjunction with individual liberty was integrally related to the seventeenth-century Whig philosophy of John Locke. In fact, it is often claimed that Locke's conception of property rights were so firmly established in American attitudes at the outset of the New World's journey into independence that it facilitated the transition of the United States into a capitalist society. There are good reasons to suppose that Locke's view of property and ownership had a palpable appeal to eighteenth-century Americans who were situated in a society that was both horizontally and vertically fluid. Locke specifically incorporated individual property rights within his overall scheme of natural law. In his view, man had a natural right to what he had produced from the land and other resources through the mixture of his own labour. Just as a man's body belonged to him, so the result of the work performed by it also belonged to him. The value of his labour, therefore, entitled him to the property produced by it. The individual ownership of property amounted to a basic right both to enjoy it and to exclude others from its possession. The theme of property underlined the operating premise in Locke's natural rights exposition: that an individual's right was synonymous with a capacity to uphold the law of nature against the intrusions of other individuals.

It is true that Locke laid down certain provisos and qualifications to this central right, which, it has been argued, did not clarify the position so much as, generate a series of insoluble problems concerning the individual's relationship with the rest of society.[6] For example, Locke proceeded from the principle that all God's creatures and creations were his property and, as such, the property entitlement each person has in relation to others is subject to the property that God has in everything. Because of this, Locke's exposition upon individual appropriation

---

[1] The Pennsylvania Constitution (1776), Articles 1, 8. See www.yale.edu/lawweb/avalon/states/pa08.htm.

[2] James Madison, 'Federalist Paper No. 10', in Alexander Hamilton, James Madison, and John Jay, *The Federalist Papers*, introduced by Clinton Rossiter (New York: Mentor, 1961), p. 78.

[3] Ibid., p. 79.   [4] Ibid.   [5] Ibid.

[6] According to Locke, the right to appropriate property is governed by the need to leave enough for the sustenance of others; by the amount that an individual can consume or exploit before the produce deteriorates; and by the extent of the property that a man can engage with his own labour.

is conditioned by a retentive regulatory interest on the part of the originating political society. It has also been claimed that Locke's concern for property has been misconstrued in that he did not confine property to external possessions. According to this view, by emphasizing that 'man has a property in his own person',[7] Locke wished to underline the proposition that each individual had the proprietorship of universal natural rights in his own possession. Such property could not be disowned; neither could it be expropriated by others. Despite the different interpretative constructions and irrespective of Locke's own true position, the fact remains that Locke's philosophy became identified with the rights of personal property and with the ethos of possessive individualism.[8]

It is evident that many eighteenth-century Americans were very much drawn to Locke. 'Most Americans...absorbed Locke's work as a kind of political gospel'.[9] His 'ideas formed an important element in the system of thought that exerted so much influence upon the Founding Fathers'.[10] The noteworthy point is that Locke's ideas were a system. They came as a package embracing such powerful themes as liberty, contract, consent, natural rights, revolution, limited government, dispersed authority, and private property. To many in the eighteenth century and in the formative years of the American republic, it was property, which was the central component of Locke's system and upon which all the other parts were dependent. Through Locke, individual liberty and property ownership came to have the same root. The ideal of individual liberty was defined and secured by the practical attribute of private property. It was because property was seen as being indistinguishable from freedom that Madison was prepared to acknowledge that government was 'instituted no less for protection of the property than of the persons or individuals'.[11]

To America's burgeoning class of merchants and entrepreneurs as well as its mass of small farmers and self-employed artisans, Locke's philosophy was influential because it conformed to the outlook and opportunities of early America. But it is seen as being more than just a set of supportive ideas, concomitant with an expanding social order. Because Locke's political philosophy was so persuasively rational, so intellectually accessible, and so practically relevant to the era of the Founding Fathers, it is widely thought to have been instrumental in setting the United States on a course of historical development, which would lead ineluctably to a capitalist order of accumulated

---

[7] John Locke, *Two Treatises of Government*, introduced by Peter J. Laslett (Cambridge: Cambridge University Press, 1967), p. 305.

[8] See C. B. Macpherson, *The Political Theory of Possessive Individualism: Hobbes to Locke* (Oxford: Clarendon Press, 1962).

[9] Carl Becker, *The Declaration of Independence: A Study in the History of Political Ideas* (New York: Peter Smith, 1933), p. 27.

[10] William A. Williams, *The Contours of American History* (New York: W. W. Norton, 1988), pp. 29–30.

[11] James Madison, 'Federalist Paper No. 54', in Alexander Hamilton, James Madison, and John Jay, *The Federalist Papers* (New York: Mentor, 1961), p. 339.

wealth, industrial organization, decentralized government, and a delimited state.[12]

Notwithstanding the leverage and authority of Lockian principles, other factors were also influential in the transformation of American society into a wealth of private possession. The 'Commonwealthman' tradition that informed so much of English radicalism in the early eighteenth century and which remained influential in late-eighteenth-century America emphasized the virtues of the reputed 'ancient constitution' of Saxon England. The Norman Conquest had allegedly shattered the idyll of Saxon liberty and replaced a system of freehold tenure, a free parliament, and a militia force with the 'yoke' of feudal tenure and baronial power. The 'Commonwealthman' tradition revived the social critiques of republican apologists like James Harrington who in *Oceana* (1656) had advocated a more equitable social order secured by a wide distribution of landed property. Since property to Harrington was synonymous with power and independence, a redistribution of property would necessarily contribute to the political stability of the republic.[13]

The importance of property to liberty was also reflected in the development of English common law. In seventeenth-century England, common law in conjunction with the development of parliamentary representation for the landed gentry fostered a highly progressive model of private landed property. This was further developed in the American colonies. Settlers proceeded upon the premise that landownership could simply be bought. Although feudal tenure remained in principle, for all practical purposes land grants and purchases were made under 'fee simple' arrangements which allowed for as near an approximation to absolute possession as permitted under common law. In contrast, settlers in the New World's French and Spanish colonies had to accommodate themselves to the principle that the lands remained by right in the direct possession of the sovereign. As such, any usage of the land continued to be closely dependent upon the feudal prerogatives of royal power.

Other factors were pertinent in the development of wealth as an organizing principle of society. The Protestant themes of work as a spiritual calling, or worldly ascetic, and of wealth as an outward sign of both individual virtue and God's grace were influential in promoting and legitimizing the accumulation of possessions. The rise of commercial, industrial, and financial interests in the late eighteenth century gave further stimulus to the contemporary liberal outlook of open markets, free trade, economic self-interest, and minimal government intervention and in the cause of wealth creation, capital aggregation, and social benefit. Significant though all these factors may have been, they were secondary to what must rank

---

[12] The definitive statement on this theme is provided by Louis Hartz, *The Liberal Tradition in America: An Interpretation of American Political Thought Since the Revolution* (New York: Harcourt Brace Jovanovich, 1955).

[13] See Caroline Robbins, *The Eighteenth-Century Commonwealthman: Studies in the Transmission, Development and Circumstance of English Liberal Thought from the Restoration of Charles II until the War with the Thirteen Colonies* (Cambridge, MA: Harvard University Press, 1959); J. G. A. Pocock, 'Machiavelli, Harrington, and English Political Ideologies in the Eighteenth Century', *William and Mary Quarterly*, vol. 22, no. 4 (1965), pp. 549–83.

as the central features of America's narrative of original wealth and extraordinary enrichment.

LAND

Land was the basis of America's wealth during its formative period from independence through to the establishment and consolidation of the republic. Law was the main source of possession at a time when American concepts and values relating to wealth were being refined into operational principles. Moreover, land was a resource in massive abundance. It not only acted as a magnet to expansionary settlement and frontier communities, but offered the prospect of a unique form of social chemistry in the form of an open-ended project of liberal replication. Instead of population pressure and scarcity exposing the imprecision and anomalies of post-revolution arrangements, the availability of land acted as a release mechanism that permitted most of the unresolved problems to remain satisfactorily unattended in the light of a progressively increasing land mass. Population movement, land purchase, and military action had pushed the jurisdiction of the United States to the Pacific and the Rio Grande by the middle of the nineteenth century. Most of the major figures in the American revolution had been heavily involved in the drive to appropriate 'virgin lands' to themselves and their estates before independence. After the break with Britain, the new elites continued to act on the model of property accumulation. It was clear during this pivotal time that how the bonanza was managed would influence the nature and course of American society.

When Thomas Jefferson became president in 1801, he wanted to use the federal government's stewardship of the territories to extend and refine his radical conception of an American democracy. In contrast to the patrician elites who favoured a natural aristocracy of landed estates, President Jefferson wanted the new lands to be distributed as widely as possible in order to secure his vision of a society of Saxon yeoman farmers with a stake in defending society and in abiding by its laws. Prior to becoming president, he had placed great emphasis on the need 'to free Virginia of laws that made inherited property unalienable. . . . He felt freedom was impossible in Europe, so long as the land was frozen in feudal molds of entail',[14] which locked land into unalterable estates of fixed inheritance. The need to open land and wealth up to a wider ownership fuelled his enthusiasm in 1803 for the Louisiana Purchase, which doubled the territory of the United States and established the basis for the subsequent expansion of America.[15] It was also

[14] Garry Wills, *Inventing America: Jefferson's Declaration of Independence* (Garden City, NY: Doubleday, 1978), p. 233.

[15] See Marshall Sprague, *So Vast, So Beautiful a Land: Louisiana and the Purchase* (Columbus, OH: Ohio University Press, 1991); Andro Linklater, *Measuring America: How an Untamed Wilderness Shaped the United States and Fulfilled the Promise of Democracy* (New York: Walker, 2002); Roger G. Kennedy, *Mr. Jefferson's Lost Cause: Land, Farmers, Slavery and the Louisiana Purchase* (New York: Oxford University Press, 2003).

Jefferson who determined that the federal government's ordinance survey should facilitate the division of land into 6 × 6 mile square sections. These could then be subdivided into 40-acre units, thereby, opening the property market to a mass of individual purchases. Further opportunities for wide distribution were afforded through the provision of part down payment and credit schemes. In 1862, the Homestead Act allowed anyone to occupy a lot of 160 acres and to keep it as long as a cabin was constructed and the land worked for five years.[16]

The cumulative effects of these devices were many and far-reaching. In some respects, they succeeded in achieving the objectives of their designers. The subcontinent was settled extraordinarily quickly through land grants and sales. Jefferson's vision of a property-owning democracy was partly realized with a profusion of small farms served by small towns. Land consumption also induced something of a social revolution. Instead of a pyramidal-vertical distribution of land holding, the United States pioneered a society that was 'created, peacefully and legally, around a horizontal model of land distribution'.[17] In doing so, it acquired the reputation of having generated 'a property-owning society never before known in history'.[18] The profusion of landed resources offered the prospect, and in many cases the physical reality, of a broad base of property ownership. In the classical republican tradition, proprietary wealth indicated a particular type of person with a distinctive background, identity, and social status. But as Gordon Wood claims, the American republic was different in that property was quickly transformed into a 'mere material possession or capital commodity'.[19] It was not simply that anyone could own property; it was that 'everyone had the right to acquire it'.[20] Moreover, property became reputedly 'the only proper democratic means for distinguishing one man from another'.[21]

Notwithstanding the multiple stakes in society afforded by landed wealth and the related development of a law-based framework of social and economic relations, the experiment of a land-induced acceleration of territorial and settlement expansion was far from being cost-free. On the contrary, it was accompanied by severe strains to the fabric of society and to the direction of the republic's historical development. For example, the Civil War was largely attributable to the tensions created over land provision and the urgency demonstrated by both sides of the conflict to displace the other's influence in the acquisition of new lands. Contrary to Jefferson's ethos, land became a commodity and source of capital in its own right leading to a market in land sales along with the development of an entire sector dedicated to credit, banking, and mortgage services. It encouraged a black economy of land speculation, landlord absenteeism, fraud, and corruption. At the same time, the aroused public appetite for land and the legitimacy attached to its forcible appropriation produced a practical and moral myopia over the position of

---

[16] See Paul W. Gates, 'The Homestead Act: Free Land Policy in Operation, 1862–1935', in Howard W. Ottson (ed.), *Land Use Policy in the United States* (Washington, DC: Beard Books, 2001), pp. 28–47.

[17] Andro Linklater, 'Life, Liberty, Property', *Prospect*, August 2002, p. 31.

[18] Ibid., p. 29.

[19] Gordon S. Wood, *The Radicalism of the American Revolution* (New York: Vintage, 1993), p. 270.

[20] Ibid., p. 270.   [21] Ibid., p. 342.

native Americans. Coercion and dispossession were seen as simply the necessary concomitants of rightful acquisition. Landed property was assumed to produce its own morality through personal ownership and legal title. Prodigious land resources, therefore, were something of a mixed blessing. They facilitated rapid settlement and dispersed ownership, but also produced serious ramifications, which continue to create problems in American society not least because of the way that prerogative property rights rooted in land-based possession continue to influence the general character of societal relationships.

EARLY EFFECTS AND CURRENT PROBLEMS

In the new republic, landed wealth generated its own criteria of social legitimacy. But in the process it also helped to assign legitimacy to other forms of wealth that could be reduced to an entitlement to personal property, or to a posited consequence of property relationships. In some areas, the authority vested in the rights attached to private property could countermand other rights even to the extent of superseding the most basic of human freedoms. The most notorious example of this prerogative afforded to property was the existence and rationalization of slavery. Whatever human characteristics slaves were assumed to possess, they were regarded as being subordinate to their primary role not only as instruments of propertied wealth, but also as actual units of property to be owned, sold, and bought as marketable commodities.

In spite of the republic's public philosophy of human rights and equality, slavery was tolerated in many areas because it was seen as an economic necessity and a social tradition. Slavery was rationalized on the grounds that slaves were racially inferior and wholly without the means to own property. The labour theory of value did not extend to slaves because they were not fully human and, therefore, neither part of civil society nor of any conception of a social contract. The institution of slavery demonstrated how the medium of property rights could turn liberal principles into a device for unmitigated social oppression and for the systematized denial of the very human rights accepted as the core values and animating principles of the republic.

Because of its potential for sectional division, the designers of the US Constitution went to great lengths to circumvent the issue of slavery. Even so, they were forced to give passing reference to the institution, in order to achieve a consensus for the new framework of government. A twenty-year moratorium was granted on any restrictions to the importation of slaves. Furthermore, in the formula for apportioning representatives and direct taxes, a slave was counted as only three-fifths of a free person. The real protection for slavery, however, lay with the general prohibition on states on passing any 'law impairing the obligation of contracts'.[22] Similar protections for property against the federal government were included in the Fifth Amendment to the Constitution.

---

[22] *United States Constitution*, Article 1, Section 10.

The constitutional status of slaves as property was underlined by the Supreme Court in the *Dred Scott* decision of 1857. In overturning the delicate political accommodation on the expansion of slavery (i.e. Missouri Compromise), the Court reiterated the central tenet that the Constitution had authorized slavery through its obligations to protect property rights. Within the logic of the premise which held that slaves had been acquired and maintained as property, the constitutional rights of their owners could not be abrogated by other parties subsequently reconfiguring the nature of that property to make it less susceptible to the normal legal protections afforded to property. This key case, which is widely regarded as having been instrumental in precipitating the Civil War, was argued out almost entirely in terms of property law. The Court concluded that the Constitution's recognition of slaves as property was simply an affirmation of an established contractual relationship:

[T]he right of property in a slave is distinctly and expressly affirmed in the Constitution.... And no word can be found in the Constitution which gives Congress a greater power over slave property, or which entitles property of that kind to less protection than property of any other description. The only power conferred is the power coupled with the duty of guarding and protecting the owner in his rights. [23]

The moral question of slavery had been a source of growing concern and even anxiety in many sectors of society, but the humanitarian and social dimensions of the institution were successively supplanted by the collective fears of property rights being derogated and of other forms property being liable to expropriation. Ultimately, the shield of private property could not withstand the depth of sectional antipathies on this issue. It took a civil war to break down the property defence of slavery. When the slaves were emancipated it was achieved through an enforced process of liberation. Their plight may have been diminished in one sense but they still continued to suffer from a property-centred society. This was most dramatically illustrated by the rise of white violence against blacks in the aftermath of the Civil War. Black 'freedmen' were no longer seen as valuable possessions to be protected as the property of others. Instead they were viewed as being merely disowned and undisciplined individuals who, when beaten or lynched, carried no property costs at all.

Another problem in the ethos of private property came with the onset of a national industrial economy. Jefferson's vision of a mainly bucolic republic of land-based wealth segmented into smallholdings was never fulfilled in a material sense. Within two generations, the balance of the economy had shifted towards manufacturing and commercial activity. By the end of the nineteenth century, advances in technology, transportation, and communications had created huge concentrations of private power and wealth. During the Civil War, the United States had 220,000 businesses. At the turn of the century, this figure had grown to over 1.1 million. Agricultural employment accounted for two-thirds of the

---

[23] *Dred Scott v. Sandford* (1857) quoted in Wallace Mendelson, *The Constitution and the Supreme Court*, 2nd edn (New York: Dodd, Mead, 1969), p. 518.

labour force in 1850. By 1900, this figure had fallen to one-third of labour force. The period witnessed the growth of corporations that offered the prospect of economies of scale in manufacturing production and capital investment. Moreover, because corporations were legally construed to be the equivalent of single individuals, their contract and property rights were protected from government intrusion. Their centralized power and social position generated the kind of political respect that is accorded to the expressions of a dominant paradigm and one with huge material resources to support its orthodoxy.[24]

This is not to say that commercial and industrial organizations were left free to operate unhindered upon a *tabula rasa* of statelessness. The business activities and property rights of corporations were often subjected to regulation by states using their extensive police powers. William Novak's work in this area underscores the depth of engagement by the states in the protection of the public interest. For much of the nineteenth century, states were highly active in regulating spheres relating to public property, public safety, and the political economy.[25] At the same time, the federal government was generating its own qualifier to the privacy of property relations. To the benefit of emerging businesses, it underwrote the development of national markets through a profusion of incentives and subsidies designed to promote the construction of various transportation and communications networks. Complex and multilayered though the economic and political development may have been during this era, its net effect was to produce unprecedented concentrations of resources under the simplifying generalization of laissez-faire dynamics, contractual freedom, and social advance.

Such was the scale and rapidity of this industrial, commercial, and financial revolution that it often overwhelmed government and regulatory structures. During the 1870s, the shift in political and legal outlooks directly challenged the traditional codes of public control. By the end of the century 'a new governmental regime was in place, and traces of the well-regulated society (past as well as contemporaneous) were being aggressively redrawn if not erased'.[26] The era heralded an entirely new social hierarchy of industrial organization that was crowned by the fabulous wealth of its entrepreneurial leaders. The emblematic extremes of the nouveau riche offered graphic affirmation of an open-ended society in which excess was not so much an incidental feature so much as a characterizing theme. The possession of wealth rationalized the making of it. Great wealth evoked notions of pushing forward the frontiers of individual autonomy and material accumulation. For example, at the end of the nineteenth century the wealth of an individual could make a significant contribution to the national economy. John D. Rockefeller's net worth at this time represented 2 per cent of the national

---

[24] See Alan Trachtenberg, *The Incorporation of America: Culture and Society in the Gilded Age* (New York: Hill & Wang, 1982), chs. 2, 3; Olivier Zunz, *Making America Corporate, 1870–1920* (Chicago, IL: University of Chicago Press, 1992); William G. Roy, *Socializing Capital: The Rise of the Large Industrial Corporation in America* (Princeton, NJ: Princeton University Press, 1999).

[25] William J. Novak, *The People's Welfare: Law and Regulation in Nineteenth-Century America* (Chapel Hill, NC: University of North Carolina Press, 1996).

[26] Ibid., p. 240.

income. During the same period, the twenty-four directors of US Steel controlled 10 per cent of America's wealth. The scale of wealth prompted one of Rockefeller's biographers to make the following observation: 'The Standard Oil Company was not, of course, a nation, but it had enough of the attributes of one'.[27]

Within such a state of social flux the imprimatur of great wealth was a demonstrable sign of status and achievement. The insecurity generated by exceptional social mobility propelled its beneficiaries into lavish forms of consumption that would reaffirm the acquisition of private property as the key indicator of social worth. If the poverty was chronic, affluence was proportionally lavish. The bloated self-hood of those who came to be known as 'robber barons' was reflected in their conspicuous consumption of everything from Roman bronzes, Merovingian jewels, Italian tapestries, and medieval armour to custom-built baronial palaces complete with coachmen and footmen in their master's personal livery. It became clear that the millionaires and monopolists of America's great leap forward had opened up an enormous gap in society. They believed their liberties to be independent of society. Some believed that the social consequences of their behaviour were utterly irrelevant. J. P. Morgan, for example, was known for his silence, his Cuban cigars, and his contempt for the public. 'I owe the public nothing', was his famous retort.[28]

According to this perspective, individual fortunes were the logical extension and chief expression of a free economy in which contractual freedom was equated with economic liberty and material progress. The momentum for exponential possession was in turn driven by the benefits of organization and output. The net effect was a social hierarchy based upon an extraordinary concentration of wealth and an ethos of heroic materialism. It could be claimed that this form of industrial organization and predatory business behaviour was tantamount to another form of slavery. It was even alleged to be crueller than slavery had been because there was no obligation to workers other than the strict terms of their contract. While slavery was hierarchical in nature, it carried with it an assumption of ordered permanence along with a notion of reciprocal bonds of mutual dependence and security. 'Wage slavery' on the other hand was impersonal, volatile, and devoid of any moral sense of conscience, duty, or limit on the part of those in positions of command.

It became increasingly evident that the economic freedom by which an employer and employee entered freely into contracts as co-equal negotiating partners was a fiction. The choice open to workers was very often either that of poorly paid work in bad and even dangerous conditions or that of penury and starvation. The problem of labour costs that were adjudged to be uneconomic was resolved simply by summarily discarding those workers who had become surplus to requirements. The encouragement of individuals to satisfy

[27] See David F. Hawke, *John D.: The Founding Father of the Rockefellers* (New York: Harper & Row, 1980), p. 163.

[28] Quoted in Matthew Josephson, *The Robber Barons: The Great American Capitalists, 1861–1901* (London: Eyre & Spottiswoode, 1962), p. 441; see also Andrew Sinclair, *Corsair: The Life of J. Pierpoint Morgan* (Boston, MA: Little Brown, 1980).

their reputedly instinctive quest for self-promotion over other individuals, combined with the derogation of the concept of society as a self-conscious and self-determining community into an agglomeration of individual appetites, reached a point where these precepts came into question. The abuses and excesses of this age of rampant individualism generated a series of reform movements that prompted some revisions to America's public philosophy to allow greater regulation of the market.

For most of the twentieth century, the relationship between the consequences of private property and the public interest claims of decentralization and democracy has been recognized as a significant pressure point in American society. By the 1930s, it was widely argued that the evolution of the modern corporation had effectively divorced ownership from control and, in the process, had created conditions under which it could be asserted that corporate property did not warrant the same level of protection as that afforded to genuinely private property.[29] In essence, the scale of corporate property and power could be said to generate a prima facie right to curtail property rights in the public interest. A number of notable incursions into corporate activity have been made by state governments and particularly by the federal government during the twentieth century. Regulatory assaults upon corporations have served to underline the principle that the legitimacy of corporate power is not solely dependent upon its property rights. The status of corporations remains contingent upon their social authority that embraces an acceptance of some measure of social responsibility, collective awareness, and government regulation.

Even though the rights of corporate wealth are no longer absolute and corporations' freedom of action has been limited, the balance of interests remains firmly weighted in favour of property. The configuration of corporate America has continued to be one of takeovers, mergers, and monopolies in the pursuit of efficiency and rationalization as protection against the insecurities of competition. The 1990s witnessed an extraordinary resurgence in business wealth. It coincided with a period of deregulation, disinflation, tax-cuts, investment incentives, and a prolonged stock market boom. As a consequence, the decade was marked by a widening gulf between those with most wealth and those with the least. In a period from the early 1940s to the late 1970s, 30 per cent of total income in the United States went to the highest 10 per cent of earners. By the end of the 1990s, that share had risen to over 40 per cent. In 1979, the average income of the highest earning 5 per cent of families was eleven times that of the lowest 20 per cent of families. In 1999, that gap had widened to a multiplier of nineteen. Even though the economy only doubled in size during the 1990s, the income and assets of the 400 wealthiest families in America grew tenfold.[30] The scale of increase in private wealth inflated

---

[29] Adolf A. Berle and Gardiner C. Means, *The Modern Corporation and Private Property* (New York: Macmillan, 1932).

[30] Figures drawn from Kevin Phillips, *Wealth and Democracy: A Political History of the American Rich* (New York: Broadway, 2002); Thomas Pikkety and Emmanuel Saez, *Income Inequality in the United States, 1913–98*, National Bureau of Economic Research, Working Paper No. W8467 (September 2001), http://www.nber.org/papers/w8467.

the shares of national income at the top end to levels unseen since the 1920s. It also coincided with the most dramatic increase in inequality since the rise of the 'robber barons' a century before.

Economic inequality is not unique to the United States amongst western industrial societies but the scale of the gap is exceptional. In the late 1990s, it has been shown that the top 0.01 per cent of income earners (i.e. 13,000 individuals) received more than 3 per cent of all the income in the United States.[31] During a period when this sector was increasing its share of the wealth, over 30 million Americans were living in poverty.[32] At a time of sustained economic growth (i.e. 1996–8), at least 10 per cent of households in eighteen states and Washington, DC, were considered by the Department of Agriculture to be 'food insecure', i.e. either going hungry or not having consistent access to good food.[33] In 2002, the number of individuals living below the poverty line was 34.6 million, which represented 12.1 per cent of the population.[34] When these poverty indicators are factored into the shares of national income, it is clear that the United States has a divide between rich and poor that is significantly larger than those encountered in Europe. By 2005, the profile on distribution had worsened still further. The US Census Bureau reported that top fifth of American households accounted for 50.4 per cent of all income in 2005. This was the largest proportion of wealth to be assigned to the top sector since the Bureau started tracking the data in 1967.

And yet, despite the magnitude of income differentials, very little public or political pressure has been exerted to reduce the gap. Numerous appeals to reformulate notions of ownership and responsibility have been made in the past, but they have always come up against the deep attachments surrounding the private and exclusionary nature of property. Herbert McCloskey and John Zaller have made a close observation of these appeals and of the lack of response generated by them in American society:

The lack of impact of these appeals on the abstract notions of private property held by American people is, however, striking. Even under the changed conditions of the industrial age, most Americans continue to adhere to the traditional conception of property as the bulwark of individual freedom and the source of economic well-being.[35]

J. K. Galbraith also notes that the disparity in incomes in the United States is 'not a matter that occasions serious dispute'.[36]

---

[31] Figures from 'Pigs, Pay and Power', *The Economist*, 28 June 2003.

[32] On average, nearly 40.9 million people were poor in a given month in 1996. By 1999, the number of people classified as poor had fallen to 34.8 million.

[33] Damian Whitworth, 'Millions of Americans "Are Going Hungry"', *The Times*, 15 October 1999.

[34] US Census Bureau, http://www.census.gov/hhes/poverty/poverty02/table1.pdf.

[35] Herbert McCloskey and John Zaller, *The American Ethos: Public Attitudes toward Capitalism and Democracy* (Cambridge, MA: Harvard University Press, 1984), pp. 139–40.

[36] J. K. Galbraith, *The Culture of Contentment* (London: Penguin, 1992), p. 26.

CONCLUSION

A residual element of the American republican tradition retains a partial suspicion of moneyed wealth. Jefferson had once warned that the citizens of the new republic were likely to forget their rights and to 'forget themselves' except in the 'sole facility of making money'.[37] As a consequence, they would 'never think of uniting to effect a due respect for their rights'.[38] But in the main, the moral legitimacy of individual wealth has far outweighed the reservations over the effects of wealth upon republican virtue and civic identity. The acquisition of wealth and the ownership of property are still taken to be the hallmark of personal energy and achievement. It is the 'stress placed on achievement in America' that fosters 'an acceptance of relatively large differences in pay among those of varying skills, responsibility, and power'.[39] Marked rises in personal fortunes are tolerated as signs of the existence of social mobility and the absence of a fixed hereditary structure of social stratification. However contentious these conclusions may be, they form a backdrop of impulses and attitudes in which conspicuous enrichment tends to be equated with reward for occupational achievement in a competitive environment.

[T]he central type of achievement is in business, manufacturing, commerce, finance; and since traditionalized social hierarchies, fixed estates, and the established symbols of hered- itary rank have had only a rudimentary development, there is a strong tendency to use money as a symbol of success. Money comes to be valued not only for itself and for the goods it will buy, but as symbolic evidence of success and, thereby, of personal worth.[40]

Surveys into the attitudes and self-image of the most affluent members of Ameri- can society complement the views of those further down the scale. Large majori- ties of the affluent assert that they originally came from poor, lower, or middle class families; that they had to work through college; and that their success was more than anything else directly attributable to a willingness to work hard.[41]

It is precisely because of this outlook that a circular dynamic presents itself. The belief in the absence of historically established reference points in American society fosters insecurities amongst even the rich which in turn produce overcom- pensatory behaviour in the search for social recognition and peer esteem. In *The Theory of the Leisure Class* (1899), Thorstein Veblen pointed out that the wealthy do not accumulate wealth in order to consume goods. On the contrary, they

[37] Thomas Jefferson, 'Notes on the State of Virginia', in Merrill D. Peterson (ed.), *The Portable Thomas Jefferson* (Harmondsworth, UK: Penguin, 1977), p. 213.

[38] Ibid.

[39] Seymour M. Lipset, *The First New Nation: The United States in Historical and Comparative Perspective* (New York: W. W. Norton, 1979), p. 326.

[40] Robin Williams, *American Society: A Sociological Interpretation* (New York: Knopf, 1963), p. 421.

[41] See the Surveys of Affluent Americans conducted for the US Trust. In particular, note that only 10 per cent of respondents cited inheritance as their source of wealth in 'The "Roots" of the Affluent', US Trust, http://www.ustrust.com/ustrust/html/knowledge/WealthManagementInsights/SurveyofAffluentAmericans/RootsoftheAffluent.html.

engage in 'conspicuous consumption' in order to display their accumulation.[42] Those who criticize this aspect of American society draw attention to what they see as the 'civil religion of money'[43] and the excessive concern that is generated by the need to display it in the form of compounded possession and accredited social position.[44] The alacrity with which the super-rich disclose the magnitude of their personal fortunes to those publications like *Fortune* and *Forbes* that produce lists of individual wealth is a reflection of the competitive drive for cultural standing in a milieu of wealth creation.

The equanimity with which economic inequality is regarded in American society is drawn from several contributory factors. These include the continuing salience of the 'American dream' of upward mobility in which the opportunity for self-improvement is accepted as a given feature of social life. In a survey for Fox News in 1998, for example, 72 per cent of respondents agreed with the proposition that if individuals work hard, they can still achieve the American dream of making a decent living, owning a home, and sending their children to college.[45] Only one-third of Americans thought it unlikely that they would one day be rich.[46] Tolerance of inequality and even of the poorest becoming proportionally poorer is linked to the perception of American society being dynamic and fluid.

These attitudes coincide with increasing evidence of a decline in social mobility during the period of sustained economic grounds in the 1990s which was expected to herald a surge of intergenerational transfers into the middle classes. Instead, the strongest economy for thirty years not only failed to restore upward social mobility to the levels achieved in the 1940s and 1950s but actually witnessed a further decline in the movement from the impoverished sector to improved economic and social positions.[47] The various research indicators on the effects of the 1990s boom, and of the period of growth since the 2001 recession, have led Paul Krugman to conclude that 'the distribution of income in the United States has gone right back to the Gilded Age levels of inequality'. Krugman continues:

Very few children of the lower class are making their way to even moderate affluence. This goes along with other studies indicating that rags-to-riches stories have become vanishingly rare, and that the correlation between fathers' and sons' incomes has risen in recent decades. In modern America, it seems, you're quite likely to stay in the social and economic class into which you were born.[48]

---

[42] Thorstein Veblen, *The Theory of the Leisure Class: An Economic Study of Institutions* (London: Allen & Unwin, 1925).

[43] See Lewis H. Lapham, *Money and Class in America: Notes and Observations on Our Civil Religion* (London: Pan, 1989).

[44] For example, see Paul Fussell, *Class: A Guide through the American Status System* (New York: Touchstone, 1983), chs. 1, 2, 5.

[45] Fox News survey quoted in Irwin Stelzer, 'Land of Plenty Feels no Envy as Rich get Richer', *Sunday Times*, 8 March 1998.

[46] Ibid.

[47] For an effective review of recent research in this field, see Aaron Bernstein, 'Waking Up from the American Dream: Meritocracy and Equal Opportunity are Fading Fast', *Business Week*, 1 December 2003.

[48] Paul Krugman, 'The Death of Horatio Alger', *The Nation*, 5 January 2004.

And yet notwithstanding the evidence of inequality popular opinion continues to be attracted to the idea of prospective wealth.

In their study of the repeal of the estate tax which was the most progressive element of the US tax system, Michael Graetz and Ian Shapiro (2005) demonstrate how a measure to limit the transfer of inherited wealth aroused a popular movement to abolish it.[49] The campaign to come to the aid of the wealthiest in American society drew effectively upon the need to preserve the fortunes of those who have yet to make them. A Time/CNN poll on the estate tax issue in 2000 demonstrated just how persuasive such an appeal can be in an aspirational culture. The poll revealed that 39 per cent of Americans believed that they were either in the wealthiest 1 per cent or would be there 'soon'.[50] This level of perceived potential was also discernible in the rise of what the Bush administration termed the 'investor class'. This referred not merely to the expansion in the sector of small investors during the Reagan, Bush, and Clinton years, but to the surge in the numbers who believed that through their ownership of limited assets and investments they had entered a different class. A Zogby poll in March 2005 found that as many as 46 per cent of respondents identified themselves as part of the 'investor class'.[51] It was consistent with this background that the popular and successful campaign to diminish the estate tax was referred to as 'a triumph of hope over envy', as well as 'a popular recognition of the very real successes of the 1980s and 1990s'.[52]

Another factor in the maintenance of the American epic of temporary privation in the cause of ultimate achievement is provided by the legendary narratives of assimilation. The culture of immigration and successive waves of achievement in which initial poverty is accepted as a rite of passage constitutes a powerful component to the conception of America as a rising ladder of prosperity, status, and achievement. Like those who are rich, the poor are regarded as the chief architects of their own position. In a market-driven society, skills, talents, energies, and merits are assumed to fund their own level in the equilibrium of inputs and rewards within the social order. The persistently impoverished are interpreted as persistent failures. Culpability is primarily personal. Class analyses depending upon concepts of fixed social orders and structural hierarchies continue to have little leverage in a society with a strong middle class identity, rising middle class standards of living, and a largely pro-business public discourse.

In a survey for the American Enterprise Institute, the pattern of responses showed that compared to Britain where large majorities believe it remains a class society, 70 per cent of Americans refute the assertion that their society is

[49] Michael Graetz and Ian Shapiro, *Death by a Thousand Cuts: The Fight over Taxing Inherited Wealth* (Princeton, NJ: Princeton University Press, 2005).

[50] Quoted in Nancy Gibbs and Michael Duffy, 'Bush and Gore: Two Men, Two Visions', *Time*, 6 November 2000.

[51] John Zogby, 'Investors for Bush', *Opinion Journal from the Wall Street Journal*, 15 March 2005, http://www.opinionjournal.com/editorial/feature.html?id=110006425.

[52] Amity Shlaes, 'Death Tax—the Great Cross-Party Unifier', *Financial Times*, 18 April 2005.

one of 'haves' and 'have-nots'.[53] Accordingly, in the same survey, 75 per cent of Americans oppose legislation limiting the amount of money any individual can earn.[54] The neo-liberal orthodoxies of contemporary American society have served further to reinforce an attitudinal structure that has always been hostile to programmes of overt redistribution. The public tolerance or ambivalence in respect to the presence of wealth does not mean that the prerogatives of the property always triumph over public values. However, what it does mean is that alternative values will always have to confront this attachment to private property and to take account of the conditioning features of its fundamentalist prescriptions.

The promise of property provides much of the cohesion to an aspirational society. Property rights continue to force the pace in respect to fostering or justifying derivative rights against incursions upon property. For this reason, the discretion of state governments to impose planning or environmental restrictions upon private property remains very limited. The use of firearms by individuals defending their own property against intruders is largely accepted on the grounds that property ownership implies the further right to protect property, even at the cost of life. The instinctive legitimacy of property rights has in many instances led to a property-based ethos being extended to whole areas of public life through an inertial drift. This can produce outcomes that are open to serious dispute on ethical grounds. Biotech companies, for example, have developed genetically modified organisms for the purposes of commercial development and, in the process, have claimed exclusive patent rights over subspecies of organic life. Property rights have even been extended to the human genome where genetic signatures have been patented by genomic companies.[55] Their acquisitions raise questions over the extent to which individuals effectively have ownership of their own gene base.

Private property continues to evoke close associations with freedom, individualism, and republicanism.[56] Nevertheless, the legal privileges and public legitimacy afforded to property do have limits and it is in the political sphere that the definition and location of those limits are argued out in a continual debate over the relationship between private possession and the public interest.

---

[53] Everett Carll Ladd and Karlyn Bowman, *Attitudes toward Economic Inequality* (Washington, DC: AEI Press, 1998).

[54] Ibid.

[55] For the issues raised by these developments, see A. M. Chakrabarty, 'Patenting of Life-Forms: From a Concept to a Reality', in David Magnus, Arthur L. Caplan, and Glenn McGee (eds.), *Who Owns Life?* (Amherst, NY: Prometheus, 2002), pp. 17–24; Ari Berkowitz and Daniel J. Kevles, 'Patenting Human Genes: The Advent of Ethics in the Political Economy of Patent Law', in Magnus, Caplan, and McGee (eds.), *Who Owns Life?*, pp. 75–98; Mark J. Hanson, 'Patenting Genes and Life: Improper Commodification?', in Magnus, Caplan, and McGee (eds.), *Who Owns Life?*, pp. 161–74; Wangari Mathai, 'The Linkage between Patenting of Life Forms, Genetic Engineering and Food Insecurity', http://www.genet-info.org/-documents/AfricaGMOsPatents.pdf.

[56] See Richard Pipes, *Property and Freedom* (New York: Vintage, 2000), pp. 228–36, 240–81.

4

Democracy

INTRODUCTION

Democracy is a notoriously complex and variable value. The meaning of democracy is invariably dependent upon processes of historical experience and cultural construction. The United States occupies a distinctive position in this matrix of contingent interpretation and mediation. American democracy is widely perceived, particularly in the United States itself, as amounting to a quintessential model of democratic order. The ubiquitous claim is that the United States is the one nation authentically dedicated to the principles and practices of democracy. Just as democracy has been a generic characterization of American society, so the United States is often depicted as providing the signature expression of democracy in the contemporary world. Because of this ascribed symbiosis, democracy in America is subjected to the continual strain of grand presumptions and sweeping claims.

Democracy is usually accepted not only as a central article in the American faith, but one that is wholly consistent with other tenets of the creed such as liberty, individualism, property, and equality. The appeal and authority of democracy are rooted in conceptions of American history and social development. The United States has traditionally taken pride in being the country of the heroic 'common man' whose sense of rank and history had been eroded by the experience of the New World leaving its recipients free from traditional sources of authority. As a result, American democracy is often portrayed as a corollary to the type of open-ended freedom that threw large numbers of people into circumstances of literal self-government. Democracy in America, therefore, is commonly conceived to be the natural outgrowth of America's own peculiarly informal and egalitarian conditions in a society much given to the belief that its institutional arrangements have been the inevitable and self-evident consequences of its own extraordinary historical and geographical condition. Against this backdrop, democracy in America has become something of a truism and one that is necessarily derived from the Founding Fathers and their Constitution, which in the succeeding years came to be identified as the source of America's 'deliberative democracy'.[1]

---

[1] See Cass R. Sunstein, *Designing Democracy: What Constitutions Do* (New York: Oxford University Press, 2001), pp. 44–5, 239–43; Cass R. Sunstein, 'Still the Framers' Constitution?', *Common Place*, vol. 2, no. 4 (July 2002), http://www.common-place.org/vol-02/no-04/author/.

And yet, in the same way that democracy itself is in reality a highly complex phenomenon, so America's association with it is far from being as simple and straightforward as it is so often reputed to be. On the contrary, it is afflicted by a profusion of qualifications, tensions, and contradictions. In fact it can be said that the United States probably exemplifies, rather than clarifies, the problematic features endemic in the operation of liberal democracy. The United States typifies the contingent and multidimensional nature of democracy's meaning both as an abstract principle and as a functioning system of government. In effect, the United States offers a particular, and conspicuous, expression of democracy, but at the same time its very prominence as an apparent exemplar of democratic organization throws into relief the inherent ambiguities and even the divisive properties of the democratic ethos. In 2001, a prestigious set of interpretive essays was published on the history of American political development and the character of state building and policy formulation during the course of the republic. Significantly, the collection was gathered together under the title of *Contesting Democracy*.[2] It underlined the fact that American society is distinguished not only by a profound and intuitive attachment to democracy as a defining feature of American identity, but by a series of tensions over the differing implications of such a social creed.

DEMOCRATIC LOGIC AND REPUBLICAN ANXIETIES

To the extent that it is true to say that American political arrangements and attitudes are derived from the Founding Fathers and their federal Constitution, then it is equally true to say that those gentleman scholars, lawyers, and merchants of the eighteenth century bequeathed a distinctive ambivalence over democracy to later generations of Americans. Whilst it would be quite wrong to ascribe a uniform outlook to so varied a group of men, it is true to say that amongst them was a strong element of distrust and even disquiet over the prospect of America developing into a democracy. The Founders' misgivings over democracy were based on the traditional belief that democracy was a social order separate from, and different to, aristocracy and monarchy. Democracy was a component of society. Like the other two components, it was dangerous to allow any one social order to become dominant.

According to classical theory, 'simple governments' were invariably oppressive governments. A preponderance of monarchy would lead to despotism, a preponderance of aristocracy would produce oligarchy, and a preponderance of democracy would run into violent anarchy. In order to prevent pure constitutional forms from degenerating into tyranny, classical theorists like Plato, Aristotle, and Polybius advocated the incorporation and mixture of the different social orders into government. This arrangement would maximize the virtues of each, while

---

[2] Byron E. Shafer and Anthony J. Badger (eds.), *Contesting Democracy : Substance and Structure in American Political History, 1775–2000* (Lawrence, KS: University Press of Kansas, 2001).

minimizing their respective vices. It was Polybius in particular who pushed mixed government to the point where it became a deliberate institutional device to achieve a balance between the three classes of society. In effect, the three social units were to be directly translated into government through separate class-based institutions. Each would share in the process of government and at the same time promote a genuine mixture of class interests in government.[3]

These Greek- and Roman-based theories were revived by Machiavelli in the early sixteenth century, and from then on they increasingly became the currency of reform and dissent in the political and constitutional turbulence of the seventeenth and eighteenth centuries. The term 'mixed government' suffered from a host of different interpretations supporting a variety of positions and lending legitimacy to a diverse set of social and political developments. It was complicated by the emergence of the 'separation of powers' doctrine which was similar with respect to its emphasis upon the dynamics of interaction, but different in that it depended upon separate institutions geared to abstract governmental functions, instead of on explicitly class-based institutions representing a mixture of social orders. Over time, these two doctrines became closely bound up with one another so that the notion of separate governmental functions came to have class connotations, while mixed government's ancient rationale of balance came to characterize the underlying theme of separated institutions.[4]

By the eighteenth century, balance had become the touchstone of constitutional propriety and authority even though it was by no means certain what balanced government consisted of or how it might be achieved and maintained. In only very general terms was the composition of constitutional balance understood and agreed upon. What was sufficiently certain to become dogma was that in one form or another the British constitution's pastiche of powers, branches, institutions, and traditions had developed into a stable equilibrium which reputedly accounted not only for Britain's national and commercial success, but for the preservation of her subjects' liberties.[5]

The American colonists were part of this British culture and believed their own freedoms to be derived from the British constitution's genius for balance and stability. John Adams, for example, described the British constitution as 'the most perfect combination of human powers in society which finite wisdom has yet contrived and reduced to practice for the preservation of liberty'.[6] This was no empty flattery but representative of a common and genuine conviction. Such was their belief in balanced government that the concept became a key instrument in the colonists' opposition to Britain in the revolutionary crisis. It is clear from the

---

[3] F. W. Walbank, *Polybius* (Berkeley, CA: University of California Press, 1972).

[4] W. B. Gwyn, *The Meaning of the Separation of Powers: An Analysis of the Doctrine from its Origins to the Adoption of the United States Constitution* (New Orleans, LA: Tulane University Press, 1965); M. J. C. Vile, *Constitutionalism and the Separation of Powers* (London: Oxford University Press, 1967); Garry Wills, *Explaining America: The Federalist* (New York: Penguin, 2001), chs. 11, 12.

[5] Vile, *Constitutionalism and the Separation of Powers*, ch. 5.

[6] Quoted in Bernard Bailyn, *The Ideological Origins of the American Revolution* (Cambridge, MA: Belknap Press, 1967), p. 67.

Declaration of Independence that the Americans were challenging Britain on the basis of balanced government by claiming that George III and the King's party in Parliament had disrupted the equilibrium of the British constitution and, in doing so, had undermined the traditional liberties of the colonists.[7]

Even during the period after independence when the new states were experiencing their initial euphoria over popular sovereignty, legislative supremacy, and contractual consent, they were nevertheless unable or unwilling to extricate themselves from the sanctions and prescriptions of balanced government. Confronted with the prospect of constructing new frameworks of government, Americans were aware of the need to reconcile the avowed simplicity of their new republicanism with the ambiguity and complexity of balanced government. Their concern for the heritage of equilibrium was reflected in their acute consciousness of the absence of the additional social orders (i.e. aristocracy and monarchy) required to construct a balanced government.[8]

The new state constitutions expressed that tension. They incorporated the radical principles of increased manhood suffrage, majority rule, natural rights, government by consent, and a rigid separation of powers, which was made thoroughly compatible with the central feature of a dominant legislature. However, the constitutions were also notable for their retention of many of the structural features associated with colonial government. Not the least of these was the principle of bicameralism. In the end, most states followed the dictates of antiquity or the sanctions of the British constitution and established upper chambers, the membership of which usually required some form of additional property qualification.[9] Even if these chambers did not compromise the principle of legislative supremacy, they certainly qualified the principle of majority rule. Furthermore, they facilitated the reintroduction of the old balanced government framework of internal checks and balances. Thomas Jefferson, for example, declared the need for Virginia to have a second chamber made independent in some way from the people. It is true that in two states, Pennsylvania and Virginia, the democratic principle of a single chamber was adhered to, but even here the chief American advocate of unicameralism, Benjamin Franklin, hoped for and trusted in the emergence of a natural aristocracy of public-spirited and virtuous men who would check the factionalism and self-interest of the assembly.

It is clear that the old norm of balanced government still exerted a very strong influence in the reputedly radical period following the War of Independence.

---

[7] It should be noted that many radical Whigs and dissenters in Britain also supported the American cause on precisely the same grounds. See Kevin Phillips, *The Cousins' Wars: Religion, Politics, and the Triumph of Anglo-America* (New York, NY: Basic Books, 1999), chs. 3–6.

[8] See Correa Walsh, *The Political Science of John Adams: A Study in the Theory of Mixed Government and the Bicameral System* (New York: Knickerbocker Press, 1915), pp. 37–59, 74–9; C. Bradley Thompson, *John Adams and the Spirit of Liberty* (Lawrence, KS: University Press of Kansas, 2002). For more on the specific linkages between the Founders' task of constitutional formulation and the influences of Machiavelli and Poybius, see John Adams, *A Defence of the Constitutions of Government of the United States of America (1787–1788)*, Da Capo Press Reprint edn (New York: Da Capo, 1971), chs. 27, 30, 31.

[9] Gordon S. Wood, *The Creation of the American Republic, 1776–87* (Chapel Hill, NC: University of North Carolina Press, 1969), pp. 207–22.

Moreover, this influence was to become even stronger, so that by 1787 when the constitutional convention met at Philadelphia, the Founding Fathers regarded the enhancement of constitutional checks and balances as one of their highest priorities. Although the new constitution continued to emphasize the separation of powers as the structural basis to government, the principle's rationale was modified into a system of contending powers more closely related to the old self-regulatory format of mixed government.[10] If Americans in their newly independent states saw 'themselves creating mixed republics, with the democratic element, the lower assemblies playing a very dominant role',[11] then the Founding Fathers' constitution 'was a retreat from the democratic efforts of the states'.[12] To Madison, small republics, with their tight linkage between majority opinion and governmental power, were tantamount to factions, which like any other faction could not be trusted to serve the general welfare.

The Founding Fathers were no democrats in the modern sense of the word. For the most part, they shared the same anxiety experienced by many of their countrymen: that 'democracy was far from "noble"—it was unspeakable, unthinkable, and accursed'.[13] The record of the state governments during the 1780s had served only to heighten these concerns. During that period, several assemblies had felt the full force of hosts of small property owners who were underprivileged and ill-educated. Many of the founders believed individual liberty to be at bay in the ominous shadow of these restive masses. 'The people it seemed were as capable of despotism as any prince; public liberty was after all no guarantee of private liberty'.[14] Indeed, in conditions of insurgent democracy, republican liberties were more likely to be abused and usurped. Even the sober-minded James Madison had no doubt that pure democracies 'have ever been spectacles of turbulence and contention; have ever been found incompatible with personal security or the rights of property; and have in general been as short in their lives as they have been violent in their deaths'.[15]

And yet, the formal origin and basis of political authority in the new states was clearly founded upon those principles of social contract and popular consent formally expressed in the Declaration of Independence. Madison summed up the problems confronting the Founders in the following way: 'To secure the public good and the private rights against the danger of . . . a [majority] faction, and

[10] See Arthur O. Lovejoy, 'The Theory of Human Nature in the American Constitution and the Method of Counterpoise', in Arthur O. Lovejoy, *Reflections on Human Nature* (Baltimore, MD: Johns Hopkins University Press, 1961), pp. 37–65.

[11] Gordon S. Wood, 'Democracy and the Constitution', in Robert A. Goldwin and William A. Schambra (eds.), *How Democratic is the Constitution?* (Washington, DC: American Enterprise Institute, 1980), p. 8.

[12] Jon Roper, *Democracy and Its Critics: Anglo-American Democratic Thought in the Nineteenth Century* (London: Unwin Hyman, 1989), p. 35.

[13] Max Savelle, *Seeds of American Liberty: The Genesis of the American Mind* (Seattle, WA: University of Washington Press, 1948), p. 321.

[14] Wood, *The Creation of the American Republic*, p. 410.

[15] James Madison, 'Federalist Paper No. 10', in Alexander Hamilton, James Madison, and John Jay, *The Federalist Papers*, introduced by Clinton Rossiter (New York: Mentor, 1961), p. 81.

at the same time to preserve the spirit and the form of popular government, is then the great object to which our inquiries are directed'.[16] Those Founders who were classicists knew that the new republic would need the restraining hand of an aristocratic elite and the virtue and public-spiritedness of America's patrician families. They also knew that there was no chance of formally investing such a social order to perform that stabilizing function in an ostensibly egalitarian world. But the many Founders who were also men of the Enlightenment knew that individual liberty was not merely the logical precondition and objective of rational government. It was also deemed to be a universal natural right and, therefore, an iron law of human existence theoretically immune to the mere will and opinions of others. Practice might be made to conform to theory through the judicious application of 'political science' by which the systematic empirical knowledge of government and political forces might be deployed to enable government both 'to control the governed; and in the next place oblige it to control itself'.[17] Madison relied on what he termed 'auxiliary precautions'[18] to keep government in its place by a combination of structural fragmentation, institutional dynamics, and formal limitations.

A COMPOUND REPUBLIC

A complex political and historiographical debate has been established over the extent to which the founding of the American republic represented either a break with pre-existing republican traditions, or a continuation of these themes in a revised form. Whether or not the American Revolution, and its aftermath, can be characterized as a 'republican synthesis' remains a matter of interpretive conjecture.[19] What is clear is that the framework of government established by the Founding Fathers produced a number of significant variations to the classic premises of republican thought. For example, instead of relying upon the basic unit of a city state with a citizenry in close proximity to itself, the designers of the constitution pressed for a federation of states with a strong national government that would incorporate all citizens under a separate and a universal conception of consent and identity. In place of a direct or pure democracy, the Founders embraced with enthusiasm the functional need for a system of representation for the transmission of views and preferences. Representative government was

[16] Madison, 'Federalist Paper No. 10', p. 80.

[17] James Madison, 'Federalist Paper No. 51', in Hamilton, Madison, and Jay, *The Federalist Papers*, p. 322.

[18] Ibid.

[19] See Bernard Bailyn, *The Ideological Origins of the American Revolution* (Cambridge, MA: Belknap, 1967); Wood, *The Creation of the American Republic, 1776–87*; Robert E. Shalhope, 'Toward a Republican Synthesis: The Emergence of an Understanding of Republicanism in American Historiography', *William and Mary Quarterly*, 3rd series, vol. 29, no. 1 (January 1972), pp. 49–80; Robert E. Shalhope, 'Douglass Adair and the Historiography of Republicanism', in Douglass Adair, *Fame and the Founding Fathers*, ed. Trevor Colbourn (New York: W. W. Norton, 1974), pp. xxv–xxxv.

claimed to be essential to governing a large society, which the Founders were intent upon increasing in scale and, thereby, rendering it even more dependent upon the logistics of representation.

Republics had a tradition of merging the public and the private spheres. In the American construction of republicanism, the rule of law was emphasized to the point where the private realm was protected against incursions from the public domain of government. Classical republican doctrines had a strong association with civic virtue, but the American founders were not prepared to depend upon the presence or development of virtue for the maintenance of their republic. Instead of public-spirited disinterest, they depended upon a multiplicity of active interests operating through a governmental framework based on consent. Even if virtue could not be assured it was intended that vices would cancel each other out to the benefit of the public interest.[20] Within the construction of the US Constitution lay a suspicion and even a dread of raw democracy displacing the refinements of republicanism. To Madison, it was evident that republican identity could not rely upon civic virtue because factionalism and the impulse to subvert the public interest for private gain were 'sown in the nature of man'.[21] Accepting the premise that the causes of factions could not be removed without destroying the liberty upon which they depended, Madison reasoned that the solution lay in controlling their effects. The Founders' views reflected the widespread anxiety of the post-colonial elites towards the threat of democratic disorder.

The framers of the Constitution were well aware that the political and intellectual ferment of the revolutionary era had been conditioned to a greater or lesser extent by currents of republican thought that stretched back to the traditions of English dissent in the seventeenth and early eighteenth centuries—and arguably back to the republican doctrines of Machiavelli and Polybius.[22] They were also conscious that the Anti-Federalists would use republican traditions to allege that the federal constitution amounted to a usurpation of state power by a distant, disconnected, and centralized national government with no civic foundation or intimate dependency upon the people. These opponents remained wedded to the notion of an active and open public sphere in which governance would be based less upon an institutional structure and more upon the outcomes of a public discourse.[23] They were also aware that many of the state constitutions retained key elements of small republican governance (e.g. multiple executives, elected judges,

[20] Garry Wills, *Explaining America: The Federalist*, chs. 13, 22–4, 28, 29.

[21] Madison, 'Federalist Paper No. 10', p. 79.

[22] Caroline Robbins, *The Eighteenth-Century Commonwealthman: Studies in the Transmission, Development and Circumstance of English Liberal Thought from the Restoration of Charles II until the War with the Thirteen Colonies* (Cambridge, MA: Harvard University Press, 1959); J. G. A. Pocock, 'Machiavelli, Harrington, and the English Political Ideologies in the Eighteenth Century', *William and Mary Quarterly*, 3rd series, vol. 22, no. 4 (October 1965), pp. 549–83; Lance Banning, The *Jeffersonian Persuasion: Evolution of a Party Ideology* (Ithaca, NY: Cornell University Press, 1980); William J. Connell, 'The Republican Idea', in James Hankins (ed.), *Renaissance Civic Humanism: Reappraisals and Reflections* (Cambridge: Cambridge University Press, 2000), pp. 14–29.

[23] Herbert J. Storing, *What the Anti-Federalists Were For: The Political Thought of the Opponents of the Constitution* (Chicago, IL: University of Chicago, 1981); Saul Cornell, *The Other Founders:*

office rotation check). The same republican impulse would later lead to the states adopting measures like the initiative, referendum, and recall in the cause of greater community rule.

The founding elites of the late eighteenth century accepted the political prudence of taking republicanism into account. The Founders therefore acknowledged, or were constrained to give recognition to, the contemporary resonance of such republican themes as civic participation, public integrity, and the moral fulfilment of a self-governing community. And yet, they remained fearful of the democratic implications of classical republicanism set within a context of revolutionary ferment, social agitation, high political expectations, and a generation steeped in ideological engagement over natural rights and consent. While the designers of the federal constitution were politically adept enough to realize the need for self-government through consent to be established as a foundational principle, they were at the same time intent upon confining its effect to the tenets of their own conception of republicanism.

Gordon Wood argues convincingly that the Founders and their supporters 'had to work within the egalitarian and populist currents flowing from the revolution'.[24] Accordingly, they employed the language of democracy and rooted all the offices and institutions of the state in 'the people'. Sean Wilentz also points out that despite their public indictments of popular excess, when 'the delegates convened in secret session, the temper of the times seeped into the room' with the result that they invented a structure of government that 'would not permit those natural aristocrats to speak only with each other'.[25] Nevertheless, their architecture remained conditioned by their anxieties over the logical foundations of the state. The objective was to limit the potential for democratic indiscipline through sober republicanism. This was to be secured by balanced institutions all ostensibly derived from the people, but whose effect would be to disaggregate democracy, to direct the state's power to that of self-limitation, and to permit the emergence of a natural aristocracy in the guise of democratic leadership. Within this remit, democracy had to be configured as an affliction with the same moral standing as corruption.

Pure democracy was widely equated with civil unrest and popular agitation, which in turn was regarded as being synonymous with a form of republican corruption. *The Federalist Papers* contain many negative allusions to democracy. With such a form of government, the danger to liberty would come as much from the 'use of violent remedies' taken by government as from the 'ferment and outrages of faction and sedition in the community'.[26] Legislative assemblies could not be entrusted with the public welfare because their memberships were

---

Anti-Federalism and the Dissenting Tradition, 1788–1828 (Chapel Hill, NC: University of North Carolina Press for the Omohundro Institute of Early America, 1999).

[24] Wood, 'Democracy and the Constitution', p. 16.

[25] Sean Wilentz, *The Rise of American Democracy* (New York: W. W. Norton, 2005), pp. 32, 39.

[26] Alexander Hamilton, 'Federalist Paper No. 21', in Hamilton, Madison, and Jay, *The Federalist Papers*, p. 140.

'sufficiently numerous to feel all the passions which actuate a multitude'.[27] The greater the size of an assembly, the greater would be the probability not only of an 'ascendancy of passion over reason', but also of an increasing component of members with 'limited information' and 'weak capacities'.[28]

On the same principle, the more multitudinous the representative assembly may be rendered, the more it will partake of the infirmities incident to collective assemblies of the people. Ignorance will be the dupe of cunning, and passion the slave of sophistry and declamation.[29]

In designing the federal constitution, it was therefore important to secure a 'republican remedy for the diseases most incident to republican government'[30]– namely the 'mischiefs of faction'[31] and the prospect of government authority being usurped by violent democratic forces fired by a 'rage for pauper money, for an abolition of debts, for an equal division of property, or for any other improper or wicked project'.[32]

Madison's solutions for a constitutional settlement were in many respects putative responses to the threat of direct democratic pressures. It was hoped that by channelling popular opinion through elected representatives, their wisdom and experience would produce enlightened and just decisions based upon the true interest of the nation. The small size of the Senate as well as the higher qualifications for senatorial office offered the prospect of patrician sobriety. A strong presidency also indicated a need for central stability. The system of checks and balances, the federal–state tension, the principle of bicameralism, the concept of a large sprawling republic of fragmented interests also contributed to the crowd control requirements of popular sovereignty.

Republicanism would be the antidote to the factionalism and majoritarianism of a democracy that could turn liberty into oppression. It was Madison who underlined the threats emanating from liberty as well as those engendered by power: 'liberty may be endangered by the abuses of liberty as well as by the abuses of power'.[33] It remains significant that although the Founders theorized over 'the people' as a unitary entity and as the source of constitutional sovereignty, they never made direct appeals to the people for mass political action. From the 'multiple traditions' standpoint, this omission was strategic in nature as it prevented any disruption in the established hierarchies of civic status or in the prevailing patterns of contemporary social exclusion. But even though many sectors of the population were legally marginalized into inferior status or into propertyless

---

[27] James Madison, 'Federalist Paper No. 48', in Hamilton, Madison, and Jay, *The Federalist Papers*, p. 309.

[28] James Madison, 'Federalist Paper No. 58', in Hamilton, Madison, and Jay, *The Federalist Papers*, p. 360.

[29] Ibid., p. 360.   [30] Madison, 'Federalist Paper No. 10', p. 84.

[31] Ibid., p. 81.   [32] Ibid., p. 84.

[33] James Madison, 'Federalist Paper No. 63', in Hamilton, Madison, and Jay, *The Federalist Papers*, p. 387.

non-persons,[34] the allusions to 'the people' as a unified abstraction, nevertheless, had a prudential appeal. In such circumstances, the usage of 'the people' in elite discourse was instrumental in resolving different claims to post-revolutionary legitimacy. Edmund S. Morgan argues that the notion of popular sovereignty was taken up primarily as a useful fiction that allowed the few to remain in a position to govern the many. By associating governance with liberty for all, the Founders were able to secure consent for the constitutional scheme of central powers and disaggregated institutions.[35] In this light, it is equally noteworthy that the term democracy never appears in the US Constitution.

AMERICAN DEMOCRATIZATION

The Founders' quest to integrate the abstraction of popular sovereignty into a republican framework of political aggregation and governmental boundaries was a finely wrought device. It succeeded in establishing an organization of governing institutions and in providing them with an operational rationale and legitimacy. The price of such an achievement, however, was a bequest of anomalies and ambiguities surrounding the meaning and value of democracy. The subtleties and nuances inherent in the Founders' creation were highly effective in producing a consensus capable of installing a new system of government. At the same time, their opaque relationship to popular pressures was to be a source of rich political dispute in a society driven by rapid expansion, immigration, and the mass movement of people.

During the nineteenth century, the United States changed from a mainly agrarian society with ideals of a settled social order to an urban industrialized flux of mass production and consumption. In what had been a socially driven transformation, democracy had become synonymous with the popular and egalitarian nature of societal development. Democracy was assumed to be the leitmotif of a developing, mobile, and open-ended society. Nevertheless, the sheer scale and energy of the compulsive drive to develop resources, create wealth, and form settlements and cities generated a host of questions relating to the nature of the relationship between republicanism principles, constitutional government, and democratic forces.

According to this perspective, democracy can be taken as a generic characterization of America's development into an enlarged nation state and mass society. In America, the term democracy, and its usages, have a collective property that can incorporate a profusion of experiences and conditions into an allegedly unified process of emancipation and self-government. Accordingly, democracy can be taken as an extension of individual autonomy, a form of social self-determination,

---

[34] Gary B. Nash, *The Unknown American Revolution: The Unruly Birth of Democracy and the Struggle to Create America* (New York: Viking, 2005), pp. 366–456.

[35] Edmund S. Morgan, *Inventing the People: The Rise of Popular Sovereignty in England and America* (New York: W. W. Norton, 1989), pp. 239–87.

a challenge to established hierarchies, an instrument of nation building, a de facto cultural condition, and a set of prescriptive ideals and norms guiding the direction of social change. In such a context, American history can be, and repeatedly has been reduced not only to a narrative of the democratic process but also to a recurrent theme of successive democratization. Just as the rise of the United States as a continental power coincided with the intensification of democratic values and arrangements, so one acquired an interdependency with the other, and with it a tendency to equate democratic change with the constitutional continuity.

The early period of the republic was marked by a general movement away from the patrician influence of the tidewater elites towards the weight of humanity in the backcountry and by those who, by force of emigration, were pushing the frontier outward to the West. The Founding Fathers, the Federalists, and the Anti-Federalists had all operated on the premise that voting rights should be dependent upon freehold property ownership. The availability of public land for settlement now set in motion a process in which the franchise was widened until property qualifications carried so little sense of distinction that they quickly became redundant. During the 1830s, nearly all property-based qualifications to voting were phased out, leaving most white men able to vote in local, state, and national elections. The irreversible shift away from the traditional centre of gravity in American society allowed for the development of mass-based and election-oriented parties. The implications of such an adjustment quickly became evident in the 'Jacksonian Revolution' which heralded a step change in the development of organized participation within the structure of American democracy.

Andrew Jackson was certainly no Virginian patrician. He was not even of Anglo-Saxon stock. He was a westerner with Scotch-Irish parentage and in 1829 he became the first geographical and social outsider to secure the presidency. It was he who established the 'spoils system' by which a president's supporters were rewarded with offices, thereby, rendering the federal government more responsive to changing patterns of public support. Jackson also encouraged the development of the 'long list', which transformed large numbers of state and local offices into elective positions. These changes, together with the popular election of members of the Electoral College, the onset of party conventions, and the development of national campaign organizations, appeared to set American politics on a course of democratic progression.[36] Political parties in the early republic played a particularly important role in defining and maintaining a national arena of political authority. They were instrumental in channelling conflict into the political structures instead of allowing it to degenerate into insurrection or secession. The parties also accommodated and encouraged the rise of mass politics and the

[36] See John H. Aldrich, *Why Parties?: The Origin and Transformation of Political Parties in America* (Chicago, IL: University of Chicago Press, 1995), ch. 4 ; Robert V. Remini, *Andrew Jackson and the Course of American Democracy 1833–45*, vol. III (New York: Harper & Row, 1984), chs. 8, 16–18, 22; Robert V. Remini, *The Legacy of Andrew Jackson: Essays on Democracy, Indian Removal, and Slavery* (Baton Rouge, LA: Louisiana State University Press, 1988), chs. 3–5, 9, 11; Harry L. Watson, *Liberty and Power: The Politics of Jacksonian America* (New York: Noonday Press, 1990), chs. 6, 8.

demands for popular mechanisms of consent and participation. In performing these roles, party-based democracy became an integral part in state building and national integration.[37]

The speed and orderliness of such a transformation can imply the existence of a continuity between the intensification of democracy and the Founders' original design of government. Just as new states were formed from territories through the procedures enumerated in the federal constitution, so it could be argued that the constitution facilitated the transition to democracy. Because the Founders had created a medium through which democracy could develop into a prevailing ethos, so the original architects could be retrospectively credited with having laid the foundations of a proto-democracy that, with time, progressed into a developed democracy.

The susceptibility of those foundations to a social transformation of democratic attitudes and impulses is examined to full effect in Alexis de Tocqueville's *Democracy in America*. It was during the Jacksonian period that de Tocqueville collected the material for his landmark assessment of the New World's experimentation with a social system in which both a monarchy and an aristocracy were conspicuously absent. This exposition upon the scale and viability of democracy within an evolving order became a classic text on the challenge of democracy both to the notion of traditional hierarchy and to the assumptions of individual freedom.

In contrast to European societies, America lacked the social differentiation for any recognizable form of mixed government. According to de Tocqueville, democracy had spread throughout society in a process of unified cause and effect. His social and cultural observations of the sweep of American democracy remain pertinent today not just because of their considered accuracy but because of their evaluative content. While acknowledging the highly developed forms of individualism, de Tocqueville also alluded to a darker underside of personal freedom in such an unstructured context. This was the phenomenon of isolation and, with it, a propensity and even need to defer to the force of common opinion. In America, de Tocqueville observed that it is 'of the very essence of democratic governments that the empire of the majority is absolute; for in democracies, outside the majority there is nothing that resists it'.[38] As a consequence, the majority frequently displayed 'the tastes and the instincts of a despot'.[39]

In effect, de Tocqueville was seeking to demonstrate the existence of an illiberal logic to a democracy in action. He believed that democracy was inclined to a form of unrestrained coercion because no alternative source or centre of power was available that could contain democracy to within a set of preformed

---

[37] William N. Chambers, 'Party Development and the American Mainstream', in William N. Chambers and Walter D. Burnham (eds.), *The American Party Systems: Stages of Political Development* (New York: Oxford University Press, 1967), pp. 3–32.

[38] Alexis de Tocqueville, *Democracy in America*, translated, edited, and introduced by Harvey C. Mansfield and Delba Winthrop (Chicago, IL: Chicago University Press, 2000), p. 235.

[39] Ibid., p. 250.

boundaries. Democracy had an unavoidable predisposition to favour the interests of the greater number over those of the few:

The majority in the United States therefore has an immense power in fact, and a power in opinion almost as great; and once it has formed on a question, there are so to speak no obstacles that can...delay its advance, and allow it the time to hear the complaints of those it crushes as it passes.[40]

Just as individualism could be transformed into a prudential conformism, so through the dominion of majoritarianism, democracy had the potential for an omnipotence to rival the absolutist regimes of Europe. It is true that de Tocqueville was writing for a French audience with a willing scepticism towards the excesses of democracy. It is equally the case that de Tocqueville 'took many of his views from the last remnants of the Feds, who supplied him with what he thought necessary to democracy, a moderating counter to extreme egalitarianism'.[41] Accordingly, he tended to adopt the critical attitude of the Federalists towards the behaviour and policies of leaders like Jackson. De Tocqueville regarded such leaders as political opportunists who shamelessly subordinated themselves to majority positions. In his defence, it can be said that de Tocqueville's portrayal of American democracy approximated to a new democratic order brought into existence by mass political parties. Michael Schudson points out that citizen behaviour under these conditions was governed more by symbolic acts of ethnocultural or communal affiliation than by exercises in reasoned choice.[42] At the same time, it has to be acknowledged that the basis upon which de Tocqueville made his analysis was partial from the point of view of those social categories which were not included in the contemporary conception of citizen-voters (e.g. women, slaves, tenant farmers, indigenous populations). Notwithstanding the question of the author's possible bias, his work stands as both a signature study of the adaptability of the republic's early political structures to the rise of democracy, and a pioneering inquiry into the problematic aspects of democratic rule.[43]

By the time of the Civil War (1861–5), the strains over sectionalism and territorial expansion had become defined as a crisis of popular sovereignty. The cause of saving the union and the Constitution was widely depicted as the need to preserve the integrity of a democratic polity. The legitimacy of popular government became the value to which President Abraham Lincoln appealed as the basis for mobilizing the North against the South's secession, and for seeking to create a point of reconciliation to the two sides. The triumph of the Union forces allowed the conflict to be defined according to the North's preferred criteria and

---

[40] Ibid., p. 237.

[41] Garry Wills, 'Did Tocqueville "Get" America', *The New York Review of Books*, 29 April 2004.

[42] Michael Schudson, *The Good Citizen: A History of American Civic Life* (New York: Free Press, 1999).

[43] See Jack Lively, *The Social and Political Thought of Alexis de Tocqueville* (Oxford: Clarendon Press, 1962), chs. 3–5; Larry Siedentop, *Tocqueville* (Oxford: Oxford University Press, 1994), chs. 3, 4; Harvey C. Mansfield and Delba Winthrop, 'Editors' Introduction', in De Tocqueville, *Democracy in America*, pp. xliii–lxxvii.

the peace to be commemorated as a victory for the American nation and for American democracy. Although Lincoln had remained wary over the use of the term democracy, he had been instrumental in defining the causes and objectives of the Civil War in terms of unrepresentative and illiberal minorities being confronted by the legitimacy of majority rule rightly motivated by principle and justice. It was a battle over what could, and what could not, be legitimately conceived as popular sovereignty. During this pivotal period in American development, the claims of popular self-rule were explicitly attached to liberal principles. Against the backdrop of secession and slavery, the fusion of democratic forms and liberal ethics was secured in such a way that each was assumed to be the agency of the other.

At the outset of his presidency, Lincoln had asserted that the only alternatives to popular sovereignty were either anarchy or despotism. He reiterated the value and meaning of rightful government: 'A majority held in restraint by constitutional checks and limitations, and always changing easily with changes of popular opinions and sentiments, is the only true sovereign of a free people'.[44] During the Civil War, Lincoln's iconic address after the Battle of Gettysburg (1863) alluded to the Union army's efforts to ensure that 'a government of the people, by the people, for the people, shall not perish from the earth'.[45] Lincoln's public credo established that it was popular sovereignty which had been at stake in the nation's turmoil. The union was defended and secured in the name of such a sovereignty. The government and society to emerge from the war were reconfigured as a functioning national democracy rightfully dominant and now secure from any serious challenge. Popular government had been cast as the victim. Now it was the victor in a newly nationalized democracy. Thereafter, the themes of nation and democracy became inseparable from one another.

The Civil War's climactic affirmation of popular self-rule allowed democracy to become fixed as a guiding motive and central objective of American development. Democracy now acquired a constructed continuity stretching back to the social ease of frontier communities and to the early Congregationalist assertions of local ecclesiastical self-rule. As part of this process, the Founders became the retrospective forefathers of American democracy. The sense of a continuum stretched into the future as well. Emergent problems were interpreted as democratic in nature. As such, they required democratic solutions usually in the form of devices to enhance the processes of democracy. Just as democracy became an assimilative summation of experience embracing a compendium of positive values and attitudes, so it also achieved the status of being both an instrument and a state of existence. Governmental reforms were, and continue to be, couched as forms of democratic progression. As a result, advances in democratic techniques or arrangements have

---

[44] President Abraham Lincoln, 'Inaugural Address, 4 March 1861', in Kenneth M. Dolbeare (ed.), *American Political Thought*, 2nd edn (Chatham, NJ: Chatham House, 1989), p. 305.

[45] President Lincoln, 'The Gettysburg Address', Gettysburg, Pennsylvania, 19 November 1863, http://showcase.netins.net/web/creative/lincoln/speeches/gettysburg.htm.

been proposed and accepted on the basis of established democratic norms, and on the need to strengthen, or to reclaim, the foundations of democracy under altered conditions.

The history of the United States, therefore, has been punctuated by periods of intense democratic consciousness and reform set within a gradualist process of democratic consolidation. These signal changes have included enactments to establish the direct election of senators, to introduce devices to enlarge the scope of direct democracy (e.g. primary elections, initiatives, referenda, and recalls), to extend the franchise to women and to those over 18 years in age, to reduce electoral inequities relating to minorities, and to reform the sources and usages of campaign contributions in the electoral process. The evolving nature of America's signature democracy has become a testament to its unfinished condition. It leads James Fishkin to make the following evaluation:

American democracy continually recreates itself in the name of one vision or another of the democratic idea.... Changing institutions so that, somehow, they better speak for the people has been a continuing American preoccupation, a distinctly American process. Ironically, democratic change has itself been a source of continuity in our political identity.[46]

As a result of this history and these developments, the United States can be perceived as a society engaged in a course of exponential democratic growth. Democracy is not only preeminent in the language and concepts relating to the nature, origins, and purposes of political authority in America, it dominates the visible appearances and tangible arrangements of government. Democracy has become an axiom of American identity:

Most citizens assume that the American political system is consistent with the democratic creed. Indeed, the common view seems to be that our system is not only democratic but perhaps the most perfect expression of democracy that exists anywhere.... To reject the creed is to reject one's society and one's chances of full acceptance in it—in short, to be an outcast.... To reject the democratic creed is in effect to refuse to be an American.[47]

After two world wars and a prolonged cold war in which the United States identified itself as the cradle and citadel of democracy with a mission to make the world 'safe for democracy',[48] America has emerged today with the conviction that it is not only the first modern democracy but also the supreme exemplar of a functioning democracy in a modern mass society.

---

[46] James Fishkin, *The Voice of the People: Public Opinion and Democracy* (New Haven, CT: Yale University Press, 1995), p. 17.

[47] Robert Dahl, *Who Governs? Democracy and Power in an American City* (New Haven, CT: Yale University Press, 1961), pp. 316–17.

[48] President Woodrow Wilson, 'War Message', p. xxx, 2 April 1917, http://www.lib.byu.edu/%7erdh/wwi/1917/wilswarm.html.

PROBLEMATIC PROPERTIES

The United States' identity as the model democracy has not been devoid of controversy and challenge. The special prominence and asserted qualities of American democracy have attracted a profusion of critiques both in respect to the internal state of the US democratic system and in relation to what America demonstrates about the performance and viability of democracy in general. In effect, if the United States is an exemplar of democracy, it is necessarily also an exemplar of its problematic properties. Probably the most common indictment relates to the state of the connection between liberty and democracy. Democracy was assimilated into a largely liberal culture in which government would be conducted through consent but would also be expected to protect the market relations and property rights of a liberal social order. This would be a democracy constrained and conditioned by the prevailing public ethos in which it functioned. By the same token, it was a democracy that protected and promoted liberal values in an apparently seamless symbiosis. Nevertheless, the conjunction between individual spheres of action and the public sphere of democratic force is always a highly problematic relationship which never achieves a state of final settlement. The United States is no exception. Its politics reverberates to the sound of disputes over the nature and location of the boundary between individual rights and legitimate claims of government acting in the name of popular sovereignty. The friction generated by the tectonic movement between these two conceptual and normative forces will be a recurrent theme of this study.

Many additional issues emanate from America's attachment to democracy. These also impact upon other ideas and their compounds in the composition and conduct of American politics. Enumerated below are some of the main critiques of American democracy. These have been particularly significant either in the formation, or in the service of, political ideas that have shaped debate, organized political movements, and even dissuaded citizens from political activity.

Critique 1: Thin Democracy

The way that American democracy has developed to serve the interests of a highly individualized, and even atomized, society is said to have produced a 'thin democracy' geared to the introversion of liberal priorities. The chief casualty of such a development is the social dialogue and community identity of a qualitatively 'strong democracy'. The latter is characterized by a more citizen-centred way of life in contrast not only to the limited and periodic engagement of electoral activity but to the formalism of representative government.[49] In this light, the magnitude of the electoral process does not make a qualitative difference to the end result. It results in a form of protective democracy in which social inequities are

[49] Benjamin R. Barber, *Strong Democracy: Participatory Politics for a New Age* (Berkeley, CA: University of California Press, 1986).

preserved; bureaucratic continuities are maintained; representational claims are confined; and where democracy is reduced to the procedural requirements allowing for a choice of governments rather than a device for self-government.[50] Far from promoting the expansion of public participation in decision-making, American democracy is criticized for encouraging civic passivity on the part of individuals who no longer have any serious objection to being marginalized by unelected leaders and experts promoting the public good.[51]

Critique 2: Institutional and Electoral Immobilism

In one respect, American democracy fosters an array of choice through the profusion of candidates and the multiplicity of elections. But in another respect, such choices can be seen as either self-negating in their aggregate effect or essentially false in nature. Multiple elections can be said not only to divide voters from workable solutions to public issues, but also to separate voters from each other by channelling electoral choice into irreconcilable strands of left and right positions that in effect contracts the political agenda and disfranchises the electorate.[52] The outcome can be one of institutional deadlock, 'divided government', and systemic dysfunction which 'prevent the nation from settling the questions that most trouble it'.[53] This in turn induces a deepening distrust over the conduct and utility of politics.[54] The prolonged and confusing nature of successive election campaigns is also cited as a cause of voter fatigue and citizen disorientation:

What could be said of an election process that is easily the world's most time consuming, cumbersome, and expensive? What words would apply to a system that saddles citizens with unnecessary burdens, teases them into activity before brushing them aside, and arbitrarily excludes many of them—sometimes whole states—from having a meaningful voice in its outcomes.[55]

---

[50] See Joseph A. Schumpeter, *Capitalism, Socialism, and Democracy*, Harper Colophon edn (New York: Harper & Row, 1975), chs. 11, 12.

[51] See John R. Hibbing and Elizabeth Theiss-Morse, *Stealth Democracy: Americans' Beliefs and How Government Should Work* (New York: Cambridge University Press, 2002).

[52] See E. J. Dionne, Jr., *Why Americans Hate Politics: The Death of the Democratic Process* (New York: Touchstone, 1992).

[53] Ibid., p. 11.

[54] See Joseph S. Nye, Philip D. Zelikow, and David C. King (eds.), *Why People Don't Trust Government* (Cambridge, MA: Harvard University Press, 1997); James Sundquist, *Constitutional Reform and Effective Government* (Washington, DC: Brookings Institution, 1986); Morris Fiorina, *Divided Government*, 2nd edn (Boston, MA: Allyn & Bacon, 1996); Byron E. Shafer, 'The Two Majorities and the Puzzle of Modern American Politics: Economic Development, Issue Evolution, and Divided Government, 1955–2000', in Shafer and Badger (eds.), *Contesting Democracy: Substance and Structure in American Political History, 1775–2000*, pp. 225–49.

[55] Thomas Patterson, *The Vanishing Voter: Public Involvement in an Age of Uncertainty* (New York: Knopf, 2002), p. 184.

Critique 3: Disproportional Representation

In a democracy that lays such weight upon representation, the American system is criticized not only on compositional grounds in terms of under-representation (e.g. women, blacks, and other minorities) and over-representation (e.g. small states in the Senate and the Electoral College), but also on numerical grounds with an ever-widening ratio of population to representatives. The anomalies are legion but the ratio of constituents to the House of Representatives of the United States is illustrative. In 1900, the 391 members of the House represented 76 million American citizens. By 2000, the 435 House members had come to represent over 281 million Americans. The ratio of representative to the represented had grown from 1:194,000 to 1:647,000. In sum, the weight given to representative inequity as a principle of minority protection leads ineluctably to a system of substantive inequality set within a context of democratic principle.[56]

Critique 4: Party Deficit

The two main parties are genuinely national organizations but they fail to produce sufficient cohesion, or to generate sufficient popular mobilization, that would allow them to claim electoral mandates and to enact organized programmes of policy. National political parties are recognized as important constituent features of democratic governance but equally they are criticized for failing to fulfil their potential for structuring government through programmatic cohesion and organized consent. Moreover, political parties are generally considered to be in long-term decline, leaving representative democracy to be increasingly disoriented by candidate-centred appeals for office and the onset of the 'permanent campaign'.[57]

Critique 5: Differential Responsiveness

American democracy is regularly accused of being insufficiently responsive to public needs and social problems. By the same token, it is also accused of being too responsive to popular opinion and to volatile shifts in public mood at the expense of long term democratic values.[58] But undoubtedly the most common indictment

[56] See Robert A. Dahl, *How Democratic is the American Constitution?* (New Haven, CT: Yale University Press, 2002); George C. Edwards, III, *Why the Electoral College Is Bad for America* (New Haven, CT: Yale University Press, 2004).

[57] Martin P. Wattenberg, *The Rise of Candidate-Centered Politics* (Cambridge, MA: Harvard University Press, 1992); Dick Morris, *The New Prince: Machiavelli Updated for the Twenty-first Century* (Los Angeles, CA: Renaissance, 1999); Norman J. Ornstein and Thomas E. Mann (eds.), *The Permanent Campaign and Its Future* (Washington, DC: AEI Press, 2000); George C. Edwards, III, *Governing by Campaigning: The Politics of the Bush Presidency* (New York: Longman, 2006).

[58] See Robert Nisbet, 'Public Opinion against Popular Opinion', in Bruce Miroff, Raymond Seidelman, and Todd Swanstrom (eds.), *Debating Democracy: A Reader in American Politics* (Boston, MA: Houghton Mifflin, 1997), pp. 115–25.

is that democratic government in America is excessively responsive to the society's major power centres and vested interests at the expense of the public interest.[59] The relationship between corporate resources within the electoral process and the composition of political agendas, policy outcomes, and legal action arouses particular concern.[60]

Critique 6: Civic Disengagement

American democracy may be distinctive in respect to the number of elective offices and the volume of elections and referenda, but it is also distinguished by poor rates of participation, low turnouts, weak party identification, and a low level of civic action.[61] Moreover, strong correlations exist between on the one hand poor turnout and participation rates, and low income and educational levels on the other.[62] Similarly, it is claimed that the profusion of advocacy groups and professionally managed agencies have displaced the traditional membership activities of civic groupings, leaving an eroded institutional space for community action in public affairs.[63]

Critique 7: Countermajoritarian Traditions

The constitution's checks and balances can be said not merely to restrict the formation of majority factions, but to resist and distrust any majorities that might form. The system's capacity to foster jurisdictional disputes, procedural delays, structural disaggregation, and even institutional deadlock allows minorities to frustrate even veto majority coalitions. The structural and procedural complexity of the legislative process together with the additional centres of political negotiation and challenge provided by the executive and judicial branches, and by the federal system mean that the location of democratic accountability is diffused and therefore indeterminate.

[59] See Frances F. Piven and Richard A. Cloward, *Why Americans Still Don't Vote: And Why Politicians Want It That Way* (Boston, MA: Beacon, 2000); Michael J. Parenti, *Democracy for the Few* (Belmont, CA: Wadsworth, 2001).

[60] Elizabeth Drew, *The Corruption of American Politics: What Went Wrong and Why* (Woodstock, NY: Overlook Press, 1999); Anthony Gierzynski, *Money Rules: Financing Elections in America* (Boulder, CO: Westview, 2000); Mark Green, *Selling Out: How Big Corporate Money Buys Elections, Rams Through Legislation, and Betrays Our Democracy* (New York: HarperCollins, 2002).

[61] See Seymour M. Lipset, 'Malaise and Resiliency in America', *Journal of Democracy*, vol. 6, no. 3 (July 1995), pp. 4–18; Martin P. Wattenberg, *Where Have All the Voters Gone?* (Cambridge, MA: Harvard University Press, 2002).

[62] See Raymond E. Wolfinger and Steven J. Rosenstone, *Who Votes?* (New Haven, CT: Yale University Press, 1980); Ruy A. Teixeira, *The Disappearing American Voter* (Washington, DC: Brookings, 1992); Sidney Verba, Kay Schlozman, and Henry E. Brady, *Voice and Equality: Civic Voluntarism in American Politics* (Cambridge, MA: Harvard University Press, 1995).

[63] See Theda Skocpol, 'Unravelling from Above', *The American Prospect* (March–April, 1996), pp. 20–5; Theda Skocpol, *Diminished Democracy: From Membership to Management in American Civic Life* (Norman, OK: University of Oklahoma Press, 2003).

Critique 8: Procedural Democracy

It can be claimed that America's advance into universal manhood suffrage came too quickly. In effect, it preceded the nation's transformation into an industrialized mass society. As a result, democratic politics has retained both its associations with the notion of landed citizenship and its discomfort with opening up fundamental questions into the structure of contemporary society and the distribution of power within a capitalist economy. The emphasis upon rights of participation, the machinery of the voting system, and the formalities of decision-making provide grounds for complaint that American democracy is primarily procedural rather than substantive in nature, i.e. that democracy is embodied more in the input of electoral and decision-making processes rather than in the substance of the output.

Critique 9: Government by Minority Interests

Over the course of much of its historical development, American democracy is reputed to have been instrumental in the repression of various minorities on the basis of several categories of ascribed inequality (e.g. race, ethnicity, religion, gender). In more recent times, the balance is widely perceived to have swung towards a disproportionate accommodation of previously marginalized groups. The tolerant attitude to minorities is thought to generate an excessive minority consciousness that can lead interests to regard themselves, and to behave, as beleaguered minorities requiring special protection and particularized benefits. As a consequence, the 'silent majority', or vacuous majority, becomes exploited by coercive minorities. This in turn is said to produce a dynamic in which increasing numbers of groups press for increasingly more sectional benefits. Governments seek to appease such minorities in order to stay in office. The price of such appeasement, however, is a declining ability on the part of government to make priorities, to manage the economy, and to prevent its own fragmentation. This dynamic is claimed to produce an expansion of governmental activity on the one hand and a damaging reduction of governmental authority on the other.[64]

Critique 10: Constitutional Dependency

The United States is widely regarded as being synonymous with democracy to the extent that its democratic credentials are considered to be central to its identity. And yet, the foundation and operation of its democracy are 'based on an avowedly pessimistic conception of human nature, assuming that people cannot be trusted

---

[64] Theodore J. Lowi, *The End of Liberalism: Ideology, Policy, and the Crisis of Public Authority* (New York: W. W. Norton, 1969); Samuel P. Huntington, 'The Democratic Distemper', in Nathan Glazer and Irving Kristol (eds.), *The American Commonwealth—1976* (New York: Basic Books, 1976), pp. 9–38.

with power'.[65] Paradoxically, the distinctive element of the American system of democracy is 'not how democratic it is but rather how undemocratic it is, placing as it does multiple constraints on electoral majorities'.[66] This might be termed a constitutional democracy but it raises the issue of whether the constitution is framing democratic behaviour or confining it to a form of conduct with which it cannot be entrusted to comply through its own volition.

Critique 11: Post-Electoral Syndrome

Although elections are central to the claims and legitimacy of representative democracy, government actions have become only marginally related to the outcomes of elections. In addition to the fact that most seats are safe and that membership turnover of legislative seats is normally very low, the policy impact of elections are confined in scope through the action of political incrementalism, budgetary inertia, policy networks, log-rolling arrangements, and court decisions. Furthermore, it is alleged that in an increasingly 'post-electoral' era, alternative arenas and forms of political conflict are marginalizing the role of elections in the political process. Political forces can increasingly exert pressure through judicial proceedings, legislative investigations, and media revelations to achieve significant effects without recourse to campaigns of voter mobilization.[67] As a result, elections have become 'less effective as ways of resolving political conflicts. . . . Today's political struggles are frequently waged elsewhere, and critical policy choices tend to be made outside the electoral realm'.[68]

Critique 12: The Irrational Crowd

Some observers view the public as composed of rational individuals with coherent policy preferences, a developed sense of the public good, and a capacity for collective deliberation based upon reason operating within a community of rights and obligations.[69] This benign conception of democracy, however, is

[65] Fareed Zakaria, 'The Rise of Illiberal Democracy', *Foreign Affairs* (November/December 1997), p. 39.

[66] Ibid.

[67] Benjamin Ginsberg and Martin Shefter, *Politics by Other Means: Politicians, Prosecutors, and the Press from Watergate to Whitewater* (New York: W. W. Norton, 1999).

[68] Theodore J. Lowi and Benjamin Ginsberg, *American Government: Freedom and Power*, 5th edn (New York: W. W. Norton, 1998), p. 264.

[69] See James Q. Wilson, 'Interests and Deliberation in the American Republic, or Why James Madison Would Have Never Received the James Madison Award', *PS: Political Science and Politics* (December 1990), pp. 558–629; Benjamin I. Page and Robert Y. Shapiro, *The Rational Public: Fifty Years of Trends in Americans' Policy Preferences* (Chicago, IL: University of Chicago Press, 1991), chs. 1–3, 10; James S. Fishkin, *Democracy and Deliberation: New Directions for Democratic Reform* (New Haven, CT: Yale University Press, 1991), chs. 6, 8; Benjamin R. Barber, 'An American Civic Forum: Civil Society between Market, Individuals, and the Political Community' (prepared for the SPPC Conference on 'Community, Individual, and the State', Palo Alto, CA, October 1994); Bruce Ackerman and James

often marginalized by an altogether darker vision of democratic realism which is marked by a fundamental scepticism towards the competence and judgement of the citizenry in arriving at its decisions.[70] Although the United States is characterized by an undisputed cultural attachment to the principle of popular sovereignty, it has nevertheless exhibited signs of caution over the capacity of individual citizens to engage attentively and reasonably with contemporary issues.

In the late nineteenth and early twentieth centuries, progressives were renowned for their advocacy of popular democracy. However, many of them were more impressed by its instrumental value as a reform device rather than by its intrinsic value in allowing the maximum autonomy for popular opinion. These reservations often produced an equivocation over the full implications of using democratic pressures to secure social change. In particular, their middle class 'misgivings toward immigrants, labor unions and women's suffrage accentuate[d] the boundaries within which many progressives hedged their democratic faith'.[71] The drive for rational social action in the public interest was not always seen as being consistent with democratic processes. Walter Lippmann believed that 'average citizens . . . had lost mastery of their minds; they could no longer make the kind of informed, rational judgments required to make popular sovereignty work. Only the rule of experts, of men like himself, could render government in the United States effective and just'.[72] This jaundiced view of democracy is reiterated by more contemporary analysis which suggests that democratic values, civil liberties, and political tolerance exist to much higher degree in the elite sectors of society than they do amongst the general public. The operation and ethical integrity of democracy, therefore, is said to be dependent upon the disproportionate social influence of elites and elite attitudes.[73]

The fear of impulsive, prejudicial, and irrational attitudes having an immediate bearing upon decision-making has been revived in response to the recent trends towards direct democracy in the form of petitions, referenda, and citizen action politics.[74] These processes underline the enduring problem relating to the wisdom

---

S. Fishkin, 'Deliberation Day', in James S. Fishkin and Peter Laslett (eds.), *Debating Deliberative Democracy* (Oxford: Blackwell, 2003), pp. 7–30.

[70] For a review on both sides of the debate, see Elliot Abrams (ed.), *Democracy: How Direct? Views from the Founding Era and the Polling Era* (Lanham, MD: Rowman & Littlefield, 2002).

[71] Peter G. Filene 'An Obituary for "The Progressive Movement"', *American Quarterly*, vol. 22, no. 1 (1970), p. 27.

[72] Gary Gerstle, 'The Protean Character of American Liberalism', *The American Historical Review*, vol. 99, no. 4 (October 1994), p. 1055.

[73] See Herbert McCloskey, 'Consensus and Ideology in American Politics', in Raymond E. Wolfinger (ed.), *Readings in American Political Behaviour*, 2nd edn (Englewood Cliffs, NJ: Prentice-Hall, 1970), pp. 381–410; W. Russell Neuman, *The Paradox of Mass Politics: Knowledge and Opinion in the American Electorate* (Cambridge, MA: Harvard University Press, 1986), chs. 1–3, 8.

[74] See D. Magleby, 'Direct Legislation in the an States', in David Butler and Austin Ranney (eds.), *Referendums around the World: The Growing Use of Direct Democracy* (Washington, DC: AEI Press, 1994), pp. 218–57; Shaun Bowler, Todd Donovan, and Caroline Tolbert (eds.), *Citizens As Legislators: Direct Democracy in the United States* (Columbus, OH: Ohio State University Press, 1998).

and consent of the masses.[75] The central question that is posed is whether the issues are 'too complex or too muddy and voters will have neither the time nor expertise to be able to vote intelligently. This is especially the case given that they seemingly cut off from the familiar voting cues of party and incumbency when it comes to voting on the very wide range of propositions'.[76] While the reactions to this inquiry can vary considerably, it is significant that the issue of direct democracy brings to the surface substantive questions relating to the depth of democratic attachment, the integrity of democratic processes, and the utility of self-government.

CONCLUSION

These complaints and critiques reveal considerable confusion over the composition of American democracy, i.e. not only what American democracy consists of but what it should consist of to be both authentically American and authentically democratic. This leads to a number of differing perspectives as to the type of democracy that is actually present in the United States. American democracy is variously characterized as a liberal democracy, a constitutional democracy, a federal democracy, a national democracy, a representative democracy, a participatory democracy, a popular democracy, a majoritarian democracy, and a pluralist democracy. Sometimes the separate properties of these constructions will be seen as being compatible with one another. But very often they will not. At this point, conflicts can arise, for example, between the rights of local democracy and the authority of national democracy, or between the force of the majority and the democratic privileges of a minority. Disagreement and debate can be said to be 'crucial to democracy not just because it leads to better decisions but because it helps to create better citizens'.[77] But democratic debate also extends to jurisdictional and demarcation disputes within the processes of democracy as well as to the meaning and principles of a democratic order.[78]

Democracy implies an interpretive license to lay claim to what democracy is and how it should be applied both in the performance of democratic polity and in the democratic performance of the polity. This is particularly so in the United States where the imprimatur of democracy is so central to the acquisition and maintenance of legitimacy. Political debate is suffused with references to the means and ends of democracy as well as to its forms and essences, and its

---

[75] Shaun Bowler and Todd Andrew Donovan, *Demanding Choices: Opinion, Voting, and Direct Democracy* (Ann Arbor, MI: University of Michigan Press, 1998), chs. 1, 2, 9.

[76] Shaun Bowler and Todd Donovan, 'California's Experience with Direct Democracy', *Parliamentary Affairs*, vol. 53, no. 4 (October 2000), p. 649.

[77] Bruce Miroff, Raymond Seidelman, and Todd Swanstrom, 'Introduction', in Miroff, Seidelman, and Swanstrom (eds.), *Debating Democracy*, p. 2.

[78] For example, see Daniel Lazare, 'America the Undemocratic', *New Left Review*, vol. 232 (November/December 1998), pp. 3–40.

ideals and operational realities. The axiomatic assumptions of democracy in the United States can distort, and even conceal, the nature of the governing process. Political and social phenomena can be defined and redefined as derivatives, or as reconfigurations, of an intrinsic democratic existence. The connection between the perceived state of American democracy and the integrity, and even security, of American society remains a very close one. So much so, that critiques with titles like *Diminished Democracy, Downsizing Democracy, Democracy Matters,* and *American Democracy in Peril* constitute salutary warnings about the state of the social fabric in the United States.[79] This does not mean that the calls for change in the name of democracy are heeded because the prescribed solutions themselves are contested on democratic grounds. While the medium of democratic discourse remains pre-eminent, it does not afford any universally accepted criteria for arriving at solutions to the problems posed.

What is evident from the contested nature of American democracy is that empirical assessments of its performance are not only guided by normative judgements but are themselves vehicles of disputes between and amongst other ideas with competing claims upon American priorities. The theme of democracy in American political culture may have the reputation of open-ended assimilation and of being able to reduce everything to its own terms. Nevertheless, such a reputation is often secured on the basis of process rather than substance. In such a context, democracy can be seen more as an instrumental value rather than an intrinsic principle. The more balanced perspective is one in which democracy has a substantive but not exclusive hold on American consciousness. Democracy has continually to confront other values and in particular it has to contend with a rival claimant to the mantle of popular sovereignty. It is to that source of rivalry that the analysis will now proceed.

---

[79] Theda Skocpol, *Diminished Democracy: From Membership to Management in American Civic Life* (Norman, OK: University of Oklahoma Press, 2003); Matthew A. Crenson and Benjamin Ginsberg, *Downsizing Democracy: How America Sidelined its Citizens and Privatized its Public* (Baltimore, MD: Johns Hopkins University Press, 2002); Cornell West, *Democracy Matters: Winning the Fight Against Imperialism* (New York: Penguin, 2005); William E. Hudson, *American Democracy in Peril: Seven Challenges to America's Future* (Chatham, NJ: Chatham House, 1995).

5

The Rule of Law

INTRODUCTION

In a political culture that is highly rules-bound and rules-related, a particular reverence is accorded to the value of law as the lynchpin of social, economic, and political arrangements. 'A government of laws not of men' was one of the rallying cries of the period of the Constitution's formation and it has remained a universally evoked ideal of American government. The rule of law is celebrated as an axiom of good government, as the essence of legitimacy, and as a natural analogue to individual rights and liberties. Nowhere is the rule of law more valued as an overriding principle of governance and as an accurate characterization of governing practice than in the United States.

In a minimalist sense, the rule of law refers to the concept of government working exclusively through law rather than through custom, or tradition, or personal prerogative. The rule of law implies that government is devoid of arbitrary action and decision based simply upon coercive promulgation. In the same way that governmental authority is based upon law, its policies and decisions are expected to be reducible to legal forms. Under the rule of law, the processes of government should be indistinguishable from the legal process. Governing through law is the equivalent of governing by reference to the outcomes of a genuine and representative process of legislation in which the government implements the collective act of the law-making body.

A rule of law system carries the following premises:

- Law should be public and ascertainable.
- Any encroachment upon the liberty of an individual must be lawful in that (i) government action should be supported by law; (ii) no outside or arbitrary interference should compromise the process; and (iii) a person should only be arrested for a clear breach of law.
- Prior to any punishment, a breach of law must be established before an impartial tribunal working according to the due process of law.
- The administration of justice must operate under the principles of equality before the law and the equal protection of the law.
- Justice should be regarded as an end in its own right. Judges need to interpret the law as it stands and should be uninfluenced by outside considerations or forces.

The United States prides itself as a model of the rule of law and one that sets the standard for other systems. Its tradition of strong legislatures acting as the first branch of government combined with its highly advanced legal culture is widely seen as embodying the essence of a genuine rule of law. Nothing better exemplifies the American reverence for both the law and the due process of law than the political status afforded to the US Constitution.

THE CONSTITUTION

In a political society formed through legal dispute and established by a political settlement expressed in terms of lawful authority, great value is attached to the constitutions of individual states and in particular to the overarching position of the constitution of the federal government. The federal constitution typifies the dependence of the political system upon the institutional arrangements and processes founded through the law of the constitution. In the United States, the Constitution provides the basic framework of the federal government. Institutions are defined and established, their roles and functions are specified, and their relationships to one other are given constitutional expression. The intention was to provide a clear and comprehensible anatomy of government in which the identity and dynamics of the component elements were made sufficiently explicit to constitute a limitation upon the reach of the state.

Given that the 'most ancient, the most persistent, and the most lasting of the essentials of true constitutionalism ... [is] the limitation of government',[1] the US Constitution offers a classic depiction of a government confined by the agency of constitutional definition. By providing a fundamental point of reference relating to the operation of government, the Constitution affords an opportunity for aggrieved parties to challenge the actions of government on the basis of being inconsistent with constitutional prescription. A disjunction between the *de jure* formality of the Constitution and the *de facto* actions of the United States government, or part of the government, allows for a claim of unconstitutional conduct on the basis of an unauthorized use of power. In this respect, constitutionalism provides the fullest expression of a rule of law because it incorporates the principle that the government not only makes laws and is in fact the exclusive provider of laws, but is itself subject to the law—i.e. governmental authority is attributable to, and accountable to, the Constitution's rules and procedures. As a consequence, the federal government operates on the understanding that it is not above the law. It is obliged to ensure that its policies and actions conform to the principles and stipulations of a sovereign constitution. In essence, governmental decisions are required both to produce and to follow law.

---

[1] Charles H. McIlwain, *Constitutionalism: Ancient and Modern*, rev. edn (Ithaca, NY: Cornell University Press, 1947), p. 22.

The Founders' objective of a government of constitutional constraint that would structure the relationships between the individual and the state, and between the different institutions and levels of governments, was not made solely dependent upon a legally determined framework of due process. In addition to the principle of limitation by specified definition, the Constitution has relied upon other sources of restraint. For example, power was explicitly divided amongst spatial (i.e. federalism) and functional (i.e. separation of powers) units of government. This was rationalized as a way of generating a mechanism of competitive interplay between institutions that would ensure a self-perpetuating dispersal of power and the preservation of individual liberties.

The framers of the Constitution were concerned that the general welfare and public interest could be endangered by the mobilized prejudices of the general population and by the agitation of the public into turbulent and impulsive majorities. It led them to justify the variously negotiated components of power as a unified scheme of checks and balances in the cause of limited government. As a consequence, the federal division of sovereignty between the national and state governments—which was largely the result of both political bargaining and a realistic appraisal of the strength of state authority—was given the same ulterior motive as the separation of powers scheme amongst the legislative, executive, and judicial branches of the national government. The Constitution's chief architect, James Madison, explained that under its auspices the rights of the people would be afforded a 'double security'.[2] Power relinquished by the people was 'first divided between two distinct governments, and then the portion allotted to each subdivided among distinct and separate departments' of government.[3]

The constitutional organization of political authority afforded legitimacy to the concept of a self-regulating mechanism that would constrain government through a continual process of checks and balances. In this guise, the Constitution's limitation of government was achieved not merely by the precision of legal definition, but by an arguably autonomous set of dynamics.[4] These were dependent upon the inexactitude of institutional boundaries and the endlessly contestable nature of institutions with rival claims to disputed powers.

Another supplementary restraint in American constitutionalism is derived from the individualistic and contractarian basis of law in the United States. The controlling premise was that individuals were invested with natural rights prior to, and independent of, any succeeding formation of government. In the American case, the precondition of natural rights to the formation of a political order led to the establishment of a Bill of Rights as an integral part of the constitutional settlement. These first ten amendments to the Constitution were proposed by the Founders' opponents. They believed that the political rights to be defended by the new structure should be made explicit. The Anti-Federalists were not prepared

---

[2] James Madison, 'Federalist Paper No. 51', in Alexander Hamilton, James Madison, and John Jay (eds.), *The Federalist Papers*, introduced by Clinton Rossiter (New York: Mentor, 1961), p. 323.

[3] Ibid.

[4] Michael G. Kammen, *A Machine That Would Go of Itself: The Constitution in American Culture* (New York: St. Martin's, 1993), chs. 1, 2.

to rely solely on the provisions of the new Constitution or upon Madison's self-limiting mechanics.[5] They wanted further guarantees to protect the states and their citizens from the incursions of a central government. The logic of their addendum to the Constitution was grounded in the proposition that if one of the central objectives of the new governing arrangements was the preservation of rights, these liberties should not be left to inference but be clearly declared as reserved and entrenched areas of civic and individual autonomy.[6] Instead of depending upon enumerated powers, due process, or self-limiting mechanisms, the Bill of Rights provided a delineated outer boundary to federal government action.[7]

In the Bill of Rights, individual rights demarcate the limits of the federal government's reach. In doing so, they also underline the overall purpose of the governing arrangements and the defining property of American constitutionalism. A recurrent textual theme, therefore, is the juxtaposition and even equation of prohibitions upon government activity with the existence and maintenance of individual rights. The prevention of government action in specified areas is presumed to leave liberty intact as a residual resource. The First Amendment, for example, prohibits Congress from making laws that would restrict the freedom of speech and of assembly. It also restricts governmental action against the freedom of the press and the rights to religious worship. Most of the remaining amendments formalize traditional common law rights against the government (e.g. fair trial procedures, the right to bear arms, rights against unreasonable searches and seizures). Together, these stipulated guarantees have become the chief monument of American individualism. The Bill of Rights bears testament to the accepted equivalence of liberties *from* government with liberties *through* government. As the final element to the project of constitution formation, the Bill of Rights offers a fail-safe precaution against the actions of even a deliberately constructed constitutional government. In doing so, the Bill of Rights has become a central reference point for the liberal distrust of authority and has thus been instrumental in fostering an advanced culture of rights in the United States.

TRADITION OF HIGHER LAW

All these sources and techniques of constitutional constraints are themselves dependent upon an essential point of anchorage. This is the understanding and

[5] Herbert J. Storing, *What the Anti-Federalists Were For: The Political Thought of the Opponents of the Constitution* (Chicago, IL: University of Chicago Press, 1981).

[6] It should be underlined that another rights-based objective of the federal Constitution was that of states' rights. These were also cited as being served and protected by the Bill of Rights.

[7] See Benjamin F. Wright, Jr., *American Interpretation of Natural Law: A Study in the History of Political Thought* (Cambridge, MA: Harvard University Press, 1931); Ernest Barker, 'Natural Law and the American Revolution', in Ernest Barker (ed.), *Traditions of Civility: Eight Essays* (Cambridge: Cambridge University Press, 1948), pp. 263–355; Morton White, *The Philosophy of the American Revolution* (Oxford: Oxford University Press, 1981), ch. 4.

acceptance that the Constitution incorporates a form of higher law. In the words of Edward S. Corwin, the notion of natural law is predicated on the existence of certain '[p]rinciples of right and justice which are entitled to prevail' on the basis of 'their intrinsic excellence...regardless of the attitude of those who wield the physical resources of the community'.[8] Corwin continues:

Such principles were made by no human hands.... They are eternal to all Will as such and interpenetrate all Reason as such. They are eternal and immutable. In relation to such principles, human laws are...merely as record or transcript, and their enactment an act not of will or power but one of discovery and declaration.[9]

The US Constitution and the constitutions of the individual states draw upon and reveal the depth of the American tradition of higher law. The Declaration of Independence and the subsequent revolutionary war against the British Empire were explicitly justified by references to the existence of a realm of natural law. This could be comprehended by reason and logic to the point of providing an ethical standard by which the colonial administration could be assessed and denounced. Natural law offered an independent dimension of political authority that allowed critics to step outside the confines of tradition and history as well as the limitations of British constitutional dispute. Natural law allowed dissenters to immerse themselves in the simplifying logic of a universal and contractual purpose.

When Americans came to organizing their own constitutions and in particular their own national or federal constitution, they invested them with allusions to natural law. In doing so, they attributed to these constitutions the political status of higher law. The establishment of the US Constitution as the 'supreme law of the law of the land'[10] was based upon the currents of natural law with which Americans had become familiar, and to which they had become increasingly attached, during the eighteenth century. The Constitution would be the law to control other laws.

In spite of the rise of mass democracy in the nineteenth century, the American tradition of higher law was not only sustained but developed in the range of its application. In fact, this period witnessed a popular fusion of constitutionalism with widespread political participation. Americans affirmed the Constitution 'as the primary doctrine of their democratic faith'.[11] In effect, 'beneath society, its customs and institutions, a law existed that men did not make. This law outlined the patterns of both individual and social life'.[12] Notwithstanding the rise in the twentieth century of a vast central government variously characterized as the positive state, the regulatory state, or the national security state, the higher law tradition has continued to the present day. Moreover, it has fostered an expectation

---

[8] Edward S. Corwin 'The "Higher Law" Background of American Constitutional Law', Part 1, *Harvard Law Review*, vol. 42, no. 2 (December 1928), p. 152.

[9] Ibid. [10] *United States Constitution*, Article VI, Clause 2.

[11] Ralph H. Gabriel, *The Course of American Democratic Thought*, 2nd edn (New York: Ronald Press, 1956), p. 14.

[12] Ibid.

that higher law not only shapes human authority but can also challenge it. The working premise is 'that "out there" lurk discoverable standards to judge whether public policies infringe on human dignity'.[13] This perspective is reflected in the now conventional belief that the Constitution is ethically superior to government and that, in comparison to ordinary laws, the Constitution is the law of superior obligation.

In sum, the US government is seen as subject to, and accountable to, the Constitution. In this way, the legitimacy of the government is, ultimately, dependent not simply on its political record, but on the extent to which it is adjudged to have conformed to the Constitution. The distinction between the Constitution and the government remains central to American politics. The Constitution maintains its distance through its close association with the virtues of higher law. The 'indebtedness of American constitutional law to natural law [and] natural rights concepts for its content in the field of private rights is vital and well-nigh all-comprehensive'.[14] The government's constitutionality is only in part determined by the fact that it is composed of those institutions and powers stipulated in the Constitution and by the necessity of having to conduct itself through the complex and self-limiting procedures laid down in the document. The American conception of constitutionality is not confined to structural and procedural propriety. It is the status of the Constitution as the facilitating agency or even the physical embodiment of a natural and immutable order of rational and moral authority which allows it to add the Constraining force of its corporate imprimatur to the limitations of its component parts and dynamics.

Because the US Constitution is infused with a moral code of a genuine and determinable higher law, it has acquired an iconic status in American society. This has occurred not simply because of what it contains but also because of what it represents and evokes. The leading jurist Robert Bork describes it in the following terms: 'It has been and remains an object of veneration, a sacred text, the symbol of our nationhood, the foundation of our government's structure and practice, a guarantor of our liberties, and a moral teacher'.[15] The exceptional appeal of the Constitution in American society is founded upon a range of factors. The ideals that are specified or implied by its contents have become central to the language of American political discourse. As a result, the Constitution remains the key point of reference for the legitimization of positions, actions, and decisions.

Another factor is the Constitution's capacious facility for either accommodating widely divergent views or at least giving the impression of having the potential of incorporating different constructions. The Constitution's sheer longevity as the foundation of a highly stable political system and spectacularly affluent

---

[13] Walter F. Murphy, 'Constitutions, Constitutionalism and Democracy', in Douglas Greenberg, Stanley N. Katz, Melanie B. Oliviero, and Steven C. Wheatley (eds.), *Constitutionalism and Democracy: Transitions in the Contemporary World* (New York: Oxford University Press, 1993), p. 6.

[14] Edward S. Corwin, *Presidential Power and the Constitution: Essays by Edward S. Corwin*, ed. and intro. Richard Loss (Ithaca, NY: Cornell University Press, 1976), p. 21.

[15] Robert Bork, *The Tempting of America: The Political Seduction of the Law* (London: Sinclair-Stevenson, 1990), p. 351.

society also adds to its lustre as a symbol and agency of continuity. In addition is the Constitution's enduring popularity as an alternative dimension to the often prosaic and occasionally disreputable realm of political exchange and electoral calculation. Accordingly, the Constitution continues to act as an outlet of anti-politics. It offers a medium of sweeping declarations, fundamental ideals, and principled abstractions. Together, they imply the accessibility of a transcendent justice at one remove from politics and secure in the integrity of an American essence manifested in a substantive higher law.[16]

So close is the identity of the Constitution with that of the American nation that the two entities are often regarded as being indistinguishable from one another. The establishment of the Constitution not only marked the creation of the American republic but it also defined the character of its subsequent history and political ethos. As a result, the American nation is conceived in constitutional terms while American nationalism is seen as the derivative of American constitutionalism. National crises are, therefore, equated with constitutional crises. By the same token, American victories are identified as occasions when the Constitution has prevailed over adversity. In the words of Hans Kohn, 'it represents the life-blood of the American nation, its supreme symbol and manifestation'.[17] The attribution of such a coexistent identity can be disputed on a range of grounds stretching from the assertion that the Declaration of Independence has a prior claim to represent the inception of the American nation,[18] to the view that the nation is a variable construction of social and cultural properties which defies a singular point of origin and identity.[19] Notwithstanding these objections, the cult of the Constitution has been sufficient to lead to a close association with the idea of a nation under law and to the Constitution as the most recognized 'symbol of nationhood, of continuity, of unity and common purpose'.[20]

Integral to its identity with the American nation has been the Constitution's capacity to absorb and to symbolize those values and ideals with which the United States has been most closely associated. In this sense, it can be said that the Constitution

draws its lasting strength not from what it says but from what it is: the embodiment of the idea by which the United States was constituted—a nation without even a name to which

[16] Corwin, 'The "Higher Law" Background of American Constitutional Law, pp. 149–85; *idem*, 'The "Higher Law" Background of American Constitutional Law', Part 2, *Harvard Law Review*, vol. 42, no. 3 (1929), pp. 365–409; *idem*, 'The Natural Law and Constitutional Law', in Loss (ed.), *Presidential Power and the Constitution: Essays by Edward S. Corwin*, pp. 1–22; Henry S. Commager, 'Constitutional History and the Higher Law', in Conyers Read (ed.), *The Constitution Reconsidered* (New York: Columbia University Press, 1938), pp. 225–45.

[17] Hans Kohn, *American Nationalism: An Interpretive Essay* (New York: Macmillan, 1957), p. 8; see also Kammen, *A Machine That Would Go of Itself*, chs. 3, 14.

[18] For example, see President Abraham Lincoln, 'First Inaugural Address', 4 March 1861, http://showcase.netins.net/web/creative/lincoln/speeches/1inaug.htm.

[19] For example, see Michael Lind, *Next American Nation: The New Nationalism and the Fourth American Revolution* (New York: Free Press, 1996).

[20] Alexander M. Bickel, *The Least Dangerous Branch: The Supreme Court at the Bar of Politics* (Indianapolis, IN: Bobbs-Merrill, 1962), p. 31.

emotions could cling, like England, France, Italia or Hellas, and yet from its beginning appealing to the imagination of men as the first nation to identify itself and to have been identified by others with an idea. To become an American has always meant to identify oneself with the idea.[21]

The idea or ideas in question—whether the emphasis is given to liberty, equality of rights, individual freedoms, or popular sovereignty—serve to render the Constitution as a foundation of social and ideological cohesion for a turbulent and rapidly developing country, whose potential for disintegration would otherwise have been considerable. As Ralph B. Perry put it: 'history affords few parallel instances of a state thus abruptly created, and consciously dedicated to a body of ideas whose acceptance constitutes its underlying bond of agreement'.[22] That initial agreement has been successively reaffirmed with the result that the Constitution now not only 'provides the most important symbol of national regime identity...it represents—and to some extent is—the regime'[23] itself. In other words, the Constitution's original 'triumph as a pure reflection of the American ideology—the political idea given governmental form'—has now been extended to the point where it is actually perceived as the 'embodiment of the country's most fundamental political values'.[24] In this respect, the Constitution typifies the commonly held proposition that America's exceptionalism as a society is both founded upon, and expressed through, the rule of law.

SUPREME COURT AND CONSTITUTIONAL JUDGMENT

Americans have generally deferred to the principle that it is judges who ought to provide the final answers as to what the Constitution has within it. This is what de Tocqueville meant when he said that 'there is almost no political question in the United States that is not resolved sooner or later into a judicial question'.[25] It is the courts that provide authoritative interpretations of the Constitution. The Supreme Court is considered to be the ultimate arbiter of the Constitution, not simply because it is the last in a long line of constitutional dispute, but because the asserted truth of the Constitution is more persuasively revealed by senior judges who appear at least to have less political concern than any other sector of society. It is for this reason that the Supreme Court is regarded as America's 'supreme symbol of the rule of law'.[26]

[21] Kohn, *American Nationalism*, pp. 8–9.
[22] Quoted in Everett C. Ladd, 'The Constitution as Ideology', *Dialogue*, No. 79 1/1989.
[23] Donald J. Devine, *The Political Culture of the United States: The Influence of Member Values on Regime Maintenance* (Boston, MA: Little, Brown, 1972), p. 88.
[24] Ladd, 'The Constitution as Ideology'.
[25] Alexis de Tocqueville, *Democracy in America*, trans., ed., and intro. Harvey C. Mansfield and Delba Winthrop (Chicago, IL: Chicago University Press, 2000), p. 257.
[26] Bork, *The Tempting of America*, p. 349.

In the landmark precedent of *Marbury v. Madison* (1803), Chief Justice John Marshall addressed the two key questions of the Constitutional system. First was the issue of when a statute law, or an executive action, that was deemed to be inconsistent with the Constitution could continue to stand. Marshall answered that it could not. Even an enactment of the US Congress could not be allowed to have precedence over the Constitution:

Certainly all those who have framed written constitutions contemplate them as forming the fundamental and paramount law of the nation, and consequently, the theory of every such government must be, that an act of the legislature, repugnant to the constitution, is void.[27]

In other words, bad laws were considered to be no laws at all. The second issue concerned the question of the relative weightings of constitutional interpretation. All parties to any dispute had their own constructions of the Constitution. The question here was who or what should have the final judgement upon the constitutionality of laws or actions. Again, Marshall had no doubt that because the Constitution was in essence law and because it was 'emphatically the province and duty of the judicial department to say what the law is',[28] it was the necessary prerogative of the Supreme Court to provide the judgment upon such issues. In effect, the Constitution as higher law required the highest levels of judicial interpretation.[29]

The position of the Supreme Court has afforded a social status and political power to American judges that are unsurpassed outside the United States. These professional custodians of the Constitution attempt both to preserve and to extend the principle that constitutionality is not a matter of construction but of elucidation. In the words of Arthur S. Miller:

The dominant ideology of the American legal profession is 'legalism'. Law is separated, in this conception, not only from morals but also from politics. Law is considered to be 'there'—separate and apart from the rest of society, a discrete entity amenable to analysis as such.[30]

According to this perspective, law can be elicited through the application of neutral principles of adjudication. American judges have encouraged the citizenry not only to view the Constitution as an 'ideal floating above [their] heads'[31] but also to accept that only judges can finally transmute the ideal into the material reality of hard decisions and concrete pronouncements.

In laying claim to be the arbiters of the Constitution, the American judiciary has worked to fuse its own identity and its own protection with the solemn majesty of the Constitution. Thus the Constitution has received a voice and an institutional expression. Judges portray themselves as having to 'interpret and apply

---

[27] *Marbury v. Madison*, 1 Cr. 137 (1803).   [28] Ibid.

[29] See William E. Nelson, *Marbury v. Madison: The Origins and Legacy of Judicial Review* (Lawrence, KS: University Press of Kansas, 2000), chs. 3–5, 9.

[30] Arthur S. Miller, 'The Politics of the American Judiciary', *Political Quarterly*, vol. 49, no. 2 (April–June 1978), p. 200.

[31] Kohn, *American Nationalism*, p. 67.

the constitutional order by deductive decision-making, applying its generalities to the specific problems of everyday life'.[32] This has the effect of continually enhancing the status of law in American society and, in particular, of securing the position of the Constitution as an evocation of high values and supreme authority. For many, the interdependency of the judiciary and the Constitution has meant that while constitutional law is celebrated as 'evidently and necessarily the rock on which the American nation is built', judges are acknowledged as having a similarly exalted status as agents 'participating directly and explicitly and actively . . . in the endless process of making the American nation'.[33] In Ronald Dworkin's words, 'the courts are the capitals of law's empire, and the judges are its princes'.[34]

The privileged position that the Supreme Court holds in determining the validity of law in relation to the Constitution has permitted the justices to intervene in areas that are not only politically sensitive but also morally contentious. The judiciary has often been accused of unnecessary and excessive activism. Its critics claim that it has deliberately followed an agenda of sweeping political reform and of engaging in the practice of 'discovering new rights in old places'.[35] The Court has a capacity for proactive adjudication that can displace established policy, disrupt devices of political accommodation, and even intrude into areas too controversial for conventional law-making. The exercise of such a role and the intensity of the responses to it are exemplified by the case of *Roe v. Wade* (1973).[36]

This case amounts to one of the Court's most ambitious attempts to reach an accommodation of values and interests. In the case, the Court sought to reach a position of equilibrium between rival claims. On one side were the claims of those women who asserted a right of personal choice over whether to have an abortion. On the other side were those who supported the rights of democratically elected state legislatures to ban abortion within their own areas of jurisdiction. In this highly charged issue, individual rights were confronted by clear expressions of public will within a context of intransigent moral fundamentalism. Even though the Court acknowledged the 'sensitive and emotional nature' of the abortion issue and the way that it aroused 'vigorous opposing views' and 'seemingly absolute convictions', the justices believed that their task was to 'resolve the issue by constitutional measurement, free of emotion and of predilection'.[37]

In effect, the Court attempted a middle course 'consistent with the relative weights of the respective interests involved'[38] by investing both sides of the issue with constitutional legitimacy at different periods of time during a pregnancy. The Court found that in the first three months of pregnancy a woman's right to choice

---

[32] Philip Allott, 'Making Sense of the Law: Lawyers and Legal Philosophy', *The Cambridge Review*, vol. 108, no. 2297 (1987), p. 66.

[33] Ibid.   [34] Ronald Dworkin, *Law's Empire* (London: Fontana, 1986), p. 407.

[35] Alan Ryan, 'The British, the Americans, and Rights', in Michael J. Lacey and Knud Haakonssen (eds.), *A Culture of Rights: The Bill of Rights in Philosophy, Politics, and Law—1791 and 1991* (Cambridge: Cambridge University Press, 1991), p. 390.

[36] *Roe v. Wade*, 410 US 113 (1973).   [37] Ibid., 116.   [38] Ibid., 165.

was protected by the guarantees of individual liberty contained in the Fourteenth Amendment. This right of privacy—implied by the individual rights enumerated in the Constitution and now extended to abortion—was not, however, an absolute right. As the fetus developed, the interest of the state grew in respect both to the mother's health and to the 'potential human life'[39] within the womb. From between three and six months, the state could regulate abortion procedures as long as they related to maternal health. The Court felt that the state's interest became compelling after six months when the potential for life outside the womb had been reached. For the final three months of pregnancy, the state 'in promoting its interest in the potentiality of human life may, if it chooses regulate, and even proscribe abortion except where it is necessary, in appropriate medical judgment, for the preservation of the life or health of the mother'.[40]

Far from resolving the abortion issue, the Court's position in *Roe v. Wade* has in many ways aggravated it.[41] The decision generated an intense legal and political controversy. Far from resolving the issue by 'constitutional measurement', the Court seems in many ways to have aggravated it. The judgment has been criticized by many constitutional lawyers for the presumption of the Court in striking down a series of anti-abortion state laws on the grounds of an asserted right to privacy that is not mentioned in the Constitution.[42] The decision has also aroused a storm of ferocious, and at times violent, political protest. On some occasions, it seemed that the *Roe v. Wade* decision had not only approached the limits of constitutional arbitration, but had actually surpassed them.

The effect of decisions like *Roe v. Wade* brings into focus the much wider issue of how the rule of law is operationalized. The Supreme Court performs a functional role and enjoys considerable institutional prestige as the vehicle of constitutional determination. Such is its pivotal position in the hierarchy of rules in an advanced legal culture that the key question no longer pertains to whether the Court should establish the Constitution's meaning but to *how* it arrives at such decisions. The descriptive and prescriptive nature of analysis into the methodology of judgment has fostered a major debate in this area.[43] It has also contributed to the ongoing

---

[39] Ibid.   [40] Ibid.

[41] See Faye D. Ginsburg, *Contested Lives: The Abortion Debate in an American Community* (Berkeley, CA: University of California Press, 1989); Laurence H. Tribe, *Abortion: The Clash of Absolutes* (New York: W. W. Norton, 1992); Barbara H. Craig and David M O'Brien, *Abortion and American Politics* (Chatham, NJ: Chatham House, 1993); Mark Graber, *Rethinking Abortion: Equal Choice, the Constitution and Reproductive Politics* (Princeton, NJ: Princeton University Press, 1999).

[42] Another constitutional controversy which the Court failed to resolve was the point at which life was formed in the womb. The Court refused to enter into this discussion and so left the question of the personal rights of the unborn wholly unaddressed. It thereby hoped to avoid the thorny problem of whether abortion might be challenged on the same Fourteenth Amendment grounds as the Court had just used to validate a woman's right to choose an abortion.

[43] See Walter F. Murphy, 'Constitutional Interpretation: The Art of the Historian, Magician, or Statesman?', *Yale Law Journal*, vol. 87, no. 8 (July 1978), pp. 1752–71; John H. Ely, 'Constitutional Interpretivism: Its Allure and Impossibility', *Indiana Law Journal*, vol. 53 (Spring 1978), pp. 399–448; John H. Ely, *Democracy and Distrust: A Theory of Judicial Review* (Cambridge, MA: Harvard University Press, 1980); Jesse H. Choper, *Judicial Review and the National Political Process: A Functional Reconsideration of the Role of the Supreme Court* (Chicago, IL: University of Chicago Press, 1980); Jack

controversy over the position of the courts within a democracy, and by extension the problematic relationship between the constitutional sovereignty of government under legal constraint and the popular sovereignty of rule by consent.

CONSTITUTIONALISM AND DEMOCRACY

The role of the Supreme Court serves to underline the deep ambiguity between constitutionalism and democracy. More often than not these two terms are used together as if they were mutually inclusive entities. But while constitutional democracy is commonly taken to be a seamless unity, their respective properties are rooted in different traditions and carry different implications. The judiciary in the United States continually has to straddle these two seminal concepts and to remain aware of their capacity for inducing strain and even tension. The Supreme Court in particular is placed in the difficult position of having to be conscious of both traditions and to be cognizant that its role and authority are dependent upon fusing a working accommodation between constitutional integrity and democratic sensitivity. Nevertheless, the Court always remains vulnerable to the charge that it is a conspicuous anomaly in a functioning democracy because in essence it embodies a fundamental clash of values.

Defenders of the Supreme Court can point to a set of constitutional provisions that not only condition and constrain its freedom of action, but also link it to the democratic process. For example, judges are appointed by a combination of the president and the Senate, the court is dependent upon cases brought to it on appeal, its decisions can be altered by changes in the Court's personnel or by shifts in judicial outlook, judges can be impeached, and decisions can be overruled by constitutional amendment. It is also important to note that judgments usually allow for discretionary action by other governmental agencies; multiple opinions in a Court decision reflect a breadth of constitutional diversity that can accommodate democratic divisions; and, more often than not, Supreme Court decisions reaffirm and consolidate the legitimacy of the state and federal governments.

N. Rakove, *Interpreting the Constitution: The Debate over Original Intent* (Boston, MA: Northeastern University Press, 1990); Antonin Scalia, 'The Rule of Law as a Law of Rules', *University of Chicago Law Review*, vol. 56, no. 4 (Fall 1989), pp. 1175–88; Christopher Wolfe, *Judicial Activism: Bulwark of Liberty or Precarious Security?* (Lanham, MD: Rowman & Littlefield, 1997); Mark Tushnet, *Taking the Constitution Away from the Courts* (Princeton, NJ: Princeton University Press, 1999); Robert J. McKeever, *Raw Judicial Power? The Supreme Court and American Society*, 2nd edn (Manchester: Manchester University Press, 1995), ch. 2; Antonin Scalia, *A Matter of Interpretation: Federal Courts and the Law* (Princeton, NJ: Princeton University Press, 1998), pp. 3–48; Jack W. Nowlin, 'Judicial Power and the Withering of Civil Society', in Christopher Wolfe (ed.), *That Eminent Tribunal: Judicial Supremacy and the Constitution* (Princeton, NJ: Princeton University Press, 2004), pp. 118–40; Jeremy Waldron, 'Judicial Review and Republican Government', in Wolfe (ed.), *That Eminent Tribunal*, pp. 159–80; Jamin B. Raskin, *Overruling Democracy: The Supreme Court vs. the American People* (New York: Routledge, 2003); Cass R. Sunstein, *Radicals in Robes: Why Extreme Right-Wing Courts Are Wrong for America* (New York: Basic Books, 2005).

In addition, the Supreme Court has developed a set of conventions in judicial self-restraint that normally minimizes the Court's intrusions into the governing process and confines its constitutional constructions to the narrowest available terms.[44]

Yet, notwithstanding these structural and attitudinal devices, the Supreme Court regularly arouses intense opposition to its decisions, which is usually translated into vehement indictments of the Court's undemocratic and even anti-democratic character. Critics point to the unelected and, therefore, allegedly unaccountable nature of the institution. The lifetime tenure of the justices, together with the ethos of judicial independence, permit the Court to interpose itself directly between the democratic process and policy outcomes. In doing so, it can substitute its views, or rather the opinions of five of the nine justices, for those of democratically elected decision-makers operating in representative institutions. The complaint that the Supreme Court supplants the popular mandates and policy judgments of democratically elected representatives has been a familiar refrain in many political disputes.

For example, after much of his New Deal programme was invalidated as unconstitutional, President Franklin D. Roosevelt denounced the Supreme Court in 1937 for 'acting, not as a judicial body, but as a policymaking body'.[45] He claimed that it had 'improperly set itself up as a third House of the Congress...reading into the Constitution words and implications which are not there and which were never intended to be there'.[46] His ill-fated reform to increase the number of justices on the bench in order to achieve a Court that better reflected the needs and responsibilities of modern government was prompted by what he regarded as the judicial contempt for his popular mandate and by extension the American public: 'The courts, however, have cast doubts on the ability of the elected Congress to protect us against catastrophe by meeting squarely our modern social and economic conditions.'[47] In effect, President Roosevelt portrayed the Court's attitude towards the New Deal as a crisis of democratic government.

Today, the Supreme Court is still attracting criticism for the way that its powers of adjudication can leak into the areas of law-making and policy formulation. Complainants range from dissident justices opposed to the doctrines and precedents of judicial activism on the grounds of democratic legitimacy[48] to the

---

[44] See Ashwander v. Tennessee Valley Authority, 297 US 288 (1936); Alexander M. Bickel, 'The Supreme Court, 1960 Term—Foreword: The Passive Virtues', Harvard Law Review, vol. 75, no. 1 (1961), pp. 40–79; Philippa Strum, The Supreme Court and 'Political Questions': A Study in Judicial Evasion (Tuscaloosa, AL: University of Alabama Press, 1974); Frederick Schauer, 'Ashwander Revisited', Supreme Court Review (1995), pp. 177–224; Cass R. Sunstein, One Case at a Time: Judicial Minimalism on the Supreme Court (Cambridge, MA: Harvard University Press, 2001).

[45] President Franklin D. Roosevelt, 'On the Reorganization of the Judiciary', 9 March 1937, http://www.geocities.com/americanpresidencynet/chat09.htm.

[46] Ibid.   [47] Ibid.

[48] Antonin Scalia, A Matter of Interpretation: Federal Courts and the Law, ed. Amy Gutmann (Princeton, NJ: Princeton University Press, 1997), pp. 3–48, 129–50.

more robust indictments of those whose interests are adversely affected by Court decisions. The latter is typified by the impassioned denunciation of the federal judiciary in an editorial for the National Right to Life Committee: 'The pro-abortionists' appetite for using the courts to thwart the will of the people is as voracious as it is undemocratic. Given that they have seeded the courts with many justices who see the world through a prism of judicial activism, this comes as no surprise'.[49]

The Court itself regards its remit to be one that necessarily requires it to review and at times to contest the validity laws passed and actions taken by elected office-holders—even those laws and actions that may accurately reflect the configuration of public opinion. This is the power that Justice Felix Frankfurter described as attracting a 'jealous eye' because the Court could serve to 'prevent the full play of the democratic process'.[50] This view is particularly pertinent to the Supreme Court's usage of the 'due process' clause in the Fourteenth Amendment to apply an increasing number of the Bill of Rights' prohibitions to the states. In what has been widely cited a 'second bill of rights', or the 'nationalization' of the Bill of Rights, the Court has developed a prodigious volume of precedents and jurisprudence in support of the federal government's right to intervene against local and state actions that are deemed to be contrary to the fundamental rights of citizenship.[51] In limiting the discretionary freedom and democratic autonomy of the state governments, the federal courts have assumed a hugely important role in structuring policy in a profusion of issue areas (e.g. criminal justice procedures, free speech, racial segregation, affirmative action, religious observance, sexual discrimination, privacy, pornography, homosexuality, abortion, and assisted suicide). The progressive incorporation of the Bill of Rights into the Fourteenth Amendment and, thereby, into a more standardized conception of civil liberty has led not only to local majorities being directly countermanded by federal judges but also paradoxically to a vast expansion in the supervisory infrastructure of the national government.

The spectre of the Supreme Court confronting democratically elected government is not, however, confined to the local and state sectors of governance. While it has been far more reticent over explicitly challenging the authority of Congress or the Presidency, the Court will occasionally underline its prerogative in determining whether the elected branches of the federal government have superseded their authority. In the case of *United States v. Eichman* (1990),[52] for example,

---

[49] Dave Andrusko, 'Getting It Done', *National Right to Life Committee Newsletter*, http://www.nrlc. org/news/2004/NRL03/getting_it_done.htm.

[50] *West Virginia State Board of Education v. Barnette*, 319 US 624 (1943), 650.

[51] See Richard C. Cortner, *The Supreme Court and Second Bill of Rights: The Fourteenth Amendment and the Nationalization of Civil Liberties* (Madison, WI: University of Wisconsin Press, 1980); Raoul Berger, *Government by Judiciary: The Transformation of the Fourteenth Amendment* (Cambridge, MA: Harvard University Press, 1977); Michael J. Perry, *The Constitution in the Courts: Law or Politics?* (New York: Oxford University Press, 1994), chs. 8, 9; Henry J. Abraham and Barbara A. Perry, *Freedom and the Court: Civil Rights and Liberties in the United States*, 8th edn (Lawrence, KS: University Press of Kansas, 2003).

[52] *United States v. Eichman*, 496 US 310 (1990).

the Court confronted the US Congress over its decision to pass the Flag Protection Act. This made defacing or damaging the US flag a criminal offence. The Court acknowledged that the legislation may have been a popular measure but then went on to add that this property represented neither a compelling argument nor a criterion of constitutionality.

[T]he Government's interest cannot justify its infringement on First Amendment rights. We decline the Government's invitation to reassess this conclusion in light of Congress' recent recognition of a purported 'national consensus' favoring a prohibition on flag burning.... Even assuming such a consensus exists, any suggestion that the Government's interest in suppressing speech becomes more weighty as popular opposition to that speech grows is foreign to the First Amendment.[53]

It is cases like these that fuel resentment against the courts and foster criticism that judicial activism is excessive, unwarranted, disproportionate, and fundamentally undemocratic. It is claimed that the extraordinary status of the Supreme Court makes it not only a de facto third house of the legislature empowered to engage in judicial policy-making, but also a monument to the way in which American democracy continues to be restricted by a rule of law that allows judges to supplant democratic opinion with expressions of constitutional fundamentalism.

The *de jure* position of the legal profession is one in which law is found by impartial judges using neutral instruments of interpretation. The *de facto* process, however, is one of divergent premises, conflicting constructions, and discernible biases. If the United States has a strong tradition of higher law, it also possesses a developed strand of sociological jurisprudence and legal realism that relates law closely to its social context—to the point where it is deemed that 'legal institutions and doctrines are instruments of social control'.[54] Even Supreme Court justices can be aware that their role is not always confined to that of passively discovering law. For example, in his dissent to the controversial *Miranda v. Arizona* decision, Justice Byron White made it clear that the Court was not merely making law in this case. It 'underscore[d] the obvious'[55] that the Supreme Court makes law in most of its decisions.

[T]he Court has not discovered or found the law in making today's decision, nor has it derived it from some irrefutable sources; what it has done is to make new law and new public policy in much the same way that it has in the course of interpreting other great clauses of the Constitution. This is what the Court historically has done. Indeed, it is what it must do and will continue to do until and unless there is some fundamental change in the constitutional distribution of governmental powers.[56]

In the American constitutional system, the classic depiction is that a policy has to go in search of law in order to achieve legitimacy. According to many observers

---

[53] Ibid., 311.
[54] Roscoe Pound quoted in Alan Hunt, *The Sociological Movement in Law* (London: Macmillan, 1978), p. 15.
[55] *Miranda v. Arizona*, 384 US 436 (1966), 531.   [56] Ibid.

and participants, the reality is that judges allow law to pursue policy positions. In other words, judges actively search for the most appropriate legal precedent or interpretation, in order to isolate the right law to suit the purposes of the judgment. This leads to charges that the courts reconfigure the rule of law in ways that may coincide with movements in public opinion, but by the same token may also supersede or frustrate expression of democratic will. Justice Antonin Scalia, for example, believes that the latter is the more likely because of the 'common law mindset'[57] that has afflicted much of the Supreme Court's work over the past fifty years. Scalia finds this approach to be objectionable on principle because it increases the scope for interpretive licence at the expense of the actual text of the laws passed by the people's representatives: 'It is simply not compatible with democratic theory that laws mean whatever they ought to mean, and that unelected judges decide what that is.'[58]

In the view of Alexander Bickel, the 'root difficulty is that judicial review is a countermajoritarian force in our system'.[59] When the Supreme Court declares legislative enactments or executive acts to be unconstitutional, 'it thwarts the will of representatives of the actual people of the here and now; it exercises control, not in behalf of the prevailing majority, but against it', and for this basic reason it can be concluded that 'judicial review is undemocratic'.[60] It was Bickel's view that federal power 'ultimately becomes irresponsible, because the electoral process is insufficient as a link between this remote, immense government and the concerns of the people with whom it deals with'.[61] The reaction against this development had produced legitimate forms of localism and devices of participatory democracy. To Bickel, the nature of the Supreme Court was 'in fundamental contrast' to this trend because the Court is 'inherently an institution of the federal government'.[62] As a consequence, it has a centralizing function that is 'counter to the basic drive for group and local self-government'.[63]

The same strand of democratic scepticism is evident in Louis Fisher's critique of the way that the separate identities of the Constitution and the Supreme Court have converged with one another: '[To] accept the two as equivalent is to relinquish individual responsibility and the capacity for self-government'.[64] By allowing the judges to have a monopoly over authoritative constitutional decisions, the public is abdicating its responsibilities for exercising citizenship. 'When the Court issues its judgments', Fisher believes that 'we should not suspend ours'.[65] The practice of judicial review may fit into an aggregate scheme of checks and balances, but in Fishers' view it is important to underline the purpose of such fragmented

---

[57] Scalia, *A Matter of Interpretation*, pp. 3–48.   [58] Ibid., p. 22.

[59] Bickel, *The Least Dangerous Branch*, p. 16.   [60] Ibid., p. 17.

[61] *Hearings before the Subcommittee on the Separation of Powers of the Committee on the Judiciary, United States Senate*, Ninetieth Congress, Second Session on the Supreme Court (Washington, DC: Government Printing Office, 1968), p. 75.

[62] Ibid.   [63] Ibid.

[64] Louis Fisher, *Constitutional Dialogues: Interpretation as a Political Process* (Princeton, NJ: Princeton University Press, 1998), p. 276.

[65] Ibid., p. 279.

power: '[W]e cannot permit judicial power and constitutional interpretation to reside only in the courts. We reject supremacy in all three branches because of the value placed in freedom, discourse, democracy and limited government'.[66] A similar point is echoed by Larry Kramer, who objects to the way that the courts, especially the Supreme Court, have effectively claimed the right to act as the authoritative source of constitutional arbitration and interpretation. In disputing the historical origins and political legitimacy of judicial review, Kramer advocates the restoration of 'popular constitutionalism' in which the public resumes its role in determining the way it is governed by a more immediate, continuous, and responsible engagement with a constitution that is effectively owned by the citizenry.[67]

In response to these critiques, a substantive democratic defence of judicial review has been advanced using a variety of arguments. Indeed '[h]eroic efforts have been made to demonstrate that judicial review is compatible with democratic theory'.[68] For example, it is possible to assert that judicial intervention is necessary in order to monitor and improve the democratic process so as to allow equal access to participation and ensure a proper adherence to procedures. Another argument for judicial review on democratic grounds relates to the need for the courts to intervene to protect minorities from discriminatory action undertaken by government. The more that states can claim to be acting on behalf of democratic consent, the greater is the likelihood that minority rights will be infringed. Justice William Brennan, for example, maintained a sceptical view of the constitutional sensitivities of impulsive lawmakers: 'Legislators influenced by the passions and exigencies of the moment, the pressure of constituents and colleagues, and the press of business, do not always pass sober constitutional judgement on every piece of legislation they enact'.[69] This increases the need for an element of government to be insulated from the democratic impulse in order to provide minorities with protection. As Justice Brennan pointed out, 'under the conditions of modern government, litigation may well be the sole practicable avenue open to a minority to petition for redress of grievances'.[70] The Supreme Court's development of the protections and guarantees of the Fourteenth Amendment against the illiberal actions of state governments has been widely interpreted as representing a central theme in the Court's contemporary usage of judicial review. Its decisions in this area have given constitutional foundation to the claims of individual and minority freedoms.[71] In doing so, the Court has reasserted the principles of pluralism and equity in the foundational framework of American democracy.

---

[66] Ibid.

[67] Larry D. Kramer, *The People Themselves: Popular Constitutionalism and Judicial Review* (New York: Oxford University Press, 2004). For more on the way that the courts have allegedly subverted democratic choice, see Gerald N. Rosenberg, *The Hollow Hope: Can Courts Bring about Social Change?* (Chicago, IL: University of Chicago Press, 1993).

[68] Choper, *Judicial Review and the National Political Process*, p. 10.

[69] *Marsh v. Chambers*, 463 US 783 (1983), 814.

[70] *NAACP v. Button*, 371 US 415 (1963), 430.

[71] Christopher Wolfe, *The Rise of Modern Judicial Review: From Constitutional Interpretation to Judge-Made Law* (New York: Basic Books, 1986), chs. 12, 13; Michael J. Perry, *We the People: The Fourteenth Amendment and the Supreme Court* (New York: Oxford University Press, 2002).

A further defence argues that the behaviour of the Supreme Court reveals a sufficiently close affinity to sustained currents of public opinion to substantiate the claim of responsiveness to popular preferences.[72] Other positions in support of judicial review tend not to concentrate upon the undemocratic properties of the Supreme Court but upon the less than democratic, and even countermajoritarian, aspects of other elements of the political system and the Constitution. In such a context, the Supreme Court can look less atypical and more symptomatic of a structure with principled reservations over the leverage of simple majorities. This kind of defence diverts attention away from the Court's credentials as an institution responsive to popular opinion. Instead, it relates to the fundamentalism of the Constitution and thereby to a normative justification of judicial review in which 'countermajoritarian judicial policy making is among the Supreme Court's legitimate, indeed essential, responsibilities'.[73] Moreover, it is because of the existence of so many checks and balances within the political system that the Court has often assumed the responsibility to take the lead in a variety of sensitive and controversial areas of public policy (e.g. sexual practices, obscenity, affirmative action, religious freedom, abortion, gay rights, gender equality, privacy, euthanasia, disability claims, and rights of free speech and expression).

The defence with probably the greatest potential for rationalizing the judicial presumption of a democratic dimension is based upon two concepts. First is the Constitution's status as a charter of people's rights. This facet is rooted not only in the Constitution's origins as an asserted product of non-state action, but in its reputation as being the property of the American public. The second concept that can be deployed in support of the Constitution and its arbiters is derived from the principle of an implicit equality of citizenship. A democracy implies the existence of a common citizenship with the same standards of rights and immunities. By extension, it can be claimed that the ethical basis of an authentic democracy infers the limitation of rule through simple majoritarian preference. This kind of argument can be based upon a minimal basis to democratic citizenship. It can also rest upon a more elevated appeal to an equivalent of Rousseau's 'general will'.[74] On both grounds, judicial activism has been justified and promoted with reference to a normative constitution with a necessarily open agenda of democratic ethics to be

---

[72] See Robert A. Dahl, 'Decision-Making in a Democracy: The Supreme Court as a National Policy-Maker', *Journal of Public Law*, vol. 6 (Fall 1957), pp. 279–95; Thomas R. Marshall, *Public Opinion and the Supreme Court* (Boston, MA: Unwin Hyman, 1989); David G. Barnum, *The Supreme Court and American Democracy* (New York: St. Martin's Press, 1993), ch. 15; see also William Mishler and Reginal S. Sheehan, 'The Supreme Court as a Countermajoritarian Institution? The Impact of Public Opinion on Supreme Court Decisions', *American Political Science Review*, vol. 87, no. 1 (March 1993), pp. 87–101. Mishler and Sheehan allude to a correlation between Supreme Court decisions and long-term trends in public opinion. However, they add the caveat that since 1981 the relationship has been disrupted by a succession of conservative to moderate appointments to the Court which over time have begun to cast doubts on the Court's level of responsiveness.

[73] Barnum, *The Supreme Court and American Democracy*, p. 310.

[74] Jean-Jacques Rousseau, *The Social Contract*, trans. and intro. Maurice Cranston. (Harmondsworth, UK: Penguin, 1968).

advanced and realized. The pursuit of government in the interests of the people, or on behalf of the people,[75] in the realization of democratic ideals can justify a high level of judicial intervention in the form of a moral imperative. Accordingly, it is openly espoused that Supreme Court judges have an obligation to act not merely as the chief source of 'our institutional common sense',[76] but as the 'educators and supervisors of the national conscience'.[77]

This asserted nexus between the Constitution as public property and the judicial articulation of democratic norms has never been wholly persuasive. On the contrary, it has been keenly contested by those who advocate a closer equivalence between democratic means and ends, and those who maintain the primacy of representative institutions and the responsibility of individuals and communities to engage in the task of self-government. Judicial activism may perform a governing function, but to sceptics of the courts' role it is at the expense of the civic integrity of the republic and its constitutional forms. Instead of encouraging the citizenry to exercise choice in the giving or withholding of consent through independent judgement, recent developments are said to have created a dependency upon the judiciary to make difficult decisions on behalf of the public. The erosion of voluntarism and the enforcement of civil morality by judicial pronouncements lead to calls for government to 'withdraw from attempting to guarantee the exercise of rights to a less ambitious and less threatening policy of securing those rights in some formal manner'.[78] According to this view, courts should not be exercising rights on behalf of the individuals who possess them. The people need a 'constitution enabling them to elevate their will into an intention and calling forth the virtues necessary to the task'.[79]

This dispute over the rightful boundaries of the courts in a democracy will continue indefinitely because it is central to the conduct of politics and the discussion of values in the American polity. What is significant about the level of contestation that such a dispute entails is its critical importance within American society. The relationship between the two concepts and the terms of their coexistence continue to have an enduring impact upon the collective consciousness of citizens and opinion leaders. To Walter Murphy, '[d]emocracy is more willing to chance injuries that can flow from majoritarian domination; constitutionalism is more willing to risk harms that can flow from restricting governmental power'.[80] An alternative construction is that while democracy reflects the force of diversity, constitutionalism offers a mediating device by which differences can be contained by a common source of connection.

---

[75] Christopher L. Eisgruber, *Constitutional Self-Government* (Cambridge, MA: Harvard University Press, 2001), chs. 2,3.

[76] Henry J. Abraham, *Freedom and the Court*, 5th edn (New York: Oxford University Press, 1988), p. 534.

[77] Choper, *Judicial Review and the National Political Process*, p. 162.

[78] Harvey C. Mansfield, Jr., *America's Constitutional Soul* (Baltimore, MD: Johns Hopkins University Press, 1991), p. 191.

[79] Ibid., p. 192.   [80] Murphy, 'Constitutions, Constitutionalism and Democracy', p. 20.

RULES AND VALUES

The brevity and ambiguity of the Constitution gives it an extraordinary capacity to absorb different positions and principles within a single unified dimension of presumptive constitutionality. It is the Constitution's lack of definition, therefore, that provides it with so many contending definitions. This makes it possible for widely differing parties to argue out their differences through the common medium of constitutional argument and construction. This does not mean that the different parties will come to agree with one another, but it does mean that they are likely to agree on how to differ from each other. The very fact that they are both using the Constitution as a central frame of reference and as a common standard of legitimacy—together with the language, words, and criteria of proof associated with constitutional argument—means that in their differences they are revealing a unified deference to constitutional arbitration. The dissent shown against individual Supreme Court decisions may well be intense but it is always directed through the Constitution and expressed in the form of alternative constructions of the Constitution.

The assimilative properties of the Constitution, together with its status as a core repository of American political legitimacy, have at various periods in American history led it to become the supreme matrix of American ideas and traditions. At a general level, it provides the medium through which values and principles confront one another and through which practical accommodations are arrived at. As ideological and social conflict is transmuted into constitutional dispute, and as political questions are transformed into legal argument, so it is that constitutional adjudication provides the format for political and ideological settlement. There is a constant need to delineate the 'appropriate parameters of that ubiquitous line between individual rights and privileges on the one hand, and societal obligations and responsibilities on the other'.[81] The need may be self-evident, but the solutions remain elusive. As Henry Abraham succinctly notes: 'There are no simple answers ... liberty and equality, *both* of which are cherished constitutional guarantees, find themselves at war'.[82] But the possibility of interim, partial, and workable solutions is dependent upon an agency of mediation. In the words of Morton Keller, the Constitution 'however tangentially and ambiguously' has 'defined the boundaries of debate over persistent, never-resolved issues in American public life'. He continues: 'The great ongoing contentions between liberty and equality, between individual freedom and social responsibility, between the nation and the states, and between the State and the citizen, have always been expressed in constitutional terms'.[83] It may be that the Constitution's wording especially lends itself to being construed in politically substantive and ideological terms. Alternatively, it is possible that political and ideological differences are simply projected onto the Constitution's language. Either way, the end result is the same: conflicting parties

---

[81] Abraham and Perry, *Freedom and the Court*, p. 9.   [82] Ibid.

[83] Morton Keller, 'Power and Rights: Two Centuries of American Constitutionalism', *Journal of American History*, vol. 74, no. 3 (December 1987), p. 675.

and values are transmuted into the same currency of constitutional propositions that require adjudication, and the provision of solutions in the form of judicial declarations as to what the Constitution contains or means.

Constitutional disputes, therefore, provide the occasions when different components of the American creed or different constructions of the creed come into direct and explicit conflict. In arbitrating between these conflicting perspectives, the Supreme Court has to use the Constitution to weigh not merely the merits of the constitutional argument, but also the contemporary meaning and importance given to the variety of American values accommodated within the Constitution. In this respect, Supreme Court judgments are often in essence declarations of public philosophy in constitutional dress. They are declarations in which the inherent strains between American values are not so much resolved as reformulated either to reflect current conceptions of, and allegiances to, different aspects of America's liberal democracy, or else to achieve a different balance between the constituent themes of the regime.

6

Equality

INTRODUCTION

Within the revolutionary rhetoric of the Declaration of Independence lies the inspirational assertion that, as far as America was concerned, it was a self-evident truth that 'all men are created equal'. The denial by British imperial authority that American colonists had rights comparable with, and even equal to, other Englishmen generated a revolutionary fervour in the 1760s and 1770s. That fervour expressed itself in an intense and broad-ranging evaluation of the origins and nature of political authority. When the technical and jurisdictional arguments against British authority had been exhausted by the ultimate constitutional sanction of parliamentary sovereignty, the Americans resorted to the sweeping categories of natural law.

Individual liberties began to be recast as expressions of a universal condition in which the equality of rights transcended social boundaries in general and imperial relationships in particular. The political implications were profound.[1] The American assertion that their rights were equal to those of the English led to the revolutionary conclusion that they possessed the same authority as Englishmen in resisting what they regarded as the subversion of the British constitution by George III. The rallying justification of the Declaration of Independence expressed both the meaning of America's revolution and the sources of its national autonomy and identity in terms of a universal equality of rights. Such a declaration, however, proved to be double-edged.

The formal dedication to equality in the very act of American independence bequeathed a potent vein of egalitarian intent to the stated principles and purposes of American society itself. The notion of equal rights was by 'its very nature corrosive to the traditional authority of magistrates and of established institutions'.[2] The clarion call in 1776 that all men were created equal and that government was derived from their consent confirmed such iconoclasm. The Declaration at the outset established an attachment to egalitarianism which was to influence political ideas and to motivate political movements throughout American history. In the view of Straughton Lynd, for example, 'the Declaration of Independence is the single most concentrated expression of the revolutionary intellectual tradition.

---

[1] Bernard Bailyn, *The Ideological Origins of the American Revolution* (Cambridge, MA: Belknap Press, 1967), pp. 301–19.
[2] Ibid., p. 308.

Without significant exception, subsequent variants of American radicalism have taken the Declaration of Independence as their point of departure and claimed to be the true heirs of the spirit of '76'.[3] But its significance has by no means been confined to radical movements. The Declaration allowed equality to occupy a central position in the nation's own sense of its origins and meaning.

The profusion of egalitarian impulses that have sought legitimacy in the language of 1776 has given American politics a special quality. Some commentators would go further and say that the moral fervour and emotional intensity generated by the equality issue is a distinguishing characteristic of American politics. Gordon Wood has no doubts that the American Revolution not only brought the egalitarian spirit to the surface of political life but ensured that it would ramify throughout the society's subsequent development:

> The Revolution resembled the breaking of a dam, releasing thousands upon thousands of pent-up pressures.... Nothing contributed more to this explosion of energy than did the idea of equality. Equality was in fact the most radical and most powerful ideological force let loose in the Revolution. Its appeal was far more potent than any of the revolutionaries realized. Once invoked, the idea of equality could not be stopped, and it tore through American society and culture with awesome power.[4]

J. R. Pole's magisterial study of American egalitarianism leads him to the conclusion that the idea of equality retains a 'tenacity' and a 'vitality' in the United States because of 'the fact that equality had entered into the language of justice in a more explicit and more public manner than in most contemporaneous political systems'.[5] In Pole's view, the United States is distinguished by this genealogy of egalitarianism: 'As a social ideal, then as a constitutional principle, the idea of equality has a primacy in America that it generally lacks in other Western democracies'.[6] Ronald Dworkin agrees and points to the effect of the Declaration of Independence and various constitutional landmarks in establishing equality as an integral element in America's conception of fundamental law. In particular, when the Bill of Rights and the provisions of the Fourteenth Amendment are taken into account, then to Dworkin the 'scope is breathtaking' for they entail 'nothing less than that government treat everyone subject to its dominion with equal concern and respect'.[7]

The centrality of the egalitarian principle in American society is unquestioned. What does remain open to question is how that centrality is both conceived and expressed. If the United States has had wide experience of egalitarian ideas in its political culture, then it is just as true that America has had every opportunity to

---

[3] Straughton Lynd, *Intellectual Origins of the American Radicalism* (London: Faber & Faber, 1969), p. 4.

[4] Gordon S. Wood, *The Radicalism of the American Revolution* (New York: Vintage, 1993), p. 232.

[5] J. R. Pole, *The Pursuit of Equality in American History* (Berkeley, CA: University of California Press, 1978), p. 3.

[6] J. R. Pole, 'Equality: An American Dilemma', in Leslie C. Berlowitz, Denis Donoghue, and Louis Menand (eds.), *America in Theory* (New York: Oxford University Press, 1988), p. 70.

[7] Ronald Dworkin, *Freedom's Law: The Moral Reading of the American Constitution* (New York: Oxford University Press, 1996), p. 73.

come to know the prodigious complexities of equality as both a concept and as an ideal. Equality is one of the most elusive of political terms. It can assume different meanings to different people at different times. There can be different dimensions of equality applied to different categories of society. Principles like equality before the law, political equality, equality of opportunity, religious equality, gender equality, racial equality, and economic equality all have separate implications which can lead to conflicts between different forms of egalitarian claims.

For example, an equality of opportunity may allow for a rudimentary equality at the starting gate of life, but in doing so it can be used to justify the greatest of inequalities that ensue in the subsequent race for possessions and status. Alternatively, the effort to achieve even a modicum of equal opportunity will require forms of political intervention that will almost inevitably restrict the liberty of some individuals and lead to charges that they are being subjected to unequal treatment by the state. The relationships between varying dimensions of equality, therefore, can be highly problematical in terms of logical analysis, practical arrangement, and social attachments. Given that the United States has traditionally given equality a position of high natural prominence, then it is true to say that America has had more experience than most with the many ramifications of egalitarianism.

THREE OUTLOOKS ON EQUALITY

American attitudes towards equality and towards the problems raised by it have been many and varied, but they can be reduced—without undue oversimplification—to three basic positions.

Equality as Given

First, equality is simply accepted as an a priori feature and conditioning property of American society. Given the revolutionary nature of the republic's origins and the 'bottom-up' character of its democratic formation, equality is taken to be an operational premise of the American condition. In this context, the foundational significance of the Declaration of Independence is based upon its affirmation of the pre-existence of equality in terms of equal natural rights.

The egalitarian premise and with it the impulse against hierarchy have become embedded in American identity. As a result, the principle of equality is now simply incorporated into the collective litany of multiple American values. The egalitarian spirit is assimilated through an inclusive discourse that repeatedly makes reference to a cluster of values, which are cited and used interchangeably. Any inconsistencies or contradictions are nullified by the belief that such traditionally American principles as liberty, individualism, and democracy are not only compatible with equality, but generically related to it. The result is that equality is often simply regarded as part of a set of values that are interdependent upon one another to the extent of forming an integral whole of American principles. They are seen as fitting together with one another by virtue of the American experience. America's social consensus, in other words, translates into a consensus of values. The values may not be fully in accord with one another on an abstract level, but they are rendered compatible in American life by their assimilation in a unified American culture.

It is common, therefore, to find potentially conflicting values spontaneously and unselfconsciously woven together in an American context. For example, according to Henry Steele Commager, the 'New World possessed not only the most favored of natural environments; it had constituted for itself the most favored of social environments—one of freedom, toleration and equality'.[8] Daniel Bell is similarly reassuring: 'In the United States, the tension between liberty and equality, which framed the great philosophical debates in Europe, was dissolved by an individualism which encompassed both. Equality meant a personal identity, free of arbitrary class distinctions'.[9] Wood asserts that revolutionary egalitarianism set in motion a movement against established hierarchies. In doing so, it not only created the social space for the promotion of individual freedoms but fostered a widely accessible form of democratic citizenship.[10] Alexis de Tocqueville used democracy and equality in America as interchangeable categories. To him, the equality of American conditions represented the embodiment of democratic development (see chapter 4). But perhaps the most celebrated example of America's fusion of equality with other political principles came in President Abraham Lincoln's Gettysburg Address (1863), which joined together political liberty, civic equality, and national democracy into a composite American ideal. In the space of a few lines, Lincoln first gave full recognition that the nation had been 'conceived in liberty, and dedicated to the proposition that all men are created equal'. He then went to link this hybrid to a democratic conception of government, which was 'of the people, by the people, for the people'.[11]

This type of accomplished conjunction of equality with other American values is not without some foundation. From a logical point of view, it is possible to argue that liberal individualism presupposes a devolution of responsibility and power outward to all persons on the basis of their equal status as citizens. Liberties in this sense follow on as a corollary of equal rights. Democracy similarly can be seen as an extension of the equality of individual rights and as the necessary expression of the belief that all individuals possess an intrinsic worth and a right to share in their own government. Equality, to W. H. Riker, is 'simply an insistence that liberty

[8] Henry S. Commager, *The Empire of Reason: How Europe Imagined and America Realized the Enlightenment* (London: Weidenfeld & Nicolson, 1978), p. 102.

[9] Daniel Bell, 'The End of American Exceptionalism', in Nathan Glazer and Irving Kristol (eds.) *The American Commonwealth—1976* (New York: Basic, 1976), p. 209.

[10] Wood, *The Radicalism of the American Revolution*.

[11] Abraham Lincoln, 'The Gettysburg Address', 19 November 1863, http://showcase.netins.net/web/creative/lincoln/speeches/gettysburg.htm. See also Gary Wills, *Lincoln at Gettysburg: The Words That Remade America* (New York: Simon & Schuster, 1993), chs. 3, 4.

be democratic, not the privilege of a class'.[12] According to these terms of reference, egalitarianism has been an American ideal, and like other American ideals, it has been achieved as part of a collective package of principles without the evident need for choices or priorities to be made between the respective components.

Equality as Process

The second view of equality which is common in the United States is to see it not as the self-evident anchorage of a republic but as a prospective condition to which social and legislative energies should be directed. Equality in this respect pertains to a prescriptive principle of motivation. Accordingly, the egalitarian terms of the Declaration of Independence are seen as a substantive promise of equality in American life. The assertion evoked at the birth of the nation that 'all men are created equal' has acted as a continuing standard of social evaluation, as a crusading manifesto of protest and reform, and as an agenda for American progress. This view of American equality does not regard egalitarianism as a descriptive generalization of American society, so much as a requirement to rekindle the radical spirit of 1776 in the context of current conditions.

Egalitarianism, according to this perspective, is a living ethical idea with profound political implications. As a value requiring sustained and intensive social activity to ensure its translation into reality, the proponents of substantive egalitarianism realize that such an ideal demands the recognition that other American political principles may not always be consistent with the drive towards equality. To press for equality in America, therefore, can be controversial for it can risk the appearance of damaging rifts amongst American ideals, and generate a need for choices to be made between them. In effect, equality has the capacity to disrupt the contractual basis of the liberal state by challenging the implicit order of its priorities.

Historical experience, for example, has shown that democracy can be used not merely to reflect the equality of individual rights, but to restrict such rights in the cause of a social equality that limits, and even, denies personal liberty. In the same vein, the pursuit of equality can fly directly in the face of a democracy that is content with an established structure of inequality in society. The same de Tocqueville who regarded American equality as being synonymous with American democracy was under no illusion that the two were interchangeable categories. Neither equality nor democracy would always be necessarily consistent with political liberty. Although 'equality in its most extreme degree' could become 'confused with freedom',[13] de Tocqueville was clear that they remained distinguishable from one another: 'The taste that men have for freedom and the one they feel for

---

[12] W. H. Riker, *Democracy in the United States*, 2nd edn (New York: Macmillan, 1965), p. 20.

[13] Alexis de Tocqueville, *Democracy in America*, trans. ed., and intro. Harvey C. Mansfield and Delba Winthrop (Chicago, IL: Chicago University Press, 2000), p. 480.

equality are in fact two different things, and I do not fear to add that among democratic peoples they are two unequal things'.[14]

He believed that the hybrid conditions of American equality and democracy posed a direct threat to liberty. To de Tocqueville, the problem with democratic government in America was not its weakness but 'its irresistible force'. What he found repugnant was not 'the extreme freedom' that reigned there but rather 'the lack of a guarantee against tyranny'.[15] Because the egalitarian logic of American democracy allowed the majority to draw 'a formidable circle around thought', de Tocqueville claimed that he knew of no other country where there was 'less independence of mind and genuine freedom of discussion'.[16]

If egalitarianism can create a dissonant presence within America's liberal democratic consensus, it can also be attractive as an instrument of political complaint—especially when it can be claimed to be an active derivative of the American Revolution. Egalitarian principles have been frequently invoked by American dissidents for this very reason. Egalitarian rhetoric has successfully animated such political movements as the Jacksonian Democrats, the slavery abolitionists, and the Populists. The generalized conception of American equality can be drawn upon to underline the disjuncture between historical principle and egalitarian formalism on the one hand, and the contemporary and empirical denial of equality on the other. Demands that these two dimensions should reach a closer approximation to one another have been a continuing theme in American politics. The desired states of equality (i.e. equality of opportunity, legal equality, economic equality) and the manner of their acquisition may well have varied greatly, but this does not detract from the fact that egalitarian principles can and have been effectively used to mobilize American protest and to define reform objectives.

Equality in the Breach

After the promise of equality comes the evidence of its apparent denial. This represents the third common conception of egalitarianism in the United States. The allusions to the prospect of, and the aspiration to, a condition of equality are normally mixed with a recognition that there exists in America a glaring discrepancy between the principled premise and the factual presence of equality.[17] The abstract attachment to egalitarianism does not translate easily into concrete measures of equality in a society which, in every other respect, is renowned for its emphasis upon individual incentives, private aspirations, and personal liberties. This does not necessarily mean that the American commitment to equality is fraudulent. It means that it is conditioned and qualified at any time by expressions of equality—each one of which is susceptible to a variety of meanings sufficient

[14] Ibid., p. 480.   [15] Ibid., p. 241.   [16] Ibid., p. 244.
[17] For example, see Rogers M. Smith, *Civic Ideals: Conflicting Visions of Citizenship in US History* (New Haven, CT: Yale University Press, 1999).

to accommodate the social existence of diversity, hierarchy, and even inequality within a construction of general equality.

The American ambivalence towards its own ideal of equality was even evident during the revolutionary period when Americans appeared to be most dedicated to the precepts of egalitarianism. At the very time when the American revolutionaries were dedicating themselves to the principle of republican equality, it was clear that the equality they had in mind was a general equality of moral esteem. The revolutionary leaders had no intention of denying what they regarded as the inevitability of natural inequalities and the consequent formation of a natural hierarchy of talents, skills, and virtues. 'By republicanism the Americans meant only to change the origin of social and political pre-eminence, not to do away with such pre-eminence'.[18] Even the Founding Fathers, who have often been accused of serving their own propertied interests by devising a central and protective government, were so concerned that a strong government could be corrupted into creating unnatural, unwarranted, and undesirable inequalities that they saw it was as much in their interests to have a government of limited powers, as it was to have one of extensive powers. Equality in this sort of context referred to the equal accessibility of rights that would allow individuals to rise and fall in station in such a way as to reflect their true merit and natural capacity. 'The peculiarities of social development in the new world had created an extraordinary society, remarkably equal yet simultaneously unequal, a society so contradictory in nature that it left contemporaries puzzled and later historians divided.'[19]

The puzzlement and divisions have remained. In some respects, late eighteenth-century America can appear to be thoroughly egalitarian in spirit. The era witnessed the destruction of the American Tories, the prevention of an established church, the formal abandonment of separate social orders, the prohibition of any titles of nobility or other forms of hereditary privilege, and the provision of guaranteed equal liberties against government in the various charters of rights included in the constitutions of the new states.[20] In other respects, the period can be said to be far removed from being egalitarian. Voting was limited to white males with a variety of age, property, and residence qualifications. Women were excluded from all political activity. Slavery was condoned by the Constitution. The indigenous Indian population was regarded as being outside the law. And indentured servants might have to survive as semi-slaves for many years in order to fulfil their contractual obligations.[21] This cultural duality over equality was epitomized in the American attitudes to rank and hierarchy. Americans found the pretensions of social distinction quite detestable, yet at the same time it was undeniable that they coveted the symbols of social status and prestige.[22]

---

[18] Gordon S. Wood, *The Creation of the American Republic, 1776–87* (Chapel Hill, NC: University of North Carolina Press, 1969), p. 71.
[19] Ibid., p. 73.   [20] See Ibid., chs. 4–6, 8, 9.   [21] See Smith, *Civic Ideals*, chs. 3–7.
[22] See De Tocqueville, *Democracy in America*, pp. 187–90, 326–48, 546–53, 563–76.

It could be said that 'the American revolution introduced an egalitarian rhetoric into an unequal society',[23] where it has stayed ever since. While this rhetoric has not been without long-term significance, its immediate effect was to emphasize equality for the purpose of a libertarian rush for the new sources of individual inequalities in the social and economic spheres of a rapidly developing country. To a historian like Martin Diamond, it is important that we should not be misled by the language of the Declaration of Independence into believing it ever had anything at all to do with a call for equality. To Diamond, it was always first and foremost a charter of political liberty: 'The Declaration does not mean by "equal" anything at all like the general human equality which so many now make their political standard.... The equality of the Declaration.... consists entirely in the equal entitlement of all to the rights which comprise political liberty, and nothing more'.[24] Notwithstanding the debates over the meanings and motivations behind the Declaration, the history of much of the nineteenth century leaves little doubt as to how the 'equality' of the Declaration was interpreted and used at the time.

In the early nineteenth century, 'equality of opportunity' rose in prominence to become an accepted orthodoxy. In a period of industrial and commercial development, such equality acquired a validity which was drawn directly from the social mobility and economic expansion of Jacksonian America. In this early American period of small-producer capitalism, it was widely assumed that individualism and equality could be fused together within the emancipating medium of economic activity. A basic legal equality, combined with an equality of access to the market, was thought to carry the potential for a wide distribution of goods and positions.[25] To many egalitarians in this period, hierarchy and inequality were derived from the dimension of government regulation and political privilege. The economic sphere by contrast offered a levelling culture of trade, exchange, and emancipation. Equal process in the form of an unregulated market would yield an equality of outcomes. Economic equality, therefore, would serve to counteract the static hierarchy of self-perpetuating political power and structured coercion. Accordingly, Jacksonians believed that because government intervention would always have a distorting influence upon the market, it would necessarily create new inequalities or deepen pre-existing inequalities.

By the end of the nineteenth century, the egalitarian benevolence of the unregulated market was no longer such a plausible construction. The availability of cheap land and new settlements had been integral to the small-producer model of capitalism but now that stimulus to mobility into the substantive equality of proprietorship had been drastically diminished. Corporate capitalism demonstrated that the dynamics between economic and political spheres could be reversed, allowing economic inequalities to be translated into political power. In this period, free enterprise and competition had been extended, or corrupted, to produce vast

---

[23] Pole, *The Pursuit of Equality in American History*, p. 13.

[24] Martin Diamond, 'The Declaration of Independence and the Constitution: Liberty, Democracy and the Founders', in Glazer and Kristol (eds), *The American Commonwealth—1976*, pp. 48–9.

[25] Wood, *The Radicalism of the American Revolution*.

economic empires and natural monopolies, along with well-established business and financial elites and a burgeoning industrial working class. Notional equality had surrendered to huge inequalities in wealth, status, and prospects. In many quarters, economic opportunity was interpreted as a fiction that simply provided a legitimizing pretext for capital accumulation (see pp. 65–7). The original egalitarian impulse of liberal capitalism had been turned in on itself and America's greatest achievement of economic growth had come to coincide with the country's most vivid contradiction of equality.

Ultimately, the disparities in wealth and status led to a radical revision of the balance between equality of opportunity and equality of result. This produced a shift in the conceptual correlation between government action and social benefit. Governments as expressions of the popular will and the public interest now competed with the market as the chief agency of equity. This process of adjustment continues to the present day. Equality of opportunity, therefore, has both procedural and substantive expressions. Benefits and costs accrue to different parties with divergent views on the meaning of equality and the legitimacy of the measures taken in its name. While the concept of equality enjoys a high level of generalized approval in the United States, the exact nature of its implications remains open to question.[26] It is when the idea has to be factored into policy priorities that equality produces intense disagreements 'over just what it is that is to be equalized'.[27]

The American ambivalence over equality is illustrated by these three outlooks upon the subject. No single view of equality exists in the United States. This is partly because of the elusive nature of what equality means in any unified abstract sense. As noted above, equality can alter in relation to any category of society (e.g. economics, religion, race, gender). 'Equalities' can clash with other 'equalities'. The mercurial nature of American equality, however, is also due to the fact that the United States' experience of equality as an ideal and as an issue has varied so much over its history. In contrast to some of the other central values in American politics (e.g. liberty, individualism, democracy), the status of equality can be said to have fluctuated quite markedly during America's development.

To Pole, equality in the first half of the nineteenth century was reduced to an equality of opportunity—'an imperfectly digested notion which actually conflicted with other egalitarian precepts'.[28] After the Civil War, the idea of equality 'advanced far beyond the heroic rhetoric of revolutionary times'[29] only to fall away as 'egalitarians lost their grip on American developments more completely than ever before'.[30] Following the Second World War, equality was 'out of its box

---

[26] See John Schaar, 'Some Ways of Thinking about Equality', *The Journal of Politics*, vol. 26, no. 4 (November 1964), pp. 867–95; Douglas Rae with Douglas Yates, Jennifer Hochschild, Joseph Morone, and Carol Fessler, *Equalities* (Cambridge, MA: Harvard University Press, 1981).

[27] Thomas Sowell, *A Conflict of Visions: Ideological Origins of Political Struggles* (New York: Quill, 1987), p. 122.

[28] Pole, *The Pursuit of Equality in American History*, p. 2.

[29] Ibid., p. 176.   [30] Ibid., p. 2.

again'[31] and given close attention as 'a central and definitive object—a social aim to be achieved'.[32] From his observations of the Supreme Court, Henry J. Abraham concluded that the period covering the 1960s to the 1980s had witnessed scenes of open warfare between 'liberty and equality, both of which are cherished constitutional guarantees'.[33] In Abraham's view, these conflicts posed the 'question whether liberty, at least to some extent, had been taking a proverbial licking from equality'.[34]

Equality as a driving political force appears, therefore, to wax and to wane in American society. This apparent variability further compounds the complexity attached to the idea of equality, as its meanings become heavily dependent upon its changing salience as a political issue. At different times, it is more likely than not that equality will be construed as (i) simply an integral feature of the American consensus, or as (ii) a promise of substantive change, or alternatively as (iii) a promise more honoured in the breach than in the observance. In this respect, it is just as plausible for the same group, and even for the same person, to concur with each of the three views of American equality at different times, as it is for any group or individual to hold consistently to one or other of these three perspectives.

RACE: FRAMING THE GRIEVANCE

Nothing better exemplifies the complexity surrounding the meanings of, and attachments to, American equality than what has been not only the most fundamental dispute in American history and society, but the most grievous challenge to America's egalitarian credentials. The dispute in question is known as America's 'racial problem'. The problem has remained rooted in the fact that America's black population is derived from its original condition of enforced enslavement. As the only sector of American society which had patently never opted voluntarily to emigrate to America and which had arrived in the New World as officially designated forms of property, the historical position of black Americans has been uncertain, provisional, and, at times, precarious.

One of the great ironies of the Declaration of Independence was that it included a charter of universal rights propounded by the great libertarian, Thomas Jefferson, who himself kept slaves. Jefferson was entirely typical of his class of landed estate owners in the South. Along with many of his contemporaries, he mixed a liberal idealism with the retention of social hierarchy entailing a supportive structure of slave labour. Jefferson's position was synonymous with a context in which the 'most radical claims for freedom and political equality were played

---

[31] Ibid., p. 292 (box).   [32] Ibid., p. 3.

[33] Henry J. Abraham, *Freedom and the Court: Civil Rights and Liberties in the United States*, 5th edn (Oxford: Oxford University Press, 1988), p. 9.

[34] Ibid.

out in counterpoint to chattel slavery, the most extreme form of servitude'.[35] In other words, the 'equality of political rights, which is the first mark of American citizenship, was proclaimed in the accepted presence of its absence'.[36] Jefferson opposed slavery in theory but believed that the security of the whites and the preservation of republican government required the continuation of the South's 'peculiar institution'. Jefferson thought that one day the slaves would be emancipated, but that the two races would never form a single society: 'Nothing is more certainly written in the book of fate than these people are to be free. Nor is it less certain that the two races equally free, cannot live in the same government. Nature, habit, opinion has drawn indelible lines of distinction between them'.[37]

Emancipation eventually came in the middle of a Civil War, which was a conflict between the social and economic interests of American sections, occasioned by, and symbolized by, the issue of slavery. President Lincoln declared the Emancipation Proclamation in 1863, but it contained none of the egalitarian tones of the Declaration. Despite his reputation for having freed the slaves, Lincoln never expressed any support for the principle of a social or political equality between the races. The terms of the Emancipation Proclamation made it quite clear that the motive had been one of military and diplomatic necessity. The Civil War bequeathed a notional equality and freedom upon a race which had been remorselessly conditioned to systematic subordination. Thereupon began a process by which Americans sought to reconcile old habits with new expectations.

At first, the prognosis looked very promising. The Civil War had freed American society from the divisive curse of slavery. President Lincoln had grounded the renewal of the union in the theme of equality: an equal basis to relations between sections, regions, and interests; the unifying experience of common sacrifice; and a comparable point of equity between whites and blacks in the form of the abandonment of enforced servitude. The Republican radicals in Congress spearheaded the movement to give civic substance to the freedom of the ex-slaves. The Thirteenth, Fourteenth, and Fifteenth Amendments to the Constitution were intended finally and conclusively to raise the ex-slaves to a position of equal citizenship with guaranteed rights and, in particular, the right to vote, by which other rights might best be maintained. To drive the point home the Fourteenth Amendment contained an unprecedented directive to the states not to 'make or enforce any law which shall abridge the privileges or immunities of citizens of the United States'; nor to 'deprive any person of life, liberty, or property without due process of law'; nor to 'deny any person within its jurisdiction the equal protection of the laws'.

The Civil War amendments were designed to prevent the South from slipping back into its old prejudices. The 'Black codes', pursued by the old confederate

---

[35] Judith Shklar, *American Citizenship: The Quest for Inclusion* (Cambridge, MA: Harvard University Press, 1991), p. 1.

[36] Ibid.

[37] Library of Congress, Thomas Jefferson, Autobiography Draft Fragment, 27 July 1821, *The Thomas Jefferson Papers, Series 1, General Correspondence,* http://memory.loc.gov/cgi-bin/query/P?mtj:1:./temp/~ammem_E09D.

states immediately after the Civil War, had already limited the property rights of blacks and prevented any ex-slaves from holding public office, from voting in elections, and from serving on juries. The new constitutional amendments, as well as the federal army of occupation in the South, helped to provide an environment in which America's new black citizens might exercise the rights of citizenry. It was from the late 1860s up to the mid-1870s that the course of black advance flourished in the South. States from the old confederacy even sent sixteen blacks to the House of Representatives and two to the US Senate during this period. It would be another 120 years before southern black representation on this scale would be repeated in the US Congress.[38]

Following the period of Reconstruction, the South was permitted to lapse back into institutionalized racism. The new consciousness of equal rights and liberties, which the Civil War had done so much to promote, declined into a steady acceptance of a social structure characterized by impregnable privileges, inviolable property rights, and entrenched inequalities. By the end of the century, the South was awash with 'Jim Crow' laws through which blacks were effectively disenfranchised and reduced to segregated second class citizenship. The Supreme Court had effectively eviscerated the Fourteenth Amendment of its meaning and force.[39] Most significantly in the *Plessy v. Ferguson* (1896)[40] decision, the Court condoned segregation by stating that the races could be constitutionally separated as long as the facilities provided were equal. As the Court showed very little interest in determining *how* equal they needed to be, the South was able to provide separate facilities that were equal instead to the level of esteem that blacks were held in by the mass of southern whites.

The collapse of black citizenship had become so endemic that by the turn of the century a black leader like Booker T. Washington had conceded that civil equality for blacks should be postponed to allow rights and reputation to be earned incrementally. Black emancipation had been secured as a result of a military calculation in the Civil War and civil freedom had been accelerated through a top-down political process that had placed southern blacks in an essentially artificial position. A form of equality had been bestowed by whites. Now it was being withdrawn through the same means. The solution for Washington was for blacks to achieve social and economic status before making political claims to equality.[41]

---

[38] Eric Foner, *Reconstruction: America's Unfinished Revolution, 1863–77* (New York: Harper & Row, 1988); Congressional Research Service, 'Black Members of the United States Congress: 1870–2005' (Washington, DC: Congressional Research Service/Library of Congress, 2005), Congressional Research Service, http://www.senate.gov/reference/resources/pdf/RL30378.pdf.

[39] In the *Civil Rights Cases*, 109 US 3 (1883), the Supreme Court established a narrow construction of the Fourteenth Amendment. 'No state ... shall deny to any person ... the equal protection of the laws' was taken to mean that only states, in the form of state officials acting under state law, were subject to the prohibitory clauses of the Amendment. Private discriminatory practices, therefore, were outside the scope of the Amendment and, as such, the US Congress had no power in these circumstances to enforce the provisions of the Amendment.

[40] *Plessy v. Ferguson*, 163 US 537 (1896).

[41] See Louis R. Harlan, 'Booker T. Washington and the Politics of Accommodation', in John Hope Franklin and August Meier (eds.), *Black Leaders of the Twentieth Century* (Champaign, IL: University

The condition of black Americans would then be ameliorated by the dynamics of progress in American society. 'It is at the bottom of life we must begin, and not at the top',[42] Washington advised. 'The wisest among my race understand that the agitation of questions of social equality is the extremest folly, and that progress in the enjoyment of all the privileges that will come to us must be the result of severe and constant struggle rather than of artificial forcing'.[43]

A particularly virulent feature of the legal discrimination between the races was the statutes outlawing sexual relations between blacks and whites. Between 1880 and 1920, twenty states, both northern and southern, passed new anti-miscegenation laws or strengthened old ones. They were derived from conventions and statutes established during the period of slavery. They had been based not only upon long-standing cultural taboos but also on the need to preserve the integrity of property rights and inheritance law. The original laws had been intended to protect white women from black slaves. Their purpose was not to protect black women from their white male owners. On the contrary, any children ensuing from a relationship between a black woman and a white man would not inherit the free status of the latter but would instead be confirmed as slaves. After the Reconstruction, Southern states developed a highly bureaucratic concern over racial purity and the requirement for individuals to be classified on racial grounds. Individuals were categorized according to blood ancestry rather than by appearance or self-definition. Fractions of mixed blood were sufficient for an individual to be designated 'Negro' or 'coloured' on birth and death certificates. Even though blacks may have been freed from slavery, these categorizations and anti-miscegenation statutes ensured that they were not to be socially liberated from the stigma assigned to their genetic composition.[44]

In the early twentieth century, the South had become the dark continent of the American mind.[45] Behind the official edifice of legal segregation lay a vast hinterland of unofficial restrictive practices, social discrimination, administrative trickery, selective treatment, and outright intimidation. The brutality of white supremacy was most chillingly symbolized by the local practice of summary lynch law for 'troublesome niggers'. A conservative estimate places the number of blacks who were victims of lynching between 1880 and 1917 at over 2,500. Many of these incidents were witnessed by large crowds who had been organized through advance publicity given in local newspapers. The events were often orchestrated by the Ku Klux Klan which ensured that the violence was ritualized and prolonged

of Illinois Press, 1982), pp. 1–18; Cary D. Wintz (ed.), *African American Political Thought, 1890–1930* (Armonk, NY: ME Sharpe, 1996), pp. 21–83.

[42] Booker T. Washington, Speech to the Cotton States and International Exposition (Atlanta, GA), 18 September 1895, http://historymatters.gmu.edu/d/39/.

[43] Ibid.

[44] See Rachel F. Moran, *Interracial Intimacy: The Regulation of Race and Romance* (Chicago, IL: University of Chicago Press, 2003).

[45] C. Vann Woodward, *The Origins of the New South, 1877–1913* (Baton Rouge, LA: Louisiana State University Press, 1951), chs. 13, 14; C. Vann Woodward, *The Strange Career of Jim Crow*, 3rd edn, rev. (New York: Oxford University Press, 1974), pp. 67–109.

through humiliation and mutilation before the hanging and incineration during or after it. Criminal liability for such unofficial forms of capital punishment was waived through the customary fiction that the perpetrators were unknown. At a more fundamental level, lynching was for all practical purposes not regarded as a crime. These acts of communal brutality, which were often arbitrary in origin, represented not only a ferocious backlash against black presumption of equality, but constituted a dramatic deterrent against attempts to question the South's form of social control. There could be no clearer manifestation of the extent to which blacks had been subjugated by a white community totally secure in its assumption of superiority, and in its local power to convert that assumption into violent activity.[46]

The South's pattern of social discrimination and economic exploitation continued largely undisturbed into the 1940s and 1950s. Even the federal government reflected the general malaise concerning the social status and legal position of black Americans. Desmond King gives graphic illustration of the way that the federal government actively underwrote the practice of discrimination in both its enactments and its mode of operation. It was 'a fundamental feature of the US government before the 1960s that its own internal organization was segregated. The entrenchment of segregated race relations in the Federal government could not but define in part the character of the American polity'.[47] And yet, in spite of the formidable practice of officially sanctioned discrimination and diminished citizenship, a growing consciousness of, and even concern for, the deprivations of southern blacks could be discerned. American consciences began to be disturbed by what Gunnar Myrdal termed the 'American Dilemma'[48]—the dilemma of the coexistent commitment to equality and to white superiority. The inconsistencies, contradictions, and even hypocrisy of such a dichotomy began to become uncomfortably evident as knowledge of southern practices became more widespread and, thereby, more open to outside condemnation. Where there was interest, so also was there opportunity.

RACE: EQUALITY AS INTEGRATION

The person who did most to exploit that opportunity and who came to embody the strategy most widely employed by black reformers was Martin Luther King, Jr. King supported the legal assault upon segregation conducted by organizations

---

[46] See W. Fitzhugh Brundage (ed.), *Under Sentence of Death: Lynching in the South* (Chapel Hill, NC: University of North Carolina Press, 1997); Philip Dray, *At the Hands of Persons Unknown: The Lynching of Black America* (New York: Random House, 2002).

[47] Desmond King, *Separate and Unequal: Black Americans and the US Federal Government* (Oxford: Clarendon Press, 1997), p. 16.

[48] Gunnar Myrdal, *An American Dilemma: The Negro Problem and American Democracy* (New York: Harper, 1944). See also Stephen Brooks, *America through Foreign Eyes: Classical Interpretations of American Political Life* (Oxford: Oxford University Press, 2002), ch. 4.

like the National Association for the Advancement of Colored People. They had been successful in undermining the structure of 'separate but equal' facilities for different races by proving that the facilities offered were usually far from equal and were occasionally non-existent. In the celebrated *Brown* v. *Board of Education of Topeka* (1954)[49] decision, the Supreme Court had even overturned the *Plessy* v. *Ferguson* formula in public education by declaring that separate educational facilities were 'inherently unequal' and, therefore, were a denial of 'the equal protection of the law guaranteed by the Fourteenth Amendment'.[50] Despite these victories, King felt that the protracted process of legal reform was a necessary but not a sufficient means to achieve change. He believed that the examination of legal meaning was no substitute for a political challenge to segregation.

King's Southern Christian Leadership Conference in conjunction with organizations like the Student Nonviolent Coordinating Committee and the Congress of Racial Equality believed in direct collective action against segregation in an attempt to mobilize public opinion, to change attitudes, and to undermine the political foundations underpinning segregation. As an avowed pacifist and as a realist who knew the limits of black power in the South, King's main tactic was that of passive resistance. His boycotts, 'sit-ins', and 'sit-downs' were very effective in placing the onus of response on the authorities. If no action was taken, then the protesters would achieve a moral victory over local segregation ordinances; alternatively, by enforcing the law, the authorities exposed the normally concealed violence of racism in beatings and arrests. King became a master of publicity, juxtaposing non-violent piety on the part of the defenceless and dispossessed with the traditional southern discipline of police dogs, whips, and water cannon. The results of these televised set-piece confrontations outraged white middle-class opinion in the North and prepared the ground for action by the federal government.[51]

King succeeded in projecting the civil rights issue, with its egalitarian overtones, into a position of national prominence in the late 1950s and early 1960s. The issue succeeded in claiming mass attention and King determined that the mobilization of political interest and sympathy should be turned into concrete legislative achievement at the highest level.[52] He knew that the power of the white majority in the South could only be restrained to the advantage of the black minority, if it were to be challenged by a prevailing national majority in the federal government. King succeeded in appealing to this wider audience by couching his radicalism in conservative terms. He had an astute sense of how American history

[49] *Brown* v. *Board of Education of Topeka*, 347 US 483 (1954).

[50] *Brown* v. *Board of Education of Topeka*, 347 US 495.

[51] See Hans Walton, Jr., *The Political Philosophy of Martin Luther, King, Jr.* (Westport, CT: Greenwood, 1971), chs. 3–5; David J. Garrow, *Bearing the Cross: Martin Luther King, Jr. and the Southern Christian Leadership Conference* (London: Jonathan Cape, 1988); Mary King, *Mahatma Gandhi and Martin Luther King: The Power of Nonviolent Action* (Paris: UNESCO Publishing, 1999), chs. 2, 4.

[52] See Adam Fairclough, *To Redeem the Soul of America: The Southern Christian Leadership Conference and Martin Luther King, Jr.* (Athens, GA: University of Georgia Press, 2001); Adam Fairclough, *Better Day Coming: Blacks and Equality, 1890–2000* (New York: Penguin, 2002), chs. 11–13.

and American values could be made to serve the cause of civil rights. He regularly wrong-footed the opposition by seeking to 'out-Americanize' them with reference to the Declaration of Independence, to the role of universal rights in the American Revolution, and to the Bill of Rights.

For over a century, sceptics had disputed the validity of the 'deferred commitment to equality' by which the Declaration of Independence had not only been given a comparable status to the US Constitution but had in effect been made a constituent part of it.[53] King, however, insisted upon establishing a seamless connection between the two and enfolding both into a conception of the American dream. The egalitarian tones of the Declaration were repeatedly conjoined to the promise of American life. In his sermon on the American dream, King located its force in the 'majestic words of the Declaration'[54] that 'all men are created equal'. He dwelt repeatedly on the meaning and significance of this assertion:

It's a great dream. The first saying we notice in this dream is an amazing universalism. It doesn't say 'some men,' it says 'all men.' It doesn't say 'all white men,' it says 'all men,' which includes black men. It does not say 'all Gentiles,' it says 'all men,' which includes Jews. It doesn't say 'all Protestants,' it says 'all men,' which includes Catholics. It doesn't even say 'all theists and believers,' it says 'all men,' which includes humanists and agnostics.[55]

King then used this fundamental premise to underline the disjunction between the ideal and the reality of American equality. Thereupon, the case was made for America to engage in a moral revival and that would lead to a greater appreciation of the social value of all human life:

I submit to you...that there is dignity in all work when we learn to pay people decent wages. Whoever cooks in your house, whoever sweeps the floor in your house is just as significant as anybody who lives in that house....And that means that every man who lives in a slum today is just as significant as John D., Nelson, or any other Rockefeller.[56]

In his celebrated 'I Have a Dream' address to the great civil rights rally in 1963, King invoked the theme that he had repeatedly associated himself with during the campaign for racial equality. He assured his listeners that his dream was 'deeply rooted in the American dream'. To King, the nation had to 'rise up and live out the true meaning of its creed: "We hold these truths to be self-evident; that all men are created equal." '[57] King's renewed revelation of the radical implications of America's traditional principles prompted a previously reluctant President

---

[53] See Eugene D. Genovese, 'The Slaveholders' Contribution to the American Constitution', in Eugene D. Genovese (ed.), *The Southern Front: History and Politics in the Cultural War* (Columbia, MO: University of Missouri Press, 1995), pp. 114–28.

[54] Martin Luther, King, Jr. 'The American Dream', sermon delivered at the Ebenezer Baptist Church, Atlanta, Georgia (4 July 1965), http://www.stanford.edu/group/King/sermons/650704_The_American_Dream.html.

[55] Ibid.   [56] Ibid.

[57] Martin Luther, King, Jr., 'I Have a Dream Speech' (28 August 1963), http://www.americanrhetoric.com/speeches/Ihaveadream.htm.

Kennedy to work for the most ambitious civil rights bill in a hundred years. In addressing the problem of civil rights, Kennedy himself found that it was difficult to avoid the egalitarian ramifications of the issue.

This nation was founded by men of many nations and backgrounds. It was founded on the principle that all men are created equal, and that the rights of every man are diminished when the rights of one man are threatened. We are confronted primarily with a moral issue. It is as old as the Scriptures and is as clear as the American Constitution. The heart of the question is whether all Americans are to be afforded equal rights and equal opportunities; whether we are going to treat our fellow Americans as we want to be treated. . . . Now the time has come for this nation to fulfil its promise. The events in Birmingham and elsewhere have so increased the cries for equality that no city or state or legislative body can prudently choose to ignore them.[58]

It was said that 'no other chief executive had ever talked that way about human rights in America'[59]; and that 'no President had ever before so forcefully recognized the moral injustice of all racial discrimination'.[60] King and his followers, therefore, had succeeded not only in establishing civil rights as a key issue on America's political agenda; they had set the terms and vocabulary of the ensuing political debate.

King's objective was that of integration. He regarded the US race issue to be not merely a social problem for America's black community but a moral problem for American society as a whole and, in particular, for the integrity of its avowed political principles. American freedom and equality—not just black freedom and equality—would be secured by the full admission of blacks to the mainstream of American society. In criticizing white behaviour, therefore, King was not condemning the principles of American democracy but offering the opportunity of their total vindication by allowing blacks their rights to full and equal participation in a basically sound and—in every respect other than race relations—even an admirable society.

RACE: CLOSING THE GAP VERSUS SPLITTING THE DIFFERENCE

It has to be pointed out that the measured arguments and assured optimism of the integrationists were not shared by all sectors of the black community. Those who experienced the *de facto* segregation and discrimination in the racial ghettoes of America's northern cities were impressed neither by King's appeals to Christian love and to the better nature of whites, nor by the assault upon the *de*

---

[58] President John F. Kennedy, 'We Face a Moral Crisis', in Henry S. Commager (ed.), *The Struggle for Racial Equality: A Documentary Record* (New York: Harper & Row, 1967), pp. 164–6.
[59] Herbert S. Parmet, *JFK: The Presidency of John F. Kennedy* (Harmondsworth, UK: Penguin, 1984), p. 267.
[60] Theodore C. Sorensen, *Kennedy* (London: Pan, 1965), p. 549.

jure segregation provided by the Civil Rights Acts of 1964, 1965, and 1968.[61] On the contrary, they believed that white racism was a deeper and far more endemic cultural condition than any civil rights legislation could ever relieve. To these embittered victims of hard-core urban racism, the problem of race was not a product of the failure to translate American values into actuality. It was, instead, the natural extrapolation of such values.

Leaders (e.g. Malcolm X, Huey Newton, Eldridge Cleaver, Stokely Carmichael) denounced the objective of integration as a bogus and even malicious digression from the real nature of the black predicament.[62] African-Americans needed to retain and to enhance their consciousness as a separate community with its culture and identity. In this light, black integration was a chimera. White tolerance would never extend to the point of racial equality. More serious than this problem was the damage that would be incurred within the black community in even attempting such an objective. In effect, the fight for integration would come at the price of the disintegration of African-American culture. The followers of black power in the 1960s identified closely with contemporary revolutionaries in Africa and Latin America, who were engaged in what were described as racial wars against imperial power. The black power movement projected the same struggle onto America, and regarded the black community as a colonial entity needing to wrest its independence from the white imperialism of the United States. Instead of integration with what was seen as a degenerate and even fascist white culture,[63] the black power ethos was centred upon a rejection of American values and the need for a physical separation of the black race into self-governing communities. In order to secure the superiority of black culture and virtue from the contamination of white greed and cruelty, nationalist leaders sought to transform a class consciousness into a revolutionary insurrection.

Even though the visions of Black Nationalism never materialized, the movement's leaders were successful in showing how the drive for racial equality could

---

[61] The Civil Rights Act of 1964 was a landmark measure that laid the foundations for other legislative enactments and for the judicial extension of rights. The Act (i) reduced the restrictions on voting registration and on literacy tests in particular; (ii) it outlawed a set of employment practices whenever they were based on race, colour, religion, national origin, or sex; (iii) it improved the ability of the federal government to hasten the desegregation of public schools; and (iv) it barred discrimination in public accommodations when such discrimination and segregation was supported by state laws or official action, when interstate travellers were being served, or when a substantial portion of the goods sold or entertainment provided had moved in interstate commerce. The Voting Rights Act of 1965 intensified the drive against discriminatory voting practices in the South by providing for the federal registration of voters and for the federal supervision of elections in seven southern states.

[62] See Malcom X, *The Autobiography of Malcom X* (New York: Grove, 1965); Malcom X, *By Any Means Necessary*, 2nd edn (New York: Pathfinder, 1992); Malcom X, 'From Basic Unity Program: Organization of Afro-American Unity', in William L. Van Deburg (ed.), *Modern Black Nationalism: From Marcus Garvey to Louis Farrakhan* (New York: New York University Press, 1997), pp. 108–15; Stokeley Carmichael and Charles V. Hamilton, *Black Power: The Politics of Liberation in America* (New York: Vintage, 1967); Eldridge Cleaver, *Soul on Ice* (New York: Dell, 1968); Bobby G. Seale, *Seize the Time* (New York: Random House, 1970); Manning Marable, *Race, Reform and Rebellion: The Second Reconstruction in Black America, 1945–82* (London: Macmillan, 1984), ch. 5.

[63] See George D. Jackson, *Blood In My Eye* (New York: Random House, 1972).

assume forms different to that provided by the prevailing conception of integration. In particular, they underlined the way that a purely legal and technical approach to the problem not only overlooked the issue's manifold moral dimension, but underestimated the durability of social attitudes and the significance of racial consciousness. But in giving a more complex construction to racial equality, Black Nationalist perspective raised just as many questions over equality as the integrationist position. It is arguable, for example, that the Black Nationalists revealed an ambivalence, and even a discomfort, over egalitarianism that ultimately propelled them into a flat rejection of equality on the grounds of the racial superiority of blacks and the need for the races to be kept apart from one another.[64] Mainstream opinion was repelled by what was taken to be the misuse of egalitarian principles, drawn from the Declaration of Independence, to assert the existence of an indigenous and immovable imperium. Such opinion resented the Black Nationalists' dismissal of an albeit nominal civic equality, and their rejection of an aspirational social equality, in favour of an outlook that privileged social division over assimilation.

King and his civil rights coalition were highly critical of the Black Nationalist message.[65] They dismissed it as a tragic paradox. In opposing white values, the nationalists were accused of imitating the worst of them: exclusion, arrogance, and violence. The integrationists found that they were being increasingly squeezed not only by black fundamentalists but also by many white sympathizers who were tiring of the theme of successive reform. The latter group believed that the passage of landmark civil rights legislation had served the logic of its advocates and had redressed the imbalance in favour of an equal opportunity to participate in the political process. The integrationist reformers, however, regarded the civil rights advances as only the beginning of a continual process of readjustment. King continued to claim special treatment for a sector of the population that had suffered generations of special discrimination against its interests. Arguably, the outcome was a frightened, passive, and apathetic people quite ill-suited to the aggressive self-assertiveness of pluralist politics. But the claim for special consideration raised a host of problematic issues over the meaning and place of equality in the United States.

Many of King's detractors felt that the civil rights campaign was divisive because it drew attention to the inequalities in American life, and because it attributed such inequalities to a structural and deliberate practice that conferred continuous advantages on some to the direct detriment of others. This was offensive to many white Americans. It amounted to a flat denial of the basic egalitarian

[64] See E. U. Essien-Udom, *Black Nationalism: The Search for an Identity* (Chicago, IL: University of Chicago Press, 1995), chs. 3, 4, 6, 10; Van Deburg (ed.), *Modern Black* Nationalism; Michael C. Dawson, *Black Visions: The Roots of Contemporary African-American Political Ideologies* (Chicago, IL: University of Chicago Press, 2003), ch. 3.

[65] For a full examination of the divisions between Martin Luther King and Malcolm X, see James H. Cone, *Martin & Malcolm & America: A Dream or a Nightmare* (Maryknoll, NY: Orbis Books, 1992); David Howard-Pitney, *Martin Luther King, Jr., Malcolm X, and the Civil Rights Struggle of the 1950s: A Brief History with Documents* (New York: St. Martin's Press, 2004).

assumptions of American life. More significantly, it sought to discredit the diversities in wealth and social position that were seen as endemic in a free society and the natural result of an interplay of different skills and talents. Sceptics of the civil rights drive pointed out that *inequalities* were a condition and consequence of freedom and that to try to convert them into a singular state of *inequality* was an attempt by black people to evade personal responsibility for their own position.

King, for his part, always insisted that he wanted blacks to be assimilated into America's liberal democratic culture as individuals. He regarded the advocates of violence as strategically misguided:

Sometimes they talk of overthrowing racist state and local governments and they talk about guerrilla warfare. They fail to see that no internal revolution has ever succeeded in overthrowing a government by violence unless the government had already lost the allegiance and effective control of its armed forces. Anyone in his right mind knows that this will not happen in the United States.[66]

But King also considered the proponents of violent reaction as engaging in a moral miscalculation. The impulse for destruction revealed 'a desire for self-destruction, a kind of suicidal longing'.[67] In King's view, this kind of behaviour was a symptom in its own right of a chronic lack of black self-esteem. Accordingly, the black man had to 'boldly throw off the manacles of self-abnegation and say to himself and to the world, I am somebody. I am a person. I am a man with dignity and honor. I have a rich and noble history.'[68] The way to achieve this was not for black leaders to advocate 'the same destructive and conscienceless power that they have justly abhorred in whites'. What was required was a strategic change that would 'bring the Negro into the mainstream of American life as quickly as possible'.[69]

Even up to the point of his assassination in 1968, Dr. King maintained that the ultimate demand of the blacks was their acceptance by whites into American society. But, in order to acquire the entry qualification of equality of opportunity, it was necessary for blacks to be helped collectively by government intervention. King always sought to escape from the paradox of seeking unequal treatment in the pursuit of an equality (i.e. an equality of opportunity) that would justify sustaining a system of inequalities. Although he attempted to tie his appeals for equality to demands for liberty, it was always a difficult hybrid to keep alive. If he gave emphasis to equality, he threatened the liberty of those who would be required to accommodate such equality. If he stressed liberty, then the equality argument always risked being turned on its head and for equality to be seen as nothing more than the equal availability of a right to be unequal.

[66] Martin Luther King, Jr. 'Where Do We Go from Here?', Presidential Address to the Southern Christian Leadership Council, 16 August 1967, http://www.hartford-hwp.com/archives/45a/062.html.
[67] Ibid.   [68] Ibid.   [69] Ibid.

RACE: AFFIRMATIVE ACTION ON THE EDGE

The main problem that King and others had in respect to equality of opportunity lay in the insufficiency of minimal legal rights to create a fully integrated
society. This was a theme that was given extraordinary emphasis during the mid-
1960s when American liberalism ventured into the theme of accelerated equality
through direct federal intervention. President Kennedy's intervention into the civil
rights debate in 1963 may have been noteworthy at the time, but within a period
of only two years, President Lyndon Johnson was prompted into publicly engaging
with the challenge of reducing the level of material inequality experienced by the
black community. He struggled with the different dimensions and implications of
the equality issue set within a mainstream of procedural liberalism. To President
Johnson, it was important to secure and advance civil rights but in his celebrated
Commencement Address at Howard University in June 1965 he made it clear that
the establishment of such freedoms would not necessarily resolve the problems of
inequality.

Negative liberty was described by the president as being insufficient. The
enabling features of positive freedom had to be conjoined to the drive for equality.

[I]t is not enough just to open the gates of opportunity. All our citizens must have the ability
to walk through those gates. This is the next and the more profound stage of the battle for
civil rights. We seek not just freedom but opportunity. We seek not just legal equity but
human ability, not just equality as a right and a theory but equality as a fact and equality as
a result. . . . To this end equal opportunity is essential, but not enough.[70]

President Johnson was adept at articulating the systemic nature and the 'seamless
web'[71] of society's historic prejudice. He gave dramatic expression to the need for
reform in the field of racial equality. But even Johnson, during this belle époque of
American liberalism, encountered difficulties in avoiding the gravitational force
of those norms that combined progress and justice with the self-regulatory
ethos of individual achievement in which '[e]ach could become whatever his
qualities of mind and spirit would permit'.[72] Government activism was deemed
necessary to offer protection on behalf of a minority or class of persons. This
would not only prevent them from falling further into a condition of structured
inequality, but would provide the basis for a defensible variation in the social
profile of black Americans.

Other agencies also sought to break the spiral of racial prejudice, economic
deprivation, and social disadvantage. None more so than the Supreme Court
under Chief Justice Earl Warren (1963–9). The Warren Court repeatedly endorsed
the principle that the federal government should not simply be confined to eliminating the negative features of inequality and discrimination, but should be acting

---

[70] President Lyndon B. Johnson, 'Commencement Address' given at Howard University,
Washington, DC, June 4, 1965, http://www.lbjlib.utexas.edu/johnson/archives.hom/speeches.hom/
650604.asp.

[71] Ibid.   [72] Ibid.

as the chief instrument through which a positive condition of equality might be secured.

Its concern was to serve the value of equality and to incorporate that value more deeply in the Constitution. While the structure was never completed, the blueprint was clear. The Court was moving toward the creation of constitutional guarantees of national basic minimums in education, housing, subsistence, legal services, political influence, birth control services, and other facets of the modern welfare state for all persons regardless of race.[73]

Education was once again identified as the primary agency of social re-engineering with the effect that it re-emerged at the epicentre of political controversy. The abandonment of discriminatory practices in higher education, for example, would not necessarily guarantee more places for blacks and, as such, would not ensure a more diversified racial profile in the future structure of American elites. More positive measures were required to achieve proportionate racial balances and these were actively pursued in particular by the Supreme Court under Chief Justice Warren Burger (1969–86). Ultimately, the response to this problem came in the form of racial quotas and other devices of affirmative action designed to create a representative mix in those centres of education that were pivotal to substantive provision of equal economic opportunities.

The governing rationale of this strategy was that the extraordinary history of slavery and subjugation required exceptional forms of action, in order to disrupt the self-perpetuating dynamics of its social consequences. Opponents adopted a different perspective. Samuel Huntington typifies the reaction from those who felt that such measures contradicted the American creed. As soon as the Civil Rights Acts had been secured, Huntington noted that black leaders 'stopped demanding rights common to all American citizens and instead began demanding governmental programs to provide material benefits to blacks as a distinct racial group'.[74] The pressure to use government to facilitate an economic equality of outcome led to civil rights reforms being reconfigured 'to mean the opposite of what they said and through these interpretations launched a frontal assault on the Creed's principle of equal rights for all that had made the new laws possible'.[75]

The introduction of affirmative action into higher education provoked in its turn an intense opposition. Critics complained that affirmative action not only flew in the face of America's culture of individual achievement and personal freedom, but was contrary to the educational ethos of meritocracy. Many white applicants felt that their places in universities and colleges had been forcibly forfeited to black applicants with inferior qualifications. They complained that they

---

[73] Martin Shapiro, 'The Supreme Court: From Warren to Burger', in Anthony King (ed.), *The New American Political System* (Washington, DC: American Enterprise Institute, 1978), p. 200. See also Morton J. Horwitz, *The Warren Court and the Pursuit of Justice* (New York: Hill & Wang, 1999), chs. 2, 3, 5, 6; Lucas A. Powe, Jr., *The Warren Court and American Politics* (New York: Belknap Press, 2000), chs. 9–17.

[74] Samuel P. Huntington, *Who Are We? America's Great Debate* (London: Simon & Schuster, 2004), p. 148.

[75] Ibid.

had been penalized on grounds of race, which in their view was tantamount to 'reverse discrimination'. In effect, measures designed to diminish inequalities were themselves being challenged on egalitarian grounds. In a twist of historical irony, disappointed whites appealed to the courts for redress through the provisions of the Fourteenth Amendment.[76] In the landmark case of *Bakke v. Regents of the University of California*[77] the Supreme Court invalidated the fixed quota system used by the University in its admissions policy on racial minorities groups. At the same time, the Court approved the principle and purpose of affirmative action in general terms. It permitted the use of race as a consideration but not the sole or overriding factor in the admission process.

Far from resolving the issue, affirmative action has remained a source of polarizing controversy. In the 1990s, those opposed to the principle began to exert considerable leverage. In 1995, the University of California abandoned the usage of race, religion, sex, colour, ethnicity, or national origin in its admission procedures. In 1996, the University of Texas followed suit. Through a direct democracy initiative (Proposition 209), California outlawed the usage of affirmative action not only in the areas of public employment and public education but also in the allocation and management of all state and local government contracts.[78] Twenty-five years after the Bakke case, affirmative action was still being disputed at the highest levels of government.

In June 2003, the Supreme Court revisited the principle of affirmative action in two cases arising from the admissions procedures of the University of Michigan (UM). The university was challenged on the grounds that it operated a de facto quota system that unfairly advantaged under-represented minorities. The position of the university was that race amounted to only one of many selection criteria and that the state had a compelling interest in achieving a diverse student body. Its critics claimed that UM's procedures were discriminatory and, therefore, amounted to having denied applicants the opportunity to compete on an equal basis. In opposing the UM and advocating the usage of 'race neutral' policies, the Bush administration underlined the importance of America's need to make a 'special effort to make real the promise of equal opportunity for all'.[79] The Supreme Court's response was a measured one. In a case related to the Law School, the Court decided in favour of UM and its right to give consideration to race in the admission of students.[80] In another case based upon the practices of UM's College of Literature, Science, and the Arts, the Court found that the University

---

[76] Terry H. Anderson, *The Pursuit of Fairness: A History of Affirmative Action* (New York: Oxford University Press, 2004), ch. 4.

[77] *Bakke v. Regents of the University of California*, 553 P.2d 1152 (1976).

[78] Proposition 209 was passed by 54 per cent of voters in California on 5 November 1996. The key section of the text reads: 'The state shall not discriminate against, or grant preferential treatment to, any individual or group on the basis of race, sex, color, ethnicity, or national origin in the operation of public employment, public education, or public contracting.'

[79] 'President Bush Discusses Michigan Affirmative Action Case', 15 January 2003, http://www.whitehouse.gov/news/releases/2003/01/20030115-7.html.

[80] *Grutter v. Bollinger*, 539 US 306 (2003).

was in breach of the 'equal protection of the laws' clause. In this case, the usage of a points system and the weighting given to race within it were considered to be too mechanical and insufficiently sensitive to other factors in an applicant's overall profile.[81] The fine lines of the Court's interpretation of equal opportunity were reflected in the split nature of both decisions.

After a period of thirty years of social experimentation with affirmative action, a reaction to its working premises has become commonplace. At the outset of the twenty-first century, the utility of intervention in the egalitarian cause of anti-discrimination is regularly subjected to a range of established critiques. Some complaints settle upon implementation problems, the issue of middle-class bias, and the legitimacy of focusing upon groups rather than individuals. Other critiques centre upon claims that affirmative action programmes have actually exacerbated the very problems of racism that they had been designed to alleviate. Alternative views are provided by those who claim that affirmative action programmes are no longer necessary as they have in essence succeeded in achieving their goals of breaking the cycle of discrimination and disadvantage.[82] The work of Abigail and Stephan Thernstrom, for example, attempts to show that access to opportunity has been widened to allow racial minorities as much scope for social advance as those in the traditional mainstream. Accordingly, 40 per cent of black Americans now consider themselves to be middle class with 42 per cent owning their own homes and a third living in suburbia. As a consequence, the need for preferential remedies can now be considered to have passed into history.[83]

Others disagree and point to the continued racial differences in average earnings, career opportunities, housing conditions, professional entry rates, and life expectancy levels. In *The State of Black America 2005* (2005),[84] the National Urban League (NUL) reported that in a series of economic and social sectors (e.g. economic, health, education, social justice) blacks remained at levels conspicuously lower than those of their white counterparts. According to the NUL's aggregate measure of status, blacks achieved an overall level of only 73 per cent of the position held by whites. The divide widened considerably to 57 per cent when the measure was limited to economic status. Even more noteworthy was the category of wealth formation that included home values and equity. This indicator revealed that the median net worth of blacks ($6,166) was ten times less than it was for whites ($67,000).

The Thernstroms counter these types of charges by claiming that education remains the key to any remaining problems. Their point of reference is the claim that high educational test scores lead to middle class prosperity—irrespective of racial background. In particular, they advocate the need to improve the motivation

---

[81] *Gratz v. Bollinger*, 539 US 244 (2003).

[82] For a review of the debates, see Francis J. Beckwith, *Affirmative Action: Social Justice or Reverse Discrimination?* (New York: Prometheus, 1997); Anderson, *The Pursuit of Fairness*.

[83] Stephan Thernstrom and Abigail Thernstrom, *America in Black and White: One Nation, Indivisible* (New York: Simon & Schuster, 1999).

[84] National Urban League, *The State of Black America 2005: Prescriptions for Change* (New York: National Urban League, 2005), www.nul.org/publications/SOBA/2005SOBAEXCSUMMARY.pdf.

and commitment of poor young blacks in a society where the career patterns of white and black graduates are now claimed to be comparable in earnings and opportunity. The cycle of black poverty is not seen to be the result of discrimination so much as the failure of schools to exert tough discipline, to concentrate on basic skills, and to raise the expectation of individuals.[85] By preparing poor blacks for what they see as an essentially non-discriminatory adult world of open opportunity, the Thernstroms believe that simple schooling can break the cycle of impoverishment far more effectively than any schemes of social improvement based upon quotas or preferences. In their work on educational opportunity, Abigail and Stephan Thernstrom exemplify the competitive motivation, individual choice, and personal progress both in conditioning American attachment to equality and in underlining American ambiguity over whether equality is a basic form of social existence or a condition to be secured.

The complex legacy of the Fourteenth Amendment, and the issue of racial inequality which it addressed, remains a continuing point of tension that conditions American approaches to the relationship between acceptable and unacceptable diversity. The ramifications of the Fourteenth Amendment typify the limitations of an enactment with egalitarian intentions set within a context of liberal democratic impulses. The issue of racial or other forms of exclusion is most effectively raised on structural grounds of inherent inequality and unwarranted minority status. However, in establishing such a case, the redress is necessarily couched in terms of legitimized forms of preferential treatment and with it the assignment of social and historical culpability to individual members of the majority, together with the material costs of the remedial action. In this way, interventionist measures to counter inequality can risk compounding original injustices with a form of compensatory injustice translated to other citizens. This can risk inducing a state of renewed intransigence and a claim of discrimination on the part of those who are required to accept the main burden of ameliorating the consequences of the past. On the other hand, interventionist measures can also be criticized for using racially conscious programmes to incorporate a disadvantaged minority successfully into the American mainstream—and in doing so to replicate and deepen the legitimacy of those hierarchies and inequalities that are sanctioned by reference to an openly pluralist society.

THE FEMINIST CHALLENGE TO EQUALITY

Controversies like those over affirmative action serve to suggest that the passage of equality is at best intermittent. Some would claim that it is reversible. But what may have been lost in terms of pace over the past twenty-five years has more than been made up for in terms of proliferation. The ideas and arguments of equality

---

[85] Abigail Thernstrom and Stephan Thernstrom, *No Excuses: Closing the Gap in Racial Learning* (New York: Simon & Schuster, 2004).

that were originally formulated and popularized in the civil rights campaigns of the 1950s and 1960s have been used to great effect by other minorities in search of group rights. Once the idea of equality had been re-established in the public domain, it was said to have 'multiplied and divided like the sorcerer's apprentice's broom'.[86] Political grievances and demands have increasingly assumed the form of egalitarian complaints. The pursuit of equal rights has fostered campaigns for political and legal action to correct alleged discrimination against such groups as Hispanics, Asian Americans, and Native Americans. The most vociferous and the farthest reaching of these challenges have centred upon the position of women in American society.

The current feminist movement, for example, originated in the 1960s when the civil rights campaign led to a heightened awareness of discrimination in other areas. Women's groups pressed not merely for equal pay for equal work, but for a re-evaluation of the comparable worth to society of different jobs, and particularly of those occupations traditionally dominated by women (e.g. teaching, nursing, office work). The cause of equality in hiring and promotions within the workplace progressed with the Supreme Court's willingness to accept sex discrimination cases under the rules of the 1964 Civil Rights Act. The Court also approved of Congressional measures viewing women as a 'protected class' requiring affirmative assistance.[87] In this context of greater sensitivity towards the problems of sexual discrimination, the movement in favour of formalizing equal rights through a constitutional amendment gathered pace. However, the pressure for a constitutional guarantee that rights would not be denied or abridged by any form of sexual discrimination also underlined the problematic nature of legal enactments in such an area of policy.

A constitutional amendment establishing the principle of equal rights for women, Equal Rights Amendment (ERA) had first been introduced into the US Congress in 1923. After languishing there for almost half a century, Congress eventually passed the amendment in 1972. The battle to secure the agreement of the required three-quarters of the states lasted for ten years but in the end the ERA campaign failed to achieve the necessary level of consent. The ERA ran into opposition on several fronts but the most damaging counterargument was that the amendment would have generated a large volume of legislation and litigation authorizing increasing governmental intervention in the spheres of private action and social diversity. The ERA episode typifies one of the central problems in seeking to enact laws to promote greater equality. Attempts to reduce or eliminate unfair discrimination also risk undermining other forms of discrimination or exemption that may be to the benefit or security of an affected minority (e.g. protection of women from hazardous types of employment; the provision of separate facilities in public places). As a result, a tension always exists 'between

[86] Pole, *The Pursuit of Equality in American History*, p. 292.
[87] The landmark case in this field is *Johnson v. Transportation Agency*, 480 US 616 (1987). See also Clare Cushman, *Supreme Court Decisions and Women's Rights* (Washington, DC: CQ Press, 2000), chs. 3, 4, 6–9.

women's political claims for equality because everyone is the same, and women's claims for special treatment because women and men are not similarly situated in society, the polity and the economy'.[88]

The ERA issue brought to the surface the objections of women who believed that gender differences offered protections and privileges based upon the concept of a fixed essence of womanhood. The proponents of this 'essentialist feminism' formed their own organization (Concerned Women for America) to challenge the objectives of the ERA and the claim of the Amendment's chief sponsor (National Organization for Women) to speak on behalf of American women. The STOP ERA movement benefited from feminist essentialism and organized a successful campaign against constitutional change. Phyllis Schlafly, the founder and leader of the STOP ERA, was particularly effective in making egalitarian arguments in opposition to a purportedly egalitarian reform. Schlafly persistently reiterated the theme that equal outcomes do not necessarily coincide with either the intentions or the consequences of equal rights advocates. In deploying the defence of civil liberties against the claims of civil rights, she was also able to arouse suspicions that the federal government was attempting to impose equality and, in doing so, create a new inequality between the government and the people. The ERA was depicted as a liberal device in engineering society from the top down, thereby, strengthening the federal hierarchy under the pretext of weakening another hierarchy.[89]

The feminist campaign for equal rights has drawn attention to an important problematic dimension in the pursuit of equality within a liberal democratic culture. The emphasis upon an equity of rights under the rule of law leads to a specific perspective on the issue of inequality: that the problem, and therefore the solution, are defined in terms of legal or legislative redress to improve the equality of access to society's protections and to its avenues of advancement. In the same way that equality is seen to be a process of incremental movement, so the substance of such reform responses is interpreted as being process-based. Their rationale is one of enhancing the integrity of the claims that hierarchies are based upon merit operating within a medium of fair and open competition. Feminist writers have subjected the assumption of an equal race of competitive individualism to close critical scrutiny. They use the perspective drawn from their collective experience of sexual discrimination to question the meaning and veracity of equal opportunity.

In addition, feminist critiques press the logic of disadvantage to structural conclusions that pose profound challenges to the customary presumption of equitable solutions offered by liberal democratic reform. In this perspective, the social world occupied by women is one of a barely concealed inequality. It is based on a culture of gendered distinctions and a repressive regime of internalized

[88] Georgia Duerst-Lahti, 'Enter Women: Modest Changes in US Politics', in Philip J. Davies (ed.), *An American Quarter Century: US Politics from to Vietnam to Clinton* (Manchester: Manchester University Press, 1995), p. 135.

[89] Donald T. Critchlow, *Phyllis Schlafly and Grassroots Conservatism: A Woman's Crusade* (Princeton, NJ: Princeton University Press, 2000), chs. 8–10. See also Gilbert Y. Steiner, *Constitutional Inequality: The Political Fortunes of the Equal Rights Amendment* (Washington, DC: Brookings Institution, 1985); Jane J. Mansbridge, *Why We Lost the ERA* (Chicago, IL: University of Chicago Press, 1986).

norms that systematically discriminate against the position of women as equals in both the public sphere of politics and civil affairs, and in the private sphere of social and personal relationships. Accordingly, women are identified as being the subject of a set of socially constructed expectations. As a result, they are assigned roles that accumulate into an orthodoxy of beliefs, ideas, and traditions related to a bifurcation of gendered identities. Even in a culture that gives high status to individualism and equality, it is asserted that gender divides citizens through the agency of physical, social, and cultural attributes. These convert differences into a hierarchy of structured inequality that is strongly resistant to substantive change. Such a feminist outlook identifies gender as permeating the entirety of American society and politics.[90]

Given this conception of cultural hierarchy, in which choice and opportunity are limited by both external and internal constraints, the conventional panacea of widening the legal access to a process of individualized success or failure is seen to constitute a false prospectus. Radical feminists claim that even to attempt to compete within such a male-dominated medium is wholly to misunderstand the nature of women's social predicament. The problem identified by this kind of feminism is one of a concealed or disguised dominance of men over women not only within individual contexts, but through social attitudes and institutional behaviour which are deeply aligned to the preservation of male power. In this light, the women's cause is that of a liberation movement designed to eliminate the social isolation of women and to raise awareness of their predicament as an oppressed class. Radical feminists combine their analyses of gender discrimination in public policy and the law with declarations of gender oppression in private contexts. Both dimensions are said to be suffused with structural patriarchy and with a basic aversion either to acknowledge inequality or to work towards a substantive condition of gendered equality.

Far from challenging the system, demands for equal rights legislation are interpreted as merely condoning and reinforcing the deeper substructure of inequality that drives the framework of discrimination throughout the rest of the system. Within this perspective, the law's reputation for equity and neutrality within a liberal order is rejected as false. Moreover, the liberal principle of maintaining a distinction between the public sphere and the private sphere means that the latter is left mainly unregulated. This is to the disadvantage of women who are subjected to a system of subordination within this sphere of social action. The historical exclusion of women from the public sphere merely exacerbates the position and leads to law being denounced not only as implicitly patriarchal in nature but

---

[90] See Catharine A. MacKinnon, *Feminism Unmodified: Discourses on Life and Law* (Cambridge, MA: Harvard University Press, 1988); Susan Faludi, *Backlash: The Undeclared War against American Women* (New York: Crown, 1991); Gisela Bock and Susan James (eds.), *Beyond Equality and Difference: Citizenship, Feminist Politics and Female Subjectivity* (New York: Routledge, 1992); Marshall, Catherine (ed.), *Feminist Critical Policy Analysis* (London: Falmer Press, 1997); Andrea Dworkin, *Life and Death: Unapologetic Writings on the Continuing War against Women* (New York: Free Press, 2002), pp. 60–72, 126–68, 179–96.

motivated by an impulse to maintain, reinforce, and conceal its dominion.[91] As such, the law 'can thus purport to guarantee equality, while simultaneously denying it'.[92] Equality in this sense of legal rights becomes synonymous with preventing any substantive change to a legal system that perpetuates social bias and gendered roles. Accordingly, the pursuit of equal rights can be seen as 'legitimizing discrimination through the language of equality'.[93] Not for the first time, the freedom of inquiry that a liberal society fosters has produced a diagnostic account of hierarchical formation and power relations that conventional liberal politics can neither assimilate nor even adequately address.

 This argument has some parallels with the essentialist viewpoint that the position of women is qualitatively different to other 'minorities'. Both perspectives are based upon the presumption that gender is not only the most important aspect of identity but that it is an essentially non-negotiable property which is not susceptible to the solutions offered by pluralist politics. Essentialist and radical feminists both harbour suspicions of liberal democratic 'solutions'. They are concerned that liberal politics can only react to discrimination within the circumscribed template of equal rights. Such equality is regularly denounced as the instrument of greater inequality. Essentialists claim that this kind of legal levelling is blind to the special category status of women that requires legal boundaries. Radicals on the other hand assert that the campaign for equal rights is merely a form of appeasement. Accordingly, aspiring to the appearance of legal equality represents a chimera that substitutes superficial change for a fundamental assault upon the systemic forms of social oppression that transcend legal rights. The joint nature of these perspectives is evocative of the Black Nationalist perspective in the 1960s when the themes of cultural exceptionalism and radical critique were combined to produce a hybrid rejection of mainstream egalitarianism.

In spite of the critiques of essentialist and radical feminists, and despite the defeat of the ERA, equality feminists have succeeded in extending the reach of women's rights over the past thirty years with numerous examples of rights-based solutions being specifically advanced to address the issue of gender inequality.[94] Even in the private sphere, there has been increasing recognition that the Fourteenth Amendment can and should provide relief against the failure of the state to provide 'equal protection' against the private sovereignty of patriarchal power in

---

[91] See Katharine T. Bartlett and Rosanne Kennedy (eds.), *Feminist Legal Theory: Readings in Law and Gender* (Boulder, CO: Westview Press, 1991); D. Kelly Weisberg (ed.), *Feminist Legal Theory: Foundations* (Philadelphia, PA: Temple University Press, 1993); Catherine A. Mackinnon, 'Difference and Dominance: On Sex Discrimination', in Michael D. A. Freeman (ed.), *Lloyds Introduction to Jurisprudence*, 6th edn (London: Sweet & Maxwell, 1994), pp. 1081–91; Patricia A. Cain, 'Feminism and the Limits of Equality', in Freeman (ed.), *Lloyds Introduction to Jurisprudence*, pp. 1106–15.

[92] Nadine Taub and Elizabeth M. Schneider, 'Perspectives on Women's Subordination and the Role of Law', in David Kairys (ed.), *The Politics of Law: A Progressive Critique* (New York: Pantheon Books, 1982), p. 123.

[93] Taub and Schneider, 'Perspectives on Women's Subordination and the Role of Law', p. 134.

[94] See Dorothy M. Stetson, *Women's Rights in the USA: Policy Debates and Gender Roles*, 3rd edn (London: Routledge, 2004).

the home. Abuses of power that had previously remained immune to challenge by public authorities are now increasingly subjected to regulatory and legal review.[95]

Statutes and court decisions relating to sex discrimination have markedly improved the rights-based position of women in fields ranging from employment to education, and from abortion and reproductive rights to credit, insurance, and pension equity. Moreover, the issue is accepted as one requiring sustained political and legal attention as part of a progressive process of gender sensitive equality. Whether the passage of such reforms has been primarily attributable to the force of legal argument and electoral pressure, or to the analytical critique and rallying rhetoric of feminist advocacy, the effect has been to deepen the rights-based culture of American politics.

In some respects, it may be claimed that the immense advances made by women in high-value sectors in society (e.g. the professions—especially those associated with higher education) is indicative of a shift in attitudes towards a greater equity of opportunity. Nevertheless, the generative properties of such a momentum owe much of their leverage to the way that equality in this field has increasingly been transposed into the parameters of legally discernible and enforceable rights. The principle of an ostensibly self-regulating system of equal opportunity had earlier been widely cited as a device which had maintained, and arguably disguised, a framework of social, economic, and political inequality. Now its potential for facilitating equity in the public sphere is increasingly accepted as an operational feature of social exchange—conditioned as it is by a due process of rights recognition.

INEQUALITIES IN THE RECOGNITION OF INEQUALITY

The collective impetus of rights claims by women as well as by the black community has increased the currency and leverage of a rights-centred language in political argument. Civil rights remedies to gender and racially related grievances have created an accumulation of precedents that afford opportunities to other sectors in the furtherance of their interests. The multiple pursuits of equal rights in a rights-based culture have many ramifications. Groups have been established with collective claims to having been discriminated against. They have used this experience to assert the right of an entitlement to redress on a class basis. These actions have led, for example, to anti-discrimination provisions being applied by the federal government in relation to a set of identified categories (e.g. religion, national origin, age, physical handicap, and sexual orientation).

---

[95] See Laura A. Otten, *Women's Rights and the Law* (Westport, CT: Praeger, 1993), chs. 5, 9, 10, 11; Robin West, *Progressive Constitutionalism: Reconstructing the Fourteenth Amendment* (Durham, NC: Duke University Press, 1994); Michael Perry, *We the People: The Fourteenth Amendment and the Supreme Court* (New York: Oxford University Press, 1999), ch. 5; Garrine P. Laney, *Violence against Women Act: History and Federal Funding* (Washington, DC: Library of Congress; Congressional Research Service, 2005).

The sphere of sexual orientation has provoked intense controversy because, in seeking to ensure the 'equal protection of the laws' to gays, the federal government along with several state governments have been accused of making exceptional provisions for what is essentially a self-selected group. Critics claim that such a group is established through lifestyle choice and not through inherent characteristics. Moreover, in trying to remove discrimination against gays by reference to equality, governments are accused of giving tacit consent to a form of sexual activity that many local majorities find morally objectionable.

The contention here is that references to equality are being used not only to countermand democratic opinion but to legitimize activities and actively promote arrangements which, it is asserted, have little or no relevance to notions of civic egalitarianism.[96] The proponents of gay rights on other hand assert that homosexuality not only has a genetic foundation but is integrally connected to the identity of an individual. As a consequence, gay rights activists look to governments and to the courts to establish rights comparable to those extended to other minorities such as blacks (e.g. franchise guarantees) and women (e.g. abortion rights). The logic of projecting the rights of privacy and the equal protection of the laws to gay men and lesbians, however, has had to confront the distinction between minimal toleration and the active acceptance of full gay rights with their manifold implications in respect to civil rights, social benefits, property law, and tax structures. In effect, what may be tolerated in the private sphere does not necessarily translate into legal equivalence of traditional social arrangements in the public sphere.[97]

Although most states had repealed, or effectively suspended, their anti-sodomy laws before the Supreme Court invalidated them in 2003,[98] this does not mean that gays have been relieved from many other discriminatory measures in relation to such areas as employment, inheritance, and immigration. The multiple campaigns to reduce or abolish many of these restrictions have been symbolized by the pressure for same sex marriage or civil unions to have full legal recognition on the grounds that to deny it would be tantamount to denigrating gays as second class citizens for sexual behaviour that is no longer regarded as illegal.[99] But pressure can be exerted in more than one direction. For example, the legal and constitutional arguments in favour of the equal recognition of gay unions have had to contend with the expressions of public opposition made in referenda. In 2004, voters in eleven states considered propositions that would amend their state constitutions to protect established legislative prohibitions on gay and lesbian civil unions. The aim was to prevent any current or future judicial action calling for the legal recognition of such unions. In all eleven states, voters overwhelmingly

---

[96] See the policy positions adopted by the Family Research Council, http://www.frc.org/file. cfm?f=SEARCH_RESULTS&text_search=gay+marriage&tg=PP.

[97] Andrew Sullivan, *Virtually Normal: An Argument about Homosexuality* (New York: Vintage, 1996).

[98] *Lawrence and Garner v. Texas*, 539 US 558 (2003).

[99] See Yuval Merin, *Equality for Same-Sex Couples* (Chicago, IL: Chicago University Press, 2002); K. Kersch, 'Full Faith and Credit for Same-Sex Marriages', *Political Science Quarterly*, vol. 112, no. 1 (Spring 1997), pp. 117–36.

supported the usage of constitutional amendments to entrench the majoritarian position against same sex marriages or partnerships.[100]

The debate over gay rights, therefore, revolves around disputes between individual and collective rights; contentions over the claims of privacy and the force of majoritarian opinion, social tradition, and religious doctrine; and divisions over different understandings of the meaning, remit, and application of equality.[101] Gay rights, or rather the contingencies and limits of such rights, underline the complexity of the logic surrounding the theme of equal rights set within a social context where equality is seen both as a foundational precept but also an interpretable frame of reference.

The invocation of the Fourteenth Amendment on behalf of minorities allegedly excluded from mainstream society has fostered two main forms of scepticism. The first is one of imprecision and disorder in the law. As government agencies and courts have responded to the varied contexts of individual claims by different groups, the law has expanded its remit on 'due process' and 'equal protection' but in a variety of ways that does not allow for a clear and uniform rationale. Robert Bork describes the confusion in the following terms:

> The court's present law of equal protection is unsatisfactory because there is no adequate explanation for the choice of groups entitled to equal protection or for the differing degrees of protection it affords to the various groups. Thus, the Court has stated that some legislative distinctions ... require strict scrutiny while others ... deserve only minimal scrutiny. But the Court's various members have gone on to articulate various and varying intermediate levels of scrutiny for distinctions made as to other groups.... The result has been an incoherent body of case law.[102]

In essence, the attempt to achieve greater equality has arguably produced an increased level of inequity.

The second complaint pertains to an asserted shift in the burden of proof relating to the issue of inequality. According to this view, the test of discrimination has been relocated from the sphere of process to that of result. Instead of having to demonstrate an intention to discriminate and, thereby, prove the presence of a direct link from cause to effect, it is increasingly alleged that the process has been reversed allowing discrimination to be inferred by the nature of the outcome.

---

[100] The eleven states were Arkansas, Georgia, Kentucky, Michigan, Mississippi, Montana, North Dakota, Ohio, Oklahoma, Oregon, and Utah.

[101] See James W. Button, Barbara A. Rienzo, and Kenneth D. Wald, *Private Lives, Public Conflicts: Battles over Gay Rights in American Communities* (Washington, DC: Congressional Quarterly Press, 1997); Mark Strasser, *The Challenge of Same-Sex Marriage: Federalist Principles and Constitutional Protections* (Westport, CT: Praeger, 1999); George W. Dent Jr., 'The Defense of Traditional Marriage', *The Journal of Law and Politics*, vol. 15 (Fall 1999), pp. 581–644; Gary Chartier, 'Natural Law, Same-Sex Marriage, and the Politics of Virtue', *UCLA Law Review*, vol. 48 (August 2001), pp. 1593–632; Lynn D. Wardle, ' "Multiply and Replenish": Considering Same-Sex Marriage in Light of State Interests in Marital Procreation', *Harvard Journal of Law & Public Policy*, vol. 24 (Summer 2001), pp. 771–814; Thomas C. Caramagno, *Irreconcilable Differences?: Intellectual Stalemate in the Gay Rights Debate* (Westport, CT: Praeger, 2002).

[102] Robert Bork, *The Tempting of America: The Political Seduction of the Law* (London: Sinclair-Stevenson, 1990), p. 330.

In effect, where the results are unequal, the operating presumption is that these amount to a prima facie body of evidence inferring the existence of discriminatory practice. While it is true that survey research and social indicators have been used in support of legislation against discrimination, the appearance of differential patterns of achievement do not necessarily prompt egalitarian responses. In a culture with such a strong attachment to individualism and pluralistic diversity, there remain significant limits to the call for equal protection even in the face of the most flagrant inequalities.

This response was graphically underlined in a Supreme Court judgement on capital punishment where the petitioner based his defence upon the suggestion of a generic racial bias in the administration of the death penalty in the state of Georgia.[103] The petitioner, Warren McCleskey, was a black man who had been convicted of murder and sentenced to death. He appealed against the punishment on the grounds that the sentencing process had been administered in a racially discriminatory manner. In support of his appeal, McCleskey introduced a piece of social research. It showed that in Georgia the incidence of the death penalty revealed the existence of two significant variables. The Baldus Study disclosed that individuals who murdered whites were more likely to be sentenced to death than persons who murdered blacks; and that black murderers were more likely to be sentenced to death than whites convicted of murder. The statistical disparities did not offer direct proof of discrimination but did establish a differential pattern of probabilities relating to the racial profile of capital punishment decisions.[104]

McCleskey's lawyers sought to infer an inequality of process from the unequal configurations of outcomes. The Supreme Court rejected the appeal not merely because the appropriateness of an individual's punishment could not be gauged by a statistical inference from a collective study, but because the discretion that allows for variable outcomes is an integral and valuable part of the court process:

Where the discretion that is fundamental to our criminal process is involved, we decline to assume that what is unexplained is invidious. In light of the safeguards designed to minimize racial bias in the process, the fundamental value of jury trial in our criminal justice system, and the benefits that discretion provides to criminal defendants, we hold that the Baldus study does not demonstrate a constitutionally significant risk of racial bias affecting the Georgia capital sentencing process.[105]

The judgement reflected the judiciary's concern over the issue of racial discrimination but also epitomized the conditioning liberal context of equal opportunity that permits a diversity of outcomes—even in questions of life and death.

---

[103] *McCleskey v. Kemp*, 481 US 279 (1987).

[104] David C. Baldus, George G. Woodworth, and Charles A. Pulaski, *Equal Justice and the Death Penalty: A Legal and Empirical Analysis* (Boston, MA: Northeastern University Press, 1990).

[105] *McCleskey v. Kemp*, 481 US 279, 313 (1987).

A MERCURIAL FUNDAMENTALISM

Just as it is customary to begin discussions on American equality with references to the Declaration of Independence, so it is traditional to end them with allusions to the continuation of barriers to complete social equality. Rogers M. Smith, for example, describes inequality as a wholly authentic tradition within American society. Hierarchy, exclusion, and discrimination have arguably been sustained 'even at the cost of violating doctrines of universal rights'.[106] When these structures of differential status are taken into account, Smith has no doubt that 'the flat plain of American egalitarianism mapped by Tocqueville and others suddenly looks quite different'. He notes:

We instead perceive America's initial conditions as exhibiting only a rather small, recently leveled valley of relative equality nestled amid steep mountains of hierarchy. And though we can see forces working to erode those mountains over time, broadening the valley, many of the peaks also prove to be volcanic, frequently responding to seismic pressures with outbursts that harden into substantial peaks once again.[107]

The 'multiple traditions' outlook is one that has particular relevance for the value of equality precisely because such a perspective advances the uncomfortable proposition that ascribed inegalitarianism amounts to both a separate system of ideas and a conscious tradition of civic life. Ideals, therefore, cannot be reduced to an amorphous prospectus that is necessarily inclusive of equality. On the contrary, it is the principle of equality which is said to reveal that American ideals contradict one another and will continue to do so because of the recurrent visceral appeal of notions of ascriptive hierarchy.

Insidious and even pernicious though these infringements of equality may be, they do not invalidate every measure, condition, or achievement of egalitarianism that have occurred in American society. In many instances, the abridgements of equality are thrown into high relief by the egalitarian suppositions of America's ideational heritage. The single criterion of an unqualified and undifferentiated equality is perhaps too unrealistic a standard by which to evaluate a society's attachment to egalitarianism. It overlooks the fact that no society has ever approximated a condition of equality and it ignores the proposition that such a state of existence is materially impossible to attain. It also fails to recognize that many other political principles and values may be jeopardized in any pursuit of substantive equality. Because Americans choose to value equality in conjunction with other norms like individualism, liberty, democracy, and capitalism, this does not mean that America's egalitarian attachments are somehow fraudulent and hypocritical, or permanently subsumed under a blanket of propertied freedoms and cultural hierarchies.

---

[106] Rogers M. Smith, 'Beyond Tocqueville, Myrdal, and Hartz: The Multiple Traditions in America', *The American Political Science Review*, vol. 87, no. 3 (September 1993), p. 550.
[107] Ibid.

Wood maintains that shortly after the Declaration of Independence, the United States became 'the most egalitarian nation in the history of the world, and it remains so today, regardless of its great disparities of wealth'.[108] Pole observes the same apparent disjunction in his claim that nineteenth-century Americans 'wanted a society run on equal principles without wanting a society of equals'.[109] Similarly, Verba and Orren discern the presence of an ambiguity by which Americans today 'can agree on equality only by disagreeing on what it means'.[110] These measured assessments are far from being forms of mere sophistry. They accurately convey the difficulty both of conceiving a fusion between equality and liberty in the abstract and of describing a society that attempts to give comparable stature to two values which are notorious not only for being mutually exclusive, but also for being absolutist in nature. Because the United States often appears to give greater weight to liberty and its associated values and because equality requires a great deal of conscious and active effort in its pursuit, then it is easy to derogate the importance of egalitarianism in American history and society. It is evident that the effort to match social change to the high rhetoric of American equality has often been absent—leaving a conspicuous discrepancy between ideal and fact as a consequence. It is just as evident that equality of opportunity has often been used as a pretext for the continuation of gross inequalities.

Moreover, equality often suffers from an unfavourable comparison with liberty. In contrast to freedom, which is customarily depicted as open-ended, emancipatory, and unstructured, equality retains associations with government-induced structures, a reduction of diversity, and the enclosure of liberty. As a result, equality has been interpreted as a primary value in the rational and formal foundations of the republic but one that is more often than not derogated to that of a secondary and contingent value in the standard operating conditions of American political exchange. With its allure of imprecision, freedom has a direct and sensory appeal to the imagination. Equality on the other hand has an absolutist property or a totalizing aspiration that connotes such an unworkable calculus that its meaning is necessarily circumscribed by provisos, caveats, and exemptions.

This outlook amounts to a misrepresentation of the political potential residing in the value of equality. The commonly cited conclusions upon the marginal and conditional nature of equality fail to take account of the visceral nature of the egalitarian impulse in the United States. The customary circumspection surrounding equality in practice should not obscure the remarkable extent to which egalitarianism can stir the American spirit and mobilize political forces in its wake. The nature of American politics provides considerable opportunity for the principle of equality to be introduced into the consideration of political proposals. Once part of the debate and once established in the vocabulary of political discourse, its effects are not easily restricted in scope and can be quite unpredictable.

---

[108] Wood, *The Radicalism of the American Revolution*, p. 233.

[109] Pole, 'Equality: An American Dilemma', in Berlowitz et al. (eds.), *America in Theory*, p. 76.

[110] Sidney Verba and Gary R. Orren, 'The Meaning of Equality in America', *Political Science Quarterly*, vol. 100, no. 3 (Fall 1985), p. 397.

Whether this is interpreted as a consequence of a discourse, or as an indication of a competing culture, the net effect is one in which the mainstream authority of personal liberty and democratic rights remains under constant challenge. In fact, 'the individualistic way of life has repeatedly come under fire in the United States from egalitarians who condemn individualism for isolating the individual from the community, dimming the sense of collective purpose, damning the springs of civic virtue, and creating unconscionable inequalities'.[111]

The reference point of egalitarianism generates an ongoing and open-ended debate within American society on the boundary between what are acceptable forms of inequality and what are not. Within this shifting remit, extensive resources become committed to arguments over the claims for, and the feasibility of, equality in different areas of social life. If equality is a contingent value, then American society is renowned for its enduring inquiries into the conditions upon which the nature and extent of equality is dependent in a free society. It is the sheer force of this egalitarian tradition in American politics that lies behind the prodigious efforts that have been made in the United States to create frameworks that will secure, maintain, and extend an equality of rights for its citizens. The ramifications of this egalitarian impulse stretch far into the hinterland of other American values and attachments and, as a result, it possesses a presence in many of the themes and issues reviewed in this study.

---

[111] Richard J. Ellis, *American Political Cultures* (New York: Oxford University Press), p. 5.

7

Morality

INTRODUCTION

American identity has always been closely bound up with its position and role in an intensely moral universe. Cultural observations of the past have invariably given prominence to the moral tenor of social intercourse in the American republic. Contemporary analyses of the animating properties of the American society continue to make the link between public action and historical purpose on the one hand and high moral consciousness and advanced moral aspiration on the other. American public life is pervaded by a profusion of moral reference points and by a drive to justify attitudes and actions through recourse to moral criteria. It is this level of moral consciousness in political exchange and argumentation that marks the United States out from other western democracies and which gives the conduct of American politics its distinctive character.

At this point, it should be acknowledged that moralism per se is not a value in itself. What is moral or not moral will be dependent upon both the current definition of certain fundamental values and their contemporary status within society. Morality in this respect is a contingent category dependent upon changing conceptions of moral right and wrong. The inclusion of moralism in this study reflects the dominant dimension associated with the usage of moral terms, language, and standards in American politics. It relates to a medium of exchange based upon an underlying belief in the centrality and accessibility of right, and in the significance of principle, virtue, and truth in the conduct of public life. The nature and effect of moralism as a component value in American politics, therefore, are drawn less from the substance or authority of individual principles and more from the generic approach towards the idea of a prescriptive moral order within the public sphere. In essence, as far as this study is concerned, moralism is a feature that relates primarily to an *attitude* towards values, to their place in society, and to their usage in politics. As Robin M. Williams points out, when observers of the United States assert that Americans tend to see the world in moral terms, they 'do not mean mere conformity to the detailed prescriptions of a particular moral code, but rather to a systematic moral orientation by which conduct is *judged*'.[1]

This moral dimension is evident in the prodigious range of phenomena and styles that invest American society with a distinctive predisposition towards locating high principle and ethical judgement within social processes and political

---

[1] Robin Williams, *American Society: A Sociological Interpretation* (New York: Knopf, 1963), p. 424.

issues. As a consequence, in the same way that America is widely depicted as possessing inherently moral origins and purposes, so the United States itself is characterized as being the derivative of a moral epic and, in essence, the equivalent of a moral construct. America's historical development has been marked to such an extent by moral claims, disputes, and crises, that its progress as a society has been closely associated with allusions to moral value as the motivating force and distinguishing signifier of an allegedly exceptional dynamic. The volatility and fervour of America's moral consciousness leads James Morone to place it not at the margins of society but at the very centre of America's historical processes. He refers to moral conflict as having literally made America.[2] It is unremarkable, therefore, that American leaders are conspicuously uninhibited in the way they publicize their moral credos and underpin their objectives through reference to the sincerity and relevance of their inner convictions. The themes of moral health, or alternatively moral crisis, have a pervasive presence in American public debate.[3] They not only support a flourishing market in studies and guides into moral behaviour,[4] but also sustain an impassioned debate over the importance of moral education and the development of strong moral character.[5]

Strangers to the United States consider the moral tenor of its political discourse to be noticeably divergent from other western democracies. Whether it is the Washington march of 600,000 male 'promise keepers' rededicating their consciences to their wives and children, the bombing of family planning clinics in response to the 'abortion holocaust', the suspension of stem cell research on ethical grounds, or the lurid inquests into President Bill Clinton's sexual behaviour, the subtext remains the same. This can be described as both an impulse and a capacity to impute great moral significance to political differences. The judgmental tenor of addressing issues in terms of high virtue and moral degradation can lead to deep ethical dichotomies and to conditions of political impasse. It is even said that the United States is beset by a politics of moral intransigence in which issues are polarized between the respective claims of secular humanism and religious ethics to be the authentic source of moral integrity.[6] This is not to infer that all or most political issues are argued out through a medium of moral outrage. But many either are or remain susceptible to being so. It might be claimed that moral disputes amount to politics pursued by different means. But this would be a misrepresentation because the moral and political spheres are so thoroughly intermixed that they remain largely indistinguishable from one another.

---

[2] James Morone, *Hellfire Nation: The Politics of Sin in American History* (New Haven, CT: Yale University Press, 2003).

[3] For example, see Charles Murray, *Losing Ground: American Social Policy, 1950–1980: 10th Anniversary Edition* (New York: Basic Books, 1999); Francis Fukuyama, *The Great Disruption: Human Nature and the Reconstitution of Social Order* (New York: Free Press, 2000).

[4] For example, see James Q. Wilson, *The Moral Sense* (New York: Free Press 1993).

[5] For example, see William J. Bennett, *Book of Virtues: A Treasury of Great Moral Stories* (New York: Simon & Schuster, 1993).

[6] See Noah Feldman, *Divided by God: America's Church–State Problem—and What We Should Do about It* (New York: Farrar, Straus & Giroux, 2005), chs. 5, 6.

American politics closely reflects these undercurrents of moral anxiety and fervour. Political debate resonates with references to the need to create, or to rediscover, or to defend the good society in both senses of the term. Issues relating to the place of personal and public virtue, the role of individual conscience in the polity, the significance of good and evil, and the relationship between ideals and self-interest all continue to inform political debate in the United States. As a consequence, the public sphere is distinguished for its developed interest in the morality of politics and politicians and in the spectacle of exposure, scandal, and retribution. The way in which moral consciousness and moral issues suffuse the presentation and consideration of political phenomena is widely considered to be unusual and even exceptional. It has led Seymour Martin Lipset to conclude that 'America is the most moralistic country in the world'.[7] He asserts that the United States is distinguished by 'intense morally based conflicts about public policy, precisely because its people quarrel sharply about how to apply the basic principles of Americanism they purport to agree about.... [G]iven the emphasis on moralism, American politicians define interest issues as well as value conflicts in ethical terms.'[8] With moral compulsion comes faith and this too is thought to mark America out from other comparable societies. Jonathan Raban for one has no doubts on this score:

No culture in the world has elevated 'faith', in and of itself, with or without specific religious beliefs, to the status it enjoys in the United States. Faith—in God, or the future, or the seemingly impossible, which is the core of the American Dream—is a moral good in its own right. In no other culture is the word 'dream' so cemented into everyday political language, for in America dreams are not idle, they are items of faith.[9]

This highly charged approach to issues can lead to intense divisions, but it can also produce a common point of moral reference that allows adversarial parties to engage with one another on the basis of a shared attachment to the importance of moral agency.

'IN GOD WE TRUST'

The origins and resources of this highly developed moral sensitivity are both numerous and varied. They are also deeply contested in respect to their historical lineage and social significance. It can be claimed that the moral imperium of American society is the result of a deeply entrenched ideological consensus upon liberal values that originated in an eighteenth-century attachment to Locke's philosophy of natural rights and social contract. If America's high moral consciousness is attributed to a widely held liberal ethos, this can also be interpreted

---

[7] Seymour M. Lipset, *American Exceptionalism: A Double-Edged Sword?* (New York: W. W. Norton, 1996), p. 27.
[8] Ibid.   [9] Jonathan Raban, 'Pastor Bush', *The Guardian*, 6 October 2004.

as a product not of eighteenth-century rationalism, but more as an expression of a continuing classical republican tradition. This set of values can be traced from Aristotle and Cicero through Machiavelli in the sixteenth century and James Harrington in the seventeenth century to English radical dissenters in the eighteenth century and, thence, to the revolutionaries and constitution builders in America. Classical republicanism conjoined the ideals of private virtue and public engagement. According to this perspective, a liberal morality was derived less from the aggregate effect of emancipated self-interest and more from a cultural reflex of a citizenship working for, and animated by, the public good.

Other constructions can give emphasis to more abstract conceptions of moral conduct such as the notion of a universal law and the proposition of natural rights; or the idea that the moral faculty is based upon rational exposition; or the belief that moral principles are identified through the senses and, therefore, by intuition rather than by reason. Another dimension to the nature of moral inquiry centres not so much upon the discernment of good and virtue, so much as on the need to underline the significance of wrongs, vices, corruption, degradation, restraints, and duties. In the American tradition, there is not only a marked aversion to private vice being translated into public vice, but a well-documented attachment to mechanistic arrangements by which the avarice and self-interest of individuals are made to counteract one another for the safety and moral enhancement of the republic. But of all the varied roots of America's moral ecology, there is one which is always given historical and cultural prominence. It draws upon and gives focus to a rich variety of cognate traditions and developments; it gives expression to a range of distinctive moral impulses; it touches upon and relates to a profusion of issues in the field of moral inquiry; and it exemplifies the continued salience and reach of moral considerations in American public life.

Religion and its suppositions, associations, and claims constitute one of the most enduring traditions of social existence in the United States. 'Investment in religious freedom plays a foundational role in the American system of government and way of life that is unparalleled elsewhere'.[10] Amanda Porterfield's description may be a stark assessment but it is an entirely typical perspective within the United States. Religion is accepted as having been instrumental in the early formation of American settlement and in the intellectual and normative context of the republic's establishment. Just as religious attitudes and attachments have continued to influence the nature of America's historical identity and social purpose, so religious themes and associations still penetrate the public consciousness and inform political debates and controversies. In the United States, religious groupings provide a rich medium of moral sentiment and ethical concern that not only contributes to the structuring of civil society, but constitutes an agency of intermediation between the realms of public action and private autonomy. The pluralistic and idiomatic properties of America's diverse religious organizations can and have been deployed both as a force of cultural conservatism and as

---

[10] Amanda Porterfield, 'Introduction', in Amanda Porterfield (ed.), *American Religious History* (Malden, MA: Blackwell, 2002), p. 4.

a instrument of political transformation.[11] Religious affiliations and arguments remain salient in the United States because of the moral authority that they can generate, and also because of the way that religious traditions can be construed as being analogous to many of America's most revered political and social principles.

The United States is noted for the multiplicity of its religious organizations. While these are located predominantly in the Judeo-Christian tradition, there can be little doubt that the primary focus of religious consciousness in America has historically lain within the Protestant experience. It is an arguable proposition that in the United States, Protestantism achieves its fullest contemporary expression.[12] The logic of individual conscience driving an array of personalized and group-based relationships with God, that are not dependent upon either ecclesiastical organization or episcopal authority, has been extended to its furthest point in America. Given Protestantism's structural and theological predisposition towards sectarian fragmentation and the individual access to grace, then the United States is in many respects *the* Protestant community. Its traditions of voluntary association, decentralized structure, and faith-based salvation have generated a widespread cultural condition in which Protestant attitudes and principles possess a reach far beyond the confines of purely religious categories. For example, it can be claimed not only that the 'average American thinks of formal religious observances in Protestant terms', but that in general the 'public rituals of the republic are Protestant rituals' and that the Protestant ethic provided the 'moral bedrock on which republican institutions were built'.[13] The cultural influences of Protestantism are manifold and complex but one in particular warrants closer attention because of its reputation as a defining influence upon the social and moral foundations of America.

Puritanism is widely acclaimed to represent that platform of principles and impulses *from* which America developed intellectually, and *to* which much of its subsequent developments can be related back in terms of its original Puritan principles.[14] The Puritans sought to extinguish the established church's elaborate and allegedly excessive structure of intermediation between God and man, and

---

[11] Martin E. Marty, *Pilgrims in Their Own Land: 500 Years of Religion in America* (New York: Penguin, 1985); Catherine L. Albanese, *American Religions and Religion*, 2nd edn (Belmont, CA: Wadsworth, 1992); William R. Hutchison, 'Diversity and the Pluralist Ideal', in Peter W. Williams (ed.), *Perspectives on American Religion and Culture* (Malden, MA: Blackwell, 1999), pp. 34–47; Edwin S. Gaustad and Mark A. Noll (eds.), *A Documentary History of Religion in America to 1877*, 3rd edn (Grand Rapids, MI: Wm. B. Eerdmans, 2003).

[12] See Sydney E. Ahlstrom, *A Religious History of the American People* (New Haven, CT: Yale University Press, 1972). For a contrary view that challenges the dominance of Protestantism as the only main organizing theme of American religious history, see Catherine Albanese, *America: Religion, and Religions*, 2nd edn (Belmont, CA: Wadsworth, 1992).

[13] Quoted in 'The Protestants and the Others', *The Times Literary Supplement*, 22 December 1972.

[14] See Perry Miller, *Puritanism and Democracy* (New York: Vanguard, 1939); Perry Miller, *The New England Mind: From Colony to Province* (Cambridge, MA: Harvard University Press, 1953); Larzer Ziff, *Puritanism in America: New Cult in a New World* (New York: Viking, 1973); Sacvan Bercovitch, The *Puritan Origins of the American Self* (New Haven, CT: Yale University Press, 1991); Andrew Delbanco, *The Puritan Ordeal* (Cambridge, MA: Harvard University Press, 1989).

thereby restore the relationship to one of Augustinian simplicity. As a result of this mission, they came to be strongly associated with the principles of Christian liberty, Congregational self-government, reason in the service of God, contractual obligation, and planned Christian commonwealth. In the process, Puritans engaged in fiercely argued criticism of established hierarchies and conventions.

The Puritan emphasis lay with the priority of personal conscience and with the corresponding need for individuals to keep a direct and 'short account' with God. This was consistent with their dogmatic belief in the pervasive and all-encompassing presence of God in the world, and in the absolute sovereignty of God's mind in providing the form and purpose of everything within the world. In this construction of reality, man had been made in God's own image, but original sin had incurred retribution so severe as to consign a now depraved and corrupt humanity to eternal damnation. In God's infinite mercy, however, the Puritans believed that He had relented and had selected some of mankind (i.e. 'the regenerate') to embody partial redemption through the revealed agency of His grace.[15]

The New England Puritans were in many respects the ultimate expression of John Calvin's conception of a select minority. They had sought to create a new social order based upon the purified principles of God's law within an enriched moral context drawn from a direct relationship with the divine. In forming their covenant with God in the wilderness, the Puritans compounded the virtue of their self-imposed exclusion with the seclusion of a literal new Eden or new Zion that served to reflect their moral elitism back upon them. Puritanism was not simply a religious phenomenon. It possessed strong psychological and emotive properties that are described by Max Savelle as 'a mood, a subjective, introspective mood, that worked itself out in religion, and from that into society, politics, ethics, philosophy, literature and art, in the first half of the seventeenth century'.[16] Savelle concludes that Puritanism's dynamics could be described as 'probably the high water mark of the Protestant revolt'.[17]

In fleeing from the religious pressures of England and in espousing religious tolerance in America, the Puritans were always vulnerable to the charge that they had replaced one set of restrictions with another of their own making. In one respect, it could be claimed that they had made their arduous journey into physical insecurity and deprivation in order to exercise their religious beliefs and build the kind of commonwealth that Oliver Cromwell had failed to establish in England after the Civil War (1642–5). In another respect, the Puritans can be seen as exerting a specific and at times repressive moral order upon their communities in which civil rights would be dependent upon religious belief and behaviour. The classical defence was that any individual was entirely free *not* to travel to New

---

[15] Miller, *The New England Mind*, ch. 1.
[16] Max Savelle, *Seeds of American Liberty: The Genesis of the American Mind* (Seattle, WA: University of Washington Press, 1948), p. 27.
[17] Ibid.

England to join them. Social discipline was of central importance to the Puritans because of their insistence that they were being continually judged by a scrutinizing God who was always close at hand. The Puritans operated on the premise that they had formed a contractual arrangement with the Almighty. By pledging their obedience to His revealed will, God would protect and support them. Those in the community who violated the covenant risked incurring damnation not only upon themselves, but on the entire community. This was a social universe packed with signs and portents, and with ever-present prospect of moral gains and losses. As a consequence, the 'society of saints' was necessarily active in perceiving sin and in punishing sinners—even to the extent of banishment or execution.

The social and normative tensions that lay at the heart of this experiment to create a theocratic state were exacerbated by the demographic and pluralizing strains of increased immigration, diversifying colonialization, and theological disputation. In the terms of its original prospectus, and its material and organizational profile, the history of New England Protestantism is chiefly a narrative of decline. Nevertheless, in terms of intellectual traditions, social attitudes, and religious impulses, Puritanism has remained a noteworthy influence in many aspects of contemporary American culture. For example:

- To the New England Puritans, the world was a flawed and corrupting place from which they had dramatically departed in order to form their own settlements as isolated yet wholly exceptional monuments to biblical ordinance and divine grace. In such a context, they generated an identity of being a chosen people with a necessarily special mission to create an ideal polity that would act as a working model of the reformed church. Because America would become a guide for the rest of Christendom, it needed to be aware of its great purpose as 'city upon a hill', where the 'eyes of all people are upon us'.[18]

- With a judgemental God as an immediate and intimate reference point in the Puritans' conceptual landscape, locating the existence of sin and rooting it out became an imperative social requirement. This was necessary not merely of the individual soul, but for the continuing integrity of the community and its security against the wrathful presence of God.

- The 'errand in the wilderness'[19] that was undertaken by the Puritans led to an intense search for signs of God's grace. As a consequence, it became a Puritan principle to invest success in survival, settlement, and material progress with a legitimacy drawn from the presumption of divine revelation and favour.

- The Puritans devised communities that were geared to continuous moral appraisal. The high standards of moral expectations were combined with low thresholds of tolerance for symptoms of moral failure or decline. Such was the significance of moral health that the Puritans were accustomed to looking

[18] John Winthrop, 'A City upon a Hill: A Model of Christian Charity', http://www.pbs.org/wgbh/pages/frontline/shows /apocalypse/primary/ciudad.html.
[19] See Perry Miller, *Errand into the Wilderness* (New York: Harper & Row, 1956).

closely at and beneath surface conditions in order to assess the presence of right and wrong. For example, as late as 1850, Henry Adams reflected upon how he had been shocked at leaving the disciplined certainties of Boston to be confronted by what he saw as the grotesque state of the antebellum South. He realized later 'that he had been unconsciously trained to fuse physical and moral geography, to know that bad roads meant bad morals'.[20]

- The Puritan community was a geographical and theological outlier that was invested with a central spiritual significance. Similar dualisms were apparent in the Puritans' corresponding preoccupations with both virtue and evil; in the fusion of their existential anxieties over the inner self with their intrusive behaviour as guardians of public morality; and in their fascination with the metaphysical world as well as the physical realm.

- Just as the Puritans gave emphasis to the conscious experience of individual regeneration, so they underlined the utility of revived personal spirituality in the creation of civil society. By the same token, they attributed social and behavioural problems to forms of moral decay requiring revivals or forms of spiritual replenishment to reverse the processes of corruption.

Even though the coherence of Puritanism dissipated through the pre-revolutionary epoch, it played a critical role in fostering a wider American Protestant community that has both influenced and adapted to a wide variety of religious traditions and experiences. The Puritan tradition remains a conspicuous component of American culture and finds expression in a variety of themes and phenomena. They include an attachment to moral intensity, scriptural truths, and biblical prophecy; a pietist inclination to distrust worldliness and to resent the interference of hierarchical structures with the essentially personal relationship with God's will; a fundamentalist reaction against the perceived cultural and moral decline of society through the concerted assault by secular forces upon 'God's own country'; and a susceptibility to the idea of social redemption and renewal through periods of spiritual revival and appeals for the 'remoralization' of society.[21] The influences of these and other elements of Puritanism will be addressed in other parts of this study.

While Protestantism has constituted the historical mainstream for much of America's past, it has never achieved the status of a singular established church and it has not been immune to the challenge of alternative theological traditions and religious experiences. In addition to the fissiparous energies within Protestantism that led to the formation of a rich diversity of denominations, the course of American development also occasioned the rise to prominence of the Catholic and

---

[20] Quoted in Larzer Ziff, *Puritanism in America*, pp. 125–6.
[21] For example, see David E. Harrell, *All Things Are Possible: The Healing and Charismatic Revivals in Modern America* (Bloomington, IN: Indiana University Press, 1975); Edward Ashbee, ' "Remoralization": American Society and Politics in the 1990s', *The Political Quarterly*, vol. 71, no. 2 (April 2000), pp. 192–201; Malise Ruthven, *Fundamentalism: The Search for Meaning* (Oxford: Oxford University Press, 2004).

Jewish faiths in the United States. More recently, America's religious endowments have been further enhanced by the emergence of other religious affiliations and by the onset of a prolific range of faith-based organizations offering different forms of spiritual replenishment (e.g. Buddhism, Islam, Mormonism, Hinduism). All these religious, and quasi-religious, establishments offer their own designs for philosophical inquiry and personal fulfilment. Nevertheless, they have all been influenced by the idiosyncratic properties of American Protestantism and, in particular, by the traditions of non-conformism, ecclesiastical segmentation, and spiritual autonomy. The American construction of religion is of the fringe, made central in a process that makes non-conformity the established norm. The effect is one of advanced religious pluralism founded upon constitutional guarantees of religious tolerance and freedom of religious worship.

This level of religious licence has contributed America's characteristic state of religious licentiousness. The United States supports over 2,000 different religious denominations. At least once a month, more than 60 per cent of American citizens attend a service at a church, chapel, temple, or mosque. Public surveys reveal the strength of social attachment to religious beliefs and values. Nine out of ten Americans are recorded as believing in God, with a comparably large majority continuing to affirm a belief in the concept or doctrine of sin.[22] While 82 per cent of Americans clarify themselves as Christian,[23] 46 per cent claim to be 'born again Christians'.[24] Nearly nine out of ten Americans (88%) believe that religion is important in their lives with 61 per cent saying that it is very important.[25] In giving reasons for America's historical success, 65 per cent regard the operation of God's will as a major factor.[26] In similar vein, 58 per cent agree that the strength of American society is based on the religious faith of its people.[27] Accordingly 61 per cent believe that 'children are more likely to grow up to be moral adults when they are raised in a religious faith',[28] while two-thirds agree with the proposition that religion can 'answer all or most of today's problems'.[29]

These levels of religious attachment are thoroughly atypical in terms of the trends in social development. In most cases, a close correlation exists between societies experiencing a process of industrialization, modernization, urbanization,

---

[22] Gallup Organization, 'Religion & Values', 29 April 2003. http://www.gallup.com/subscription/?m=f&c_id=13416.

[23] The Pew Research Centre for the People and the Press, in association with the Pew Forum on Religion and Public Life, 'Americans Struggle with Religion's Role at Home and Abroad', 20 March 2002, http://people-press.org/reports/display.php3?PageID=385.

[24] CNN/USA Today/Gallup Poll, 9–10 December 2002, http://www.pollingreport.com/religion.htm.

[25] Ibid.

[26] The Pew Research Centre for the People and the Press, 'Technology Triumphs, Morality Falters', 3 July 1999, http://people-press.org/reports/display.php3?ReportID=57.

[27] The Pew Research Centre for the People and the Press, in association with the Pew Forum on Religion and Public Life, 'Americans Struggle with Religion's Role at Home and Abroad'.

[28] Ibid.

[29] CNN/USA Today/Gallup Poll, 9–10 December 2002, http://www.pollingreport.com/religion.htm.

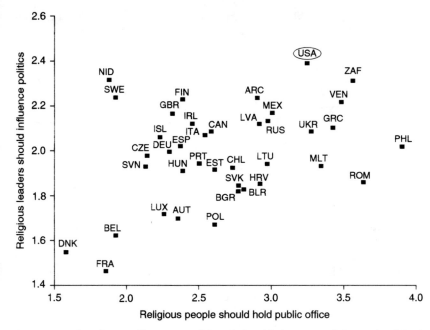

Figure 7.1. Values for two dimensions of the relationship between religion and politics in thirty-eight selected countries

Source: World Values Survey (2004) (http://www.worldvaluessurvey.org/Upload/5_madrid%20def%20version%20med%20tabeller%20och%20figurer.pdf)

and material advance on the one hand and the onset of a more secular and rationalist outlook on the other. In the United States, this trend line is reversed, leaving American society standing alone as a highly advanced industrialized nation with an exceptionally durable pattern of religious observance (see Fig. 7.1).

RELIGION AND POLITICS

It is not simply the sheer scale of religious activity in the United States that is noteworthy. More significant is its penetration into society and into the political realm. In contrast to nearly every other western democracy, God remains a ubiquitous reference point in American culture. This is reflected in the widespread usage of biblical quotations and allusions as a means of appeal to a common code of ethics. It is also illustrated in the way that public figures regularly invoke the Almighty as the reason for their success in their fields of endeavour. In American culture, God is habitually employed as an instrument of comprehension, prescription, and legitimacy. American politicians in particular are strongly oriented towards using resources in order to cultivate religious constituencies and themes for the purposes of political mobilization.

Within such a context, political activity often reflects not only distinctly religious themes, but also the agendas of politically attuned religious expression. Just as many mainline churches were involved in the campaigns for civil rights in the 1960s and for a nuclear freeze in the 1980s, so grassroots evangelical movements like the Moral Majority and the Christian Coalition have sought to exert pressure in the political arena and to engage actively in the various campaigns to alter court decisions in such areas as school prayer, gay rights, and abortion.[30] Polling organizations have recognized the impact of such activity upon the conduct of contemporary politics. The Pew Center for the People and the Press, for example, reached the following conclusion in June 1996:

Religion is a strong and growing force in the way Americans think about politics. It has a bearing on political affiliation, political values, policy attitudes and candidate choice. Its increasing influence on political opinion and behavior rivals factors such as race, region, age, social class and gender.[31]

This cross migration of religious and political themes is especially conspicuous in relation to the US presidency. The representational and symbolic resources of the office are heavily dependent upon the presidency's capacity to give expression to the nation's self-conception of a society with religious meaning and moral purpose. Given that American identity is strongly attached to the national responsibility of moral leadership in the world, it has become a cultural expectation that the presidency should be occupied by a leader that can exemplify, articulate, and also personify the ideals of public virtue. Accordingly, presidents have become adept at drawing upon, and appealing to American society's sense of its inherent values. Barbara Hinckley describes their behaviour:

[T]hey engage in moral—and explicitly religious—activity. Literally they preach, reminding the American people of moral and religious principles and urging them to conduct themselves in accord with these principles. They lead prayers, quote from the Bible, and make theological statements about the Deity and His desires for the nation. We know...that the public perceives presidents as altruistic and benevolent: They are the

---

[30] See A. James Reichley, *Religion in American Public Life* (Washington, DC: Brookings Institution, 1985); A. James Reichley, *Faith in Politics* (Washington, DC: Brookings Institution, 2002), chs. 6, 7; Hugh Heclo and Wilfred M. McClay (eds.), *Religion Returns to the Public Square: Faith and Policy in America* (Baltimore, MD: Johns Hopkins University Press, 2003); Kenneth D. Wald, *Religion and Politics in the United States*, 4th edn (Lanham, MD: Rowman & Littlefield Publishers, 2003); E. J. Dionne, Jean B. Elshtain, and Kayla M. Drogosz (eds.), *One Electorate under God: A Dialogue on Religion and American Politics* (Washington, DC: Brookings Institution, 2004).

[31] The Pew Research Centre for the People and the Press, 'The Diminishing Divide: American Churches, American Politics', 25 June 1996, http://people-press.org/reports/display.php3? ReportID=126.

moral leaders and high priests of the American society.... [P]residents themselves are contributing to the impression and indeed consciously cultivating it.[32]

Presidents regularly employ the language of moral crisis and moral solution, in order to transform political issues into themes more susceptible to moral appeal and social cohesion. When the violent disturbances over civil rights in the South during the early 1960s threatened to degenerate into serious social disorder, President John F. Kennedy defined it as a 'moral crisis' for the country and the people. In a televised national address, he urged every American to examine their consciences and to make a moral choice: 'Those who do nothing are inviting shame as well as violence. Those who act boldly are recognizing right as well as reality'.[33]

Personal virtue and public morality are closely connected dimensions in American public life. The private backgrounds and value systems of individual presidents are integral elements in how political leadership is assessed and evaluated. The moral commitment of leaders to the policies they espouse is seen as a crucial component of political success. Effective presidents have been categorized as those who 'reached beyond simple transactional politics to persuade people that what they wanted was the right thing to do, for its own sake'.[34] As a consequence, presidents are often assigned to, or become closely associated with, the role of being the 'primary source of moral agency in American politics'.[35] Just as a multitude of moral expectations are invested in the presidential office, so presidents seek to complete the circle by offering a national point of moral reference.

Within such a context of intensive moral sentiment, presidents are rarely diffident in claiming the licence to speak on behalf of America's moral inheritance or even in embodying its moral identity. It is thought politically prudent to do so. President George W. Bush has been particularly adept at using this genre of moral conscience and religious inflection. For example, in vetoing his first bill after five years in office, President Bush gave emphasis to the moral nature of the decision and his responsibility as a moral guardian for the nation. The Stem Cell Research Enhancement Act (2005) would have lifted a ban on the federal funding of new embryonic stem cell research. In the president's judgement, the legislation crossed 'a moral boundary' that a 'decent society need[ed] to respect'.[36] In the search for new medical advances, it was necessary to subject the ethics of biotechnology to

---

[32] Barbara Hinckley, *The Symbolic Presidency: How Presidents Portray Themselves* (New York: Routledge, 1990), p. 73.

[33] President John F. Kennedy, 'We Face a Moral Crisis', June 1963, in Henry S. Commager (ed.), *The Struggle for Racial Equality: A Documentary Record* (New York: Harper & Row, 1967), p. 164.

[34] Erwin C. Hargrove, *The President as Leader: Appealing to the Better Angels of our Nature* (Lawrence, KS: University Press of Kansas, 1998), p. 174. See also Marvin Olasky, *The American Leadership Tradition: Moral Vision from Washington to Clinton* (New York: Free Press, 1999).

[35] Erwin C. Hargrove, 'Presidential Leadership: Skill in Context', *Politics and Policy*, vol. 30, no. 2 (2000), p. 211.

[36] President George W. Bush, 'President Discusses Stem Cell Research Policy' (19 July 2006), http://www.whitehouse.gov/news/releases/2006/07/print/20060719-3.html.

the criteria of national morality: 'America must never abandon our fundamental morals.... I will not allow our nation to cross this moral line. I felt like crossing this line would be a mistake, and once crossed, we would find it almost impossible to turn back.' He continued: 'Our conscience and history as a nation demand that we resist this temptation. America was founded on the principle that we are all created equal, and endowed by our Creator with the right to life. We can advance the cause of science while upholding this founding promise'.[37]

President Bush has also typified the convention of fusing national purpose with moral leadership.[38] In declaring a war against terror, his speeches dwelt repeatedly upon the morality of the American people and nation set within a moral universe of good and evil. The president underlined the centrality of both 'moral clarity'[39] in national leadership and the 'moral purpose of American influence'.[40] These virtues were considered vitally important because of the need to affirm that America possessed a redemptive role in the world and with it an 'obligation ... to stand for morality and virtue in the face of evil and terror'.[41] President Bush effectively rallied the nation by reflecting its moral presumptions back on itself: 'Our Nation was built on a foundation of sound moral principles'.[42] As a consequence, it was necessary for the national leadership to discriminate between moral and immoral nations. For the president, the choice was simple: 'nations are either with us or against us in the war on terror'.[43] He made no apology for drawing the difference in such stark terms:

Some worry that it is somehow undiplomatic or impolite to speak the language of right and wrong. I disagree. ... There can be no neutrality between justice and cruelty, between the innocent and the guilty. We are in a conflict between good and evil, and America will call evil by its name.[44]

It is entirely consistent with this fusion of personal moral expression, public policy, and national meaning that one of President Bush's predecessors should dispute the Bush administration's political outlook with an equally fervent moral statement.

[37] President Bush, 'President Discusses Stem Cell Research Policy'.

[38] For an illustration of President Bush's view upon the role of personal faith in public service, see Stephen Mansfield, *The Faith of George W. Bush* (New York: Tarcher/Penguin, 2003), chs. 5–8; George W. Bush, *George W. Bush on God and Country: The President Speaks Out about Faith, Principle, and Patriotism*, ed. Tom Freiling, (Fairfax, VA: Allegiance/Faith Works, 2004).

[39] For example, see President Bush 'Proclamation by the President, National Character Counts Week' (20 October 2003), http://www.whitehouse.gov/news/releases/2003/10/20031020.html

[40] President Bush, 'Remarks by the President in the Commencement Address to the United States Coast Guard Academy', New London, CT (21 May 2003), http://www.whitehouse.gov/news/releases/2003/05/20030521-2.html.

[41] President Bush, 'Proclamation by the President, National Character Counts Week' (23 October 2001), http://www.whitehouse.gov/news/releases/2001/10/20011023-23.html

[42] Ibid.

[43] President Bush, 'President Bush Calls for new Palestinian Leadership' (24 June 2002), http://www.whitehouse.gov/news/releases/2002/06/20020624-3.html.

[44] President Bush, 'Speech by the President at the Graduation Ceremony at West Point' (1 June 2002), http://www.whitehouse.gov/news/releases/2002/06/20020601-3.html.

In *Our Endangered Values: America's Moral Crisis* (2005), President Jimmy Carter draws attention to an alternative set of morally influenced positions on international law traditions and upon the Christian ethos of compassion, inclusion, and tolerance.[45]

The narrative and symbolic tradition of investing political themes with moral content is illustrated to its fullest extent in presidential inaugural addresses. As a ritual, an inaugural ceremony represents not only the culmination of a protracted electoral process, but also a rededication of the republic and its governing ethos. In giving an inaugural address, a new president provides a singular focal point to embody what it is that unites the American people as a collective entity. Just as the outcome of a presidential election is suggestive of a personal journey and transforming experience on the part of the winner, so an inaugural speech is strongly associated with a revival of the political process and a reaffirmation of American identity. In such a context, it is highly significant that presidents almost invariably enlist the concept, imagery, and active intervention of God to give force to the moral urgency and grandeur of the presidential task.

For example, in his first inaugural address, President Ronald Reagan made open reference to the religious character of the occasion: 'I am told that tens of thousands of prayer meetings are being held on this day, and for that I am deeply grateful. We are a nation under God, and I believe God intended for us to be free'.[46] He went on to make the following suggestion: 'It would be fitting and good, I think, if on each Inauguration Day in future years it should be declared a day of prayer'.[47] The theme of God's intentions for America was reiterated in his second address when he exhorted his audience to 'raise our voices to the God who is the Author of this most tender music'. He prayed that God would 'continue to hold us close as we fill the world with our sound—sound in unity, affection, and love—one people under God, dedicated to the dream of freedom that He has placed in the human heart'.[48]

President Clinton appealed to the revivalist tradition to invest his presidency with the tone of a new beginning and a spiritual-political challenge: 'From this joyful mountaintop of celebration, we hear a call to service in the valley. We have heard the trumpets. We have changed the guard. And now, each in our way, and with God's help, we must answer the call'.[49] President Bush, on the other hand, gave emphasis to the supernatural dimension of America's inherent moral story. He set in overtly biblical tones: 'We are not this story's author, who fills

---

[45] President Jimmy Carter, *Our Endangered Values: America's Moral Crisis* (New York: Simon & Schuster 2005).
[46] President Ronald Reagan, *First Inaugural Address*, 20 January 1981, http://www.bartleby.com/124/pres61.html.
[47] Ibid.
[48] President Ronald Reagan, *Second Inaugural Address*, 20 January 1985, http://www.bartleby.com/124/pres62.html.
[49] President Bill Clinton, *First Inaugural Address*, 21 January 1993, http://www.bartleby.com/124/pres64.html.

time and eternity with his purpose.... This work continues. This story goes on. And an angel still rides in the whirlwind and directs this storm'.[50] Whatever the specific nature of the parable or message, presidents are always aware of the need to call upon God for support in the discharge of their presidential duties. President Franklin Roosevelt, for example, asked 'divine guidance' to help him in the cause 'to give light to them that sit in darkness'.[51] In similar vein, President Richard Nixon requested 'your prayers that in the years ahead I may have God's help in making decisions that are right for America'.[52]

It is evident that in claiming to occupy a space between the people and government, presidents find it prudent to draw upon religious themes. They do so not only to underline the integrity of the republic and, thereby, to supplement their own legitimacy as leaders, but also to reassure their audience that they have the vision and virtue to claim an intermediary role between the republic and God. At the same time, they have been instrumental in the development of the nation as a civil religion that embraces widespread moral expectations and a unifying ethos of values. Whether the concept of a civil religion relies upon the presence of an explicit substructure of religious attachment or whether the cultural reverence conferred upon national beliefs and symbols gives it the status of religious equivalence,[53] the fact remains that presidents have a central role in giving voice to the idea of a common code of public ethics.

RELIGION AND THE MORAL FOUNDATIONS OF DEMOCRACY

The explicit and implicit intermingling of religion and politics in the United States generates a host of serious questions relating not just to the appropriate status of religion within the structure of America's constitutional order, but also to the role of religion in a modern liberal polity. The classic issues that have always surrounded the relationship between religious morality and politics can in the main be reduced to the following themes:

- The extent to which law and public policy are based on a 'universal' morality and ethics, and the extent to which they should be.

[50] President George W. Bush, *Inaugural Address*, 20 January 2001, http://www.bartleby.com/124/pres66.html.

[51] President Franklin D. Roosevelt, *Second Inaugural Address*, 20 January 1937, http://www.bartleby.com/124/pres50.html.

[52] President Richard M. Nixon, *Second Inaugural Address*, 20 January 1973, http://www.bartleby.com/124/pres59.html.

[53] Martin E. Marty, *The New Shape of American Religion* (New York: Harper, 1959); Robert N. Bellah, 'Civil Religion in America', in *Daedalus, Journal of the American Academy of Arts and Sciences*, vol. 96 (1967), pp. 1–21; Martin E. Marty and Edith L. Blumhofer, 'Public Religion In America Today', The Martin Marty Center/The Institute for the Advanced Study of Religion at the University of Chicago, http://marty-center.uchicago.edu/research/publicreligion_today.shtml.

- Accepting that morality has a place in politics, the degree to which this morality should be grounded in religious values.

- The point at which the application of religious values to government policy becomes the equivalent of a state supporting religion.

- The extent to which the supporters of a religious outlook have a legitimate right to try and exert influence in the political sphere, and if they do, the techniques that can be considered appropriate to achieve such an objective.

In respect to liberal democracy, the issues tighten around the role and legitimacy of religion in an order that is based upon consent, autonomy, and freedom, and where authority is centred upon secular processes, values are purportedly drawn from a civic morality and the state is constructed on the logic maximizing the principle of neutrality.

The founders of the American republic were acutely aware of the need to immunize civil society from the destructive effects of religious animosities. They were also conscious of avoiding the contrary vice of an established national church that might offer unity but at the expense of creating not only a transcendent moral authority but an alternative socio-political power centre. It is also worth noting that many of the Founders were Deist[54] rather than explicitly Christian in their philosophical convictions, and their morality was expressed more specifically through their membership of Masonic orders. On the other hand, they appreci-ated the religious roots of liberal history and the fundamental importance of reli-gious toleration in the contemporary ethos of civil rights. Moreover, the founders in varying respects acknowledged the functional value of religious discipline, education, and ethical guidance in the maintenance of even a republican order. President George Washington, for example, asserted in his Farewell Address that of 'all the dispositions and habits to political prosperity, religion and morality are indispensable supports'. He concluded that 'reason and experience both forbid us to expect that national morality can prevail in exclusion of religious principles'.[55]

At the national level, the *de jure* solution to this dualistic outlook was to aggre-gate religious tolerance with a clear separation of church and state. In effect, the federal constitution outlaws any official establishment of religion by the state while at the same time allowing for the 'free exercise' of religion. This duality is not as internally consistent as it first appears. The freedom of religious practice can lead to forms of public recognition and support by democratic institutions responding to constituency preferences. By the same token, the strict separation of church and state may have effects that can be interpreted as restricting religious freedom and even as militating against religious practice.

It needs to be noted that during the nineteenth century and for much of the succeeding century, the wall of separation doctrine had traditionally been softened

---

[54] This refers to the acceptance of a supreme god who is revealed more by nature and reason rather than by revelation, scripture, or religious doctrine.
[55] Quoted in William A. Galston, 'Public Morality and Religion in the Liberal State', *PS* (Fall 1986), p. 811.

at the local level by a de facto arrangement. This centred upon a latitudinarian approach to the issue that allowed local communities to assert their religious preferences in the formulation of public policy. The quasi-establishment of religion at this level was taken to be a concomitant of the states' police powers in support of a well-regulated society and in defence of common law principles of governance: 'Morality in this tradition was not a private, individual, or discretionary matter. Rather, it was a responsibility of government and a quid pro quo of community membership'.[56]

The collective infusion of moral virtue into the regulations, provisions, and pre-requirements of office-holders in state and local governments proceeded largely unhindered over the first 160 years of the republic.[57] However, as the remit of the federal government expanded through the nationalization of the Bill of Rights through the Fourteenth Amendment, local traditions of religiously informed public policy and moral suasion began to be cited as prima facie breaches of the First Amendment strictures on the establishment of religion. Since the 1950s, the Supreme Court has taken upon itself to examine this section of the Bill of Rights in respect to local practices. This has taken the form of reviewing the jurisdictional character of the religious clauses and of investigating the logic of the separation principle within subcultures where a nexus has developed between religiously guided morality, public policy, and democratic consent.[58]

In approaching this issue, the Court has been aware that the principle of separation is less a solution and more a device establishing the rules of engagement for questions generated by the interplay of private tolerance and public restriction. Despite the sensitivity of the issues surrounding the theme of religious freedom, the Court has progressively intervened in the area of local choices, established practices, and public subsidies in respect to religious priorities and moral codes. In a series of controversial cases, the Supreme Court has challenged the legitimacy of majoritarian actions against the right of particular religious sects (e.g. absolving Jehovah Witnesses and members of the Amish community from various citizen obligations on grounds of religious conviction[59]), while at the same time

---

[56] William J. Novak, *The People's Welfare: Law and Regulation in Nineteenth Century America* (Chapel Hill, NC: University of North Carolina Press, 1996), p. 154.

[57] Note should be made of efforts in the late nineteenth century aimed at restricting the freedom of local communities in offering de facto support to religious institutions. Campaigns surrounding the adoption of 'Blaine Amendments' or Blaine provisions in state constitutions were a case in point. These were primarily aimed at the prevention of government assistance being granted to private educational establishments with religious affiliations. Ironically, many of these campaigns were supported by local Protestant churches which were particularly concerned over the emergence of concentrations of Roman Catholics within individual communities. See Philip Hamburger, *Separation of Church and State* (Cambridge, MA: Harvard University Press, 2002), ch. 11.

[58] See Steven D. Smith, *Foreordained Failure: The Quest for a Constitutional Principle of Religious Freedom* (New York: Oxford University Press, 1999), chs. 6–8; John Witte, Jr., *Religion and the American Constitutional Experiment* (Boulder, CO: Westview, 2000), chs. 4–8.

[59] For example, see *West Virginia State Board of Education v. Barnette*, 319 US 624 (1943); *Wisconsin v. Yoder*, 406 US 205 (1972).

strengthening the wall of separation between the state and those mainline faiths that have a prima facie claim to prevailing social currency.

In these cases, the Court has had to tread a fine line between protecting the principle of neutrality, while not confining or obstructing the freedom of religious worship. In its decisions, the Court has pointed out that while vigorous political debates are 'normal and healthy manifestations of our democratic system', political conflict based upon religion was 'one of the principal evils against which the First Amendment was intended to protect'.[60] The Court's approach has been to operate on the assumption that religion is sectarian in nature and that religious denominations in essence constitute a plurality of competing sects: 'The sectarian character of the Holy Bible has been at the core of the whole controversy over religious practices in the public schools throughout its long and often bitter history'.[61] Consequently, it is important on equity grounds that the Court should not allow any of the constituent sects to acquire a relative advantage over the others through its relationship with the state. In essence, the 'government must be neutral when it comes to competition between sects'.[62]

According to this perspective, any breach of this neutrality would have widespread social and political repercussions because what may be 'today a trickling stream may all too soon become a raging torrent'.[63] By the same token, the 'highways of church and state relationships are not likely to be one-way streets'.[64] Defending religion from the state is as necessary as protecting the state from religious doctrine: 'The history of many countries attests to the hazards of religion's intruding into the political arena or of political power intruding into the legitimate and free exercise of religious belief.'[65] The Supreme Court's attentiveness to the wall of separation issue is driven by the stated conviction that the condition of neutrality is discernible, accessible, and necessarily even-handed: '[W]e cannot accept that the concept of neutrality, which does not permit a State to require a religious exercise even with the consent of the majority of those affected, collides with the majority's right to free exercise of religion'.[66]

This position continues to be strongly contested not just on sectarian grounds of perceived grievance or bias, but on the conceptual ground that neutrality will always be open to dispute in terms of latent intent and actual consequence. Apart from the issue of the judges' own impartiality in relation to the Court's judgments on what can be regarded as neutral, and what cannot, it can be argued that all positions—including that of neutrality itself—are highly subjective in nature. As such, it can also be asserted that they are equally highly moral in content because

[60] *Lemon v. Kurtzman*, 403 US 602 (1971).

[61] *School District of Abington Township, Pennsylvania, et al. v. Schempp et al.*, 374 US 203 (1963).

[62] *Zorach v. Clauson*, 343 US 306 (1952), 314.

[63] *School District of Abington Township, Pennsylvania, et al. v. Schempp et al.*, 374 US 203 (1963), 225.

[64] *Lemon v. Kurtzman*, 403 US 602 (1971), 623.   [65] Ibid.

[66] *School District of Abington Township, Pennsylvania, et al. v. Schempp et al.*, 374 US 203, (1963), 225–6.

of the morally contentious properties of the issue. Opponents of the Supreme Court's decisions in such morally contentious areas as school prayer, sexual behaviour, and abortion claim that the judiciary is not acting in a neutral manner. They assert, moreover, that adjudication can never be neutral in effect.

Apart from the counterargument that court decisions in such a sphere amount to a paradoxical restraint of freedom and democracy by an agency of central government, the Court's opponents complain that its profession of neutrality merely disguises a process that is divisive and damaging to civic autonomy and identity. The view of the religious right movement, for example, is that in such cases the Supreme Court deliberately employs the language of neutrality in order to rationalize its bias in favour of secular humanism and against the forces of biblical authority, religious conviction, and social tradition. The indictment of the federal court's philosophy by such an organization is based on analytical grounds (i.e. the reductionist position that no pronouncement in moral areas can ever be neutral or amoral in effect), but more particularly upon the normative position that there is an interdependency between the sphere of public and private morality, and that this should be cultivated for the benefit of society. The perspective of the religious right and similar movements in this field draws upon a common impulse in American society to connect social complexity with moral simplicity. In the same way that multidimensional forms of social dysfunction are depicted as signs of moral decay, so the solution to these attributed disorders is habitually translated into the need to return to a prior condition. During such a designated period, it is alleged that there once existed a closer alignment of citizenship with moral consciousness and religious faith.

The inference of a direct linkage between the integrity of society's processes and the presence of a prevailing moral anchorage has normative connections that stretch from the Puritan ethos of social existence having to be judged on the criteria of communal purpose, to the contemporary communitarians who stress the importance of social cohesion, solidarist virtues, and the socially constituted nature of individuals. But the relationship between social and moral dispositions is not confined to traditionalist or normative perspectives. It has featured strongly in many empirically based analyses of the American condition.

Alexis de Tocqueville employed a sociological analysis to demonstrate the mutually supportive nature of religion and politics. In his view, religion was a powerful determinant of personality, behaviour, and social structures. De Tocqueville declared that the trend in democratic societies is towards individual autonomy, self-absorption, and material gratification at the expense of spiritual awareness, social perspective, and civic obligation. Religious nations, he concluded, are 'naturally strong in precisely the spot where democratic peoples are weak; this makes very visible how important it is that men keep to their religion when becoming equal'.[67] But in America, he observed that religious organizations had achieved a balance between running with the grain of a democratic

---

[67] Alexis de Tocqueville, *Democracy in America*, trans., ed., and intro. Harvey C. Mansfield and Delba Winthrop (Chicago, IL: Chicago University Press, 2000), p. 419.

society, while at the same time retaining the capacity to provide a basis for moral standards, a community dimension, and collective self-control. The sectarian character of American religious practice did not constitute a threat to republican institutions. Instead, they offered a countervailing force to the prevailing values of material self-advancement. Religion helped to counteract the excesses and abuses of liberal acquisitiveness: 'The principal business of religions is to purify, regulate, and restrain the too ardent and too excessive taste for well-being' and to persuade individuals 'to enrich themselves only by honest means'.[68]

More recently, Robert Bellah et al. have reiterated the social utility of this nexus between religion and politics. They see the value of religious consciousness not simply as a check upon possessive individualism but as a means of offering an alternative sense of personal identity, and as a way of recovering the roots of community life within an increasingly mass society. To Bellah et al. the 'great contribution' that the church community can offer is 'its emphasis on the fact that individuality and society are not opposites but require each other'.[69] They continue:

The church idea reminds us that in our independence we count on others and helps us see that a healthy, grown-up independence is one that admits to healthy, grown-up dependence on others. Absolute independence is a false ideal. It delivers not the autonomy it promises but loneliness and vulnerability instead. Concomitantly, the church idea remands us that authority need not be external and oppressive. It is something we can participate in.[70]

Drawing on the National Congregations Study (1998),[71] Mark Chaves analyses the work and social effect of America's 300,000 congregations. Their mix of collective worship, religious education, spiritual expression, and cultural activities lead him to conclude that religious congregations are the most ubiquitous, diverse, and energetic of America's voluntary associations.[72]

On a wider scale, it can be claimed that the deleterious effects of modernity upon communal action and social morality can be moderated, and even partially reversed, by the cohesive properties of broad-based religious communities. George A. Kelly, for example, underlines the interconnectedness of religion and politics as two distinct but overlapping control systems in human society. The processes of secularization, therefore, undermine not only religious tradition but also the moral authority of political institutions and processes. To Kelly, morality is necessarily inseparable from politics: 'Traditionally, religion has animated it, law has given it a shell to inhabit, opinion has calibrated it, and politics has been domesticated by its force and persuasion'.[73] The erosion of religious attachment

---

[68] Ibid., p. 422.

[69] Robert Bellah, Richard Madsen, William M. Sullivan, Ann Swidler, and Steven M. Tipton, *Habits of the Heart: Americans in Search of Themselves* (New York: Harper & Row, 1985), pp. 246–7.

[70] Ibid., p. 247.

[71] Inter-University Consortium for Political and Social Research, 'National Congregations Study, 1998', http://webapp.icpsr.umich.edu/cocoon/ICPSR-STUDY/03471.xmL

[72] See Mark Chaves, *Congregations in America* (Cambridge, MA: Harvard University Press, 2004).

[73] George A. Kelly, *Politics and Religious Consciousness in America* (New Brunswick, NJ: Transaction, 1990), p. 250.

has been assisted by a liberal state working with a false prospectus of neutrality. In Kelly's view, the outcome has been one of a decline in American civic morality, with little prospect of a new public ethic emerging from the privatizing aftermath of a Judeo-Christian order in the process of collapse.

These diagnoses and prognoses are themselves representative of a society that retains a deeply moral identity, and continues to be preoccupied with the cultural force and social significance of the moral perspective. Just as American history is portrayed and marked by great moral disputes (e.g. slavery, human rights), so America's conception of its history and social dynamics are guided by an underlying premise of moral purpose. The precise definition of that purpose, and the means of sustaining or fulfilling it, is the subject of continuing dispute in which the vocabulary and idioms of religious faith remain prominent. As we see elsewhere in this study, the ramifying cultural conflicts surrounding this issue of America as a civil religion both inform and influence not only the role of other values in American political debate, but also the way in which they are fused together into differing compounds.

8

Progress

INTRODUCTION

The United States places a high degree of value upon both the idea and the material reality of progress. The concept of progress is highly esteemed as a descriptive fact of American society and also as a normative prescription conjoined to western modernity. In the United States, change is conceived as being largely synonymous with vitality, purpose, and direction. It is regarded as an integral and imperative feature of an open society. As a consequence, American discourse is studded with references to the benevolence of change, to the primacy of the future over the past and the present, and to the importance of 'moving forward'. The instinctive prejudice against such terms as 'old fashioned', 'regressive', 'immobile', and 'outmoded' is a reflection of the cultural attachment to progress. Political, economic, and social forms of progress are generally thought to occur in tandem and, especially so, in a social order like that of the United States which is traditionally geared to the emancipation of human potential for individual action and collective enterprise.

Progress has become the grand characterization of American flux. It ranks as both an apologia and a rationale for successive reconfigurations of social existence. In many respects, progress constitutes the only way of rationalizing the shifting contours of such a mutable society. Furthermore, by giving form and purpose to change, progress lends legitimacy to altered states of existence. As a consequence, progress becomes a way of observing the transformational scale of America's pattern of human settlement as well as its economic expansion and its rise to military pre-eminence. The presumption of, and faith in, the rationalizing presence of progress also constitutes a means of understanding and ascribing value to a complex of permanent movement. In fact, it is largely because mutability is so central to American history and society that progress has acquired such a high status as a concept of organization and meaning. Frances FitzGerald's celebrated observation on this theme typifies the predominant outlook: 'Americans see history as a straight line and themselves standing at the cutting edge of it as representatives for all mankind. They believe in the future as if it were a religion'.[1] It is no exaggeration, therefore, to claim that American exceptionalism is closely associated with the theme of progressive change. The United States is seen as being not only particularly susceptible to the supposition of historical progress, but also

[1] Frances FitzGerald, *Fire in the Lake: The Vietnamese and the Americans in Vietnam* (London: Macmillan, 1972), p. 7.

peculiarly representative of the potential for, and the actual realization of, cumulative and purposive change. In America, the ameliorative properties of progress are widely conceived as being an inevitable feature of social life because of the way that the United States is seen as being bound up with an ineluctable historical process which combines evolutionary forces with a benevolent determinism.

AMERICAN ENLIGHTENMENT

The American adherence to the value of progress is strongly rooted in the association between the Enlightenment and America's early period of republican formation. During this era, enlightened reason had become an intellectual tradition central to America's historical understanding of its emergence as an emancipated social entity. Just as intellectual assertion had fuelled the drive towards political independence, rational inquiry had shaped the structure and dynamics of the republic's constitutional settlement. A cultivated theme of American historiography gives special status to the force of Newtonian natural philosophy and to the spirit of analytical reason that radiated from science outwards to the full gamut of human activity.[2] Far from the Enlightenment being an intrinsically European departure in thought and practice, it is widely contended that the peculiarly liberating conditions of the New World in the eighteenth century made Americans particularly susceptible to the progressive prospectus of Enlightenment ideas.

It can be argued that the fluid conditions within America generated something more significant than a non-European addendum to the Enlightenment. It has been claimed that the United States represented a social and political point of culmination of the Enlightenment's fundamental precepts. Theoretical experimentation and intellectual hope in Europe had become material innovation and hope fulfilled in the protean circumstances of the New World. In Bernard Bailyn's view, the 'political and social ideas of the European Enlightenment have had a peculiar importance in American history'.[3] To Bailyn, these ideas were more 'universally accepted in eighteenth-century America than in Europe'.[4] In America, they 'were more completely and permanently embodied in the formal

---

[2] See R. D. Mosier, *The American Temper: Patterns of Our Intellectual Heritage* (Berkeley and Los Angeles, CA: University of California Press, 1952), pp. 85–155; Henry F. May, *The Enlightenment in America* (New York: Oxford University Press, 1976); D. H. Meyer, 'The Uniqueness of the American Enlightenment', *American Quarterly*, vol. 28 no. 2 (Summer 1976), pp. 165–86; I. B. Cohen, 'Science and the Growth of the American Republic', *Review of Politics*, vol. 38, no. 3 (July 1976), pp. 359–98; Adrienne Koch (ed.), *The American Enlightenment: The Shaping of the American Experiment and a Free Society* (New York: George Braziller, 1980); J. R. Pole, 'The Enlightenment and the Politics of the American Nature', in Roy Porter and Mikulás Teich (eds.), *The Enlightenment in National Context* (Cambridge: Cambridge University Press, 1981), pp. 192–214; Darren Staloff, *Hamilton, Adams, Jefferson: The Politics of Enlightenment and the American Founding* (New York: Hill & Wang, 2005).

[3] Bernard Bailyn, 'Political Experience and Enlightenment Ideas in Eighteenth-Century America', *American Historical Review*, vol. 67, no. 2 (1962), p. 339.

[4] Ibid.

arrangements of state and society'.[5] Because they were 'less controverted [and] less subject to criticism and dispute, they have lived on more vigorously into later periods' and have as a result been 'more continuous and intact' in their social currency.[6]

Peter Gay reiterates the same theme. The Founders and their contemporaries were distinguished by a common belief in the opportunity and need for America to engage in the 'human program of the Enlightenment applied'.[7] Henry Steele Commager is similarly convinced of America's status as the place where the Enlightenment was 'realized and fulfilled'.[8] Whereas the Old World imagined and formulated the Enlightenment, it was the 'Americans who not only embraced the body of Enlightenment principles, but wrote them into law, crystallized them into institutions and put them to work'. To Commager, this exercise in intellectual emancipation was a realization of the Enlightenment: 'That, as much as the winning of independence and the creation of the nation, *was* the American Revolution.'[9] According to this view, American society in the eighteenth century achieved, through the force of conscious and self-willed reason, an advanced level of civilized tolerance, material progress, and political freedom. So much so, it could be claimed that the New World rather than the Old World truly embodied both the spirit and the objective of the Enlightenment. As a consequence, the interaction of enlightened progress and progressive Enlightenment became a basic presumption of American life. Most European *philosophes* had an 'almost uncritical faith in progress', but this outlook 'tended to be an intellectual abstraction or an aesthetic ideal'.[10] In America, on the other hand, progress was accepted as a living ideal and one that continues to be regarded as 'practical, material, immediate, and equalitarian [*sic*]'.[11]

The theme of the American Enlightenment and the extent to which it represented a totality of belief that displaced tradition, mystique, and ancestry remains a contested issue.[12] What is less contentious is the extent to which the Enlightenment faith in the existence of rationally discernible laws of nature and in the application of knowledge to human improvement became a core characteristic of American development. This was typified in the industrial expansion of the United States in the nineteenth century. During this period, America benefited from the exploitation of successive breakthroughs in science and technology

---

[5] Ibid.   [6] Ibid.

[7] Peter Gay, 'The Applied Enlightenment?', in E. M. Adams (ed.), *The Idea of America: A Reassessment of the American Experiment* (Cambridge: Ballinger, 1977), p. 12.

[8] Henry S. Commager, *The Empire of Reason: How Europe Imagined and America Realized the Enlightenment* (London: Weidenfeld & Nicolson, 1978), p. ix.

[9] Ibid.   [10] Ibid., p. 37.   [11] Ibid.

[12] For example, see Robert A. Ferguson, *The American Enlightenment, 1750–1820* (Cambridge, MA: Harvard University Press, 1997). In a historically sensitive study, Ferguson underlines the significance to the American Enlightenment of the constitutional traditions of colonial America, the Whig political theory of historical process, the influence of English common law, and the religious undercurrents of reform Protestantism. Ferguson also distinguishes a conservative component to the Enlightenment that was manifested in a regard for progress in the form of harmony, unity, control, and order.

(e.g. steel production, railroad construction, telegraph communication, canal building, mining technology, steamship design, and agricultural machinery). This allowed American history to be characterized as a process by which 'a rustic and in large part wild landscape was transformed into the site of the world's most productive industrial machine'.[13] As a result, technological progress and even 'technological determinism [became] an inescapable aspect of the modern American way... [and] an implicit American assumption'.[14]

The imagery and power of the machine came to dominate the role of America as a continental society and a world force. The usage of science and technology was so instrumental in the acceleration of America's settlement and development that the machine became an integral feature of the American identity. Mechanistic concepts, values, and metaphors penetrated American culture and were assimilated as conventional criteria of perception and normative assessment. Even the Constitution became instinctively defined in terms of a system of mechanistic energy in which institutions and powers operated in accordance with a stated order of mechanical sequence and with a precise pattern of interlocking dynamics.[15] Given the pronounced attachment to mechanical terms of reference, the distinction between the belief that the constitutional framework resembled a machine and the view that it possessed real mechanical properties often became lost to view. This lack of discrimination prompted Woodrow Wilson to exhort Americans to disavow the fixed perspective of an eighteenth-century constitutional machine in favour of an evolutionary conception of the political system. Government was 'not a machine, but a living thing' that fell under the 'theory of organic life'.[16] Like the rest of society, governments had to adapt to changing environmental conditions and in doing so they were 'accountable to Darwin, not to Newton'.[17]

'ALL GROWS BETTER'

The successive demonstrations of nature's susceptibility to ordered manipulation and reasoned control, and the ability of an industrial order to secure continued material and social progress generated a demand for this triumph of science and technology to receive its own rational explanation in the form of a general theory. This was provided by Herbert Spencer who located social progress within an

[13] Leo Marx, *The Machine in the Garden: Technology and the Pastoral Idea in America* (Oxford: Oxford University Press, 1964), p. 343.

[14] G. M. Ostrander, *American Civilization in the First Machine Age: 1840–1940* (New York: Harper & Row, 1970), p. 228.

[15] See Michael Kammen, *A Machine That Would Go of Itself: The Constitution in American Culture* (New York: Knopf, 1986); Michael Foley, *Laws, Men and Machines: Modern American Government and the Appeal of Newtonian Mechanics* (London: Routledge, 1990).

[16] Woodrow Wilson, *The New Freedom: A Call for the Emancipation of the Generous Energies of a People*, intro. William E. Leuchtenburg (Englewood Cliffs, NJ: Prentice-Hall, 1961), p. 42.

[17] Ibid.

overarching framework of cosmic cause and effect. Advances within industrial and social organization were part of a universal dynamic within nature. In Spencer's view, the development of the universe had been characterized by a succession of transformations of unstable homogeneous entities to complex heterogeneous arrangements. The physical, organic, and social fields all demonstrated the corroboration of the presence of such a natural law of linear development and purposive change.[18]

Spencer rationalized the disruption and disorientation of accelerated industrialization by refracting change through the prism of a general movement in nature towards an ordered complexity. Social progress was characterized by a movement away from monolithic, static, and oppressive arrangements towards plural, dynamic, and freely adaptive organizations. The former were destined to decay, while the latter were assured of the same natural pre-eminence which had been acquired by the heterogeneous entities in the physical and biological fields. To Spencer, the state was not the climax of social organization. It was a restrictive and regressive anachronism. It obstructed progress by diminishing the effect of natural and spontaneous forces working towards the heterogeneity that would assure advance. Spencer had no doubt that only the perversions of nature could, and would, pass away. All forms of life and culture were necessarily subject to the universal drive that would reduce deficiencies and unfitness in favour of an adaptive evolution to the conditions of existence. Like the rest of nature, society evolved towards a higher order of organization and achievement.

Retrograde or recessive elements in society would, in Spencer's view, necessarily degenerate and disappear in order to allow human arrangements to reach the adaptive capacity required to fit their conditions of existence. With each individual 'having freedom to use his powers up to the bounds fixed by the like freedom of others', then, according to Spencer, 'there is maintained the vital principle of social progress; inasmuch as, under such conditions, the individuals of most worth will prosper and multiply more than those with less worth'.[19] Although Spencer believed that social progress was dependent upon a competitive struggle, his liberalism operated on the premise that different interests were ultimately compatible with one another. Just as conflict could, and would, be resolved by society evolving to a higher condition of material and moral improvement, so progress would be marked by an increasingly organic basis of mutual interest.[20]

---

[18] See Herbert Spencer, *Herbert Spencer: Structure, Function and Evolution*, ed. Stanislav Andreski (London: Michael Joseph, 1971), pp. 55–104; David Wiltshire, *The Social and Political Thought of Herbert Spencer* (Oxford: Oxford University Press, 1978), ch. 8; H. Stuart Jones, *Victorian Political Thought* (Houndmills, UK: Macmillan, 2000), pp. 74–81.

[19] Herbert Spencer, 'The Coming Slavery', in Alan Bullock and Maurice Shock (eds.), *The Liberal Tradition* (Oxford: Clarendon Press, 1967), p. 185.

[20] Spencer, *Herbert Spencer: Structure, Function and Evolution*, pp. 107–47; Wiltshire, *The Social and Political Thought of Herbert Spencer*, ch. 9; John W. Burrow, *Evolution and Society: A Study in Victorian Social Theory* (Cambridge: Cambridge University Press, 1966), pp. 196–227.

The theme of cultural transformation had exercised philosophes like A. R. J. Turgot and the Marquis de Condorcet in the eighteenth century.[21] Condorcet in particular had sought to systematize the notion of progress through the study of epochs of human history. While the status of progress as a general law of human nature received close attention during the Enlightenment, the operational dynamics of progress as a natural phenomenon remained unknown. It was Spencer who offered a scientific explanation of progress and in the process afforded the material conditions of advancement a renewed moral legitimacy as the essence of a natural order of evolution. This conjunction of high theory and palpable social resonance allowed Spencer to enjoy extraordinary popularity in the United States in the late nineteenth century. It was not merely that his theory suited the interests and pretensions of the new industrial warlords, or that his theory of cosmic progress gave meaning and respect to the social mobility of the rising commercial classes in general. It was that the principles associated with Spencer's laissez-faire liberalism appeared to explain the sudden onset of industrial power and technological innovation, while at the same time rationalizing the discriminatory effect of 'fitness' as the necessary instrument of a generic social progress. He popularized the phrase the 'survival of the fittest' and integrated it into a totality of explanation that took evolutionary theory out of the organic realm and applied it uniformly across all areas of development.

Spencer's American reputation was assisted by William Graham Sumner who not only elucidated some of Spencer's more obscure theorizing, but also sought to incorporate the new economic licentiousness specifically into the American tradition of individual liberty. While Spencer had been a popularizer of science, Sumner in turn popularized the work of Spencer for an American audience. In particular, Sumner developed the linkage between the Darwinian notion of biological fitness and the possession of private property. While Spencer concentrated more on the beneficent consequences of evolutionary change, Sumner was more directly prescriptive over the necessarily robust nature of the evolutionary processes. Property rights to Sumner were the pre-eminent means and signs of progress. In effect, Sumner extracted the illiberal implications of Spencer and prioritized the realism of a competitive property-based struggle over the formalism of constitutional law and individual rights as the motive force of civilization.[22]

It was during this period that Spencer's evolutionary philosophy was portrayed as modern realism in the service of American optimism. It fitted into an increasingly conventional American historiography that categorized the United States as a cumulative development away from feudal anachronism, royal despotism, cultural superstition, and religious intolerance. The cosmology of Herbert Spencer situated the United States in the forefront of human progress and, in doing so,

---

[21] See Robert Nisbet, *History of the Idea of Progress* (London: Heinemann, 1980); Richard Bronk, *Progress and the Invisible Hand: The Philosophy and Economics of Human Advance* (London: Warner, 1998), ch. 6.

[22] See Robert G. McCloskey, *American Conservatism in the Age of Enterprise, 1865–1910: A Study of William Graham Sumner, Stephen J. Field and Andrew Carnegie* (New York: Harper & Row, 1964); Louis Auchincloss, *The Vanderbilt Era: Profiles of a Gilded Age* (New York: Scribner's, 1989).

helped to turn American notions of advance away from a displacement of the past and more towards a triumphant epitome of a modernizing civilization. Spencerian conceptions of social advance tapped into, and in turn, cultivated an emerging American identity centred upon an exceptionalism of progress. According to this view, 'science and technology have developed in this country, unhindered by European traditions and privilege, and are bound to make for a newer and higher type of civilization'.[23] Morris Cohen goes on to point out that Spencer 'stirred the popular imagination as few intellectual achievements had done since the rise of Copernican astronomy'.[24] In the process, Spencer offered not merely hope for progress but the certainty of its existence and continuation: '[I]nstead of doing away with all teleology, the evolutionary philosophy itself became a teleology, replacing bleak Calvinism with the warm rosy outlook of a perpetual and universal and upward progress.'[25]

During this ground-breaking period of industrial growth, material transformation and rising affluence, capitalism became fixed as the touchstone of American modernity and progress. Economic liberty and the free market had had a galvanizing effect upon both the physical and the moral basis of the social order. Progress was increasingly attributed to an evolutionary imperative that found its outlet in a compulsive medium of self-seeking materialism through which society measured its dynamic energies and secured its advances. Even though Darwin's theory contained no inference that evolutionary processes led to qualitative improvement, Social Darwinism successfully fused the concept of evolution to the idea of progress through the insinuation of a historical process of human progression. A plutocratic oligarchy that had self-evidently been responsible for foundational change could plausibly be portrayed as both the agency of progress and the proof of its existence. To a ruthless entrepreneur like Andrew Carnegie, whose rapid enrichment had promoted him to an elite position of social authority, the ethos generated its own vindication as a natural law and a moral benefit. Upon reading Spencer, Carnegie said: 'Light came as in a flood and all was clear. . . . Not only had I got rid of theology and the supernatural but I had found the truth of evolution. "All is well, and since all grows better" became my motto, my true source of comfort'.[26] Carnegie felt vindicated. His working priorities could now be affirmed as ethical principles.

In this consummate epoch of capitalism, more was synonymous with better. As a consequence, American expanding economy constituted the main solution to all problems. As a consequence, just as growth became a primary value, so social advances became seen as largely a derivative of a freely developing economic order. The paradigm of progress and the dominion of its needs have resonated throughout the twentieth century. The imperative of progress as a defining rationale for decision-making and identity has remained in place. In America, progress

---

[23] Morris R. Cohen, *American Thought: A Critical Sketch* (New York: Collier, 1962) p. 78.
[24] Ibid., p. 326.   [25] Ibid.
[26] Quoted in Harold J. Livesay, *Andrew Carnegie and the Rise of Big Business* (Boston, MA: Little, Brown, 1975), pp. 74–5.

continues to constitute the main basis for American optimism and for the nation's self-belief as the vanguard of the West.

THE PROBLEMATIC NATURE OF PROGRESS

Even though America has an inherent allegiance to the theme of progress and its status as a New World condition, both the idea and its material expression raise a profusion of questions over its meaning and identity. The United States is often cited as the defining embodiment of progress. Equally, it is also employed to demonstrate the contestable dimensions of progress.

The concept of progress has always generated philosophical and empirical disputes.[27] It is, for example, dependent upon an acceptance of a set of premises relating to the mutability of society and to a linear development over time that imposes order and direction upon change. In such a template, history is no longer a mere succession of events. It approximates more to an autonomous temporal process moving towards a purposeful projected outcome. The cumulative pattern of change works through time in such a way as to make advance and improvement interchangeable categories. Despite the fact that in this construction, progress becomes synonymous with the supposed virtues of evolution, the adaptive nature of the evolutionary process has no necessary relationship to the idea of advance: 'In the natural world, later evolutionary adaptations are not necessarily superior to their predecessors in any objective sense other than their ability to survive. Nature has no necessary direction or purpose which it can lend, by analogy, to history'.[28] Progress as an idea that fuses purposeful change with successive improvement, therefore, depends upon the extent to which it is treated as a fact, i.e. upon the will to construct an impression of movement and advance from the evidence of change. In other words, although progress is explicitly reliant upon the physical evidence of change, it remains a value-loaded term that requires a normative consensus for change to become interpreted as a historical process guided by an implicit point of culmination.

Far from having a factual logic, progress remains a tautological device in so far as its premises and conclusions are interwoven with one another. As a consequence, in analytical terms progress continues to constitute an uneasy hybrid of fact and value in which each becomes defined in terms of the other. At a substantive level, this can lead to every development being couched as progress simply on grounds of movement towards an objective that is assumed to exist by the very presence of movement itself. This form of inertia can also lead to the abuse of progress and even to its corruption in the form of reaction disguised as an advance.

---

[27] See Nisbet, *History of the Idea of Progress*; Bronk, *Progress and the Invisible Hand: The Philosophy and Economics of Human Advance*; Leo Marx and Bruce Mazlish (eds.), *Progress: Fact or Illusion?* (Ann Arbor, MI: University of Michigan Press, 1996).

[28] Bronk, *Progress and the Invisible Hand*, p. 55.

By the same token, in another context, progress is clearly an idea dependent upon time, but also one which cannot be wholly determined by the passage of time without becoming meaningless. Time is a necessary but not a sufficient condition. Progress is often confused with time. It certainly requires time but time is not a generative and purposive process in its own right. Differences also exist between the concept of progress that simply extrapolates change into a projected future state, and the more substantive and deductive view of progress that conceives of a desirable end and then relates and assesses the present directly in terms of such a conscious purpose. Further confusion exists in the way progress is used in political argument. Sometimes progress is regarded as the end that is served by new developments, while on other occasions it is taken to be the process or agency of change itself.

Possibly the greatest source of discord relating to the theme of progress emanates from its associations with reliable knowledge set against the problem of how that knowledge should be used. During the Enlightenment, it was recognized that the revelation of nature's laws yielded a wealth of useful and usable information. Nevertheless, it did not, and could not, offer moral guidance over the uses to which such knowledge could be put. 'To the extent that the laws of nature were to be discovered' they were ultimately in the category of being 'purely descriptive'.[29] They might disclose the 'ordered relations of phenomena' but they also underlined the limitations of such knowledge and the fact that 'nature and reason did not say *how* to live'.[30] The greater the faith that was vested in the pursuit of knowledge, the wider was the gap in devising an ethical direction within the abundance of data. Notwithstanding these constraints, some *philosophes* believed that an objective moral science could be formulated to close the gap. Others either depended upon the ameliorative consequences of progress offering its own solution, or were content to leave the issue in a state of obscurity. This factual-normative disjunction within progress has remained in existence since the eighteenth century. At times it is given due recognition but for the most part, it remains concealed, or at best, left in a state of suspended ambiguity.

Many of these concerns over progress and its prerogatives were evident during the belle époque of America's industrial leap forward in the late nineteenth century. The excesses of the period prompted complaints that the definition and means of progress had become the subject of a technological determinism and a Darwinian view of society both of which privileged unsocial behaviour for the sake of net material gains. As social forms were re-conceptualized in terms of struggle and conflict, so the idea of liberty risked becoming diminished to that of a secondary value. Freedom was in jeopardy of becoming a facilitating device in the drive for technological advance, or in the service of a construction of natural selection. The prospect of rights being subsumed within an overall assessment of social utility was a real threat. Private property was already conceived as being rightfully

[29] Thomas Hankins, *Science and the Enlightenment* (Cambridge: Cambridge University Press, 1985), p. 6.
[30] Ibid.

possessed by those who were self-evidently fit to own it by the mere fact of having it. The concentration of property, and rights based upon property, became further rationalized as a scientific and moral prerequisite of progress. The individuals who survived and prevailed through the competitive struggle were those who, by their own definition, were fit to do so. Those who were declared to be naturally the most fit could reveal their fitness only through the medium of a competitive struggle. Progress and the triumphant industrialist, therefore, tended to be defined and validated in terms of each other. The tautology was evident but also compelling.

Ultimately, the persuasiveness of this conception of progress was reducible to power. The magnitude of the economic forces unleashed by industrialization revealed how republican language and ideals could be transformed into the supportive adjuncts of an unequal and, arguably, amoral social arrangement. The hugely corrupting and self-serving inequities of laissez-faire capitalism were subsequently identified as imbalances rather than as necessary elements in a harmony of progress. Individuals had been encouraged to satisfy their reputedly instinctive quest for self-promotion over other individuals. Similarly, the concept of society as a self-conscious and self-determining community had been reduced to an agglomeration of individual appetites. Now what had been taken to be operational facets of progress were increasingly subjected to critical challenge. In particular, it became increasingly clear that the freedom of contract by which labour and wages were regulated did not necessarily produce an equitable balance of interests in a largely unregulated industrial setting. Economics of scale often produced a pattern of non-negotiable arrangements that left workers with few if any choices other than to accept the conditions offered to them. The only other feasible option was even less attractive: that of subsistence or marginal agriculture in an economic sector where new land resources had become drastically depleted.

The abuses and excesses of this age of individualism generated a series of reform movements and prompted serious revisions in America's public philosophy. The pragmatist school of theorists, for example, stressed the importance of knowledge as an instrumental value to be used to ameliorate social problems in a spirit of openness and experimentation. In contrast to the Social Darwinist view of society, pragmatists operated on the assumption that humanity was not part of any closed or predetermined natural order.[31] Radical utopian writers like Henry George and Edmund Bellamy encouraged their readers to subject the state of contemporary society to critical evaluation through the consideration of sweeping alternatives.[32]

[31] Andrew Feffer, *The Chicago Pragmatists and American Progressivism* (Ithaca, NY: Cornell University Press, 1993); John Patrick Diggins, *The Promise of Pragmatism: Modernism and the Crisis of Knowledge and Authority* (Chicago, IL: University of Chicago Press, 1994), chs. 3, 4, 8; Alan Ryan, *John Dewey and the High Tide of American Liberalism* (New York: W. W. Norton, 1995), pp. 19–34, 189–225; Louis Menand, *The Metaphysical Club* (London: Flamingo, 2002), pp. 285–95.

[32] John Thomas, *Alternative America : Henry George, Edward Bellamy, Henry Demarest Lloyd and the Adversary Tradition* (Cambridge, MA: Belknap Press, 1983); Matthew Hartman, 'Utopian Evolution: The Sentimental Critique of Social Darwinism in Bellamy and Peirce', *Utopian Studies*, vol. 10, no. 1 (1999), pp. 26–41. Samuel Haber, 'The Nightmare and the Dream: Edward Bellamy and the Travails of Socialist Thought', *Journal of American Studies*, vol. 36, no. 3 (December 2002), pp. 417–40.

The Social Gospel movement encouraged the revival of Christian social ethics.[33] Social theorists, like Herbert Croly, sought to regenerate a sense of solidarism in society. Heavily influenced by Hegelian historicism and idealism, Croly pressed for popular sovereignty to be redefined in terms of a collective directional will that was derived from the asserted historical and moral fact of an underlying and all-inclusive American community.[34]

The development of the social sciences at the end of the nineteenth century also contributed to a trend of perceiving the person as being social in essence. Traditional American individualism had mainly conceived of society as an atomized collection of mutually independent agents. Contemporary social science shifted the balance towards a view that men and women are primarily social creatures who are shaped not only by an outside physical environment, but by an interior environment of social values, beliefs, and practices.[35] Social psychology, in particular, developed a paradigm which reconstituted the Darwinian category of an organism from the basis of an isolated and competitive individual to that of a complex structure of interdependent and cooperative components. According to this science, neither the individual nor society pre-existed the other. They both presupposed each other so that the community was as natural a feature of life as was the individual. It was this organic community of individuals which represented the base unit of human evolution and the medium through which mankind could progress to a higher plane of development and fulfilment.[36]

One of the chief consequences of this altered perspective of evolution was the belief that humanity had been able to mould society through conscious invention and regulation from within. Evolution in this form, therefore, could be construed

[33] Ronald C. White, Jr., and C. Howard Hopkins, *The Social Gospel: Religion and Reform in Changing America* (Philadelphia, PA: Temple University Press, 1976); Walter Rauschenbusch, *Christianity and the Social Crisis* (Louisville, KY: Westminster/John Knox Press, 1991), chs. 4–7; Jacob H. Dorn, *Socialism and Christianity in Early 20th-Century America* (Westport, CT: Greenwood Press, 1998); Susan Curtis, *A Consuming Faith: The Social Gospel and Modern American Culture* (Columbia, MO: University of Missouri Press, 2001).

[34] See Charles Forcey, *The Crossroads of Liberalism: Croly, Weyl and the Progressive Era, 1900–1925* (New York: Oxford University Press, 1961), pp. 3–51; David W. Noble, 'Herbert Croly and American Progressive Thought', in John P. Roche (ed.), *American Political Thought: From Jefferson to Progressivism* (New York: Harper & Row, 1967), pp. 259–83.

[35] For more on the influence of contemporary sociologists and economists (e.g. Richard Ely, Franklin Giddings, Simon Patten, and Albion Small) on the development of this outlook, see James Livingston, *Pragmatism and the Political Economy of Cultural Revolution, 1850–1940* (Chapel Hill, NC: University of North Carolina Press, 1997), ch. 3; Olivier Zunz, *Why the American Century?* (Chicago, IL: University of Chicago Press, 2000), ch. 2; Jeffrey Sklansky, *The Soul's Economy: Market Society and Selfhood in American Thought, 1820–1920* (Chapel Hill, NC: University of North Carolina Press, 2002), ch. 6.

[36] Lester F. Ward, *Psychic Factors of Civilization* (New York: Ginn, 1892); Charles Horton Cooley, *Social Organization: A Study of the Larger Mind* (New York: Charles Scribner's Sons, 1909); Henry S. Commager, *The American Mind: An Interpretation of American Thought and Character Since the 1880s* (New York: Bantam, 1970), ch. 10; Peter J. Bowler, *Evolution: The History of an Idea* (Berkeley, CA: University California Press, 1984), ch. 10; Eldon J. Eisenach, *The Lost Promise of Progressivism* (Lawrence, KS: University Press of Kansas, 1994), chs. 3, 6; Sklansky, *The Soul's Economy*, chs. 6, 7.

as an active assertion of collective will, rather than merely a fatalistic experience of blind purposeless forces acting upon society. The emphasis laid upon the creative consciousness in evolutionary progress by influential figures like Lester Ward made a marked impression upon progressive thought. For example, it is widely regarded as having been a major source of inspiration behind the experimental activism of the New Deal and its various reformist derivatives throughout the century.[37]

Although progress retained its allure as a standard of social achievement, it became increasingly seen as a highly contingent and contestable category of value. It was no longer assumed that progress was cumulative in character. Economic progress, for example, could not be relied upon to draw political, social, and moral progress in its wake. On the contrary, it was apparent that one form of progress would often be secured at the expense of another. Because the means to achieve progress in one area of social life may not be accepted as necessarily the way to secure in a different social sector, there could be no one-to-one relationship of cause and effect covering all fields of social existence. Progress was still served by reasoned inquiry, science, and technology, but it remained at root a subjective entity.

PROGRESS AS AN AMERICAN VALUE

In spite of its contested nature, progress has remained a distinctive point of cultural reference in the United States. It provides a guiding assumption and a conditioning expectation of American life. A strong belief exists in the presence of an underlying course to American development in which the United States is both the chief facilitator of progress and its prime beneficiary. This predisposition towards constructing change as progress with net benefits for all is typified by Bill Gates and his vision of the future. The founder of Microsoft is a committed advocate of the social virtues accruing from successive advances in information technology (IT). His outlook is one of complete optimism in which the dynamics of IT would create a social transformation in the way that people communicated with one another. In 1995, Gates offered a detailed prospectus of 'the road ahead'[38] and the need to adapt to the future of 'a new mediated way of life'.[39] Gates had no doubt that everyone was 'watching something historical happen' which would 'affect the world seismically, rocking us in the same way the discovery of the scientific method, the invention of printing, and the arrival of the Industrial Age did'.[40] To the originator of Microsoft, this was a development to be welcomed and to which humanity had to make the necessary adjustments: 'I'm someone who

---

[37] Max J. Skidmore, *American Political Thought* (New York: St. Martin's Press, 1978), p. 167.
[38] Bill Gates with Nathan Myhrvold and Peter Rinearson, *The Road Ahead* (London: Viking, 1995).
[39] Ibid., p. 5.   [40] Ibid., p. 273.

believes that progress will come no matter what, [and that] we need to make the best of it'.[41]

A similar conception of ineluctable forces in the service of a known future of improvement is given by Francis Fukuyama in his celebrated thesis on the end of history. This rationalization of the post-cold war condition was immensely influential in the 1990s because it offered an explanation in the form of a prospectus of progression. Fukuyama's optimism in the therapeutic properties of an uninhibited and unrestrained form of liberal progress quickly came to be qualified by a renewed appreciation of the classic caveats of progress. Developments that in some respects could be classified as advances could also engender new problems, or a repetition of old problems in new guises. Notwithstanding the United States' apparent triumph over the threat of a state-centred and expansionary communism, the disappearance of a genuine alternative to liberal capitalism brought in its wake a profusion of anxieties over the dominance of private economic forces over the politics of the public interest. The globalizing economy and the growing hegemony of transnational corporations threatened a loss not only of individual autonomy but also of national sovereignty. Progress risked being defined purely in terms of market forces, profit margins, and stock values.[42] As concerns grew over rising income inequality, civil disorder, moral malaise, and political apathy, objections were increasingly lodged against the suppositions and drives of progress.

In this context, the Enlightenment's own problems with the concept of progress were revived. The accumulation of knowledge about nature and the increased ability to manipulate and control nature could not offer a comparably precise set of rules that might offer moral guidance over how such resources might be used. In the contemporary era of neo-liberal dogmas, the fusion of modern science and technology with industrial and commercial disciplines offers an ethos of progress but without a corresponding set of ethics. The Enlightenment had also highlighted another paradox: as science increasingly demonstrated a determinate universe, humanity was increasingly revealed as possessing little in the way of an open future. Science in this sense promised no emancipation, only a more advanced understanding of humanity's own predetermined and permanent predicament. Even in the current epoch of systems management and information revolution, progress can still be interpreted as having the same price in terms of a reduction of individual autonomy and an increasingly fatalistic view of human vices and social dysfunction.

This is a theme that has been developed most recently by John Gray, who challenges the idea of progress not only as a mythical delusion but as a fatal form of hubris.[43] In spite of the exponential advances in science and technology, Gray asserts that human beings remain biologically and psychologically static. In terms of those criteria most commonly associated with progress, humanity is, and

---

[41] Ibid., p. 11.

[42] See Martin Wolf, *Why Globalization Works* (New Haven, CT: Yale University Press, 2004); Jagdish Bhagwati, *In Defense of Globalization* (New York: Oxford University Press, 2005).

[43] John Gray, *Heresies: Against Progress and Other Illusions* (London: Granta, 2004), chs. 1–8.

will always remain, flawed to such an extent that it subverts the very concept of progress. Humans are unable to match the sophistication of technology with social structures and decision-making systems that are in any way commensurate with the resources they are seeking control. The end result is not one of inevitable progress but that of self-destruction through the retention of irrational instincts and unconscious drives.

The chief tenet of the Enlightenment is that the growth of knowledge is the key to human emancipation. No true believer in the Enlightenment would ever question that article of faith. Yet at the close of the 20th century, faith in progress through the growth of knowledge itself looks irrational. In fact, there is no consistent, enduring link between the adoption of modern science and technology on the one hand and the progress of reason in human affairs on the other. If anything, new technologies can give a new lease of life to the side of human nature that is not and will never be rational.[44]

Far from being a cause for assured optimism, the spirit of the Enlightenment to Gray should lead to the recognition of intrinsic uncertainty and renewed pessimism in the course of human affairs.

Set against this background, the United States at the end of the twentieth century began to rediscover the nineteenth-century debates surrounding the legitimacy and costs of corporate wealth-creation and the need for social responsibility to be promoted and for the public interest to be protected. These anxieties have become a continuing theme in the new century's absorption with the neo-liberal vision of free markets and the spread of democracy. The human and moral costs of industrialized and globalized progress have been reflected in the renewed reservations over unfettered capitalism, corporate enrichment, international capital flows, environmental degradation, consumer myopia, and democratic stagnation.[45] Such disquiet can evoke systemic critiques based upon, and focused on, the regressive potential of progress—especially when there is increasing evidence of a generic disconnect between economic growth and human well-being.[46]

These indictments feature America's cultural attachment to the idea of progress as a prime cause of social deterioration. The antagonism against ill-considered economic expansion, acquisitive individualism, and self-seeking priorities has almost invariably been expressed as an assault upon the cultural imperatives of progress.[47] Within this construction, republican virtue and civic character are depicted as the chief casualties of a morally neutral liberalism that displaces the authority and cohesion of community with the soulless technocracy of 'big

---

[44] John Gray, 'The Myth of Progress', *New Statesman*, 9 April 1999.

[45] For example, see Robert Reich, *The Future of Success: Work and Life in the New Economy* (London: William Heinemann, 2001), chs. 4, 5, 7, 10.

[46] Bronk, *Progress and the Invisible Hand*, chs. 7–12.

[47] See John Gray, *False Dawn: The Delusions of Global Capitalism* (New York: New Press, 2000), ch. 5; William Hutton, *The World We're In* (London: Little, Brown, 2002), chs. 4, 6; Noreena Hertz, *The Silent Takeover: Global Capitalism and the Death of Democracy* (New York: HarperCollins, 2003), chs. 3–6, 9.

government' and the amoral blight of consumer capitalism in which the only value is that of greater demand.[48]

Insightful and evocative though these principled assessments may be to the predicament of American modernity, they nevertheless amount to a radical scepticism that is usually distinguished for lying well outside the conventional bounds of the mainstream. Even in the face of evident misgivings over its reach as an idea and as a rationale, progress continues to be strongly correlated to other core liberal values—freedom, reason, enlightenment, civilization, and the advancement of humanity. Critics who attempt to make a case for establishing a conflict between progress and other American values find it difficult to challenge the orthodox view that progress is an integral feature of the American experience. In spite of the many indictments of progress' presumptions and the numerous critiques of the way that it is said to create division and alienation within society, the belief in the substantive worth of progress continues to exercise a forceful hold upon the American perceptions and value-judgements. The social mobility and material potential that allows the next generation to have the realistic expectation of surpassing the achievements and acquisitions of the previous generation remains a pivotal narrative of the American experience. Personal and specific progression is assumed to be a condition that occurs concurrently with society's historical and generic progression.

In terms of American principles, progress ranks as a characteristic ideal and one that is widely seen to be both a defining condition and an achievable objective. So embedded is progress in America's conception of the good society that even when social and economic developments are brought into question, they are more likely than not to be interpreted as corruptions of progress. These require corrective action, very often in the form of devising alternative constructions of progress. On occasion, these will involve the need to pursue progress through the medium of explicit appeals to the past, and in particular to a 'democratic faith' in the idea of America's progress being based upon providence.[49]

In a society built upon movement, the theme of progress retains its legitimizing rationale. As a consequence, it is not only a conditioning factor in the formation of political argument but also a recognized object of value that attracts controversies, debates, and competing interpretations. Progress can generate a host of conceptual disputes. It is possible to regard it as a purely derivative value, or as a collective condition rather than a principle, or as a relativistic term, or as a static and self-enclosed tautology. At the same time, progress is associated with a variety of themes and properties which have their own priorities. While liberty, for example, is widely accepted as an iconic value in its own right, the proponents or apologists for progress have very often seen it more as an instrumental value serving the ultimate purpose of improvement. In other contexts, progress is accepted as a

---

[48] See Christopher Lasch, *True and Only Heaven: Progress and Its Critics* (New York: W. W. Norton, 1991); Michael J. Sandel, *Democracy's Discontent: America in Search of a Public Philosophy* (Cambridge, MA: Belknap Press, 1998).

[49] George Bancroft, *Literary and Historical Miscellanies* (New York: Harper & Brothers, 1855), pp. 415–26.

principle of comparable status with other core elements of America's credo. Like liberty, progress appeals to an aspiration to be emancipated from limits. Like democracy, progress also offers solutions in terms of itself. In the United States, the problems of democracy are conventionally interpreted as being resolvable through the provision of greater democracy. Similarly, any social and economic difficulties attributed to the passage of progress are generally taken to be improved by further progress.

9

Order

INTRODUCTION

The conspicuous public attachment to liberal principles in the United States often overlooks, and even conceals, the issue of order within American society. Commentaries upon the utility and value of social order often reveal a fundamental ambiguity in basic attitudes. Order can on occasion simply be taken as a self-evident and axiomatic premise to any form of stable political activity. Liberal politics in particular can be seen as being necessarily dependent upon a basically settled social order. On other occasions, order can be reconfigured into a countervailing force that provides an appropriate balance against the extremes of libertarian emancipation from social norms and traditions.

The United States is no exception to this dualistic pattern. At one level, the notion of order can be reduced to simply an analogue of a self-stabilizing society. Whether the cohesion is seen as being drawn from the attributed general presence of republican virtue, or from an ideological consensus on liberal principles, or from the premise of a basic compatibility of liberal interests, the interpretive effect is one of an autonomous solidarity. Another quite different conception of America's social and political stability comes from the asserted need for a distinctive value and agency to protect public order and maintain individual security. In this construction, order is not necessarily a corollary of liberty, or of liberal society, so much as a corrective response to its drives and value. American history has been marked by both these outlooks. As a result, they have left a fractured legacy on the issue of stability and on the threats posed not only by disorder but also by an excess of social order.

The classic strategic technique of creating a workable reconciliation between these opposing conceptions of order has been to work with an understanding of a balanced coexistence. But even though an asserted equilibrium offers a beguiling impression of symmetry, it does not resolve the inherent tension within this interplay between order from above and order from below. Equilibriums can operate in more than one way. A self-regulating balance between a multiplicity of interests and resources can simply be assumed to exist within an open society. By the same token, a balance can also denote a force constraining the fissiparous properties of liberal individualism and personal emancipation. The concept of equilibrium can be used either to give recognition to the existence of a fundamental order upon which liberal licence is necessarily based, or to underline the need for a more secure anchorage to counteract the centrifugal energies of a liberal society. Both these dimensions of balance have been evident in the course of America's development, but they were particularly prominent in the originating experiences of the republic when the issues of order and security became established as questions of long-standing significance.

FOUNDATIONS OF ORDER

It was noted in Chapters 1 and 4 that the American Revolution was rationalized through an ideological medium that privileged the liberation from the Crown as the climactic and decisive solution to the colonists' grievances. The social and military mobilization required to challenge British authority was rooted in the theme of emancipation and in the cohesion formed by the transformation of the Crown from a protective agency into an asserted source of oppression and corruption. The success of the War of Independence appeared to offer grounds for concluding that the social integration required to fight a successful war of resistance could be translated into the creation of a satisfactory scheme of governance. But the cohesion derived from war and from the undifferentiated promise of emancipation was not easily extended into post-war conditions that were characterized by inflated and conflicting expectations.

Eventually, the pressure for a more consolidated form of government was sufficient to create a movement to amend the Articles of Confederation. The Articles had given the newly emergent states a notional form of collective administration but for much of the 1780s it had become clear that this loose confederation represented a solution to the immediate post-revolution requirement of decentralization and the supremacy of the individual states. Increasingly, the Articles of Confederation were not seen to be the answer to the problems of long-term governance. Under this loose arrangement, the separate states were able to operate their own monetary systems, raise their own armed services, and devise their own trading practices and foreign policies, and the potential for decentralization to deteriorate into unstable fragmentation became a widespread issue of concern.[1]

The Founding Fathers who formulated the US Constitution in 1787 were prompted by a variety of motivations but the theme common to all of them and the one given most prominence in their advocacy of the new Constitution was that of security. Although their distance from Britain had been a strategic advantage during the colonial disputes and the War of Independence, the American states were now not only relatively isolated but also situated in a region of competing imperial powers. In addition to undermining the already limited powers of the centre, the states appeared intent upon subverting each other's

---

[1] See Gordon S. Wood, *The Creation of the American Republic, 1776–1787* (Chapel Hill, NC: University of North Carolina Press, 1969), chs. 9, 10; Jack N. Rakove, *The Beginnings of National Politics: An Interpretive History of the Continental Congress* (Baltimore, MD: Johns Hopkins University Press, 1982), chs. 11–14; Richard B. Morris, *The Forging of the Union, 1781–1789* (New York: Harper & Row, 1987), chs. 4–6, 8, 10.

claims to sovereignty through a largely unregulated competition in which each sought positional advantage over their respective neighbours. This had the effect of restraining trade and undermining the development of an integrated American market for goods and services. In doing so, it risked reducing the prosperity that had allowed the American colonists to challenge the imperial authority of Britain. Most serious of all was the fear of communal, or intercommunal, violence. Shays's Rebellion exemplified the fear of sudden eruptions of social upheaval. A collapse in the management of national credit, combined with a decline in trading activity and a tax increase to pay for war loans, prompted an uprising of farmers in Massachusetts.[2] Although the rebellion was quickly put down, it highlighted the potential for social conflict and the conspicuous absence of any credible military force at the national level to provide security guarantees. Shays's Rebellion was symptomatic of a much deeper dread: the possibility of an interstate war, a catastrophic slave revolt, or an incursion by one of the imperial powers encouraged by America's economic and military weaknesses.

The Founders were highly successful in taking up this theme of insecurity and disorder. They built upon the fear that decentralization could become a vehicle for disintegration unless an antidote could be devised to reverse the problem. In devising a US constitution, the Framers sought to create, or ostensibly recreate, a cohesive response to a security challenge. The result was a compound of attributed balances. The states were now depicted as being in equilibrium with the federal government. At the same time, the federal authority was conceptualized as facilitating a balance between the states. The overall purpose of the adopted scheme was one in which liberty would be harmonized with order, and individual rights reconciled with collective security. This theme of order was no mere qualifying proviso to that liberty. It was a central objective in its own right. It was significant that in the stated objectives listed in the preamble to the US Constitution, the need to 'insure domestic tranquillity' and to 'provide for the common defense' preceded the requirement of securing the 'blessings of liberty'.

The defence of the Constitution expounded in *The Federalist Papers* makes successive references to the theme of either the 'crisis at which we are arrived'[3] or the dangers that would be incurred if an effective federalism were not achieved. Human nature could not be trusted to produce prudent and virtuous outcomes within government. Powers would always be abused because of the 'caprice and wickedness'[4] of men. They were seen to be 'ambitions, vindictive and rapacious'.[5] The Founders, in general, shared a concern over the likely behaviour of individuals even in a republic: 'They accepted the mercantile image of life as an eternal

---

[2] See Leonard L. Richards, *Shays's Rebellion: The American Revolution's Final Battle* (Philadelphia, PA: University of Pennsylvania Press, 2003).

[3] Alexander Hamilton, 'Federalist Paper No. 1', in Alexander Hamilton, James Madison, and John Jay, *The Federalist Papers*, introduced by Clinton Rossiter (New York: Mentor, 1961), p. 33.

[4] James Madison, 'Federalist Paper No. 57', in Hamilton, Madison, and Jay, *The Federalist Papers*, p. 353.

[5] Alexander Hamilton, 'Federalist Paper No. 6', in Hamilton, Madison, and Jay, *The Federalist Papers*, p. 54.

battleground, and assumed the Hobbesian war of each against all; [yet] they did not propose to put an end to this war, but merely to stabilize it, and make it less murderous'.[6] Arguably, it would be more accurate to describe the attitude as dualistic in which virtue and venality were recognized as coexisting features in personality: 'As there is a degree of depravity in mankind which requires a certain degree of circumspection and human distrust, so there are other qualities in human nature which justify a certain portion of esteem and confidence'.[7] Nevertheless, there was a conspicuous concern over the security ramifications of such a dualism in which passion could 'wrest the sceptre for reason'.[8] It was underlined that safety was the first object and responsibility of government.

James Madison referred to the 'absolute necessity of the case; to the great principle of self-preservation; to the transcendent law of nature and of nature's God, which declares that the safety and happiness of society are the objects at which all political institutions aim and to which all such institutions must be sacrificed'.[9] An effectively organized government on a national scale was taken to be the best guarantee against hostility from abroad and instability at home. At the same time, such a government posed a danger to American liberties through its ability to amplify human nature: '[W]hat is government but the greatest of all reflections on human nature?' Madison asked. 'If men were angels, no government would be necessary.' He concluded that in framing a new polity, 'you must first enable the government to control the governed'.[10] Madison was keenly aware that the price of a social order backed by concerted government action was high. Nevertheless, it was one which he and other Founders considered worthy of the risk to republican liberty.

CHALLENGE OF 'CLEAR AND PRESENT DANGERS'

Whether this theme of order and its origins in the Constitution is treated as an explicit value or as an implicit condition, the net effect has been to permit intrusive government action into the private sphere of individual liberty on the grounds of preventing disorder. The fear of insufficient order has legitimized an array of extraordinary governmental measures directed towards known or suspected dangers to the republic. On some occasions, repressive action has been categorized as a

---

[6] Richard Hofstadter, *The American Political Tradition and the Men Who Made It* (London: Jonathan Cape, 1967), p. 16; see also George Mace, *Locke, Hobbes, and the Federalist Papers: An Essay on the Genesis of the American Political Heritage* (Carbondale, IL: Southern Illinois University Press, 1979).

[7] James Madison, 'Federalist Paper No. 55', in Hamilton, Madison, and Jay, *The Federalist Papers*, p. 346.

[8] Ibid., p. 342.

[9] James Madison, 'Federalist Paper No. 43', in Hamilton, Madison, and Jay, *The Federalist Papers*, p. 279.

[10] James Madison, 'Federalist Paper No. 51', in Hamilton, Madison, and Jay, *The Federalist Papers*, p. 322.

proportionate response to a manifest threat to social stability. On other occasions, such action has been depicted more as a precautionary device directed against a possible threat. On all occasions, the measures have amounted to a serious and substantive addendum to the more overt value system of freedoms and rights, and of limited government and the rule of law that normally characterize the aims and purpose of American government.

The following selected examples provide an illustration of the lengths to which the federal government has gone to preserve order at the clear expense of liberty. Within ten years of the establishment of the US Constitution, Congress had passed the Alien and Sedition Acts (1798). These measures empowered the president at his own discretion to expel or imprison any foreigner who was adjudged to be objectionable to the administration. The enactments also permitted American citizens to be fined or imprisoned if they were deemed to be acting in a way that would defame, or bring into disrepute, the president or any other part of the government. Under the terms of the legislation, over twenty editors of Republican newspapers were fined and jailed.[11]

In 1919, amidst a wave of strikes, industrial violence, and bombings, the federal government actively promoted a 'red scare' amongst the American public. The government made sweeping allegations of communist infiltration and subsequently launched a series of highly repressive and indiscriminate series of mass arrests. The Palmer raids, named after A. Mitchell Palmer the Attorney General, led to the detention of more than 6,000 suspected trade union activists, political radicals, and communists. In one night in January 1920, over 4,000 alleged communists were arrested in thirty-three cities. Even though the raids produced very little evidence of revolutionary activity and practically no results in respect to arms, they nevertheless led to mass detentions, property seizures, and deportations. William Leuchtenburg sums up the episode in the following terms: 'Not for at least half a century, perhaps at no time in our history, had there been such a wholesale violation of civil liberties'.[12]

Another episode worthy of note occurred during the Second World War. In March 1942, an executive order of President Franklin Roosevelt authorized the removal of 112,000 Japanese Americans from their homes on the west coast to a series of inland 'relocation centres'.[13] The decision was based upon a claim of military necessity. It was feared that the west coast would be invaded by Japan and that individuals of Japanese descent might seek to give aid and support to

[11] See Geoffrey R. Stone, *Perilous Times: Free Speech in Wartime from the Sedition Act of 1798 to the War on Terrorism* (New York: W. W Norton, 2004), ch. 1.

[12] William E. Leuchtenburg, *The Perils of Prosperity 1914–32* (Chicago, IL: University of Chicago Press, 1958), p. 78; see also David H. Bennett, *The Party of Fear: The American Far Right: From Nativism to the Militia Movement* (New York: Vintage, 1995), pp. 183–98; David J. Goldberg, *Discontented America: The United States in the 1920s* (Baltimore, MD: Johns Hopkins University Press, 1999), chs. 2, 3; Frederick L. Allen, *Only Yesterday: An Informal History of the 1920's* (New York: Perennial/HarperCollins, 2000), chs. 2, 3.

[13] See Peter Irons, *Justice at War: Story of the Japanese–American Internment Cases* (Berkeley, CA: University of California Press, 1993); Erica Harth (ed.), *Last Witness: Reflections on the Wartime Internment of Japanese Americans* (New York: Palgrave Macmillan, 2003).

such an incursion. As there was no time to check every person, all Japanese Americans were removed even though over 70,000 of them were full US citizens. The Supreme Court reviewed the action over two years after the event when there had been adequate time to reach a clearer understanding of the ill-considered and intemperate nature of the action. Nevertheless, the Court found the exclusion order to be constitutional on the grounds of military urgency. Those justices dissenting from the majority decision regarded the action as a clear and unnecessary violation of constitutional rights. Justice Murphy called the exclusion order a 'legalization of racism'. He continued: 'Racial discrimination in any form and in any degree has no justifiable part whatever in our democratic way of life. It is unattractive in any setting but it is utterly revolting among a free people who have embraced the principles set forth in the Constitution of the United States.'[14] Such views, however, could not withstand the prevailing opinion that the action had been legitimate because the 'properly constituted military authorities...felt constrained to take proper security measures'.[15]

The cold war provided another rationale for a range of restrictive measures. The 1950 Internal Security Act, for example, required the registration of all communist organizations, prevented the entry into the United States of any individual suspected of belonging to a totalitarian organization, and provided internment for communist sympathizers in the event of national emergencies. Under the Immigration and Nationality Act 1952, the Attorney General was empowered to deport aliens and naturalized citizens if their activities were deemed to be 'prejudicial to the public interest, safety, or security'.[16] These and many other measures revealed the 'volatility of popular opinion, the growing capacity of the State to repress dissent, and the frailty of civil libertarian thought and action in the United States'.[17]

The extent to which a sense of emergency could overwhelm liberal democratic precepts was illustrated by the case of *Dennis v. United States* (1951). The Truman administration prosecuted a group of suspected communists under the terms of the Smith Act (1940). This was a Second World War security measure that had originally been designed to apprehend and prosecute Nazi sympathizers. The legislation made it a criminal offence to teach or to advocate the overthrow of the United States government. It made no distinction between the advocacy of action and any action undertaken in the pursuit of the stated cause. Now it was being invoked in peace time. The action was regarded as highly controversial because it made no distinction between advocacy and action. It raised profound questions over civil liberties and in particular over the rights to free speech.

---

[14] *Korematsu v. United States*, 323 US 214 (1944), 242.   [15] Ibid., 223.

[16] Immigration and Nationality Act 1952, Section 235 ('Inspection by immigration officers; expedited removal of inadmissible arriving aliens; referral for hearing'), http://uscis.gov/lpBin/lpext.dll/inserts/slb/slb-1/slb-22/slb-4991?f=templates&fn=document-frame.htm#slb-act235.

[17] James T. Patterson, *Grand Expectations: The United States, 1945–1974* (New York: Oxford University Press, 1996), p. 179.

The Supreme Court used the case to examine and to develop the theme of what constituted a 'clear and present danger'. Even in such a contentious case when the claims of constitutional liberties were pitted directly and explicitly against the claims of an unspecified security threat, the Supreme Court clearly privileged the latter. In the view of the majority of the Court, nothing was 'more certain in modern society than the principle that there are no absolutes'. Accordingly, speech was 'not an absolute, above and beyond control by the legislature'.[18] The Court's position therefore was one of judgment within a context of perceived threat. In such a situation, speech could not be qualitatively distinguished from action: 'To those who would paralyze our Government in the face of impending threat by encasing it in a semantic straitjacket we must reply that all concepts are relative'.[19] Free speech had to be assessed on the basis of contingencies related to order and security. The Court pointed out that the 'analysis disposes of the contention that a conspiracy to advocate, as distinguished from the advocacy itself, cannot be constitutionally restrained, because it comprises only the preparation'. In the opinion of the Court, it was 'the existence of the conspiracy which creates the danger....If the ingredients of the reaction are present, we cannot bind the Government to wait until the catalyst is added'.[20]

RESPONDING TO TERRORISM

The United States was confronted by a different threat to its security after the terrorist attacks in September 2001. The shock of those events prompted an immediate response in the form of the Patriot Act 2001. The legislation was over 300 pages in length. Only a few members of Congress had read it before voting into law a series of sweeping measures designed to increase the police powers of the federal government and to revise the rules under which they operate. The Patriot Act signaled a marked departure from previous anti-terrorist measures in two main ways. First was the shift in emphasis from standard law enforcement objectives of arrests and convictions to one of preventing any recurrence of the casualties and destruction occasioned by al-Qaeda. Second was the operational premise that terrorism could no longer be construed as an exclusively overseas threat. It was now recognized as having a domestic dimension that meant the authorities had to have the kind of freedom of manoeuvre which US intelligence agencies normally possessed only outside the country. The outcome has been a series of often loosely drafted measures, complemented by assertions of state power based upon executive prerogative.

Under these new rules, law enforcement agencies have been given enlarged powers of surveillance, arrest, and detention over both immigrants and citizens.

---

[18] *Dennis v. United States*, 341 US 494 (1951), 508.
[19] Ibid.   [20] Ibid., 511.

For example, the Patriot Act allows the US Attorney General to authorize the indefinite detention of non-citizens who have not been convicted of any crime if the Attorney General has reason to believe their release 'endangers the national security of the United States'.[21] The Act also allows the government to subject non-citizens facing deportation for minor visa and other immigration violations to indefinite imprisonment.

The most controversial aspect of the 'war on terror' was not specifically related to the Patriot Act or to the treatment of individuals within the United States. Even so, it was to have a powerful symbolic significance in the status given to civil liberties in the national emergency. Prisoners captured in Afghanistan or suspected of having al-Qaeda connections were held in isolation at the US naval base in Guantanamo Bay, Cuba. The 660 detainees from forty countries were neither given POW status nor charged with any particular crime. By being designated 'enemy combatants', they were denied access to both lawyers and the legal process. They were to be kept in isolation for an indefinite period on grounds of national security. The administration's position was that because they were not American citizens and were not detained on US territory, they could be held indefinitely until the point when they could eventually stand trial by military tribunal. It appeared that these high-profile prisoners would not only be devoid of rights and have no form of redress or appeal, but would also be liable to the death penalty.

The magnitude of these powers has alarmed civil libertarian organizations, which claim that the array of measures mounted against the terrorist threat is both excessive and ill-conceived. The American Civil Liberties Union, for example, has raised numerous objections (i) over the secrecy surrounding the identity and allegations relating to numerous Arab and Muslim detainees; (ii) over the selective enforcement of immigration law based upon race, ethnicity, and national origin; and (iii) over the way that restrictions upon civil liberties have been established without time limits and with little or no requirement to establish a connection to anti-terrorism. The ACLU has taken particular exception to the exclusion of anti-terrorism measures from due process safeguards and from judicial review. In March 2002, Anthony Romero, the Executive Director of the ACLU, publicly stated his concern over what he described as the 'government's apparent dismissal of the idea that our society can and must be both safe and free'. Mr. Romero concluded: 'Checks and balances are the cornerstone of our democracy.... The Founders put the judiciary in place to protect our rights, a role they can't play if Congress explicitly forbids them from even reviewing ... law enforcement actions'.[22]

Widespread anxiety has been registered both inside and outside the United States over the severity of the current security regime and over the way that

---

[21] *Uniting and Strengthening America by Providing Appropriate Tools Required to Intercept and Obstruct Terrorism (USA PATRIOT ACT) Act of 2001*, Section 236A. (a) (3) (B).

[22] Quoted in 'On Eve of Sixth-Month Anniversary of September 11th, ACLU Says Terrorist Attacks Have Changed American Law, Society', 8 March 2002, http://www.aclu.org/NationalSecurity/NationalSecurity.cfm?ID=9944&c=24

civil liberty concerns have been marginalized by the Bush administration.[23] In March 2003, *The Economist* pointed out that the enhancement of police powers risked propelling the United States into a new area of exceptionalism: 'America is not the only democracy to have reduced the legal constraints on its policemen since the terrorist attacks of 2001. But the change in the balance between liberty and security is especially striking in the United States'.[24] *Index on Censorship* agreed that since 11 September 'virtually every aspect of human rights protection in the United States has been called into question'.[25] The new powers threatened to 'impose permanent constraints on the fundamental freedoms central to most Americans' conception of their country'.[26] It could be said that the robust response to the terrorist threat by the administration was a direct consequence of the fact that the United States had been the target of the 9/11 attacks. Equally significant, however, has been the historic fear within America that its liberal democracy can be vulnerable to the traditions of tolerance that characterize it. American anxieties can be aroused over the appearance of weakness in the face of a resolute enemy with the capacity to exploit the space reserved for individual rights for the purpose of inflicting grave disorder within society. American identity is closely tied to its self depiction as a model of liberty. And yet, its cultural sensitivity over the potential abuse of freedom has established a tendency within the United States for the value of order to be periodically, yet explicitly, privileged over the claims of civil liberty.

ORDER AS A CONSTITUTIONAL PRINCIPLE

The lengths to which the United States government has been prepared to go in order to maintain American security, even at the expense of reconfiguring the Constitution, is best exemplified by the accumulation of presidential power in the field of foreign policy. The presidential office is clearly an integral feature of the Constitution's logic of reciprocal checks and balances. And yet in this field, the presidency through custom, usage, precedent, and asserted force of necessity has fundamentally altered the nature of the Constitution. Whether it is treaty-making powers, or decisions to commit American forces to war, or in restrictions upon civil liberties, or exercises in covert action and secret intelligence, the presidency has acquired an authority that can transcend the formalism of the Constitution. The rationale is one of preserving the spirit and framework of constitutional

---

[23] David Cole and James X. Dempsey (eds.), *Terrorism and the Constitution: Sacrificing Civil Liberties in the Name of National Security* (New York: New Press, 2002); Danny Goldberg and Robert Greenwald (eds.), *It's a Free Country: Personal Freedom in America after September 11* (New York: RDV Books, 2002).

[24] 'A Question of Freedom', *The Economist*, 8 March 2002.

[25] Michael McClintock, 'The Trials of Liberty', *Index on Censorship*, vol. 32, no. 3 (July 2003), p. 88.

[26] Ibid.

government, while at the same time having access to extraordinary powers in order to achieve the objective.

Under the pressure of international instability and domestic insecurity, the presidency has evolved from its origins to emerge as the chief agency and operating rationale for maximizing the value of order within a system normally character-ized by structured disorder. The scale and status of the modern presidency has in large measure been derived from the recognition of an imperative need: the func-tional requirement to react purposefully in response to perceived security threats and to provide the means to ensure that public safety and national security are not compromised by inaction or indecision. The presidency's capacity to generate its own supplementary powers has been assimilated into the constitutional tradition of the United States.[27]

Even the Supreme Court has had to acknowledge that a literal interpretation or strict construction of the Constitution cannot accommodate the responsibilities of the modern presidency. Interpretive licence has become a prerequisite to the constitutional legitimation of the presidency. On some occasions, the pressure to rationalize presidential authority takes the form of a claim of intrinsic powers lodged within the constitutional infrastructure of the chief executive's position. In the case of *In re Neagle* (1890), for example, the Court declared that the president's basic constitutional duty of 'faithfully executing the laws' could not be limited to the express terms contained in Acts of Congress or in US treaties. The Court made reference to 'the rights, duties and obligations growing out of the constitution itself, our international relations, and all the protection implied by the nature of the government under the constitution'.[28]

Through this kind of argument, powers could be elicited or extrapolated from the substantive meanings and interior logic of the original grants. On other occasions, the argument was driven more by a response to the force of external circumstances. For example, in *The Prize Cases* (1863), the Court was asked to pass judgment on President Lincoln's decision to blockade southern ports in the absence of a formal declaration war by Congress. Such was the level of danger confronting the republic that the Court did not detain itself in drawing out the implied powers of Article 2. The very nature of the emergency not only created its own momentum for executive action, but prompted a recognition that under cer-tain conditions executive prerogative possesses a legitimacy that is not reducible to the Constitution:

[T]he President is…bound to resist force with force. He does not initiate the war, but is bound to accept the challenge without waiting for any special legislative authority. And whether the hostile party be a foreign invader, or states organized in rebellion, it is none

---

[27] Louis Fisher, *Presidential War Power* (Lawrence, KS: University Press of Kansas, 1995), chs. 5–8; Louis Henkin, *Foreign Affairs and the United States Constitution*, 2nd edn (Oxford: Oxford University Press, 1997); Harold H. Koh, *The National Security Constitution: Sharing Power after the IranContra Affair* (New Haven, CT: Yale University Press, 1990), chs. 3, 5, 6; Mark J. Rozell, *Executive Privilege: Presidential Power, Secrecy, and Accountability*, 2nd edn (Lawrence, KS: University Press of Kansas, 2002); Joseph A. Pika and John A. Maltese, *The Politics of the Presidency*, 6th edn (Washington, DC: CQ Press, 2006), ch. 10.

[28] *In re Neagle*, 135 US 1 (1890), 64.

the less a war.... [In] this greatest of civil wars,... [t]he President was bound to meet it in the shape that it presented itself, without waiting for Congress to baptize it with a name.[29]

By far the most significant decision in this area came in 1936 when the Supreme Court reacted to the increased levels of international tension by affording the presidency an unprecedented level of executive power in the conduct of foreign relations. The Court explicitly drew attention to the force of circumstance and to the prerogative right of the president to react to them. As a consequence, the president was afforded 'a degree of discretion and freedom from statutory restriction which would not be admissible were domestic affairs alone involved'.[30] The Court concluded that the president possessed a 'very delicate plenary and exclusive power ... as the sole organ of the federal government in the field of international relations'.[31] The judgment in *US v. Curtiss-Wright Export Corporation* represented an extraordinary piece of constitutional metamorphosis. The principle of shared and concurrent powers, which lies at the heart of American constitutionalism, was largely superseded in this area to one of prescribed presidential management. In the opinion of one noted commentator, the *Curtiss-Wright* decision expanded a theory in which the presidency possessed 'a secret reservoir of unaccountable power' that flowed from the concept of external sovereignty rather than from the Constitution. As a consequence, it amounted to 'the furthest departure from the theory that [the] United States is a constitutionally limited democracy'.[32]

Ever since 1936, presidents have referred to the *Curtiss-Wright* decision as the basis of their independent authority in foreign affairs. The decision has never been reversed or revoked. On the contrary, it has been embellished and refined. During the cold war, *Curtiss-Wright* provided the main support to the presidential claim of a unified command structure commensurate with the extremity of the threat posed by communist forces. Judicial silences, evasions, and deferments in the area of presidential foreign policy-making have preserved the force of *Curtiss-Wright* and, with it, the legitimacy of a de facto corrective to the Constitution. In sum, the Court decision and the case law surrounding it remain a testament of the extent to which the normal interplay of constitutional dynamics and values have been suspended, and even superseded, by the perceptions of a Hobbesian external world characterized by threat, insecurity, and disorder.

A significant concomitant of this executive impulse towards order and stability has been a tolerance of presidential initiative and an expectation that presidents will maximize the office's powers even to the extent of stretching the Constitution in the name of security. Great presidents are regarded as being synonymous with strength and with the need to deploy force. Those presidents characterized as 'great' are distinguished by 'their mastery of events, their influence on history,

---

[29] *Prize Cases*, 67 US 635 (1862), 669.
[30] *United States v. Curtiss-Wright Export Corp.*, 299 US 304 (1936), 320.   [31] Ibid.
[32] David Levitan, 'The Foreign Relations Power: An Analysis of Mr. Justice Sutherland's Theory', *Yale Law Journal*, vol. 55, no. 3 (April 1946), p. 493.

their shaping of their country's destiny...their ability to magnify their own department, and their own powers, at the expense of other branches'.[33] As a consequence, presidential eminence is strongly equated with the phenomenon of leadership conviction prevailing over opposition and even initial public hostility in order to pursue security purposes in the public interest. An integral de facto element of the presidential role, therefore, is to force the issue of public safety and national security against a constitutional system designed to minimize the opportunities for decisive governance.

SOCIAL CONTROL AND CONSPIRACY

The value of order, and the emphasis upon sustaining and protecting it, is not confined to the top-down directions of government. Order is also a derivative of social organization and attitudes. The United States has long been associated with the phenomenon of social consensus and with the sense of spontaneous order that accompanies a uniform outlook upon basic principles and priorities. Many observers of the United States have gone further and noted that the basic agreement on general principles has either led to or is a sign of a deep unanimity in social thought and behaviour. This in turn has prompted considerable speculation over whether such a convergence is more apparent than real. It may be more important for individuals to give the impression of value consensus rather than to base their behaviour upon actual conviction. Whatever the nature of the motive forces, the inertial force of social conformity has often fostered an extraordinary degree of order.

It was Alexis de Tocqueville who first drew attention to the paradox of social restriction and sanction existing within a philosophical context dominated by references to social liberty and personal emancipation. He observed that in America, majority opinion represented a potent restriction on the freedom of discussion and even upon the individual's independence of mind. In such a society, the weight of orthodoxy reflected the presence of 'only a single power, a single element of force and success, and nothing outside it'.[34] Many others have followed this theme and 'repeatedly commented on how effectively Americans [have] regulated one another through the presence of collective judgement'.[35] American individualism may feature the epic properties of a 'rejection of the state' and an 'impatience

[33] James M. Burns, *Presidential Government: The Crucible of Leadership*, (Boston, MA: Houghton Mifflin, 1966) p. 81. See also Marc Landy and Sidney M. Milkis, *Presidential Greatness* (Lawrence, KS: University Press of Kansas, 2000); Thomas E. Cronin and Michael A. Genovese, *The Paradoxes of the American Presidency*, 2nd edn (New York: Oxford University Press, 2004), pp. 86–96; James Taranto, 'What Makes a President Great?', *Opinion Journal* from *The Wall Street Journal*, 10 June 2004, http://www.opinionjournal.com/pl/?id=110005196.

[34] Alexis de Tocqueville, *Democracy in America*, trans., ed., and intro. Harvey C. Mansfield and Delba Winthrop (Chicago, IL: Chicago University Press, 2000), p. 244.

[35] John Higham, *Strangers in the Land: Patterns of American Nativism, 1860–1925* (New York: Atheneum, 1968), p. 205.

with restraints upon economic activity' but in terms of mundane existence and everyday behaviour 'it has not tended to set the autonomous individual up in rebellion against his social group'.[36]

This corporate impulse is assisted by the opportunities for localized solidarity afforded within the legal order of American federalism. It is also supported by the fervour with which claims are made on behalf of the proposition that a moral order requires rules of enforcement. As a consequence, the freedom of conscience in America does not always experience the sovereign dimension that is often attributed to it. On the contrary, the legislative history of the United States is said to constitute the 'most thorough oversight of personal behaviour in the Western industrial world'.[37] According to Michael Woodiwiss:

Tens of thousands of federal, state and local laws have attempted to enforce morality by prohibitions on alcohol, gambling, prostitution and drugs, plus strict censorship and a host of more trivial restrictions. ... The intention was to end all behaviour that a Protestant culture defined as sinful and non-productive. Persuasion and education were not enough: Americans had to be coerced by law into a virtuous and healthy way of life.[38]

The concept of an intuitive moral order placed at risk by those perceived as occupying a different, darker, and more dangerous moral universe is, according to James Morone, the chief organizing theme of American history.[39] Over the course of 500 years, American history has been repeatedly marked by a series of concerted reactions against what is seen to be a condition of social and moral disorder. The responses can take many forms, but they have usually been centred upon the enactment of restrictive and repressive measures designed to restore communities to a prior state of equilibrium. The persistent nature of this insurgent demand for order in accordance with a fixture of value has always invariably led to racist and nativist action being taken against those classified as outsiders.

Even Louis Hartz's celebrated elegy to American liberalism had to acknowledge that the avowed unity of principle had an illiberal underside. Hartz's interpretation of American society and history sought to fuse together the primacy of liberal principles with the evident existence of a collective temperament that was neither susceptible to critical self-examination nor tolerant of open challenge: 'At the bottom of the American experience of freedom, not in antagonism to it but as a constituent element of it, there has always lain the inarticulate premise of

---

[36] Robin Williams, *American Society: A Sociological Interpretation* (New York: Knopf, 1963), p. 451; see also Edward A. Ross, *Social Control: A Survey of the Foundations of Order* (New York: Macmillan, 1918).

[37] Michael Woodiwiss, *Crime, Crusades and Corruption—Prohibitions in the United States, 1900–1987* (London: Pinter, 1988), p. 1.

[38] Ibid. See also William J. Novak, *The People's Welfare: Law and Regulation in Nineteenth Century America* (Chapel Hill, NC: University of North Carolina Press, 1996).

[39] James A. Morone, *Hellfire Nation: The Politics of Sin in American History* (New Haven, CT: Yale University Press, 2004).

conformity.... This then is the mood of America's absolutism: the sober faith that its norms are self-evident'.[40]

A range of factors have been cited to account for America's exceptional social conformity. For example, it has been attributed to the outcome of a process in which population increase, combined with the limited reach of government during a period of territorial expansion, fostered a dependence upon self-organized order working through public opinion and social expectations. Alternative explanations give weight to the social and cultural diversity of American society generating its own countervailing force in the form of a unifying medium for social exchange, shared standards, and common identity. Other constructions focus more on the compulsive nature of conformity within a highly mutable society lacking clear hierarchies and traditional stratifications of class. In such a context, the key to even minimal success lay in aligning oneself to any emergent structure of social approval and acceptance.

Central to all these accounts, however, is a dynamic which is particularly evident in American society. This is the attitudinal ambiguity that accompanies the principle of social liberty. The extraordinary prominence given to freedom both as a normative principle and as an empirical assumption in American society has fostered a set of concomitant anxieties over the actual or possible ramifications of such a fluid social entity. The mutable, and even amorphous, nature of society in the New World can offer prodigious opportunity, but to many this protean and open-ended quality also provokes disorientation and intimidation. If liberty can confer individual challenge, then the American notion of a highly developed form of liberty within society can generate commensurate levels of anxiety. These are often translated into palpable fears: the fear of social rootlessness; the fear of rapid change without direction; the fear of disorientation from any point of reference; and the generic fear of disorder.

Such fears were often fused with a view of the social order that was perceived to be highly mutable, therefore, fragile in nature. A liberal society could be construed as being particularly susceptible to misuse by those who are intent upon undermining the social order, in order to advance their own interests and dogmas. The natural corollary of such a view is the need for drastic action to save society from itself; in essence to form a counterconspiracy to confront the source of the disorder. Accordingly, a profusion of measures and movements have been designed to counteract the presumed existence of forces subverting a conception of America that is regarded as 'correct', or 'normal', or 'natural'. These reactive strategies have come in a prodigious variety of forms. Nevertheless, they all rely for their effect upon a form of identity politics in which groups are demarcated as strangers whose status in civil society is marginalized and whose claims to citizenship are deeply contested on grounds of being unacceptably different.

The referent category of abnormality has ranged from blacks, Catholics, homosexuals, and Jews to radicals, communists, recent immigrants, and illegal aliens.

---

[40] Louis Hartz, *The Liberal Tradition in America: An Interpretation of American Political Thought Since the Revolution* (New York: Harcourt Brace Jovanovich, 1955), pp. 57–8.

The reactions to these perceived threats have been equally varied. The classic technique of social control in these circumstances has been the direct approach of taking measures either to restrict, exclude, and deport those categorized as 'undesirable', or to ensure that selected minorities are maintained in a position of social subordination by limiting their citizenship rights and deliberately diminishing their sense of civic identity. The systemic character of the discrimination has been described as a pervasive and defining ideology of America's civic history.

[W]hen restrictions on voting rights, naturalization, and immigration are taken into account, it turns out that for over 80 per cent of U.S. history, American laws declared most people in the world legally ineligible to become full U.S. citizens solely because of their race, original nationality, or gender. For at least two-thirds of American history, the majority of the domestic adult population was also ineligible for full citizenship for the same reasons.[41]

A related but less severe response to the threat of social disorder has been to make concerted efforts to induce greater conformity to what is conceived to be the American norm. These have taken the form of civic education programmes, tighter immigration controls, and various Americanization processes in support of a melting-pot ethos aiming for a unified culture of '100 per cent Americans'.[42] Another device has relied less upon legislation and more on direct action. This can include social intimidation, political intolerance, and cultural discrimination in support of an array of nativist and illiberal impulses.[43] Both forms of reaction have as their controlling premise the belief that freedom brings with it exceptional dangers to the social fabric and to any designations of an American order.

In essence, American liberty allows for, and is in many respects blind towards, its own subversion. As a consequence, the preservation of liberty can be said to require the closest attention to those who would seek to abuse the privilege of freedom in order to undermine the social order. This linkage between enhanced freedom and a heightened state of anxiety and alertness is thought to have given American politics a distinct susceptibility towards notions of conspiracy operating within its midst. Suspicions of conspiracy have in the past been directed towards groups such as witches, Antinomians, Indians, Quakers, Mormons, Catholics, the Masons, pornographers, and the civil rights movement. More recently the emphasis has been given to Latinos, illegal immigrants, drug syndicates, agencies of the 'new world order' (e.g. the United Nations, the International Red Cross, the

[41] Rogers M. Smith, *Civic Ideals: Conflicting Visions of Citizenship in U.S. History* (New Haven, CT: Yale University Press, 1997), p. 15.

[42] Maldwyn A. Jones, *American Immigration*, 2nd edn (Chicago, IL: University of Chicago Press, 1992), ch. 9; Desmond King, *Making Americans: Immigration, Race, and the Origins of the Diverse Democracy* (Cambridge, MA: Harvard University Press 2000), chs. 3–7; Mae M. Ngai, *Impossible Subjects: Illegal Aliens and the Making of Modern America* (Princeton, NJ: Princeton University Press, 2003), chs. 1, 2; Roger Daniels, *Guarding the Golden Door: American Immigration Policy and Immigrants Since 1882* (New York: Hill & Wang, 2004), chs. 1, 2.

[43] See David Brion Davis, *The Fear of Conspiracy: Images of Un-American Subversion from the Revolution to the Present* (Ithaca, NY: Cornell University Press, 1971), chs. 6–8; Seymour M. Lipset and Earl Raub, *The Politics of Unreason: Right Wing Extremism in America, 1790–1970* (London: Heinemann, 1971); Bennett, *The Party of Fear*, chs. 10–13.

Council on Foreign Relations, the Trilateral Commission), and radical Islamists of which al-Qaeda is the most conspicuous source of anxiety. Also noteworthy has been the increased significance of the intelligence and security agencies of the federal government in the 'global war on terror'. These have offered renewed scope for the generation of distrust and suspicion on the part of those citizens who are inclined to the view that the government in Washington is in its own right a conspiracy against the public interest.

So endemic have been the references to conspiracy in the political history of the United States that Richard Hofstadter popularized the phenomenon as the 'paranoid style of American politics'.[44] The prodigious claims relating to the concealed presence of forces systematically undermining American society by exploiting its attachment to liberal principles was described by Hofstadter as 'an old and recurrent expression in our public life'.[45] The paranoid style is claimed to operate according to a necessarily conspiratorial perspective of social developments: that altered expectations constitute evidence of a conspiracy designed to compromise and ultimately to destroy a way of life. Hofstadter's observations of this aspect of American society lead him to the this conclusion:

> The distinguishing thing about paranoid style is not that its exponents see conspiracies or plans here and there in history, but that they regard a 'vast' or 'gigantic' conspiracy as *the motive force* in historical events. History *is* a conspiracy, set in motion by demonic forces of almost transcendent power, and what is felt to be needed is not the usual methods of political give-and-take, but all-out crusade.[46]

Hofstadter's classic transposition of a psychological condition to a form of collective behaviour can be disputed on grounds of analytical appropriateness.[47] It can be argued that the free exchange of ideas in a liberal society should entail the free exchange of threat recognition. Far from being an irrational or pathological response to modernity, it is possible to conceive conspiracy politics as a legitimate form of rational inquiry that seek explanations by way of extrapolating connections into patterns of phenomena. In addition, because conspiracy theorizing can provide a form of positive empowerment to those who feel most marginalized and lacking influence, it is possible to conclude that 'conspiracism ... offers community to believers'.[48]

Notwithstanding the myriad causes and consequences ascribed to those who discern the presence of conspiracies, it is evident that the discourse on conspiracy is a signal characteristic of numerous political positions and movements in the

---

[44] Richard Hofstadter, 'The Paranoid Style of American Politics', in Richard Hofstadter (ed.), *The Paranoid Style of American Politics and Other Essays* (New York: Vintage, 1967), pp. 3–40.

[45] Ibid., p. 6.   [46] Ibid., p. 29.

[47] For example, see Mark Fenster and Philip Rosen, *Conspiracy Theories: Secrecy and Power in American Culture* (Minneapolis, MN: University of Minnesota Press, 2001), chs. 1–3.

[48] Robert Alan Goldberg, *Enemies Within: The Culture of Conspiracy in Modern America* (New Haven, CT: Yale University Press, 2001), p. 260; see also see Fenster and Rosen, *Conspiracy Theories*, ch. 7.

United States.[49] They operate upon a cluster of premises relating to suspicion, concealment, dispossession, deviation, usurpation, and illegitimacy. Their strategy is based upon equating difference and otherness with that which is unintelligible, alien, and subversive. The reactive nature of the response to such an identified threat not only highlights the expectations and traditions of social conformity, but underlines the political appeal and leverage of a vulnerable social order requiring exceptional measures to ensure its protection.

CRIMINAL JUSTICE AND PRIVATE SECURITY

The United States is a highly regulated and rules-bound society. It has a very strong attachment to the rights and guarantees of the due process of the law. It also has by far the highest number of lawyers per head of any population. These characteristics help to make the United States the most litigious society in the world. At the same time, America's egalitarian, individualistic, and anti-statist impulses have fostered a culture of rule-bending and law evasion. The interior dynamics of a highly competitive and fluid society, in which the outcome of individual achievement and personal advancement is often privileged over the means employed to secure it, has supported a black economy of working around the rules. The culture of tolerance towards defying 'the system' when the system is characterized as distant, bureaucratic, and hierarchical has permitted the United States to acquire the reputation of being 'less law-abiding ... than other developed countries'.[50]

And yet, notwithstanding this populist folklore of noble outlawry and anti-elitist non-conformity, American society is also noted for its very strong reaction to behaviour that is deemed to be directly antithetical to the security of property and the safety of the person. This has fostered a fascination with direct and unmediated responses to perceived threats to the individual. Whether it is the construction of over 20,000 'gated communities' affording residential security,[51] or the widespread ownership of guns as a means of personal protection,[52] American social attitudes condone stringent reactions to disorder and legitimizes them in terms of individual responsibility, moral right, and constitutional freedom. Even though these types of measure are taken in response to an apparent breakdown in

---

[49] See Timothy Melley, *Empire of Conspiracy: The Culture of Paranoia in Postwar America* (Ithaca, NY: Cornell University Press, 1999), pp. 1–46; Goldberg, *Enemies Within*; Michael Barkun, *A Culture of Conspiracy: Apocalyptic Visions in Contemporary America* (Berkeley, CA: University of California Press, 2003), chs. 1–4, 10.

[50] Seymour M. Lipset, *American Exceptionalism: A Double-Edged Sword?* (New York: W. W. Norton, 1996), p. 289.

[51] Figures drawn from Edward Blakely and Mary Gail, *Fortress America: Gated Communities in the United States* (Washington, DC: Brookings, 1997).

[52] It is estimated that there are in excess of 250 million guns in circulation in the United States. A quarter of all American households have one or more handguns within them.

social authority, their very existence exacerbates the context of fear, polarization, and insecurity within society.

Under such conditions, unsystematized tolerance can turn to systematized intolerance. It is in these circumstances that the open-textured freedoms of a liberal society become conjoined to a commensurately closed sphere of reprimand, repudiation, and even rejection. The duality of liberal licence in coexistence with a regime of punishment and ostracism for those exceeding the boundaries of legitimate conduct is particularly stark in the United States. It is especially evident in relation to the criminal justice system. Enormous resources are expended upon arrest procedures, indictment hearings, pre-trial reports, fair trial arrangements, sentencing assessments, and rights to appeal. But set against this need to satisfy the requirements of due process is a system of punishment for the guilty that is exceptional in its scale and severity.

Prison sentences in the American justice system are often extensive in duration. The regime of imprisonment has been further compounded by the profusion of 'zero tolerance' initiatives in which laws are rigidly enforced with little or no consideration given to the contexts of the offences, or the reasonableness of the response by law enforcement agencies. Prison expansion has also been assisted by the introduction of formulaic approaches to deterrence and punishment in which mandatory minimum sentences are attached to low level offences (especially in relation to drugs) and where imprisonment is made automatic when a set number of offences are entered on a person's criminal record (e.g. 'three strikes and you're out' measures). The introduction of zero tolerance regimes of 'disorder reduction'[53] by many city police departments in the 1990s also increased the number of convictions and custodial sentences.

In addition to the severity of extended incarceration is the volume of prisoners within the system. In 2002, there was a prison population of over 2 million.[54] This represented a rise of 56 per cent in ten years. More significantly, the prison population as a proportion of the national population during the same period has risen by 39 per cent to 702 per 100,000 which now gives the United States' the highest imprisonment rate in the world.[55] The American rate of imprisonment is five times the rate in England and Wales. The equivalent rates in countries such as Mexico (156 per 100,000), Canada (116), Australia (112), Germany (91), France (85), and Japan (53)[56] all underline the atypical nature of the American profile. The United States prison population even exceeds the imprisonment percentage of Russia which until 2002 was the country with the highest recorded levels of incarceration.

Many reasons have been advanced to account for the United States' attachment to punishment through incarceration. Crime rates are on average three times

---

[53] See William Bratton, *Zero Tolerance* (London: Institute of Economic Affairs, 1997).

[54] The Sentencing Project, 'Nation's Inmate Population Exceeds 2 Million for First Time', http://www.sentencingproject.org/news/2million-pressrelease.pdf

[55] International Centre for Prison Studies, http://www.kcl.ac.uk/depsta/rel/icps/worldbrief/north_america_records.php?code=189.

[56] See International Centre for Prison Studies, http://www.kcl.ac.uk/depsta/rel/icps/worldbrief/world_brief.html

higher than those in other developed countries. The rates of violent crime are over ten times higher than those in other western industrialized societies. Even though crime rates have begun to fall from the period of rapid rises during 1960–80, the public perception of intensifying lawlessness has remained. As a result, the precautionary principle of taking action to prevent, or to deter, the occurrence of harm has been in the forefront of policy-making rationales. Fear for personal safety and for the security of private property has combined with general anxieties over the cohesion of civil society to create a climate of acceptance of a growing regime of prison punishment. Other influences are not so immediately related to the assertion of a stimulus–response to crime by elected office-holders who are vulnerable to populist solutions. The impulse to moral denunciation, the principle of retributive justice, and the theme of individual culpability all remain powerful motivating forces.

Tradition also plays a strong role. In his study of imprisonment in America since its colonial founding, Scott Christianson demonstrates that bondage of one form or another has played a pivotal role in the formation and development of the American nation. It is true that in the eighteenth century, the colonists did not share Britain's expansive attitude towards the list of capital crimes. It is also the case that in the early nineteenth century, parts of the United States had acquired a reputation for enlightened penology. Nevertheless, over the course of America's development as a whole Christianson discerns a pattern of abiding affection for imprisonment as the primary form of social control. Over the extended period of American settlement, physical and geographical emancipation went hand in hand with individual confinement as jails and prisons were always among the first public facilities to be constructed in any new towns. Once built, however, costs tended to be kept low by brutalizing regimes of isolation, deprivation, and disease.[57]

In the late nineteenth century and during the twentieth century, larger prison complexes were built by the federal and state governments. But these were also criticized for their oppressive security systems, their remote locations, and their usage of solitary confinement. The roles and functions ascribed to these institutions were reflected in the terminology used in their official titles: 'penitentiary', 'correctional institute', and 'reformatory'. Today, these facilities are home to one in every 143 American citizens. If those on parole and probation are added to the total of those in prison or under community supervision, then the overall figure in 2002 reached 6.6 million. This correlates to ratio of one in 32 adults with a current connection to the custodial element of the criminal justice system.[58]

The most exacting instrument of deterrence and retribution in any system of criminal justice is that of capital punishment. In this respect, the United States' position in comparison with other advanced industrialized states and western

---

[57] Scott Christianson, *With Liberty for Some: 500 Years of Imprisonment in America* (Boston, MA: Northeastern University Press, 2000); see also Stuart Banner, *The Death Penalty: An American History* (Cambridge, MA: Harvard University Press, 2003).

[58] BBC, 'US Prison Figures Rise', 26 August 2002, http://news.bbc.co.uk/1/hi/world/americas/2217382.stm.

democracies is even more anomalous than its regime of imprisonment. Along with China and Iran, the United States has regular recourse to the death penalty. Since individual states were permitted to reintroduce the penalty in 1976, 1,004 executions had taken place by the end 2005. The number of prisoners on 'death row' grew from 688 in 1980 to over 3,700 in 2002. The incidence of capital punishment and the public support given to it make the death penalty an integral part of the criminal justice system. It has aroused serious controversy on grounds of equity, justice, and ethics. It is claimed that the death penalty is arbitrarily imposed and capricious in nature; that it is implicated in numerous miscarriages of justice; that it has no material effect upon crime rates; and that it is morally repugnant and places the United States at variance with international law and with agreements on human rights to which the United States itself is a signatory.[59] In spite of these critiques, which have 'weakened its position in the world as a bulwark of human rights',[60] the United States' conspicuous attachment to capital punishment remains undiminished. It continues to stand as a testament to the extent to which the fear of violent crime and civil insecurity create a fundamentalist response that places an individual beyond forgiveness or redemption. A piece of folk wisdom in the old South was that 'a little lynching went a long way'. Whether its chief value today lay more in symbolism or deterrence, capital punishment has retained its position as an analogue of American social order. In effect, it invites the correlation to be drawn between advanced liberalism, high insecurity, and authoritarian control.[61]

[59] See Austin Sarat, *When the State Kills: Capital Punishment and the American Condition* (Princeton, NJ: Princeton University Press, 2001); David R. Dow and Mark Dow (eds.), *Machinery of Death: The Reality of America's Death Penalty Regime* (New York: Routledge, 2002); Amnesty International USA, 'Death Penalty', http://www.amnestyusa.org/abolish/index.do.

[60] Edmund S. Morgan in 'A Very Popular Penalty', *The New York Review of Books*, 10 April 2003.

[61] See Christian Parenti, *Lockdown America: Police and Prisons in the Age of Crisis* (London: Verso, 1999).

Part III

Compounds

10

Capitalism

FOUNDATIONAL THEMES

If the United States can be said to possess a socio-economic system with a unified basis and a unifying ethos, then it is capitalism that satisfies these credentials more than any other framework of collective activity and belief. Capitalism has not only become integrally related to the growth of the United States into a global industrial power, but in doing so has acquired an iconic property as the generic expression of American ideas and experience. Just as capitalism has played a role in giving definition to America's social identity and historical position, so the United States has emerged as the exemplar of capitalist organization and the defining reference point by which its merits and demerits as an economic and ethical system is adjudged.

Capitalism in the United States represents far more than a set of economic arrangements. It denotes an entire way of life. American capitalism draws so closely upon the indigenous values, ideals, and traditions of the republic, that the dynamics of capitalism and the United States are almost invariably depicted as being interchangeable categories. Capitalism provides a characterization of American history. It is seen as not merely a system of economic exchange but something beyond materialist and utilitarian principles. Michael Novak, for example, describes capitalism as a system with moral and spiritual foundations, which fuses together a market economy with a democratic polity and an ethical basis for social existence.[1] According to these criteria, American capitalism has often been referred to as the epitome of the capitalist ethos. By the same token, capitalism has come to embody the quintessence of America's social nature, and to explain the causes and meanings of America's success as a social force. In the words of George C. Lodge, capitalism in the United States is a 'pervasive, quasi-religious entity which...has remained unassailably the primary source of legitimacy for our institutions, whether economic, political or social'.[2] Capitalism on this scale is not merely a means to liberty, but the mark and measure of a society's very conception of liberty. As such, capitalism has become a portmanteau term that can assimilate American principles and conditions in such a way as to make them not merely compatible with, but synonymous with free enterprise. If Calvin Coolidge

---

[1] Michael Novak, *The Spirit of Democratic Capitalism*, rev. edn (Lanham, MD: Madison Books, 2000), pp. 13–186, 333–60.
[2] George C. Lodge, *The New American Ideology* (New York: Knopf, 1976), p. 11.

was accurate in stating that the 'business of America is business',[3] then it can also be said that the business of business in America has witnessed the fullest extension of such American mores as individualism, equality of opportunity, competition, economic progress, limited government, private property, social mobility, and personal rights.[4]

The assimilative properties of American capitalism are matched by its capacity to synthesize historical and social strands of American experience into an apparently seamless process of cultural accumulation. American history, therefore, is commonly portrayed as following a course that made the republic peculiarly susceptible to the tenets of economic individualism and material enrichment. The social ingredients that are customarily cited as being instrumental in the rise of America's capitalist economy include the following:

- The work ethic of ascetic Protestantism
- The Calvinistic belief in wealth as an outward sign of God's grace and of an individual's inner worth and proximity to salvation
- The profusion of natural resources in an underpopulated area
- The opportunity for capital formation through the availability of domestic resources but more especially through the transfer of capital through international investment
- The stream of immigrant labour complemented by industrial and commercial entrepreneurs drawn by the opportunities of emergent market economies
- The availability of new technologies permitting the continental land mass to be settled and developed into a national market affording national economies of scale and an accelerated rate of progress
- The influence of the Enlightenment with its emphasis upon natural rights and material progress set within a framework of legal protection
- The natural resonance of classical economics in a land whose birth had coincided with the breakdown of the mercantilist order and whose formative years had been marked by the emancipation of old structures of authority

The fusion of disparate factors has encouraged a common conception of American social consciousness: that capitalism grew up with the United States. It is seen as having drawn together an array of separate conditions and impulses to produce an exceptional society.

This idiosyncratic historical process is said to have bequeathed a comprehensive order of explanation and justification upon an otherwise volatile society with little alternative sense of coherent design. Capitalism succeeds in incorporating a number of premises and values relating to human nature, and to the preferred means and desirability of attaining certain objectives. It is this 'network of assumptions'

---

[3] Quoted in Arthur M. Schlesinger Jr., *The American as Reformer*, preface by Arthur M. Schlesinger, Jr. (Cambridge, MA.: Harvard University Press, 1968), p. 49.

[4] Peter J. Berger, *The Capitalist Revolution: Fifty Propositions about Prosperity, Equality and Liberty* (New York: Basic Books, 1986).

that effectively 'converts capitalism from a descriptive term to a prescriptive and justifying ideology'.[5] Capitalism in the United States is an enveloping ideology which has become so synonymous with the conditions of the New World that any triumph of capitalism is customarily portrayed as an affirmation of the American way. By the same token, any flaws or failures attributed to capitalism are taken very seriously because they can impugn the integrity of American principles.

THE CAPITALIST CREDO

In the abstract, capitalism refers to a form of production financed and controlled by individuals who have accumulated wealth over and above their immediate needs and who are prepared to forgo the benefits of this wealth in the expectation of receiving a greater accumulation of wealth in the future. It is assumed that privately owned capital will be directed to those schemes which can be expected to make the maximum return on the investment. Invested capital is conjoined to privately owned land and labour, which is also in search of the greatest possible gain. The result is that goods and services, together with profits and wages, are maximized and efficiently allocated by way of the price mechanism of competitive markets.

It is this reliance upon the market which makes capitalism into a system. The supposition is that underlying private economic activity is a naturally harmonious and self-regulating interaction between the factors of production expressed and secured through the market. According to capitalist theory, as long as those market forces (i.e. supply, demand, competition, and price) are not subverted or misdirected by restrictive practices, economic privileges, or outside interference, then and only then will they reach a state of equilibrium. At this point, they will realize their optimal benefit to society in allowing for the maximization of production at the minimum cost to consumers. Through the free movement of productive resources, capitalism is thought to release the full potential of a society's inner wealth and to reduce prior structures of authority and organization to the level of historical anachronisms. It is this combination of vigorous innovation and entrepreneurial aggression that Joseph Schumpeter had in mind when he described the essence of capitalism as a process of 'creative destruction'. In releasing the potential for production, capitalism could never be stationary. It amounted to a form of incessant revolution from within society.[6]

Capitalism both relies upon and validates the free play of individual self-interest, for it is only through this agency that the market can function as the unsurpassed register of social information which capitalists believe it to be. Individual self-interest, however, does not merely make for an effective repository

[5] Kenneth M. Dolbeare and Patricia Dolbeare, *American Ideologies: The Competing Beliefs of the 1970s* (Chicago, IL: Markham, 1971), p. 22.

[6] Joseph A. Schumpeter, *Capitalism, Socialism and Democracy* (New York: Harper, 1975), pp. 82–5.

of market information. It is also thought, paradoxically, to ensure the greatest material benefit to society as a whole. With every individual 'continually exerting himself to find out the most advantageous employment for whatever capital he can command, it is his own advantage...and not that of society which he has in view'.[7] Nevertheless, 'by pursuing his own interest, he frequently promotes that of the society more effectually than when he really intends to promote it'. Adam Smith's celebrated 'invisible hand'[8] promotes a social end from myopic self-concerns. In doing so, it ennobles economic individualism from merely an empirical motivation into a normative principle and an ethical arrangement.

Some defenders of capitalism would go even further and claim that because economic progress leads to the 'freedom and equality of the individual in a free and equal society,'[9] individuals have a moral responsibility to serve themselves in a calculated and uninhibited manner. As Peter Drucker points out, 'the capitalist creed was the first and only creed which valued the profit motive positively as the means by which the ideal free and equal society would be automatically realized'.[10] According to the system's apologists, capitalism is so geared towards the functional objective of sheer production that it is inherently libertarian in nature. It not only frees people from want but, in order to acquire such liberating abundance, it requires a full liberation of economic and social arrangements. To put a positive social value upon the profit motive requires the freeing of individual economic activity from all restrictions. Capitalism, therefore, has to endow the economic sphere with independence and autonomy. This means that economic activities must not be subjected to non-economic considerations but must take precedence, in order for capitalism to secure the benefits of material progress.[11]

In spite of the evident inequality implicit in the concentrations of capital needed to generate production, there nevertheless remains a strong egalitarian, anti-feudal, anti-authoritarian streak within the capitalist framework. Capitalism is purported to encourage and to reward individuals on the basis of their diligence, intelligence, talents, judgements, and entrepreneurial skills—irrespective of rank, background, or manners. In such a system, the society moves inexorably forward, not only in the material sense of goods and services, but also in the moral sense. By allowing individuals to rely on their own resources to establish their own place in society and their own sense of achievement and self-esteem, a capitalist order is thought to release human potential to the full. Capitalism in this classical perspective can be seen as being not merely a device for material production but the very touchstone of individual liberty itself.

---

[7] Adam Smith, *An Inquiry into the Nature and Causes of the Wealth of Nations*, vol. 1, textual editor W. B. Todd (Oxford: Clarendon Press, 1976), p. 454.

[8] Ibid., p. 456.

[9] Peter Drucker, *The End of Economic Man: A Study of the New Totalitarianism* (London: Basic Books/Heinemann, 1940), p. 35.

[10] Ibid.

[11] See Friedrich A. Hayek, *The Constitution of Liberty* (Chicago, IL: University of Chicago Press, 1960), ch. 3.

In making the moral case for capitalism, Michael Novak underlines the significance of invention and creativity. The 'moral genius' and defining characteristic of capitalism is that of enterprise: 'the habit of employing human wit to invent new goods and services, and to discover new and better ways to bring them to the broadest possible public'.[12] A capitalist economy, therefore, is one that is characterized not merely by expansion but by diversification. It allows societies to transform from zero-sum bases to arrangements that 'defeat envy' and which allow everyone to make gains, i.e. a life in which people are encouraged to 'attend to their own self-discovery and to pursue their own personal form of happiness'.[13] It is this focus upon the 'creation of plenty, rather than the pursuit of power' which leads Novak to claim that capitalism has 'found a better way than any other system to link self-interest to the advancement of the common good'.[14]

This positive view of capitalism's utility and value as a form of social organization is particularly strong in the United States. In fact, the course and status of capitalism in the world has been strongly influenced by American social and economic development. By reputation, the United States has acted out and fulfilled to the greatest extent possible the true potential of capitalism. Whenever the productive energy and social benefit of a capitalist order are placed in doubt, its apologists invariably point to the United States in the late nineteenth century as the historical proving ground for the utility of the market. By the beginning of the twentieth century, the United States had been transformed from an agrarian republic into an industrial superpower described by Arthur M. Schlesinger, Jr. as 'the capitalist fatherland' and 'the home of the world's most confident and energetic business community'.[15] What can be cited as the most spectacular advance in industrial production coincided with a time and a place of unprecedented industrial freedom.

This was a period of reputedly unrestrained capitalism because nothing compelled American capitalists to be anything other than unrestrained. Uninhibited entrepreneurs built empires in the form of huge vertically integrated companies that came to dominate major sectors of the economy. Later, American capitalism was further transformed by the emergence of what Olivier Zunz sees as a singularly American matrix of institutions based upon business, science, engineering, management, universities, research foundations, social science, market research, advertising, government agencies, and policy centres.[16] Zunz describes the horizontal synergy between these various sectors as leading to a controlling technical and managerial hegemony geared to a distinctive conception of a mass market of middle class consumption. America's 'more fluid style of interaction between

---

[12] Michael Novak, 'Wealth and Virtue: The Moral Case for Capitalism', *National Review Online*, 18 February 2004, http://www.nationalreview.com/novak/novak200402180913.asp.

[13] Ibid.   [14] Ibid.

[15] Arthur M. Schlesinger, Jr., *The Vital Center: The Politics of Freedom* (Cambridge, MA: Riverside, 1962), p. 28.

[16] Olivier Zunz, *Why the American Century?* (Chicago, IL: University Of Chicago Press, 2000).

science and industry'[17] generated a highly productive integration of social and scientific knowledge that stimulated technological and economic advance. America's industrial organization and economic development allowed it to become an established international power, to fight two world wars and finally to emerge in 1945 as a global colossus exerting vast economic and military influence. By the middle of the twentieth century, America had come to see itself as 'the classical country of classical economics'.[18] At the end of the century, it had become even more evident than before that the United States was a society which was not only 'unusually enthusiastic about capitalism'[19] but had 'an exceptional faith in capitalism'.[20]

THE AMERICAN MARX

The technological and productive scale of America's capitalist order has coincided with a deepening conviction in the ineluctable progression of capitalism in the New World. The United States has acquired the reputation of being 'the home of rapid, unceasing capitalist modernization and unceasing change'.[21] Against this backdrop, capitalism is seen as both the dominant engine of modernity and also the pre-eminent agency of its explanation. Capitalism has benefited not only from a particular construction of American core values, but from the way that this selective assemblage of emphases has been incorporated into a coherent belief system that can account for the past and legitimize the present.

The appeal of capitalism as the primary form of American economic organization, the chief source of social unity, and the defining expression of American liberal principles is epitomized by the work of Louis Hartz. In one of the most influential treatises on American society, Hartz sought to embed capitalism decisively into America's past as an immutable and inescapable tradition. In doing so, he attempted to confirm the capitalist order of the mid-twentieth century as the authentic outcome of a process of historical progression. In effect, Hartz used capitalism to systemize American history and society into an exclusive analytical entity capable only of validating capitalist priorities.

Hartz took John Locke as his point of departure and used Locke's theory of property rights as the basis of his historiography. To Hartz, Locke's conception of property as a natural right became firmly established in American attitudes

---

[17] Zunz, *Why the American Century?*, p. 6.

[18] Eric Bentley (ed.), *Thirty Years of Treason: Excerpts from Hearings before the House Committee on Un-American Activities, 1938–1968* (London: Thames & Hudson, 1972), p. 935.

[19] John Micklethwait and Adrian Wooldridge, *The Right Nation: Why America is Different* (London: Allen Lane, 2004), p. 305.

[20] Ibid., p. 306.

[21] Anatol Lieven, *America Right or Wrong: An Anatomy of American Nationalism* (London: HarperCollins, 2004), p. 93.

at the outset of the colonial era. To the burgeoning class of merchants and entrepreneurs, as well as its mass of small farmers and self-employed artisans, Locke's philosophy was considered to be highly influential because it conformed to the outlook and opportunities of the early settlers. America not only attracted individuals with strong attachments to toleration, free agency, and entrepreneurial innovation, but offered the prospect of abundant land and other natural resources. According to Hartz, class antagonisms and political polarities had failed to develop because social conditions had spontaneously produced 'an absolute and irrational attachment'[22] to Lockian ideas. Hartz believed that 'the historic ethos of American life, its bourgeois hungers [and] its classlessness'[23] was the living embodiment of Locke and, as such, the entire range of the nation's social relationships was inevitably pervaded by Lockian principles. The result was a consensus centred upon Locke's propertied liberalism—'for a society which begins with Locke, and...stays with Locke...has within it, as it were, a self-completing mechanism which ensures the universality of the liberal idea'.[24]

Hartz subordinates all social tensions to the underlying American unity of bourgeois competition and the cultural reverence shown towards property and capitalist enterprise. 'The magic alchemy of American life', he asserted, 'transform[ed] passive peasants into dynamic liberal farmers [and] proletarians into incipient entrepreneurs'.[25] All aspects of American history and society served only to confirm, to Hartz, the extent of America's extraordinary moral unanimity. The constitutional restraints of the Founding Fathers, for example, had only been able to survive in such dynamic surroundings because of the 'compulsive impact of a single creed'.[26] The unanimity of Lockian liberalism marked the existence of a society with only one estate. This ensured that no one sector would feel permanently frustrated, or discriminated against, by the Constitution's checks and balances. America's 'reality of atomistic social freedom'[27] and the 'compulsive power of Locke made..."success" and "failure"...the only valid ways of thought'.[28] Hartz portrayed America as locked tight within an overwhelming uniformity which Americans could not transcend and from which they could not escape. They remained entrapped by Locke's central value of property aspiration and, accordingly, could not help but be permanently engaged in the 'relentless running of the Lockian race'.[29]

In Hartz's work, all social conflict is necessarily reduced to that arising from mere differences of emphasis or technique. As a consequence, the existence of fundamental social dichotomies is precluded as is the possibility of them ever occurring in the New World. In this perspective, major political failures in America have been due to attempts to introduce European ideologies into the

---

[22] Louis Hartz, *The Liberal Tradition in America: An Interpretation of American Political Thought Since the Revolution* (New York: Harcourt Brace Jovanovich, 1955), p. 6.

[23] Ibid., p. 206. [24] Ibid., p. 6. [25] Ibid., p. 122. [26] Ibid., p. 211.

[27] Ibid., p. 62. [28] Ibid., p. 219. [29] Ibid.

United States. Alexander Hamilton's eighteenth-century elitism, the aristocratic pretensions of the early nineteenth-century American Whigs, the feudal reaction of the antebellum South, and the collective programmes of industrial radicalism were automatically doomed as they were simply incompatible with the liberal mainstream of American society. They were hopeless attempts to break the American consensus into artificial fragments and to attach European labels and analytical forms to the parts. American conditions—especially the lack of an anti-industrial right wing and the absence of a class-conscious peasantry or proletariat—produced, in Hartz's view, a wholly invincible consensus that excludes any basis for fundamental conflict and, therefore, for any ideological divisiveness.

Hartz can be reconfigured into the American Marx. This is not just because he provides a systematic conception of society that depends primarily upon economic forces and relationships, but because he introduces a deterministic quality to the analysis. He endeavours to define the United States as a society wholly dependent upon its own iron laws of materialistic development. To Hartz, the United States is set upon its own pathway of history which essentially is a combination of economic advance on the one hand, and social and philosophical immobility on the other. Hartz's laws produce an America sustained in a static and timeless world of capitalist harmonies, self-regulating balances, and consensus politics. In this way, Hartz is the prince of American exceptionalism. 'In a brilliant analysis of the relationship between social structure and ideology,'[30] Hartz provides a coherent social and economic framework that transforms a basic American wish to be seen as different to the rest of the world into a systematic exceptionalism, rendering the United States immune to European categories of analysis and to European lines of development.

For these reasons, it would perhaps be more accurate to see Hartz as America's antidote to Marxism. Instead of class antagonisms and social contradictions, Hartz portrays America's social consensus as being ubiquitous and permanent. The faith in possessive and competitive individualism is so deep that, in America, capitalist principles are seen simply as being self-evident axioms. America's instinctive allegiance to capitalism may well have led to the 'atrophy of the philosophic impulse'[31] but, to Hartz, this ensures the maintenance of American capitalism against all challenges. Furthermore, it is predetermined to prevail for, in Hartz's view, America possesses the unique characteristics which allow capitalism to sustain itself indefinitely. While it is true that Hartz's thesis can be criticized on several fronts, what is significant about it is the durability of its appeal. It successfully encapsulates America's historical development in terms which can comprehensively accommodate all of the supposed and actual origins of American

---

[30] John P. Diggins, *The American Left in the Twentieth Century* (New York: Harcourt Brace Jovanovich, 1973), p. 147; see also Diggins, 'Knowledge and Sorrow: Louis Hartz's Quarrel with American History', *Political Theory*, vol. 16, no. 3 (August 1988), pp. 355–76.

[31] Hartz, *The Liberal Tradition in America*, p. 285.

capitalism into one inevitable social order. Under these terms, the pantheon of American principles (e.g. liberty, individualism, constitutionalism, democracy, rights, property, competition, equality) can all be made to seem integral to one another by being reduced to, and expressed through, capitalism. They can all be assimilated as instrumental in the creation of a singular society uniquely characterized by the capitalist impulse.

Hartz reformulates American history and society into a persuasive depiction of a continuity of American experience centred upon the organizing agency of capitalism. The interdependency of historical construction and contemporary interpretation may be criticized for its circular quality but this should not detract from the scale and reach of Hartz's within American society. The very receptivity of Hartz's portrayal of consensus to American audiences has in itself helped to lend weight to the thesis that capitalism is synonymous with American attitudes; that it amounts to an accurate evocation of America's past; and that it constitutes the essence of American exceptionalism.

Although the Hartzian thesis was no doubt influenced by the ideological cohesion of the cold war and by the need to root American solidarity within a durable historical continuity, the theme of a consensus formed around liberal capitalism continues to resonate throughout American society. Hartz's notion of a 'self-completing mechanism'[32] of liberal values found another expression in Francis Fukuyama's thesis on the 'end of history' which envisaged a generic condition of liberal democracy and capitalism as the culminating condition of humanity's cultural evolution.[33] The model and dynamics of Fukuyama's predictive exposition bore such a strong resemblance to Hartz's conception of America's social development that 'the end of history' was often criticized for proceeding upon the basis of an identifiably American model of modernity.

At the turn of the century, American culture gave many indications of being just as Hartzian in outlook as it had been in the 1950s. With the political and intellectual collapse of viable alternatives to liberal capitalism, the dynamics and virtues of the market underwent a dramatic revival. The 1990s, in particular, marked a period of exponential confidence in the beneficence of capitalism and the progressive force of a business civilization. Numerous analysts and commentators constructed persuasive arguments that fused the market with the legitimizing features of democracy, liberty, progress, and individual fulfilment.[34] The changing public conception of the relationship between the state and the market revolved around the liberating themes of privatization and a market that offered not merely

---

[32] Ibid., p. 6.

[33] Francis Fukuyama, *The End of History and the Last Man* (London: Penguin, 1992).

[34] For example, see Jeffrey Bell, *Populism and Elitism: Politics in the Age of Equality* (Washington, DC: Regnery Gateway, 1992); Daniel Yergin and Joseph Stanislaw, *The Commanding Heights: The New Reality of Economic Power* (New York: Simon & Schuster, 1998); Robert Kiyosaki and Sharon L. Lechter, *Rich Dad, Poor Dad: What the Rich Teach Their Kids about Money That the Poor and the Middle Class Do Not* (New York: Warner, 2000).

a medium of exchange but an instrument of popular empowerment. Thomas Frank uses the term 'market populism' to convey the metamorphosis:

The market and the people—both of them understood as grand principles of social life rather than particulars—were essentially one and the same. By its very nature the market was democratic, perfectly expressing the popular will through the machinery of supply and demand, poll and focus group, superstore and Internet. In fact, the market was *more* democratic than any of the formal institutions of democracy—elections, legislatures, government. The market was a community. The market was infinitely diverse, permitting without prejudice the articulation of any and all tastes and preferences. Most important of all, the market was militant about its democracy.[35]

The propagandizing creed of the 'new economy' was highly successful and revealed the susceptibility of American opinion to the drives and disciplines of a capitalist ethos. As the market became increasingly equated with a de facto democracy and as government agencies were exhorted to adopt business practices, the hegemony of capitalism was depicted as a universal force of nature to which individuals and nations had to adjust. Within the 'Washington consensus', there was no room for economic dissent. In exactly the same spirit with which Hartz had adumbrated the orthodoxy of cold war unity, there was no alternative because no alternative was deemed necessary: '[E]ven as Americans marveled at the infinite variety of the Internet and celebrated our ethnic diversity, we were at the same time in the grip of an intellectual consensus every bit as ironclad as that of the 1950s'.[36]

WHY THERE IS NO SOCIALISM IN THE UNITED STATES

The United States' self-image as an exceptional society rests heavily upon its belief in being exceptionally capitalist in its outlook and priorities. Nothing better exemplifies the dynamics of this identity than the long-running debate on why the history of the United States is conspicuously devoid of socialism.[37] This controversy, which has generated an enormous literature, proceeds upon the central

---

[35] Thomas Frank, *One Market under God: Extreme Capitalism, Market Populism and the End of Economic Democracy* (London: Vintage, 2002), p. 29.

[36] Thomas Frank, 'The Rise of Market Populism: America's New Secular Religion', *The Nation*, 30 October 2000.

[37] The question was originally posed and popularized in Werner Sombart's *Why Is There No Socialism in the United States?*, intro. C. T. Husbands (White Plains, NY: M. E. Sharpe, 1976). The question relates to a *general* absence of socialism in the United States. It should not be forgotten that pockets of socialist politics existed in immigrant communities. Socialist newspapers were often the most popular periodicals in immigrant neighbourhoods and socialist activists were notable local politicians. See Paul Buhle, *Marxism in the United States: Remapping the History of the American Left* (London: Verso, 1987). But the appeal of radical class politics and socialist movements was particularly prominent in areas of America's farmland. See Lowell K. Dyson, *Red Harvest: The Communist Party and American Farmers* (Lincoln, NE: University of Nebraska Press, 1982); James R. Green, *Grass-Roots Socialism: Radical Movements in the Southwest, 1895–1943* (Baton Rouge, LA: Louisiana State University Press, 1978).

premise that the United States has no tradition of socialist politics. It has not even developed a mass-based working-class political party. According to basic Marxist theory, an industrialized society like the United States should, by the universal laws of historical materialism, have generated the sort of class antagonisms that would have inevitably produced a progressive drive towards socialism. Socialism in this sense constitutes a reaction to, and a development of, advanced capitalism.

Even without the dogmas of Marxist theory, developed capitalist societies have generally been drawn towards an increased consciousness of the disparities in wealth. This in turn has created an impulse, amongst concentrations of industrial workers in particular, to press for greater social equality and, accordingly, for the public ownership and control of major sectors of the economy. The accelerated advance of American capitalism, together with the rapacity of American industrialists, led even Marx himself to believe that the United States might be the first country to undergo a socialist revolution. In *Das Kapital*, Marx explained how the 'most developed country shows to the less developed the image of their future'.[38] In 1881, he viewed the United States as the country in the vanguard of the capitalist development. He observed that in the United States 'the capitalist economy and the corresponding enslavement of the working class [had] developed more rapidly and shamelessly than in any other country'.[39] And yet apart from some localized and temporary penetrations, America's Socialist Party and associated groups have continually failed to disturb the edifice of American capitalism. The reasons offered for what is often purported to be an aberration of world history are legion. They can be divided into two main groups. First are the socio-economic causes; second are the political–constitutional causes.

The socio-economic factors include the frontier, which acted both as a safety valve for propertyless workers and as a continuous drain on the working population of the eastern cities, with the result that the labour supply remained limited and industrial wages were kept high. The relative affluence and mobility of American workers compared with their European counterparts was thought to have made them far less receptive to radical politics and far more interested in moving up the ladder of social status in the Horatio Alger tradition.[40] Even amongst those workers who were not so taken with the individualist promises of success, and who favoured greater solidarity with one another, found that any collective consciousness stopped at racial, ethnic, and religious barriers. The American labour force was notoriously splintered by such animosities, which were marked by divided neighbourhoods and segregated settlements. Divisions were perpetuated at the workplace by Protestant and Catholic discrimination, by factories split into ethnic and racial enclaves and by strictly defended barriers dividing the skilled from the unskilled workers. As the Irish communities, for example, solidified in their areas

---

[38] Quoted in Mandy Garner, *Times Higher Education Supplement*, 3 November 2000.

[39] Karl Marx, 'Letter to Friedrich Sorge' (30 June 1881), in Karl Marx and Friedrich Engels, *Letters to Americans, 1848–1895* (New York: International Publishers, 1963), p. 129; see also Harvey Klehr, 'Marxist Theory in Search of America', *The Journal of Politics*, vol. 35, no. 2 (May 1973), pp. 311–31.

[40] See Sombart, *Why Is There No Socialism in the United States?*, pp. 61–106; see also Loren Bariz, *The Good Life: The Meaning of Success for the American Middle Class* (New York: Knopf, 1989).

with their own customs, schools, and churches, so the Jewish communities, for example, did likewise. Neither grouping would be very receptive to the idea of joining forces against an abstract economic system in a campaign that might well jeopardize their jobs and their opportunities for advancement in a society with little or no provision for social welfare or economic security.[41]

The general belief is that at the very time when a working-class consciousness might have developed in the United States (i.e. 1880–1920), the socialist movement was stillborn because American society offered a mass culture of individual progress and consumption. The cultural norm of equal opportunity provided a meritocratic rationale for the disparities in wealth and, with it, a further suppressant to the development of any class solidarity stretching across other cultural divides. In addition to the processes of 'embourgeoisement', American society was distinguished by a permanent and identifiable black underclass that further defused the dissatisfaction of the poor whites and dissuaded them from any egalitarian radicalism that would risk eroding the racial barrier.

The political–constitutional factors lay emphasis upon the United States' traditional attachment to popular sovereignty and to individual rights and liberties. In particular, the extension of the male franchise in the early nineteenth century is thought to have eliminated a major source of social grievance. In European countries it was precisely the lack of political participation through a limited franchise that helped to harden class lines and to give focus to broader-based social and industrial complaints. Because the American worker had already been enfranchised before the onset of full industrialization and, therefore, prior to the possible emergence of a proletariat, it meant that American workers were denied the stimulus which may have drawn them together and prompted the formation of mass-based, autonomous organizations to serve their collective interests.

Once weakened in this way, it is thought that industrial labour was maintained in its fragmented form by a variety of political and constitutional circumstances. These include (i) an established two-party system that militated against the emergence of a third component; (ii) the Populist movement's exacerbation of sectional antipathies between the agrarian West and the industrial North which prompted a generation of northern workers to vote for the Republican party; (iii) the divisive effects of interest-group politics and of a governmental structure dedicated to checks and balances; (iv) the Constitution's values of limited government, civil liberties, and individual rights which were thoroughly analogous to the capitalist dogmas in society at large; (v) the disaggregative effects of the federal structure which meant that 'there was, in effect, no national pattern of law, legitimization or repression to confirm a socialist critique'[42]; (vi) and not least, the explicit antagonism shown towards left-wing sympathizers and radical groups in the

---

[41] See Mike Davis, 'Why the US Working Class is Different', *New Left Review*, No. 123 (September–October 1980), pp. 3–46.

[42] Theodore J. Lowi, 'Why is There No Socialism in the United States? A Federal Analysis', *International Political Science Review*, vol. 5, no. 4 (1984), p. 377.

impulsive 'red scares' of the 1920s and 1950s when socialists were openly subjected to intimidation, persecution, and social ostracism.[43]

Socialists also had to battle against the central rationale of the American political system: the prevention of a centralized oppressive state whose coercive capacity could be co-opted by minority interests intent upon maximizing their strategic advantages to the detriment of the public interest. This suspicion of an overarching central power is a major theme in Seymour Martin Lipset's study of the noted non-appearance of socialism in the United States. In *It Didn't Happen Here: Why Socialism Failed in the United States* (2000),[44] Lipset draws particular attention to the influence of the Protestant tradition in the American conception of power and liberty. The Protestant impulse is one of freedom of self-organization and denominational affiliation. In contrast to many European cultures where established churches possessed highly institutionalized and hierarchical structures, American Protestant organizations were highly localized and fissile in nature. Their social and intellectual environment was one of animosity towards distant and coercive churches, and a corresponding emphasis upon voluntary association and membership retention in a highly competitive matrix of sectarianism. Socialism, therefore, not only stimulated America's anti-central impulses, but also aroused its hostility to the imposition of large organizations laying claim to doctrinal prerogatives and collective discipline. In this context, the socialist cause was not assisted by the fact that so many of its proponents and potential beneficiaries were drawn from the masses of southern and eastern European Catholics who had migrated to the United States in the late nineteenth and early twentieth centuries.

This variety of ascribed causes and the differing emphases given to them have generated a considerable volume of scholarly debate.[45] It is not necessary on this occasion to appraise the relative merits of the separate arguments. What is important to note is the extraordinary attention given to this theme in American history and the conspicuous satisfaction in what seems to be the incontrovertible condition of 'no socialism'. While those on the left lament the failure of socialist movements to embed themselves in an American identity or in a characteristically American philosophy,[46] the mainstream reaction has generally been one of cultural satisfaction with the avoidance of mass-based socialist politics and programmes.

Americans have traditionally taken pride in the view that its society has distinguished itself as the bulwark of freedom. More often than not, this condition is characterized by the celebrated absence of what has been widely regarded

---

[43] Robert J. Goldstein, *Political Repression in Modern America from 1870 to the Present* (Cambridge, MA: Schenkman, 1978), chs. 5, 9.

[44] Seymour M. Lipset, *It Didn't Happen Here: Why Socialism Failed in the United States* (New York: W. W. Norton, 2000).

[45] See John H. M. Laslett and Seymour M. Lipset (eds.), *Failure of a Dream? Essays in the History of American Socialism* (Garden City, NY: Anchor, 1974); Jerome Karabel, 'The Failure of American Socialism Reconsidered', in Ralph and John Saville (eds.), *The Socialist Register, 1979* (London: Merlin, 1979), pp. 204–28.

[46] John P. Diggins, *The Rise and Fall of the American Left* (New York: W. W. Norton, 1992).

in American society as a European affliction. According to this viewpoint, the historical dearth of socialist forces in the United States is conclusive proof that America is different from other industrialized states. For most of the last century, the freedom preserved in the New World has been defined as the freedom from socialism. In effect, American identity is closely calibrated with the cultural escape from socialism and from its supposed leviathan of authoritarian state controls and central intervention, of property expropriation, and of redistributed wealth to those with no moral right to it. America's preference for capitalism over socialism serves to exemplify the American antipathy towards the state, which is deep enough to be sustained even when the state purports to embody the collective interests and purposes of the American public. Against this background, the United States has not simply celebrated its traditional animus towards socialism. It has portrayed itself as the defining antidote to the socialist presumption of an inevitable reconfiguration of society.

WHERE THERE IS 'SOCIALISM' IN THE UNITED STATES

America's celebration of capitalism as a counterweight to socialism and as a rebuttal of Marxism has undoubtedly contributed towards the civic integration of the United States. Nevertheless, the instinctive identity of Americans as non-socialists raises a number of problematic points that strike at the very heart of American capitalism and of the public's attachment to it. Some of these points relate to general analytical difficulties over socialism. For example, since socialistic attitudes in history have not correlated with any one set of objective economic preconditions, then 'failure' of American socialism should not perhaps be seen as a deviant case of social development. The affluence and mobility of American workers, therefore, might just as well have led them to socialism as to capitalism.[47] Furthermore, since the motivation to Marxist socialism is recognized to be as much a consequence of feudalism as it is of capitalism, then America's lack of an *ancien régime* may well be more responsible than capitalism for its lack of socialism.[48] This would hardly rank as a refutation of Marxism—it might conceivably represent a vindication of it.

The main point raised by the controversy over American socialism is that it always tends to overlook the possibility of socialist elements and objectives already present in American society. A plausible argument can be made that the main reason for the lack of an explicitly socialist movement or agenda in the United States is not that America is fully capitalist, but that it is only partly capitalist in that it possesses several socialist characteristics which make it comparable to other western democratic countries. Even in the nineteenth century the picture is

[47] See C. T. Husbands' introductory essay in Sombart, *Why Is There No Socialism in the United States?*, pp. xxiii–xxvii.
[48] Hartz, *The Liberal Tradition in America*, pp. 6, 78, 178–200.

ambiguous. It was during this era that American capitalism became renowned for its apparent ability to reconstruct the republic's social and economic organization over and against weak and undeveloped forms of governance. But it has been shown that the period was marked by an extensive infrastructure of state and local regulation in an array of areas pertaining to property, markets, licensing, transportation, and contracts.[49]

In the twentieth century, the United States developed into a sophisticated mixed economy with a public sector accounting for 40 per cent of the country's gross national product. After the watershed of the Great Depression and President Franklin Roosevelt's reaction to it in the form of the New Deal programme, the United States developed into a positive state with a massive permanent infrastructure of controls, regulations, subsidies, contracts, benefits, entitlements, insurance facilities, and loans. Keynesian economics—which assumed that markets were not naturally self-regulating and that they required government intervention to manage the level of demand within the economy—had once been thought to be dangerously subversive. By the end of the Second World War, the United States had formally accepted Keynesianism. In the Employment Act of 1946, the federal government was obliged to take all the necessary steps 'to promote maximum employment, production and purchasing power' in the economy. By 1971, even a conservative Republican president felt able to declare that 'I am now a Keynesian in economics', shortly before imposing a sweeping programme of wage, price, and rent controls on the American economy.[50]

The growth of, and the acknowledged need for, government expenditures and even deficit financing has led America to an enhanced realization of the past and especially of the historic role of the state in the rise and development of early American capitalism. Contrary to common reputation, the formative period of American capitalism was not an idyll of pure competition and unbridled enterprise amongst the self-employed. Early entrepreneurs very often acquired their wealth by extracting privileges and subsidies from the governments of the day. Even in the early years of the republic, government sanctioned the formation of monopolies and promoted their activities.[51] Federal and state governments also supported and financed entrepreneurial activity through land grants, 'internal improvements' (e.g. roads, canals), tariffs, and security measures. It is now accepted that the development towards the regulation of business by government was instigated as much by industry as by social reformers. In order to prevent ruinous competition and to stabilize prices and markets, and even to offset the

---

[49] William J. Novak, *The People's Welfare: Law and Regulation in Nineteenth Century America* (Chapel Hill, NC: University of North Carolina Press, 1996).

[50] See Daniel Yergin and Joseph Stanislaw, *The Commanding Heights: The Battle between Government and the Marketplace That Is Remaking the Modern World* (New York: Simon & Schuster, 1998), pp. 60–4; Rowland Evans and Robert Novak, *Nixon in the White House: The Frustration of Power in the White House* (New York: Vintage, 1972), p. 372.

[51] For example, see Marshall E. Blume, Jeremy J. Siegel, and Dan Rottenberg, *Revolution on Wall Street: The Rise and Decline of the New York Stock Exchange* (New York: W. W. Norton, 1993); see also Novak, *The People's Welfare*.

prospect of more radical measures especially at the state level, business supported federal regulation through such agencies as the Interstate Commerce Commission, the Federal Trade Commission, and the Federal Reserve Board.[52]

This partnership between government and business has grown in scale to the point where the two elements are now virtually indistinguishable from one another. On the one hand, federal regulations have ramified into such a profusion of areas within American society (e.g. securities, credit, advertising, the environment, occupational safety, car design, nuclear hazards, drug testing) that the entire polity is often termed the 'regulatory state'. On the other hand, business has direct access to government, possesses a virtual veto on governmental proposals wholly adverse to business interests, and benefits from the government's position of being the largest purchaser of goods and services in the country. The close interdependency of the public and private sectors means that industries remain reliant upon the governmental supervision of the market. The threat of any disruption will lead to vociferous appeals to the government *not* to compromise its regulatory regimes for fear of creating instability and giving outsiders a competitive advantage. It is true that deregulation has been a popular cause in both political and business circles over the past twenty-five years. Nevertheless, it is equally true that much of this deregulation has been directed to areas that have come to be seen as sources of excessive restraint upon enterprise activity (e.g. environmental protection, workers' rights, health, and safety). As the mission statement of the National Association of Manufacturers (NAM) makes clear, the conventional reliance by business upon government intervention for market stability and industrial security remains very much intact:

The NAM's mission is to enhance the competitiveness of manufacturers by shaping a legislative and regulatory environment conducive to U.S. economic growth and to increase understanding among policymakers, the media and the general public about the vital role of manufacturing to America's economic future and living standards.[53]

When the 'regulatory state' is combined with the volume of federal and state financed programmes in areas such as social security, welfare provision, unemployment compensation, educational support, and health care, then a case can be made that the United States has in effect followed a path very similar to that pursued in other western societies. It can be argued that the United States not only has a social democratic tradition, but possesses an active social democratic movement located primarily within the Democratic Party. The efforts of these social democratic forces in reshaping the operational context of America's capitalist economy have become so well established in the mainstream of society that the United States has acquired a reputation for having fostered a new hybrid

[52] Gabriel Kolko, *The Triumph of Conservatism: A Reinterpretation of American History, 1900–1916* (New York: Free Press, 1963).

[53] National Association of Manufacturers, 'Profile and Mission', http://www.nam.org/s_nam/sec.asp?CID=26&DID=24.

formation known as 'welfare capitalism'.[54] In effect, American capitalism is said to have undergone a profound metamorphosis and to have produced a social democratic order in everything but name. The shift in priorities is reflected in the composition of the federal budget. In 2003, $1,419.6 billion was directed to human resources. This represented 66.3 per cent of federal expenditure and far exceeded the allocation of $376.3 billion for national defense, which accounted for 17.6 per cent of federal outlays. The health budget alone ($467.8 billion) surpassed the defense sector in budgetary priorities. Over half the entire budget (51.2 per cent) was dedicated to direct transfer payments to individuals.[55]

It can be contended that these arrangements have a superior claim to Louis Hartz's epithet of 'democratic capitalism'. This is because of the attentiveness now given to the need to intervene in the market to protect and support those non-participants located on the margins of society. It is also derived from the redistributive forces that are discernible within capitalism's own contemporary dynamics. One example is provided by share ownership. In 1983, the number of Americans holding shares in companies totalled 42 million, which represented 18 per cent of the population. By 1999, the number of stockholders had risen to 79 million, thereby, increasing the proportion of the population with stocks to 28 per cent. Another example is provided by the expansion of employee ownership and profit-sharing plans in American businesses.[56] In 2003, as much as 23.3 per cent of all employees working in for-profit companies owned stock in those concerns. This represented a marked increase over the past twenty-five years. Nearly 40 per cent of for-profit companies (37.8%) now offered employment ownership plans for over 50 per cent of their employees. These devices equated to over 25 million employees having a share-related stake in their companies' performance.[57] These and other trends can be used to depict a radically different expression of capitalist organization and one that possesses a genuine adaptability to change beyond its conventional ethos of market-centred concentrations of private wealth.

Such developments can be deployed to give substance to the proposition that America's capitalist order has achieved socialist objectives by alternative means. These modern assimilating properties associated with the terms 'popular capitalism' or 'democratic capitalism' or the 'ownership society' serve to complement an older depiction of America. This relates to the legendary notion of the New World offering a form of substitute socialism[58] based upon a naturally occurring

---

[54] Stuart D. Brandes, *American Welfare Capitalism, 1880–1940* (Chicago, IL: University of Chicago Press, 1976).

[55] US Census Bureau, *Statistical Abstract of the United States: 2003*, pp. 322–3.

[56] It is estimated that in 2005 there were 11,500 Employee Stock Ownership Plan (ESOP) schemes, stock bonus plans, and profit sharing plans primarily invested in employer stock. As many as ten million employees were thought to be registered under these schemes. See The National Center for Employee Ownership, 'A Statistical Profile of Employee Ownership (November 2005)', http://www.nceo.org/library/eo_stat.html.

[57] Figures from The National Center for Employee Ownership, 'A Statistical Profile of Employee Ownership (November 2005)'.

[58] Michael Harrington, *Socialism* (New York: E. P. Dutton, 1972), pp. 111–18.

condition of social inclusiveness and, with it, a sense of equality and mobility greater than that found in the class-bound societies of Europe.[59]

THE LIMITS OF AMERICAN CAPITALISM'S ADAPTATIONS

The capacity of American capitalism to adapt to contemporary forces and to assimilate shifting social priorities raises the question of whether it has out-evolved the customary tenets of a capitalist order and whether it is engaged in the creation of a post-capitalist formation. The extent to which capitalism can adapt to produce a qualitatively different order of economic and social relationships is perhaps best illustrated by the post-cold war era. During the 1990s, capitalism was widely perceived to have emerged as the supremely predominant ideology. Nevertheless, at the same time, it was generally thought that the price of capitalist pre-eminence had been one of close regulation, social provision, and 'corporate social responsibility'. In effect, capitalism might be said to have been conditioned out of its old excesses.

The extraordinary surge in information technology (IT), and the dramatic rise in dotcom companies that were intent upon exploiting the Internet for commercial use, seemed to underline the contemporary energy and vitality of a reconfigured capitalism. Just as the Internet itself had cultivated a culture of accessibility and disintermediation between customer and corporation, so the organization of dotcom companies led the way in open-textured and horizontally designed management structures that were evocative of the egalitarian spirit of the 'information super highway'. Informality, iconoclasm, and dissolving hierarchies fused together with the ambition of knowledge-based IT industries and a stock market that appeared to be locked into a continual ascent, all served to add credence to the claims of a 'new economy'. The new economy was propagated as clean and almost effortless abundance in which the 'business cycle was a thing of the past, as were imperfect information, predatory monopolies, tyrannical bosses and the eight-hour workday'.[60] In such a context, post-materialist values appeared to have found their economic expression.

The 1990s confirmed that the United States possessed not only the strongest economy in the world but the most entrepreneurial economy in terms of business start-ups, small company employment, and the proportion of the stock market accounted for by companies less than ten years old. And yet despite the gains and successes of America's economic performance during this period, the evidence of a new industrial order can only be described as at best mixed. For every indicator of transformation, there exists another suggesting that the problematic ingredients of capitalism have remained in existence. This period, for example, was marked

---

[59] Peter d'A. Jones, *The Consumer Society: A History of American Capitalism* (Harmondsworth, UK: Penguin, 1965), p. 259.

[60] Thomas Frank, 'Talking Bull', *The Guardian*, 17 August 2002.

not just by economic advances but by widening inequalities, large-scale mergers, job losses through outsourcing and downsizing, and a wholly unsustainable rise in share values that brought in its wake a highly damaging stock market collapse in 2001. The boom time of the 1990s was a period when the remuneration packages of top managers rose from 42 times more than the average employee in 1980 to more than 400 times the average in 2000. The overriding priority of their work was to sustain the market value of their companies' shares. Given the dynamics of the stock market, any announcement of large-scale job losses by a company usually resulted in a commensurate rise in share values based not so much upon the development of new markets or company growth, but upon the appearance of efficiency savings and, thereby, of enhanced earnings.

The internal strains within capitalism were typified by two particular events. First was a series of sudden and spectacular share value collapses combined with the exposure of corporate malfeasance at the very highest levels of management. The scale of these losses in 2002 was gargantuan and affected such major corporations as Enron, WorldCom, Tyco, GE, and Qwest. The collapses also led to several celebrity chief executive officers (CEOs) (e.g. Bernie Ebbers of World-Com, Dennis Kozlowski of Tyco, Kenneth Lay of Enron, Jack Welch of GE, and Joseph Nacchio of Qwest) facing investigations and criminal proceedings over allegations of conflict of interest, bookkeeping deception, money laundering, false accounting, insider training, conspiracy, and fraud.[61] The overall impact of these compounded shocks was immense. For example, when the shares in the giant WorldCom Corporation ceased trading at 83 cents—after a high of $64.50—the company had to lay off its 17,000 workforce and announce that its pension scheme had been largely destroyed. The slump in shares had cost investors $175 billion. After Ebbers had resigned as CEO, it was revealed that he owed the company $366 million in low-interest loans. The sensational nature of the charges gave a highly damaging and public insight into the normally discreet world of corporate finance and management culture.

The revelations of the conflict of interest pervading the matrix of directors, auditors, stock analysts, and investment bankers created the most severe corporate crisis in seventy years and prompted immediate calls for reform by the Bush administration and the Congress. The most conspicuous element of the crisis, and the one that generated the harshest of indictments, was the lavish but largely undeclared pay-outs and perquisites given to the CEOs. These benefits came on top of their very substantial stock option portfolios. They were originally designed to tie pay to company performance but they became instead instruments of market manipulation for individual gain. The crisis revealed that many CEOs and senior directors regarded the maximization of their personal fortunes as more important than protecting the incomes and pensions of their companies' employees and investors. In effect, the CEOs were shown to have been instrumental both

[61] For example, see Brian Cruver, *Anatomy of Greed: The Unshredded Truth from an Enron Insider* (New York: Carroll & Graf, 2002); Frank Portnoy, *Infectious Greed: How Deceit and Risk Corrupted the Financial Markets* (New York: Times Books, 2003).

in inflating the stock market bubble and in exacerbating its collapse by selling their shares to make the optimum gains before the downturn affected all the other principal parties. The episode generated sufficient condemnation for *Time* magazine to conclude that the amount of 'red ink on the moral balance sheet' meant that 'a fat slice of corporate America ha[d] been ethically bankrupt for years'.[62] The duplicity and apparent greed of these professional managers raised serious questions not just over the standards of corporate finance, but also over the moral substance of corporate activity and, in particular, the legitimacy of the market in senior executive salaries, benefits, and incentive packages.

The second example that served to symbolize the ambiguities of American capitalism at the turn of the century was the anti-trust suit filed against Bill Gates and Microsoft in 1998. Although Gates and his company exemplified the libertarian style of the new economy, he vigorously defended his near monopoly position in the personal computer software market. His west coast informality belied his status as the richest individual in America. He was not just an apologist for IT; he had become its popular talisman. Gates's national and international status as an entrepreneur was said to have reinvigorated America's self-belief in its capacity to be at the cutting edge of technology innovation and application. Nevertheless, as Gates and Microsoft achieved greater prominence, they came under increasing scrutiny and were revealed to be not quite the benign force that they depicted themselves to be. Microsoft was accused of pursuing a highly aggressive market strategy that included allegations of unfair trading practices (e.g. predatory pricing, blatant copying, commercial reprisals, compromising the integrity of competing products) in the pursuit of monopoly power.

Microsoft's attempt to squeeze access to the Internet through the installation of its browser with the Windows format finally prompted action to be taken against the company. In an increasingly knowledge-based society, Gates was accused of trying to assume a monopolistic control of the market relating to the production, distribution, and exchange of information. The consumer champion, Ralph Nader, argued that Americans should not be deceived by the public interest blandishments of Gates. His language was redolent of the excesses of the Gilded Age:

Just imagine the data possession that this a company will have, the invasion of privacy potential. Imagine the influence over government. Domination, ever growing, is the goal...an octopus may have a few tentacles. This company has dozens of tentacles, and then off each tentacle there are lots more mini-tentacles.[63]

To Nader and many others, Gates was no different to the 'robber barons' of the later nineteenth century for whom self-restraint in the pursuit of market position, profit, and power was neither comprehensible nor desirable.

---

[62] Daniel Kadlec, 'WorldCon', *Time*, 8 July 2002.
[63] Quoted in John Carlin, 'Bill Gates Beware, America's Consumer Champion Is on to You', *The Guardian*, 18 November 1997.

The American economy remains the largest and most successful in the world. The 1990s witnessed not only the biggest stock market bubble in the nation's history but also a 69 per cent increase in its GDP. American capitalism continues to act as a model of productive enterprise and as an object of international emulation. Since the end of the cold war, western capitalism has become a guiding and enforceable orthodoxy. This has occasioned a marked shift within international institutions towards a neo-liberal project of economic reform and a pattern of globalization based upon open markets and free trade. During this period, the United States has presented itself as the spearhead of liberal capitalism and as the epitome of Francis Fukuyama's 'end of history'. America's subsequent economic dominance has even led to assertions that it was capitalist consumerism rather than political democracy which was responsible for the collapse of communism.[64]

The United States' vindication of capitalism, however, has not been translated into an unqualified affirmation of the virtues, or even the reality, of fair and legal competition. On the contrary, 'it is remarkable how remote much of the world's largest economy has become from free market Darwinism'.[65] The efficiency and success of corporate capitalism is contested on the grounds of its own criteria and principles. Far from demonstrating the integrity of free markets, open competition, and entrepreneurial risk, America's corporate structures are criticized for diminishing competition, dispersing responsibility, acting unethically, and transferring risks to the taxpayer in the form of public guarantees, government subsidies, tax breaks, and emergency bail outs. Complaints are also levelled against corporations for the structure and standards of their internal governance. The combination of concentrated management and widely dispersed shareholding generates extensive opportunities for the abuse of financial and commercial power. The interdependency of managers, directors, auditors, and consultants have created institutional structures that are accused not only of failing to provide transparency and accountability, but of prejudicing the interests of investors and even the value of the enterprises themselves. These systemic flaws lead some analysts to conclude that the formal arrangements of private ownership in the corporate sector do not correspond to the operational realities of their actual conduct. In effect, it can be claimed that capitalism at this advanced level is distinguished by the absence of effective ownership.[66]

Criticism is also directed against the way corporations seek to break down the distinction between private and public sectors. Whether it is through lobbying and campaign contributions, or the creation of government–industry networks of cooperation, or the force of corporations' economic and social position, it is commonly alleged that government has been systematically penetrated by corporate interests. The resultant symbiosis has been described as 'crony capitalism' because of the way informal connections can effectively subvert open market formalities.

[64] Gary Cross, *An All-Consuming Century: Why Commercialism Won in Modern America* (New York: Columbia University Press, 2000), chs. 1, 5, 6.
[65] John Plender, 'America, Land of the Not-So-Free Market', *Financial Times*, 25 July 2003.
[66] Robert Monks and Allen Sykes, 'Capitalism without Owners', Centre for the Study of Financial Innovation (London: Central Books, 2002).

The administration of President George W. Bush in particular has been accused of establishing a 'cash-and-carry model' of market–state relations, 'where government has served less and less as a brake on corporate behavior and more and more as its auxiliary'.[67] Another term regularly employed during the Bush administration has been the 'good-old-boy network'. To Michael Lind, this did not represent an 'abuse of traditional southern capitalism; it *was* traditional southern capitalism'.[68] During this period, it was claimed that business and government had become indistinguishable from one another. Robert Reich, for example, complained in 2001 that the corporate sector was not even encountering resistance from government: 'There's no longer any countervailing power in Washington. Business is in complete control of the machinery of government.... It's payback time, and every industry and trade association is busily cashing in'.[69]

To critics like Nader, these dynamics are structural in nature rather than the symptoms of a particular administration. As a consequence, they cannot be classified as abuses of the system because the system itself is said to constitute an abuse of the public interest which is essentially reconstructed into an extension of corporate interests. Nader employs the more systemic term of 'corporate socialism' to depict the foundational dependency of American capitalism upon the protective embrace of government. According to Nader, 'corporate socialism' describes the way that the 'privatization of profit and the socialisation of risks and misconduct is displacing capitalist canons'. He continues:

> This condition prevents an adaptable capitalism, served by equal justice under the law, from delivering higher standards of living and enlarging its absorptive capacity for broader community and environmental values. Civic and political movements must call for a decent separation of corporation and the state.[70]

The social penetration and economic power of corporations is a familiar theme to those who regard them as the defining feature of modern capitalism. They are seen to reflect, reinforce, and extend the logic of capitalist priorities into the value structures and even the psychological states of individuals. In the same way that corporations can epitomize the market drives of profit and share value maximization, so it can be alleged that they are compelled to commercialize as many components as possible of the private sphere. It is the corporations' attachment to their own self-interest and to overcoming any limits to their growth that leads to criticism of their ethical standards and even to speculation over whether they possess principled criteria by which to operate as a responsible social institution. Joel Bakan concludes they do not. On the contrary, he claims that corporations

---

[67] Molly Ivins and Lou Dubose, *Bushwhacked: Life in George W. Bush's America* (London: Allen & Busby, 2004), pp. xiii, 16.

[68] Michael Lind, 'The Texas Nexus', *Prospect*, April 2003.

[69] Robert B. Reich, 'Corporate Power in Overdrive', *New York Times*, 18 March 2001; see also Common Cause, 'Just Watch' campaign (http://www.commoncause.org/justwatch/default.cfm) and Public Citizen's monitoring of the Bush administration's relationships with corporate donors, http://www.whitehouseforsale.org/.

[70] Ralph Nader, 'Corporate Socialism', *Washington Post*, 18 July 2002.

strive for positions of unaccountability and, in doing so, have a characteristic 'penchant for breaking legal rules'.[71] To Bakan, such an outcome is embedded within the obsessive logic and institutional culture of corporations. 'The corporation, after all, is deliberately designed to be a psychopath: purely self-interested, incapable of concern for others, amoral, and without a conscience—in a word, inhuman'.[72]

The relationship between freedom, the market, equality, democracy, morality, progress, and the social order is a problematic one. The concept of the 'invisible hand' offers a primarily utilitarian justification of the free market but it resolves neither the issue of capitalism's moral legitimacy nor the moral foundation of a state based upon market principles. It is possible that the market, and the economic institutions created by the market, generate an aggregate public good which is entirely separate from any consciously motivated objectives of individual participants drawn from their private moral senses. On the other hand, if this rationale is extended too far it can transform the concept of liberty into a wholly instrumental value rather than an intrinsically moral principle in its own right.[73] The principle of equality can also come under strain when the distribution of wealth and rewards within a capitalist society is taken into account. Just as the disparities in income tend to rise in periods of market deregulation and economic growth, so the rationales of material progress, productive efficiency, and free trade tend to be positioned in support of the classic liberal proposition of equality as the equal right to become unequal.

American capitalism in particular has a reputation of vigorous market discipline in which inequalities become synonymous with freedom of movement, social mobility, and a responsive social order based upon talents and skills. A competitive society is portrayed as one that allows some to rise and others to fall in line with economic merit and individual application. As Bill Emmott makes clear, the fundamental value assigned to economic liberty remains a strong feature not just of American capitalism but also of America's own sense of social identity. Emmott notes that 'America's great peculiarity is its relative lack of concern about the ills of what critics call "unregulated market capitalism" and fans just call "capitalism"'.[74] In American society, the market is seen as an intrinsically benevolent force. It is true that the United States is similar to many other modern economies in that trade unions press for improved pay and conditions, and that pressure is brought to bear on private enterprise by a regime of regulations and monitoring requirements. But despite these shared characteristics,

---

[71] Joel Bakan, *The Corporation: The Pathological Pursuit of Profit and Power* (London: Constable & Robinson, 2004), p. 58.

[72] Ibid., p. 134.

[73] See Norman Barry, 'The New Liberalism', *British Journal of Political Science*, vol. 13, no. 1 (January 1983), pp. 93–123; Stephen L. Newman, *Liberalism at Wits' End: The Libertarian Revolt against the Modern State* (Ithaca, NY: Cornell University Press, 1984), ch. 6.

[74] Bill Emmott, *20:21 Vision: The Lessons of the 20th Century for the 21st* (London: Penguin, 2004), p. 39.

the United States remains significantly different to its economic contemporaries in the cultural adherence it maintains to the principles and rigours of capitalism:

Entrepreneurs can go bankrupt with little or no stigma, companies can hire people this year and fire some of them next year when they realize that they have made a mistake. The result is an extraordinary capacity for innovation and reinvention, for the pursuing of new opportunities and new fortunes. That has long been an American advantage relative to other rich countries.[75]

It is the 'tolerance of capitalism's harshness' that represents one of the key factors that has not only 'made America the exceptional economy that it has been for the past century' but has allowed the United States to develop an 'exceptional character' that is 'vital to America's self-image'.[76]

The perception of capitalism in the United States is, therefore, a mixed one. America's particular brand of capitalism can rationalize extensive material wealth and technological innovation, whilst also offering a conception of social justice and a foundational defence of liberty within an economic sphere of competitive and possessive individualism. At the same time, it can provide a legitimizing device for gross inequality and static social structures. It can also facilitate the usage of corporate power to subvert both the ideal of a citizen-based democracy and the prospect of a conscious formulation of the public interest. Corporate behaviour can arouse suspicion that capitalism's balances are not as self-regulating and collectively beneficial as they are often purported to be. Political pressure is periodically mounted against 'special interests' that are accused of abusing their economic position and corrupting the political process. At a more fundamental level, capitalism can be criticized for failing to satisfy its own criteria of legitimacy. Whether it is the limitations, or 'imperfections', of the market in facilitating choice and efficiency—or the lack of any necessary connection between economic growth and the incidence of more broad-based societal and moral benefits—or the way that constant organizational restructurings and delayerings both generate and conceal new forms of inequality, the American economic system can be said to risk evolving 'in many different ways toward a capitalism with an inhuman face'.[77]

Nevertheless, in the main, the political economy of the capitalism system remains fundamentally unchallenged. Just as American history and identity are tied to the primitive epics of free enterprise, so too many American values have been assimilated within capitalism for it to be subjected to sustained cultural indictment. Even in the depth of the crisis over corporate corruption in 2002, President Bush was able to categorize the problem as one of egregious dishonesty on the part of individuals. In signing into law a hastily constructed reform package designed to restore confidence to the markets, he reaffirmed the ethos of 'honest

---

[75] Emmott, *20:21 Vision*, p. 40.   [76] Ibid., pp. 45–6.

[77] Frederic L. Pryor, *The Future of U.S. Capitalism* (Cambridge: Cambridge University Press, 2002), p. 367; see also Benjamin M. Friedman, *The Moral Consequences of Economic Growth* (New York: Knopf, 2005); Richard Sennett, *The Culture of the New Capitalism* (New Haven, CT: Yale University Press, 2006).

enterprise'.[78] Such a virtue he said lay at the heart of a 'great economic system that provides opportunity to all' and which constitutes 'a strength of our country, and a model for the world'.[79] Such an episode revealed the capacity of capitalism in providing the interpretative framework for its own critique and for its own resolution to a defined problem. It is a capacity which, as Chapter 11 will demonstrate, has other applications.

[78] President's remarks upon signing the Corporate Corruption Bill, 30 July 2002, http://www.whitehouse.gov/news/releases/2002/07/20020730.html.
[79] Ibid.

11

Pluralism

FOUNDATIONAL THEMES

Americans have an abiding fascination with the relationships between the one and the many. The Great Seal of the republic features an eagle bearing the legend 'e pluribus unum' ('out of many, one'). The dominant theme is that of unity coexisting with multiplicity—the single shield fusing thirteen columns within a single restraining bar; the solitary eagle grasping thirteen arrows in one of its talons; the pyramid of thirteen levels. The shield was designed to give symbolic representation to the idea of a federal polity in which a union of discrete states could simultaneously operate within their own respective spheres of sovereignty. The precise nature of the relationship between the federal government and the states was a matter of conjecture and has remained a perennial source of competing interpretations. Nevertheless, the controlling conception of the federal union is one of a generalized aggregate whose dynamics allow for reciprocal restraint and collective structure.

The meaning and usage of pluralism is suggestive of the same fusion of opposites that is redolent of the tensions and balances of federalism. The capitalist ethos of market competition and the price mechanism is also strongly evident in the working premises of pluralism which place great weight upon the interaction of diverse political forces and the collective benefit of their cumulative activities. In effect, pluralism is a view of politics that is based upon two fundamental elements. First, it is seen to be a direct derivative of America's evident freedom of political expression and association. Second, it is drawn from the perceived presence of a bounded entity that not only accommodates the multiplicity of political actions but is in turn served by the underlying unity of their attachment to the marketplace. As a result, pluralism carries the suggestion of an inversion of the Great Seal's motto 'out of one, many'.

Pluralism incorporates the principle of democracy through its recognition that the only legitimate source of sovereignty is located in the people. Given the segmentation of society into a profusion of groups, it is not accurate, necessary, or desirable to invest the mantle of popular sovereignty in any particular governing authority. No one government or one centre of government can ever claim rightfully to possess an unequivocal and unified mandate from the people. It can only vouch for a particular set of minorities whose group interests coincide with the policy priorities of the government, or at least the governing institutions in question. Because the constitutional structure is itself fragmented into a schema of checks and balances with multiple veto points, the group nature of politics means that democratic governance is necessarily one of a continued process of adjustment. Complex coalition-building within multiple levels and units of government fits in with the constitutional dogmas of fragmented and constrained power. At the same time, this form of open-ended political bargaining is seen as having the functional value of maximizing opportunities for peaceful conflict resolution to the mutual benefit of all the parties to a conflict.

In this respect, pluralism can provide a general characterization of American politics and government. It recognizes the heterogeneity of American society with its multiplicity of social, ethnic, and religious cleavages. It combines the evident profusion of political groups and a citizenry actively engaged in associational life with the clear evidence of a decentralized political system requiring extensive intergroup consultation and negotiation to reach any agreement over policy. As a result, 'decisions are made by endless bargaining; perhaps in no other national political system in the world is bargaining so basic a component of the political process'.[1]

Pluralism is not confined, however, to being merely a descriptive summary of American politics. It also ranks as a comprehensive system of cause and effect which serves to account for all the relationships and processes between society and government. Pluralism, therefore, does not simply propound the existence of interest groups engaged in political decision-making. It assumes the property of a general law of political existence by presupposing that all the constituent elements of political activity are ultimately reducible to the base units of group interests, group motivations, and group demands. Bargaining is not just a distinguishing characteristic. It represents an elemental feature of political accommodation and, as such, is always present in policy-making because all interests are thought to exert a force through the mere fact of their physical presence in the process.

According to Robert Dahl, writing at the high tide of the pluralist model of politics, 'a central guiding thread of American constitutional development has been the evolution of a political system in which all the active and legitimate groups in the population can make themselves heard at some crucial stage in the process of decision'.[2] The end product of such a mechanistic conception of politics is the belief that whatever emerges from the process is, by definition, an expression of an equilibrium acquired through the autonomous dynamics of group interests and group power. Instead of being simply a type of political accommodation, therefore, pluralism in this classical form is tantamount to a sovereign self-regulatory system of political benefit. It offers the same liberal dynamics of a capitalist market in which the competitive behaviour of individual agencies supposedly leads to an automatic equilibrium of economic benefit between parties based upon their market advantages and disadvantages. Moreover, just as capitalism is widely cited as satisfying key criteria of a liberal order, so is pluralism equally suffused with

---

[1] Robert A. Dahl, *A Preface to Democratic Theory* (Chicago, IL: University of Chicago Press, 1956), p. 150.
[2] Ibid., p. 137.

references to its structural and cultural associations with equality of opportunity, market rationality, natural rights, democratic participation, the rule of law, and the conjunction of diversity within consensus.

PLURALIST REALISM AND THE RECONFIGURATION OF DEMOCRACY

The currency of pluralism as an authentic and defensible exposition of American political conduct is based firmly upon the evidence of observation. The sheer profusion of groups and the palpably group-based nature of so much political activity constitutes the perceptual basis for a field of vision that sees groups operating everywhere and accounting for everything. Within this perceptual range, any interest in the United States, no matter how inconsequential or marginal, creates for itself a group formation to protect and advance the position of those whom they represent. In addition, citizens are encouraged not merely to categorize themselves as one of a group or a composite of several groups, but to support the interests of such groups with uninhibited civic enthusiasm. Group formations pursue their interests vigorously. They coalesce with other groups as long as their interests are served by such a strategy. By the same token, groups also compete with one another in the recruitment of members and in the promotion of substantive interests. Moreover, they confront and oppose other groups whose objectives are seen as being detrimental or antagonistic to their own.

Because the regulatory state has become so central to the functional operation of a complex society, groups gravitate towards governing structures in order to maximize their leverage in the matrix of policy-making and programme implementation.[3] Groups gravitate towards government in the firm belief that they have the right to exert whatever force they can command in the furtherance of those interests they represent. Political groups take advantage of the large numbers of entry points in the American system of checks and balances. The cellular compartments of power acknowledge, receive, and give access to minorities as minorities. Operating explicitly as groups and pursuing group interests, they can penetrate deep into government without having to aggregate themselves into a broader party organization in order to maximize their chances of influencing the course and content of political decision-making.

In the same way that interest groups reach deep into government structures, administrative departments and agencies come to rely upon such groups not just for information but for substantive consultation and for the prior clearance of policy proposals. The interdependency relationships lead to indeterminate boundaries between governmental structures and non-governmental organizations.[4] In

---

[3] See James Q. Wilson, *The Politics of Regulation* (New York: Basic Books, 1980).

[4] See David Vogel, *Kindred Strangers: The Uneasy Relationship between Politics and Business in America* (Princeton, NJ: Princeton University Press, 1996), chs. 4, 10.

many respects, units of the executive branch have to operate like interest groups to achieve their objectives within a fragmented system of contending institutional authorities. Such is the profusion of groups and the ferocity of the politics between them that even government departments and agencies must lobby for their programmes and budgets to the extent that they can become indistinguishable from the other group interests.

The group culture of American politics has attracted a great deal of attention and has been the subject of concerted political analysis and interpretation. It has revealed an exotic ecology of group activity with great variations in organizational bases, operational strategies, governing objectives, and sources of influence.[5] Nevertheless, the persuasiveness of the pluralist conception is not confined to the documented bulk of interest group behaviour. Pluralism is also supported by cultural arguments and normative claims. For example, the profusion of groups in American society carries with it a historical legitimacy born out of the early acknowledgements of group activity in the new republic. In the 1830s, Alexis de Tocqueville noted with considerable interest that 'Americans of all ages, all conditions, all minds constantly unite'.[6] These were not limited to 'commercial and industrial associations' but extended to 'a thousand other kinds'[7] of organization. He regarded this impulse to form associations as distinctive feature of American life:

As soon as several of the inhabitants of the United States have conceived a sentiment or an idea that they want to produce in the world, they seek each other out; and when they have found each other, they unite. From then on, they are no longer isolated men, but a power ... that speaks, and to which one listens.[8]

While political action in other countries occasionally involved the formation of associations, Americans 'seem to see in it the sole means they have of acting'[9] within the political realm.

De Tocqueville's political sociology underlined the significance of group behaviour in relation to an emergent culture that had its roots in individual autonomy and local identity, in the rights of free expression and association, and in the need for collective security against distant centres of authority. To de Tocqueville, the extraordinary number and range of associations represented a defining characteristic of a democratic order. They also constituted a form of civil society that to a large extent amounted to a counterweight to a government devoid of the customary constraints of an aristocratic or patrician class. No government as far as de Tocqueville was concerned should have a monopoly of power—or even the

---

[5] See Jeffrey M. Berry, *The Interest Group Society*, 3rd edn (Boston, MA: Addison-Wesley, 1997); Kenneth M. Goldstein, *Interest Groups, Lobbying, and Participation in America* (Cambridge: Cambridge University Press, 1999); Allan J. Cigler, Burdett A. Loomis, and A. B. McKillop (eds.), *Interest Group Politics*, 6th edn (Washington, DC: CQ Press, 2002).

[6] Alexis de Tocqueville, *Democracy in America*, trans., ed., and intro. Harvey C. Mansfield and Delba Winthrop (Chicago, IL: Chicago University Press, 2000), p. 489.

[7] Ibid.   [8] Ibid., p. 492.   [9] Ibid., p. 490.

potential access to such a monopoly. As a consequence, associations had to 'take the place of the powerful particular persons whom equality of conditions'[10] had largely swept aside. De Tocqueville, therefore, looked with favour upon political associations who were 'so to speak the only powerful particular persons who aspire to regulate the state'.[11]

A similar transition from the descriptive to the prescriptive is evident in the work of James Madison. His reputation as the chief architect of the United States Constitution gives his views on the ubiquitous presence of groups in America particular resonance. In *The Federalist Papers*, Madison discusses the bases of political motivation and action. To him, factions were an integral feature of the human condition. The 'latent causes of faction' were 'sown in the nature of man'. As a consequence, mankind had a 'propensity... to fall into mutual animosities'.[12] In the view of Madison and many of the other defenders of the Constitution, political groupings were a sign of republican freedom but, at the same time, they also constituted the chief threat to republican liberty. *The Federalist Papers* are replete with references to the dangers of group formations. Groups were seen as magnifiers of individual appetites and drives for self-advancement at the expense of the collective good, and of the rights and freedoms of others. There was always 'reason to fear that the pestilential breath of faction may poison the fountains of justice'.[13] It was, therefore, deemed essential to guard against 'those violent and oppressive factions which embitter the blessings of liberty'.[14] As a result, the Constitution had first and foremost to be a 'cure for the diseases of faction'.[15]

Even though political groupings represented a direct threat to the integrity of republican government, they were also construed to be part of the solution: 'The regulation of these various and interfering interests forms the principal task of modern legislation and involves the spirit of party and faction in the necessary and ordinary operations of government.'[16] Madison's classic response to the challenge of freely forming groups in a republic was to argue for a system of representative government that would minimize their worst excesses, and enlarge the potential for the mutual control of the groups by each other. By enlarging the republic, Madison believed that it would make American freedom more secure because it would reduce the likelihood of a majority faction ever taking form.

Extend the sphere and you take in a greater variety of parties and interests; you make it less probable that a majority of the whole will have a common motive to invade the rights of other citizens; or if such a common motive exists, it will be more difficult for all who feel it

[10] De Tocqueville, *Democracy in America*, p. 492.

[11] Ibid., p. 499. See also Richard Boyd, *Uncivil Society: The Perils of Pluralism and the Making of Modern Liberalism* (Lanham, MD: Lexington Books, 2004), ch. 6.

[12] James Madison, 'Federalist Paper No. 10', in Alexander Hamilton, James Madison, and John Jay (eds.), *The Federalist Papers*, intro. Clinton Rossiter (New York: Mentor, 1961), p. 79.

[13] Alexander Hamilton, 'Federalist Paper No. 81', in Hamilton, Madison, and Jay (eds.), *The Federalist Papers*, p. 484.

[14] James Madison, 'Federalist Paper No. 45', in Hamilton, Madison, and Jay (eds.), *The Federalist Papers*, p. 288.

[15] Hamilton, 'Federalist Paper No. 81', p. 375.   [16] Madison, 'Federalist Paper No. 10', p. 79.

to discover their own strength and to act in unison with each other. . . . [I]t may be remarked that, where there is a consciousness of unjust or dishonourable purposes, communication is always checked by distrust in proportion to the number whose concurrence is necessary.[17]

The implication of this point is that Madison was prepared to forego the prospect of majority government in preference to a system which would openly rely instead upon minority politics, in a system formally designed to produce a form of reciprocal restraint between active groups. The rationale of fragmentation and mutual limitation was further embedded in the framework of governance by Madison's inclusion of the states and the federal union as integral parts of a generalized conception in institutional pluralism. This underlying objective of security through dissonance has become increasingly evident over time. Dahl, for example, expressly draws out the inferences of Madison's position to demonstrate that Madisonian democracy was counter majoritarian in nature and purpose. In addition to the barriers to, and deferments of, direct democracy, Madison's institutional architecture is also blamed for the active prevention of majority rule at the national level of government.[18]

In this respect, the chief architect of the US Constitution would appear to have given his imprimatur to pluralism and to have established the foundation upon which twentieth-century pluralist politics would emerge in its finished form. 'The pluralist characterization . . . thus has a long and respectable intellectual history'.[19] Beginning with the Founding Fathers and 'carried into effect by the provision of the document they produced, it is little wonder that this image should have such ideological power by now, or that it should be effective in shaping the American political style'.[20] Even though factions were seen as a danger to the republic, Madison's view was that their irrepressible energies could be channelled into a form of competitive interplay that would generate a pattern of reciprocal control.

Analysts like de Tocqueville and Madison laid the foundations for the full development of a pluralist conception of politics that became closely associated with the figures of Arthur Bentley, David Truman, and Robert Dahl in the twentieth century. 'Classical pluralism' systematizes the role and status of groups within the polity. Within this scheme of thought, groups become central to the structure and operation of the political system. More significantly, they are taken to be the sole and exclusive constituent of political activity and explanation. Under this rubric, society is defined as nothing other than a collection of distinct, yet interrelated and interacting parts. The constituent units amount to an amalgam of interests. Interests may compete and conflict with one another. They may, on the other hand, simply transcend one another. But together, they have a cultural identity

---

[17] Ibid., p. 83.

[18] Dahl, *A Preface to Democratic Theory*; Robert A. Dahl, *How Democratic is the American Constitution?* (New Haven, CT: Yale University Press, 2002).

[19] Kenneth M. Dolbeare and Murray J. Edelman, *American Politics: Policies, Power and Change*, 2nd edn (Lexington, MA: D. C. Heath, 1974), p. 257.

[20] Ibid.

and share an agreed form of social conduct through which they achieve a state of coexistence. Within this framework, the criterion of democracy is satisfied less by direct participation and voluntary action, and more by the presence of multiple fragmented interests together with the political equilibrium that is taken to be the outcome of group interplay.

To the pluralist, these social units do not add up to an integrated and corporate whole. Nor do they accumulate to form a stratified social and political hierarchy. The value of such units lies in their provision of social and political diversity that prevents any aggregation of interests developing into a permanent form of class dominion. The pluralist conception of society, therefore, sees a vast profusion of group interests represented and embodied by political groups, none of which has the power to prevail over the rest. Because they are obliged to accommodate one another by extensive negotiations, it ensures that no one centre of sovereign power can emerge.[21] It is conceded that some groups will have better opportunities, resources, and organizational skills with which to compete for political commodities. Nevertheless, it is also the case that other less advantaged groups will have alternative sources of political leverage (e.g. voting strength, publicity, withdrawal of labour, or political support) that they can deploy against their notional superiors. The result is claimed to be an open competition for government that is fairer than other systems of rule. It is also claimed to constitute a highly responsive form of government, in which power is never static, but always remains at the mercy of ceaseless bargaining and of constantly changing coalitions of attentive minorities.

Such a view of the nature and origins of political life exerts substantial pressure on the integrity of democratic terms like majority rule, popular consent, public interest, and electoral mandate. Majority rule becomes a misnomer for rule by minorities, while popular consent is converted into either a nonsensical myth or a basic agreement on the rules of engagement for group conflict. The public interest loses much of its meaning because in an environment of competitive group interests it becomes difficult to conceive of a set of overriding interests that would attract the support of the entire public.[22] As for an electoral mandate, the pluralist vision sees politics as a permanent election in which interests are continually vying with one another in order to maximize their resources in the political marketplace.

---

[21] See Arthur F. Bentley, *The Process of Government* (Cambridge, MA: Belknap Press, 1908); David Truman, *The Governmental Process* (New York: Knopf, 1951); Robert A. Dahl, *Who Governs?* (New Haven, CT: Yale University Press, 1961); Nelson W. Polsby, *Community Power and Political Theory* (New Haven, CT: Yale University Press, 1963). For a commentary on the background and development of pluralism, see Gregor McLennan, *Marxism, Pluralism and Beyond: Classic Debates and New Departures* (Oxford: Polity Press, 1989), pp. 17–56.

[22] This view is challenged by Brian Barry, in particular, who asserts the necessary existence of at least some interests which are common to all members of society. See Brian Barry, *Political Argument* (London: Routledge & Kegan Paul, 1965), chs. 11, 12; Theodore Lowi, *The End of Liberalism: Ideology, Policy and the Crisis of Public Authority* (New York: W. W. Norton, 1969).

It is the notion of the democratic state itself, however, which is the heaviest casualty. The pluralist emphasis upon group interests as the engine room of politics tends to transform the government's role into one of being merely a broker between conflicting group demands. In the pluralist framework, government institutions become the medium through which group interests negotiate and arrive at accommodations with one another. The government is the arena within which the marketplace is situated. As such, the government embodies the 'rules of the game'. It regulates the marketplace in order that it should retain and even extend its efficiency in the exchange of power and influence. As a result, the state is not only fragmented in terms of its structure and sovereignty, but it possesses no authority independent of the groups that inhabit its interior. The state becomes little more than a facilitative device, i.e. a neutral balance of social demands. The only legitimate source of sovereignty remains with the people, but in the pluralist vision, the people can never translate that sovereignty into government because they are congenitally fragmented into so many minorities that even a unified majority, acting on behalf of the people, would be impossible to form. As a result, sovereignty which rests, however notionally, with 'the people' is never conclusively mobilized or channelled into direct or positive representational authority at the governmental level. Democracy in thus transmuted into a minimalist and procedural construct that echoes Joseph Schumpeter's definition of the democratic method as that 'institutional arrangement for arriving at political decisions in which individuals acquire the power to decide by means of a competitive struggle for the people's vote'.[23]

THE LIMITS OF PLURALISM

In the same way that pluralism is defended on empirical, cultural, and normative grounds, it is criticized on precisely the same basis. Listed below is a selection of the major critiques of pluralism:

Critique 1: Historical Overgeneralization

Critics complain that James Madison's statements on the subject of groups have been misunderstood by pluralists. His remarks are said to amount only to a set of partial recommendations and were not part of some comprehensive theory of political activity, or a description of an iron law of political experience. Accordingly, it is misleading to try and substantiate modern conclusions with false notions of the Founders' original intentions. It has been pointed out that

---

[23] Joseph Schumpeter, *Capitalism, Socialism and Democracy* (New York: Harper, 1947), p. 269. See also Robert A. Dahl, *Polyarchy: Participation and Opposition* (New Haven, CT: Yale University Press, 1971).

Madison's comments about groups never amounted to a generalized and comprehensive theory about the character of American politics. In particular, it is claimed
that the reputed 'father of American pluralism' never believed that the interplay
of groups would lead to an automatic and benevolent state of equilibrium. On
the contrary, it is thought that Madison believed and hoped that groups would
neutralize one another and allow enlightened and rational statesmen to fill the
breach of public leadership.[24]

Critique 2: Group Inequality

Despite the fact that pluralism is reliant upon a market-based conception of
politics, it does not take into account the empirical repercussions drawn from the
evident lack of equity between groups in terms of access, information, resources,
and competitive capacity. Pluralists are criticized for engaging in a tautology where
a balanced output is inferred from a balanced input, which is in turn attributed
from the defined characteristics of the outcome. Pluralism conceals the fact that
the inequalities existing in society are not plural in nature but can conceivably
accumulate into one unified and overarching inequality. As a consequence, there
can be no assumption of a natural harmony of interests and a balance of social
power. Pluralism is reliant upon the presence of countervailing forces but these
cannot always be assumed to exist on a sufficient scale to ensure that powerful
interests are constrained.

Critique 3: Privileging Stability and Passivity

Pluralists are accused of overexaggerating the capacity of intergroup competition
to produce a spontaneous equilibrium and a self-regulating form of social justice. In advocating the priority of procedural justice over more abstract notions
of substantive justice,[25] a pluralist outlook tends to foreclose the possibility of
politics becoming an arena for equity, emancipation, and progress. By postulating
the self-sufficiency of the interplay between groups, pluralists tend to preclude the
need for broad social movements in politics. In doing so, they are said to deter
political participation and to rationalize political passivity, voter apathy, and civic
indifference. It can be argued that pluralist logic equates citizen inactivity and
silence with consent and satisfaction, rather than with alienation and exclusion.
Pluralism neither explains nor envisages the need for substantial social change.
This is because pluralism essentially equates social stability and political effectiveness with the status quo.

[24] See Gordon S. Wood, 'Democracy and the Constitution', in Robert A. Goldwin and William
A. Schambra (eds.), *How Democratic is the Constitution?* (Washington, DC: American Enterprise
Institute, 1980), pp. 11–12.
[25] See Robert Dahl, *Democracy and Its Critics* (New Haven, CT: Yale University Press, 1989),
pp. 164–7, 303–12.

Critique 4: Obstructing Majority Rule

The fundamental axiom of pluralism is that '[i]nstead of a single center of sovereign power, there must be multiple centers of power, none of which can be wholly sovereign'.[26] Pluralism's dependence upon a decentralized and organizationally complex structure of self-governing groups arguably has the effect of diminishing governmental responsiveness to majority demands and social needs in favour of an absent sovereignty and a notion of the public interest that is a derivative of nothing more than perpetual group conflict. In legitimizing interest group activity in politics, pluralism undermines the organizational integrity of party organizations, retards the formation of stable majorities, and reduces the prospect of majority rule and, therefore, of self rule. Because pluralism encourages the proliferation of groups within government, it is said to create an excess of demand, a 'hyperpluralism' of congested group behavior, and a gridlock of government colloquially referred to as 'demosclerosis'.[27]

Critique 5: Social Fragmentation

In endorsing the active presence of minorities as the basis of political life, pluralists are said to promote a condition of mutual animosity between groups and, in the process, to disincentivize the formation of a governing majority. Intemperate group behaviour is replicated in institutional stasis leading to judicial intervention not merely to establish a common policy framework in many contentious areas but also to bring groups into some form of reasoned debate and political engagement. Left to themselves, group identities and attachments can fester into polarized attitudes and traditions that can be oppressive in content and even inconsistent with democratic values.[28]

Critique 6: Contextual Myopia

Pluralism underestimates the role of the state as an autonomous entity and as an active agency in the exercise of power. Pluralism is also criticized for ignoring the role of dominant ideologies, corporate realities, structural constraints, objective interests, and social consciousness in conditioning the nature of the issues requiring decisions.[29] The empirical claims made on behalf of pluralism can be disputed on the grounds either of possessing a highly selective evidence base, or of

[26] Robert A. Dahl, *Pluralist Democracy in the United States: Conflict and Consent* (Chicago, IL: Rand McNally, 1967), p. 67.

[27] See Jonathan Rauch, *Government's End: Why Washington Stopped Working* (New York: Public Affairs, 1996), chs. 3, 6, 8.

[28] See Cass R. Sunstein, *Designing Democracy: What Constitutions Do* (New York: Oxford University Press, 2001), chs. 1, 3.

[29] See E. E. Schattschneider, *The Semisovereign People: A Realist's View of Democracy in America* (Hinsdale, IL: Dryden 1972); Lowi, *The End of Liberalism*; Peter Bachrach and Morton S. Baratz, 'Two

adopting a willfully superficial outlook that is satisfied with surface appearances to the detriment of substantive and structural inquiry.

Critique 7: The Devaluation of Democracy

By redefining democracy to fit the stark 'realities' of a mass society, it is alleged that pluralism emasculates democracy of its ideals, aspirations, and purposive nature. The ethical and moral content of 'classical democracy' or civic republicanism is said to be subordinated by pluralists who give priority to an instrumental conception of social management and a largely value-free conception of democracy,[30] i.e. one in which it becomes merely a governmental process for arriving at decisions with a minimum of popular participation. Pluralism can be construed as having replaced the principle of equality between individuals by a posited equilibrium between organizations. In giving emphasis both to the latter and to the prevention of democracy being co-opted by majoritarian force, it is claimed that pluralists have overlooked how these precautions have made American democracy less egalitarian than other western democracies.

The chief complaint made by Marxist and elite theorists is that pluralists have simply misunderstood their own evidence. They are accused of being so distracted by the phenomenology of groups that they have become unable to discern the structural forces operating at depth within society. The argument here is that pluralist realism, which roots politics and political arrangements within a matrix of social forces, fails to extend the analysis to the more controversial areas of class and systemic inequality. This criticism centres upon the adopted unit of analysis. In locating their reductionism in groups rather than in broader and more cohesive entities, pluralists overlook the political biases that frame agendas, shape decisions, and dispose the 'rules of the game' towards selective ends. In possessing what critics describe as a one-dimensional view of power, pluralists fail to perceive that the state has not so much a passive or neutral presence as a highly active and coercive role in promoting the interests of a ruling class or dominant elite. Worse still, pluralists are alleged to cloak those in positions of power inside a palpably unequal society with an authority based upon a distortion of democratic terminology and meaning.[31]

faces of power', *American Political Science Review*, vol. 56, no. 4 (December 1962), pp. 947–52; W. A. Kelso, *American Democratic Theory* (Westport, CT: Greenwood, 1978); Charles Lindblom, *Politics and Markets* (New York: Basic Books, 1977).

[30] See Jack L. Walker, 'A Critique of the Elitist Theory of Democracy', *American Political Science Review*, vol. 60 (June 1966), pp. 285–95.

[31] See C. Wright Mills, *The Power Elite* (Oxford: Oxford University Press, 1956), chs. 1, 12, 13; John F. Manley, 'Neo-Pluralism: A Class Analysis of Pluralism I and Pluralism II', *American Political Science Review*, vol. 77, no. 2 (June 1983), pp. 368–83; John F. Manley, 'Class and Pluralism in America: The Constitution Reconsidered', in John F. Manley and Kenneth W. Dolbeare (eds.), *The Case against the Constitution* (New York: M. E. Sharpe, 1987), pp. 101–19; Thomas R. Dye and Harmon Zeigler, *The Irony of Democracy: An Uncommon Introduction to American Politics*, 13th edn (Belmont,

Pluralists generally respond to such critiques by claiming that their position is not falsifiable on the evidence available. Moreover, the assertions of a cohesive, conscious, and pre-eminent class or elite are unproven. Their claims to empirical rigour in studying how decisions are made and which actors have a discernible presence lead them to reiterate their view that the political universe is tightly packed with interacting groups. Pluralists point to the absence of class-based movements or parties in the American system. They also claim that the lack of substantive change in a democratic society is necessarily related to a dearth of discernible demand for it. Just as difficulties in the objective interests of separate parties to an issue can only be demonstrated by actual disagreements, so a convergence in objective interests is only revealed through the manifest integration of groups to a level where they lose their separate identities and distinctive agendas.

In response to the complaints over their democratic credentials, pluralists underline that their conception of political dynamics is based upon a bottom-up approach in which political forms and processes are driven by social forces. The argument is also made that theirs is the only feasible expression of democratic rule which is available in a large, complex, and interdependent society. It is said that pluralism simply extends liberal democracy from the scale of the individual to that of the group and that it optimizes America's democratic norms in an age of large organizations and bureaucratic centralism.[32] Competition among social groups for advantages in the fragmented system of government helps to maintain the dispersal of power in the government and, thereby, perpetuates the competitiveness for positions and benefits. A government of multiple and interacting minorities is seen by pluralists as providing not only an enhanced form of representation but also an assured means of preserving the democratic character of the regime.

The issue of campaign finance reform illustrates the pluralist argument against an external frame of reference for democratic authenticity. Campaign contributions are manifestly unequal and lead to public perceptions that they buy influence within government commensurate with the size of financial support. Notwithstanding the evident disparity in different types of contributions, reform has been very difficult to achieve. The robust measures included in the 1974 amendments to the Federal Election Campaign Act (1971) were passed in the wake of the Watergate scandal and created a regime of limits upon political contributions and campaign expenditures. Nevertheless, its impact has been limited. The legislation produced a number of unintended consequences (e.g. the rise of political action committees). Significant sections of the reform were also circumvented in practice. Most significantly, the Supreme Court declared parts of the 1974 reform to be unconstitutional.[33] The Court's opinion echoed pluralist premises, priorities, and prejudices. The limitation of political contributions and campaign expenditures may have been a social good in the abstract but it was fraught not only with the

CA: Wadsworth Publishing, 2006), chs. 1, 4; Michael Parenti, *Democracy for the Few* (Belmont, CA: Wadsworth Publishing, 2001).

[32] For example, see Geraint Parry, *Political Elites* (London: George Allen & Unwin, 1969), p. 125.

[33] *Buckley v. Valeo*, 424 US 1 (1976).

difficulties over how it could be achieved and through what agency, but also with the dangers of tampering with liberties in the pursuit of an arguably impractical objective. Limiting political spending by law was deemed to be denial of free speech and, therefore, an unconstitutional violation of the First Amendment.

In the view of the Court, imposing a ceiling upon personal or independent campaign expenditures 'fails to serve any substantial governmental interest' and represents a restriction that 'heavily burdens core First Amendment expression'.[34] Moreover, just as the First Amendment protects the freedom of association, so it could be construed that the only satisfactory answer to the problem of campaign spending lay in the Madisonian dynamics of 'extend[ing] the sphere' of competing entities:

> The First Amendment denies government the power to determine that spending to promote one's political views is wasteful, excessive, or unwise. In the free society ordained by our Constitution, it is not the government, but the people—individually, as citizens and candidates, and collectively, as associations and political committees—who must retain control over the quantity and range of debate on public issues in a political campaign.[35]

In this decision, the Supreme Court gave an intuitive endorsement to the pluralist presumptions (i) that groups should be seen as interchangeable with individuals in the basic foundations of a democratic polity; and (ii) that by extension the outcomes of elections are legitimate extensions of the self-regulating claims of intergroup mechanics.

The ubiquitous nature of pluralist terms of reference does not mean that pluralism is impervious to all critiques and that its position cannot be amended. Like capitalism, pluralism is renowned for its capacity to adapt to changing conditions and differing arguments. For example, even though the pluralist position provides an effective counter to any hierarchical conception of the public good being exerted through the political system, it is acknowledged by pluralists that this safeguard comes at a considerable price. The main problem is that of aggregating dispersed interests into coalitions that can redress the balance against those interests that are well organized and highly resourced. The separation of political institutions in this respect can create severe difficulties for political parties in acting as coalitional brokers, or in creating centres of effective governance. To Robert Dahl, the rights of citizens to advance their necessarily diversified demands should be given improved guarantees. By the same token, institutions should be made more responsive to the expressed preferences of the citizenry in general and to their efforts in organizing coalitions of distinct interests.[36]

The most significant adaptation of pluralism has probably occurred in its relationship to the evidence supporting the presence of elites in American politics. The central pluralist position is to deny the existence, or at least proof of the existence, of an integrated elite. In order to preserve the integrity of this position, pluralists have adapted their perspective to incorporate the evident disparities of power and influence between those at the senior levels of organizations on the one hand and

---

[34] *Buckley v. Valeo*, 424 US 1, 48 (1976).   [35] Ibid.

[36] See Robert A. Dahl, *The New American Political Disorder: An Essay* (Berkeley, CA: Institute of Governmental Studies Press, 1994).

the general public on the other. Pluralists concede that there are elites: not one or a few elites, but many of them. They head responsive and open-ended organizations in which personnel can rise and fall, ideas can circulate, and opinions can be brought to bear at the top. Each elite, therefore, is a democratic expression of the people and interests within its organization. Instead of taking elites as proof of a horizontal integration of hierarchies, the 'democratic-elitist' or 'polyarchical' position is to see elites in their vertical context of separate and competitive democratic organizations.[37] It is these multiple elites who are said to secure the liberal nature of the regime and to make the potentially dangerous disruption from illiberal mass participation less of a threat to the political equilibrium.[38]

Those who adopt a more sceptical approach to pluralism remain unimpressed. They claim that 'polyarchy' amounts to an inversion of classical democratic theory because the 'masses, not elites, become the potential threat to the system and elites, not masses, become its defender'.[39] Arguably, the conjunction of democracy with elitism strips away any remaining pretence that pluralists may have had towards democracy.

The political passivity of the great majority of the people is not regarded as an element of democratic malfunctioning, but, on the contrary, as a necessary condition for allowing the creative functioning of the elite.... While embracing liberation it rejects, in effect, the major tenet of classical democratic theory—belief and confidence in the people.[40]

Other sceptics point to political pluralism as being benignly mainstream yet opaquely abstract at the same time. The net outcome is said to be one in which the old moorings of local associations and voluntary action have been replaced by a profusion of condoned differences operating impersonally at a distance. From its modern inception at the beginning of the twentieth century, pluralism became 'a way for most Americans to preserve multiple identities by leaving the relationship among them undefined. Turning the art of equivocation into a national ideology was no easy task' but, as Olivier Zunz notes, pluralism became 'the new middle way'.[41] This is because it offered an acceptable understanding of political life at the expense of a reliance upon a highly functional yet studiously ambiguous notion of social reality:

Pluralism has played a significant part in the lives of twentieth-century Americans as a guide, no matter how amorphous, that has allowed us to manage our right to be 'different'. It has been an act of accommodation, born of necessity, with admittedly shallow philosophical roots and limits to its application.[42]

---

[37] See Peter Bachrach, *The Theory of Democratic Elitism* (Boston, MA: Little, Brown, 1967); Robert A. Dahl, *Polyarchy* (New Haven, CT: Yale University Press, 1971).

[38] See Chapter 4 note 73 and Chapter 14 notes 44 and 45.

[39] Bachrach, *The Theory of Democratic Elitism*, pp. 8–9.

[40] Ibid., pp. 32, 94. For a sustained denial that apathy is both inherent and necessary to a stable democratic order, see Carole Pateman, *Participation and Democratic Theory* (Cambridge: Cambridge University Press, 1970).

[41] Olivier Zunz, *Why the American Century?* (Chicago, IL: University of Chicago Press, 2000), p. 134.

[42] Ibid., pp. 134–5.

Even the revised iterations of pluralism remain highly contentious. Pluralism is still seen as being so closely analogous to the traditional objective of liberal equilibrium that its responses are thought to be inadequate either for the collective needs of the public interest or for the particular requirements of constituent minorities.

CULTURAL PLURALISM AND MULTICULTURALISM

The adaptive but also the problematic nature of pluralism is illustrated in the many controversies surrounding multiculturalism which have been prominent in the United States since the 1980s. The term relates to the various measures taken to acknowledge the diverse nature of America's changing patterns of immigration and to give recognition to the social heritage afforded by the presence of Afro-Americans, Native Americans, and other marginalized minorities in the historical development of the United States. Multiculturalism takes many forms and embraces many claims. Its origins are located in the early twentieth century when large-scale immigration led to a renewed concern over the optimum relationship between America's tradition of assimilation and a growing realization that modern America was composed of a plurality of increasingly conscious groupings based upon race, religion, language, ethnicity, culture, and even gender. It was during this period that Horace Kallen popularized the term 'cultural pluralism' to convey the idea of an internal federation of different cultures set within a national context and a common ethos of American values and mutual tolerance. Throughout the twentieth century, this integrative conception of cultural coexistence has been prominent in the examination of the role of social diversity and national pride in the maintenance of civic stability.[43] Cultural pluralism reflects an approach towards difference that incorporates fragmentation and heterogeneity as being analogous to American freedom and American democracy.

An altogether different variant of cultural plurality is one that has now become more closely identified with the generic term of multiculturalism. The emphasis here is on alienation, exclusion, and rejection of assimilation both as a factual condition and a normative principle. In line with this perspective, social existence and cultural redemption can only be secured by discarding the American mainstream either as a model of emulation, or as a defensible—or even a valuable—basis of commonality. The advocates of this form of multiculturalism 'hold that racism, conquest, and empire have so compromised the American nation that its virtue

[43] For example, see Nathan Glazer and Daniel P. Moynihan, *Beyond the Melting Pot: The Negroes, Puerto Ricans, Jews, Italians, and Irish of New York City*, 2nd edn (Cambridge, MA: MIT Press, 1970); Lawrence Fuchs, *The American Kaleidoscope: Race, Ethnicity, and the Civic Culture* (Hanover, NH: Wesleyan University Press, 1990); John Higham, 'Multiculturalism and Universalism: A History and a Critique', *American Quarterly*, vol. 45, no. 10 (June 1993), pp. 195–219; Nathan Glazer, *We Are All Multiculturalists Now* (Cambridge, MA: Harvard University Press, 1997).

or goodness cannot be salvaged'.[44] Gary Gerstle completes the indictment on the fraudulent character of common reference points:

Thus, not only have these multiculturalists denounced assimilationist strategies as simply covers for programs of racial, male, bourgeois, or heterosexist domination, but they have refused to acknowledge that an alternative strategy of belonging would redeem the nation and its civic nationalist promise. They do not believe that their aspirations can be realized as long as they are bound by ties of affection or coercion to the American nation. They want instead to see the American nation exposed, weakened, and even broken up.[45]

Multiculturalism in these hands extends the logic of one-half of the cultural pluralism equation to the point where plurality becomes unbounded by any recognition that the American nation and the cultural entities of America are reconcilable with one another.

Between these two polar expressions of multiculturalism lays a vast hinterland of inquiries, speculations, critiques, paradigms, and devices surrounding the issue of cultural consciousness and its place in the uniform practices and policies of the United States. From its roots in the social and intellectual movements surrounding the civil rights revolution of the 1960s—and proceeding apace through the 1970s and 1980s—the impulse towards underwriting diversity has been evident both in the allowances made to different cultural groupings and in the critical self-examination of institutions in respect to their ethno-racial or cultural biases. Responses have varied from legal protections for cultural minorities to organizational projects designed to raise levels of consciousness over sensitive areas of cultural distinction; and from increased provision of public bilingualism for Spanish-speaking Americans to policy shifts in naturalization procedures, employment practices, educational admissions, and curricula content.

Multicultural activity has been directed not merely towards creating affirmative action programmes or increasing minority representation; multiculturalism has also been instrumental in reflecting what the United States has come to represent to many of its citizens who have suffered from exploitation and exclusion by dominant institutions. Underpinning much of this activity has been a dynamic between a deepening politics of identity and recognition on the one hand and an increasing disposition to challenge the hegemony of an Anglo-American culture based upon white, male, Christian, heterosexual, and middle-class characteristics on the other. It is this challenge to the concept of a dominant culture with claims to universal values and transcendent truths that provides much of the leverage for the notion of a genuinely inclusive society where space exists for minorities to pursue their own conceptions of moral truth and the good life.[46]

---

[44] Gary Gerstle, *American Crucible: Race and Nation in the Twentieth Century* (Princeton, NJ: Princeton University Press, 2001), p. 350.
[45] Ibid.
[46] Ronald Takaki, *A Different Mirror: A History of Multicultural America* (Boston, MA: Back Bay Books, 1993); David Theo Goldberg (ed.), *Multiculturalism: A Critical Reader* (Oxford: Blackwell Publishers, 1995); Glazer, *We Are All Multiculturalists Now*.

Desmond King locates the surge of multicultural expression firmly within American history and in particular the measures taken to impose a single American identity through the selective immigration and educational reforms during the early part of the twentieth century.[47] To King, multiple traditions were always part of American society. The actions taken to marginalize these traditions and the groups associated with them, in conjunction with the historical neglect of alternative traditions and minority experiences, led to a delayed but vigorous reaction against the narrow conception of American authenticity. It is not merely the recognition that the United States is 'composed of groups other than a dominant white-based elite but that those groups' distinctions and diverse traditions were fostered and formed in the very development of the polity and contributed to that polity's development. The two cannot be separated'.[48] Actions and policies that promote multiculturalism, therefore, do not reflect a sudden emergence of diversity but rather an attempt to redefine American democracy and to reformulate the power relationships between the different peoples of the United States.

Many parallels exist between multiculturalism and the operating principles of pluralism. Apologists for pluralism would experience an immediate resonance with Bhikhu Parekh's definition of multiculturalism as something 'best understood neither as a political doctrine with a programmatic content nor a philosophical school with a distinct theory of man's place in the world but as a perspective on or a way of viewing human life'.[49] The claim that individuals are not only 'culturally embedded' and 'live with a culturally structured'[50] world, but that different cultures also benefit from interacting with one another in the same society are observations with which pluralists would find favour. They would also feel familiar with the multiculturalists' view that different cultures coexist with one another and that 'every culture is internally plural and reflects a continuing conversation between its different traditions and strands of thought'.[51] Given the pluralist focus upon differentiation and the collective benefits to be derived from the mutual adjustment between segmented and autonomously guided entities, multiculturalism can be interpreted as a valid extension to pluralism. In assigning value to a multiplicity of constituent elements, assimilative processes, and aggregated harmonies, multiculturalists can appear to subscribe to a pluralist world view of politics.

In the same way that many of the properties ascribed to multiculturalism attract comparisons with pluralism, the critiques of pluralism closely correspond to the complaints that are commonly made in connection to multiculturalism. In some respects, pluralism can be portrayed as an analogue of federalism because it facilitates a form of dispersed autonomy set within central constraints. Initially,

---

[47] Desmond King, *Making Americans: Immigration, Race, and the Origins of the Diverse Democracy* (Cambridge, MA: Harvard University Press, 2000).

[48] Ibid., p. 288.

[49] Bhikhu, Parekh, 'What Is Multiculturalism?', http://www.india-seminar.com/1999/484/484%20parekh.htm.

[50] Ibid.   [51] Ibid.

federalism embraced a strong states' rights ideology which incorporated the ideal of separate development for sectional and regional cultures. Just as pluralism can be said to give a similar priority to the constituent units of a polity, so multiculturalism can be characterized as extending the categories of sub-national existence to race, ethnicity, and gender. In acknowledging and promoting this level of differentiation, multiculturalism becomes more vulnerable to the objection most commonly lodged against pluralism: that of generating a centripetal dynamic under the guise of a rudimentary unity. Because cultural identities are both the unit of analysis and the object of value in multiculturalism, they are said to exert a disintegrative effect upon the general fabric of society. Cultural attachments carry their own truths and disciplines. It is for this reason that they can be seen as encouraging an attitude in which adherents give a higher priority to their own immediate cultural requirements than to the public interest or the common good, or indeed the need to attend to the unifying properties of a general culture. Pluralism is often criticized for its conception of society's welfare as a blind trust in which the aggregate effect of an interplay of self-interested groups generates a benign collective outcome. Multiculturalism generates similar misgivings over the absence of a developed sense of a collective identity or common purpose. In promoting the legitimacy not merely of distinctions but of non-negotiable differences, proponents of multiculturalism stand accused of ignoring, or undermining, the common bases of mediation that allow politics to operate and society to function.[52]

The multiculturalist response to such complaints is to claim that appeals to community or a common interest often represent concealed attempts to reassert or reinforce a dominant cultural hegemony. Multicultural advocates will also point out that the pluralist adherence to the 'rules of the game' is in many ways a medium of convenience that serves the purpose of advancing group interests rather than reflecting authentic bonds of solidarity. It can be argued on this basis that multiculturalism shares with pluralism an indifference, and even a hostility, towards generic social issues, and the need to organize systemic solutions to them.

The multicultural outlook and the programmes that it engenders pose a series of challenging questions relating to fundamental American values such as liberty, equality, democracy, individual rights, and national consciousness. The universalistic assumptions of liberalism, for example, are confronted by multiculturalism's central premise of qualitative differences between sectors of humanity. This friction prompts Charles Taylor to divide liberalism into two types. The first variant prescribes the same rights and degree of recognition to all citizens. The second form is more hospitable to difference and is willing to assess the norms of uniform rights and treatment in the light of the need to ensure forms of cultural survival. Based on the merits of each case, Taylor believes that it will on occasions be necessary for the principles of the first liberalism to defer to the constraints of

---

[52] See Arthur M. Melzer, Jerry Weinberger, and M. Richard Zinman (eds.), *Multiculturalism and American Democracy* (Lawrence, KS: University Press of Kansas, 1998).

the second variant. While Taylor does not prescribe a liberalism that becomes a progression of amorphous adjustment, he does see the need to strike a set of complex balances around the themes of equality of worth.[53]

Another perspective sees multiculturalism as an integral component in a pluralist revival. It is argued that this more contemporary form of pluralism draws upon the philosophical roots and analytical foundations of the early pluralists at the beginning of the twentieth century (e.g. Arthur Bentley, Mary Parker Follett, William James, Harold Laski). Their outlook is contrasted with the narrower construction of diversity that was adopted by pluralists in the post-First World War era. It is claimed that while the latter were inclined to base their understanding of group formation upon the limited dimension of economic self-interest, the former concentrated upon the manifold nature of social difference in its own right.[54] In order to move beyond the self-imposed limitations of either an absolutist conception of sovereignty or a unified social order on the one hand, or a nullity of dissolution and irrationality on the other, early pluralists referred to the diversity of actual group experiences as a way of challenging the centrality of the state in the composition of political theory. The recent renewal in theoretical interest in pluralism is said to reflect both the philosophical grounding of this early form of pluralism and the emergence of a greater appreciation of diverse and discriminating experiences within America's civil society.[55] As David Schlosberg points out, this more contemporary iteration of pluralism gives emphasis not only to the multidimensional politics of subjectivity and difference but also to the importance of communication and inclusion within such a medium.

Recognition, respect, a focus on discourse based in difference, and an acceptance of the ongoing nature of such a process are at the center of contemporary pluralist theorizing and action.... This recent focus on exclusion is certainly a central difference between the targets of earlier and contemporary generations of pluralist thought—the former more focused

---

[53] Charles Taylor, Steven C. Rockefeller, Michael Walzer, and Susan Wolf, with commentary by Amy Guttman, *Multiculturalism and the 'Politics of Recognition': An Essay* (Princeton, NJ: Princeton University Press, 1994); see also Will Kymlicka, *Multicultural Citizenship: A Liberal Theory of Minority Rights* (Oxford: Clarendon Press, 1995).

[54] See David Schlosberg, 'Resurrecting the Pluralist Universe', *Political Research Quarterly*, vol. 51, no. 3 (September 1998), pp. 583–615.

[55] William Connolly, *Identity/Difference: Democratic Negotiations of Political Paradox* (Ithaca, NY: Cornell University Press, 1991); Joshua Cohen, 'Moral Pluralism and Political Consensus', in David Copp, Jean Hampton, and John Roemer (eds.), *The Idea of Democracy* (Cambridge: Cambridge University Press, 1993), pp. 270–91; Avigale Eisenberg, *Reconstructing Political Pluralism* (Albany, NY: SUNY, 1995); James Bohman, 'Public Reason and Cultural Pluralism: Political Liberalism and the Problem of Moral Conflict', *Political Theory*, vol. 23, no. 2 (May 1995), pp. 253–79; Chantal Mouffe, 'Democracy, Power, and the "Political"', in Seyla Benhabib (ed.), *Democracy and Difference: Contesting the Boundaries of the Political* (Princeton, NJ: Princeton University Press, 1996); Chantal Mouffe, 'Deliberative Democracy or Agonistic Pluralism?', *Social Research*, vol. 66, no. 3 (1999): pp. 745–58; David Schlosberg, *Environmental Justice and the New Pluralism* (New York: Oxford University Press, 1999).

on absolutism and singularity in the theoretical realm, the latter squarely responding to exclusions in the political realm and the innovations of political movements in response.[56]

Other analysts take a less sanguine view of multiculturalism. Those whose critiques of American society are informed by class-based analyses tend to regard multiculturalism as another historical distraction from the underlying reality of corporate power and property relationships. It is said to deter the development of class consciousness and the exercise of collective action in pursuit of social justice and sustainable economic development. Some claim that multiculturalism serves corporate interests because it provides a revised form of the classical managerial technique of 'divide and rule' in terms of both production and consumption. As a consequence, equality issues become clouded in themes of liberated diversity and the sovereignty of choice.

Michael Lind posits the view that an 'overclass' with integral connections to corporate interests has actively promoted the cultural hegemony of multiculturalism in order to divide the nation through a mix of racial and sexual preference policies that effectively allow the plutocratic manipulation of free market capitalism to be maintained. To Lind, the top professionals and managers, who dominate both the economy and the main political parties, succeed in monopolizing the benefits of economic growth for themselves through a variety of measures that have had the effect of polarizing not merely the underclass but also the broad mass of the middle classes. Multiculturalism is particularly significant to Lind in this respect because of its capacity to appeal to the Left while at the same time fracturing the very constituency that could confront the power of the 'overclass' with a class-based programme of progressive policies.[57] David Rieff agrees and claims that by the early 1990s business had effectively co-opted multicultural themes for its own use. The business community was, according to Rieff, in the forefront of change by adopting a practical multiculturalism in response to the changing profile of labour resources. Because non-white labour and the role of women would become increasingly important in the twenty-first century labour market, it had become necessary to 'change the workplace in such a way as to make it more hospitable to them'.[58] Others are not convinced and believe that multiculturalism's appeal to business is primarily that of a powerful distraction from the scale of its dominance. Russell Jacoby, for example, asserts that notwithstanding the popular discourse on multiculturalism, 'Americans exist within a single consumer society'.[59] This mainstream culture of production, consumption, and entertainment is so infectiously accessible that multiculturalism's nostrums 'do not offer any real alternative to American life, leisure or business'.[60]

---

[56] Schlosberg, 'Resurrecting the Pluralist Universe', pp. 609–10.

[57] Michael Lind, *The Next American Nation: The New Nationalism and the Fourth American Revolution* (New York: Free Press, 1996).

[58] David Rieff, 'Multiculturalism's Silent Partner: It's the Newly Globalized Consumer Economy, Stupid', *Harper's*, August 1993.

[59] Russell Jacoby, 'The Myth of Multiculturalism', *New Left Review*, vol. 208 (1994), pp. 12–16.

[60] Ibid.

While egalitarian concerns over multiculturalism centre upon the fragmentation of a common frame of reference for social evaluation and action, libertarians
register their anxieties in terms of what they see as the repressive and intolerant
implications of intensive cultural allegiances. For example, Michael Berliner and
Gary Hull of the Ayn Rand Institute brand multiculturalism as the 'new racism'
because of the way it categorizes people by reference to exclusive categories of
collective identity. According to Berliner and Hull, multiculturalism is a call to
'institutionalize separatism' and to create an 'unbridgeable gulf between people,
as though they were different species, with nothing fundamental in common'.[61]
Their view is that multiculturalism is an assault upon the individual:

One cannot espouse multiculturalism and expect students to see each other as individual
human beings. One cannot preach the need for self-esteem while destroying the faculty
which makes it possible: reason. One cannot teach collective identity and expect students
to have self-esteem.[62]

Liberal and conservative traditionalists on the other hand are particularly provoked by what is deemed to be multiculturalism's disregard for the balance
between group affiliation and the value of a single unifying tradition of historical
cohesion and social aspiration. These critics feel that the national culture has been
misrepresented. They do not see it as a corrupting and coercive force. Instead,
they view it as a necessary fixture for social stability and individual aspiration. It is
this national culture of democracy and human rights that provides the licence for
groups to express their separate cultural identities. In this light, cultural pluralism
is dependent upon a central and embracing set of national values that warrant
appreciation and loyalty.

Multiculturalism thus amounts to a reversal of American history because it
overlooks the extent to which the United States has always been an experiment
in multi-ethnic nation building. This is the line adopted by Arthur M. Schlesinger
Jr. in his celebrated polemic against multiculturalism and its dismissal of America
as a transformative culture built upon common political ideals and a shared
identity.[63] Schlesinger acknowledges the Eurocentric properties of the original
melting pot concept adopted by progressives like John Dewey, Israel Zangwill,
and Jane Addams at the beginning of the twentieth century. He also recognizes
the historical and contemporary problems associated with the unresolved consequences of racial division. Nevertheless, he remains emphatic in his belief that
progress can only be achieved by adhering to the creed of a common identity
that can and has assimilated different religions, languages, races, and cultures.
Despite its inequities, the United States is in the main an open and tolerant

---

[61] Michael S. Berliner and Gary Hull, 'Diversity and Multiculturalism: The New Racism',
http://multiculturalism.aynrand.org/diversity.html; see also Walter Williams, ' "Diversity" as Dou-
blespeak for Ideological Conformity', *Capitalism Magazine*, 13 February 2002, http://www.capmag.
com/article.asp?ID=1410.

[62] Berliner and Hull, 'Diversity and Multiculturalism: The New Racism'.

[63] Arthur M. Schlesinger Jr., *The Disuniting of America: Reflections on a Multicultural Society* (New
York: W. W. Norton, 1992).

society in which the 'steady movement of American life has been from exclusion to inclusion'.[64] In Schlesinger's view if the proponents of multiculturalism succeed in inculcating the illusion that membership in one or other ethnic group is the basic American experience,[65] the outcome will be the 'disintegration of the national community, apartheid, Balkanization, tribalization'.[66] These views are shared by others who believe that attention needs to be drawn to the need to enhance a stronger awareness of a common citizenship and of a common aspiration for justice.[67]

The storms over multiculturalism and 'culture wars' have recently shown signs of diminishing in intensity, but this does not detract from the issues they raise over the nature and reach of American pluralism. Multiculturalism can be portrayed as a deviation from pluralism and even a contradiction of its tenets relating to the 'rules of the game' and the principle of negotiated conciliation. However, the themes of multiculturalism reveal a close relationship to pluralism and its accommodation between the general and particular. In fact, the debates over multiculturalism serve to give graphic illustration of the way that social problems are defined in the United States and how the responses to them are framed in terms of a cultural licence for interests and identities to be operationalized as free-standing minorities with particularistic agendas. By the same token, just as pluralist traditions require a double solution in the form of sectional agendas within a common arena of accommodation, so the critics of multiculturalism seek to move the subcultures back into a matrix of mediation and, thereby, into the self-regulating equilibria of traditional pluralist interaction.

THE 'INVISIBLE HAND' AND THE 'PUBLIC INTEREST'

The arguments over pluralism remain heated because of their salience both to the everyday conduct of American politics and to the importance of the condition and authenticity of republican ideals to the self-image of the United States. In American culture, the central values of freedom and democracy are presupposed to exist as achieved objectives by virtue of the generative properties of American conditions. This means that empirical theory has tended to have a higher priority than normative political theory. The questions which are raised come to revolve around issues like the ways in which, and the extent to which, democracy can be said to exist in the United States. The objective is to elucidate what is already there against a background of popular expectation that social reality should, and will, correspond to the democratic ideal in one form or another.

---

[64] Ibid., p. 134.   [65] Ibid., p. 112.   [66] Ibid., p. 118.

[67] See Richard Bernstein, *Dictatorship of Virtue: Multiculturalism and the Battle for America's Future* (New York: Knopf, 1994); David A. Hollinger, *Postethnic America: Beyond Multiculturalism* (New York: Basic Books, 2000).

Even though pluralism has been subjected to strong challenges on analytical, cultural, and normative grounds, it has retained its broad appeal as an explanatory framework. 'Relatively few political and social theorists would accept it in unmodified form today, though many politicians, journalists and others in the mass media still appear to do so'.[68] This is the crux of the matter, for while pluralism may well have been seriously compromised in respect of its own analytical categories, it has retained that rapport with America's prevailing political culture which gave it its early and immediate appeal. Pluralism has an immediate resonance with the mainstream field of political perception in which groups and group behaviour conspicuously occupy the foreground of political activity. While pluralism is far from being the only conception of political conduct, it does succeed in portraying the course of American politics in a way that is not only amenable to American principles, but also readily familiar with the common-sense experience of the outward forms of American political life.

It should be acknowledged that in the era of public concern over levels of social engagement and civic connection in American society, joining groups continues to be seen as a positive contribution to political participation. As was noted in Chapter 2, the volume and variety of associational life remains a distinguishing characteristic of the United States. Moreover, it can be claimed that the membership of groups does not merely serve a strictly political purpose but meets a range of psychological and moral needs on the part of individuals who would otherwise become isolated and alienated. This feature of pluralism is explored by Nancy Rosenblum who persuasively argues that in taking up membership of a group—even a paramilitary hate-organization—individuals are encouraged to make a series of personal adjustments and to cultivate a sense of social trust.[69]

In some respects, it can be said that pluralism is now a more convincing characterization of American politics than it was in the 1950s when many of the pluralist accounts were first written. Blacks, women, environmentalists, and consumers, for example, were not conspicuous participants in the pressure-group politics of the time. Today, they are prominent in the political disputes of the nation. They are part of a new pattern of group politics which, with the decline in the cohesion of American parties, has led to the rise of highly organized citizen action groups involved in 'new politics' themes or 'post-material' issues. These grass-roots organizations move group conflict directly back to the public through their strategy of creating pressure by mobilizing large numbers of people to monitor government action, lobby for reform, and vote in elections on the basis of issue-based activism.[70]

---

[68] David Held, *Political Theory and the Modern State: Essays on State, Power and Democracy* (Oxford: Polity Press, 1989), p. 44.

[69] Nancy L. Rosenblum, *Membership and Morals: Personal Uses of Pluralism in America* (Princeton, NJ: Princeton University Press, 2000).

[70] See Jeffrey M. Berry, *The New Liberalism: The Rising Power of Citizen Groups* (Washington, DC: Brookings Institution Press, 2000); Sylvia Tesh, 'In Support of "Single Issue" Politics', *Political Science Quarterly*, vol. 99, no. 1 (Spring 1984), pp. 27–44.

Citizen-funded organizations that directly contest the power of business interests have arisen.[71] These 'public interest' groups like Public Citizen, Common Cause, The Center for Study of Responsive Law, and the various states-based Public Interest Research Groups[72] claim that their objective is to make the political system more genuinely pluralist in character. They seek to achieve this by encouraging greater citizen participation in industrial policy, by establishing greater public accountability in the corporate sector, and by ensuring a countervailing force to the power of business. Such group formations can be deployed to demonstrate the reactive adaptability of pluralism through their claim to be responding to an imbalance in the matrix of group activities. The mission statement of Common Cause, for example, specifically propounds its commitment to the general welfare in opposition to the particularistic preoccupations of other groups:

Common Cause seeks by sustained and focused lobbying campaigns, grassroots activities, and other efforts ... [t]o ensure that government and the political process serve the general interest, rather than special interests; to curb the excessive influence of money on government decisions and elections ... and to protect the civil rights and civil liberties of all Americans.[73]

While it is true that such groups have often been effective in helping to create sufficient pressure for reform legislation and improved administrative regulations, it is equally true that their self-depiction as public interest groups serves to question the legitimacy of the process within which they are seeking to operate and from which they are trying to benefit. By classifying themselves as groups serving the public interest, they are in effect implying that the public interest cannot be entrusted to the normal operations of the political market. The very fact that public interest groups are required to exist suggests that the common good is not served by the interplay of political groups. The position is further exacerbated by their need to compromise within the bargaining culture of pluralism. This will define any outcome to be at variance with the public interest as outlined in the original negotiating positions of those claiming to promote the interests of all.

In the final analysis, the status of pluralism as a quintessentially American view of politics rests not just upon its intellectual accessibility or its material persuasiveness, but also upon those characteristics which make Americans exceptionally susceptible to its appeal. These would include its ambivalence over the state, the priority given to social and economic forces over political institutions, and the faith in a self-regulatory form of political stability and social justice provided by the interplay of group interests. Pluralism's assumptions of an 'invisible hand' guiding group conflict towards the unintended social benefits of market dynamics have the closest of connotations with the operational principles of capitalism. In a

---

[71] For background on the usage of 'public interest' concepts on reform, see David Vogler, 'The Public Interest Movement and the American Reform Tradition', *Political Science Quarterly*, vol. 95, no. 4 (Winter 1980), pp. 607–27.

[72] See http://uspirg.org/uspirg.asp?id2=2414&id3=USPIRG&.

[73] http://www.commoncause.org/about/mission.htm.

society lacking any strongly supported alternative conceptions of social justice—especially any requiring concerted state action in support of strongly redistributive policies—the pluralist vision, even if only by default, has remained closely associated with mainline American dispositions.

The pluralist solution is . . . a descriptive term for the way in which American government is structured to cope with . . . problems (e.g. majority rule versus minority rights, the problem of concentration of power and the problem of faction) and is, further, a set of value statements expressing the preferred American approach to such issues.[74]

What this preferred approach amounts to and what pluralism justifies is essentially a way of dealing with problems by ignoring them, i.e. by assigning them to the spontaneous benevolence of freely interacting interests. The subsequent licence afforded to group aggression regularly produces a prodigious amount of politics and a strong belief in the efficacy of politics. What it does not provide for in any great measure is the means of conscious change and adaptation. Political problems are broadly defined in terms of group solutions. The corollary is a tendency both to derogate the role of any external and active agency in the process of political accommodation and to diminish the legitimacy of guiding principles such as the public interest and the general welfare. Because pluralism can be said to devalue politics and the public realm, it subjects those advocating serious reform to the gravest of problems.

[74] John F. Manley, *American Government and Public Policy* (New York: Macmillan, 1976), pp. 24–5.

12

Liberalism

FOUNDATIONAL THEMES

Liberals in the United States are known for their hybrid character. They are embedded in the liberal traditions of America but at the same time they are driven towards a critical assessment of the outcomes and ramifications of a purportedly liberal order. By reputation and endeavour, American liberals give full recognition to the precepts of liberalism but seek to extend their logic to the point where they become a set of criteria not only for estimating the integrity and legitimacy of contemporary society, but also for constituting a prospectus for reasoned reform to ensure the continuity of the liberal spirit in altered conditions.

The advocates of liberal reform have to proceed on the basis that American society has many sources of imbalance and injustice, and that a reliance upon notions of self-regulation and market dynamics will not assure the creation of a fair or secure social order. Accordingly, liberals have mainly been distinguished by their advocacy of an interventionist state that will widen opportunity, reduce discrimination, provide protection, advance citizenship, and enhance the capital of public goods. Although the proponents of liberalism can lay claim to the foundations of the modern American state, they have always found themselves in the anomalous position of having to rationalize the central direction and social value of the positive state in a society not only with strong libertarian traditions but also with a cultural scepticism of governmental motives and competence. As a result, American liberals tend to suffer from an unstable, and at times, precarious form of legitimacy.

In making social critique and reform acceptable strategies of American political action, liberals have had to compete with their opponents on the same ground of a pre-existing liberal heritage. Like their adversaries, American liberals have had to contest the meaning of liberty, democracy, and equality in relation to rapid social and economic development. They have had to lay claims to a reconfiguration of rights, a reconstruction of opportunity, and a revision of property prerogatives. In their efforts to advance civil rights, protect civil liberties, improve social conditions, and ameliorate the extremes of an advanced capitalist order, liberals have had to appropriate key American themes and to rework them in line with strategic requirements. By doing so, they have attempted to legitimize increased governmental activity in the name of liberalization and in the cause of the public interest.

The key device has been to recontextualize the central value of liberty within American society. On this basis, it has been possible to advocate the need for the negative conception of freedom to be transmuted into a rationale for a regime of positive freedom that takes into account the de facto substance of opportunities and the capacity to exercise real choices. While this strategy has been very successful in securing a liberal agenda and in justifying the enabling role of the central government, it has also been very context-dependent. As such, the status of the liberal impulse in US politics has been highly susceptible to shifting outlooks both upon the perceived state of American freedom, and upon the current value and utility of the government itself.

Most significantly, those with liberal reform objectives have been, and continue to be, confronted by a potent and highly usable national identity based upon the axioms of nineteenth-century liberalism. In many respects, this classical form of liberalism has a more immediate and tangible association with many of America's core values. The cultural and historical attachment to such principles as rights, consent, and the rule of law were originally established, and subsequently developed, in an era when freedom was primarily associated with the notion of emancipation from traditional structures of authority. Since then, these defining principles have become embedded in America's social identity. They remain a continuing source of historical inspiration. They also constitute an affirming feature of America's self-image as an entirely new nation founded upon a direct and allegedly natural experience of liberation.

Against this background of providential beneficence and a liberal optimism in the faith of reason, the United States has retained an attachment to the claim that its society is an apparently natural and self-sustaining order of freely moving interests. This depiction of social processes has helped to legitimize the principles of both a free-market economy based upon private property and a pluralist system of political competition. So deep has been the conviction in an inevitably liberal society that America's liberal principles and values risk becoming conventional to the point of being axiomatic formalities. They can imply a state of existence that is regarded as objectively authentic and rightly immune to changing circumstances and conditions—even to the point of jeopardizing the very existence of a liberal society.

Those who are termed liberals and that which is known as liberalism in this contemporary context refer to those individuals who, and to that spirit which, regard the classical model of liberalism to be at fault. The notion of a society and an economy functioning as a self-regulating equilibrium is seen as complacent, myopic, and conservative in effect. Modern American liberals believe that traditional American values and procedures are sound. Nevertheless, it is claimed that the pervasive nature of classical liberalism's comforting ethos can often conceal the effects of vested interests and atrophied thought. The integrity of liberal values is seen to be constantly at risk through the effects of liberalism's own social orthodoxy. The identified danger is one of a damaging state of public disillusionment in which liberal dogmas give legitimacy to social conditions that are evidently at variance with the spirit and understanding of the original foundation of American liberty.

Liberal reform comes from the impulse to dissent from the inequities of the political and social order. To be more precise, the reformist spirit emanates from a reaction to the aggregations of privilege, power, and wealth, to the limits placed upon individual opportunities and to the racial, ethnic, regional, and economic divisions that afflict society. Modern liberals are reformers who believe that conventional American thought on capitalism and pluralism serves to deny the critical and emancipatory roots of old liberalism and to prevent the adaptation of liberal principles to the changed conditions of modern society. Liberal reformers do not seek the repudiation of American values as much as their full realization. According to this perspective, contemporary capitalist–pluralist society is seen as failing to live up to its avowed values of freedom, opportunity, democracy, progress, and equality. It is even seen to be directly militating against such objectives by imposing a closed order of vested interests and explanations upon a rapidly receding open society.

Furthermore, it is claimed that this traditional liberal society cannot transcend its own limitations without the external stimulus, or conscious agency, of governmental direction. The autonomous processes of capitalism and pluralism cannot generate of their own accord the necessarily strategic perspective by which purposeful change can be planned and achieved. This is not least because the very autonomy of the established economic and political processes is widely regarded to be one of the chief virtues of those self-same processes. Reform liberals believe that the American political system is designed to leave problems in an unresolved state. The pluralist outlook is one which regards democracy as simply a process of conflict management by which the competing demands of group interests produce effective, if arguably amoral, accommodations. These partial solutions amongst private interests are, to reformers, merely superficial measures which reflect the imbalance of power in American society and which serve to perpetuate the spiral of conditions that is responsible for the permanency and depth of America's social problems.

For liberal reformers to acquire political leverage in a pluralist system, they have to criticize either explicitly or implicitly the contemporary state of American freedom. Because the tradition of liberalism is so central to the nation's identity, such an indictment can generate the mobilizing force required for political change. By the same token, to question the current integrity of American freedom carries the risk of creating a disconnection between reform and the nation's foundational principles. The customary method of avoiding this problem is to root the reform impulse in the original materials of the New World (e.g. the spirit of dissenting Protestantism, the inheritance of the Enlightenment, the attachment to natural law and individual rights) and in the cumulative character of America's reactions to successive crises (the War of Independence, the Civil War, economic depressions, the two world wars).[1] However, this technique only ever constitutes a partial and contingent solution to the reformers' persistent problem with substantiating the authenticity of a liberal critique of a self-professed liberal society.

---

[1] For example, see Arthur M. Schlesinger, Jr., *The American as Reformer* (Cambridge, MA: Harvard University Press, 1950).

It is the very proficiency of the liberals' critical faculties and diagnostic skills which throws into relief their plight of being reformers in a society that tends to see itself as already libertarian in character. As reformers rather than radicals, and as realists intent upon avoiding the fate of American socialists, liberals do not step outside the political and economic system, so much as step back from it. They remain in the liberal mainstream through their attachment to civil liberties, reason, individual opportunities, private property, and even pluralist democracy. The drive is to open up the processes of government, to increase participation, to restore the balance in a capitalist economy, and to remove injustices in favour of a more substantial equality. At the same time, liberal reformers are constrained by the need to work within and through the prevailing system, and by the need to contend with the profound equivocation that has traditionally surrounded American dissent and reform. The nature of the liberal predicament is revealingly reflected in the variability of strategies and contingencies used to support the objective of reform in modern American history.

THE POPULIST INSURGENCY

The populist movement that emerged in the 1880s marked the first organized reaction against the transformation of the United States from a rurally based agrarian order to one of an urbanized mass society with large-scale immigration and an exponential growth of corporate power and monopoly capital. The populist position was permeated by the depiction of antagonistic interests and a society increasingly riven by polarized evaluations of American development. Populism marked a new era in which the consequences of an irretrievably industrialized and urbanized society were causing sufficient strain to produce political dissent and protest. It was also generating an intense debate into the meaning, value, and challenges of modernity in the New World. In this context, it was entirely appropriate that the Populists should represent that section of America which had experienced the most severe disruption to its identity and status, i.e. those whose livelihood and living patterns were dependent upon the farms and agricultural communities of the South and the West.[2]

The volatility of land values and the high dependency upon cash crops combined with an intensifying culture of rural indebtedness and credit dependency existed alongside severe natural challenges and the profiteering activities of railroad, banking, and merchant interests. The smouldering discontent that had produced the Farmers' Alliance and a variety of cooperative purchasing and marketing schemes eventually produced a conflagration of dramatic protest that culminated in the formation of the Populist Party in 1892. The new party's

---

[2] See William F. Holmes, 'Populism: In Search of Context', *Agricultural History*, vol. 64 (Fall 1990), pp. 26–58; David B. Griffiths, *Populism in the Western United States, 1890–1900* (Lewiston, NY: Edwin Mellen, 1992).

progress was sweeping in its condemnation of those contemporary conditions which permitted 'the fruits of the toil of millions' to be 'stolen to build up colossal fortunes for a few ... [who] in turn despise the republic and endanger liberty'.[3] The populist programme was equally radical in its proposals. Its solutions were national in character. It proposed that the federal government should nationalize all railroad, telegraph, and telephone systems; seize land held by corporations that are 'in excess of their actual needs'[4]; reduce working hours; establish the unlimited coinage of silver as an anti-inflation measure; and redistribute wealth through the introduction of a graduated income tax.

The Populist Party attracted over a million votes in the presidential election of 1892. This was sufficient to disturb the two main parties. By 1896, the Democrats had co-opted enough of the populist cause to kill off the new party. The Democrats not only endorsed the principle of free silver which had become a panacea to the debt-ridden Populists, but also nominated William Jennings Bryan whose rural background, agrarian rhetoric, and western prejudices were guaranteed to appeal to Populist voters. The Populists endorsed the Democratic platform and promptly disappeared as a political organization. The Democrats succeeded in drawing off the populist sting but, in doing so, alienated much of its working-class urban constituency. This in turn led to a sectional division of the national party system and to a prolonged period of Republican hegemony.[5]

The populist movement illustrates a number of the problems that have conditioned liberal reform in the United States. First, because the populists primarily represented a provincial movement of rural indignation, they encountered great difficulties in enlarging their constituency within the framework of national politics.[6] In their original declaration of 1892, the Populists sought to cultivate a joint rural and urban constituency based upon a conception of labour common to agricultural and industrial workers. This reciprocity, however, was always very difficult to develop without endangering the Populists' natural supporters in the western and southern farmlands. The scale of popular agitation in these areas was in itself attributable to a deep and habitual suspicion of the city. To an indebted farmer, it was the city that symbolized the impersonal forces of corporate capitalism and the depraved character of much of contemporary American society. The sectional nature of the populist movement gave it a distinctive power base and with it a clear programme for reform. But depth was secured at the expense of breadth in a political system that required extensive coalition building and extraordinary

---

[3] 'The Populist Party Platform' (1892), http://www.wwnorton.com/eamerica/media/ch22/resources/documents/populist.htm.

[4] Ibid.

[5] Walter D. Burnham, *Critical Elections and the Mainsprings of American Politics* (New York: W. W. Norton, 1970), chs. 3, 4; Peter H. Argersinger, *Populism and Politics: William Alfred Peffer and the People's Party* (Lexington, KY: University Press of Kentucky, 1974), ch. 8; Peter H. Argersinger, *The Limits of Agrarian Radicalism: Western Populism and American Politics* (Lawrence, KS: University Press of Kansas, 1995).

[6] For the importance of rural isolation as a motivating force in the populist movement, see James Turner, 'Understanding the Populists', *The Journal of American History*, vol. 67, no. 2 (September 1980), pp. 354–73.

majorities to achieve substantial legislative movement at the federal level. In the end, the mutual interests of the agrarian populists and the urban proletariat could not surmount the geographical, cultural, and sectional barriers to their political integration. The Populists could not overcome their suspicion of an urban work-force, which in so many respects represented another facet of precisely that trend towards urban organization and centralization which the Populists resented so much.[7]

The second problem posed by the Populists was the fact that their radicalism was mobilized around a desire to return to a golden age—or at least their con-struction of such an age—when American yeomanry, honest toil, family farms, and agrarian riches were the attributed lifeblood of the republic.[8] For much of the nineteenth century, farmers had been central to America's notion of social and national identity. They were celebrated not only as the source of natural and righteous wealth, but also as the basis of Protestant virtue and American individ-ualism. Despite the apparently progressive content of their programme, therefore, the populist reforms were largely driven by a wish to retreat from modernity. The mobilizing messages of the populist movement were those of regression into an allegedly simpler, more equal, and increasingly virtuous past. While the populist conception of freedom was one of liberation from a new and threatening order, their sense of democracy was governed by the impulse to turn it into an interest-based instrument of social assault and cultural correction.

A final characteristic of the populist movement that is significant in the Amer-ican tradition of liberal reform lay in the manner of its demise. It declined sud-denly in the face of a rapid upturn in the farming economy from 1898 through to the First World War. As farmers experienced an unprecedented period of prosperity, their radicalism turned to an endorsement of group politics. The Populists' strength of radicalism had come from their economic base and the economic foundations of their analysis and reform programme. Their weakness was commensurate to their recovery within the established parameters of the capitalist economy. To a critic of liberalism like Christopher Lasch, the populists were 'incurable individualists who did not see the need for counter-organization against the power of organized wealth'.[9] According to this view, their lack of ide-ological consciousness meant that they failed to understand either their historical opportunity or their social meaning. Ultimately, attempts made by the Populists to accommodate their reforms within the conventional operations of the political process ended with their assimilation into the prevailing priorities of the capitalist economy.[10]

---

[7] See Greg Hall, *Harvest Wobblies: The Industrial Workers of the World and Agricultural Laborers in the American West, 1905–1930* (Corvallis, OR: Oregon State University Press, 2001).

[8] Michael Kazin, *The Populist Persuasion: An American History* (Ithaca, NY: Cornell University Press, 1998), chs. 1, 2.

[9] Christopher Lasch, *The Agony of the American Left* (Harmondsworth, UK: Penguin, 1973), p. 18.

[10] See also Michael Pierce, 'Farmers and the Failure of Populism in Ohio, 1890–1891', *Agricultural History*, vol. 74 (Winter 2000), pp. 58–85; Stephen Kantrowitz, 'Ben Tillman and Hendrix McLane,

Richard Hofstadter concludes that in failing to extend their notions of social conflict into a fully developed framework of irreconcilable class division, the Populists revealed an inner conformity to the tradition of American capitalism. In contrast to historians like Frederick Jackson Turner and John Hicks who regarded populism as another expression of frontier idiosyncracy and pioneering primitivism,[11] Hofstadter placed populism in the universal American mould of entrepreneurial capitalism. While illustrating the difficulties of attempting to secure the reform of a liberal capitalist framework without being absorbed by it, this judgement is possibly too dismissive. The populist movement not only set in motion a reform agenda but also demonstrated the effectiveness of employing the past, with its appeal to traditional virtues, in the service of contemporary critique and a programme dedicated to liberalization.

THE PROGRESSIVE MOVEMENT

The progressive movement became a significant force in American society during the first two decades of the twentieth century. During this time, the United States experienced many of the social and economic strains that were evident in other advanced industrialized countries. The Progressives did not have the same focus or programmatic clarity as the Populists had possessed in the 1890s. On the contrary, the Progressives were representative of an era that was defined by a general ferment of social criticism and political agitation. The manifold nature of complaint and unrest gave the progressive movement a heterogeneous and elusive character. Progressives were normally entangled in a profusion of objectives, motives, and priorities.[12] As a consequence, it is difficult to detect any single strand of progressive thought and action. Because of this very diversity, it is doubtful whether Progressive reformers ever constituted anything as coherent as a political movement. Nevertheless, they did possess a number of distinguishing characteristics.

Progressives were predominantly drawn from the middle classes of small businessmen, independent traders, middle managers, clerical workers, and salaried

Agrarian Rebels: White Manhood, "The Farmers", and the Limits of Southern Populism', *Journal of Southern History*, vol. 66 (August 2000), pp. 497–524.

[11] Everett Walters, 'Populism and Its Significance in American History', in Frank O. Gattell and Allen Weinstein (eds.), *American Themes: Essays in Historiography* (New York: Oxford University Press, 1968), pp. 325–37.

[12] See Peter G. Filene, 'An Obituary for "The Progressive Movement"', *American Quarterly*, vol. 22, no. 1 (1970), pp. 20–34; Arthur S. Link and Richard L. McCormick, *Progressivism* (Arlington Heights, IL: Harlan Davidson, 1983); Steven J. Diner, *A Very Different Age: Americans of the Progressive Era* (New York: Hill & Wang, 1998); John W. Chambers, II, *The Tyranny of Change: America in the Progressive Era, 1890–1920*, 2nd edn (New Brunswick, NJ: Rutgers University Press, 2000); Glenda E. Gilmore (ed.), *Who Were the Progressives?* (New York: Palgrave Macmillan, 2002); Michael McGerr, *A Fierce Discontent: The Rise and Fall of the Progressive Movement* (New York: Oxford University Press, 2005).

professionals.[13] They were mostly orientated to city life and, as such, they were particularly sensitive to those urban ills which were threatening to subvert both the fabric of the new cities and the ideals of the American republic. Progressives were dismayed at the social and cultural disruption produced by the millions of new immigrants who flooded into the cities in record numbers between 1905 and 1914. Progressives were concerned over the 'merger boom' when individual corporations began to dwarf not merely their competitors but also the financial structure and political integrity of state governments. Progressives were further alarmed by the raw power and corrupt practices of the citywide political machines. These were highly proficient at consolidating the new sources of political power in the vote-ridden slums and at exploiting their relationships with business interests to produce unprecedented levels of corruptly procured political funds.

These concerns and anxieties bred a belief amongst the Progressives that the capitalist order was a highly productive machine, but one that was in a dangerous condition. Progressives were affronted just as much by the squalor, vice, disease, and crime of the slums as by the inflated wealth of the industrial barons and speculators. But because the middle-class Progressives felt morally obliged and materially able to do something to correct the degeneration, they were prompted to engage in political campaigns that would redirect and even redeem an affluent yet ailing society. Progressives cultivated a discourse of social critique described by Daniel T. Rodgers as 'three languages of discontent'.[14] They were categorized according to the challenges that confronted both the dynamics of contemporary society and the traditional associations between liberty and democracy: '[T]he first was the rhetoric of antimonopolism, the second was an emphasis on social bonds and the social nature of human beings, and the third was the language of social efficiency'.[15] Interwoven within these three strands of dissent was the urgent need for social reassessment and political action.

The Progressives were noted in particular for their passionate interest in exposure and revelation. This was not confined to the famous 'muckraking' articles of Lincoln Steffens and Ray Stannard Barker.[16] It was extended to a general fascination for the realism that lay behind the formalities of social principles and practices. Charles Beard sought to strip away the edifice of American history by revelations of economic conflict, while Vernon Parrington worked to expose what he took to be the continuous ideological conflict between the forces of enlightened progress and the forces of blind reaction.[17] In the same vein, US law and even the US Constitution were being similarly reduced to the new realism of economic

---

[13] Diner, *A Very Different Age*, ch. 6. Richard L. McCormick, 'The Heart of Progressivism Was the Ambition of the New Middle Class to Fulfill Its Destiny Through Bureaucratic Means', in Gilmore (ed.), *Who Were the Progressives?*, pp. 77–102.

[14] Daniel T. Rodgers, 'In Search of Progressivism', *Reviews in American History*, vol. 10, no. 4 (December 1982), p. 123.

[15] Ibid. See also Diner, *A Very Different Age*, ch. 8.

[16] Cornelius C. Regier, *The Era of the Muckrakers* (Gloucester, MA: Smith, 1957).

[17] Richard Hofstadter, *The Progressive Historians: Turner, Beard, Parrington* (London: Jonathan Cape, 1969).

drives and vested interests. The assault upon formalism was such that politics was no longer seen as the medium of individual rights and popular self-government. It was increasingly perceived to be a system in which underlying group interests generated the material substance of political activity and the mutual adjustment of such interests embodied the reality behind the institutional processes of the political system.[18]

Alongside the revelation and condemnations were sets of prescriptive and normative schemes by which the American world would be righted. Publicists like Frederic C. Howe and William Allen White produced popular works advocating reform. Analysts and theorists like Louis Brandeis, Walter Weyl, Herbert Croly, and Walter Lippmann attempted to combine contemporary material conditions with current intellectual perspectives to produce accounts of social explanation and guidance for reform in an age increasingly collectivist in character and, therefore, requiring conscious and purposeful action.[19] The consolidation of industrial organization had thrown into disarray the traditional nexus between American anti-statism and a traditional economic order based upon individualized property and personal virtue. The corporation had now effectively depersonalized the economic order and, in doing so, 'removed the economy...from the control of a personal code'.[20] Arthur M. Schlesinger, Jr., describes the dynamic faced by Progressive critics:

Impersonality produced an irresponsibility that was chilling the lifeblood of society. The state consequently had to expand its authority in order to preserve the ties which hold society together. The history of governmental intervention has been the history of the growing ineffectiveness of the private conscience as a means of social control. The only alternative is the growth of the public conscience, whose natural expression is the democratic government.[21]

Progressive analysts and reformers preferred to work through the medium of mutual interests and common values. They gave emphasis to the mobilizing force of unity rather than to sectional or social divisions. In this spirit, they made continual references to the 'public interest' and the 'public good'.

Progressive intellectuals...sought to define values that all Americans could endorse: reform, progress, good government. The Progressives abhorred social division and refused to define the battle in class terms. Instead they chose specific targets of protest—party

[18] See Arthur F. Bentley, *The Process of Government* (Cambridge, MA: Belknap Press, 1908); Henry S. Commager, *The American Mind: An Interpretation of American Thought and Character Since the 1880s* (New York: Bantam, 1970), pp. 317–43.

[19] Charles B. Forcey, *The Crossroads of Liberalism: Croly, Weyl, Lippmann and the Progressive Era, 1900–1925* (New York: Oxford University Press, 1961); Melvin I. Urofsky, *Louis D. Brandeis and the Progressive Tradition*, ed. by Oscar Handlin (Boston, MA: Little, Brown, 1981); David E. Price, 'Community and Control: Critical Democratic Theory in the Progressive Period', *American Political Science Review*, vol. 68, no. 4 (December 1974), pp. 1663–78.

[20] Arthur M. Schlesinger, Jr., *The Vital Center: The Politics of Freedom* (Cambridge, MA: Riverside, 1962), p. 176.

[21] Ibid.

bosses, corrupt industrialists, arrogant corporate leaders—and attacked their behavior, not their interests.[22]

Progressive reform, therefore, had the character of an aggregate response to a multiplicity of problems. The aggregation was based upon the rationalism of social analysis and the presumption of a common code of moral value. To David Thelen, the collaborative tenor of progressivism was its chief distinguishing characteristic: 'When the Progressive era is put against the backdrop of the growth of industrialism in America, the remarkable fact about the period is its relative freedom from social tensions....Not competition but cooperation between different social groups...was what distinguished progressivism'.[23]

The pragmatic nature of the progressive mindset generated a profusion of reform practitioners ranging from social welfare workers and city missionaries devoted to the social gospel, to public administrators and activists intent upon revising the structure of city, state, and national governments. Whether the motives of all these progressive elements were drawn primarily from a human concern for the poor, from a moral outrage at city life, or from a desire for a more efficient use of resources, the end result was a reform-conscious era. It produced a stream of legislation in areas such as working conditions, maximum hours, minimum wages, child labour practices, unemployment compensation, social insurance, municipal ownership of utilities, and direct taxation. These social and economic reforms by which government sought to provide a more equitable distribution of wealth were accompanied by several changes to the political structure (e.g. secret ballot, primary elections, women's suffrage, initiative recall, and referendum) in an effort not only to secure the passage of reform proposals but also to prevent government itself from coagulating into blocks of aggregate interests.

Like the Populists, the Progressives were beset by varied cross-pressures that served to complicate the nature of liberal reform. On the one hand, the Progressives have been described as fervent democrats seeking to widen political participation and to enhance the value of citizenship. On the other hand, they were often characterized as elitists intent upon deploying methods of public administration and the force of executive government to provide technocratic means of advancing the public interest. In addition, Progressives have been described as both reformers and conservatives, for while advocating social change in the name of progress. Progressivism 'was also an effort to realize familiar and traditional ideals under novel circumstances'.[24] It was always difficult to ascertain whether the Progressives viewed the past as an open objective to be retrieved, or simply as a disguise under which a new age would be levered into place. As a result, there were always problems in determining whether old or new means were being used in an old or new spirit to further old or new principles.

[22] William Schneider, 'Understanding Neoliberalism', *Dialogue*, vol. 22, no. 4 (1989), p. 5.

[23] David P. Thelen, 'Social Tensions and the Origins of Progressivism', *The Journal of American History*, vol. 56, no. 2 (1969), p. 335.

[24] Hofstadter, *The Age of Reform*, p. 213.

This ambiguity was particularly acute in respect to the central problem of the appropriate action to be taken in response to the industrial, commercial, and financial conglomerates that were known at the time as 'the trusts'. On the one side were those who believed that the trusts were the inevitable consequence of technological progress and capitalist development. Because they provided the base of American prosperity and social advance, it was believed that they should be recognized as legitimate and, thereupon, regulated by government in a cooperative partnership. Theodore Roosevelt supported this corporatist outlook. His programme in 1912 was duly entitled the New Nationalism.[25]

Roosevelt had been particularly influenced by Herbert Croly's *The Promise of American Life*.[26] Croly typified that facet of the progressive movement which drew its inspiration from Hegelian historicism and idealism. Croly believed that America was declining into disorder and that it was essential to regenerate its social unity out of the corrosive forces of alienation, fragmentation, and inequality. Croly sought to combine America's traditional attachment to democracy with the conscious development of a popular sovereign will embodying the ideal purpose of an underlying absolute and all-inclusive American community. A cooperative commonwealth would be created through the absorption of the individual within the natural and moral fact of the nation's higher reality, and through the central direction of individuals by a government representing their collective purpose and their totality as a national entity. Croly implied that the old libertarian aims of Thomas Jefferson were now to be achieved through the centralist means of Alexander Hamilton's statism.[27] Roosevelt regarded this strategy as the only way forward and, as a result, sought to align progressivism with vigorous federal government, along with an enhanced nationalist fervour and an enriched executive leadership.[28]

The views of Roosevelt and Croly were disputed by Woodrow Wilson who was Roosevelt's rival for the loyalties of the Progressive reformers. While Roosevelt believed that a benevolent state would act as regulatory balance to the increasingly centralized economy, Wilson's brand of progressivism conceived of balance in terms of government rolling corporate power back into a prior state of competitive

---

[25] See Arthur A. Ekirch, *Progressivism in America: A Study of the Era from Theodore Roosevelt to Woodrow Wilson* (New York: New Viewpoints, 1974), chs. 8–10; Walter Lippmann, *Drift and Mastery: An Attempt to Diagnose the Current Unrest*, with a revised introduction and notes by William E. Leuchtenburg (Madison, WI: University of Wisconsin Press, 1985); John M. Cooper, *Pivotal Decades: The United States, 1900–1920* (New York: W. W. Norton, 1992), chs. 2–4.

[26] Herbert D. Croly, *The Promise of American Life* (New York: Capricorn Books, 1964); Herbert D. Croly, *Progressive Democracy* (New York: Transaction, 1998).

[27] Byron Dexter, 'Herbert Croly and the Promise of American Life', *Political Science Quarterly*, vol. 70, no. 2 (June 1955); David Levy, *Herbert Croly of the New Republic: The Life and Thought of an American Progressive* (Princeton, NJ: Princeton University Press, 1985); Edward A. Stettner, *Shaping Modern Liberalism: Herbert Croly and Progressive Thought* (Lawrence, KS: University Press of Kansas, 1993); Eldon J. Eisenach, *The Lost Promise of Progressivism*, 2nd edn (Lawrence, KS: University Press of Kansas, 1994), ch. 6.

[28] George E. Mowry, *Theodore Roosevelt and the Progressive Movement* (New York: Hill & Wang, 1960), pp. 131–82; Ekirch, *Progressivism in America*, pp. 157–61.

interplay.[29] The more sentimental and moralistic position of Wilson was based upon the view that irrespective of the trusts' productive value and economies of scale, they remained fundamentally illegitimate and, therefore, had to be dismantled. He believed that for government to attempt to regulate the trusts was sheer folly. It would condone and ratify the trusts' position, which had been built up unfairly and inefficiently through every possible technique for evading fair and free competition. Moreover, it would require a mammoth state apparatus to regulate the expanding monopolies. This would not only further endanger American liberty through a concentration of governmental power, but would also make it likely that the trusts would acquire even greater power—enough to ensure that the corporate poachers would always be able to maintain control of the government gamekeepers.[30]

Wilson believed that Jeffersonian liberty could only be revived by *reversing* the process of combination and by seeking to return to a fairer and more competitive age of smaller units. 'When I am fighting monopolistic control, therefore, I am fighting for the liberty of every man in America'.[31] Roosevelt was economically radical in the role he saw for a government and business partnership but at the same time he was politically conservative in not wanting to create an anti-business base that would allow such a partnership to be an equitable undertaking. Wilson's moral repugnance for corporate power and big government mixed political radicalism with an economic conservatism that looked to the past in order to respond to fundamental social change. Wilson won the 1912 presidential election with his New Freedom programme. Although he had beaten Roosevelt, it is instructive to note that during his administration, Wilson departed from his laissez-faire principles and came to adopt the New Nationalism programme of his rival. By the end of his administration, Wilson had built up an extensive regulatory structure at the federal level. He had had to come to terms with the necessity of 'big government'. Even though he claimed that it was merely the best route back to individualism, competition, and opportunity, he could not deny that government was being made compatible with, and even integral to, the cause of personal liberty.[32] Wilson would not be the last reforming president to become more radical with the experience of government.

In the end, the Progressives succeeded in passing much of the Populists' agenda into legislation.[33] The Progressives never approved of the sectional motivations or

---

[29] Ekirch, *Progressivism in America*, ch. 14; Cooper, *Pivotal Decades: The United States, 1900–1920*, chs. 6, 7.

[30] Arthur S. Link, *Woodrow Wilson and the Progressive Era, 1910–1917* (New York: Harper & Row, 1954), pp. 1–80.

[31] Woodrow Wilson, *The New Freedom: A Call for the Emancipation of the Generous Energies of a People*, introduction and notes by William E. Leuchtenburg (Englewood Cliffs, NJ: Prentice-Hall, 1961), p. 125.

[32] Richard Hofstadter, *The American Political Tradition: And the Men Who Made It* (London: Jonathan Cape, 1967), pp. 251–7.

[33] Elizabeth Sanders, '[M]ost of the National Legislative Fruits of the Progressive Era Had Their Unmistakable Origins in the Agrarian Movements of the 1870s, 1880s, and 1890s', in Gilmore (ed.), *Who Were the Progressives?*, pp. 43–76.

the divisive and acrimonious style of the Populists. Their battle with 'the interests' looked to the Progressives too much like a battle between class units. As long as the populist programme seemed fired with prairie vitriol, the Progressives were not inclined to support it. But once the content of that programme was cast in the light of the Progressives' own rational analysis and moral judgement, the proposals looked to be necessary and sensible. It was this dispassionate rationality and the concern for a nebulous 'public interest', however, that became the chief source of criticism levelled at the Progressives. Progressivism acquired a reputation for technocratic efficiency and with it a reservation over popular democracy in any sense of unqualified legitimacy or collective autonomy that might compromise the rationality or social justice of government action. The middle-class nature of the progressive movement failed to root its reforms deep into popular consciousness and public sympathy. The progressive middle-class wish was to suspend the conflict between corporate capitalism and working-class radicalism by reference to a 'neutral state' and to the existence of an overriding common interest, which would be represented quite naturally by the moderate middle classes.

Progressivism continues to evoke controversy over its nature and influence upon American liberalism.[34] For example, Progressives are often criticized for their emphasis on enacting preventative measures and deferring difficult choices. It is claimed that they failed to make a systematic and positive adjustment to a new industrial age. H. W. Brands concludes that what the Progressives 'essentially lacked was a *positive* conception of government'.[35] Although they succeeded in laying the basis for a regulatory state, 'almost none of them...had even a glimmering of what would characterize modern liberalism: a state where government didn't simply prevent evil but actively promoted good'.[36] In such a light, progressivism can be seen as largely a series of separate responses to an industrial order whose problems were offensive but which, in affluent times, hardly seemed potentially chronic. In its attempt to moderate class antagonisms and to preserve traditional concepts of good citizenship against the excesses of a self-regarding liberalism, Michael McGerr claims that the progressive movement possessed a fundamental ambivalence over the use of the people as the centrepiece of authority in an expansionary state. McGerr refers to a 'fundamental paradox'[37] within progressivism:

To battle the rich and their political satellites, progressives rallied 'the people' and supported a clutch of reforms intended to open up political participation.... But a narrow definition of 'the people' dictated antiparticipatory reforms as well.... The progressives' political strength was their ability to project the 'people' against the powerful; their political

---

[34] For example, see Arthur Mann (ed.), *The Progressive Era: Liberal Renaissance or Liberal Failure?* (London: Holt, Rinehart, & Winston, 1963); John Chamberlain, *Farewell to Reform: The Rise, Life and Decay of the Progressive Mind in America*, 2nd edn (Chicago, IL: Quadrangle Books, 1965).

[35] H. W. Brands, *The Strange Death of American Liberalism* (New Haven, CT: Yale University Press, 2001), p. 18.

[36] Ibid.   [37] McGerr, *A Fierce Discontent*, p. 216.

weakness was their willingness to...keep so many Americans out of the battle against privilege.[38]

Eric Foner, on the other hand, acknowledges many of the Progressives' limitations but arrives at a different judgement concerning their bequest. To Foner, Progressives propagated the idea that freedom had to be dislodged from its traditional equation with limited government and laissez-faire economics. The theme of liberty had required, and received, an amended interpretation as a positive and socially rooted concept. To the 'traditional notion of individualism and autonomy, Progressives wedded the idea that such freedom required the conscious creation of the social conditions for full human development'.[39] To this end, the progressive movement helped to give 'freedom a modern social and economic content and established an agenda that would continue to define political liberalism for much of the rest of the century'.[40]

THE ROOSEVELT LEGACY

The pivotal point in the development of American liberalism remains the New Deal. The frenetic experimentation and improvization of President Franklin D. Roosevelt's reform programme amounted to a profound shift not only in the balance of the federal system, but also in the relationships between American society, the state, and the individual. The role and responsibility of federal government was in essence reconfigured into a centre of proactive intervention geared towards economic management, financial regulation, and social welfare. The rise of the positive state and the redefinition of liberal values were prompted by the catastrophic collapse of the American economy during the Great Depression. This had followed a prolonged period of unprecedented affluence during which the dogmas of laissez-faire dynamics and free-market capitalism had received the kind of material expression that amounted to a triumphant affirmation of a self-regulating economy. The Great Depression seriously distorted America's faith in economic progress.

The New Deal is the generic term given to an array of reform initiatives taken by the Roosevelt administration in response to the chronic consequences of the Depression. The New Deal's relentless inventiveness and pragmatic innovation generated a volume of regulatory powers and government interventions that surpassed the level of central direction achieved during the First World War. For example, the market in stocks and securities came under government supervision through the Securities and Exchange Commission. The banking sector was

[38] McGerr, *A Fierce Discontent*, p. 216.

[39] Eric Foner, *The Story of American Freedom* (New York: W. W. Norton, 1998), p. 153.

[40] Ibid., pp. 160–1; see also R. Laurence Moore, 'Directions of Thought in Progressive America', in Lewis L. Gould (ed.), *The Progressive Era* (Syracuse, NY: Syracuse University Press, 1974), pp. 35–54; Thomas K. McCraw, 'The Progressive Legacy', in Gould (ed.), *The Progressive Era*, pp. 181–201.

brought under firmer regulatory control at the same time that the Federal Deposit Insurance Corporation underwrote the deposits of those solvent banks selected by Washington to provide the basis for a stronger banking system. The National Industry Recovery Act sought to restore industrial production by government-sponsored codes of competition that allowed whole industries to fix prices and wages. In response to the farming crisis, the Agricultural Adjustment Act aimed to stimulate America's rural economy by paying farmers to limit their production, and thereby to break the cycle of overproduction and underconsumption.

In addition, the federal government intervened to lower interest rates and to reduce power and transportation charges as part of a wider strategy to halt deflation, increase the circulation of resources, and widen purchasing power in order to boost business confidence, generate investment, and revive economic activity. The New Deal also engaged in enormous public works schemes to stimulate industrial production (e.g. the Civil Works Administration) and to provide jobs for the unemployed (e.g. the Civilian Conservation Corporation). Relief for the destitute was provided by expanded public assistance and, ultimately, by the landmark Social Security Act, which established the provision of both a contributory social insurance scheme and a back-up of a non-contributory set of welfare arrangements for the needy, the aged, the blind, and for families with dependent children. As part of its strategy to make labour an equal partner within industry, the administration sponsored legislation that led to the establishment of workers' rights to organize into unions and to bargain collectively for improved pay and conditions.[41]

In essence, the New Deal conclusively altered the national government's position in American society. It marks the time when the federal government came to assume a basic responsibility for the state of the American economy and for the welfare of the citizenry. The vast expansion of the federal sphere was widely interpreted as a redistribution of political power in favour of a national democracy capable of liberating government from the concentration of corporate wealth, reducing the property rights of vested interests, and responding to the needs of the underprivileged. The net effect of the New Deal measures not only 'transformed the relationship of the federal government to the economy and the citizenry' but also 'established much of the agenda of modern American liberalism'.[42]

It is precisely because the New Deal is seen as a pivotal period of American history that it arouses such fierce debate amongst different advocates, each desiring to claim the programme, and to establish its legitimacy, for their own political purposes. The problem of the New Deal is heightened by its very association with

---

[41] William E. Leuchtenburg, *Franklin D. Roosevelt and the New Deal, 1932–1940* (New York: Harper & Row, 1963); Anthony J. Badger, *The New Deal: The Depression Years, 1933–1940* (New York: Hill & Wang, 1989); Frank Freidel, *Franklin D. Roosevelt: A Rendezvous with Destiny* (Boston, MA: Back Bay, 1991), chs. 7–16; William E. Leuchtenburg, *The FDR Years: On Roosevelt and His Legacy* (New York: Columbia University Press, 1995); chs. 1–3, 5–7; Alan Brinkley, 'The New Deal Experiments', in William H. Chafe (ed.), *The Achievement of American Liberalism: The New Deal and Its Legacies* (New York: Columbia University Press, 2003), pp. 1–20.

[42] Foner, *The Story of American Freedom*, p. 201.

American liberal reform. Just as the New Deal is regarded as the watchword of American liberalism, so the nature of that liberalism is closely bound up with the character of the New Deal and of the society it brought into being. This dual identity, however, serves to clarify neither party. Put bluntly, there remains so much controversy over the origins and purposes of the New Deal because of the volume of dispute over the meanings and aims of contemporary liberalism. Likewise, the debate over the latter is fuelled by the ambiguities of the New Deal programme, which supposedly represents the fullest expression of liberal reform.[43]

Many questions are raised by the New Deal. For example, whether there was one continuous New Deal or two quite separate New Deal programmes—the first based upon economic recovery and institutional stability (e.g. the National Industrial Recovery Act), and the second geared towards social radicalism in the form of expanded social provision (e.g. the Social Security Act) and increased industrial regulation. Another question hinges upon whether the New Deal ever contemplated economic planning, or whether the emphasis lay inevitably upon emergency and experimental measures. Another debate centres upon the New Dealers' attitudes to corporate capitalism. The New Deal seemed to alternate between two philosophies and their supportive factions within the administration. On the one hand was the New Nationalism approach defended by individuals like Rexford Tugwell and Adolph Berle. This group accepted economic concentration but called for its supervision in the public interest. On the other hand were those like Thomas Corcoran and Felix Frankfurter who adhered to the New Freedom position of reversing contemporary trends in an effort to restore competitive markets.[44] As a consequence, President Roosevelt's legacy in this area has remained a mixed one. Lastly, there is an intense dispute over the extent to which the New Deal represented the culmination of a continuous reform tradition encompassing both the Populist and Progressive movements, or alternatively a decisive break from that tradition into an altogether more modern and more social-democratic dimension.[45]

All these questions remain unanswered. Within the New Deal there were visionary planners as well as exponents of 'meat and potatoes' liberalism. There were also pragmatists and technocrats and moralists. President Roosevelt's own ideological ambiguity further served to complicate the nature of the New Deal. Some measures were evocative of the class-based radicalism of the Populists (e.g. the

---

[43] See Richard S. Kirkendall, 'The New Deal As Watershed: The Recent Literature', *The Journal of American History*, vol. 54, no. 4. (March 1968), pp. 839–52; Jerold S. Auerbach, 'New Deal, Old Deal, or Raw Deal: Some Thoughts on New Left Historiography', *The Journal of Southern History*, vol. 35, no. 1. (February 1969), pp. 18–30; Alan Brinkley, *Liberalism and Its Discontents* (Cambridge, MA: Harvard University Press, 2000), chs. 2–4; Sidney M. Milkis and Jerome M. Mileur (eds.), *The New Deal and the Triumph of Liberalism* (Amherst, MA: University of Massachusetts Press, 2002); Jim Powell, *FDR's Folly: How Roosevelt and His New Deal Prolonged the Great Depression* (New York: Crown Forum, 2003).

[44] Joseph P. Lash, *Dealers and Dreamers: A New Look at the New Deal* (Garden City, NY: Doubleday, 1988); see also Leuchtenburg, *Franklin D. Roosevelt and the New Deal, 1932–1940*, chs. 2, 3.

[45] See Hofstadter, *The Age of Reform*, ch. 7; Eric Goldman, *Rendezvous with Destiny* (New York: Knopf, 1972), pp. 328–73. Leuchtenburg, *The FDR Years*, chs. 8, 9.

rights of labour, progressive taxation), while others seemed more like derivatives of the progressive concern over business concentration and the prevention and punishment of its abuse (e.g. the dissolution of the holding companies in public utilities). On the other hand, the New Deal's emphasis on realism, organization, technology, efficiency, and practical results gave it a distinctive character all of its own. The programme had a free-wheeling quality of breaking down barriers in the cause of material improvements, rather than being overtly concerned with the righteousness of techniques or with the aesthetic defects and moral costs of large economic or political organizations.

The end result was a massive government structure of regulations, controls, and provision which, for all its positive achievements and popularity, had never been fully thought through or rationalized in terms of a conscious or coherent revision of public philosophy. Liberalism's legendary response to the historical crisis of the Great Depression had not produced the anticipated metamorphosis of the state's role in modern society. Instead, the New Deal bequeathed a proliferation of assorted programmes and agencies whose only *raison d'être* was their utility in ameliorating conditions and the public's acceptance of their need to exist. By the end of the Second World War, the infrastructure of the New Deal had simply been accepted as an enduring necessity devoid of solid reflection or a reasoned foundation. Its apparent success and indispensability had become its own justification.

The continuing relationship between the historical meaning of the New Deal and the social nature of American liberalism creates profound problems for the latter. In some respects, the New Deal can be seen as revolutionary in that it ushered in a Keynesian structure of economic management, a welfare state, a modern system of social and economic regulation, and a centralization of power within the American federation. But because such a transition was made under the anaesthetic of emergency measures, unpremeditated proposals, and temporary solutions, the revolution—if such it was—came more by sleight of hand than by any conscious assimilation of collective action and social purpose.[46]

In another respect, the New Deal can be represented as a conventionally conservative response to the greatest crisis in American capitalism. The character of the New Deal and of its modern bequest was dominated by a desire to work with business to save capitalism from itself and to preserve the prevailing structure of private property, free enterprise, and the profit system. President Roosevelt himself was always quite adamant that this was to be the overriding objective. To him, the economic system and the ethos of free enterprise were integral features of American democracy. He was deeply critical of the excesses and abuses of what he termed the 'princes of property',[47] but he resisted using these extremes to construct a general characterization of the economic order: 'I am not prepared to say

---

[46] Hofstadter, *The American Political Tradition*, pp. 324–38.
[47] President Franklin D. Roosevelt, 'The Commonwealth Club Address' (23 September 1932), in Kenneth M. Dolbeare, *American Political Thought*, 2nd edn (Chatham, NJ: Chatham House, 1989), p. 508.

that the system which produces them is wrong'.[48] The leaders of major industrial and financial corporations needed to appreciate the social responsibilities of their power. In return, the federal government could revive confidence, increase demand, and stimulate economic activity. In his stock campaign speech during the 1936 presidential election, Roosevelt celebrated his government's record in responding to a crisis that 'all the combined forces of private enterprise had failed'[49] to correct. The interventions undertaken by the administration were repeatedly defended in terms of protecting the aggregate store of individual liberty within American society. The emphasis was on the rehabilitation of business enterprise by government action: 'The wheels of business began to turn again; the train was back on the rails. Mind you, it did not get out of the ditch by itself; it was hauled out by your Government'.[50]

In the final analysis, the New Deal did not succeed in returning the American economy to high growth, low unemployment, and mass consumption. It was the Second World War that provided the stimulus to full economic recovery. The peacetime emergency was ultimately resolved by the defence-related demands of wartime production, economic mobilization, and social planning. Although the instruments of central government grew exponentially through the systemic character of the war effort, they were directed less towards explicitly liberal objectives and more towards the imperatives of national security.

LIBERAL DISTURBANCES

The Second World War compounded the reactive impulses of the New Deal with a state of national emergency requiring exponential increases in the federal government's penetration of American society. The war had been fought in the cause of what President Roosevelt had termed the 'Four Freedoms' (freedom of speech, religious freedom, and freedom from both want and fear). National security and international power projection thereby became bound up with the reformist prospectus of the New Deal. The resultant mix could be rationalized as an internally consistent programme. Alonzo Hamby points out that 'as World War II made relations with the rest of the world a central concern of American life, the New Deal tradition became internationalized. It envisioned a world role for the United States—active global leadership in the drive for a world community organized around liberal democratic values'.[51] However, the war also heralded a change in socio-political conditions that were not always conducive to the cause of liberal reform.

[48] President Roosevelt, 'The Commonwealth Club Address'.
[49] President Roosevelt, 'Campaign Address' (1936), in Dolbeare, *American Political Thought*, p. 512.
[50] Ibid., p. 513.
[51] Alonzo L. Hamby, *Liberalism and Its Challengers: FDR to Reagan* (New York: Oxford University Press, 1985) p. 5.

Given the specific contingency basis of the justification for the scale of government intervention during the New Deal and the Second World War, the question arose of whether the infrastructure of federal regulation could survive the cessation of hostilities and the evident recovery of the American economy. If the New Deal had largely been conceived as a response to an economic emergency, then, as the economy achieved an unprecedented level of sustained growth during and after the war, it could be argued that the problems of economic insecurity that had haunted the 1930s had now been largely laid to rest. In previous periods of expanded government activity, the passing of an emergency had been followed by a process of retrenchment prompted by the desire to return to a prior state of existence. Following the war, various appeals to the past and campaigns for a revival of laissez-faire were combined with calls for demobilization and international disengagement. But just as the cold war effectively ruled out any serious reversal of America's global role, so the 1950s witnessed the endorsement and consolidation of the New Deal's infrastructure of economic management and the social regulation.

The defeat of Robert Taft by Dwight Eisenhower for the Republican leadership represented the triumph of pragmatic centrism over a doctrinal attachment to minimal government. Eisenhower's subsequent tenure as president disappointed many who had waited for a generation to roll back the New Deal and to isolate it as an experiment that had outlived whatever marginal utility it had once possessed. Although President Eisenhower remained sceptical of the effectiveness and value of government intervention as an instrument of social improvement, he possessed a traditional conservative respect for those New Deal reforms that were now considered to have become satisfactorily entrenched in society and, thereby, absorbed into people's expectations. He was not inclined to disturb a settled social order by engaging in Taftite retreats on domestic policy. The administration was not required to defend the measures of the New Deal and the Fair Deal,[52] 'but merely to accept their immutability, as a matter of political necessity'.[53] The effectiveness of liberalism had achieved a conventional status and was even being cited as constituting a dominant intellectual tradition. President Eisenhower operated within its parameters and helped to institutionalize its precepts by extending social security benefits, increasing public works programmes, and using federal funds to finance the construction of an interstate highway network.

Even though the 'Eisenhower consensus' evoked notions of an end of ideology within an increasingly suburban political culture, the pressure for liberal reform remained. It is true that much of the reform programme in the late 1940s and the 1950s was derived from the established agendas of the New Deal. It is also true that liberalism during this period suffered from an 'identity crisis' that emanated

[52] President Harry Truman's Fair Deal programme of reforms was generally considered to be an extension to the liberal agenda of the New Deal.
[53] Emmet J. Hughes, The *Ordeal of Power: A Political Memoir of the Eisenhower Years* (London: Macmillan, 1963), p. 333.

from the strains of its post-war ascendancy.[54] The 'corporate liberalism' of Keynesian economic management, market stability, and national security infrastructure was not always in accord with the civic moralism and social welfare traditions of 'insurgency liberalism'. The former gave a higher priority to inflation control, middle-class security, and anti-communism. The latter not only professed a greater interest in those on the margins of society and in civil rights, but also retained the class-based front of the 1930s that embraced a more conciliatory view of the Soviet Union.[55] Notwithstanding these undercurrents of strain, the progressive ethos of liberalism continued to produce a reform agenda geared towards deepening and extending the framework of social protection and provision.

Yet, in spite of the general assimilation of the New Deal into the fabric of national tradition, and the liberal orientation of the post-war social order, the liberal agenda of the period was almost invariably frustrated by the institutional friction between a Democratic Congress and a Republican presidency, and by the existence in Congress of a 'conservative coalition' of Republicans and Southern Democrats. The difficulties of achieving reform were further compounded by the national cohesion of cold war absolutism, the rising significance of race as a reform issue, and the increasing salience of economic performance and states' rights as defining themes of liberal critique. While Congressional Democrats and their allies continued to press for a series of reform measures (e.g. civil rights, Medicare, aid to education, minimum wage increase), their efforts were largely in vain.[56] Even when the Democrats secured the presidency, they found that President John F. Kennedy's New Frontier programme fared little better than President Harry Truman's Fair Deal had done in the late 1940s. Many concluded that the systemic properties of the American political system now militated against large-scale legislative reform. According to this perspective, because institutional divisions and minority veto points were instrumental in maintaining the inertial forces of established programmes, they necessarily excluded innovative shifts in the distribution of priorities and resources.

When the breakthrough came, it occurred on such a scale and produced such a volume of legislation that it was to have the most profound consequences for the stature and authority of reform liberalism within American society. An exceptional array of factors emerged in the 1960s to provide a favourable context for liberal reform. The combination included the cultural shock of President Kennedy's assassination, the prodigious legislative skills of President Lyndon B. Johnson, the Democrats' landslide victory over Senator Barry Goldwater in the 1964 presidential election, the resurgence of the American economy, and the

---

[54] Alonzo L. Hamby, *Beyond the New Deal: Harry S Truman and American Liberalism* (New York: Columbia University Press, 1973); see also Robert J. Donovan, *Tumultuous Years: The Presidency of Harry S Truman, 1949–1953* (New York: W. W. Norton, 1982).

[55] Norman D. Markowitz, *The Rise and Fall of the People's Century: Henry A. Wallace and American Liberalism, 1941–1948* (New York: Free Press, 1973); Brian Waddell *The War against the New Deal: World War II and American Democracy* (DeKalb, IL: Northern Illinois University Press, 2001).

[56] James L. Sundquist, *Politics and Policy: The Eisenhower, Kennedy and Johnson Years* (Washington, DC: Brookings, 1968).

recognition that the United States needed to enhance its credentials as a progressive society in the cold war competition for third-world allegiance. These and other influences all contributed to an aggregate drive to fulfil a substantial part of a liberal agenda that had been advocated over the previous quarter century.

This was a period when public trust in the integrity and utility of government was high. It was also a time when President Johnson was able to revive the New Deal notion of a 'concurrence of interests'. His strategy was to diminish the significance of division (e.g. race, class, regional, party) in the currency of political exchange. He sought to operate on the premise that all legitimate American interests were by their very nature reconcilable to one another. His theme of consensus politics working in concert to achieve a 'Great Society' found resonance in a political system that was suddenly becoming responsive to presidential leadership, to legislative action, and to policy change. During the 89th Congress (1965–6), President Johnson secured the passage of over 180 legislative proposals including measures in areas that had previously been regarded as being too controversial to allow for Congressional action (e.g. the 'war on poverty', the Voting Rights Act, the Elementary and Secondary Education Act, as well as the Medicare, Medicaid, and Headstart programmes).

It is now a familiar narrative that this triumph of liberalism was rapidly followed by a spectacular descent from which the reformist sprit of affirmative government has still to recover. At one level, the problems generated by this stream of legislation were those of coordination, coherence, and consolidation. Governmental overload was exacerbated by internal divisions in the Democratic Party, by mid-term losses in 1966, and by a fracturing of the political consensus that had permitted President Johnson to act as the facilitator of a national democracy. At another level, President Johnson's liberal experimentalism and governmental activism became bound up in a syndrome of abrasive scepticism and social dislocation. The reaction may have been induced by the sheer pace of change, or the realization that the high expectations of reform could not be fulfilled. Alternatively, it may have been due more to the resourcing problems posed by the coexistence of high social spending with financing the Vietnam War. Whatever the reasons for the response, the effect was one in which numerous negative properties were attributed to either the intentions or the consequences of liberal activism.

Just as the violently deteriorating condition of the Vietnam War became known as 'Johnson's war', so did the rising indicators of inflation, drug abuse, crime, pornography, racial tension, urban decay, campus dissidence, political radicalism, and violent direct action become collectively characterized as 'Johnson's society'. This had far-reaching effects upon the society's conception of its own stability: 'In the broad American public, there was a widespread sense of breakdown in authority and discipline that fed as readily on militant political dissent as on race riots and more conventional crime'.[57] Although many of the critiques of

---

[57] Philip E. Converse, Warren E. Miller, Jerrold G. Rusk, and Arthur C. Wolfe, 'Continuity and Change in American Politics: Politics and Issues in the 1968 Election', *American Political Science Review*, vol. 63, no. 4 (December 1969), p. 1088.

American society were directed towards liberal values and programmes, the mere existence of such ferocious criticism tended to shift middle-class opinion away from a defence of the liberal establishment and towards a loss of confidence in its authority for having generated such a disaggregation of American culture. It appeared that as President Johnson's reformist consensus was splitting apart, the New Deal coalition itself was breaking up. It seemed as if the American consensus was crumbling away under the corrosive forces of political disruption and social polarization. The noble causes and inflated promises of liberalism had apparently sunk into a morass of body counts in Saigon, ostentatious sex, psychedelic escapism, and a reprehensible 'imperial Presidency'.[58]

The sense of disintegration and crisis also generated a profusion of radical critiques of American culture. This was the belle époque of the New Left when its analytical and normative expositions of American democracy's chronic failures not only reflected popular concerns but also attracted furious public condemnations. The New Left's indictments of a repressive, coercive, and homogenized society were applied with equal vigour to the prescriptions and programmes of American liberalism. According to those on the New Left, liberals were an integral part of the structural problems of corporate power, social hierarchy, bureaucratic unresponsiveness, and cultural deprivation. What was seen as a volatile mix of technological progress and economic abundance coexisting with poverty, isolation, alienation, and misery required the kind of enlightenment into the potential human development, social community, and participatory democracy that American liberals were incapable of bringing into existence. Liberals, therefore, found themselves besieged on both sides of a widening and increasingly rancorous spectrum of political opinion.[59]

Since the late 1960s, the demise of American liberalism has been a recurrent theme in the political debate of the United States. Arguments circulate on when and how it was eclipsed, and on the likelihood or otherwise of its revival. Out of these discussions, one overriding core conclusion becomes clear. Namely, that liberalism fell from grace as a result of a series of factors ranging from a growth of economic insecurity to the onset of middle class tax revolts, from populist insurgencies against a 'liberal establishment' to the anxieties over the decline in social cohesion, and from a resurgence of patriotic social defensiveness to various backlashes over the consequences of reform measures. Just as liberalism lost the

---

[58] See Marvin E. Gettleman and David Mermelstein (eds.), *The Great Society Reader: The Failure of American Liberalism* (New York: Vintage, 1967); Godfrey Hodgson, *In Our Time: America from World War II to Nixon* (London: Macmillan, 1976), chs. 13–25; Allen J. Matusow, *The Unravelling of America: A History of Liberalism in the 1960s* (New York: Harper & Row, 1984); Robert Dallek, *Flawed Giant: Lyndon Johnson and His Times, 1961–1973* (New York: Oxford University Press, 1999), chs. 6–10; Arthur M. Schlesinger, Jr., *The Imperial Presidency* (London: Deutsch, 1974), chs. 7–11; Otis L. Graham, Jr., 'Liberalism after the Sixties: A Reconnaissance', in Chafe (ed.), *The Achievement of American Liberalism*, pp. 293–326.

[59] Kenneth M. Dolbeare and Patricia Dolbeare, *American Ideologies: The Competing Beliefs of the 1970s* (Chicago, IL: Markham, 1971), ch. 6; George Katsiaficas, *The Imagination of the New Left: A Global Analysis of 1968* (Boston, MA: South End Press, 1987), chs. 4–6; Van Gosse, *The Movements of the New Left, 1950–1975: A Brief History with Documents* (New York: St. Martin's Press, 2004).

intellectual high ground, so was its power base progressively eroded through regional realignments within the Democratic Party, through the weakening of the labour movement, and through the dealignment of much of the blue-collar sector into 'Reagan Democrats'. The appeal and authority of reform liberalism were further undermined by the decline of public trust in government. Because America's reform ethos had been state-centric in its programme and development, it was always susceptible to the traditions of visceral anti-statism in American society. While different strands of emphasis within liberalism became increasingly evident and discordant, the emergence of new cross-cutting issues (e.g. environmental protection, minority rights, abortion, strategic arms limitation) further confounded the lack of precision and consistency in the liberal project.

The collective memory of the 1960s became defined by the spectre of spiralling government costs, exponential rises in entitlements, and prodigious evidence of maladministration and government incompetence. The post-Watergate presidency of Jimmy Carter exemplified both the turmoil within the liberal constituency and the debilitating effect of severe socio-economic problems coexisting within an anti-Washington framework of public impulse and political rhetoric. The reaction against liberalism in the 1970s is well documented[60] but the scale of the retrenchment can be overstated. The decade witnessed a succession of reform advances in areas such as environmental protection, consumer rights, campaign finance, gender discrimination, workplace safety, desegregation, criminal justice, and abortion reform.[61] At the same time, it is fair to add that many of these achievements were rooted in the agendas of the 1960s. While the momentum of reform was continued through various administrative, regulatory, and judicial regimes, the cutting edge of political advocacy rooted in federal activism was sharply diminished. Despite the reduced political momentum for a reform agenda, the liberal imagination remained active. It was a period that witnessed a deep interest in, and a concern for, the state of liberalism. This was reflected in the extraordinary prominence given to John Rawls's innovative treaties on the required principles of social justice.

In *A Theory of Justice* (1971),[62] Rawls set out to revive liberal political philosophy by constructing a systematic framework of political thought and social ethics based upon a foundation of moral argument. In essence, Rawls sought to reinstate the notion of justice in the form of fairness as the primary organizing principle of social existence and public morality. The project was grounded in

---

[60] See Peter N. Carroll, *It Seemed Like Nothing Happened: The Tragedy and Promise of America in the 1970s* (New York: Holt, Rinehart, & Winston, 1982); Jonathan Rieder, *Canarsie: The Jews and Italians of Brooklyn against Liberalism* (Cambridge, MA: Harvard University Press, 2005), ch. 8; Steve Fraser and Gary Gerstle (eds.), *The Rise and Fall of the New Deal Order, 1930–1980* (Princeton, NJ: Princeton University Press, 1989).

[61] Hugh Davis Graham, 'Civil Rights Policy in the Carter Presidency', in Gary Fink and Hugh D. Graham (eds.), *The Carter Presidency: Policy Choices in the Post-New Deal Era* (Lawrence, KS: University of Kansas Press, 1998), pp. 202–23; Hugh Davis Graham, 'Legacies of the 1960s: The American "Rights Revolution" in an Era of Divided Governance', *Journal of Policy History*, vol. 10 no. 3 (1998), pp. 267–88.

[62] John Rawls, *A Theory of Justice* (Oxford: Oxford University Press, 1971).

Rawls's dissatisfaction with the precepts of utilitarianism. These assumed that justice could be encompassed by a general calculation of interests through which the
overall welfare of society would be maximized. Rawls believed that this approach
marginalized the social value and theoretical status of individuals and with it the
central importance of rights as a point of normative anchorage. It was also seen as
overlooking the deep inequalities inhering in economic and social structures and
the way in which such entrenched forms of unfairness could be, and very often
were, sustained by the state.

Rawls's proposed solution lay neither in a calculus of aggregate impersonal
benefit, nor in an improved device for political bargaining. His axiomatic point
of departure was the value assigned to individual liberties and to an equality of
legal rights and social entitlements. Providing and protecting this putative equality
should be the primary business of the state. The inequalities in the distribution of
wealth and power could only be construed as just when they could reasonably
be expected to benefit those least advantaged in society. Under the 'difference
principle', some inequalities would be acknowledged as the concomitants of an
open and prosperous society. However, they have to be justified as legitimate
derivatives of the contractual agreement in which the least advantaged would
accept that the talented should have a larger share of society's resources—but only
as long as the latter gave the former some part of their additional wealth.

Despite raising a host of philosophical, conceptual, and logistical problems,
Rawls's theory succeeded in giving fresh contemporary impetus to the discussion
of classical themes such as obligation, citizenship, equality, rights, and justice.
The theory aimed to establish a way of reconciling not only different interests
within a society but also the different claims associated with liberty and equality.
Rawls's ideal of justice was designed to minimize the disadvantages of those who
suffered from their position within social structures—a position which they had
not chosen and for which they could not be held to be culpable: 'For us the
primary subject of justice is the basic structure of society, or more exactly, the way
in which the major social institutions distribute fundamental rights and duties
and determine the division of advantages from social cooperation.'[63] The moral
emphasis upon the social context of justice led Rawls's theory to become interpreted in many quarters as a rationale for the welfare state, progressive taxation,
and social democracy. Although Rawls himself was critical of some elements of
free-market liberalism, his view of the system most likely to optimize his scheme of
justice remained an open question. Nevertheless, this did not prevent a profusion
of scholars and commentators from debating the merits and demerits of his
theory in relation to contemporary politics. In doing so, they helped to establish
a Rawlsian framework within which many social issues and reasoned arguments
concerning fairness acquired a social currency and a structured connection to
reform liberalism in the United States.

Notwithstanding the intellectual cogency and cultural penetration of Rawls's
exposition of justice as a rights-based construction of social fairness, the late 1970s

---

[63] Rawls, *A Theory of Justice*, p. 7.

were marked by a widely cited turn to the right. The chief rallying point for the forces of conservatism was the liberals' attachment to the federal government as the traditional and primary agency of social improvement:

> However real or imagined their grievances, people found government—big, interventionist and tax-consuming—a convenient scapegoat. . . . By 1980 the liberal center, lacking both intellectual coherence and a viable political and economic strategy, confronted a conservative movement ready and eager to challenge it for power.[64]

The subsequent Reagan ascendancy forced many reformers to engage in a thorough reassessment of liberal strategy away from the New Deal–Great Society legacy. 'Neoliberals' like Paul Tsongas and Gary Hart advocated a 'post-ideological' liberalism that would no longer be wedded to high-taxation and high-spending government but would be concerned more with fluid approaches to new problems. Priority was given to the problem of America's economic health in a world of finite resources, de-industrialization, and budgetary constraints.[65] Neoliberals not only distanced themselves from established New Deal agendas but also aligned themselves to new issues (e.g. bureaucracy, environmental protection, industrial planning, consumer choice, deregulation, drug abuse, technology, and nuclear power) that cut across the old dualities of the New Deal.[66] These reformers wanted to combine a concern for social issues with a realistic appreciation of the central importance of the economy and the need for government to support the private sector through technology, investment, education, skills training, and a range of public–private partnerships. This kind of liberalism privileged managerial competence and economic growth rather than freedom or justice.

So concerted was the Democratic Party's attempt to distance itself from the negative properties of the 1960s that its presidential candidate in 1988 refused either to defend liberalism or to be in any way associated with what had become known as the 'L-word'. As a leading neoliberal, Michael Dukakis was highly conscious of the way that liberalism had acquired a social stigma with which it was possible to smear a political opponent. Governor Dukakis's campaign deliberately steered away from the discussion of social values. After repeatedly denying that he was a liberal, Governor Dukakis dropped his non-ideological guard at the very end of his campaign. He attempted to invigorate his flagging campaign with an injection of cautious liberal statements. Although he finally and reluctantly associated himself with the 'L-word', Dukakis failed to mobilize the Democratic vote. In the process, he demonstrated a 'disastrous inability to express any definition of "liberal values" likely to allure voters or even persuade them that here was a man of principle'.[67]

---

[64] William C. Berman, *America's Right Turn: From Nixon to Clinton*, 2dn edn (Baltimore, MD: Johns Hopkins University Press, 1998), pp. ix, 59.

[65] Paul Tsongas, *The Road from Here: Liberalism and Realities in the 1980s* (New York: Knopf, 1981).

[66] For the divisions in the liberal ranks, see James H. Duffy, *Domestic Affairs: American Programmes and Priorities* (New York: Simon & Schuster, 1978) and Randall Rothenberg, *The Neoliberals: Creating the New American Politics* (New York: Simon & Schuster, 1984).

[67] Alexander Cockburn, 'The L-Word in Crisis', *New Statesman and Society*, 4 November 1988.

The terms of Dukakis's endorsement of liberalism seemed like the final affirmation of a post-liberal age.

The state of reform liberalism, and the mix of ideas and traditions used to support it, remained in an ambiguous position for the rest of the century. Although the Democrats occupied the White House from 1993 to 2001, the Clinton administration did not achieve any major social and economic reforms. President Bill Clinton had only become electable by accommodating himself to the predominant currents of conservative priorities. He had begun his national political career as chairman of the Democratic Leadership Council (DLC), which was an organization committed to reversing the institutionalized liberalism of the Democratic Party's main constituencies. The DLC, together with its derivative organization, the Progressive Policy Institute, worked to create an alternative centre of gravity within the party. This would allow the Democrats to reshape their public philosophy, to realign themselves to the centrist perspectives, and to strengthen the cohesion of the party by weakening the grip of its liberal advocacy groups.[68]

From his position as the DLC chairman, Clinton had been instrumental in devising a 'New Democrat' philosophy for government. The New Democrats advocated deficit reduction, free trade, fiscal discipline, economic revitalization, and infrastructure investment. By acknowledging the productive value of the market, the New Democrats sought to develop a 'third way' that could combine deregulation and economic growth with liberal guarantees and social supports.[69] The impulse behind this movement was to 'eradicate the Democrats' vulnerabilities with the electorate' and to strengthen the party's proximity to 'nationalist values'.[70] The New Democrats pursued their objective by working to decrease 'the party's identification with the poor ... with traditional welfare state mechanisms ... [and] with the cultural avant-garde'.[71] New Democrats referred to the 'forgotten middle classes' and to the need for government to be responsive to mainstream values and public impulses in the formulation of social and foreign policy. In government, the third way was widely criticized as less of a defining ideology and more of a political and electoral strategy.

At first, Clinton was widely suspected of being a closet liberal with a radical agenda of government expansion.[72] But after the high-profile failure of his health-care plan and the historic scale of his party defeat in the 1994 mid-term elections, Clinton's gravitational compass moved inexorably to the right. He subsequently found a role and a considerable source of political capital in engaging in rearguard defences against the Republican assaults upon the infrastructure of the positive

---

[68] Kenneth S. Baer, *Reinventing Democrats: The Politics of Liberalism from Roosevelt to Clinton* (Lawrence, KS: University Press of Kansas, 2000).

[69] For a concise explanation of the DLC's conception of the third way, see DLC, 'The Hyde Park Declaration: A Statement of Principles and a Policy Agenda for the 21st Century', 1 August 2000, http://www.ndol.org/ndol_ci.cfm?cp=1&kaid=86&subid=194&contentid=1926.

[70] Bert A. Rockman, 'Leadership Style and the Clinton Presidency', in Colin Campbell and Bert A. Rockman (eds.), *The Clinton Presidency: First Appraisals* (Chatham, NJ: Chatham House, 1996), p. 329.

[71] Rockman, 'Leadership Style and the Clinton Presidency', p. 329.

[72] Elizabeth Drew, *On the Edge: The Clinton Presidency* (New York: Simon & Schuster, 1994).

state. But not even President Clinton could withstand the pressure exerted by the Republican insurgents for welfare reform in 1996.[73] It is true that welfare reform had been a key component of the New Democrats' prospectus for government. But now that the Democrats had lost control of the Congress and the political agenda, President Clinton was widely expected to convert the issue into a symbolic rallying point in the defence of mainstream Democratic values. But instead of vetoing the Republicans' robust reform imposing strict time limits to the governmental support assigned to the poorest sector of society, President Clinton signed the legislation into law. The welfare system had been 'the issue that conservatives had most successfully used against liberals for a quarter of century'.[74] Even so, the President's 'decision was perhaps the most controversial for liberals, of Clinton's years in office'.[75]

President Clinton's re-election in 1996 was not the harbinger of any further liberal experimentation. On the contrary, his leadership was reconfigured into giving expression to the limits of government and, thereby, to the limits of liberalism according to the New Deal conception of amelioration and security through direct government action. President Clinton himself flagged this theme in his second inaugural address. He attempted to stake out a position for government that was more equivocal and circumscribed than the customary position adopted by Democratic presidents:

Government is not the problem, and government is not the solution. We—the American people—we are the solution.... As times change, so government must change. We need a new government for a new century—humble enough not to try to solve all our problems for us, but strong enough to give us the tools to solve our problems for ourselves; a government that is smaller, lives within its means, and does more with less.[76]

The faded splendour of the century's liberal constructions was further underlined by President Clinton's successor as Democratic Party leader. Vice-President Al Gore's main role within the Clinton administration had been to pursue the 'reinvention of government' programme. By demonstrating the extent to which waste, fraud, and abuse had become integral parts of the public sector, Gore had sought to create a constituency for the rationalization of government.

As the Democratic Party's presidential candidate in 2000, Gore declared his allegiance to those aspects of government that had a proven functional value and a wide constituency. On these grounds, he undertook never to 'threaten the promise of Social Security'.[77] To Gore, family values meant 'putting both Social Security

---

[73] Michelle Cottle, 'Reforming Welfare Reform: Clinton Signed the Bill; Now Conservatives and Liberals Alike Have Work To Do If We Want it To Succeed', *Washington Monthly*, November 1996; Gwendolyn Mink, *Welfare's End* (Ithaca, NY: Cornell University Press, 1998), ch. 2.

[74] Joe Klein, *The Natural: The Misunderstood Presidency of Bill Clinton* (London: Hodder & Stoughton, 2002), p. 152.

[75] Ibid., p. 153.

[76] President Bill Clinton, Inaugural Address, 20 January 1997, http://search.eb.com/elections/pri/Q00147.html.

[77] Acceptance speech at the 2000 Democratic National Convention, 17 August 2000, http://www.al-gore-2004.org/gorespeeches/08172000d.htm.

and Medicare in an iron-clad lockbox where the politicians [could not]...touch them'.[78] On the other hand, Gore remained a New Democrat. Two weeks before the election, he drew a clear line between his candidacy and the collective memory of American liberalism:

> I don't ever want to see another era of big government....In this tale of two candidates, I'm the one who believes in limited government, and I have believed in it long before it was fashionable to do so in the Democratic Party. I don't believe in it that there's a government solution to every problem. I don't believe any government program can replace the responsibility of parents, the hard work of families or the innovation of industry.[79]

This outlook bore eloquent testimony to the way in which the Democrats as the traditional party *for* government could no longer be regarded as the natural party *of* government.

LIBERAL COMPLAINTS

American liberalism has been reported as being dead or dying for over thirty years. At one level this represents a gross overstatement. Big government remains big. The federal, state, and local government budgets account for over 30 per cent of GDP. The federal government, for example, continues to offer a profusion of programmes providing protection against loss of income as a result of retirement, prolonged disability, death, or unemployment. Other programmes give federal support in areas such as medical care, housing, education, food purchases, energy expenses, children's welfare, vocational rehabilitation, and public health services. Federal spending on human resources not only exceeds 65 per cent of federal outlays but also outranks defence expenditures by a factor of over three to one.[80] Even during a period when Republican insurgents in Congress conducted a sustained assault against social spending, President Clinton managed to secure the passage of a number of new, if limited, social programmes. Yet, notwithstanding the evident infrastructure of affirmative government and the accepted need for state supervision and regulation in American society, liberalism retains its stigma and continues to be subjected to political critique.

The complaints against liberalism come in a variety of forms. One particularly significant strand is derived from the widespread perception that liberalism has been not only the rationalizing philosophy behind the emergence of central government but also the defining feature of that government's contemporary dynamics. To the extent that Washington can be characterized as an establishment, it is almost invariably depicted as a liberal establishment. This fusion of identities has reputedly afforded enormous political and social leverage to the 'liberal elite'

[78] Acceptance speech at the 2000 Democratic National Convention.

[79] Al Gore, quoted in Brands, *The Strange Death of American Liberalism*, pp. 171–2.

[80] US Census Bureau, *Statistical Abstract of the United States* (2005), http://www.census.gov/prod/2005pubs/06statab/fedgov.pdf.

and has allegedly worked to consolidate and extend the liberal agenda in government. But while the principles of progressive reform may have been advanced by the positional advantage of liberal themes and priorities in government, the connection to the state has also brought with it allegations that the symbiosis has resulted in illiberal outcomes.

The very construction of the liberal state in the 1930s was built upon the notion that the federal government could act as a neutral agency in mediating between powerful organized interests. Nevertheless, its effectiveness in performing this role meant that it drew these interests into the orbit of government. As these organizations became component parts of an emergent scheme of governance, other interests inevitably followed in order to stake their claims and seek security for their priorities in the expanding policy framework of the federal government. It is argued that this set in progress a dynamic which inflated the scale of government while at the same time depleting its independence and undermining its claims to act in accordance with autonomous rationality and social justice. In *The End of Liberalism*, Theodore Lowi describes how reformers in government did not so much exercise power as parcel it out to special interests.[81] This practice bought support and cooperation. But, according to Lowi, such a strategy also led inexorably to a vacuity of public policy and to a culture of dependence within government upon clusters of large, institutionalized, and unassailable interests. Today, interest groups do not merely penetrate government; they in effect reconstitute it through the aggregate effect of their needs. The liberal attachment to pluralist theory leads, in Lowi's view, to a complacency that relies upon spontaneous, natural balances to secure the common interest. The consequence is one of chronic, and even corrupt, disarray within government which leads to a decline in political competence and public trustworthiness.

Michael Sandel takes a slightly different view of the liberal ascendancy in government. By acting in the role of a neutral arbiter between competing interests, he claims that government is preoccupied with ensuring that interests do not encroach upon each other's individual rights. The net effect of this dominant 'procedural liberalism' is a myopic concern for the processes of competition for resources at the expense of any overarching conception of the public good. The liberal interplay of interests may facilitate political participation but only at the instrumental level of marginal gains and losses. High activity is secured at the expense of moral vision and, with it, a deterioration in civic engagement and collective action.[82] Michael Tomasky takes a different view. In contrast to Sandel who believes that the New Deal largely eclipsed the republican ethos of the common interest, Tomasky claims that republicanism had been a distinctive theme in President Roosevelt's administration but that since then it had been superseded by modern liberalism's concern for social justice, cultural differentiation, and

[81] Theodore J. Lowi, *The End of Liberalism: Ideology, Policy, and the Crisis of Public Authority* (New York: W. W. Norton, 1969).

[82] Michael J. Sandel, *Democracy's Discontent: America in Search of a Public Philosophy* (Cambridge, MA: Belknap Press, 1998).

the expansion of rights. For Tomasky, it is now necessary for liberals to realize that they have become disconnected from the civic republican tradition which had been the foundation of liberal programmes from the New Deal to the Great Society. In having become too remote and too detached from society, contemporary liberals could no longer advance any realistic rationale for collective action and had, as a result, become conspicuously reticent over advocating forms of state intervention. Thus, liberals are said to have lost touch with what Tomasky describes as liberalism's 'philosophical principle—that citizens should be called upon to look beyond their own self-interest and work for a greater common interest'.[83]

When these types of criticism are taken in tandem with the indicators associated with the 'culture of contentment'[84] and the tax resistance of the consolidating middle classes, the cutting edge of liberalism can appear to have been eroded into institutional complacency. The very success of liberal measures can be said to have fostered a middle class shocked at the iconoclasm of the New Deal and its successor programmes. By the same token, it can be claimed that the sheer expansion of liberal government has created its own political constituencies, its own institutional clients, and its own budgetary inertia geared to defending settled patterns of federal expenditure. On this basis, liberal forces are often indicted for maintaining government programmes irrespective of need or performance; for claiming privileges and exclusions in the same way as any other self-perpetuating elite; and for creating a state that is far from neutral in either its methods or its outcomes.

Another strand of complaint centres upon the alleged redundancy of the liberal agenda. The charge made is either that the reform agenda has largely been completed and socially assimilated, or that its experimentation in social engineering has been shown to be a failure. With both indictments, the conclusion is one in which liberalism is confronted with severe political, social, technical, and moral limitations. Set against a background of declining public trust in government, an increasing resistance to tax increases, and a growing acceptance of the intractability of social problems and of the limits of political action, the cause of liberal reform can be seen as having entered a cul-de-sac. Just as liberalism has reputedly lost its intellectual force, so are its advocates accused of facilitating a process of successive adjustments to prevailing social realities. Given liberalism's traditional association with the principles of rational enquiry and social progress, the loss of intellectual energy and authority, together with the preoccupation with retrospective debates, have in many respects amounted to a negation of the liberal prospectus for eliciting improvement through organized intervention.

Far from being identified with progress, American liberals have become associated with regression and with the bequest of ideological and government failure. Instead of defining a pathway to an improved future, liberalism is now often perceived to be locked into the conditions of the 1960s and even the 1930s. The

---

[83] Michael Tomasky, 'Party in Search of a Notion', *The American Prospect*, May 2006.

[84] J. K. Galbraith, *Culture of Contentment* (Harmondsworth, UK: Penguin, 1993).

capacity of liberalism for reform has also been affected by its historical connection to crises and emergency responses. While the critical circumstances of war, depression, and social disarray are powerful agencies of political mobilization, the reform programmes which they generate can often suffer from an attenuated legitimacy. Liberal measures enacted during abnormal times and presented as temporary devices of social amelioration or economic management are vulnerable to challenge when conditions return to normal, or when it can be claimed that conditions have degenerated further into abnormality. A liberal programme that is dependent upon a national mood for its inception is equally susceptible to a change of mood. The critical atmosphere that may have ushered in a period of liberal reform can quickly transfer itself to the liberal measures themselves and to their sponsors. The need to publicize the future benefits of reform, and even to oversell the product, in order to maximize the chances of enactment has generated overexpectations in the past and, with them, a high level of disenchantment with liberalism's record. In this respect, liberalism is criticized not merely on the grounds that its programme has been fulfilled and found wanting, but also that its agenda was always flawed in design and durability.

Divisions within liberalism offer further sources of disaffection. Liberals are often characterized as the agents of the large state in which government intervention is equated with efficiency, progress, and equity. The authentic picture, however, is much more opaque because of the trend towards civil liberties and issues of social and personal emancipation. These more recent priorities 'cannot be subsumed within the rubric of interventionist government'. Foner continues: 'Ironically, decline of confidence in the state during the 1980s and 1990s strengthened public commitment to such liberal values as freedom of expression and women's right to make their own decisions concerning sexual relations and reproduction'.[85] This enlargement of liberalism to encompass the personal rights of autonomy against the state often sits uneasily alongside efforts to secure rights through the state. Moreover, the contemporary reliance upon the judiciary to nullify state and local majority decisions further distances liberalism from its earlier commitment to political democracy and popular support.

Other sources of strain also remain evident. While some liberals have always given priority to the theme of education and moral improvement for those on the margins of society, others have been less oriented to the individual aspect of a democratic citizenship and more disposed to a national configuration of democracy allowing for economic reorganization and social progress through the enlightened technocracy of central government. This historical division has resonance with the more contemporary tension between the priorities associated with macro-level economic management on the one hand and the segmented nature of reformist advocacy groups pressing for particular social benefits on the other which can seriously disrupt liberal agendas—especially in an era when tax and spending levels remain a highly sensitive political issue. Another basis for discord is provided by the presence of extensive structural programmes

---

[85] Eric Foner, 'Reasons for Thinking That War is a Good Thing', *London Review of Books*, 27 June 2002.

dedicated to ameliorating middle-class insecurities, existing alongside liberal efforts to intervene on behalf of the excluded and dispossessed where the problems are most severe but where the scepticism over the effectiveness and even legitimacy of government action is at its highest.

The depth of social grievance and complaint as a basis for political action accounts for another dimension of differentiation. The populist strand of fundamental critique and class-infused invective against corporate power and privilege remains an intermittent but potent element of liberal dissent. Yet it is an attribute that those who closely identify with the progressive approach find highly objectionable. The DLC, for example, openly acknowledges its progressive pedigree and vigorously condemns 'the populist tendency to indiscriminately attack corporations as inherently corrupt or regard a market economy as an inherent obstacle to social justice'.[86] Accordingly, the New Democrats have to be watchful of populist efforts to use corporate scandals in order 'to restrain competition, to punish innovation, to expand government at the expense of the private sector, and to constrain economic growth'.[87]

The reform impulse is also distracted by what is seen as a disconnect between the required rhetoric of the need for, and the feasibility of, change set against the perceived reputation of liberal action in compounding social problems and diminishing the authority of government in the process. Liberals have had to 'face unprecedented government problems, which ... have come about under the auspices of impeccably liberal government'.[88] At the same time, they have also had to deal with the increasing dealignment of the New Deal constituency under the pressure of socially conservative impulses, ethnic and racial enmities, as well as a renewed differentiation between rural, small town, and suburban interests on the one hand, and cosmopolitan and inner city concerns on the other. These points of difference, and the political context within which they occur, underline the classic distinction within reform liberalism between the ethical desire to improve society and the strategic need to secure power. J. K. Galbraith summarizes the nature of the dilemma:

On one side are those who would accommodate [and] show that we on the Left are people with whom the comfortable can be secure. No new and disturbing initiatives. Caution in the United States about the acceptability of the liberal label itself. Or alternatively, there are those who propose that there be an uncompromising assertion of still relevant social goals—the goals of greater equality in income and enjoyments, attention to the many holes in the social fabric of the welfare state and ... the terrible problems of homelessness, other deprivation and general social disaster in our big cities.... [I]t is a division between those who, in this comfortable world, make the concessions that they believe are necessary to

---

[86] Democratic Leadership Council, 'Idea of the Week: Progressivism, Not Populism', *New Democrats Online*, 12 July 2002, http://www.dlc.org/ndol_ci.cfm?kaid=131&subid=207&contentid=250645.

[87] Ibid.

[88] Daniel P. Moynihan, *Counting Our Blessings: Reflections on the Future of America* (Boston, MA: Little Brown, 1980), p. xx.

win power and those who, speaking for the uncompleted agenda of the welfare state and specifically for those still left outside, are committed to comforting the afflicted, however this afflicts the comfortable.[89]

Notwithstanding their strategic and purposive differences, both the types of liberals described by Galbraith have generally found it prudent to give their support to measures that are categorized as being essential to the nation's defence. Whether it is due to a need to overcompensate for their criticism of American society or for their perceived empathy for others, or whether it is symptomatic of an action-oriented and even authoritarian outlook upon the role of government, American liberalism has had a close historical association with US military intervention and war. The sustained priority of high military expenditure inevitably leads to a disjunction between liberal aspiration and liberal achievement in the sphere of restricted budgets. Recently, the emphasis upon national security and the war on terror has meant that liberal support for emergency measures have contributed to a substantive restriction upon civil liberties and personal freedoms. Indeed, the spectre of new security threats has prompted some to call for a liberal realignment. This would combine social reform, economic programmes, and greater equality with an unequivocal position on the challenge of global terrorism and the need to recognize it both as an existential threat and as a genuine form of totalitarianism. In an effort to recreate the cold war liberalism of the Americans for Democratic Action and its supporters, Peter Beinart, for example, believes that liberals must not divide on the issue of Jihadism in the way they became split over Vietnam in the 1960s. Instead, they are called upon to pool their resources into a coordinated response of liberal idealism, pragmatism, and realism. This would involve social and economic proposals as well as forms of international cooperation and institutional development in a concerted programme of robust 'liberal anti-totalitarianism'.[90]

It is possible to claim that American liberalism is an inherently mixed compound. On the other hand, it can be argued that its hybrid qualities have been externally imposed by the eclectic choices of supporters and voters, creating in the process a variety of liberal constructions. American liberalism's deficiencies in ideological coherence can be cited as evidence of its ability to 'survive and thrive, in no small measure because of the willingness and ability of American liberals to reconfigure their creed'.[91] Either way, liberalism is criticized for its lack of consistency, clarity, and vision. It is susceptible to the charge that it has no agreed moral priority and, as a result, remains suffused in ambiguity in respect to both its means and ends.

The predicament facing American liberal reformers bears a close relationship to the problems that have always confronted those who have tried to secure

[89] J. K. Galbraith, 'The Death of Liberalism', *The Observer*, 26 March 1989.

[90] Peter Beinart, *The Good Fight: Why Liberals—and Only Liberals—Can Win the War on Terror and Make America Great Again* (New York: HarperCollins, 2006).

[91] Gary Gerstle, 'The Protean Character of American Liberalism', *The American Historical Review*, vol. 99, no. 4 (October 1994), p. 1073.

improvements within a culture based upon traditions of historical emancipation and presumptions of individual freedom. Reform proposals necessarily have to be situated within the liberal tradition. Solutions have to be based upon the very precepts of American identity, which can arguably be claimed to be the source of the problems requiring attention. The nature of this predicament is well established but it can be claimed that its problematic properties have deepened in time. The reform agendas and bequests of the populist and progressive movements have now persisted for more than a century. On this basis, reform liberalism might be considered to have become either a settled tradition in its own right or an integral constituent of a national tradition. Yet, liberalism retains its egregious reputation. Whether it is because liberal reforms are associated with cultural division, elitist privilege, historical failure, or the interventionist state, the term 'liberal' continues to have a pariah status in the popular vocabulary of American politics.

Most candidates for elected public office still take great care in avoiding the disparagement of the 'L-word'. Given that only two in ten Americans classify themselves as liberal,[92] the circumspection demonstrated by candidates is well founded. It reflects the contemporary notoriety attached to liberals and even the doubts over liberalism's legitimacy as a reform ethos. Some indications suggest that the liberal reform impulse might be undergoing a revival. For example, citizen action groups in support of progressive causes have increased their penetration into public debate and government decision-making.[93] The increased profile of progressive think tanks (e.g. Center for American Progress, Progressive Policy Institute, Rockridge Institute, New York Progressive Network, Democracy Alliance) has also contributed to the promotion of liberal analysis and policy agendas. In addition, there are indications of a greater salience to liberal alternatives and in particular to the need for a more critically aware conception of how a market economy operates and how it could be made to facilitate a more equitable and engaged society.[94] Moreover, demographic sectors that have traditionally leaned towards the liberal wing of the Democratic Party are projected to create an emergent majority within the next decade.[95] Notwithstanding these current or future developments, the suspicion of liberalism remains an enduring feature of American politics. Liberals have suffered from the custodial disputes over the definition and usage of national values. It is to liberalism's main detractors and tormentors to whom we will now turn in order to demonstrate the pivotal significance of this ideological competition for America's values matrix.

---

[92] The Gallup Organization, 'Most Americans Identify as Either Conservative or Moderate', 11 November 2003, http://www.galluppoll.com/content/?ci=9691.
[93] Jeffrey M. Berry, *The New Liberalism: The Rising Power of Citizen Groups* (Washington, DC: Brookings Institution Press, 2000).
[94] Douglas S. Massey, *Return of the 'L' Word: A Liberal Vision for the New Century* (Princeton, NJ: Princeton University Press, 2005).
[95] John B. Judis and Ruy Teixeira, *The Emerging Democratic Majority* (New York: Scribner, 2004).

13

Conservatism

FOUNDATIONAL THEMES

Throughout American history, the logic, legitimacy, and status of conservatism have been subjected to recurrent patterns of critique. These challenges to the presence and plausibility of American conservatism are almost invariably based upon the operational premise that the American republic is an intrinsically liberal construction. The foundation of the United States is closely bound up with an explicit reaction against the imperial position of the British Crown and its supportive structure of Toryism in the form of a landed aristocracy with inherited estates, legal privileges, and a static stratification of society. Given that, its identity remains so integrally connected to the authority of liberal principles that the United States can appear to be a society wholly at variance with the precepts of conservatism. Moreover, the United States is often taken to be a society that is actively characterized by its generic incompatibility with conservatism. Arguably, social mobility and liberal opportunity have given the United States a historical capacity for emancipation not least from the kind of constraints that in more traditional cultures embed the individual into a social stasis of established authority and hierarchical stability.

It was the United States' departure from the European norm of conservative traditionalism that provided the motive force of Louis Hartz's celebrated assertion of an all-embracing liberal consensus as the defining characteristic of American civilization.[1] The initial absence of feudalism and an *ancien régime* in American society had permitted liberalism to acquire an uncontested monopoly status in the public philosophy and individual mindsets of an uninhibited bourgeois culture. Laissez-faire capitalism built upon the civil libertarian implications of the republic's foundations and further encouraged the abandonment of any notion of a fixed social order. It was not simply that individualism increasingly supplanted those corporate community values that were traditionally the preserve of conservative institutions. It was that individual enrichment and social mobility were potentially correlated with the operational ideals of the American republic. Just as property ownership was regarded as a natural right, so was the conferral of property upon individuals through the operation of the market the basis of a constantly mutating pattern of social relationships. America lacked a feudal conception of class

---

[1] Louis Hartz, *The Liberal Tradition in America: An Interpretation of American Political Thought Since the Revolution* (New York: Harcourt Brace Jovanovich, 1955).

relations and responsibilities. As a result, it was deemed to be devoid of the kind of anti-industrial right wing and class-consciousness peasantry or proletariat that might have fostered a polarizing opportunity for a conservative alternative to the liberal alternative mainstream.

Hartz reasoned that in America's conceptual landscape, conservatives could only ever be a derivative of the liberal consensus. The claim was that American conditions had effectively merged conservatism into liberalism, so that a secular unity had been produced in which American conservatives were condemned to conserving liberal traditions. As a consequence, 'anyone who dared to use conservatism in order to refute liberalism would discover instead that he had merely refuted himself'.[2] Hartz's calculus was designed for one outcome: to demonstrate that a social consensus in American conditions could only ever be an expression of liberal principles and priorities.

Notwithstanding the acclaimed prominence of America's foundations, it is possible to advance the claim that a liberal ascendancy cannot, and does not, incorporate every position and condition in the interplay of American political argument. In fact, over the last quarter of the twentieth century, it has been the conservatives who have dominated public debate and who have been pre-eminent in the formulation of political ideas and policy agendas. Far from being subsumed within the parameters of a liberal orthodoxy, conservatives have been in the vanguard of alternative ideas, radical programmes, and iconoclastic initiatives. Conservatives have contested the prevailing constructions of American values and the conventional priorities of liberal-based policies. By organizing grass-roots movements, establishing think tanks, managing lobbying campaigns, advocating policy shifts, and securing electoral leverage, conservatives have become the most conspicuous feature of American politics in terms of intellectual engagement and ideological conviction. In effect, they have set out to redefine the moral and historical basis of the liberal mainstream. Thus, American conservatives have sought to offer a genuine and culturally authenticated alternative to the notion of a singular disposition.

Although conservatives have exerted enormous pressure upon the established configurations of policy and policy-making in the United States over the past twenty-five years, their efforts have been marked more by their extraordinary diversity rather than by the evidence of any unified doctrinal or sociological basis.[3] Self-styled conservatives and their policy solutions have been drawn from traditionalists and libertarians, law-and-order advocates and free-market ultras, corporate financiers and Southern evangelicals, patrician Wasps and tax-cutting suburbanites, and disillusioned intellectuals and blue-collar populists. Such a rich ecology offers breadth of vision and political energy. By the same token, it also generates a confusion of discordant impulses and mixed messages. This leads

---

[2] Hartz, *The Liberal Tradition in America*, p. 151.

[3] William F. Buckley, Jr. (ed.), *American Conservative Thought in the Twentieth Century* (Indianapolis, IN: Bobbs-Merrill, 1970); William F. Buckley, Jr. and Charles R. Kesler (eds.), *Keeping the Tablets: Modern American Conservative Thought* (New York: Harper & Row, 1988); Charles W. Dunn and J. David Woodard, *The Conservative Tradition in America* (Lanham, MD: Rowman & Littlefield, 2003).

to complaints that a proliferation of conservative dissent amounts to neither a coherent system of thought nor a settled programme of action. Nevertheless, it is this very plurality of conservative principles and impulses that not only underlines the usage of values in American political argument, but also demonstrates the dependency of political debate upon the contested meanings of ostensibly settled reference points of social principle. American conservatives may exhibit a bewildering profusion of stances and preferences, but a substantial proportion of this diversity can be reduced to the derivatives of two seminal traditions. Although they intersect one another and their themes draw upon each other, there exists a clear sense of differentiation in terms of first principles, ideological priorities, and attitudinal traditions.[4]

ORGANIC CONSERVATISM

Organic or traditional conservatism is the term used to describe the attempt to locate a conservative ethos within a culture of historically sanctioned customs and norms. This form of conservatism conceives of society as an integrated whole. While the separate parts and categories of society can be discerned and even analysed, a society's basic nature can only ever be comprehended as an organic unity from which each part derives its function and purpose. The components of a society are likewise only to be understood in terms of their relation to the entirety of society.

The basic consequence of this holistic conception is that society is accepted as a corporate entity, which not only exists historically prior to the individuals within it, but is ethically superior to them as well. According to this perspective, societies, like organisms, are products of history and experience. Their very existence is proof of their evolutionary success and of their moral virtue in a world of constant turbulence and danger. The traditional structure and behavioural conventions of such societies, therefore, are to be valued in their own right as embodiments of survival. Guiding principles are derived from history, religion, natural law, and tradition. They are sustained through instinct, sentiment, and practice.

This form of conservatism has always been strongly associated with European politics. Drawn from the social forms and certainties of various *anciens régimes*, European conservatism has had a strong tradition of accepting the historical bequest of classes, ranks, and hierarchy within society. Such stratification is believed to be essential to the very continuation of society. Traditionalist conservatives place their trust in the security offered by social experience within what is conceived to be a dangerously fragile system of civilized order. In such a context, the highest attainment and the lowest levels of barbarism are divided by the finest of margins. The course of history to this mindset is not one of assured progress

---

[4] See George Carey (ed.), *Freedom and Virtue: The Conservative/Libertarian Debate* (Lanham, MD: University Press of America, 1984).

but rather a cautionary tale of delicate inheritance secured from the tragedies of human error and conceit.

Societies may engage in forms of enhancement, but to the traditionalist there is always a price to pay because an unqualified improvement is a chimera. The benefits of progress have to be carefully judged in relation to the inevitable costs of change. Although this kind of conservatism possesses a powerful attachment to the society in existence, it does not subscribe to the idea that such a society has reached perfection or that it could ever attain perfectibility. On the contrary, traditionalist conservatives are cautious, suspicious, and fatalistic. Their belief in humanity's inner drives towards greed, violence, and destruction and in the limitation and fallibility of human reason leads them to the conclusion that the human condition is inherently imperfect. On this basis, traditionally minded conservatives adhere to the security of order and to the obligations that are necessary to its preservation. They refute the claims of reason, progress, rights, democracy, and equality as delusions serving only to threaten the delicate bonds of civilization and to risk a subsequent descent into the barbarism of anarchy or tyranny. Traditionalists conserve out of an instinct for continuity and because of an anxiety over the cost of any ostensible improvement.

The values and principles defended in this sort of conservatism have generally been thought by Europeans to be common to western civilization as a whole. However, in the United States this premise could not be so easily assumed. American experience and conditions appeared to be diametrically opposed not just to this type of conservative tradition, but to any conservative tradition. America's political independence and cultural autonomy, together with its avowed principles of liberty, progress, democracy, and reason, and its celebration of natural rights, contractual government, and individual autonomy within a self-made society, seemed to be wholly incompatible with the spirit of conservative sentiment.

To Sheldon Wolin, the predicament of the American conservative has been highly problematic because of the society's affinity with progress through capitalism. Conservative traditionalists may have offered eulogies to artisan virtue, Sunday observance, community cohesion, and individual responsibility, but their appeals had become increasingly plaintive set against the driving forces of modernity.

[C]onservative bankers, businessmen, and corporate executives were busy devitalizing many local centers of power and authority, from the small business and family farm to the towns and cities. They created the imperatives of technological change and mass production which have formed the attitudes, skills, and values of the worker; and erased most peculiarities of place, of settled personal and family identity; and made men and women live by an abstract time that is unrelated to personal experience or local customs.[5]

The outcome has posed a 'formidable challenge to the conservative imagination': a 'traditionless society that conserves nothing; ruling groups that are committed

---

[5] Sheldon Wolin, 'The New Conservatives', *The New York Review of Books*, 5 February 1976.

to continuous innovation; social norms that stigmatize those who fail to improve their status; incentives that require those who move up must move away'.[6]

Several strategies have been employed to resolve the problem of establishing an acceptable foundation for traditional conservatism within a self-consciously liberal culture. Three devices in particular have been prominent and they can best be conveyed by examining the views of three key individuals in the development of American conservative thought during the middle of the twentieth century. All three had to contend with the challenge of differentiating a clear basis of conservative value in the American mainstream which at the time was characterized by the prevailing doctrines of cold war liberalism.

The strategy employed by Russell Kirk was simple and direct. He made an explicit attempt to recreate a European form of conservatism on American soil. His campaign to infuse American life with an organic prescription for order, authority, and mystique would have been instantly recognizable to a European traditionalist.[7] Kirk saw no necessary connection between a balance of interests within society and the need for a particular set of political institutions. A monarchy or an aristocracy might just as easily secure such an equilibrium. Moreover, according to Kirk, these political estates would help to give authenticity to the idea of a fixed order of social rank: 'What really matters is that we should accept the station to which "a divine tactic" has appointed us with humility and a sense of consecration'.[8]

Many fellow-conservatives felt that Kirk's conservative prospectus belonged to a different time (i.e. the eighteenth century) and to a different place (i.e. Europe). He had attempted to universalize organic conservatism into a single timeless model and then to embed the construct within a social identity that was based upon difference to the point of exceptionalism. In trying to provide a comprehensive statement on the way tradition can and should act as the guiding principle of social conduct, Kirk had shown just how problematic such a proposition could be in the American context. Against the historical spirit of traditionalist conservatism, Kirk invoked the liberal presumption of individual choice and social autonomy to create a prefabricated conservatism that could be absorbed within another tradition. His vigorously organic form of conservatism led paradoxically to claims that his prospectus represented a dissociation with the American experience and to an 'unhistorical appeal to history' and to a 'traditionless worship of tradition'.[9]

Peter Viereck's solution to the source of an authentic American traditionalism was to privilege cumulative experience over notions of an idyllic past age or a fixed

---

[6] Ibid.

[7] Russell Kirk, 'Prescription, Authority and Ordered Freedom', in Frank S. Meyer (ed.), *What is Conservatism?* (New York: Holt, Rinehart and Winston, 1963), pp. 23–40; Russell Kirk, *The Conservative Mind: From Burke to Eliot*, 7th edn (Washington, DC: Regnery Gateway, 1986); see also Russell Kirk, 'The Essence of Conservatism', http://www.kirkcenter.org/kirk/essence-1957.html.

[8] Russel Kirk, 'The Problem of the New Order', in Buckley, Jr. (ed.), *American Conservative Thought in the Twentieth Century*, p. 367.

[9] Peter Viereck, 'The Philosophical "New Conservatism" (1962)', in Daniel Bell (ed.), *The Radical Right* (Garden City, NY: Anchor, 1963), p. 188.

social order. Viereck was not concerned with trying to attach American conservatism to an overarching western tradition, or to a permanent system of moral and social absolutes. He was largely indifferent towards the argument that American conservatism needed to be based upon an indigenous historical continuity which, in his opinion, the passage of American history could not support. What Viereck viewed to be of central significance were the habits of mind that were drawn simply to what were taken to be traditions in a contemporary context. He gave emphasis not to what traditions *were* in some objective sense, but what they had *become.*

In the context of organic conservatism, Viereck pointed out the importance of the adaptation of tradition, in order for tradition to be preserved in a changing world and especially in America, whose world was always changing faster than elsewhere. As a consequence of this adaptive and evolutionary outlook, Viereck was prepared to approve of what had become an 'increasingly conservatized New Deal liberalism'.[10] In his view, the true conservative ought to cherish the New Deal reforms because they had become an integral part of American society. Time had lent legitimacy so that a 'now middle-aged New Deal' had 'become conservative and rooted'[11] and, therefore, worthy of preservation as a development of integral value.

While conservative advocates like Viereck offered a mantle of Burkean consolidation to the quest for an operational American tradition, the problems with a liberal mainstream persisted. It was possible to criticize such conservatives on the conservative grounds that they were engaging in a form of liberal relativism and disguising it as a search for a core conception of society. They could also be accused of ignoring the status and the consequences of the liberal norm in American society. Clinton Rossiter was particularly significant in this respect because he set out to confront the issue of liberal orthodoxy head on. He recognized it and engaged with it on the same terms as Hartz. However, unlike Hartz, he did not claim that liberalism and conservatism enveloped one another to produce a single undifferentiated whole. Instead, Rossiter used American history to substantiate the argument that there has existed a long-established duality of ideas and impulses in American society.

On the one hand, Rossiter conceded that the American political tradition was basically liberal in form because of the way it gave emphasis to progress, liberty, democracy, equality, and individualism. On the other hand, Rossiter claimed that such a tradition had only remained viable with the coexistence of a 'deep strain of philosophical conservatism'.[12] This was embodied in the American adherence to conservative principles such as tradition, loyalty, unity, patriotism, morality, constitutionalism, religion, higher law, property, and community. Without this conservative element in American history, the attachment to liberal principles would not have been tempered into the stability and order for which America

---

[10] Viereck, 'The Philosophical "New Conservatism" (1962)', p. 188.   [11] Ibid., 198.
[12] Clinton Rossiter, *Conservatism in America: The Thankless Persuasion*, 2nd edn (New York: Vintage, 1962), p. 73.

had become renowned. Conservative principles, therefore, had provided the corrective force that prevented liberalism from realizing its potential for internal contradictions and destabilizing excess. In the United States, the 'unquestioning devotion to a whole series of inherited ideals and institutions'[13] had 'kept reform like almost everything else, within the bounds of tradition and reality'.[14] In terms of everyday political conduct, Rossiter had no doubt that conservative intuition was predominant.

In any showdown between liberalism and conservatism in American political thought, Liberalism wins out nine times out of ten. In a showdown between liberalism and conservatism in American political practice, conservatism wins out almost as monotonously. We have long-standing habit of doing political business and carrying on social relations in a conservative way.[15]

Notwithstanding his claims for the historical and social authenticity of conservative values in America, Rossiter was not disposed to assert the existence of a conservative parity with liberalism.

Even though he made an extensive case for the existence and influence of conservative principles in American history, Rossiter found it difficult to characterize the phenomenon as a singular and exclusive tradition. His argument was based wholly upon tradition, but his conclusion avoided the term.[16] The refusal amounted to a form of denial because in effect he made a convincing argument for an indigenous conservative tradition but at the same time revealed a conspicuous refusal to give it recognition. Rossiter could neither make the American consensus conservative in nature nor satisfactorily disestablish American conservatism from the liberal mainstream to give the American conservative tradition an autonomy and an identity completely its own. In alluding to a tradition that dare not speak its name, Rossiter reflected not only the conformity of his era but also the cultural prejudice against the term 'conservative'. Traditionalism, unity, patriotism, constitutionalism, and other elements of America's stable order were to Rossiter 'profoundly conservative principles'.[17] But political pragmatism appeared to have intervened at this point: '[W]e might label them conservative if it were not for the open contempt that our mind has displayed toward the conservative faith.'[18]

For nearly half a century, American conservative thought, and particularly the advocacy of an organic traditionalism, was confronted by the historical foundations of American liberalism compounded by the political momentum of successive liberal reform. From the New Deal era to the 1970s, the ideological initiative lay with the generation that had developed the organizing and protective power of the positive state. In 1951, Lionel Trilling had reached the conclusion that

---

[13] Ibid., p. 75.   [14] Ibid., p. 84.   [15] Ibid., p. 78.

[16] In this respect, he stood out from other conservative analysts who have been less inhibited over the use of the term 'tradition'. See Allan Guttman, *The Conservative Tradition in America* (New York: Oxford University Press, 1967); Jay A. Sigler (ed.), *The Conservative Tradition in American Thought* (New York: Puttnam, 1969).

[17] Rossiter, *Conservatism in America*, p. 75.   [18] Ibid.

liberalism was so dominant that it had become essentially 'the sole intellectual tradition'[19] within the United States. He continued:

> For it is the plain fact that nowadays there are no conservative or reactionary ideas in general circulation.... [T]he conservative impulse and the reactionary impulse do not...express themselves in ideas but only in action or in irritable mental gestures which seek to resemble ideas.[20]

In 1964, J. K. Galbraith was equally confident in his assessment that liberalism had acquired the status of a ubiquitous presence: 'These, without doubt, are the years of the liberal. Almost everyone now so describes himself'.[21] Conservatism was widely seen to be a reactive impulse confined to the margins of American political debate. Ironically, conservatives occupied non-consensual positions and offered choices that the mainstream largely ignored. A senior conservative recalls that for 'nearly half a century, conservatism was or felt itself to be, in the political wilderness'. At this time, 'it became cranky and recriminatory' and many questioned whether conservatives could 'come to terms with a social reality more complex than their slogans'.[22] Yet, over a relatively short period of time, the political status of conservatism was transformed from that of a political outlier to a central governing doctrine with a durable electoral base.

Several factors have been advanced to explain the dramatic shift to a conservative hegemony. They include the public's disenchantment over Vietnam and the way that the war was conducted; the decline in economic performance combined with inflation, unemployment, and high government expenditure levels; and the breakdown in law and order, race relations, and moral conventions. New Deal liberalism and the coalition that sustained it began to unravel over the 1960s under the weight of a faltering welfare-capitalist economy and the duress of social division and political distrust. Against such a disintegrative background, conservative ideas acquired an increased currency and electoral appeal. Conservatives offered analyses, explanations, and plausible solutions. Rossiter's notion of a remedial conservatism correcting liberalism found favour with large sectors of the American public. They viewed the conservative response as a means by which some sense of autonomy over social and economic processes might be restored through the force of alternative perspectives.[23]

The stimulus of increased social dislocation, economic stagnation, and Soviet adventurism fostered a ferment of conservative activity. A defining theme was that reform liberalism had not so much failed in its policy prospectus as had

---

[19] Lionel Trilling, *The Liberal Imagination: Essays on Literature and Society* (Harmondsworth, UK: Penguin, 1970), p. 9.

[20] Ibid.

[21] Quoted in John Micklethwait and Adrian Wooldridge, 'For Conservatives, Mission Accomplished', *Sooner Thought*, 18 May 2004, http://www.soonerthought.com/archives/000672.html.

[22] George Will, *Statecraft as Soulcraft: What Government Does* (London: Weidenfeld & Nicolson, 1984), p. 130.

[23] See Jonathan Schoenwald, *A Time for Choosing: The Rise of Modern American Conservatism* (New York: Oxford University Press, 2002); John Micklethwait and Adrian Wooldridge, *The Right Nation: Why America is Different* (London: Allen Lane, 2004).

succeeded in revealing its dysfunctional capacity for political overreach and in overlooking the fragility of the social order. Many of the complaints against the liberal ascendancy settled upon the critique that social engineering and experimentation had inherent limits. Society could not be regarded as possessing an endlessly mutable basis. As such, it could be expected to assimilate a range of premeditated reconfigurations without any negative ramifications.[24]

Organic conservatives were swift to make allusions to a breakdown in political authority and to draw on the contemporary state of disarray to underline the value of society's historical and traditional foundations. They condemned liberal government for having condoned and encouraged a culture of minority privileges over public interest concerns. This kind of self-serving myopia was cited as having disrupted the processes of public policy and fragmented the Democratic Party into a proliferation of segmented clienteles. Their pursuit of minority rights denied any opportunity for a grand vision that could counter the centrifugal energies of liberal self-interest in the cause of social cohesion or even cultural unity.

This concern for the contemporary state of the social fabric was reflected in the work of Robert Nisbet. In *Twilight of Authority* (1976), Nisbet despaired over the deterioration of authority as political communities, social classes, families, and churches had been marginalized by a central state devoid of traditional social ligaments. The decline of these agencies not only reduced the level of integration and meaning in social existence, but also failed to replace the structures of authority with anything resembling a holistic construction of legitimacy. On the contrary, the only substitute were forms of dislocated and alienated power, complemented by an intellectual scepticism that, in Nisbet's view, had no conception of the need to support a belief system.[25] Samuel Huntington was another who criticized the way that government had been turned into an amoral service agency of special interests. What authority it still possessed had to be secured by the multiple appeasement of continual coalition-building. The leverage of sectional interests had progressively displaced the community-based agencies that supported the cultural interest of an overarching authority. To Huntington, this dynamic had produced in the 1960s a condition which he termed 'democratic distemper'. This referred to the expansion of governmental activity on the one hand and the simultaneous reduction of governmental authority on the other. By the end of the 1970s, this had led to the paradoxical situation of Americans 'progressively demanding and receiving more benefits from their government and yet having less confidence in their government than they had a decade earlier'. Government was deemed in effect to have become ungovernable.[26]

Another aspect of this concern over the totality and interconnectedness of society underlined the importance of a moral order. Implicit in this perspective was

---

[24] M. Stanton Evans, *The Future of Conservatism* (New York: Anchor, 1969); Barry Goldwater, *The Conscience of a Majority* (New York: Pocket Books, 1971); M. Stanton Evans, *Clear and Present Dangers: A Conservative View of America's Government* (New York: Harcourt Brace Jovanovich, 1975).

[25] Robert Nisbet, *Twilight of Authority* (London: Heinemann, 1976).

[26] Samuel P. Huntington, 'The Democratic Distemper', in Nathan Glazer and Irving Kristol (eds.), *The American Commonwealth—1976* (New York: Basic Books, 1976), p. 11.

the need of society to reiterate the significance of moral foundations. Government should be required both to embody a social hierarchy of values and to engage in the active shaping of the citizenry's moral character. This kind of conservatism assumed the existence of an objective moral order that prescribed standards of human conduct to which governments should be expected to approximate. Integral to this perspective was the belief in moral priorities and in a moral imperative to act upon them. Liberalism could not be relied upon either to acknowledge the value of deep cultural traditions or to provide any substitute for them.

Drawing upon the work of writers such as Leo Strauss, Frank S. Meyer, Joseph Cropsey and Henry V. Jaffa, these conservatives placed a central value upon the moral foundations of society and upon the virtuous circle of the good citizen and the good society. According to this perspective, society was endangered by the moral relativism of secular liberal values and by schemes of social improvement that processed individual responsibility and moral consciousness out of the equation of public policy. In this respect, authority was an instrumental value that allowed a moral purpose to be served and the moral spirit of the people to be strengthened in the light of a continual conflict between good and evil.

The outlook fostered by this reactive form of conservatism was well captured by the analyses and prescriptions of George Will. In *Statecraft as Soulcraft* (1984), he stated his objections to the way that modern liberalism privileged self-expression and emancipation over established rules and standards of excellence. Because liberals favoured the 'egalitarian principle that all desires are created equal in moral worth',[27] notions of excellence and discipline were construed as illiberal. Notwithstanding the liberal bias in support of relativism, subjectivism, and spontaneity, Will called for a 'conservative counterattack, in law and culture and elsewhere, in the name of those forms of excellence which, as the Founders said, a free society especially presupposes'.[28] Just as there were bad moral arguments and outcomes, so were there also good ones, and it is these which Will believed was the responsibility of the government to promote.

[I]t is not compelling persons to act against their settled convictions; it is not a collision of wills, the state's and the citizen's. Rather, it is a slow, steady, gentle, educated and persuasive enterprise. Its aim is to dispose citizens toward certain habits, mores and values, and to increase the probability that persons will choose to will certain things.[29]

To Will, the objective was 'not to make society inhospitable to pluralism, but to make pluralism safe for society'.[30] In the same way that the 'continuance of the citizenry's moral profile is a matter of political choice', conservatism had to operate on the understanding that 'authority grows organically from the rich loam of social mores and structures'.[31]

Traditionalist conservatives like Nisbet and Will reflected a widespread concern over the state of American society and an anxiety that its cohesion and moral

---

[27] Will, *Statecraft as Soulcraft*, p. 90.   [28] Ibid.   [29] Ibid., p. 94.   [30] Ibid.
[31] Ibid., p. 95.

basis could no longer be taken for granted. Increasingly, conservative dissenters found that their expositions on authority, order, and morality were acquiring a critical leverage over the priorities of the liberal mainstream. Nevertheless, the more inroads they made into the profile of Washington agendas, the greater became the realization that their challenge had to be shared with another form of conservatism that occupied quite a different set of nuances upon American values.

INDIVIDUALISTIC CONSERVATISM

The other main organizing principle of American conservatism gives primacy not to the community and its web of evolving traditions, but to the individual and the need to protect personal liberties from the encroachment of constraining structures and doctrines. Individualistic conservatives have a powerful attachment to nineteenth-century liberalism and to the central questions relating to the foundation and purpose of the state. These issues possess a sustained immediacy to such conservatives because of their emphasis upon the recent origins of American society and because of their conviction in the New World's basic condition as a state of nature. The pre-existence of freedom in America is the key conditioning factor to this conservatism. Although the formation of government is taken to be a basic necessity for the security of society, it remains a contingent institution whose role is to preserve and maximize individual freedom to the fullest possible extent within a social setting. The criterion of optimizing liberty remains the sole priority and evaluative standard for such conservatives. Their preoccupation is one of scrutinizing the boundary between the state and individual, and of ensuring that the burden of proof for altering the relationship falls upon the state to establish legitimate reasons for increasing its remit.[32]

Individualistic conservatives accept that the United States is a mass society that can no longer depend wholly upon a vision of primitive freedom. Nevertheless, their belief in the contractual nature of political authority leads them to attribute enormous instructive value to capitalism in the organization of a free society. In the same way that the contractual ethos finds an extended resonance in the framework of capitalism, a capitalist order of property distribution is seen to offer a convincing rationale for a free society operating on the basis of full contractual freedom. It is for this reason that individualistic conservatives tend to take the period most closely associated with the productivity of laissez-faire capitalism (1875–1910) as the defining model of individual liberty and social advance. This was a period when the remit of government was weighted towards a minimal intervention in the economy. The absence or removal of restraint not only reduced the chances of political authority being abused but also allowed

[32] See David Boaz, *Libertarianism: A Primer* (New York: Free Press, 1997), pp. 27–58, 94–104, 148–211; Charles Murray, *What It Means To Be a Libertarian: A Personal Interpretation* (New York: Broadway Books, 1997), pp. 18–44, 60–79, 124–38, 143–56.

the natural dynamics, productive forces, and social benefits of the market to be maximized to reach a state of optimum synergy. The degree of economic liberty was regarded as the litmus test for all other liberties. Political liberty, therefore, was assumed to be reliant upon the condition of economic freedom embodied in a freely competitive market and in the absolute freedom of contract between any two parties.

Modern individualist conservatives take this era as their point of reference because to them it provides absolute standards of social and political prescription. Laissez-faire capitalism and the operation of the free market continue to offer a heroic vision of modernity to these conservatives. It is this period that the Cato Institute, for example, has in mind when it describes free-market capitalism as 'the most progressive, dynamic, and ever-changing system the world has ever known'.[33] To conservatives of this persuasion, the values of the economic organization and human possibilities released by capitalism are regarded as timeless and universal in character. Successive deviations from this model on the part of misguided or malign reformers have not invalidated these principles of early capitalism. On the contrary, their appeal has been enhanced by the cumulative claims that the positive state has not only failed to provide solutions to America's social economic problems, but has in fact served to exacerbate them. This is the reason why the Cato Institute dedicates itself to the need to 'broaden the parameters of public policy debate to allow consideration of the traditional American principles of limited government, individual liberty, free markets and peace'.[34]

Individualistic conservatives draw their inspiration not only from the idealized era of laissez-faire capitalism but from a reaction against the explicitly illiberal regimes that were formed during the historical experiment of communism. This strand of conservatism celebrates the work of F. A. Hayek who persistently warned Western governments during the cold war that they had to avoid the 'road to serfdom'[35] which would be the inevitable result of an incremental drift away from the free market. Hayek made a direct connection between economic freedom and political liberty. The management and planning of the economy by the state, therefore, posed huge risks to society.

Hayek's warning had two bases. First, government intervention compromised the efficient operation of a self-regulating mechanism of demand, supply, and price levels. The market remained the only means by which the sheer volume of information or changing individual demands could be systematically processed in an immediate and responsive way. The second threat posed by state interference was an ethical objection to the restriction of individual freedom. In seeking to displace the technical proficiency of the market, the state would always attempt to compensate for its lack of information and responsiveness by imposing abstract and subjective notions of fairness and social justice. Such rationalist exercises were misplaced and thoroughly dangerous. Their failures would always lead to

---

[33] The Cato Institute, 'Statement of Principles', http://www.cato.org/about/about.html.
[34] Ibid.
[35] F. A. Hayek, *The Road to Serfdom* (London: Routledge & Kegan Paul, 1944).

greater and more coercive attempts to impose a centrally directed system of resource allocation. The result would lead to the economic and moral bankruptcy of totalitarianism. According to Hayek, therefore, the free market was both an embodiment of free choice and a preventative measure that kept tyranny at bay.[36]

This concern for the overriding importance of liberty had a deep cultural appeal in the United States where the theme was further refined into an ideological frame of reference. Milton Friedman, for example, popularized the view that post-war government programmes and expenditures had already demonstrated the damage to freedom of market manipulation and social intervention by central government. Since a free market and a free political order are interdependent entities, any government intrusion in one would always destabilize the other. By intervening in both sectors at the same time, Friedman believed that liberal reformers had placed the condition of natural liberty in double jeopardy. To an individual like Friedman, laissez-faire capitalism was both the direct expression of freedom and also the chief means of ensuring its continuation. The freedom of the market necessarily had a prior claim over the requirements or contingencies of other areas of society. Political freedom in Friedman's view had a relationship of dependency upon the economic freedom of individuals making multiple choices in an open market.[37]

The connections between market capitalism and freedom, and between fundamental precepts of human nature and social ethics, are also forcibly pursued in the work of Ayn Rand. Proceeding on the basis that reason is necessarily the only guide to individual action and the sole means of ensuring an individual's survival as a person, the process of politics represents a quest for a social system that optimizes individual freedom and rights. Rand's sustained assault upon the state was explicitly derived from a philosophical-ethical foundation.[38] From this basis, it was possible to postulate that individuals exist for their own sake and that the pursuit of their own happiness was a moral obligation with the highest priority. Governments could neither take on, nor take over, such a pursuit. They could assist in the securing of rights and in managing the different spheres of rights between separate individuals, but in the main governments constituted one half of a permanent dichotomy between freedom and statism. To Rand, self-ownership and free action could not and should not be differentiated from free trade and the free property of capitalism. She objected to capitalism being defended on ameliorative or altruistic grounds. Capitalism had a moral justification but it had nothing whatever to do with collective notions of the public interest. In Rand's view, capitalism's moral rationale was rooted in the fundamental reality

[36] See Fritz Machlup (ed.), *Essays on Hayek* (London: Routledge & Kegan Paul, 1977); John Gray, *Hayek on Liberty* (Oxford: Robertson, 1984).

[37] Milton Friedman, *Capitalism and Freedom* (Chicago, IL: University of Chicago Press, 1962); Milton Friedman and Rose Friedman, *Free to Choose* (New York: Harcourt Brace Jovanovich, 1980).

[38] Donna Greiner and Theodore Kinni, *Ayn Rand and Business* (New York: Texere Publishing, 2001).

of human existence and in the asserted power of reason to elicit and extrapolate the requirements for pure survival.[39]

Another exercise in creating a countervailing ethos to liberal reform and the positive state came with Robert Nozick's *Anarchy, State and Utopia* (1974).[40] This amounted to an assault upon the post-war consensus that freedom and social justice were reconcilable through redistributive and welfare programmes. In many respects, it was conceived and subsequently cited as an explicit response to John Rawls's *A Theory of Justice* (1972).[41] In what was in essence a systematic re-enactment of John Locke's theory of individual rights, private property, and the state, Nozick repeatedly concluded that any interference with individual choice amounted to coercion. His premise was that everything begins with, and is consequently rooted in, individuals and their rights to liberty. Nozick accepted that individual rights should afford a floor of equal status. But once this basic condition is satisfied, the need is eliminated for any ceiling to be imposed upon the unequal outcomes that inevitably attend the exercise of personal freedom. Accordingly, the role of the state should be limited to that of a night watchman in protecting citizens against violence, theft, and fraud and in enforcing contracts and property rights. Assuming any additional roles would be to exceed its remit: 'The minimal state is the most extensive state that can be justified. Any state more extensive violates people's rights'.[42] All attempts to enhance the claims and responsibilities of the state through pretexts such as social justice, collective rights, or national sovereignty are fraudulent in that they only serve to disguise coercion and the contraction of liberty.

According to Nozick, for a state to sustain its legitimacy, it has to possess the least capacity for force consistent with the maintenance of rights. If a state were to intervene to reduce inequalities, therefore, it would have nullified its *raison d'être*. It would have destroyed liberty by unjustly infringing upon property rights, in order to bring about a state of affairs different from that produced by the free trade of property holdings. Nozick points out that whenever a state pursues a policy of equality, even in accordance with the most altruistic motives, it inevitably subverts its own foundations. The position is further compounded by Nozick's assertion that egalitarian schemes are not only ethically questionable, but also operationally problematic. They are said to break down through the operation of free choice by individuals who will always attempt to circumvent an imposed pattern of social justice. Nozick's conception of an atomized society reduced to a stark basis of individual freedoms and property holdings afforded a fundamentalist calculus, through which almost every government action could be condemned on principle.

Anarchy, State and Utopia is in many respects an unconservative tract of political thought. It is highly libertarian in content and rationalist in its manner of

---

[39] Ayn Rand, *Capitalism: The Unknown Ideal* (New York: Signet Books, 1986); Mimi Reisel Gladstein, *The New Ayn Rand Companion* (Westport, CT: Greenwood Press, 1999).

[40] Robert Nozick, *Anarchy, State and Utopia* (Oxford: Blackwell, 1974).

[41] John Rawls, *A Theory of Justice* (London: Oxford University Press, 1972).

[42] Nozick, *Anarchy, State and Utopia*, p. 149.

construction. It eschews any ideas of justice based upon religion or natural law and it dispenses with any concern for the social bonds of mutual and collective obligation. Nevertheless, its iconoclasm appealed to those who were frustrated with the perceived heavy-handedness of government and who felt that they were paying the price of a social benefit that was in effect a forcible expropriation. Nozick's exposition was highly influential in the way it provided a fully developed expression of individualist conservatism in a period when such conservatism no longer seemed reactionary or shameless, but appeared to present logical alternatives and even the prospect of solutions.[43]

Theorists like Hayek, Friedman, Rand, and Nozick have enjoyed widespread notoriety in the United States because of the way they combine cultural instincts with elegant reasoning. Their systematically reasoned expositions of first principles are significant in their own right, but they are also important for the way their themes create a resonance within American society. The strong American impulse towards anti-statism and anti-establishment scepticism is well served by such extensive critiques. The libertarian character of the analysis both reflects a deep undercurrent of social attitudes and contributes towards a radical right theme in much of America's public life. The advocacy of contractual restraints upon the state, the advancement of free-market dynamics, and the libertarian thrust against hegemonic structures and doctrines have found a particularly receptive audience in parts of the Republican Party. The effect of these same impulses, and their affinity with the iconoclastic outlook of libertarian intellectualism, has also fostered the development of alternative political movements with adventurous policy agendas.

The Constitution Party, for example, adopts a fundamentalist approach to the problems of American society and the 'mess in Washington'.[44] Its project is to reclaim the principles of the Constitution which it claims 'have been abandoned by our political establishment'.[45] In order to reverse 'America's slide into lawlessness, corruption and tyranny',[46] it is necessary to restore the government to its 'proper balance'[47] and to its rightful role of preserving and promoting individual liberty. The party's principles expressly coincide with the foundational themes of the Constitution itself. It asserts that the original objective of the government was to protect individual rights which included the 'freedom to own, use, exchange, control, protect, and freely dispose of property'.[48] The lessons of history had made 'clear that left unchecked, it is the nature of government

---

[43] See Jeffrey Paul (ed.), *Reading Nozick: Essays on Anarchy, State and Utopia* (Oxford: Basil Blackwell, 1982); Jonathan Wolff, *Robert Nozick: Property, Justice and the Minimal State* (Oxford: Polity, 1991).

[44] Constitution Party, 'Party Programme (2003)', http://www.constitutionparty.com/pr03.htm.

[45] Constitution Party, 'A Brief History of the Constitution Party', http://www.constitution-party.com/party_history.php.

[46] Ibid.   [47] Ibid.

[48] Constitution Party, 'Constitution Party National Platform', http://www.constitution-party.com/party_platform.php.

to usurp the liberty of its citizens and eventually become a major violator of the people's rights'.[49] Accordingly, it was necessary to stop and to reverse the processes of government expansion and usurpation. By eliminating income tax, sales taxes, estate taxes, gasoline taxes, and the Internal Revenue Service, the federal government would be downsized to a format consistent with its original purpose. The corollary would be a restoration of liberties to individuals and local communities. The libertarian logic of the Constitution Party leads it to advocate the abandonment of the welfare state with the same animus against government as it reflects in the party's proposals to repeal the Patriot Act, the Homeland Security Act, and the National Security Act because of the way that they enable government agencies to conceal their activities and to undermine the freedoms of citizens.

The same unequivocal hostility to government is also reflected in the formation and guiding principles of the militia movements. The sense of government as a direct threat both to personal liberty and to national security is conveyed in their mission statements which draw on themes of dispossession and popular sovereignty to legitimize the claim for an alternative and countervailing force for the benefit of American society. The common view is that just as 'all power is inherent in the people', so the 'greatest system of checks and balances exists with the people'.[50] Whether it is the decline of public trust in government, or a symptom of the eroded autonomy of individuals and communities, the militia movements offer a combination of pioneering self-reliance with political primitivism that is directed against government-sponsored enemies. The purist libertarian conclusion is that government is the greatest threat of all. Direct action, therefore, is required to defend the people against its government:

The usurpation of our Constitution and Bill of Rights has awakened many Americans to the dangers of lawless government and people are catching on to the fact that the problems in America today are coming out of Washington, D.C. and their own State House—not the rural areas and backwoods of their State.[51]

Given the conviction that the 'domestic enemies of the Constitution . . . are found in every institution and sector of our society', and that Washington can be equated with 'gangster government',[52] the logic of the diagnosis is pressed to its conclusion of radical and direct action. In this way, the citizen militias are a characteristic product of libertarian reasoning in which the logic of critical analysis is driven to the point of identifying a solution that is in exact accordance with the parameters of the stated problem. When the imperative of these first principles is combined with the normative force of America's legendary state of first existence, the result is one of an enriched appeal to the simplicities of a recoverable past.

---

[49] Constitution Party, 'Constitution Party National Platform'.

[50] http://texas-militia.us/main/content/view/32/42/.

[51] http://www.indianamilitia.homestead.com/Milandyou1.html

[52] http://www.constitution.org/mil/adversaries.htm

THE CONSERVATIVE MATRIX

The doctrinaire nature of individualistic conservatism is its strength. It provides an absolutist position of core convictions based upon a notion of historical endowment drawn from a period when the state had only a rudimentary presence in society. By offering a counternarrative to modern political development, individualistic conservatism affords a framework of critique in which elements of modernity can be opposed as heretical breaks with the past. This type of conservatism has a tendency to view politics as an epic encounter and a continual moral struggle between the baseline of liberty and the corrupting force of government. The relationship between the two is assumed to be a strict zero-sum conflict of values. In reflecting upon, and in celebrating the past, individualistic conservatives use history as a way of directing public attention to certain values that are closely associated with a previous era or, more accurately, with the idea of a period that reputedly epitomizes the American spirit. The intention is to underline what appears to have been lost, but at the same time to demonstrate what can be reclaimed through the force of human will and moral courage.

It is evident that major tensions exist between the evolutionary character of organic conservatism and the conservative instinct that is inclined to value a fixed regime of fundamentalist positions. Traditionalists give emphasis to order, authority, continuity, duty, moral purpose, and social cohesion. They are sceptical of the laissez-faire outlook and of its faith in the reliability of self-regulating social dynamics. In organic conservative thought, religious and moral values are often given a higher priority than the claims of individual liberty. While property rights and the notion of a natural aristocracy are common to both, the traditionalist conception of hierarchy is closely tied to a more settled social order than that envisaged by the market dynamism of the libertarians. This is witnessed by the equanimity shown by someone like Kirk towards differences within society. Because a natural hierarchy exists in society, inequalities should be seen as 'occasions for positive virtue, if accepted with a contrite heart'.[53] He continues:

> That some men are richer than others ... and that some are more educated than others is no more unjust, in the great scheme of things, than that some undeniably are handsomer or stronger or quicker or healthier than others. This complex variety is the breath of life to society, not the triumph of injustice. ... Without inequality, there is no opportunity for charity, or gratitude; without differences of mind and talent, the world would be one changeless expanse of uniformity.[54]

In general, organic conservatives acknowledge the importance of individual liberty both as an ethical value and as an instrument of progress but are not prepared to concede that freedom represents either the supreme cultural tradition or the primary prescriptive standard by which social developments and government

---

[53] Kirk, 'The Problem of the New Order', in Buckley, Jr. (ed.), *American Conservative Thought in the Twentieth Century*, p. 367.
[54] Ibid.

actions are judged. The libertarian thrust of individualistic conservatives arouses suspicion amongst organic conservatives that freedom is being used to legitimize a form of rootless materialism that violently erodes the traditional patterns of social hierarchy. Organic conservatives tend to believe that the unreflective drives of libertarians are likely to lead to social distortions in which recent patterns of wealth are progressively strengthened, leading to an exacerbation of social discord and a widening of those social and economic differences that threaten the cultural fabric of America.[55]

To a traditionalist cast of mind, individualistic conservatives can appear to be not merely ahistorical but anti-historical in their demands for time to be reversed and for America to be projected back to a selected era of social harmony and economic prosperity. Because of their abrasive contempt for the consequences of accumulated experience, these individualistic conservatives are said to challenge the present from a position of wanting to recreate the past. Their antagonism towards tradition has in the past earned them the reputation of being described as 'pseudo-conservatives'.[56] Certainly, organic conservatives are wary of the impulsive fundamentalist character of many on the radical right of individualistic conservatism. Traditionalists speculate upon whether these individualistic conservatives have a closer approximation to reform liberals than to conservatives. It can be claimed that individualistic conservatives and liberal reformers both fail to appreciate the limitations of politics and the restricted opportunities for ordered change.

At a temperamental and intellectual level, organic conservatives have a greater affinity with the philosophical principles and historical properties of classical political thought than is the case with their libertarian counterparts. Organic conservatives tend to draw upon the classical traditions of examining the definitions, ideals, and practicalities of the right way of life. These take into account the unchangeable nature of humanity, but also the central importance of social harmony and individual virtue within the limits of that nature. By adopting a classical outlook in terms of both historical perspective and transcendent existence, organic conservatives are able to suggest that individualist conservatism was formed from, and remains attached to, a narrowly constructed base. Within this context, it is possible to claim that the libertarian prospectus was derived from one atypical historical period (i.e. the Enlightenment) that had temporarily overlooked the moral limitations and behavioural continuities of human nature. Because complexity as well as evil would always persist in human society, the eternal and problematic question of virtue could never be resolved by liberalization or any other one-dimensional panacea. The classical outlook ensured that for many organic conservatives, order and virtue would remain paramount over the demands of freedom in a flawed world of moral imperfectability. The political pertinence of Strauss in this particular sphere is based precisely on this element of the threat of modernity and liberal democracy not only upon the proper

---

[55] Viereck, 'The Philosophical "New Conservatism" (1962)', pp. 185–207.

[56] Richard Hofstadter, *The Paranoid Style in American Politics and Other Essays* (New York: Vintage, 1967), chs. 2–4.

consideration of moral values and the categories of classical antiquity, but also upon the organic integrity of a society capable of withstanding challenges to its principles.[57]

Those who subscribe to the position of individualistic conservatism remain equally sceptical of organic conservatives. Traditionalists are often criticized for their attachment to the status quo. In some quarters, this is equated with appeasement towards the consequences of accumulated liberal intervention. Some libertarian conservatives even draw parallels between traditionalist conservatism and socialism. Murray Rothbard, for example, always stressed the contrast between libertarianism and conservatism, and to this end he urged his readers to regard conservative traditionalists as the real adversary:

[Historically] conservatism was the polar opposite of liberty; and socialism, while to the 'left' of conservatism, was essentially a confused, middle-of-the-road movement. ... Socialism, like [classical] liberalism and against conservatism, accepted the industrial system and the liberal *goals* of freedom, reason, mobility, progress, higher living standards for the masses, and an end to theocracy and war; but it tried to achieve these ends by the use of incompatible, conservative means: statism, central planning, communitarianism, etc.[58]

While organic conservatives tend to be concerned about the fragility of the state, libertarian anxieties are directed towards the growing incursions of a state whose basis is one of cumulative and increasingly irresistible power. To a libertarian like Rothbard whose proposals included the privatization of the police and national defence forces, the mobilization of values had to confront head-on the exigencies of this kind of historical drift. They had to oppose the statist habits and hierarchical presumptions of society's traditional stratification.

Individualistic conservatives complain that instead of using a prior state of existence to generate forms of emancipation, traditionalists are consumed by, or entrapped in, the processes of history. They are accused of failing to understand the forces through which a free society organizes itself, and in particular the progressive dynamics of economic power. Those who align themselves with the libertarian ethos of individualistic conservatism tend to view traditionalist conservatives as too elitist, too passive, and too inhibited to engage in a counter-revolution against government. While organic conservatives give weight to continuity and gradualism, individualistic conservatives are disposed to call for a state of emergency and for action to be taken commensurate with the perceived presence of crisis. Within these debates, iconoclasts like Barry Goldwater and Ronald Reagan pitted themselves as much against the assimilative properties of traditionalist conservatives as they did against the prospectus of liberal reform.[59]

---

[57] Leo Strauss, *The City and Man* (Chicago, IL: University of Chicago Press, 1964).

[58] Murray Rothbard, *Left and Right: The Prospects for Liberty* (Washington, DC: Cato Institute, 1979), pp. 6–7.

[59] Rick Perlstein, *Before the Storm: Barry Goldwater and the Unmaking of the American Consensus* (New York: Hill & Wang, 2002); Kiron K. Skinner, Annelise Anderson, and Martin Anderson, *Reagan, In His Own Hand: The Writings of Ronald Reagan That Reveal His Revolutionary Vision for America* (New York: Touchstone, 2002); Craig Shirley, *Reagan's Revolution: The Untold Story of the Campaign That Started It All* (Nashville, TN: Nelson Current, 2005).

Senator Goldwater notoriously admonished his own party in his 1964 presidential campaign that 'extremism in the defence of liberty [was] no vice'.[60] In a similar tone, Reagan flatly asserted at the outset of his presidency that government was the problem rather than the solution. Both succeeded in disrupting the conservative mainstream and in injecting libertarian energy into its agendas.

It is this libertarian insurgency which traditionalists find particularly difficult because it demonstrates the destabilizing potential of a freedom that attacks the source of its own social and moral standing. To Peter Berkowitz, the 'self-subverting tendencies' of freedom give rise to an apparent paradox.

> Freedom depends upon a variety of beliefs, practices, and institutions that are weakened by the increasingly forceful reverberations of freedom throughout all facets of moral and political life. Some more traditional conservatives will say that such weakening is the baleful and inevitable consequence of modern freedom.[61]

Berkowitz is unimpressed with such an argument because it overlooks the self-regulating dynamics of freedom. Berkowitz typifies the commonly held supposition amongst individualistic conservatives that freedom provides its own solutions. An expansion of freedom is thought to release its potential for indigenous order. In fact, 'the very same circumstances that unleash freedom's self-subverting tendencies also create opportunities for the exercise of the liberal spirit's self-correcting powers, which primarily consist of the free mind's ability to understand its interests well and devise measures to secure them'.[62] Organic conservatives are not convinced that extreme liberty induces its own discipline and they remain concerned over the Jacobin language and adversarial outlook of those conservatives who urge the need for historical discontinuity.

The views of Berkowitz echo attempts made in the past to achieve a synthesis or 'fusion' between these two constituent elements of American conservatism. In the 1960s, for example, Meyer sought to meld the two strands together by arguing that freedom was an individual objective that could best be achieved within an ordered social setting. Meyer recognized the libertarian priority that freedom was the primary political objective, but he drew out a concomitant responsibility that invested liberty with a requirement to foster virtue through persuasion and example.[63] To the organic conservatives, he acknowledged their objections to the rise of an insurgent central state over American society, but he pointed out that they needed to give due attention to the coercive nature of inherited structures and traditional communities. The communal imposition of virtue was to Meyer as serious a critique as the libertarians' reputation for sharply

---

[60] Barry Goldwater, 'Acceptance Speech to the Republican Party Convention, 1964', http://www. washingtonpost.com/wp-srv/politics/daily/may98/goldwaterspeech.htm.

[61] Peter Berkowitz, 'The Liberal Spirit in America', *Policy Review*, no. 120 (August/September 2003), p. 41.

[62] Ibid., p. 47. For another attempt to reconcile American traditionalism with the libertarian thrust of minimal government, see Murray, *What It Means To Be a Libertarian*.

[63] Frank Meyer, *In Defense of Freedom: A Conservative Credo* (Chicago, IL: H. Regnery, 1962).

distinguishing law from morality. The solution to both complaints was a synthesis of the two traditions that proceeded upon the assertion of their interdependence upon one another. Meyer sought to strengthen the fusion by enfolding it within a form of American exceptionalism by claiming that the conditions and traditions of the New World had fostered a form of conservatism that was separate and independent from the experience of European conservatism. His drive to create a basis for a conservative coalition that could unite against the common enemies of communism and reform liberalism was well conceived in terms of practical politics. Nonetheless, Meyer's exposition upon the mutual inclusiveness of the two traditions was generally considered to be an intellectual failure and one that was widely condemned by traditionalists and libertarians alike.[64]

While the threat of communist expansion and collective coercion proved to be a durable source of social solidarity at the level of national endeavour, it did not subdue the tension between these two generic expressions of American conservatism. Despite the changes in international conditions—or arguably because of them—the struggle between traditionalists and libertarians continue to fuel many of the internal debates within the conservative movement. Thus, they contribute to the energy and vivacity of contemporary American conservatism. Each side disputes the foundations and doctrinal ramifications of the other. Each seeks to establish primacy of its own conservative credentials and to shift the balance of the conservative movement decisively in accord with its own principles. And each has a cultivated antipathy towards the pragmatism of mainstream conservatism which, in the view of both organic and individualist conservatives, has been responsible for the unprincipled drift of conservatism into the state-centric and socially disruptive policy regimes of successive liberal administrations.

On the libertarian side, the cause has been promoted by a range of organizations such as the Cato Institute, the Ludwig von Mises Institute, the Heritage Foundation, the Institute for Humane Studies, and the John Randolph Club. Libertarian views and analyses have been projected into the public realm by journals (e.g. *Journal of Ayn Rand Studies*), magazines (e.g. *Reason, Liberty*[65]) and websites (e.g. www.libertarian.org). Organic conservatives also have their outlets of propagation which have contributed to conservative debates and to the overall struggle over conservative identity (e.g. Family Research Council, Institute for Communitarian Policy Studies, Center for the Community Interest, and Ethics and Public Policy Center). Because organic conservatism is more instinctive and attitudinal in its origins, outlooks, and tone, it has less of a tradition of intellectual analysis and systematic exposition. By the same token, it has often suffered from being temperamentally associated with the predispositions of mainstream conservatism.

---

[64] See Kevin J. Smant, *Principles and Heresies: Frank S. Meyer and the Shaping of the American Conservative Movement* (Wilmington, DE: ISI Books, 2002).

[65] *Liberty* defines itself as a 'journal of culture and politics written from a classical liberal point of view' (see http://www.libertyunbound.com/); it should not be confused with *Liberty Magazine*, which is devoted to the cause of religious freedom.

This has created internal tensions which have led to various attempts to make some of the roots and implications of organic conservatism not only more explicit but also more stridently expressed.

The most controversial element of this development has been the emergence of what has become known as 'paleoconservatism'. In their desire to draw out the deep historical and even mystical elements of conservative attachment, paleoconservatives have adopted several highly reactionary positions. Individuals like Pat Buchanan, Samuel Francis, and Paul Gottfried, and outlets such as *The American Conservative, The American Cause,* and *Chronicles Magazine* have deliberately distanced themselves from the evolutionary norms of traditionalist conservatism. Their critiques vary but they tend to centre upon the racial and ethnic identity of the United States, the historical presence of an innate social order; and the cultural threats posed by the federal government and the welfare state. Against accusations of being pre-modern or even anti-modern in outlook, paleoconservatives press for restrictions on immigration, a rollback of multicultural programmes, the decentralization of the federal polity, the restoration of controls upon free trade, a greater emphasis upon economic nationalism and isolationism in the conduct of American foreign policy, and a generally *revanchist* outlook upon a social order in need of recovering old lines of distinction and in particular the assignment of roles in accordance with traditional categories of gender, ethnicity, and race. Perhaps the most succinct illustration of the paleoconservative outlook is conveyed by the works of its chief polemicist Buchanan: *Right from the Beginning* (1988); *The Great Betrayal: How American Sovereignty and Social Justice Are Being Sacrificed to the Gods of the Global Economy* (1998); *The Death of the West: How Dying Populations and Immigrant Invasions Imperil Our Country and Civilization* (2002), and *State of Emergency: The Third World Invasion and Conquest of America* (2006).[66]

In their various forms, the organic and individualist strands of conservatism account for much of the dissonant energy that characterizes American conservatism. The distinctive outlooks and contentions of these two conservative variants have considerable ramifications in the organization of political argument and action both within the conservative movement and in the wider public sphere. However, while many groupings and positions have their roots in one or other of these perspectives, this is not to say that all conservative viewpoints are reducible to the derivatives of a clear bipolar distribution. On the contrary, a number of conservative phenomena and organizations are complex compounds that draw upon both strands in idiosyncratic ways. Two of the more significant melds are illustrated below.

---

[66] Patrick J. Buchanan, *Right from the Beginning* (Boston, MA: Little, Brown, 1988); Patrick J. Buchanan, *The Great Betrayal: How American Sovereignty and Social Justice Are Being Sacrificed to the Gods of the Global Economy* (New York: Little, Brown, 1998); Patrick J. Buchanan, *The Death of the West: How Dying Populations and Immigrant Invasions Imperil Our Country and Civilization* (New York: Thomas Dunne, 2002); Patrick J. Buchanan, *State of Emergency: The Third World Invasion and Conquest of America* (New York: Thomas Dunne, 2006).

THE RELIGIOUS RIGHT

The term 'religious right' refers to an amalgam of issue advocates and organizations that rose to political prominence in the 1980s and that have continued to
pursue an active agenda of religiously inspired proposals designed to recalibrate
public policy back towards a condition of moral integrity. The proponents of religious right give priority to the kind of 'hot button' issues that most elected office-
holders normally try to evade due to the polarizing properties of the disputes
that they generally arouse in the public sphere. The issues embrace controversial
themes such as abortion, school prayer, gay rights, childrearing, public education,
and government funding for the arts. Supporters of the religious right seek to
place these issues at the centre of political debate. They do so not only to present
politics as a series of moral dichotomies, but also to lend credence to the idea of
a deep moral crisis afflicting the nation. These religious groups claim that they
are uniquely able to act as society's moral barometers and to offer morally based
solutions commensurate with the apocalyptic scale of the identified problems.[67]

By identifying themselves with concepts like the 'silent majority', or 'God's
people', the religious right organizations offer a collective ministry to the nation
and a way of mobilizing large numbers of people who would otherwise be political
non-participants. Reacting to the sense of moral malaise in society, and to the
emergence of localized groups centring upon the issue of 'family values', leaders
like Jerry Falwell and Pat Robertson formed umbrella organizations to pull the
disparate elements of religious protest together. These agencies drew upon, and
encouraged the development of, an evangelical revival. Traditionally, evangelicals
have tended to avoid political engagement because they regard society as being
permeated with evil. Organizations like Moral Majority, Religious Roundtable,
Focus on the Family, and the Christian Coalition, however, have actively solicited
evangelical support and directed it to a public crusade for moral values.[68]

Significantly, the religious right has also fostered an alliance between evangelicals and conservative Catholics. This was pioneered in the early 1990s by several
religious leaders from both denominations who wished to create a Christian
'solidarity in opposition to the forces of unbelief'.[69] Father Richard Neuhaus,

---

[67] Michael Lienesch, 'Right-Wing Religion: Christian Conservatism As a Political Movement', *Polit-
ical Science Quarterly*, vol. 97, no. 3 (1982), pp. 403–25; Robert C. Liebman and Robert Wuthnow
(eds.), *The New Christian Right* (Hawthorne, NY: Aldine, 1983); A. James Reichley, 'Religion and the
Future of American Politics', *Political Science Quarterly*, vol. 101, no. 1 (Spring 1986), pp. 23–46; A.
James Reichley, *Faith in Politics* (Washington, DC: Brookings, 2002), pp. 289–303, 329–36; Martin
Durham, *The Christian Right, the Far Right and the Boundaries of American Conservatism* (Manchester:
Manchester University Press, 2000), pp. 105–25.

[68] Jerry Falwell, *Listen, America* (New York: Doubleday, 1980); Michael Cromartie (ed.), *No Longer
Exiles: The Religious Right in American Politics* (Washington, DC: Ethics and Public Policy Center,
1992); Michael Cromartie (ed.), *Disciples and Democracy: Religious Conservatives and the Future of
American Politics* (Washington, DC: Ethics and Public Policy Center, 1995); Ralph Reed, *Active Faith:
How Christians Are Changing the Face of American Politics* (New York: Free Press, 1996).

[69] 'A Statement of Evangelicals and Catholics Together: The Communion of Saints', *First Things*,
vol. 131 (March 2003), http://www.firstthings.com/ftissues/ft0303/articles/sect-saints.html.

together with the Institute on Religion and Public Life and its journal *First Things*, was especially prominent in establishing a basis for cooperation in the form of the 'Evangelicals Catholics Together' (ECT) organization.[70] The ECT movement has been significant not only in developing a spiritual and theological basis for joint action over social issues, but also in giving the Catholic East European element of the conservative coalition a base through which to express its religious and moral objections to the state of American society.

Increasingly, religious groups with mass memberships have sponsored forms of mass political action. They have engaged in an intense lobbying campaign to increase voter registration, to support candidates for public office, and to promote Christian values within society.[71] The Christian Coalition, for example, has defended its record of political action in terms of having had a 'continual impact on America's political discourse'[72] and thus 'returning a sense of cultural ownership to Christian citizens nationwide'.[73] The religious right not only became an integral part of the 'new right' in the last quarter of the twentieth century, but it also typified the theme of a conservative movement independent of party structure and institutional support. Its mix of evangelist denunciation of society and the usage of modern marketing techniques (e.g. satellite broadcasting, cable television, sophisticated market targeting, and computerized mass mailing) succeeded in generating an impression that the unsophisticated mass of those with simple faith was being unfairly frustrated by godless elites.

The electoral potential of the religious right was quickly recognized by conservative strategists. As a consequence, religious right organizations became a key constituency in the Republican Party and were in the vanguard of the 'Reagan revolution'. They have been credited with a succession of defeats for liberal officeholders and with having shaped the national political agenda since the 1980s. They remain very influential and in 2001 celebrated the elevation to the presidency of George W. Bush, whom the evangelicals regarded as one of their own. President Bush for his part has responded by giving emphasis to the need for 'moral clarity' in the conduct of the presidency, by infusing his speeches and public statements with biblical references, and by setting up agencies such as the cabinet level Office of Faith-Based and Community Initiatives.[74] During the course of his presidency, it became evident that Bush's Christian commitment was neither perfunctory nor

---

[70] 'Evangelicals & Catholics Together: The Christian Mission in the Third Millennium', *First Things*, vol. 43 (May 1994), pp. 15–22; 'The Gift of Salvation', *First Things*, vol. 79 (January 1998), pp. 20–3; Charles Colson and Richard J. Neuhaus (eds.), *Evangelicals and Catholics Together: Toward a Common Mission* (Dallas, TX: Word Publishing, 1995).

[71] Steve Bruce, *The Rise and Fall of the New Christian Right: Conservative Protestant Politics in America, 1978–88* (Oxford: Clarendon Press, 1990), pp. 50–125.

[72] Christian Coalition, 'Our Vision: The New Christian Coalition: Faith with Action in the New Millennium', http://www.cc.org/vision.cfm.

[73] Ibid.

[74] See Jo Renee Formicola, *The Faith-Based Initiatives and the Bush Administration: The Good, the Bad and the Ugly* (Lanham, MD: Rowman & Littlefield, 2003); David Masci, *CQ Researcher Religion and Politics v. 14–27* (Washington, DC: Congressional Quarterly Press, 2004); Marvin Olasky,

symbolic but represented a core element of his personal philosophy and inner convictions.[75] While his reliance upon prayer and moral instincts has caused dismay in some quarters,[76] his 'faith-based presidency'[77] was a key component of his successful campaign for re-election in 2004.

Although the religious right is based upon the professed need for clear principles, the movement itself is not devoid of differing points of emphasis.[78] On the contrary, a major disjunction is discernible along the classic fault-line between supple traditionalism and fractious fundamentalism. Some elements of the religious right movement are clearly animated by the impulse towards a moral order in a society, or more particularly by the recognition that society is in jeopardy of a debilitating moral disorder. The central premises are that American society is rooted in a Judaeo-Christian tradition; that American culture is under assault from the insidious influences of liberal rationalism and 'secular humanism'; and that the causes and symptoms of this syndrome are discernible in the nation's moral and social breakdown. In the same way that there are thought to be limits to the rate at which society can assimilate forms of social engineering, it is assumed that there are genuine dangers for a society that allows religious doctrines to be redesigned into more secularized constructions.

The organic response to these threats is one of giving priority to unity through the reclamation of tradition. By rediscovering the textual foundations of theology and providing a clearer sense of a divinely sanctioned moral order, the traditionalist strand of the religious right seeks the reintegration of society. This is regarded as a wholly viable solution on the grounds that it is based upon a revival of a prior American condition; that the United States is an exceptional society; and that the advocacy and attainment of national renewal represents God's will. The restoration of a past moral order is also seen as a viable objective because it can draw upon the close affinity of religion with the traditions of American conservatism.[79] Notwithstanding these connections, the intention to place God at the formal centre of society not only creates a profusion of political challenges but also generates an ambiguity over the authenticity of the religious right's traditionalism. For example, it can be argued that the emphasis which is given to the idea of a moral past and to the need to restore it through a moral revival casts doubts upon the evolutionary character of organic adaptation. It can be

---

Compassionate Conservatism: What It Is, What It Does, and How It Can Transform America (New York: Free Press, 2000).

[75] For an illustration of President George W. Bush's view upon the role of personal faith in public service, see Stephen Mansfield, *The Faith of George W. Bush* (New York: Tarcher/Penguin, 2003), chs. 5–8; George W. Bush, *George W. Bush on God and Country: The President Speaks Out about Faith, Principle, and Patriotism* (Fairfax, VA: Allegiance Press, 2004).

[76] For example, see Ron Suskind, 'Without a Doubt', *New York Times*, 17 October 2004.

[77] Ibid.

[78] For an impressive examination of the internal debates within the Christian Right, see Sara Diamond, *Not by Politics Alone: The Enduring Influence of the Christian Right* (New York: Guilford Press, 2000).

[79] Kenneth J. Heineman, *God Is a Conservative: Religion, Politics and Morality in Contemporary America* (New York: New York University Press, 1998).

claimed that the radicalism of the religious right's programme on social issues amounts to a challenge upon the Constitution's separation of church and state. In its most extreme form, the ideas associated with 'Reconstructionist' theology explicitly assert the need to replace democracy with a form of 'Biblical law' that would restrict civil rights and impose a theocratic state.[80]

On the one hand, a usage of religious and spiritual injunctions may be seen as a symbolic device to produce an increased appreciation for social cohesion. On the other hand, it may also indicate a real intention to transform a particular form of religious doctrine into the only permissible substance of social unity. Whatever the motivations underpinning the religious right's employment of organic allusions, the strategy has placed severe strains upon the unifying properties of the theme. A programme that is geared to the injection of moral absolutes at the expense of settled traditions, or at least long-established social practices, in areas of personal responsibility or individual freedom (e.g. abortion, gay rights, religious observance, pornography, medical ethics) can be construed as being repressive, intolerant, and divisive. Apart from the direct challenge to the cumulative nature of constitutional jurisprudence, the policy agenda carries implications, if not of a theocratic state, at least of an established doctrinal order and a revival of an eighteenth-century Tory–church duopoly. In seeking to evoke the virtues of an older America and of a society apparently more settled within a clear public philosophy, the religious right's properties threaten to place it outside the accepted contours of America's liberal tradition. American liberty in this regard can denote a freedom to emancipate oneself from the imposition of liberal social doctrines, but at the same time to conform to an alternative conception of social order and moral sanction.

Other elements in the religious right reveal far less interest in, or concern for, tradition and organic unity. The emphasis here echoes the radical right ethos of ideological battle, fundamentalist critique, a revolt against authority, and a complete break with the past. Some of this belligerence is attributable to the absolutism of religious truth, which by its very nature is not open for negotiation. Another source is provided by the social equivalent of revelation in which complex systemic problems are attributed to a single, or at least to a simple, set of agencies of corruption and expropriation. Deviations from the expected norm of American excellence are presupposed to be the direct result of active intervention by corrupting forces. Malicious intent requires an equally concerted response on the part of those who are aware of the moral danger of appeasement.[81]

These themes of absolutism and revelation are complemented by a populist message of unjustified social exclusion and cultural deprivation. By rationalizing the social and moral discomfort of modernity with a conflict of interests between

---

[80] Frederick Clarkson, 'Theocratic Dominionism Gains Influence', *The Public Eye Magazine*, vol. 8, nos. 1 & 2 (March/June 1994), http://www.publiceye.org/magazine/v08n1/chrisre1.html.

[81] See Robert Boston, *The Most Dangerous Man in America? Pat Robertson and the Rise of the Christian Coalition* (Amherst, NY: Prometheus, 1996), pp. 63–148.

secular elites and popular Christianity, the religious right has attempted to channel diffuse resentments into a coherent theme of majoritarian liberation. The organization has clear populist overtones of elite conspiracies, moral subversion, social resentments, and the personalization of interests, issues, and politics. As part of this explanatory structure, the religious right has on occasion encouraged a vengeful attitude towards those sectors of American society that are identified as being responsible for the economic and social discomfort of the forgotten millions of lower middle-class Americans and for the subsequent dislocation of American society. The subversives generally include liberals, blacks, pacifists, feminists, federal judges, homosexuals, Jews, and urban sophisticates.[82] Even when the movement's leaders have been more inclusively benign in their outlook, 'the America to which they wish to return is a Protestant America' where—notwithstanding developments like the ECT—there is often 'very little in the mythology of "one nation under God" to which Catholics, Jews and Mormons can attach their aspirations'.[83]

The extensive sources of cultural disinheritance also offer a point of access to the sphere of fundamentalism. Within this dimension, the initial indictment of specific American conditions can be widened into an altogether more sweeping condemnation of the norms and values of modern society. Fundamentalism is an international phenomenon that is present in all religious traditions. It is characterized by a pronounced sense of the need (i) to fight *back* the rise of modernism; (ii) to fight *for* a traditional world view and the identity associated with it; (iii) to fight *with* doctrinal and textual fundamentals; (iv) to fight *against* those who would subvert the divine integrity of an established order; and (v) to fight *under* the direction of God's active presence in society.[84] In the United States, this fundamentalist ethos has a close affinity with the religious right's antagonism against those who are identified as being responsible for the subversion of America's moral identity. The religious right has worked assiduously in this vein to associate itself with the fundamentalist vocation of providing a commensurate response to the extreme conditions of a chronic epoch.

Religious right organizations have been remarkably adept at translating the generic properties of fundamentalism into a style and language that can resonate with American audiences. They have worked to conflate civil dissent and democratic assertiveness with an attachment to freedom of conscience, moral restoration, and divine authority. They have also mixed doctrinal integrity with sectarian

---

[82] Daniel C. Maguire, *The New Subversives: Anti-Americanism of the Religious Right* (New York: Continuum Publishing, 1982).

[83] Steve Bruce, 'Zealot Politics and Democracy: The Case of the New Christian Right', *Political Studies*, vol. 48, no. 2 (2000), p. 267.

[84] See Martin E. Marty and Scott Appleby, 'Introduction?', in Martin E. Marty and Scott Appleby (eds.), *The Fundamentalism Project*, Vol. 1: *Fundamentalisms Observed* (Chicago, IL: University of Chicago, 1991), pp. ix–x; Nathan Glazer, 'Fundamentalism: A Defensive Offensive', in Richard J. Neuhaus and Michael Cromartie (eds.), *Piety and Politics: Evangelicals and Fundamentalists Confront the World* (Washington, DC: Ethics and Public Policy Center, 1987), pp. 245–58.

pluralism and given priority to the authenticity of experience over historical continuity.[85] The United States is a highly religious country and also the defining model
of modernity. The religious right has sought to extend the logic of this duality by
developing a pronounced fundamentalist outlook of doctrinally based aggression
in the service of an urgent and radical break from the secular world. This kind of
fundamentalism is further strengthened by its proximity to the libertarian priorities of individualistic conservatism and its revolt against governing elites. When
the latter are transfigured into secular and cultural forces intent upon removing
religious attachments and moral strictures from the public sphere,[86] the religious
right has sought to invoke both traditionalism and libertarianism in its calls for
a moral revival. The evangelical impulse has been particularly suggestive in this
respect. Its attachment to inner experience and a personal apprehension of God,
combined with the resultant privatization of faith as an individualized process of
being 'born again', have a strong resonance with the anti-institutional instincts of
the free market. The clearance of impediments and the subsequent emancipation
of the individual generate a metaphorical and political leverage. This libertarian
ingredient runs concurrently with the religious right's determination to clarify the
range of moral choices and to underline the full impact of the individual's moral
responsibility for the consequence of those choices.

The religious right straddles the complex and ambiguous terrain between
formal religious affiliation and religiously informed political behaviour. Those
seeking to use religious belief to shape electoral and policy choices have been able
to draw upon core American themes to advance their claim. The freedom from
oppression, the individualism of the soul, the democracy of a mobilized silent
majority, the rule of law as God's ordinance, and the appeal for order have all
featured as instruments of advocacy by religious right organizations. But in pursuing its themes of spiritual consciousness and social conversion, the movement
has often proceeded with an intensity that has proved to be divisive and intolerant. Its fundamentalist agenda has arguably exceeded the limits of conventional
pluralist politics and this has meant that many of its policy objectives have not
been achieved. Nevertheless, the movement retains an important role in framing
the evaluative criteria of public action and in conditioning the political agenda
to fundamental issues of moral conscience. The religious right's ability to infuse
political argument with subtexts of moral complaint and ethical critique has been
effective in creating a medium of opposition and an alternative channel of political

---

[85] See Matthew C. Moen, 'From Revolution to Evolution: The Changing Nature of the Christian
Right', *Sociology of Religion*, vol. 55, no. 3 (1994), pp. 345–57; Mark J. Rozell and Clyde Wilcox,
'Second Coming: The Strategies of the New Christian Right', *Political Science Quarterly*, vol. 111, no. 10
(1996), pp. 271–94; Clyde Wilcox, *Onward, Christian Soldiers? The Religious Right in American Politics*
(Boulder, CO: Westview, 1996); Mary E. Bendyna and Clyde Wilcox, 'The Christian Right Old and
New: A Comparison of the Moral Majority and the Christian Coalition', in Corwin E. Smidt and
James M. Penning (eds.), *Sojourners in the Wilderness: The Christian Right in Comparative Perspective*
(Lanham, MD: Rowman & Littlefield, 1997), pp. 41–56.

[86] For example, see Richard J. Neuhaus, *The Naked Public Square: Religion and Democracy in
America* (Grand Rapids, MI: William B. Eerdmans, 1984).

expression. This builds upon the traditions of republican virtue, which has not only allowed social conservatism to be equated with a transformative ethos but has also permitted the ideal of progress to be defined as a reversal of the processes of social degradation.

NEOCONSERVATISM

This form of conservatism is rarely referred to as a collective entity. Instead, it is characterized as an association of individuals who share a range of family, professional, and intellectual connections and who have, over twenty-five years, developed into a formidable centre of opinion formation. The roots of their collaborative project lay in the civil dislocation of the 1960s when, in their view, America's social consensus was undermined by excessive expectations of what government could achieve and by an intellectual vogue for new left critiques and social democratic agendas. Many of those who became neoconservatives had their origins in the Democratic Party and in the liberal reform tradition of the New Deal (e.g. Irving Kristol, Seymour Martin Lipset, Daniel Bell, James Q. Wilson, and Daniel Moynihan). Whether it was a form of disillusionment over the segmentation of government into clientele-servicing units, or whether it was the alarm over the destructive energies of an apparently dysfunctional society, the neoconservative response was to make a robust analytical claim for a thorough reassessment of public policy priorities. Their previous liberal allies in government and academia labelled them 'neoconservatives' as a term of ridicule, but the epithet was accepted by the recipients who believed that their outlook would represent a genuinely new variant of American conservatism.[87]

The neoconservatives have a strong sense of purpose, place, and identity. Their habitat is centred on a cluster of organizations located for the most part in New York City and Washington, DC. The close proximity of neoconservatives to governmental and social elites reflects both the neoconservatives' own backgrounds and their agenda of challenging policy interests with an 'in-house' feel for the political dynamics of government. In effect, they form a social and intellectual network and, on this basis, have developed their own foundations, publishing houses, journals, magazines, radio and television outlets, research institutes, and think tanks. The weight given by neoconservatives to public intellectualism makes them an unconventional component of American conservatism. But as Mark Lilla points out, their 'strategies for retaking cultural and political territory[88] lend a

---

[87] See Irving Kristol, *Neoconservatism: The Autobiography of an Idea* (New York: Free Press, 1995); Christopher DeMuth and William Kristol, *The Neoconservative Imagination* (Washington, DC: AEI Press, 1995); Mark Gerson (ed.), *The Essential Neoconservative Reader* (New York: Perseus, 1996); Jeane Kirkpatrick, 'Neoconservatism as a Response to the Counter-Culture', in Irwin Stelzer (ed.), *Neoconservatism* (London: Atlantic, 2004), pp. 233–40.

[88] Mark Lilla, 'The Closing of the Straussian Mind', *New York Review of Books*, 4 November 2004.

conservative authenticity to their critiques of the media, educational, and policy establishments.

Traditional American conservatism was anti-intellectual; neoconservatism is counter-intellectual. That is the source of its genius and influence. Unlike traditional conservatives who used simply to complain about left-leaning writers, professors, judges, bureaucrats, and journalists, the neoconservatives long ago understood that the only way to resist a cultural elite is to replace it with another. So they have, by creating their own parallel universe.[89]

That universe is composed of a tightly defined cluster of organizations in which neoconservatives congregate and exchange ideas (e.g. Project for the New American Century, American Enterprise Institute, Jewish Institute for National Security Affairs and Center for Security Policy, Heritage Foundation). The epicentre of neoconservative thought has been the journals *The Public Interest*, *The National Interest*, and *First Things*,[90] as well as the magazines *Commentary* and *The Weekly Standard*. It is from this organizational and media base that a profusion of intellectual critiques and policy initiatives have flowed for over a generation into the public domain. The effect of these public and private activities is widely cited as having been instrumental in shifting the national agenda to the right and in having reinvigorated American conservatism in general.[91]

Although neoconservatives operate across a broad spectrum of public affairs and are associated with a diversity of viewpoints, they can in the main be distinguished by a number of common themes. A developed scepticism towards the purposes and utility of liberal programmes, for example, constitutes a keynote neoconservative posture. Although neoconservatives are in the main wary of liberals who advocate government schemes of social intervention, their opposition is not based upon a fundamentalist or libertarian antagonism against the state. Instead, it is grounded in an analytical assessment of the cost–benefit ratio of government action. In many areas of public policy, neoconservatives seek to demonstrate that government programmes have not only failed to diminish social problems but have actually served to exacerbate them. In material terms, the counterproductive nature of much of government intervention is one of high cost and negligible benefit. In terms of the social fabric, government programmes are often cited as having undermined the mediating structures of social cohesion (e.g. family units, neighbourhood communities, voluntary associations), thereby screening out the requirements of individual responsibility and group respect (e.g. the welfare system). The pivotal neoconservative indictment was not simply that of policy-makers having insufficient knowledge or of having misapplied the available

---

[89] Lilla, 'The Closing of the Straussian Mind'.

[90] Although *First Things* is nominally a Catholic publication based upon the Institute on Religion and Public Life, its founding editorial board contained a number of Jewish intellectual figures.

[91] See David Brooks, 'The Neocon Cabal and Other Fantasies', in Stelzer (ed.), *Neoconservatism*, pp. 39–42; Joshua Muravchik, 'The Neoconservative Cabal', in Stelzer (ed.), *Neoconservatism*, pp. 241–57.

data. It was more a question of the inherent unreliability of social knowledge, and the limits of self-awareness in being able to recognize the deficiency.[92]

Another recurrent element of neoconservative thought is the malign influence of what is termed the 'new class'. This refers to the growing number of policy professionals and knowledge elites who are primarily upper middle class in composition and dependent upon the growth of activist government for their power, status, and wealth. They include scientists, administrators, social workers, educators, journalists, planners, health-care managers, welfare operatives, and social scientists. Neoconservatives claim that these occupational sectors constitute a highly organized apparatus that not only possesses class interests of its own but also has at its disposal the influence to service them in ways that are detrimental to the public interest. This new class is denounced by neoconservatives for developing an independent constituency within government and for exploiting it to maintain and expand government programmes irrespective of their expense, or their impact upon the community.[93]

Collectively the members of the new class are said to possess a deep-seated influence upon government and to be responsible for the durability of those policy agendas that have not resolved the problems for which they were originally put in place. This class is generally depicted as a self-perpetuating elite of liberal politicos and policy professionals whose interests are tied to the material manifestations of the liberal reform tradition. Far from being progressively oriented, the new class is dismissed as regressive and retrograde in the way it is able to persist with indefensible policy structures and to rely upon the force of bureaucratic inertia against the challenge of fresh thinking. To the neoconservatives, the new class gives physical expression to the 'liberal establishment', which is claimed to rest upon an attitude of government support devoid of any understanding either of the limitations of public action, or of the way that government intervention can deplete political authority.[94]

Although neoconservatives have a jaundiced view of government competence in domestic policy, they have a powerful attachment to the state in the field of foreign policy. They are resolved to use the state in a concerted way in order to advance American interests abroad but, more importantly, to propagate American ideals and to act on behalf of them in the international sphere. This nationalist Hamiltonian conception of government purpose originally emerged from the neoconservative objections to the new left critiques of the United States in the 1960s. A discourse on the corrupt and even fascist nature of American values was thought to be not only extreme but also dangerous in that it weakened the contribution of the United States in the wider global struggle over political

---

[92] See Nathan Glazer, 'The Limits of Social Policy', *Commentary*, September 1971; Irving Kristol, *On the Democratic Idea in America* (New York: Harper & Row, 1972), pp. 127–49; Daniel P. Moynihan, *Maximum Feasible Misunderstanding* (New York: Free Press, 1970).

[93] See Irving Kristol, *Two Cheers for Capitalism* (New York: Basic Books, 1978), pp. 25–31; Norman Podhoretz, *Breaking Ranks* (London: Weidenfeld & Nicolson, 1980), pp. 283–95; Nathan Glazer, *Affirmative Discrimination* (New York: Basic Books, 1978), ch. 6.

[94] See Irving Kristol, *Neoconservatism*.

principles. As a consequence, the classic neoconservative response in this field has been one of uninhibited ideological warfare.

Neoconservatives have a fervent conviction in the supremacy of western civilization, especially in the ethical superiority of the American variant that features liberal capitalism, Jeffersonian democracy, and national resolve. During the cold war, neoconservatives became progressively dismayed over the Soviet Union's control of Eastern Europe, its arms build-up, human rights abuses, expansionary policies, and nuclear threat to the West. The alleged weakness of the West's response, together with its adoption of containment, coexistence, and, ultimately, détente were increasingly subjected to neoconservative critiques. Their chief complaint was that the United States was engaging in a form of appeasement that legitimized a repugnant status quo. The presidency of Reagan afforded some respite to this complicity, but even his administration sought to temper ideological confrontation with negotiation and accommodation in areas such as arms control and human rights. After the cold war, the neoconservatives became even more agitated that a historic opportunity to shape the world rather than merely reacting to it was being needlessly wasted. They complained that the West's initiative was being relinquished by the Clinton administration's emphasis upon multilateral engagement, trade promotion, conflict resolution, and peaceful long-term democratization.

On George W. Bush's accession to the presidency, several neoconservatives were appointed to key positions in the new administration. From their respective vantage points in the State Department and the Pentagon, they and their allies are reputed to have exerted disproportionate influence upon policy-making in the defence and national security areas. According to this perspective, they have been able to press the neoconservative agenda in favour of the United States abandoning international treaty obligations, acting independently in the absence of collective action, and using the power of the United States to shape a world congruent with American values and interests. The agenda has been described as 'hard Wilsonianism' because its advocates 'embrace Woodrow Wilson's championing of American ideals but reject his reliance on international organizations and treaties to accomplish our objectives'.[95] The belligerent nature of neoconservatives' position reflects this expansive view of the national interest. It was one of the founders of neoconservatism, Irving Kristol, who declared that extensive nations had vital interests well beyond their borders: '[L]arge nations whose identity is ideological, like ... the United States today, inevitably have ideological interests as well as more material concerns'.[96] On both counts, neoconservatives believe that the United States is rightfully engaged in an ideological conflict which requires the strongest exertion of national will.

It has been suggested that the clarity of the neoconservative world view has been shaped by the experiences of their formative years. John Ehrman, for example, regards many neoconservatives as essentially cold war liberals. They are said to correspond to the working assumptions of President Harry S Truman, who

---

[95] Max Boot, 'What the Heck Is a Neocon?', *Wall Street Journal*, 30 December 2002.
[96] Irving Kristol, 'Can Neo-cons Break Out and Save the World?', *Sunday Times*, 24 August 2003.

combined a centrist position on state-organized social reform with a vigorous foreign policy centring upon anti-communism.[97] Other interpretations go further back and take up the Trotskyite past of seminal neoconservative figures such as Nathan Glazer, Sidney Hook, and Albert Wohlstetter.[98] On the left, the Trotskyite attachment to global change over the pragmatic and more restricted ambitions of Stalin's nationalist priorities produced a lasting legacy of revolutionary internationalism. Those neoconservatives who began on the left but who then subsequently shifted to the right are thought to have retained their revolutionary outlook.[99] Henry Kissinger observed that 'once they had changed sides, their anticommunism was intense'. Moreover, it was expressed through a 'considerable affinity for strategy honed by years of ideological warfare on the left side of the barricades'.[100] While their energetic outreach remained constant, it could now be said to have been placed in the service not of international socialism but of the exportation of democratic capitalism.

An alternative explanation of the neoconservatives' conception of their political role places the emphasis upon the philosophical influence of Leo Strauss. He had underlined the need for cohesive elites to drive policy in the light of truthful imperatives and had drawn attention to the utility of an external threat in clarifying a moral vision and the need to act upon it. Strauss advocated a greater sensitivity to the fundamental themes and universal principles of classical philosophy, in order to reveal the depth of crisis in western civilization. In denouncing the cultural relativism and nihilism of a liberal democracy that negligently propagates its own destruction, Strauss underlined the need for political character to be measured by the civic virtue required to confront the evil of tyranny in whatever form it presented itself. Straussians are sensitive to the complexity and fragility of the social order as well as to the limited mutability of the human condition and to the intractability of social problems. In this light, careful and informed thought should activate political action.[101] Any distinction between theory and practice, therefore, is seen as a false dichotomy. Just as theory is regarded as an integral part of political conflict, so is it thought vital for political action to be shaped by theory. Indeed, as Michael C. Williams makes clear, it would be difficult 'to find a contemporary position more committed to the proposition that ideas matter in politics and that theoretical commitments and debates have practical consequences'.[102]

[97] John Ehrman, *The Rise of Neoconservatism: Intellectuals and Foreign Affairs 1945–1994* (New Haven, CT: Yale University Press, 1995).

[98] Khurram Husain, 'Neocons: The Men behind the Curtain', *Bulletin of the Atomic Scientists*, vol. 59, no. 6 (November/December, 2003), pp. 62–71.

[99] Irving Kristol, *Reflections of a Neoconservative: Looking Back, Looking Ahead* (New York: Basic Books, 1983), pp. 3–13; John B. Judis, 'Trotskyism to Anachronism: The Neoconservative Revolution' *Foreign Affairs*, vol. 74, no. 4 (July/August 1995), pp. 123–9.

[100] Henry Kissinger, *Year of Renewal* (London: Weidenfeld & Nicolson, 1999), p. 106.

[101] Shadia B. Drury, *Leo Strauss and the American Right* (New York: S. Martin's Press, 1999); Anne Norton, *Leo Strauss and the Politics of American Empire* (New Haven, CT: Yale University Press, 2004).

[102] Michael C. Williams, 'What is the National Interest? The Neoconservative Challenge in IR Theory', *European Journal of International Relations*, vol. 11, no. 3 (September 2005), p. 308.

Other constructions of neoconservative cohesion make allusions to the high concentrations of Jewish intellectuals within the movement. Set against the experience of the Holocaust, these individuals are highly sensitive to the history of international inaction in relation to the protection of human rights. They are also strongly supportive of an activist foreign policy to protect the security of democracies in general and Israel in particular as it offers a regional model of democracy for the Middle East as a whole. Whatever the precise blend of factors at work in the neoconservative mindset, their net effect has been to create an influential point of advocacy in support of a foreign policy for a global battle between moral extremes.

Ostensibly it is ironic that, in a period that has witnessed a developing conservative movement, the neoconservatives have come to prominence as a small and distinct group of policy analysts and scholarly ideologues. Neoconservatives attach great significance to the concerted power of ideas and to leadership expressed through intellectual rigour. Nevertheless, their political strategy is primarily one of re-energizing the republican ideal of an active public interest and reconnecting the populous with a socially compelling conception of a national prospectus rooted in republican virtue. The neoconservative diagnosis of American society does focus upon the vacuity, decadence, and disintegration of contemporary life and is informed by a general scepticism of modernity and its effect upon communal ties, social cohesion, and moral solidity. Yet, the neoconservative outlook is not one of despair or fatalism.

Neoconservatism is oriented towards reversing the processes of individual alienation and social 'nihilism'[103] through reviving a republican identity and transforming the individual from a state of isolated self-interest to an integral part of an encompassing social order. Instead of relying upon the unidimensional categories of modern liberal-capitalism with its bounded concepts of interests and balances, neoconservatives redefine progress in terms of recalibrating American society in line with its roots in classical liberalism and civic republicanism. Some conservatives look to the sentimental comforts of a regressive patriotism, or to the more exotic appeal of European conservatism, to provide the foundations for a conservative reaction to modernity. In contrast, neoconservatives remain optimistic and progressive in their view of the American nation as both an intrinsic repository of social value and an emancipatory source of universal principle.

The neoconservatives' relationships with other parts of the conservative coalition have not been without incident.[104] Williams' observation goes to the heart of the matter: 'As neoconservatives are well aware, advocating the necessity of an ideological nationalism and a heroic politics of national greatness are likely to cause more than a little unease'.[105] The disquiet has been deepened by what is

---

[103] Kristol, *Reflections of a Neoconservative*, pp. 114–22.
[104] Adam Wolfson, 'Conservatives and Neoconservatives', in Stelzer (ed.), *Neoconservatism*, pp. 213–31.
[105] Williams, 'What is the National Interest?', p. 317.

widely seen to have been the neoconservatives' disproportionate influence upon the policy-making processes within the Republican Party and in the administration of President Bush.[106] A particularly potent source of doctrinal conflict comes from the libertarian wing of the conservative movement. Advocates of this strand of conservatism claim that neoconservatives are in essence apologists for 'big government' who have encouraged a rapid expansion of central power at the direct expense of civil liberties, individual privacy, and constitutional restraint. Far from being progressive in nature, libertarians regard the neoconservatives as a regressive and authoritarian force which seeks to reformulate conservatism under a false prospectus. Moreover, it is claimed that the privileged position of neoconservatives within the state has allowed them to 'control the debate over what western values are and by what methods they will be spread throughout the world'.[107] As a consequence, libertarians like Congressman Ron Paul refuse to integrate the neoconservative position within their conception of modern conservatism or historical processes.

Restating the old justifications for war, people control and a benevolent state will not suffice. It cannot eliminate the shortcomings that always occur when the state assumes authority over others and when the will of one nation is forced on another, whether or not it is done with good intentions. ... If the neoconservatives retain control of the conservative, limited-government movement in Washington, the ideas, once championed by conservatives, of limiting the size and scope of government will be a long-forgotten dream.[108]

Libertarians claim that there is an alternative morality and a competing conception of republican authenticity to that of neoconservatism. It is structured around the reductionist calculus relating to the asserted zero-sum duality of the individual and the state. The rationalist character of this unilinear approach to social analysis and prescription leads libertarians to dismiss the complex nuances of the neoconservatives cause as collectivist contrivances solely designed to diminish freedom. Neoconservatives for their part acknowledge the strain with libertarians who are seen to be 'conservative in economics but unmindful of the culture'.[109]

By contrast, traditionalist conservatives share much of the neoconservatives' concern for social order, community cohesion, and civic temperament. It is true that the neoconservative attachment to the positive state and to the muscular promotion of democratic values abroad presents difficulties for some traditionalists and especially for paleoconservatives whose priorities of isolationism, protectionism, and cultural enclosure sit uncomfortably with the expansive internationalism

---

[106] For an assessment of this complaint, see Zachary Selden, 'Neoconservatives and the American Mainstream', *Policy Review Online*, http://www.policyreview.org/apr04/selden.html.

[107] Honourable Ron Paul, 'Neo-Conned', Statement to the House of Representatives, 10 July 2003, http://www.house.gov/paul/congrec/congrec2003/cr071003.htm.

[108] Ibid.

[109] Irving Kristol, 'The Neoconservative Persuasion', *The Weekly Standard*, 25 August 2003.

of the neoconservatives. Patrick Buchanan has no doubts that under the 'tutelage of Jacobins who call themselves idealists',[110] President Bush has abandoned traditional doctrines of American foreign policy in order 'to embrace Wilsonian interventionism in the internal affairs of every autocratic regime on earth'.[111] To Buchanan, the penalty for breaking with tradition is dire:

A conservative knows not whether to laugh or weep. . . . We are going to democratize the world and abolish tyranny. Giddy with excitement, the neocons are falling all over one another to hail the president. They are not conservatives at all. They are anti-conservatives, and their crusade for democracy will end as did Wilson's, in disillusionment for the president and tragedy for this country.[112]

In spite of these sources of friction, many traditionalists and neoconservatives do share a close common cause in relation to the depth and seriousness of what is perceived to be America's moral crisis. The traditionalists' belief in the existence of a transcendent order to which societies should approximate finds a connection with the neoconservatives' more functional appreciation of the role of moral principles in the furtherance of community solidity. Accordingly, the need for ethical principles to be propagated and ethical standards to be adhered to in a society is given a high priority by traditionalists and neoconservatives alike.

The neoconservatives' foundational premise that America possesses a social and national significance as a historically exceptional moral entity has opened up alliances with the Christian right and other social conservatives.[113] Even though many neoconservatives have Jewish origins and, therefore, possess a strong affinity with Israel, their emphasis upon the role of morality within the political order has found a strong resonance in the agendas of more conventional centres of conservatism. It is noteworthy, for example, that a number of leading Catholic intellectuals (e.g. Michael Novak, Richard J. Neuhaus, George Weigel) have been closely associated with the neoconservatives and their robust prescriptions. The constituency of anxiety over the influence of secularism, feminism, and cultural relativism in American society have encouraged many conservatives to advocate the kind of assertive moralism within America that is comparable to the neoconservatives' moral commitment to international reconstruction. The theology of an influential sector of evangelicals, which places a high priority upon Israel's security on grounds of biblical prophecy, further underlines the common ground between the religious right and the neoconservatives.[114]

---

[110] Patrick J. Buchanan, 'The Anti-Conservatives', *The American Conservative*, 28 February 2005.
[111] Ibid.   [112] Ibid.
[113] Stefan Halper and Jonathan Clarke, *America Unbound: The Neoconservatives and the Global Order* (Cambridge: Cambridge University Press, 2004), ch. 6.
[114] Richard Popkin and David Katz, *Messianic Revolution: Radical Religious Politics to the End of the Second Millennium* (London: Penguin, 2000); Victoria Clark, 'The Christian Zealots', *Prospect*, July 2003, pp. 54–8.

CONCLUSION

The religious right and the neoconservatives account for just two compounds within the complex chemistry of American conservatism. While the conservative persuasion in the United States is often referred to in terms of contemporary cultural predominance, the nature of conservatism remains highly segmented and open to many permutations. Any attempt to assemble a political coalition of conservative forces always reveals the varied underlying ecology of American conservative thought. It is this pluralistic composition that distinguishes American conservatism and marks it out as a complex and contingent amalgam of contested properties.

In its classic guise, conservatism carries the inference of a clear set of values and priorities to be conserved. Almost by definition, conservatism implies a unified outlook and a fixed point of reference incorporating a hierarchy of ideas. American conservatism, however, exhibits properties that do not fit the traditional norms of conservative thought. As this chapter has attempted to show, conservative identity in the United States has been strained by the foundational status of liberal principles in both the conceptual and historical basis of the New World ethos. The related theme of American universalism has also imposed strains upon the conservative ethos of societal uniqueness and the organic differentiation of nations.

The core value of progress in the United States constitutes another conceptual and practical difficulty for American conservatism. The need to oppose many of the precepts of liberalism without opposing the progressive consequences of a liberal society has remained a problematic feature of conservative existence within a culture attached to the virtues of improving movement. In seeking to be associated with the liberal optimism of progress, conservatives have had to ground it within a cautionary outlook that recalibrates progress into a benefit drawn from static principles and ideally located within a construction of American society repeatedly set in a securely idealized past. On these and other grounds, American conservatives have traditionally been discomfited by the strains of being on principled grounds both American and conservative. American conservatives have to operate in a culture pervaded by liberal values. Nevertheless, they are not so immersed in the primacy of liberal principles not to be conservative. However, to the extent that they are conservative, they remain open to the criticism that they are set apart from the grain of the American tradition.

Notwithstanding these apparent cultural disadvantages, it is clear from the evidence presented in this chapter that American conservatism has not only flourished for a generation but has also arguably become the dominant force in American political argument. During the same period that the Republican Party adopted a more rigorous perspective, it also succeeded in developing an electoral coalition capable of breaking the Democratic hegemony in the Congress and of becoming the dominant force in presidential elections. The electoral effectiveness of the Republican coalition and its varied successors has coincided with the continued growth and vitality of the conservative ecology of think tanks, policy institutes, advocacy organizations, journals, and media outlets. The political confidence and mobilizing energy of the conservative sector have been symptomatic of a momentum that has not only witnessed the forcible presentation of conservative issues onto the national agenda, but has decisively shifted the centre ground to the right over the past twenty-five years.[115] To John Micklethwait and Adrian Wooldridge, the shift has been palpable and far-reaching: 'Not only has America produced a far more potent conservative movement than anything available in other rich countries; America as a whole is a more conservative place'.[116] The sense of achievement was evident in President Bush's address to the American Conservative Union on the occasion of its fortieth anniversary:

Some here tonight were there for that first meeting of the ACU in the fall of 1964. Back then...you stood behind a good man from Arizona, Barry Goldwater. You knew that the principles he represented—freedom and limited government and national strength— would eventually carry the day. And you were right.... The conservative movement has become the dominant intellectual force in American politics.... It's easy to understand why. On the fundamental issues of our times, conservatives have been right.... These convictions, once defended by a few, are now broadly shared by Americans. And I am proud to advance these convictions and these principles.[117]

Yet, in spite of the electoral and political impression made by conservative forces, conservatives have not always managed to translate their resources into a coherent programme or even into a settled pattern of preferences. On the contrary, conservative energies have constantly been dissipated by the variability exhibited in the precepts and priorities of different conservative groupings. In many respects, the conservatives' collective weaknesses have been a product of their multiple successes in the sphere of energetic and focused mobilization. But very often high value-rallying strategies and doctrinally inflated expectations are accompanied by disappointments and recriminations. The biodiversity of conservative perspectives, therefore, has been both a source of vitality and an explanation for the conservatives' own sense of continuous frustration.

The segmented nature of American conservatism was well illustrated by the Reagan coalition. At one level, it was a highly successful combination of blue-collar social conservatives centred in the Midwest; Southern-based religious conservatives; and a broadly suburban constituency of economic libertarians whose main emphasis lay in the reduction of taxes and government activity. Ostensibly, the coalition represented a 'fusionist synthesis' between the free market, social conservatism, and an enhanced military. The disciplinary effect of the cold war was another key element in the cohesion of a movement that has been described

---

[115] See William C. Berman, *America's Right Turn: From Nixon to Clinton* (Baltimore, MD: Johns Hopkins University Press, 1998); Lee Edwards, *The Conservative Revolution: The Movement That Remade America* (New York: Free Press, 1999).

[116] Micklethwait and Wooldridge, *The Right Nation*, p. 11.

[117] President George W. Bush, 'Remarks to the American Conservative Union 40th Anniversary Gala', 13 May 2004, http://www.whitehouse.gov/news/releases/2004/05/20040513-8.html.

by Jonathan Schoenwald as the culmination of a process of post-war development: 'Traditionalism, libertarianism and anticommunism all offered something for those who were inclined to believe that the country needed to change, that programs wrought by the New Deal hurt rather than helped.'[118]

But while the coalition may have been electorally effective, difficulties inevitably arose in translating it into a workable framework of government. The Reagan administration was continually divided by the differing interpretations and priorities given to the conservative project. For example, friction occurred

- *between* the moral fundamentalism of the religious right *and* the more evolutionary and pragmatic outlook of incremental traditionalists;

- *between* the class connotations of cosmopolitan intellectuals and Wall Street's Keynesian conservatives who were generally moderate, interventionist, and even progressive *and* the classless provenance of suburban insurgency against cities, bureaucracies, and government in general;

- *between* 'retrenchment conservatives' intent upon reducing government per se *and* 'empowerment conservatives' who were prepared to use market structures and taxation incentives to achieve imaginative ways of achieving social objectives and raising public services without recourse to high-expenditure bureaucracy (e.g. tax credits, vouchers);

- *between* the principled elitism of the neoconservatives *and* the populist outrage of those experiencing cultural exclusion and dispossession;

- *between* the property consciousness of big business and capital gains constituencies *and* those concerned with social cohesion and civic values;

- *between* free-traders *and* nationalistic protectionists;

- *between* the economic 'supply-siders' seeking to stimulate both the economy and government revenues *and* the free-market libertarians who wanted the economy to be stimulated in order to reduce government spending;

- *between* the free-marketeers *and* those business interests who did not want their enterprises to be liberated by 'deregulation';

- *between* evangelical and Catholic 'Main Street' conservatives animated by issues of social and ethical decline *and* patrician 'Wall Street' conservatives who privileged the stability of the economic order over political experimentation in the enforcement of morals and, finally;

- *between* the conservative working class 'Reagan Democrats' who were critical of the abuses of the welfare state *and* the individualist laissez-faire ultras who wished to turn a campaign against abuse into a holy war against the positive state that provided much of the working class with its long-term financial security.

Reagan's difficulties were symptomatic of a president who wished to base his administration firmly upon conservative principles. He found that not only were

---

[118] Schoenwald, *A Time for Choosing*, p. 12.

such principles many and varied, but that in order to transform even a fraction of them into law he necessarily had to be selective over which conservative principles he would adopt and which ones he would reject. He also had to confront the paradox of having to centralize power, in order to implement a radical programme of concerted decentralization.

Another celebrated attempt to fuse together the disparate elements of conservative support was attempted in the Republicans' 'Contract With America' (CWA) in 1994.[119] The package of proposals was designed to maximize the Republicans' conservative base by drawing upon a set of themes that could unite different conservative constituencies. The Contract included commitments to balance the budget, reform the welfare system, improve defence, protect the family, impose term limits on members of Congress, and reduce taxation and regulation. Even though the CWA was expressly formulated to avoid divisions over doctrine and priorities, the objective of establishing a post-Reagan programme of conservatism was only partially realized.

Points of contention that reflected the tidal undertows of American conservatism quickly emerged. For example, the pledge to reduce budget deficits, decrease taxes, and restrict the growth of the federal government appealed to economic conservatives. However, the economic package did little to resolve the debate between these conservatives over whether the main objective was to reduce taxes in order to achieve economic growth or to balance the budget through fiscal discipline. Social conservatives were more concerned with civil dilapidation and family values. Their priority was to strengthen society's mediating structures and to increase individual responsibility and local autonomy. But even within this field, social conservatives differed with one another. For example, some approved of the objective of government promoting moral values—albeit with doubts over the likely effectiveness of such a course of action. Others possessed a more libertarian approach that centred upon the denial of public funds in support of policies and practices that condoned a particular moral outlook. This would prevent a state sponsorship of secularism and allow Christian values within an expanded social sphere to have greater leverage.

The CWA's propositions on defence and foreign policy also sought to disguise substantive differences between conservatives. Broad statements of intent related to a stronger defence and greater independence from international organizations, however, provided only a temporary respite from the seminal conflicts between national isolationists, the proponents of democratization and globalization, and 'neo-realists' who urged cautious internationalism based upon the priority of national interest. The debates within each subfield of the CWA were compounded by priority disputes between the separate subfields. The net effect was a successful programme of electoral mobilization but one that underlined the disaggregate properties of American conservatism. It typified the profusion of themes within

---

[119] See Newt Gingrich and Dick Armey, *Contract with America* (New York: Times Books, 1994); Elizabeth Drew, *Showdown: The Struggle between the Gingrich Congress and the Clinton White House* (New York: Simon & Schuster, 1996).

a conservatism that has to endure within a prevailing liberal culture. Different diagnoses, prognoses, and solutions competed with one another amidst a mosaic of diverse objectives and methods, together with a variety of moral and technical orientations.

Similar fissures of principled positions have been evident in the conservative reactions to the presidency of George W. Bush. His 'compassionate conservatism' in areas such as education and prescription drugs has been criticized by libertarians whose concerns over the scale of federal expenditures and powers have been compounded by the rapid expansion of the national security state. President Bush's proposals for faith-based organizations to receive federal funds to provide selected social services may have been welcomed by church organizations, religious leaders, ethical theorists, and government agencies committed to the theme of moral regeneration. But the policy has raised doubts over the President's conservative priorities and, in particular, over his attitude to the intrusiveness of 'big government'. While much of his ideological constituency is committed to the economic conservatism of fiscal restraint and limited government, he does not appear to regard government reduction as an overriding priority. On the contrary, President Bush has made it clear that as long as government serves the purpose of expanding individual choice and responsibility, the scale, structure, and intrusiveness of government is not a key issue.

After ushering in some of the biggest federal programmes since the Great Society, and committing the administration to both the reconstruction of the Gulf Coast after Hurricane Katrina in 2005 and a partial privatization of the Social Security fund, fiscal conservatives have grown alarmed over the scale and projection of the federal deficit. Along with many libertarians, they claim that the White House is running a big government administration but with a small government tax base, and that the president's declarations on social conservative issues (e.g. abortion, stem cell research) only serve to distract attention from the main issue of government expansion. In addition, those with an organic disposition remain sceptical of the administration's interest in social cohesion and have shared the libertarians' dismay over the inequity of the Republican tax cuts and in particular the tax breaks for the wealthiest sectors of society. Demands for further tax reductions for the most affluent, suspension of environmental regulations, and condoning of the ineffectual policing of corrupt corporate practices have only exacerbated the anxieties felt in many sectors of mainline conservatism. Finally, while traditionalists and internationalists have been concerned over the administration's aggressive foreign policy positions, free-traders have been less than impressed with the administration's predilection for protectionist measures.[120]

The profusion of contested conservative positions is a sign of both the vitality of conservative thought and the social significance attached to the incorporation

[120] See K. R. Mudgeon, 'Nowhere To Go', *Liberty*, July 2004; George C. Edwards, III, *Governing by Campaigning: The Politics of the Bush Presidency* (New York: Longman, 2006); 'Send in the Cronies', *The Economist*, 24 September 2005; Holly Yeager and Caroline Daniel, 'Will Cracks in the Conservative Coalition Stop a Lasting Realignment of US Politics?', *Financial Times*, 13 October 2005.

of primary values within a conservative rubric. In 1952, a keynote article on American conservatism bore the subtitle 'The Forbidden Faith'.[121] The same theme was taken up by Clinton Rossiter in his 1955 study of American conservatism under the subtitle *The Thankless Persuasion*.[122] To Rossiter, the conservative persuasion in the United States had always been a historically problematic attachment. As a conservative he concluded that its status would continue to remain ambiguous within such a self-consciously republican society. But contrary to his predictions, conservatism since the 1960s has become transformed from an implicit set of understandings in support of stability and order into an altogether more explicit, assertive, and manifold social movement. Instead of constituting a partial antidote to America's historical commitment to liberal principles, conservatives have risen in confidence and now compete openly for the imprimatur of American authenticity in the medium of ideas.

It has to be conceded that the prominence and status of contemporary thought is still highly dependent upon a cultivated antagonism towards the attributed excesses and social leverage of reform liberalism. American conservatives retain their characteristically oppositionist posture, their defensive outlook against government presumption, and their antipathy towards cultural elites. They continue to rely heavily upon the central theme of a governing liberal establishment, with its entrenched policy regime, for summoning up public sympathy with the stated need for a vigorous response. Just as the civil and moral basis of society is depicted as being under assault, so are America's core values interpreted as experiencing a transmutation and even a form of corruption. The conservative impulse to preserve and defend an inheritance thereby becomes fused with a principled dispute over the contemporary resonance of America's foundational and elemental concepts.

Conservative reactiveness in support of its own alarmist references to social change and moral challenge has proved to be a very successful political strategy. However, the very responsiveness associated with American conservatism has limited its ability to achieve a position of systematic domination. Although conservatives are generally considered to have achieved a position of ideational hegemony, conservatism is far from being a supreme, autonomous, and systematic public philosophy. In sum, it remains an eclectic amalgam of sentiments and traditions that necessarily has to compete for political position on the generic grounds of freedom, democracy, and other primary values. Conservative pre-eminence is neither self-sufficient nor comprehensive in nature. It relies upon a capacity to assimilate itself to, and make full use of, a dominant liberal discourse. It also depends upon an ability to compete effectively for the political resources associated with two other notable compounds that feature the agency of instinct and temperament within the usage of ideas: namely populism and nationalism. It is these two aggregates to which our attention will now be turned.

---

[121] Raymond English, 'Conservatism: The Forbidden Faith', *American Scholar*, vol. 21 (Autumn 1952), pp. 393–412.

[122] Clinton Rossiter, *Conservatism in America: The Thankless Persuasion* (New York: Knopf, 1955).

14

Populism

FOUNDATIONAL THEMES

In the United States the term sovereignty is customarily conjoined to either one of two defining conditions. Constitutional sovereignty relates to the authority vested in the ideal and practical arrangements of securing governance under the rule of law. The corporate nature of the Constitution fuses together government structures and processes into a designated scheme for establishing government whilst restricting its reach. Popular sovereignty, on the other hand, refers to the principle that locates the ultimate authority within the republic to the people. The corollary is that notwithstanding the construction of governing institutions, the people retain their status as the fundamental source of political legitimacy. Thomas Jefferson, for example, had no doubt that popular sovereignty was the organizing principle of the American system: 'Where then is our republicanism to be found?' he asked. 'Not in our Constitution certainly, but merely in the spirit of our people'.[1] This purist construction of self-government is perhaps best exemplified by James Wilson who, as James Madison's close friend and fellow participant in the creation of the Constitution, insisted that government could be the instrument of the public. 'In our government', he claimed, 'the supreme, absolute and uncontrollable power remains in the people'.[2]

To Wilson, and to those who have subscribed since then to his interpretation, popular sovereignty has not been merely a proposition or an objective, but an accomplishment of the republic. In support of this contention it is possible to refer to the various devices and experimental measures of direct democracy that are associated with the distinctively American sensitivity towards refining the democratic process. American theories of representation reflect this anxiety over the government losing contact with the source and origin of its power. The importance of representatives giving direct expression to constituency interests and opinions was given special attention by *The Federalist Papers*. It was regarded as imperative that representatives should have an 'immediate dependence on,

---

[1] Thomas Jefferson, *The Writings of Thomas Jefferson*, vol. 10, ed. Paul Leicester Ford (New York: Putnam's, 1892–9), p. 39.
[2] James Wilson, *The Works of James Wilson*, ed. Robert G. McCloskey, vol. 2 (Cambridge, MA: Belknap Press, 1967), p. 770.

and an intimate sympathy with, the people'.[3] Frequent elections were widely supported as the best way of maintaining the integrity of the representational process. In the American republican tradition, elections were never accepted as a means of transferring authority through popular consent. They were conceived as a necessary substitute for direct democracy and a device that would enable the people to retain the ability to govern themselves. In a 'working concept of government [that] is exclusively American',[4] elections did not mark the passage of sovereignty to government, so much as the extension of republican authority to a government in which the representatives remained the people's agents.

In spite of these devices and traditions of direct democracy and delegate-centred representation, a basic tension has always remained between the acquired prerogatives of government and the basic rights of those who are being represented. Given the centrality of democracy and self-government within American political culture, the ramifications of this strain are never far beneath the surface. The progressive increase in the size and centralization of government further exacerbates the problem especially as the representational superstructure has remained largely the same over the past century. The constitutional structure of republican governance—together with its presumptions of democratic legitimacy and its claim of representativeness and responsiveness—can generate high expectations that cannot always be fulfilled. It can be argued that they can never be realized in the precise terms of the prospectus or to the complete satisfaction of all the participants in a democratic order. Notwithstanding the merits of what is, or is not, operationally feasible in terms of democratic authenticity in a mass society, the disjunctions between ideals and practice, and between anticipation and performance, create a cognitive and interpretive space within which populism can occur.

Populism is a term that can be defined in a variety of ways,[5] but in the United States it is usually employed to designate an intensive response to a perceived distortion of democracy by those operating within its structures. The beneficiaries may claim to be acting in the name of the people but they are seen as not acting in accordance with its interests. A populist movement in these circumstances is usually built upon a reactive injunction against what is interpreted to be a misuse of a cultural norm. The intensity of such a response is characterized by (i) the sweeping nature of the condemnation; (ii) the urgency ascribed to the need for corrective action in the public interest; (iii) the implied solidarity of support for direct measures; and the (iv) the innate virtue assigned to the proposed solutions. The motive force is usually provided by those sectors of society who feel a strong

[3] James Madison, 'Federalist Paper No. 52', in Alexander Hamilton, James Madison, and John Jay, *The Federalist Papers* intro. by Clinton Rossiter (New York: Mentor, 1961), p. 327.

[4] A. H. Birch, *Representation* (London: Pall Mall Press, 1971), p. 49.

[5] See Margaret Canovan, *Populism* (New York: Harcourt Brace Jovanovich, 1981); Margaret Canovan, 'Trust the People! Populism and the Two Faces of Democracy', *Political Studies*, vol. 47, no. 1 (March 1999), 2–16; Cas Mudde, 'The Populist Zeitgeist', *Government and Opposition*, vol. 39, no. 4 (Autumn 2004), pp. 542–63.

identity with the nation's history and ideals, but who believe that their society, and their place in it, is being subverted and corrupted from within. Such people tend to depict themselves as 'forgotten'. When their frustration or alienation reaches chronic levels, they become susceptible to calls for an emphatic reinstatement of their interests and principles by direct means. In these conditions, dissent is mobilized through the organizing theme of the people as both the subject of grievance and the agency of corrective reaction.[6]

The populist impulse, therefore, is an expression of the social frustration and resentment within a society which, while dedicated formally to the principles of popular sovereignty and democracy, appears to many of its citizens to be controlled by manipulative groups working against the public interest. The democratic structure of elections and consent, therefore, is seen as part of the affliction in that it provides a covering of democratic legitimacy to the continuation of the economic, social, and cultural impoverishment of the populace. As a result, populist insurgency often represents an idealized appeal to popular government at the same time as it impugns the integrity of the intermediary institutions of democratic government. Populists are inspired by the dissenting traditions and heroic folklore of American democracy. They are fired by the legitimacy and moral superiority of the people's will and by the need for it to be directly and forcibly expressed—rather than transposed into distant structures of consent.

Populism can thrive under American conditions. Populists exploit the democratic sensitivities of a nominally open society within which there is considerable potential for particularism and exclusion. By the same token, there exists a rights-based culture where the opportunities for complaint and redress are valued. Populists take full advantage of the idiomatic themes of inequality, injustice, deliverance, redemption, and fulfilment. Because liberty and order are construed as being the silent victims of a wilful infringement of American principles, radical and even retributive action is claimed as a necessity in order to recalibrate society in accordance with its authentic settings. As a consequence, American populism lays at the centre of a fractious dispute over the contested nature of the identity of the 'American people', and by extension the identity of the United States itself. It is for this reason that populism can rightfully be claimed to be the equivalent of a genuinely American fundamentalism. As Michael Kazin asserts, populism alludes to a 'vital way in which Americans have argued about politics. From the birth of the United States to the present day, images of conflict between the powerful and the powerless have run, through our civic life, filling it with discord and meaning'.[7]

---

[6] John D. Hicks, *The Populist Revolt: A History of the Farmers' Alliance and the People's Party* (Lincoln, NE: University of Nebraska Press, 1961); Lawrence Goodwyn, *The Populist Moment: A Short History of the Agrarian Revolt in America* (Oxford: Oxford University Press, 1978); Canovan, *Populism*, chs. 5, 6; Michael Kazin, *The Populist Persuasion: An American History* (New York: Basic Books, 1995); Alan Ware, 'The United States: Populism as Political Strategy', in Yves Mény and Yves Surel (eds.), *Democracies and the Populist Challenge* (Basingstoke, UK: Palgrave, 2002), pp. 101–19.

[7] Kazin, *The Populist Persuasion*, p. 1.

'SOFT POPULISM'

Government is a natural magnet for populism. This is not merely because of the advantages government can offer to those intent upon acquiring position, status, and power in society, but because government can easily be seen as a public expression of private leverage and protected privilege. Set within this kind of scepticism, government is almost invariably characterized as 'big government'. This attribution insinuates a degree of growth beyond that envisaged in a system of checks and balances, and to infer an expansive potential for abuse and misappropriation. The precise indictment of big government can vary depending upon the perceptual disposition of the observer. To those on the left of the political spectrum, Washington represents a military–industrial matrix of corporate power, social interconnections, and financial hierarchy. According to this perspective, government is used to maintain the strategic position and corporate interests of the established economic order through a vast infrastructure of restrictive practices, campaign donations, and inequitable taxation structures. To those on the right, the concept of an 'establishment' carries quite different connotations. From this quarter, the perception is one of a liberal ascendancy in which a political class drawn from government service, the media, federal beneficiaries, and cultural elites determine political agendas and ensure the continuity of a regime of high taxation, extensive intervention, and self-perpetuating liberal priorities.

What remains consistent in both constructions of the 'establishment' is the notion of Washington as a junction point for a vast network of collaborative activity and collective self-interest. In the words of Kevin Phillips, what flourishes in Washington, 'like orchids in a hothouse', is 'power, hubris and remoteness from ordinary people'. Phillips gives expression to the common frustrations over Washington:

To most Americans, Washington now seems like a fortress, more and more bloated and inefficient at a time when the rest of America has cut back and toiled to rebuild itself. The capital supports a growing, well-to-do elite of lobbyists, lawyers and other influence peddlers, while America's middle class has suffered stagnant incomes and shrinking opportunity. In an ominous number of ways, Washington has come to resemble the parasitic capital of a declining empire.[8]

It is often difficult to discern whether the notions of an American establishment are being inferred by the reputation of Washington, or vice versa. The two phenomena are repeatedly treated as interchangeable categories to give a reinforced impression of insulated power at the public's expense. The widespread presumption is that the national centre of government symbolizes a generic dearth of effective governance. In essence, the reputation of government is one of functional efficiency in producing dysfunctional effects. Its associations with stasis, paralysis, waste, fraud, inequity, and detachment generates deep-set prejudices against

[8] Kevin Phillips, 'Fat City', *Time*, 26 September 1994.

government because it is seen not only as corrupt, but also as a corrupting force to those who engage in its processes.[9]

The development of a conceptual and ethical dichotomy between the government and the people arouses a profusion of anxieties based on liberal, democratic, and moral values. These in turn support a range of different populist responses that can be divided into two main types. 'Soft populism' relates to the heightened consciousness on the part of elected office-holders, or aspirants to office, to maintain as close and conspicuous attachment as possible to their constituents and constituency interests. As a consequence, American politicians have increasingly adopted the role of 'outsiders' when campaigning for office. They do so in order to underline their claims to immunity to the temptations of Washington privileges and their intentions to remain true to the interests of the 'silent majority'. Candidates' professed non-conformism to the orthodoxy of Washington's vested interests leads to every variety of dissociation from party-based appeals and to incessant and well-publicized trips away from Washington back to the home constituencies.[10]

The most conspicuous example of this form of outsider activity comes with the increasing incidence of presidents seeking to disconnect themselves from Washington government, in order to preserve their populist credentials. While it has become customary for presidential candidates to campaign for the White House on the populist theme of political betrayal, so incumbents have had to emphasize their continuing allegiance to 'the people' by retaining government as a negative frame of reference. Accordingly, recent presidents have sought to enhance their position in Washington by creating as much distance between it and the presidency. Physical distance and political distance become synonymous with one another in this form of leadership. The strategy allows presidents to remain an integral and even a central part of government. At the same time, it affords them the opportunity to detach themselves selectively from the organizational machinery of government and, thereby, relinquish responsibility for much of what it does. This kind of leadership is at once both self-denying and self-promoting in nature. Even though presidents are, and have to be, at the centre of government, they are impelled through the logic of the populist impulse to engage in an imagery that places governmental activity in zero-sum relationship to democratic virtue. As such, presidents now have to engage continuously and visibly with the American public in order not only to maintain their popular authority when dealing with other centres of Washington decision-making, but also to give physical validity to the continued claims of representing the public interest.

The public office has developed from a position whose influence was ultimately drawn from public support, to one whose influence is now drawn almost exclusively from a continuous and intimate relationship with the public. Just as presidents seek to circumvent other institutional intermediaries in their desire to

---

[9] For example, see Charles Lewis, *The Buying of the Congress: How Special Interests Have Stolen Your Right to Life, Liberty, and the Pursuit of Happiness* (New York: Avon Books, 1998); Elizabeth Drew, *The Corruption of American Politics: What Went Wrong and Why* (Woodstock, NY: Overlook Press, 1999).

[10] For example, see Richard F. Fenno, *Home Style: House Members in Their Districts* (New York: Longman, 2002).

develop a visceral rapport with the public, so they also develop a language and a role centred upon giving expression to popular causes and private impulses.[11] The convergence of the presidency and the public to categories that are arguably extensions of each other represents the end product of a contemporary process of populist marketing.

It is no longer possible for presidents merely to use the public to complement their other leadership facilities. A president has to be popular. Moreover, he has to be prominently and enduringly popular. It is not enough for presidents simply to resort to the communications media, in order to weaken Washington's opposition to their policies. Presidents have to be incorporated into the media's handling of the news on a virtually permanent basis simply in order to maintain their position.[12] Furthermore, presidents can no longer merely claim to be the expression of the popular will. They need instead to be seen to be implanted physically within it. With this in mind, presidents are increasingly induced to exploit the mass media in order to cultivate a form of personalized leadership in the form of an individual relationship with the public. An integral element of this strategy has been the need to maintain a presidential distance from the negative reputation of Washington and, in doing so, to convey the impression of an authentic populist connection to the wider constituency of public scepticism towards government.[13]

Even though considerable resources are committed to this kind of populism, it remains for the most part a top-down strategy in which elected office-holders seek to maintain their position. It is true that successful leaders ingratiate themselves into a populist idiom with the aim of creating an abiding impression of a close correspondence with current issues and anxieties. The prudential and strategic value of such a stratagem is well founded in contemporary electoral history. It also has many repercussions on the political process. In *The New Prince*, Dick Morris describes how imperative it is now for elected politicians to accommodate

---

[11] Samuel Kernell, *Going Public: New Strategies of Presidential Leadership*, 3rd edn (Washington, DC: Congressional Quarterly Press, 1997). See also Theodore Lowi. *The Personal President: Power Invested, Promise Unfulfilled* (New York: Cornell University Press, 1985), chs. 3–6; Jeffrey Tulis, *The Rhetorical Presidency* (Princeton, NJ: Princeton University Press, 1987); Bruce Miroff, 'The Presidency and the Public: Leadership as Spectacle', in Michael Nelson (ed.), *The Presidency and the Political System*, 2nd edn (Washington, DC: Congressional Quarterly Press, 1988), pp. 271–9; K. K. Campbell and Kathleen H. Jamieson, *Deeds Done in Words: Presidential Rhetoric and the Genres of Governance* (Chicago, IL: University of Chicago Press, 1990).

[12] See John A. Maltese, *Spin Control: The White House Office of Communications and the Management of Presidential News*, 2nd edn (Chapel Hill, NC: University of North Carolina Press, 1994); Howard Kurtz, *Spin Cycle: Inside the Clinton Propaganda Machine* (London: Pan, 1998); Lawrence R. Jacobs, 'The Presidency and the Press: The Paradox of the White House Communications War', in Michael Nelson (ed.), *The Presidency and the Political System*, 8th edn (Washington, DC: CQ Press, 2006), pp. 283–310.

[13] Robert J. Donovan and Ray Scherer, *Unsilent Revolution: Television News and American Public Life, 1948–1991* (Cambridge: Cambridge University Press, 1992); Maltese, *Spin Control: The White House Office of Communications and the Management of Presidential News*; Craig A. Smith and Kathy B. Smith, *The White House Speaks: Presidential Leadership as Persuasion* (Westport, CT: Praeger, 1994); Kurtz, *Spin Cycle: Inside the Clinton Propaganda Machine*.

themselves to a public that is more volatile, suspicious, and discerning than it used to be, as well as to a media that is more hostile than was once the case. Under these conditions, elected office-holders have no collective security. They cannot depend upon party approval, or elected mandates, or even upon their political records. According to Morris, the era of traditional democracy has come to an end. Political strength now comes only from current popularity. A daily mandate has to be elicited from a state of permanent electioneering based upon intensive intelligence gathering on public attitudes, and upon making customized initiatives to appease the voters.[14] Others agree and argue that governance in the United States has become dominated by the strategies of a 'permanent campaign'.[15]

Nevertheless, even this kind of populism remains soft because it is mainly confined to style and symbolism. In effect, it is geared not so much to a solution to a democratic deficit, so much as to a form of compensation for the lack of citizen participation. As views and opinions are elicited through polling surveys and focus groups, the general public is both marginalized as a political entity and segmented into discrete cohorts at which point they can be appealed to on different grounds. In cultivating and drawing upon generalized attitudes of political dissension, soft populism can give expression to an otherwise diffuse outlook that is normally confined to passive scepticism and public lassitude. Far from mobilizing complaints into a concerted movement, those engaging in soft populism exploit the values of democratic dissent, representational equity, and procedural justice as a largely preventative measure. Populist themes are employed in order to allay the fears of elected incumbents against being displaced by challengers claiming a superior attachment to popular causes on the basis of them not being part of a Washington establishment.

The precautionary basis of soft populism can be an effective political technique but it always carries the risk of self-negation. When it succeeds, it does so only by reaffirming the public distrust of the political sphere, by creating unrealizable expectations of future political responsiveness and by establishing further precedents of populist critique for challengers to follow in the future. In effect, soft populism exploits the sense of dislocation between government and public, and, in doing so, deepens the discourse of cynicism and fatalism upon which it depends for its short-term advantage.

'HARD POPULISM'

Hard populism has a closer correspondence to the issue-based radicalism of the Populist Party in the 1890s. Like soft populism, it is drawn from the reservoir

---

[14] Dick Morris, *The New Prince: Machiavelli Updated for the Twenty-first Century* (Los Angeles, CA: Renaissance Books, 1999).

[15] See Norman J. Ornstein and Thomas E. Mann (eds.), *The Permanent Campaign and Its Future* (Washington, DC: American Enterprise Institute Press, 2000); Paul S. Herrnson, *Congressional Elections: Campaigning at Home and in Washington*, 4th edn (Washington, DC: CQ Press, 2003), ch. 10.

of populist resentments and anxieties, but the response in hard populism is altogether more challenging in perspective and action. Hard populism is characterized by a greater willingness on the part of its practitioners to engage in explicit diagnoses of perceived problems, to identify specific culpability, to propose clear solutions, and to create the political force required to achieve decisive action. These kinds of populists claim to be genuine outsiders and, therefore, in communion with the popular pulse. They have less interest in procedural probity and more concern with challenging the parameters of conventional political activity. Theirs is a visceral form of direct democracy that seeks to be liberated from the constrictions, filters, and refining devices of institutional structures. Where processes are accepted, the preference is for the kind of populist legacies that can be found in many of the state constitutions in the West and Midwest: namely the provision of petitions for the removal of elected or appointed officials, the usage of popular referenda to decide policy issues, and the legal resort to publicly induced legislative initiatives. In essence, the emphasis in hard populism is one of bottom-up insurgency that forms movements, pursues programmatic changes, attempts to circumvent or transcend traditional political arrangements, and regards its solutions as non-negotiable moral imperatives.

One of the most vivid examples of a contemporary populist movement was the sudden emergence of H. Ross Perot as a presidential candidate in 1992. His campaign was only brought into existence as a result of a television interview in which the businessman pursued the logic of his own indictment of Washington to the point of putting his name forward for consideration by the general public. Perot was resolutely independent and sought no endorsement from either major party. He presented himself as the consummate outsider with no party organization, media managers, or public financing to support his candidacy.[16] His credentials were limited to his vaunted independence, his success as a businessman, his billionaire self-sufficiency, and his stated vision of a mission to fix the system. 'People want things fixed' he stated. 'They want a guy to get under the hood of the car and fix the engine'.[17] In his view, Washington had become 'become a town filled with sound bites, shell games, handlers and media stunt-men who posture, create images, talk and shoot off Roman candles but who don't ever accomplish anything'.[18] To Perot, the 'entire political system [was] broken' because it was operated by politicians who had different agendas to that of the citizenry: 'It is run by insiders who do not listen to working people and are incapable of solving our problems'.[19] As a consequence, drastic action was required. Using a metaphor more rooted in the traditions of rural populism, he asserted that it was 'time to take out the trash and clean out the barn'.[20]

---

[16] Peter Louis Goldman, Thomas M. DeFrank, Mark Miller, Andrew Murr, and Tom Mathews, *Quest for the Presidency 1992* (College Station, TX: Texas A&M University Press, 1994), chs. 21–5.

[17] H. Ross Perot quoted in an interview with Henry Muller and Richard Woodbury, *Time*, 25 May 1992.

[18] Quoted in Ian Brodie, 'A Texas Folk-Hero Aims to Join Race', *Daily Telegraph*, 23 March 1992.

[19] Quoted in Martin Walker, 'The Postmodernist Saviour of America', *Guardian Weekly*, 7 June 1992.

[20] Ibid.

Perot excelled at tapping into the high levels of voter dissatisfaction and alien-ation. He offered sweeping solutions (e.g. campaign reform, term limits for mem-bers of Congress, and a constitutional amendment requiring a balanced federal budget) that had an immediate appeal to those who felt newly marginalized in contemporary American society. His self-professed political amateurism and apparent moral simplicity propelled him into a position where at one point in May 1992 he was leading the opinion poll ratings with 34 per cent of voters making Perot their first preference for president. Although the grass-roots campaign was unable to sustain that level of support, Perot achieved a remarkable 19 per cent of the popular vote in the election and was widely credited with having prevented the re-election of President George H. W. Bush. His meteoric success gave graphic illustration to the mobilizing capacity of a populist iconoclast. In effect, Perot had made a spectacular entry into presidential politics by giving expression to a variety of public prejudices against the generic theme of government.

A year after his dramatic entry into national politics, Perot formed his own citizen watch organization. United We Stand America (UWSA) was dedicated to working towards structural reform to break the linkages between lobbying, money, influence, fraud, and waste. The stated purpose of UWSA was 'to give the people a voice ... to re-create a government that comes from the people—not at the people'.[21] In 1995, he was instrumental in transforming the UWSA movement into the Reform Party and in 1996 he contested the presidential election as its leader. Perot was, and remains, an emblematic figure that epito-mizes the medium of populist non-conformism in the United States. He may have been more conspicuous than most recent populist figures but he is thor-oughly representative of the rich traditions and democratic dogmas of American protest.

Similar strands of populist insurgency were evident in the Contract With America (CWA) campaign in 1994. The radical right leadership of the Repub-lican Party that formulated the CWA programme did so with the intention of harnessing the citizen action ethos of the Perot organization. In an effort to forge an alliance with the 'Perotistas', the formulators of the CWA included within their charter of popular government specific proposals for a constitutional amendment to balance the federal budget and a line item veto that would allow the president to reduce the amount of pork barrel supplements to spending bills. The CWA also included a commitment to introduce another constitutional amendment designed to limit the number of terms that members of Congress could serve. This form of mandatory turnover in representation was seen in some quarters as 'a form of blind retaliation against all politicians'.[22] In fact, it had been a priority item of the Perot organization and one that exemplified its congenital distrust of the political process. The bill was appropriately entitled 'The Citizen Legislatures Act'. Even though much of the CWA did not withstand subsequent political pressures and constitutional challenges, the constructed formulae for appealing to public trust

---

[21] http://www.issues2000.org/Celeb/Ross_Perot_Government_Reform.htm.
[22] William Pfaff, 'Down with Government They Pretend to Shout', *Herald Tribune*, 11 October 1994.

was highly successful and represented a clear attempt to emulate the success that Perot had achieved in drawing upon the contemporary groundswell of popular resentment.[23]

Considerable debate surrounds the issue of the origins and nature of populism's raw materials in the American context. The attributed influences range from the traditional sectional strains between north and south, and between east and west, to rural–urban tensions as well as suburban–inner city enmities. Another major influence is the division between idealized pasts and present realities, and between the official inclusiveness of a nominal consensus and the chronic alienation of many citizens from the democratic order. Some populist strands are explicitly political in style and strategy. Other strands are more diffuse in their sense of dislocation and malaise. They possess a breadth of critical analysis over contemporary society but their political application is secondary to their *raison d'être*.

For example, radical religious organizations like the Christian Coalition of America and the Moral Majority Coalition engage in a form of cultural populism. Their moral critiques of contemporary society have an appeal to those who feel isolated by the pressures of modernity. Even though the main objective of these groups is to transcend society's deficiencies through a revivalism of Christian values, they do attempt to mobilize their members in support of certain litmus test agendas (e.g. provision of school prayer, prohibition of gay marriage). Another strand of oblique populism is provided by single-issue groups such as the National Rifle Association and the Pro-Life Movement. The nature of their social appeal and their mobilizing rhetoric is strongly suggestive of exclusion and dispossession. Notwithstanding the fact that many of these single issues have a symbolic dimension related to wider populist grievances, the political pressure exerted by these groups remain preoccupied with single themes and single sets of solutions.

Populist messages are varied in nature but they all tend to offer the kind of appeal that centres upon feelings of unwarranted exclusion. In giving public expression to private anxieties and insecurities in the form of a lost or declining order, populist themes build upon the conviction that detrimental social developments can be reversed. Objectionable trends in society can be corrected through the arousal of a democratic consciousness and a renewal of popular sovereignty. In the words of Patrick Buchanan, it was possible for the unrestrained will of the normally silent majority to 'take back our cities, and take back our culture, and take back our country'.[24]

In the 1990s, there appeared to be a profusion of raw materials for such collective restoration. This was the era that was marked by numerous references to America's angry voters who allegedly had reached 'boiling point' over their

---

[23] Daniel J. Balz and Ronald Brownstein, *Storming the Gates: Protest Politics and the Republican Revival* (New York: Little, Brown, 1996); Thomas B. Edsall, 'The Cultural Revolution of 1994: Newt Gingrich, the Republican Party, and the Third Great Awakening', in Byron E. Shafer et al. (eds.), *Present Discontents: American Politics in the Very Late Twentieth Century* (Chatham, NJ: Chatham House, 1997), pp. 136–45.

[24] Patrick J. Buchanan, speech to the 1992 Republican National Convention, 17 August 1992, http://www.buchanan.org/pa-92-0817-rnc.html.

frustration with the state of society and the political system in general.[25] During this period, the middle classes were becoming increasingly restive over the growing cost of living, the expense of the tax burden, the decline in economic expectations, and the rise in job insecurity due to technological change and globalization. As wealth became progressively concentrated in the highest sectors of income generation, and as the financing of political campaigns became increasingly dependent upon the contributions of business corporations and labour, trade, and professional associations, the incidence of public distrust and cynicism within the structure of public opinion continued to deepen.[26]

These kinds of factors made large numbers of voters susceptible to the language and promises of populist injunctions. The decade ended with the Democratic candidate for the White House, Vice-President Al Gore, basing his campaign upon an impassioned indictment of Washington's 'special interests' and the need to restore the public's ownership of the institutions of government. He faced George W. Bush, who was a self-professed outsider to Washington politics. The challenger's evident lack of political experience was marketed as being analogous both to the presence of personal integrity and to a refined sensitivity to populist impulses on tax, social morality, and national self-interest. The fact that both candidates were self-declared populists was entirely consistent with the evolution of election campaigns over the previous twenty-five years. The compulsion to base their appeals on populist grounds was a testament to the volatile nature of the electorate and its scepticism towards the conventional patterns of democratic governance. It was also a reflection of the extent to which presidential candidates (e.g. Pat Buchanan, Bill Bradley, John McCain), like so many other elected office-holders (e.g. Arnold Schwarzenegger), are expected to create a point of identity between themselves and the American public in which they act as a kind of antidote to the established processes of government.

POPULIST PARADOXES

All these different aspects to American populism, as well as the different expressions and motive influences that characterize it, demonstrate the leverage provided by the strong traditions of libertarian consciousness and collective action in

[25] Kevin P. Phillips, *Boiling Point: Democrats, Republicans, and the Decline of Middle-Class Prosperity* (New York: HarperCollins, 1994); Susan J. Tolchin, *The Angry American: How Voter Rage is Changing the Nation* (Boulder, CO: Westview, 1998); Joseph N. Cappella and Kathleen H. Jamieson, *Spiral of Cynicism* (New York: Oxford University Press, 1997).

[26] National Election Studies, *The NES Guide to Public and Electoral Behavior: Trust the Federal Government 1958–2002*, http://www.umich.edu/~nes/nesguide/toptable/tab5a_1.htm; Gary Orren, 'Fall from Grace: The Public's Loss of Faith in Government', in Joseph S. Nye, Philip D. Zelikow, and David C. King (eds.), *Why People Don't Trust Government* (Cambridge, MA: Harvard University Press, 1997), pp. 77–107; Darrell M. West and Burdett A. Loomis, *The Sound of Money: How Political Interests Get What They Want* (New York: W. W. Norton, 1999); Elizabeth Drew, *The Corruption of American Politics: What Went Wrong and Why* (New York: Overlook Press, 2000).

the United States. The diversity of popular impulses also gives graphic expression not just to the tensions within populist themes, but between those themes and other constructions of American principles.

Although populism has strong connotations of clarity and immediacy, populist themes are notoriously diffuse and open to conflicting sets of priorities. A central paradox in American populism relates to the way that its proponents manipulate their claims to both majority status and minority rights. Populists are highly critical of those minorities that operate under the auspices of an allegedly pluralist system in order to acquire or maintain a wholly disproportionate degree of power. They regard the status and leverage of such minorities as illegitimate as they do not represent the public interest and yet assume a position for acting in its name. Populists, however, make exactly the same claim and use their minority position in order to pursue it. They make full use of the system's accommodation of minority rights and privileges to participate in the political process, to register their protests, and to propagate their messages of exclusion.

Another disjunction within American populism features the assertion that democratic government has been corrupted either by a majority faction or by a minority faction that has expropriated a majority status and is operating with majoritarian powers. Either way, populists are often in the position of being implicitly counter-majoritarian in the content and language of their critique of contemporary government. The problems relating to the inequalities of exclusion are, thereby, compounded by a solution that is often couched in terms of a freedom from government, irrespective of whether that government can be characterized as majoritarian. Some analysts even go so far as to assert that substantive populist measures have been best served in American history by an elite oriented to public service and social responsibility.[27] In such a context, even majoritarianism is alleged to be a condition that can be corrupted against the public interest and the popular will.

This leads to another tension: the strain between populists and populism. Politicians who espouse populist causes are traditionally dissenters who give visceral expression to widespread frustrations and resentments. Populist politics is generally raw, unrefined, and fragmented in its differing sources and objects of disaffection. At the same time, the righteousness of the message and the authority on which it is based is derived from the unified abstraction of 'the people'. Rousseau's distinction between 'the will of all' and 'the general will'[28] is never far beneath the surface of populist politics. The anomaly of combining temporal disaffection with the spiritual allusions of one overarching conception of the people retains a disruptive influence upon the conduct of populist politics.

The problematic nature of American populism has further dimensions. One of these relates to the general identification of tradition as a defining point of

---

[27] See John B. Judis, *The Paradox of American Democracy: Elites, Special Interests, and the Betrayal of Public Trust* (New York: Routledge, 2001), chs. 2, 3.

[28] Jean-Jacques Rousseau, *The Social Contract*, trans. and intro. Maurice Cranston (Harmondsworth, UK: Penguin, 1968).

reference by which to establish and assess the state of contemporary corruption or decline. The claim of eroded tradition becomes the spur to popular mobilization. And yet, central to the American political tradition is the fabric of representative government and the interplay of democratic politics. In their avowed allegiance to tradition, populists very often overlook or dismiss the significance of intermediary institutions of opinion formation and transmission. In many instances, the traditions of party systems and governing structures are their primary objects of indictment. Notwithstanding the alacrity with which they seek to defend and revive tradition, populists tend to have a distinctly irreverent approach to political reform and do not place a high value upon working through the conventional channels of democratic politics. On the contrary, the emphasis in populism is to employ new devices to circumvent both the established processes of political mediation and the political need for such accommodation. The populist drive is one that is set upon the creation of a political force that remains largely unmediated by conventional structures and which is geared both to correcting a systemic dysfunction and to reviving a foundational ethos of social justice.

Ross Perot, for example, advocated the establishment of 'electronic town halls' that would allow the presentation of computerized referenda on a range of policy options. The results, it was argued, would carry the legitimacy of an exercise in popular sovereignty and, as a consequence, should be implemented without any intervention from politicians or judges. Such apparent simplicity, however, is far from being traditionalist in scope or intention. James Fishkin assessed the reform idea as innovative but also potentially destructive:

Electronic town meetings are just a device to step outside established political mechanisms—to abandon traditional forms of representation and elections—in order to acquire a mantle of higher legitimacy. And in the very worse case, it could be invoked towards unconstitutional ends.[29]

George Grant also concludes that such an idea comes from an anti-traditionalist pursuing iconoclastic ends: 'At first glance, the electronic town halls appear to be nothing more than a high-tech fireside chat—with a response mechanism. But it is actually a usurpation of one of the basic tenets of American checks and balances: representative government'.[30]

Another problematic theme is derived from the populist logic by which 'the people' is deployed as a unified and abstract entity for the purposes of rhetorical and political leverage. Very often the requirements of such a device allow for, and even demand, the instrumental force of an assertive leadership that can transmute the generalized entity of the people into a specific rationalization and, with it, a set of defining issue positions. Populism is a political phenomenon that is based upon a reaction to the perceived elitism of normal politics and to the abuse of power by representatives claiming the right to act on behalf of their constituents. The irony

[29] Quoted in Walter Shapiro, 'He's Ready, But is America Ready for President Perot?', *Time*, 25 May 1992.

[30] George Grant and Susan Alder, *Perot: The Populist Appeal of Strong-Man* Politics (Wheaton, IL: Crossway, 1992), p. 110.

is that populist movements in the United States are usually characterized by the flambouyance of its leaders and for their presumption in claiming to possess an inherent communion with the people.

In one sense, this development is an extension of a highly personalized conception of social dynamics. Complex structures are interpreted anthropomorhically by populists. Accordingly wilfulness and culpability require a response based upon the exertions of a leader's individual willingness to accept responsibility for the decisive action. Paradoxically, the populist denunciation of minority power becomes inverted into a licence for an extreme formation of minority power in the form of a leader's actions taken in the name of empowering the people. Ross Perot, for example, typified a process by which 'politics and government were inextricably linked and ... made indistinguishable from one another to become politics/government, the new enemy'.[31] As a political leader, he dedicated himself to a cause of anti-politics in which he was the 'only legitimate outsider who could successfully overcome that enemy'.[32] Through the agency of himself, Perot proposed to 'replace the power and decision-making abilities of politics/government with the power and decision-making abilities of the people'.[33] The phenomenon of anti-politics leadership of this kind prompts Harvey Mansfield to ruminate on the curious inversion of roles involved when a democratic leader acquires the 'task of taking the people towards a prophetic vision rather than minding the store and letting the people advance on their own'.[34] The danger posed becomes one of leadership that cannot differentiate the role of being an instrument of the people from the prerogative of being its embodiment.

But perhaps the source of the greatest strain within American populism comes from the inherent ambiguity between content and purpose on the one hand, and the medium and technique of popular appeal on the other. What may evoke a populist response will often not translate into effective or even plausible policy positions. On the contrary, the seductive potential of populist diagnoses is directly linked to the deceptive simplicities of the proposed solutions. Effective populist mobilization usually goes hand in hand with sweeping generalizations, grandiose explanations, and uncompromising stances. It is the illicit and polemical flavour of populist themes that give them their affective and often emotional appeal. Whether it is the cure-all of free silver with the original Populist Party in the 1890s, or the catch-all format of successive populist phenomena (e.g. Joseph McCarthy's anti-communist crusade, Steve Forbes' 'flat tax' movement, Pat Buchanan's campaign in support of industrial protectionism), the claim to democratic legitimacy is centred upon allowing the people to break out of the constraining structures of elite opinion and social convention. Populism becomes an antidote to repression,

---

[31] Gwen Brown, 'Deliberation and its Discontents: H. Ross Perot's Antipolitical Populism', in Andreas Schedler (ed.), *The End of Politics: Explorations into Modern Antipolitics* (Houndmills, UK: Macmillan, 1997), p. 140.

[32] Ibid., p. 143.   [33] Ibid.

[34] Harvey Mansfield, 'The Vision Thing', *Times Literary Supplement*, 7 February 1992.

including self-repression. It offers clarity over imprecision and audacity over caution.

The incautious nature of populist attraction is well illustrated by Pat Buchanan's campaigns for the presidency first within the Republican Party (1992 and 1996) and subsequently as presidential candidate for the Reform Party in 2000. Buchanan's raw, but well-articulated, critique of contemporary political conduct was a destabilizing force within the Republican Party for much of the 1990s. His outsider status and his aggressive rhetoric gave him considerable appeal both within blue collar constituencies and also amongst the salaried white collar sector. Both groups were suffering increasingly from economic insecurity through downsizing, outsourcing, and other processes of globalization. They were also taking increasing exception to the demands of multiculturalism and racial reparation.[35] The nature of Buchanan's attraction is evident from his platform in the presidential primary elections for the Republican Party leadership in 1996. It included the following measures:

- A fence to be built along the length of the US–Mexican border
- A request to Congress to pass a five-year moratorium on legal immigration
- An Executive Order abolishing federally mandated minority set-aside programmes and affirmative action plans
- The withdrawal of the United States from the World Trade Organization
- The abandonment of the North Atlantic Free Trade Agreement
- The cancellation of all US foreign aid, except for humanitarian relief
- The introduction of a 15 per cent flat tax

Given the delicate context of intra-party coalition building, such a manifesto was seen by many party strategists as being notionally popular, but also politically injudicious, and even organizationally destructive. Republican managers believed that Buchanan was seeking publicity by playing the populist card which, if successful, would subject the Republican Party to the classic populist paradox: that if Buchanan secured the leadership he would lose the election through the divisiveness of his policy prescriptions. By the same token, if he were to win the election, his policies would in all likelihood unravel as being impractical or unworkable in government. Populists are regularly accused of willing the ends but not the means. Nevertheless, the anomaly is more complex than this. They often will the means of critique and complaint but almost invariably at the expense of creating a substantive and broad-based political force.

It is for this reason that populist movements in the United States are often seen as carrying the seeds of their own decline. This is because their very success in stimulating the rapid formation of support on the basis of popular grievance against governing structures and processes have tended to create a climate of expectations that far exceeded what was possible, or even plausible, within the

[35] Patrick J. Buchanan, *A Republic, Not an Empire: Reclaiming America's Destiny* (Washington, DC: Regnery, 2002); Patrick J. Buchanan, *The Great Betrayal* (New York: Little, Brown, 1998), chs. 1–5, 13–15

exigencies of political accommodation. Populist support is soft and unsustained but even when it has been an effective instrument of protest, its signature characteristics of iconoclasm, anti-politics, and alienation have not made it into a reliable agency of political settlement. On the contrary, the impulsive attempt by populists to operationalize the ideals and processes of direct democracy in a mass society have led to serious questions over how such a vision of self-rule could ever guide any serious process of institutional reconstruction.

CONCLUSION

In his critique of Washington's culture of governmental disconnection, Kevin Phillips gives intuitive emphasis to the need for the past to be restored. Populists have a strong tendency not only to equate a previous state of existence with authenticity and virtue, but also to assume that these prior conditions are recoverable. Phillips is no exception: 'Renewing popular rule is the challenge. ... But how was it lost in the first place? And what can be done to turn back the tide?'[36] These rhetorical questions are founded upon the unexamined and, therefore, undisputed assumptions that 'popular rule' was once an established condition of social life but was then relinquished or usurped by other forces. This kind of populist nostalgia or mystique cannot withstand close scrutiny. Apart from the doctrinal disputes over the place of the citizenry during the founding of the republic,[37] the historical incidence of franchise restrictions and disenfranchisement measures based upon race, class, ethnicity, gender, age, residence, and criminal conviction render any notion of an original standard of American democracy a highly contested condition.[38]

These types of objections, however, are mostly seen as irrelevant. The populist outlook thrives more on the logic and value of popular sovereignty than on its historical validity or operational practicality. The notion of popular self-rule is given a mythic status as an integral and inherent constituent of the American experience. Populists celebrate history because it is used to lend authority for a prospective vision of the future. On the other hand, populism has a strong ahistorical character because its proponents strive to break historical continuity in order to engage in a vivid restoration of the past. History is used, therefore, but it remains subordinate to the primary thrust of populist politics: agitation and radical change in the name of the past.

The use and misuse of history is symptomatic of a more general dynamic within populist activity that confuses means and ends often to the point of making

---

[36] Phillips, 'Fat City'.

[37] See Bernard Bailyn (ed.), *The Debate on the Constitution: Federalist and Antifederalist Speeches, Articles and Letters During the Struggle over Ratification*, Parts I and II (New York: Library of America, 1993).

[38] See Alexander Keyssar, *The Right to Vote: The Contested History of Democracy in the United States* (New York: Basic, 2001).

them interchangeable. In effect, it can be claimed that whatever moves people becomes the objective of a populist movement. This can give populist causes the character of being at one and the same time both conspicuously moral in tone and amoral in purpose. Populist practitioners would certainly dispute such a claim because their appeal is based upon a reaction to the allegedly amoral nature of normal politics which, in their view, is guided by vested interests and the cash nexus of campaign contributions. The problem with this reaction is that it can too easily attribute moral value not merely to the abstraction of the people, but more significantly to their mobilization irrespective of where that insurgency may lead.

The populist accent upon the mobilization of discontent and the creation of alternative outlets of democratic expression can give populism a close association with the relief of frustration and the manifestation of repressed sentiments and prejudices. It is for this reason that populism is often accused of being a euphemism for social antipathy and political intolerance. In his work on 'multiple traditions' and different civic ideals, Rogers M. Smith strongly infers that populism and populist leaders have been at the forefront of those attempts by elites to use the ascriptive inegalitarian ideal to propagate a vision of a political community that conveys to its members an expression of their own conviction of being special and distinctive. The compulsive message of a rightful and defensive resort to a theme of inegalitarianism has often been more effective in the creation of constituencies with a renewed communal identity than those civic traditions associated with liberalism or republicanism.[39] It is because of populism's capacity to project an outward sign of inward alienation towards a perceived deterioration in the composition and identity of a social order that populism has acquired a reputation for being primarily associated with right-wing impulses and agendas. The Right has provided some of the most notorious examples of how populism can degenerate into nothing more than organized expressions of nativist intolerance, racial discrimination, religious bigotry, and chronic xenophobia.[40]

One such movement was the Ku Klux Klan, which had its origins in the racial divisions of southern society after the Civil War, but which grew into an altogether broader movement of resentment in response to the disruptive changes to rural and small-town life in America after the First World War. The Klan was more or less an open secret society, which attracted those who felt that they, and their conception of America, were being displaced by alien elements. In the cause of a higher moralism and patriotism, the Klan became a vehicle of White Anglo-Saxon Protestant fundamentalism. Its animus was widened from simple racial prejudice into a self-styled redemptive force against Jews, Catholics, liberals, socialists, communists, homosexuals, and hyphenated Americans (i.e. recent immigrants).

[39] Rogers M. Smith, *Civic Ideals: Conflicting Visions of Citizenship in U.S. History* (New Haven, CT: Yale University Press, 1999).

[40] John Higham, *Strangers in the Land: Patterns of American Nativism, 1860–1925* (New York: Atheneum, 1968); Chip Berlet and Matthew N. Lyons, *Right-Wing Populism in America: Too Close for Comfort* (New York: Guilford Press, 2000); Joseph Scotchie, *Revolt from the Heartland: The Struggle for an Authentic Conservatism* (Somerset, NJ: Transaction, 2004).

The Klan was the political embodiment of the social strains exerted upon tradi-tional Protestant communities by rapid urban and industrial growth, and by the influx of millions of European Catholic and Jewish immigrants.[41] The Klan's vio-lent excesses were always justified by the scale and malevolence of the subversion believed to be directed to the true American conditions. Although the Klan has now declined in importance since the 1950s, it retains a presence in areas of high tension and its rituals of intimidation continue to be employed as a warning to what it regards as social deviants.[42]

Another populist phenomenon was McCarthyism. This refers to the period in the early 1950s when the United States was overrun by a public paranoia that fixed itself upon the belief that American institutions and government were infested by communist agents. Senator Joseph McCarthy was the most notorious publicist of this belief and he used it to generate a heightened state of anxiety which allowed him to engage in an indiscriminate witch hunt. Unsubstantiated accusations, smears, and innuendos led to blacklists, deportations, and loyalty oaths. Despite the fact that there was no evidence of an invisible communist government or even of any widespread communist espionage and infiltration, the McCarthyite hysteria prevailed over mere fact. McCarthy was left free to browbeat and humiliate not only left-wing organizations and labour unions, but also such previously sacrosanct elements of Washington's liberal establishment as the civil service, the State Department, the Army, and the Presidential record of Franklin D. Roosevelt.[43]

Senator Joe McCarthy's accusations of governmental subversion, and the associ-ated inquisitions of the House Un-American Activities Committee, had profound consequences for the state of American civil liberties and the integrity of its constitutional protections. The excesses of the anti-communist crusade effectively smeared the historical and social reputation of populism. C. Vann Woodward describes the way that liberal intellectuals, like Richard Hofstadter, sought to account for McCarthyism in terms of what it was assumed to disclose about the behaviour of agitated masses. In their search to 'find a scapegoat for their disen-chantment with the seamy side of democracy', the liberal intelligentsia identified populists as 'apologists for provincial anti-Semitism, Negrophobia, xenophobia,

---

[41] Wyn C. Wade, *The Fiery Cross: The Ku Klux Klan in America* (New York: Simon & Schuster, 1988); David M. Chalmers, *Hooded Americanism: The History of the Ku Klux Klan*, 3rd edn (Durham, NC: Duke University Press, 1987).

[42] Patsy Sims, *The Klan*, 2nd edn (Lexington, KY: University Press of Kentucky, 1996); Raphael S. Ezekiel, *The Racist Mind: Portraits of American Neo-Nazis and Klansmen* (New York: Penguin, 1996); Worth H. Weller, *Under The Hood: Unmasking the Modern Ku Klux Klan* (North Manchester, IN: DeWitt Books, 1998), chs. 1, 2, 3; Michael Riley, 'White and Wrong: New Klan, Old Hatred', *Time*, 6 July 1992.

[43] David Caute, *The Great Fear: The Anti-Communist Purge under Truman and Eisenhower* (Lon-don: Secker & Warburg, 1978); Michael P. Rogin, *Intellectuals and McCarthy: The Radical Specter* (Cambridge, MA: MIT Press, 1967); Richard M. Fried, *Nightmare in Red: The McCarthy Era in Perspective* (New York: Oxford University Press, 1990); Albert Fried, *McCarthyism: The Great American Red Scare: A Documentary History* (New York: Oxford University Press, 1997), chs. 5–8.

crypto-fascism, paranoid conspiracy hunting, and anti-intellectualism. Since then "populism"...has been regularly used as an epithet of opprobrium'.[44] Populism can in fact raise serious doubts about the depth of attachment to liberal attitudes within a democracy, and in particular about the extent to which prejudice and intolerance can coexist with the rights of democratic expression.[45]

The most recent example of a mass-based and explicitly right-wing populist movement was George Wallace's American Independent Party. Wallace appealed to the 'little people' whose 'hard won gains...seemed threatened on the one side by Negroes and on the other by the federal government'.[46] Wallace's explicit racism appealed to Ku Klux Klan members, while his sweeping denunciation of the liberal establishment along with the federal government and its taxes drew support from those who vilified the interventionist and coercive dimensions of government. Wallace was a spokesman of the radical right. He appealed to those who had been most affected by change, i.e. those who 'were upset...by pressures toward integration, who were concerned about law and order, who reacted strongly to the changes in moral values as reflected in sexual behavior, use of drugs, the liberalization of the churches, and the like'.[47] As a result, Wallace's party was in essence a populist backlash directed against those forces in society that had made his supporters feel dispossessed, displaced, and disaffected.[48]

In contemporary America, these populist undercurrents remain clearly discernible. They are evident in the repressive tone of numerous 'talk radio' programmes and the other elements of what has been termed a contemporary 'hate culture'.[49] The militia is another expression of social resentment that resonates with the outlook and language of populism. Conspiracy theories suggesting the presence of subversive forces at work within the republic (see pp. 202–7) are taken up and acted upon with a revolutionary rigour. Militias draw on the language of colonial rebellion and the associated need to restore America to a state of popular sovereignty. In their various guises, militia organizations are driven by the stated need to save the people from its politicians and from its government.

[44] C. Vann Woodward, 'Wallace Redeemed', *The New York Review of Books*, 20 October 1994.

[45] See Herbert McCloskey, 'Consensus and Ideology in American Politics', in Raymond E. Wolfinger (ed.), *Readings in American Political Behaviour*, 2nd edn (Englewood Cliffs, NJ: Prentice-Hall, 1970), pp. 383–410; Herbert McCloskey and Alida Brill, *Dimensions of Tolerance: What Americans Believe about Civil Liberties* (New York: Sage, 1983).

[46] Christopher Lasch, *The Agony of the American Left* (Harmondsworth, UK: Penguin, 1973), p. 192.

[47] Seymour M. Lipset and Earl Raub, *The Politics of Unreason: Right Wing Extremism in America, 1790–1970* (London: Heinemann, 1971), p. 345.

[48] Jody Carlson, *George C. Wallace and the Politics of Powerlessness: The Wallace Campaigns for the Presidency 1964–1976* (New Brunswick, NJ: Transaction, 1981); Stephan Lesher, *George Wallace: American Populist* (New York: Addison-Wesley, 1994).

[49] See Gerry Spence, *Bloodthirsty Bitches and Pious Pimps of Power: The Rise and Risks of the New Conservative Hate Culture* (New York: St Martin's Press, 2006); Rush Limbaugh, 'Topic Index', http://www.rushonline.com/indextopic.htm.

The self image of the militias is one of acting as the vanguard of the public in the face of clear and present dangers.[50] Populist narratives can, and have, served the interests of small but highly committed activists who believe that their numbers are inversely proportional to the clarity of their social insight and the immensity of their historical role. In their prescription of a superior insight or revelation, the paucity of their numbers is integrally linked to the morally imperative nature of their role: to constitute the fixed essence of the people and to act as the public's real agents. As the Indiana Militia, for example, makes clear the militia and the people are 'not exclusive terms.'[51] On the contrary, it claims that they are one and the same entity: 'Citizen Militia is not a threat to the American people. The Citizen Militia IS the American people.'[52]

The same fusion of unjustified exclusion and solitary righteousness was evident in the outlook of Timothy McVeigh. In April 1995, he was responsible for the explosion that destroyed the Murrah federal building in Oklahoma City with the loss of 168 lives. McVeigh had been an archetypal angry white male who owned over twenty guns and mixed in the company of extreme right-wing survivalist and militia groups. After leaving the US army, McVeigh developed a deep revulsion of the political system as a whole. Although he was not a formal member of a militia group, he lived in Kingland, Arizona, which was a focal point for fringe survivalist militias opposed to taxation, gun laws, federal ownership of land, and other forms of Washington intervention. It is significant that McVeigh's world view appeared to be rooted in a fundamentalist attachment to constitutional rights and the need to make a stand against what he took to be the largely concealed forces of an alien and subversive government. He saw himself as a legitimate heir to the leaders of the American Revolution. He could recite the Declaration of Independence by heart and often wore a T-shirt inscribed with Thomas Jefferson's classic quotation on revolution: 'The tree of Liberty must be refreshed from time to time with the blood of patriots and tyrants.' His was a nativist combination of libertarian outrage, populist emancipation, and a demand for the imposition of an alternative order. McVeigh's justification in igniting his truck bomb was based upon a personal imperative to act on behalf of the American people not merely in resisting the government, but in actively retaliating against it: 'I decided to send a message to a government that was becoming increasingly hostile. Bombing the Murrah building was morally and strategically equivalent to the US hitting a government building in Serbia, Iraq or other nations'.[53]

More recently, right-wing populism has been criticized less for its forcible intolerance and more for its subtlety in aligning the populist message to the nuances of cultural disinheritance and identity anxiety. In this guise, populism

---

[50] Daniel Levitas, *The Terrorist Next Door: The Militia Movement and the Radical Right* (New York: St. Martin's Press, 2002).

[51] http://www.indianamilitia.homestead.com/Milandyou1.html.   [52] Ibid.

[53] Quoted in 'He Found His Future Was in Death', *Sunday Times*, 10 June 2001. See also Lou Michel and Dan Herbeck, *American Terrorist: Timothy McVeigh and the Oklahoma City Bombing* (New York: Regan Books, 2001).

is used to affirm an underlying sense of social consensus and national solidarity. Accordingly, the system of free enterprise and share ownership is reconfigured as 'market populism'.[54] By deliberately redefining populism within a cultural dimension, conservatives have successfully deployed the issue of class in relation to liberal elitism, cosmopolitan sophistication, and intellectual affectation. The explicit and implicit subtext is described as that of a righteous backlash directed towards mobilizing a social movement in support of a process of cultural reclamation.[55]

In reaction, it is not uncommon for liberals to refer nostalgically back to a period when progressive elites had the political influence and public trust to pursue the common good through imaginative leadership that addressed the needs of the disadvantaged. It is claimed that the position and status of such elites have been largely destroyed by the aggressive action by the profusion of business lobbies together with their strategy of co-opting populist rhetoric against their adversaries.[56] Not all the critics of this trend, however, are to be found on the left. Conservatives like John Lukacs have voiced concerns over the nature of contemporary American politics that echo the anxieties of de Tocqueville over the illiberal undercurrents of mass mobilization. Lukacs asserts that populist politics is regressive and destructive because it essentially appeals to crude sentiment over informed public opinion. In doing so, it debases social tradition and political stability in order to achieve a state of deranged agitation based upon a cynical manipulation of the public by a degenerate mass media. The result, to a conservative like Lukacs, is the combination of stupidity and hate that leads to an intolerant nationalism and a deep resentment of selected minorities.[57]

To concentrate exclusively upon the dark facets of populism is to give an unmeasured portrayal. Populism has suffered from its conspicuous disgraces. But it needs to be recalled that the original Populist Party in the 1890s was a highly admired movement that represented the first coherent challenge to the reach and legitimacy of corporate wealth. Populist leaders like Tom Watson, 'Pitchfork' Ben Tillman, and 'Sockless' Jerry Simpson were masters at agitation and propagandas against a foe whose immense magnitude and momentum were historically unprecedented.[58] Since then, the populist traditions in the southern and western

---

[54] Thomas Frank, *One Market under God: Extreme Capitalism, Market Populism and the End of Economic Democracy* (London: Vintage, 2002).

[55] Thomas Frank, *What's the Matter with Kansas: How Conservatives Won the Heart of America* (New York: Metropolitan/Henry Holt, 2004); Thomas Frank, 'What's the Matter with Liberals?', *The New York Review of Books*, 12 May 2005.

[56] See Judis, *The Paradox of American Democracy*, chs. 5–7.

[57] John Lukacs, *Democracy and Populism: Fear and Hatred* (New Haven, CT: Yale University Press, 2005).

[58] See Walter T. K. Nugent, *The Tolerance Populists: Kansas Populism and Nativism* (Chicago, IL: University of Chicago Press, 1963); David B. Griffiths, *Populism in the Western United States, 1890–1900* (Lewiston, NY: Edwin Mellen, 1992); William Alfred Peffer, *Populism, Its Rise and Fall*, edited and with an introduction by Peter H. Argersinger (Lawrence, KS: University Press of Kansas, 1992); Peter H. Argersinger, *The Limits of Agrarian Radicalism: Western Populism and American Politics* (Lawrence, KS: University Press of Kansas, 1995).

regions have continued to resonate with the need to maintain and develop the positive state in respect to social welfare, health, education, public works, and economic security.[59] It has to be acknowledged that this kind of populist concern for those 'regular people' and 'little guys' on the margins of society has often shared the same ambiguity over race and immigration that characterized the original Populist Party. A figure like George Wallace, for example, demonstrated an attachment to the southern populist tradition of supporting the interests of low-income blue collar workers and the rural poor. He endorsed the federal government's schemes of social benefits and entitlements at the same time that he resolutely opposed the same government's interventions over race.

More recently, left of centre populism has been undergoing something of a revival through the medium of the Internet and, in particular, the opportunities it offers for self-organizing networks of social connections and news aggregations. The popularity and responsiveness of the 'blogosphere' has allowed outfits like *Daily Kos*[60] to provide a channel of communication through which an insurgent liberal constituency can publicize unmediated views and opinions with the kind of sustained immediacy, responsiveness, and irreverence which echoes the traditional spirit of populist critique.

In sum, it is fair to conclude that populism has a mixed reputation. For over a century, the perspective and terminology of populism was strongly associated with left of centre radicalism. It was only in the 1940s, and increasingly in the final quarter of the twentieth century, that American populist discourse began to become assimilated into the conservative world view.[61] Many professional politicians and cosmopolitan elites stigmatized populism as a social disorder and as an incoherent expression of the illiterate and intolerant.[62] Others saw, and continue to view, the populist impulse as part of an entrenched historical struggle over the definition, meaning, and legitimacy of democracy in ever changing circumstances. Whether the appeal is primarily to the past or to the future, populism takes its energy and its rationale from the ideas of democratic renewal and social progress. These are set within a conception of a rightful moral order that has either been denied or expropriated by those who have made the mass feel estranged from their own political processes. In essence, democratic denial under such conditions becomes a moral affront to those who are marginalized in a society that is accustomed to the values of individual autonomy, equal rights, and civic virtue.

[59] For example, see Nancy Beck Young, *Wright Patman: Populism, Liberalism, and the American Dream* (College Station, TX: Texas A&M University Press, 2001). See also publications from *The Progressive Populist*, which 'reports from the heartland of America on issues of interest to workers, small business owners and family farmers and ranchers' and which has the foundational statement that 'people are more important than corporations', http://www.populist.com/.

[60] See http://www.dailykos.com/. See also AMERICAblog (http://americablog.blogspot.com/); Critical Acclaim (http://www.criticalacclaim.info/index.php?method=in&cat=&start=1);The Liberal News (http://www.theliberalnews.com/poor.html); Liberal Politics: US (http://usliberals.about.com/).

[61] See Michael Kazin, *The Populist Persuasion: An American History* (Ithaca, NY: Cornell University Press, 1998), chs. 9–11.

[62] See Frank Furedi, 'From Europe to America: The Populist Moment Has Arrived', *Spiked Essays*, 13 June 2005. http://www.spiked-online.com/Articles/0000000CABCA.htm.

In spite of the historical and social ambiguities that surround American populism, the contribution of populism remains a valuable component of America's democratic culture. The populist impulse can act as a potent corrective to the self-absorption of political elites and a necessary antidote to the habitual co-option of the people's name by office-holders and decision-makers. At its worst, populism can become embroiled in existential speculations over the identity of the people which can lead not so much to the moralization of politics but to the moral rejection of politics in favour of a simplified and more ominous alternative. At its best, populism offers a critical awareness of the anomalies and imbalances within a mass democracy, as well as a reformist impulse that finds expression either through a renovation of established institutions or through the provision of alternative public spheres.

15

Nationalism

FOUNDATIONAL THEMES

American nationalism remains something of counterintuitive development. Nationalism is commonly associated with a single people that have a strongly developed identity based upon a common culture, history, and language set within the context of a fixed geographical area. Although the themes and characteristics of nationalism are notoriously resistant to clear definition, the basic idea of nationalism does centre upon the convergence of a singular people and a single place. It is thought that the cultural and ethnic distinctiveness of a people is best expressed through a sense of place. By the same token, it is the homeland which is taken to be the source of a national community of common ancestry, history, traditions, and customs. The culmination of place and people lies in the development of the nation-state, in which the nation is taken as the proper basis for a viable government and the state is seen as an affirmation of the integrity and autonomy of a genuinely national community.[1]

These defining characteristics of nationalism bear little immediate relationship to the formative constituents of the United States. On the contrary, the United States appears to defy the conventional properties of national existence. Americans are renowned for being a society of immigrants from all parts of the world. In many instances, the arrival of these migrants represented a renunciation on their part of their own national connections, or at the very least a clear disengagement from their homeland societies. As a consequence, the United States developed into a society which necessarily rejected the idea that its people were bound together by common descent. Americans did not have the advantage of 'a common past with its roots in antiquity or medieval times [or] a common religion or a unique cultural tradition'.[2] They did not even have a sense of being rooted in 'a historically defined territory'.[3] Instead, American society made a virtue of its disabilities and celebrated itself as a polyglot collection of exiles from the Old World. Far from possessing a common awareness of territory or ancestry, Americans seemed to be

---

[1] See Elie Kedourie, *Nationalism*, 3rd edn (London: Hutchinson, 1966); Ernest Gellner, *Nations and Nationalism* (Oxford: Blackwell, 1983); Anthony D. Smith, *National Identity* (London: Penguin, 1991).

[2] Hans Kohn, 'Nationalism', in *International Encyclopaedia of the Social Sciences*, vol. 11 (New York: Macmillan/Free Press, 1968), p. 66.

[3] Hans Kohn, *American Nationalism: An Interpretive Essay* (New York: Macmillan, 1957), p. 3.

distinguished more by a consciousness of *not* having such attributes and of taking a positive pride in their own rootlessness and mobility.

Notwithstanding America's deficiencies in the ancient lineages of blood, language, and soil, the United States became an outstanding example of national cohesion and patriotic pride. In many ways, it has far surpassed the levels of national commitment, remembrance, and devotion found in Europe and in other areas of advanced industrial democracy. Polling organizations routinely report that Americans usually show the highest levels of national pride among western democracies. For example, in 2000 the World Values Survey recorded that 72 per cent of Americans categorized themselves as being 'very proud' of their country. This contrasted starkly with the responses given in Britain (49%), Italy (39%), Denmark (48%), France (40%), and the Netherlands (20%).[4] In a similar survey published by the National Opinion Research Center in 1998, a comparable pattern was revealed. The conclusion drawn from over 28,000 interviews in twenty-three countries was that 'Americans are prouder of their country than are any other people in the world'.[5]

The demonstrative attachment to the nation is a ubiquitous element of American culture. It is evident in the daily recitation of the oath of allegiance in schools, the high incidence of the national anthem and 'God Bless America' at public events, and the extraordinary presence of the 'Stars and Stripes' throughout the visual field of American society. What makes this expression of national fervour even more remarkable is that so much of it emanates from social convention and voluntary practice. This reinforces the impression that just as American attitudes to the nation have a cult-like quality to them, so the object of their veneration possesses the characteristics of a faith-based community or even arguably a civil religion.

The customary response of the riddle of America's national cohesion is that its unity is based upon a common allegiance to a set of ideas and principles, rather than upon any fixed cultural background rooted in a particular ancestral soil. According to Hans Kohn, America's national identity was 'born in a common effort, in a fight for political rights, for individual liberty and tolerance'.[6] What were originally English rights and traditions were transformed by the American experience into universal rights which had the 'strength to transform men of the most various pasts and descents into new men, building a common future in a new land'.[7] This was tantamount to making a nation through the acquisition of common values.

---

[4] University of Michigan, World Values Survey, survey data reported in 'Living with a Superpower', *The Economist*, 2 January 2003.

[5] National Opinion Research Center, 'Americans Are World's Most Patriotic People', 30 June 1998, http://www.norc.uchicago.edu/online/pats.htm.

[6] Hans Kohn, 'Nationalism', in Hans Kohn (ed.), *Nationalism: Its Meaning and History*, 2nd edn (Princeton, NJ: D. Van Nostrand, 1965), p. 20; see also Henry S. Commager, *The Empire of Reason: How Europe Imagined and America Realized the Enlightenment* (London: Weidenfeld and Nicholson, 1978), pp. 171–5.

[7] Kohn, 'Nationalism', in *International Encyclopaedia of the Social Sciences*, vol. 11, p. 66.

The United States indeed, virtually alone among nations, found and to some extent still finds its identity not so much in ethnic community or shared historical experience as in dedication to a value system; and the reiteration of these values, the repeated proclamation of and dedication to the liberal creed, has always been a fundamental element in the cohesion of American society. In this respect the United States has always resembled rather a secular church, or perhaps a gigantic sect, than it has the nation-states of the Old World.[8]

Against this background, America is claimed to have become the archetype of 'open nationalism'—a nation of fellow citizens from different backgrounds but with a shared allegiance to certain general principles of social and governmental organization. In this sense, America can be viewed more as an act of faith than as an arena of predestination. It is for this reason that there exists a close association between patriotic sentiment and the notion of America as a civil religion.[9] Expressions of national pride are often presented with a pronounced overlay of religious terminology. By the same token, it is common for spiritual and affective attachments to find an outlet in the patriotic pride taken in America's experiment in open-door republicanism.

American nationalism, therefore, is widely reputed not only to be based upon values but to be primarily understood and expressed in terms of these characterizing principles. The ideas in questions are those core values associated with the United States—liberty, democracy, rule of law, individual rights, progress, equality, and property. In one respect, America's tradition of 'open nationalism' provides a satisfactory account of the country's social cohesion and ideological unity. Under these ecumenical auspices, nationalism can offer a plausible explanation of how America's disparate values have been reconciled into an amalgam capable of providing both the focal point and the unifying medium for a vast immigrant culture. Just as American values seem to explain the national fervour of the United States, so the American nation appears to provide a unifying device for American values. This fusion of pluralities has a beguiling symmetry. Nevertheless, it is not as clarifying or as explanatory a construct as it first appears. As much of this study has shown, the relationships between American political ideas are highly problematic and are not easily susceptible to aggregate simplicities. By the same token, national identity in the United States is more complex in origin, nature, and consequences than the premise of open nationalism implies.

LIBERAL NATIONALISM

The prevailing self-characterization of the United States is one of liberal nationalism. The primary source of this reputation lies in the centrality of the federal

---

[8] Michael Howard, *War and the Liberal Conscience* (Oxford: Oxford University Press, 1981), p. 116.
[9] See Robert N. Bellah, 'Civil Religion in America', in Russell E. Richey and Donald G. Jones (eds.), *American Civil Religion* (New York: Harper & Row, 1974), pp. 21–44.

constitution both to the founding of the nation and to the organization and ideals of the state. From its inception, the United States was hailed as a model of limited constitutional government and expansive individual freedom. American nationhood appeared to go hand in hand with the political emancipation from an imperial order and with a formal recognition of the authority vested in the principle of popular sovereignty. The United States has been habitually depicted as the 'first new nation' because of its status as the 'first major colony successfully to break away from colonial rule through revolution'.[10] In a similar vein, America has been widely credited with having been devised and organized through the medium of liberal rationalist construction. As a consequence, the achievements of the Founding Fathers and their successors have allowed the United States to become a symbol of not just the viability of a liberal nation but of its potential in generating enormous economic and political resources.

Given that the chief theme of America's national narrative is that of westward expansion, the main challenge in the political sphere has traditionally been that of affording stability and security to a mutating territorial area. The claim to liberal nationalism has conventionally been based upon the capacity of the political arrangements to facilitate an open nationalism with an open-ended conception of the location of borders. During the nineteenth century in particular, the rapidity of expansion generated severe strains over settlements, resources, property rights, and boundary lines. In most instances, the governing institutions were able to achieve negotiated settlements based upon the notion of an equilibrium of interests within a liberal society. The ability to reach these accommodations was aided by the development of an authoritative linkage between the idea of an American nation and the legal format of the federal union. In effect, the federal constitution offered a common point of legal and national reference through which disputes could be minimized and even resolved. It provided a set of agreed criteria based upon a contractual agreement in which parties could contest the meaning and application of the original drafted document.[11]

The nexus between the American sense of nation and the constitutional nature of its governing arrangements also cultivated an organic process of enlargement for the United States. The initial founding of the republic had been marked by a constitution elevated to the 'supreme law of the land' and characterized by a fixed statement of liberal principle. Accordingly, every new accession to the union could be construed as the product of the Constitution's own indigenous processes of statehood. In this way new states were not only assimilated into the original compact through the Constitution's own rule of law, but could be construed as direct derivatives from the single point of constitutional and national origin. New states were the legal equivalent of the thirteen foundational states because they achieved statehood through absorption into the liberal values of the republic. It

---

[10] Seymour M. Lipset, *The First New Nation: The United States in Historical and Comparative Perspective* (New York: Norton, 1979), p. 15.

[11] W. James Booth, 'Communities of Memory: On Identity, Memory and Debt', *American Political Science Review*, vol. 93, no. 2 (June 1999), pp. 249–63.

can be claimed that the ethos of liberal nationalism not only secured the union but also facilitated its expansion by ensuring that each addition would necessarily represent a creation in the Constitution's own image. Moreover, the dynamic deepened with time. The greater the number of states to be authorized by the Constitution's processes, the more legitimacy accrued to the Constitution itself and by extension to the national character of the union.

The main challenge to this organic conception of federal unity came with the Civil War (1861–5). The view that the federal government could be interpreted as embodying the people in the form of a national community was used to support the idea of national growth and the central development of a continental economy. Its opponents believed that the union had never been anything other than a contract between sovereign states. As a consequence, the states retained the right to nullify acts of the federal government if any of the constituent parties believed that the terms of the federal contract had been broken.[12] These arguments over the sources of political authority, the nature of political obligation, and the meaning of federalism persisted throughout the first half of the nineteenth century. The disputed contentions only became chronic when it was clear that James Madison's vision of a multiplicity of continental interests had broken down into a polarized sectionalism of northern and southern blocs. The union had encouraged nationalism, but at the price of a threatened secession of the South into a second American nation. As the two sections hardened in attitudes, so their respective constructions of the federation and the union became irreconcilable.

In the ensuing Civil War, the northern forces ground the southern nation into military defeat. In doing so, it conclusively won the argument over the characteristics of the American union. Through the massive mobilization of men and materials on both sides, the Civil War succeeded in energizing the two sections into a heightened state of consciousness concerning their respective nations. The enormous bloodshed and devastation of the conflict ultimately directed that consciousness into the single dimension of the United States. The Civil War ended the fundamentalist arguments over federal authority and state sovereignty and, as a result, cleared the ground for the development of an uninhibited American nationalism.[13] Before the war, the United States was commonly referred to in the plural reflecting the nature of its segmented composition. Following the conflict, the federation was considered to be a unified whole. Before the war, Americans had referred to 'these United States'; after it, the terminology had changed to 'the United States'. The union had become transformed into an indissoluble and indivisible nation. This provided the scale and solidarity of American integration

---

[12] James Oakes, *Slavery and Freedom: An Interpretation of the Old South* (New York: Knopf, 1990); Eugene G. Genovese, *The Southern Tradition: The Achievements and Limitations of an American Conservatism* (Cambridge, MA: Harvard University Press, 1994); David F. Ericson, 'Dew, Fitzhugh, and Proslavery Liberalism', in David F. Ericson and Louisa B. Green (eds.), *The Liberal Tradition in American Politics* (New York: Routledge, 1999), pp. 67–98.

[13] Kohn, *American Nationalism*, ch. 3; Ralph H. Gabriel, *The Course of American Democratic Thought*, 2nd edn (New York: Ronald Press, 1956), ch. 10.

that was later to enable the United States to engage in global conflict as a major international power.

It should be pointed out that the clash between the North and the South was almost exclusively defined in terms of rival interpretations of liberal iconography. Far from rejecting the liberal principles of the North, the confederacy objected to what it regarded as the unionists' corruption of such values as free trade, property rights, and individual liberty. The northern states struggled for dominion over the meaning of liberty and democracy, and when victory came it was widely interpreted as a triumph for a union now united in its common attachment to an agreed form of liberalism.[14] President Abraham Lincoln repeatedly alluded to the victory in terms of a decisive affirmation of national values that were now to be regarded as inherent in the existence of all the American states.

To Garry Wills, President Lincoln deliberately modified the rationale of the conflict to create a second foundational process that was necessarily intellectual in character. A nation of principles could only survive by an explicit refinement of its animating ideals and by a rededication of the nation in the name of a liberalizing equality. Just as civic equity was the basis of liberalism, so under President Lincoln's tutelage the public philosophy underlying the war shifted from a simple defence of the union to a unifying appeal to national conscience.[15] In President Lincoln's view, the Civil War had become a test of whether America could emerge from the implications of its birth:

Four score and seven years ago our fathers brought forth on this continent a new nation, conceived in liberty and dedicated to the proposition that all men are created equal. Now we are engaged in a great civil war, testing whether that nation or any nation so conceived and so dedicated can long endure.[16]

The only way of lifting the nation out of conflict with itself was to convert it into a crisis of national idealism and, thereby, into a source of reconciliation around the theme of liberalism refined through national agency. In a similar vein, Eric Foner draws attention to the way that the Civil War followed on from the revolutionary War of Independence in associating military conflict with the security and refinement of liberty in the form of a freed people within a free nation. The Revolution 'created a new collective body whose members were to enjoy rights and freedom as citizens in a new political community'.[17] In the same spirit, the Civil War was rationalized as a device for correcting past inequities of citizenship. This linked the progress of freedom directly to an 'intense new nationalism' based upon the liberating 'power of the nation state'.[18]

---

[14] See J. David Greenstone, *The Lincoln Persuasion: Remaking American Liberalism* (Princeton, NJ: Princeton University Press, 1993).

[15] Garry Wills, *Lincoln at Gettysburg: The Words That Remade America* (New York: Simon & Schuster, 1993).

[16] President Abraham Lincoln, 'The Gettysburg Address', 19 November 1863, http://www.law.ou.edu/hist/getty.html.

[17] Eric Foner, *The Story of American Freedom* (New York: W. W. Norton, 1998), p. 153.

[18] Ibid., p. 98.

The common currency of liberal norms was illustrated with dramatic effect in the second half of the nineteenth century when the liberties enumerated in the Civil War amendments for newly emancipated slaves were used to defend the economic freedoms of corporate interests. As the United States became a single market and as its production, transportation, and communications systems experienced increasing levels of integration, the national dimensions of the union's existence became increasingly evident. In effect, the nation grew up alongside, and directly benefited from, the dramatic expansion of large-scale liberal capitalism and the surge in material progress derived from rationalized organization and technological innovation.[19]

The idea of an open market was analogous to the idea of an open nationalism. Economic opportunity and entrepreneurial energy encouraged the formation of new structures and fostered the general acceptance that these were self-organizing entities which, through the market, would maintain an autonomous equilibrium. The same supposition of a self-regulating dynamic of human behaviour and liberal values was evident in the development of a national identity formed through a social as well as a spatial emancipation. The United States' great leap forward into an industrial and international powerhouse was widely conceived as an outward sign of an internal symbiosis that merged the nation with the liberal nature of its foundational principles and core values. National achievements, developments, and heroes reflected the faith in a liberal democratic ethos. In like manner, the exploits of pioneers and entrepreneurs were cast in the light of nation builders taking advantage of American opportunities to produce a proliferation of further possibilities for progress.

In his study of the social construction of American historical memory, Michael Kammen examines the transition in the late nineteenth and early twentieth centuries of a country with little or no interest in the past to one in which the formative events and material artefacts of the republic's past became venerated as signs of historical evolution.[20] The 'new hunger for history' took the form of 'a self-conscious phenomenon'[21] in that it appeared to fulfil a need to create, or at least to clarify, a national identity. The result of this appetite was the establishment of a civil religion based upon a fusion of tradition and progress encased in nationalistic commemoration. The onset of flag worship and the pilgrimages to historical sites, together with the entrenchment of patriotic hymns and the endowment of libraries, universities, and museums all served to give historical grounding to the idea of a national community

This sudden emergence of the United States as a formidable national power provoked a profusion of accounts seeking to explain its transformation. Many were celebratory and triumphant in their teleological drive to explain the past

[19] See Samuel P. Hays, *The Response to Industrialism, 1885–1914* (Chicago, IL: University of Chicago Press, 1957); Olivier Zunz, *Making America Corporate, 1870–1920* (Chicago, IL: University of Chicago Press, 1992).

[20] Michael Kammen, *Mystic Chords of Memory: The Transformation of Tradition in American Culture* (New York: Alfred Knopf, 1991).

[21] Ibid., p. 100.

in terms of the present. Others were more reflective in style. For example, a strong historiographical impulse sought to ascribe the stability and security of the United States to the Founding Fathers. In the same vein, the longevity of the United States Constitution has been widely attributed to the liberal precepts of its design. Given that the Founders were confronted with having to create an entire system of government, the outcome has been successively portrayed as an Enlightenment achievement in rational thought. It is claimed that they worked on the assumption that it was possible to elicit empirically derived principles of political behaviour from which a precise and integrated framework of government could be formulated from first principles. As such, the final document could be made to seem like a 'triumph of mechanism'. This is because with few exceptions, the 'constitution-makers thought that the government they were constructing was in accord with nature's design'.[22]

Another popular theme of American liberal nationalism came in the form of attributing liberal doctrines and attitudes to the idiosyncrasies of the New World itself. The most celebrated example of an attempt to establish America's identity exclusively in conditions and experiences peculiar to the United States was Frederick Jackson Turner's frontier thesis of American society.[23] Turner's assertion concerning how a frontier of settlements advancing against a wilderness could have socially and ideologically regenerative properties proved to be a popular analysis of American liberty and democracy. Because it offered a picture of successive purification from the decadence of established social settlement, it had widespread appeal to a developing nation eagerly in search of an understanding of what was distinctively American about America. The Turner thesis was ultimately recognized as being too contrived an attempt to lodge American traditions within a purely domestic context and, in particular, a western American context. Nevertheless, the analysis exemplified the American propensity for locating its national character within a unique matrix of spontaneous liberalism set within indigenous and naturalistic contexts.[24]

Much of American nationalism is bathed in this kind of liberal triumphalism in which an autonomous and self-directed society is claimed to have transformed both itself and the world's conception of the possibilities of a free society. The social experimentation of volunteerism and choice in the construction of American society is celebrated as a liberation from the constraints of ancestral tradition, fixed orders, and limited horizons. Just as national themes and achievements are portrayed as products of freedom, so the mobilization of national endeavour in wartime has been dominated by references to the defence of liberty.

---

[22] Martin Landau, *Political Theory and Political Science: Studies in the Methodology of Political Inquiry* (Atlantic Highlands, NJ: Humanities Press, 1979), p. 76.

[23] Frederick J. Turner, *The Frontier in American History* (Huntington, NY: R. E. Krieger, 1975).

[24] Ray A. Billington, *The Genesis of the Frontier Thesis: A Study in Historical Creativity* (San Marino, CA: Huntington Library, 1971); Ray A. Billington, *America's Frontier Heritage* (Albuquerque, NM: University of New Mexico Press, 1974); Allan G. Bogue, *Frederick Jackson Turner: Strange Roads Going Down* (Norman, OK: University of Oklahoma Press, 1998).

This idea of the American nation embodying the culmination of a liberal order is reflected in the profusion of historical tracts and political commentaries that attend the mystery of how Americans produced a new nation. Henry Steele Commager typifies the genre, which takes as its premise the belief that when the United States was formed it represented a 'new kind of nationalism' and one that was 'achieved with a swiftness unprecedented in history'.[25] America had not possessed the customary ingredients of a nation in the context of the late eighteenth century (e.g. a fixed conception of a particular people; a developed sense of a historic homeland; and a settled ethnic or cultural community finding expression in a national identity). Nevertheless, in Commager's view, the apparent deficiencies of American society amounted to a collective strength in the formation of a substantive nationalism. This is because the people themselves through an 'act of will'[26] were able to form a national community: 'To an extent unimaginable in the Old World, American nationalism was a creation of the people themselves: it was self-conscious and self-generating.'[27] The actions of free citizens freely forming their own sense of national convergence and purpose further strengthened America's claim to the Enlightenment in action. Commager's convictions reflected the predominant assumptions surrounding the formative processes of American nationalism:

It was rooted not in the exhausted soil of some remote past, but in the virgin land of a new continent; it found inspiration not in dubious mythology masquerading a history...but in the public will openly proclaimed. Its institutions were fashioned...by the laws of Reason and the dictates of Common Sense. Because the United States was really new, it was free from most of those inherited ambitions and animosities which had for so long made a shambles of many of the nations of Europe.[28]

The manner of its formation and the nature of its succeeding development have remained central to the liberal credentials of a national consciousness whose boundaries are still in the main construed as open and emancipating.

The United States has constructed a pronounced sense of nationhood but it remains strongly influenced by the sanction of inheritance. American identity retains a close connection with the belief that the United States is distinguished by its variance from other nations. The United States continues to celebrate itself as a nation apart because of its professed status as the authentic extrapolation of the liberal temperament.[29] This is reflected in the conviction that

---

[25] Henry S. Commager, *The Empire of Reason: How Europe Imagined and America Realized the Enlightenment* (London: Weidenfeld & Nicolson, 1978), p. 162.

[26] Ibid., p. 163.   [27] Ibid., p. 173.   [28] Ibid., p. 175.

[29] Samuel P. Huntington, *American Politics: The Promise of Disharmony* (Cambridge, MA: Belknap Press, 1981), ch. 2; James Chace, 'Dreams of Perfectability; American Exceptionalism and the Search for a Moral Foreign Policy', in Leslie C. Berlowitz, Denis Donoghue, and Louis Menand (eds.), *America in Theory* (New York: Oxford University Press, 1988), pp. 249–61; Trevor B. McCrisken, *American Exceptionalism and the Legacy of Vietnam: US Foreign Policy Since 1974* (Basingstoke, UK: Palgrave Macmillan, 2004).

American nationalism is based upon a natural solidarity manifested through civic voluntarism and grass-roots affection. In contrast to many other societies where national attachments and rituals are enforced by dominant elites and state action, expressions of national loyalty in the United States are organized on the basis of convention and choice. Significantly, it can be claimed that in America 'promoting nationalism is a private enterprise'[30] geared to the achieved ideal of liberty.

This liberal dimension to American nationalism is translated with dramatic effect to the cultural disjunction in the United States between the nation and the state. The American nation not only remains differentiated from the state, but is often deployed to oppose the exertions of the state. Many other developments of nationalism have featured a convergence of nation and state. The United States has resisted this conflation. American nationalism has never featured the process of a people becoming the state. This is not to say that leaders and governments have desisted from using the American nation to legitimize policy and authority. The federal government, in particular, has in many ways successfully claimed the right to embody an integrated form of national citizenship and to act on behalf of the nation to promote the general welfare and the national interest. Nevertheless, the fusion of nation and state remains far from complete.

As a consequence, an integral feature of American national culture is that of freedom against the intrusion of government. Nationalism can be the preserve of the private sphere demarcated by the limited boundaries of a public sphere. American nationalism continues to suggest and to accommodate the libertarian injunction that can challenge the authority of the state. In spite of its democratic credentials, America retains a nationalist dimension of common experiences and allegiances that is separate from government. As a consequence, it is possible to act against the state without acting against the nation. In contrast, an attachment to the nation is often regarded as being positively synonymous with anti-statist sentiment. This being so, America's periodic crusades against government are normally accompanied by an arousal of national ideas, faiths, and symbols. American attitudes reveal a consistent pattern of strong patriotism but at the same time a persistent disavowal of nationalistic behaviour. The former is regarded as voluntarist and benevolent. The latter continues to be associated with state-centric excess.

CONSERVATIVE NATIONALISM

Conservative nationalism is often portrayed as having little or no role in the United States. In many instances, American identity is defined in terms of how it differs from conventional nationalism in which the emphasis is laid upon ancestral territory, language, ethnicity, and religion. American nationhood is largely

---

[30] Minxin Pei, 'The Paradoxes of American Nationalism', *Foreign Policy* (May/June 2003), p. 33.

distinguished by its reputation for youth, openness, universalism, progress, tolerance, and assimilation. By contrast, other nationalisms are seen as inherently conservative in that they are based primarily upon a backward-looking ethos dwelling upon ancient enmities, collective grievances, frustrated aspirations, and established hierarchies. Its irreverence for history and its disposition for mobility are thought to make the United States wholly incompatible with the customary characteristics of conservative nationalism. This depiction, however, can be premature and even inaccurate.

In Chapter 13, it was noted that the United States possesses considerable conservative resources that depend upon a set of traditions and impulses which privilege the values of order, stability, security, and cohesion. It can be argued that in a generic sense, nationalism is an intrinsically conservative phenomenon. Whether the conservatism is one of core values, or of instinctive temperament, the contention is that nationalism has a correlation with the past and with a respect for the authority and guidance of historical continuity. In the United States, it can be claimed that nationalism is the main outlet and agency for the articulation of conservative themes. The American nation is habitually employed by conservatives both as a medium through which to express conservative principles and as a focal point of identity from which to substantiate conservative positions.

The affinity between conservative values and the nation is illustrated by the emphasis given in American society to patriotism, national symbolism, and historical continuity. In contrast to the often iconoclastic depiction of America's revolutionary and republican origins there is a strong attachment to tradition. Whether it is the Pilgrim Fathers, the War of Independence, the formulation of the US Constitution, or the Civil War, these events and developments are celebrated as evidence of a shared past and a collective sense of national community. National myths and symbolic representations evoke strong emotional reactions and underline the instinctive, compulsive, and even irrational dimensions of national loyalty. The conservative ethos of an organic yet fragile community requiring special protection and close vigilance is reflected in the modern American preoccupation with national security even to the extent of compromising liberty for the sake of conformity. The inward nostalgia and fear of enemies combined with the non-transferable properties of indigenous experience and national character produce a form of nationalism that is not easily reduced to an aggregate of liberal principles. On the contrary, the need to restrain the force of liberal licence and emancipation has often led conservatives to embrace the nation as a vehicle for restoring order and protecting social cohesion.

Nationalism therefore poses some significant problems to the nature of America's liberal order. The unifying character of nationalism opens up the question of whether a liberal society generates a national spirit through its own principles or whether it has to rely to such an extent upon conservative supports that it compromises its own liberal origins. Louis Hartz offered an imaginative solution to this conundrum by fusing the two alternatives together into an undifferentiated whole. Over time, liberal foundations can become so deeply ingrained into the nation's consciousness that they develop their own reflexive traditions. In the American case, it is said to have produced a 'kind of nationalism found nowhere else on earth, exploding the familiar categories...a "traditionalist nationalism" that was liberal, a Burkean nationalism that was Lockian'.[31]

A different perspective is offered by the proposition that American nationalism offers a genuine alternative framework of conceptual coherence within which conservative intuition plays a central role. Instead of an all-consuming liberal tradition, this interpretation assigns a more independent status to conservative values in the currency and legitimacy of national attachment.[32] Another perspective locates the national traditionalism of the United States firmly within the concept of the nation itself. In this light, nationalism is neither a derivative nor an adjunct of liberalism or conservatism but a tradition drawn exclusively from America's experience of existing without the need for doctrinal rationalization.

Daniel Boorstin epitomizes this approach of confining the American nation to a set of values that are separate and entire to itself. To Boorstin, America did not need to acquire a theory of the nation because it had already been bestowed with a preformed conception of national existence through the immediacy of American conditions. As a consequence, '[n]o nation has been readier to identify its values with the peculiar conditions of its landscape: we believe in *American* equality, *American* liberty, *American* democracy, or, in sum, the *American* way of life'.[33] This romanticist view has fostered a 'naturalistic approach to values'[34] which in Boorstin's view is strongly reflected in American attitudes towards patriotism.

Michael Lind has followed in a similar vein. He feels that the United States has a national existence which is not dependent upon either liberal or conservative precepts. Despite being assailed by the centrifugal forces of multiculturalism, Lind points to the underlying corporate nature of a nation based upon a common culture of historical knowledge, language, habits of liberty, particular 'folkways', and styles of behaviour, as well as a heritage of laws and political institutions.[35] Lind challenges the liberal basis of America's reputation as a universal centre of open nationalism. He complains that liberal 'universalists' look to defining statements of principle as the central components of American national meaning.[36] The outlook is typified by President Lincoln's Gettysburg Address, which contained the celebrated reference to a 'nation dedicated to the proposition that all men are created equal'.[37] Lind disputes the logic of how this foundational assertion has been used: 'A nation may be *dedicated* to a proposition, but it cannot *be* a

---

[31] Louis Hartz, *The Liberal Tradition in America: An Interpretation of American Political Thought Since the Revolution* (New York: Harcourt Brace Jovanovich, 1955), p. 207.

[32] Clinton Rossiter, *Conservatism in America: The Thankless Persuasion*, 2nd edn (New York: Vintage, 1962).

[33] Daniel J. Boorstin, *The Genius of American Politics* (Chicago, IL: University of Chicago Press, 1953), p. 25.

[34] Ibid.

[35] Michael Lind, *The Next American Nation: The New Nationalism and the Fourth American Revolution* (New York: Free Press, 1996), chs. 1–5.

[36] For example, see Ben J. Wattenberg, *The First Universal Nation* (New York: Free Press, 1990).

[37] President Lincoln, 'The Gettysburg Address', http://www.law.ou.edu/hist/getty.html.

proposition.'[38] To Lind, the culture of a nation as well as its membership cannot depend merely upon the acceptance of a set of propositions: 'The United States, according to universalists, is not a nation-state at all, but an idea-state, a nationless state based on the philosophy of liberal democracy in the abstract.'[39]

Irrespective of the debates over the sources, what is significant is the extent to which American nationalism can be characterized through a conservative attachment to tradition as a value in its own right. It can be argued that the very speed of settlement and development in the United States produced a kind of historical stasis within which a conservative perspective could quickly gather pace. Because so much change could be explained by reference to an established continuity of individual behaviour and social organization, it allowed the effect of time to accelerate. Minimal settlements could rise to the status of established cities within a generation, allowing their populations to pass through the equivalent of extended social time. In like manner, political practices could quickly acquire the status of traditions drawn literally from time immemorial.

Conservative tradition, however, can be used to support, and at times to conceal, a more restrictive conception of American nationhood. This perspective draws upon a sense of the alien in defining America both in terms of what it is not and in relation to the need to protect the republic from the corrupting influence of those that are deemed to threaten its integrity. The theme of integrity in this context can, and has, carried strong ethnic, racial, religious, and gendered connotations during the course of American history. For example, the high idealism of equal rights and national citizenship that distinguished the Reconstruction era (1865–75) was followed by a reversion to racial segregation, disfranchisement, and the legalized subordination of freed blacks to a dominant white structure of regional repression.[40] During the same period, a resurgence of Anglo-Saxon sensitivities hardened the ethnocultural premises of America's national discourse. It brought in its wake a range of immigration, employment, educational, and civic measures designed to restrict the cultural penetration of Jewish and Irish ancestry; to diminish the influx of Southern and East European Catholics; and to marginalize the immigrants from East Asia.[41] Integral to the concept of the 'melting pot' was the bounded nature of the pot itself. This was not to be assimilated with the contents of the mix but would guide the construction of the immigrant nation along the lines of established priorities.[42]

Even though the United States has a long established lineage of civic nationalism, its history is punctuated with episodes of ethnic nationalism. These two representations of nationalism have starkly different properties. The premise of

---

[38] Lind, *The Next American Nation*, p. 5.   [39] Ibid., p. 3.

[40] Eric Foner, *A Short History of Reconstruction* (New York: Harper and Row, 1990); John H. Franklin, *Reconstruction: After the Civil War* (Chicago, IL: University of Chicago Press, 1961).

[41] See Lucy E. Salyer, *Laws Harsh as Tigers: Chinese Immigrants and the Shaping of Modern Immigration Law* (Chapel Hill, NC: University of North Carolina Press, 1995); Dale T. Knobel, *America for the Americans: The Nativist Movement in the United States* (New York: Twayne, 1996).

[42] See Rogers M. Smith, *Civic Ideals: Conflicting Visions of Citizenship in U.S. History* (New Haven, CT: Yale University Press, 1999), chs. 11, 12.

civic nationalism is that the nation should be composed of those who subscribe to a set of beliefs and principles irrespective of race, colour, creed, gender, language, or ethnicity. The nation in this sense is a community of equal citizens with a common attachment to a shared set of political practices and values. Since civic nationalism invests sovereignty directly in the people, it is democratic in character. Ethnic nationalism on the other hand is based upon inheritance rather than choice. Instead of individuals defining the national community, it is the nation that is the independent variable. Ethnic nationalism gives force to what divides people rather than to what may unite them. As a consequence, it tends towards authoritarian imperatives rather than to democratic consent.[43]

The reference to ethnic nationalism in the American context is not meant to imply that the authoritarian character of this kind of solidarity necessarily displaces the open-textured optimism of America's civic nationalism. It is not even suggesting that these two forms of nationalism have equal weight in the United States. However, it is undeniable that during periods of great change, or great fear, the reaction often comes in the form of a retrenchment towards the notion of a core ethnic community. It is claimed in some quarters that Americans have revealed themselves historically to be far from immune to the calls of an ethnocentric identity. On the contrary, they have been depicted as having been highly susceptible to notions of an exclusive nationalism based upon discriminatory rules of eligibility for full membership of the national community.[44]

These periodic impulses to privilege social categories over political beliefs as the qualifying determinants of American identity and citizenship are not always explicitly attached to assertions of racial, ethnic, or religious exclusion. Moreover, such claims do not usually seek overtly to contradict the principles and traditions of America's open nationalism. Nevertheless, they can generate intrusive and even authoritarian measures commensurate with what is considered to be the threat posed to the inheritance of a national community. Whether it be arrests and deportation, or nationalization procedures and loyalty oaths, the inference is one of an open nationalism that is conditional upon the ability to discriminate between those who are considered to be ideologically open to its precepts and those who are not.

Located at the extreme end of American ethnic nationalism is a resentful reaction against what is seen to be a flawed and prejudicial development of open nationalism. This type of inclusive intolerance against an exogenous cultural presence has been termed 'Jacksonian nationalism'. It draws upon the resentment of the traditional white South and the frontier regions, which in Andrew Jackson's time had produced a psychosis of fear, oppression, and defeat. The Irish and Scotch immigrants of the Southern and Western states were suspicious not only of distant government but also of distant elites who were regarded as the natural

---

[43] See Anthony D. Smith, *The Ethnic Origins of Nations* (Oxford: Blackwell, 1986); Yael Tamir, *Liberal Nationalism* (Princeton, NJ: Princeton University Press, 1993); Michael Ignatieff, *Blood and Belonging: Journeys into the New Nationalism* (New York: Vintage, 1994); Walker Connor, *Ethnonationalism: The Quest for Understanding* (Princeton, NJ: Princeton University Press, 1994).

[44] See Smith, *Civic Ideals*.

successors of the British colonial order. The Jacksonian constituency defined the national interest narrowly. The Jacksonian outlook was one of closed communities based upon race, religion, and ethnicity. As a consequence, the tradition of Jacksonian nationalism is one of a culture-fuelled belligerence against other entities that are considered to be alien forces. In contrast to the avowed universalism of the American creed, the Jacksonian tradition 'stresses closed communities defined by race, religion, and ethnicity'.[45] While the principles of democracy, justice, and more recently tolerance and pluralism mark the character of the creed, the Jacksonian tradition is 'characterized by ruthless violence against racial enemies, both by US state forces and groups spontaneously formed from local society'.[46]

Jacksonian nationalism is renowned for its defiant belligerence against enemies. It follows the spirit of Jackson's Indian wars in which massacres were regarded to be not merely acceptable but necessary instruments of cultural purification. Because Jacksonian frontier-dwellers 'neither were nor wanted to be students of multicultural diversity' and because Indian war tactics were considered to be dishonourable and unscrupulous, the Jacksonians abandoned their own restraints with the result that the 'ugly conflicts along the frontier spiralled into a series of genocidal conflicts'.[47] In the Jacksonian tradition, the spirit of the enemy had to broken completely in order to achieve security for the settlers:

It was not enough to *defeat* a tribe in battle; one had to 'pacify' the tribe; to convince it utterly and totally that resistance was and always would be futile and destructive. For this to happen, the war had to go to the enemy's home: The villages had to be burned, food supplies destroyed, civilians killed.[48]

In effect, the severity of the measures was derived from the fear and abhorrence of those who were set apart from the nation conceived as a folk community. Conservatism and destruction became two directly related elements in the furtherance of national identity. While the Jacksonian tradition may represent the severest form of American ethnocentrism, it does underline the extent to which national identity can be used in the service of conservative constructions of order, security, and ancestral attachment.

As we have seen, the conservative themes of an integrated community and cultural solidarity can be invoked by different groupings and against different groupings within America. However, it is in the international realm that those conservative attributes have their greatest leverage. The conservative constituents of nationalism are almost invariably manifested to their fullest effect in the medium of international relations when national differences and national prejudices are thrown into high relief. The United States is no exception. On the contrary, it is often accused of having a dualistic outlook in which its liberal principles are

[45] Anatol Lieven, 'Demon in the Cellar', *Prospect*, March 2004.
[46] Ibid.
[47] Walter R. Mead, *Special Providence: American Foreign Policy and How It Changed the World* (London: Routledge, 2002), p. 252.
[48] Ibid., p. 256.

exchanged for a more realistic, pessimistic, and even repressive demeanour in the conduct of its foreign policy. It is even possible to argue that American foreign policy outlook is in fact a product of deep-set domestic attitudes that are only fully expressed in respect to other societies.

In his historical analysis of American attitudes towards the rest of the world, Michael Hunt ascribes the exclusionary, hierarchical, and repressive biases of American foreign policy to an ideology 'inextricably tied up with the emergence of an American nation'.[49] It is an ideology that has been 'tested, refined, and woven into the fabric of the national consciousness' and which has been instrumental in propelling the United States 'ever deeper into the thicket of international politics and warfare'.[50] But as Hunt points out, this foreign policy ideology is far from liberal in content or tone. On the contrary, it has been distinguished by (i) the hostility shown towards revolutions that diverge from the American model; (ii) the assessment of other peoples and nations in relation to a racial hierarchy; and (iii) the presumptive sense of mission to redeem lesser cultures and facilitate their passage into civilized freedom.

The sense of national superiority...has given rise to stereotypes that diminish other people by exaggerating the seemingly negative aspects of their lives and by constricting the perceived range of their skills, accomplishments, and emotions. By denigrating other cultures as backward or malleable, these stereotypes raise false expectations that it is an easy enterprise to induce and direct political change and economical development. On encountering obstinacy or resistance, Americans...may indulge dehumanizing stereotypes that make possible the resort to forms of coercion and violence otherwise unthinkable. This pattern, first fully apparent in relations with blacks and native Americans, continues to govern American dealings with 'Third World' peoples.[51]

Anatol Lieven makes a similar point in tracing the legacy of defeat and displacement in the Jacksonian tradition. Lieven claims that the capacity for American chauvinism can be 'explained largely by the fact that the role of defeat in the genesis of nationalism resides not only in the defeat of nations as a whole, but of classes, groups, and indeed individuals within them'. He continues: 'The hatred and fear directed abroad by nationalism often emanates from hatreds and tensions at home, and this is strikingly true in the case of the United States'.[52] These kinds of assertions bear witness to the contested nature of American nationalism. They raise the prospect of conservative instincts being fully exposed in the revealing medium of foreign policy. They also pose serious questions over the extent to which America's self-defined status as a principled force in the world has been compromised by its international prominence.

---

[49] Michael H. Hunt, *Ideology and U.S. Foreign Policy* (New Haven, CT: Yale University Press, 1987), p. 171.
[50] Ibid., p. 172.   [51] Ibid., p. 176.
[52] Anatol Lieven, *America: Right or Wrong* (London: HarperCollins, 2004), p. 90.

IDEALS OUT OF THE BOX

The paramount theme in America's narrative of nationhood is that of enlargement. The capacity for westward expansion amounted to an extraordinary geographical and historical opportunity for the young republic to grow up literally by growing out. That opportunity rapidly became a guiding imperative as the nation acquired a strong expansionist ethos. Its history assumed a pattern of more land and settlements, more people and movement, and, in the process, ever more mutable frontiers. For much of the nineteenth century, the United States was a nation that had little conception of its rightful or final territorial area.

The story of the American nation generated a conjunction between the idea of progress and the visible evidence of a spatial progression across an increasing land mass. By purchase (e.g. Louisiana Territory, 1803), by treaty (e.g. Oregon Territory, 1818), by war (e.g. California and the Utah, and New Mexico Territories through the war with Mexico, 1846), by annexation (e.g. Texas, 1845), and by the continual clearance of Indians from their lands, America assumed a land mass of continental dimensions. The huge interior of the New World exaggerated the absence of any notion that America possessed a traditional and fixed national heartland. It allowed the concept of the American nation to become as expansive as the union itself. In the nineteenth century, several factors were significant in America's sense of itself as a nation. Given the early state of the republic as a young, underpopulated, and overstretched entity with poor communications and a relatively weak centre of government, it was necessary to maximize any opportunity for social cohesion. A sense of binding nationhood was of crucial significance in this respect and served further to enhance the emphasis upon common values from a common source of origin.

Another factor was related to the need for the concept of a nation to be deployed as a programmatic prescription for the expansion and progressive legitimation of American principles. By portraying America as the 'empire of reason', American nationalists could point to the moral righteousness of releasing the interior lands from the dominion of nature. Moreover, in doing so, they would allow vast numbers of people to be emancipated from poverty and dependence. The need to explain the abundance of American resources provided another dimension to the emergence of a national identity. The Enlightenment impulse to find connections between material cause and effect fostered a conception of the nation as a unique laboratory of freedom producing a commensurate liberation of natural and social resources. A more explicitly moral explanation came with the conclusion that America's natural bounty was a sign of God's grace and, therefore, a reflection of the nation's special providence in history.

The net effect of these influences was the emergence of a material advance and moral distinction that interacted with one another to produce an increasing conviction of national exceptionalism. As the idea of an idiosyncratic nation came to make sense of the past, it also served to characterize the present and to mobilize society in the pursuit of future projects and enhanced security. In American society, the developed consciousness of its extraordinary geopolitical position and its prevalent republican principles laid the foundations for a presumption of a historic role and even an intrinsic moral purpose.

Initially, this self-distinction was largely confined to the colonial tradition of grandiose preconceptions that celebrated the New World as a divinely inspired expression of historical significance. Such impulses usually took the form of an instructive parable drawn from the purity of wilderness for an otherwise sinful or backward world. Because of its unique position in providential history[53] and its acquired identity as the 'city upon a hill',[54] the New World would provide an inspirational example to the rest of mankind. This notion of America as the chosen place of excellence and the universal model for emulation had acquired a historical momentum by the end of the eighteenth century. American identity had become bound up with the notion that the 'new nation' was the proving ground which would test and demonstrate to a hopeful world the feasibility of the republican ideal.[55]

In the view of Thomas Jefferson, the establishment of a 'just and solid republican government' would act as a 'standing monument and example for the aim and imitation of the people of other countries'. Just as the transition of America into an independent condition of 'free government had excited ... the mass of mankind', so Jefferson believed that its consequences would 'ameliorate the condition of man over a great portion of the globe'.[56] This construction of America as a model or instrument of human improvement became a guiding theme in the emergent identity of the United States at an early stage in its development. According to this perspective the United States had been marked out as a moral template for humanity to emulate. America depicted itself as a social entity that exemplified the full potential of individuals to recreate their lives in accordance with their true nature. America was not merely *a* model or *a* refuge but the only model and refuge left to a world distorted by anachronistic and degenerate social structures.[57]

Later in the nineteenth century, America's inherent sense of virtuous example to others assumed a more activist disposition. The American drive to annex territories became increasingly associated with the imposition of a national mission to spread republican institutions to the furthermost reaches of the continent. Expansion became synonymous with the ennobling cause, and the onerous

---

[53] Sacvan Bercovitch, *The Puritan Origins of the American Self* (New Haven, CT: Yale University Press Yale, 1975), ch. 2.

[54] John Winthrop, 'A City upon a Hill: A Modell of Christian Charity', http://www.pbs.org/wgbh/pages/frontline/shows/apocalypse/primary/ciudad.html.

[55] Deborah L. Madsen, *American Exceptionalism* (Edinburgh: Edinburgh University Press, 1998), ch. 1.

[56] Thomas Jefferson, 'Letter to John Dickinson' (1801), quoted in *Thomas Jefferson on Politics and Government*, ch. 54: 'The Spread of Self-Government', http://etext.virginia.edu/jefferson/quotations/jeff1750.htm.

[57] Ernest L. Tuveson, *Redeemer Nation: The Idea of America's Millennial Role* (Chicago, IL: University of Chicago Press, 1968).

responsibility, of ensuring a natural American freedom within America's own state of nature.[58] To an increasing extent, America conceived itself as the chosen people selected by nature, or God, or 'nature's God'[59] to be the chosen people whose promised land would offer hope and progress to others who could be liberated by the gravitational force of an American ethos.

During the 1840s, however, the missionary prospectus was becoming more difficult to realize. Political, geographical, and logistical limitations were exerting increasing resistance to the idea of an ineluctable momentum of liberal enlightenment. In addition to the opposition posed by the more hostile reactions to white settlement on the part of western tribes of native Americans, US expansion encountered constraint in the form of the Spanish Empire in Mexico and the British imperial presence in Oregon. It was during this period that an emphasis upon the need to reconceptualize the nature of America's liberal mission was first advocated. In effect, the inertial drive to secure territory began to create a rationale based upon an aggressive imposition of American interests and priorities. The certainty attached to the progressive and enlightened nature of America's indigenous democracy started to make a forcible entry into the justificatory equation of American expansion. Forceful liberation acquired a greater currency in the American discourse on historic purpose. The logic of John Winthrop's 'city upon a hill' was extended to embrace the proposition that the United States possessed the remit to prevail over the rival claims of other parties to the westward accumulation of land.

The phrase that encapsulates this imperative of robust emancipation is 'manifest destiny'.[60] It was first deployed in 1839 by the journalist John O'Sullivan. He used it as a blanket rationale for the territorial enlargement of the United States whether by treaty, intimidation, or outright force. O'Sullivan pointed to the magnitude of American growth and concluded that this amounted to evidence of an underlying force that possessed both material and moral dimensions. To O'Sullivan, the expansion of the United States was not simply a circumstantial phenomenon. It was direct proof that the American nation was wholly unlike the nations of the Old World. It was distinguished by a special fate 'to overspread and to possess the whole continent which providence has given us for the development of the great experiment' of liberty and federated self-government'.[61] Successive enlargement, therefore, was not merely a sign that the United States would come to occupy the continent but it would do so on grounds of a moral superiority over any of its competitors.

A contemporary of O'Sullivan, William Gilpin, was even more flamboyant in his millennial prophecies of America:

<hr/>

[58] A. K. Weinberg, *Manifest Destiny: A Study of Nationalist Expansion in American History* (Chicago, IL: Quadrangle, 1963).

[59] This deist term is used in the Declaration of Independence (1776). See also Perry Miller, *Nature's Nation* (Cambridge, MA: Harvard University Press/Belknap Press, 1967).

[60] See Weinberg, *Manifest Destiny*; Anders Stephanson, *Manifest Destiny: American Expansionism and the Empire of Right* (New York: Hill & Wang, 1995).

[61] Quoted in Kohn, *American Nationalism*, p. 183.

The *untransacted* destiny of the American people is to subdue the continent—to rush over this vast field to the Pacific Ocean—to animate the many hundred millions of its people, and to cheer them upward ... to agitate these Herculean masses—to establish a new order in human affairs ... to regenerate superannuated nations ... to stir up the sleep of a hundred centuries—to teach old nations a new civilization—to confirm the destiny of the human race—to carry the career of mankind to its culminating point—to cause a stagnant people to be reborn—to perfect science—to emblazon history with the conquest of peace—to shed a new and resplendent glory upon mankind—to unite the world in one social family— to dissolve the spell of tyranny and exalt charity—to absolve the curse that weighs down humanity, and to shed blessings round the world![62]

The imprimatur of manifest destiny lent significant support to America's aggressive foreign policy goals in the 1840s. It helped to justify a claim to dominion over the contested areas of the American interior. Given the virtue of its strength and the strength of its virtue, the United States could not fail simply to prevail as the exemplar of the New World and, by implication, the proselytizing model for the Old World. To Ray Alan Billington, the moral righteousness of the American people in the middle of the nineteenth century was its own geopolitical spur. These compulsive settlers 'sincerely believed their democratic institutions were of such magnificent perfection that no boundaries could contain them. Surely a benevolent Creator did not intend such blessings for the few; expansion was a divinely ordered means of extending enlightenment to despot-ridden masses in nearby countries! This was not imperialism, but enforced salvation'.[63] Manifest destiny was essentially a one-nation doctrine justifying the consolidation of the United States to the Pacific Ocean on the grounds of a unifying set of values and a historic obligation to replicate its own ethos. It cultivated a strand of liberation ideology in America that would come to have far-reaching consequences later in the century and beyond.

During the 1890s and the early period of the twentieth century, the United States emerged as a power of global potential whose interests and security concerns had become exponential in nature. After a prolonged period of internal consolidation, the question of the rightful territorial reach of the United States was revived with an enhanced intensity. Even though the frontier was now officially declared to be closed, Turner claimed that its influence continued to have a strong bearing upon American culture. In his view, it was so ingrained in the psyche of the United States that the frontier spirit of superseding limits would necessarily find other outlets: 'That these energies of expansion will no longer operate would be a rash prediction; and the demands for a vigorous foreign policy ... for a revival of our power upon the seas, and the extension of American influence to

[62] Quoted in Henry N. Smith, *Virgin Lands: The American West as Symbol and Myth* (New York: Vintage, 1950), p. 40.

[63] Ray A. Billington, *Westward Expansion: A History of the American Frontier* (New York: Macmillan, 1949), p. 572.

outlying islands and adjoining countries, are indications that the movement will continue'.[64]

Coexisting with this outlook was the contemporary fascination with Social Darwinism and its fatalistic prescription for progress through the primary drives of aggressive competition. According to this perspective, the United States was neither culturally inclined to stand still, nor able to remain static in the evolutionary rush to international power politics. These influences were significant in the development of the US Navy and in America's penetration into an increasing number of regional economic zones. Its military interventions in the First World War, and more especially in the Second World War, confirmed the nation's status as a global power and prepared the ground for its subsequent emergence as the dominant hegemon, or lone superpower.[65] At the beginning of the twenty-first century, the US military had acquired a position in which it surpassed the size of the next ten national forces combined. The Pentagon's budget for technological research and development dwarfed that of any other power centre. Its capability in force projection was equally immense with permanent military bases straddling a host of strategic and energy sensitive areas in over fifty-five countries.[66]

Providing an overarching rationale to this transition into a global power and to America's subsequent rise to a superpower was the conception of itself as a morally distinct and instructive nation. The more extensive it became, the more security it acquired. The continuity of expansion offered a way of fusing together a territorial trend with a moral imperative. This had a direct bearing upon the relationship between patriotism and nationalism in America. Patriotism is often denoted as having a set of properties that distinguish it from nationalism. The patriotic impulse is seen as an a priori conservative attachment to a formed country that requires preservation in its current material existence. Nationalism on the other hand has strong associations with the future and with an ideal or abstract concept of the nation and its historical potential.[67] While patriotism evokes an instinctive and emotive response to tradition, nationalism has connotations of a mission and even a messianic impulse for the nation to become something more than its past. In the United States, however, patriotic affection and nationalist ambition had become interwoven with one another because of the republic's history of growth and mutation. In effect, the visceral qualities of patriotism were closely implicated with the nationalistic outlook of a future-oriented role and a compulsive moral purpose in the world.

To a society that was not only susceptible to moral injunction but appeared to require an ethical basis to its foreign policy, manifest destiny continued to offer a

[64] Frederick Jackson Turner quoted in James Chace, 'Tomorrow the World', *New York Review of Books*, 21 November 2002.

[65] Stephen E. Ambrose and Douglas G. Brinkley, *Rise to Globalism: American Foreign Policy Since 1938*, 8th edn (Harmondsworth, UK: Penguin, 1998).

[66] See Andrew Bacevich, *The New American Militarism: How Americans Are Seduced by War* (Oxford: Oxford University Press, 2005).

[67] See Kenneth R. Minogue, *Nationalism* (London: Batsford, 1967); Booth, 'Communities of Memory: On Identity, Memory and Debt'.

compulsive duality of necessary power with benign purpose. The cultural leverage associated with this avowal of national predestination elevated the American impulse for expansive liberation to the level of an inexorable and providential process. The more the United States advanced, the more compelling became the proposition that Americans had been bequeathed special rights and obligations to extend their sphere of influence over other peoples. As the prime benefactor of liberal values, such a dominion would almost invariably be to the benefit of the United States. But more significantly, such dominance could be couched as serving the interests and securing the freedoms of the recipient societies. This theme of a teleological history generating a moral sanction and explanation for America's national and international development has been highly influential in the creation of an American identity. But at the same time, it has also fomented deep controversies over the nature and usage of American power and over the ethical integrity of those principles that are employed to support it.

'EMPIRE OF LIBERTY'

The national dimension of the United States has historically been based upon growth. While this characteristic offers continuity, it can be secured at the price of perspective. Many of the deepest disputes surrounding American nationalism centre upon the extent to which a society can develop without losing its original specifications. Thomas Jefferson popularized the thesis of an 'empire of liberty' in which successive enlargement would allow the founding principles of the republic to be extrapolated and reinforced through their propagation into open space. Size would demonstrate the universality of American values. By contrast, increased size could also be interpreted as a loss of innocence allowing the republic to foster the same concerns with power politics and armed conflict as those that afflicted the Old World. In this construction, size could denote a shift in values. In essence, the idea of an American empire constituted the 'republic's permanent temptation and its potential nemesis'.[68]

An important argument for American national identity revolves precisely around this notion of whether the United States' emergence as a continental force entailed a qualitative transformation as well as a quantitative transformation. According to Arthur Ekirch, for example, the United States did indeed undergo a profound change. Over the course of the nineteenth century, its republican consciousness as an example to the world altered to one of forceful imperialism. Although the original idea of a mission had been an expansionary concept, Ekirch argues that it 'emphasized on the whole the peaceful export of American ideology and the realization of the natural rights of man through the spread of American institutions'.[69] The rallying cry of manifest destiny, however,

---

[68] Michael Ignatieff, 'Empire Lite', *Prospect*, no. 83 (February 2003), p. 36.

[69] Arthur A. Ekirch, Jr., *Ideas, Ideals and American Diplomacy: A History of Their Growth and Interaction* (New York: Appleton-Century-Crofts, 1966), p. 44.

amounted to a sea change in outlook and consequence because it 'implied expansion in a more belligerent manner'.[70] From this Ekirch develops the theme of manifest destiny into a historical disjunction in the development of the United States.

It turned the defensive and idealistic notions of isolationism and mission toward the course of a unilateral, nationalist, political, and territorial expansion. In so doing it also transposed broader, more universal values of genuine international importance—the natural rights philosophy, for example—into a narrower doctrine of the special rights of Americans over and against other peoples.[71]

Walter McDougal echoes the same theme within the rise of the United States as a continental and international power. He identifies two central and sustaining traditions in American history: the 'promised land' and the 'crusader state'.[72] While the former relates to America's initial outlook, which was to deny the outside world the opportunity to shape America's development, the latter offered the prospect of the United States being able to shape the world's future. McDougal refers to these traditions as the old and new testaments of American foreign policy. He comes to the conclusion that the 'promised land' is superior to the 'crusader state' because it is more securely embedded in American principles. As a consequence, the 'promised land' tradition offers greater coherence to America's relationship with the rest of the world.

While analysts like Ekirch and McDougal infer a form of corruption that turned the republic into an empire, other observers assert that this is a false dichotomy and that the United States was implicitly imperial in nature from the outset. The thrust of this view is one of imperial continuity: 'Although the country had been born in revolt against empire, America harboured the seeds of its own from the beginning'.[73] On the basis of its geostrategic position and the dynamics of its subsequent development, America can be construed as an entity that established itself through territorial expansion, violent expropriation, and ethnic and racial oppression.[74] Another version of this imperialist perspective leaves to one side the virtues or otherwise of the early republic. It grounds the American empire

---

[70] Ekirch, *Ideas, Ideals and American Diplomacy*, p. 44.   [71] Ibid., pp. 43–4.

[72] Walter A. McDougall, *Promised Land, Crusader State: American Encounter with the World Since 1776* (Boston, MA: Houghton Mifflin, 1998).

[73] Clyde Prestowitz, *Rogue Nation: American Unilateralism and the Failure of Good Intentions* (New York: Basic Books, 2003), p. 30.

[74] For example, see Richard Van Alstyne, *The Rising American Empire* (New York: Norton, 1960); Michael H. Hunt, *Ideology and U.S. Foreign Policy* (New Haven, CT: Yale University Press, 1987); Paul M. Kennedy, *The Rise and Fall of the Great Powers: Economic Change and Military Conflict from 1500 to 2000* (London: Fontana, 1988), pp. 228–34, 311–21; Barbara J. Fields, 'Slavery, Race and Ideology in the United States of America', *New Left Review*, No. 181 (May/June 1990), pp. 95–118; Rogers M. Smith, 'Beyond Tocqueville, Myrdal, and Hartz: The Multiple Traditions in America', *The American Political Science Review*, vol. 87, no. 3. (Sept 1993), pp. 549–66; Desmond King, *Making Americans: Immigration, Race, and the Origins of the Diverse Democracy* (Cambridge, MA: Harvard University Press, 2000).

less upon land acquisition and more upon the drives of capitalist accumulation, commercial force, and market advantage.[75]

An alternative exposition of empire diverts attention away from the origins and intentions of America's global reach, and concentrates instead upon its attributed effect as a sponsor of liberal values. Set against such a background, America has been interpreted as an evangelizing force for liberal democracy, progress, and the rule of law.[76] In this guise, the United States is seen as a nation that has transposed its own liberal ethos into the wider format of liberal internationalism. According to this criterion, the United States can be couched as the chief sponsor and main underwriter of an array of central tenets in the promotion of an international order based upon democratic peace and mutual security. These include the principles of human rights, national self-determination, equity between sovereign nations, free trade, market liberalization, open diplomacy, international organization, collective security, and international law.[77]

Following the unprecedented carnage of the First World War, the liberal idealism of Woodrow Wilson gave graphic expression to the idea of a world of sovereign nation-states working in harmony and operating through the medium of international law. As the self-professed laboratory of liberal principles, the United States was well positioned to advocate the spread of liberal democratic dynamics as a plausible and necessary solution to the need for a new international order. By giving nations the same status as individuals within a liberal order of equal rights and protections, the interplay between states could be accommodated through peaceful competition, open trade, and the rule of law. The Wilsonian ethos was one of dispensing with balance of power calculations, 'spheres of interest', and secret diplomacy in favour of a supranational solution in which stability would be secured through a commonality of liberal ethics. As a result, the world would be 'made safe for every peace-loving nation which, like our own, wishes to live its own life, determine its own institutions, be assured of justice and fair dealing by the other peoples of the world as against force and selfish aggression'.[78] To Wilson, it was not just possible for liberalism to be extended to a universal and workable system of international politics. The plan for a League of Nations represented the imperative means by which to avoid another catastrophe and to achieve 'justice to

[75] For example, see Noam Chomsky, *Turning the Tide: US Intervention in Latin America and the Struggle for Peace* (Boston, MA: South End, 1986); William A. Williams, *The Tragedy of American Diplomacy* (New York: W. W. Norton, 1991); Michael Parenti, *Against Empire* (San Francisco, CA: City Light, 1995).

[76] For example, see Max Boot, *The Savage Wars of Peace: Small Wars and the Rise of American Power* (New York: Basic Books, 2002); Niall Ferguson, *Colossus: The Price of American Empire* (New York: Penguin, 2004).

[77] For example, see Michael Mandelbaum, *The Ideas That Conquered the World: Peace, Democracy, and Free Markets in the Twenty-first Century* (New York: Public Affairs, 2002); G. John Ikenberry, 'American Power and the Empire of Capitalist Democracy', *Review of International Studies*, vol. 27, Special Issue (December 2001), pp. 191–212.

[78] President Woodrow Wilson, Address to Joint Session of Congress, 8 January 1918, http://history.acusd.edu/gen/text/ww1/fourteenpoints.html.

all peoples and nationalities, and their right to live on equal terms of liberty and safety with one another, whether they be strong or weak'.[79]

Although the United States failed to join the League and subsequently embarked upon a period of isolationism, Wilson's project remained a model of liberal extrapolation. After the Second World War, American political and military dominance was combined with its enlarged security interests to produce a revival in the themes collective security, supranational organization, and international law. The onset of the United Nations bore witness to the strand of liberal intervention that Wilson had championed as the culmination of American experience and moral vocation. Now the centrality of the United States to the international order allowed the idea of propagating and self-harmonizing liberalism across national borders to gather credence and momentum. Whether it was the United States operating unilaterally, or through the offices of the United Nations, the Wilsonian impulse of high moral self-definition and onerous obligation came to characterize the language of American foreign policy during the cold war. Alliances, pacts, and treaties between the United States and other nation-states not only demonstrated the capacity for liberal cooperation, but defined the collective outcomes as the 'free world'.[80]

With the collapse of the Soviet Union and the Eastern Bloc, the limitations to liberal extension were removed. It allowed the formation of a post-cold war world that came to be characterized by the 'Washington consensus' (i.e. privatization, deregulation, trade liberalization, labour market flexibility, budgetary austerity, deficit reduction, low taxation, and inflation control). The indictment of empire that had been a recurrent theme during the United States' orchestration of the West during the cold war now became a persistent critique of American global hegemony. The charge has been met with two mainstream responses that both serve to illustrate the depth of American attachment to the medium of liberal integrity. The first reaction is completely to disavow any parallels with imperialism on the grounds that the United States is by definition an anti-imperial construct. The values conceived in the American Revolution against the British Empire and reiterated in the idealism of President Wilson's liberal internationalism ensure that the United States could not undertake such a metamorphosis of design. It may have achieved a global pre-eminence and a hegemonic status. Nevertheless, in promoting a world order of democracy and markets, the United States' position remains set in a context of multilateral organizations and reciprocal influence.

In this respect, the American alliance system is 'not just an instrument of US domination', but has 'helped to create a stable, open political space' which gives

---

[79] President Wilson, Address to Joint Session of Congress.

[80] See Thomas G. Paterson, *On Every Front: The Making of the Cold War*, rev. edn (New York: W. W. Norton, 1979), chs. 2–7; John L. Gaddis, *Strategies of Containment: A Critical Appraisal of Postwar American National Security Policy* (Oxford: Oxford University Press, 1982), chs. 2–5; Thomas J. McCormick, *America's Half-Century: United States Foreign Policy in the Cold War and After*, 2nd edn (Baltimore, MD: Johns Hopkins University Press, 1995), chs. 4–8; Richard Crockatt, *The Fifty Years War: The United States and the Soviet Union in World Politics, 1941–1991* (London: Routledge, 1995), chs. 4–8.

both 'depth and complexity to the international order'.[81] To Joseph Nye, US preponderance has been embedded in a 'web of international institutions that allow others to participate in decisions and that act as a sort of world constitution to limit the capriciousness of American power'.[82] John Ikenberry goes further. He extrapolates from America's own experience with immigration and assimilation, and suggests that its open nationalism has created an open centre of global power: 'Built on a civic national base, the United States has pioneered a new form of multicultural and multi-ethnic political order that appears to be stable and increasingly functional with the demands of global modernization'.[83]

A second reaction has been to accept the term empire but to recast it in terms of American experience into a benign and benevolent force. Such an empire is distinguished by moral self-restraint, the soft power of cultural influence, and the voluntary nature of its reception outside the United States. Accordingly, the term 'empire' is used with irony as it represents the fullest expression of the consummate liberal nation. In the same way that an 'empire by invitation'[84] or an empire 'acquired...in a fit of absent-mindedness'[85] does not allegedly amount to an empire in the classic sense, so the United States' burden of international security obligations is not construed as the normal kind of imperial privilege. In this light, the United States is the 'reluctant imperialist' which does 'not like to act alone'[86] and prefers complex stability rather than a centrally directed order. Empire in such a context is reconfigured on the basis of American values and intentions into a metaphor for liberal expansion on the same lines as Jefferson's original hybrid of an 'empire of liberty'.

A NATION OF IDEAS

Although the United States characterizes itself as a national embodiment of liberal democratic ideas, it is universally criticized on precisely the grounds on which it assumes excellence. The core element of anti-Americanism in this respect centres upon the critique that the United States fails to fulfil its own prospectus of high principles. It is charged with exerting national sovereignty in order to undermine the self-determination of other nations. It is also claimed that it employs liberal democratic norms as a device by which to widen its influence over other societies and economies.

---

[81] G. John Ikenberry, 'Illusions of Empire: Defining the New American Order', *Foreign Affairs*, vol. 83, no. 2 (March/April 2004), p. 148.

[82] Joseph Nye, *The Paradox of American Power: Why the World's Superpower Can't Go It Alone* (New York: Oxford University Press, 2003), p. 17.

[83] Ikenberry, 'American Power and the Empire of Capitalist Democracy', p. 939.

[84] Geir Lundestad, *The American 'Empire' and Other Studies of US Foreign Policy in Comparative Perspective* (Oxford: Oxford University Press, 1990), p. 55.

[85] Charles Krauthammer, *Democratic Realism: An American Foreign Policy for a Unipolar World* (Washington, DC: American Enterprise Institute, 2004), p. 2.

[86] Gerard Baker, 'The Reluctant Imperialists', *Financial Times*, 8 September 2002.

The indictments of double standards and hypocrisy are many and severe. They range from America's record of military interventions and counterinsurgency programmes to the manipulation of markets and elections, and even the overthrow of hostile governments. Punitive expeditions, bombing campaigns, and covert operations are cited as evidence of America's insistence upon prevailing through force rather than by argument. Its hostility to radical social revolutions has led the United States to destabilize nationalist movements and disrupt emergent democracies. In many instances, American preferences have been to favour the stability of local oligarchies and authoritarian regimes offering stability and security for American investments and assets. A recent study of America's foreign interventions concluded that United States foreign policy had been 'fueled not by a devotion to any kind of morality'[87] but by a need to pursue four overriding objectives. They are cited as (i) 'making the world open and hospitable for ... globalization'; (ii) 'enhancing the financial statements of defense contractors'; (iii) 'preventing the rise of any society that might serve as a successful ... alternative to the capitalist model'; and (iv) 'extending political, economic and military hegemony ... to prevent the rise of any regional power that might challenge American supremacy, and to create a world order in America's image'.[88]

These asserted violations of liberal democratic principles are not given wide credence in the United States. This is due, in part, to a patriotic defensiveness in respect to criticism. It is also rooted in an anxiety that democratic states suffer from an inherent weakness in foreign policy, requiring corrective action in the form of a vigorous overcompensation to defend the national interest. Connected to both these responses remain the sustained cultural attachment to the conception of America as a long-term point of anchorage for democratic security and liberal values. Inequities and injustices may occur as incidental features of America's historical role. The corollary is that judgement and evaluation of American behaviour should be guided by an asserted integrity of motivations and moral purpose. The problem is that this presumption of integrity becomes so structurally incorporated into nationalist dogmas that while it evokes strong belief in the United States, it is not easily transferable to the cognitive processes of other nations.

The United States is renowned for the sense of inner conviction that can prompt Americans not only to pursue self-interest under the guise of idealism, but even to pervert its own democratic principles in the name of an overriding notion of idealized obligation. To a nation with an established identity in the elevated reaches of universal moral hierarchy, anxieties over ethical duplicity as a contradiction do not easily arise. Accordingly, when an apparent attachment to liberal democratic principles on the part of a state within an American sphere of influence threatens to produce a hostile regime, the United States tends to regard the phenomenon as an aberration. Its universalist response has often led to attempts at overturning such regimes on the grounds that they are contrary to America's national interest

---

[87] William Blum, *Rogue State: A Guide to the World's Only Superpower* (London: Zed, 2001), p. 13.
[88] Ibid., pp. 13–14.

and therefore, by American definition, contrary to the interests of the countries in question.[89] Historically, this has been a compelling argument in the United States.

The inability or unwillingness of others to subscribe to the fundamentalist logic of the 'indispensable nation'[90] has fostered a schismatic approach to the world within the United States. Those who distrust or oppose the United States and seek to reverse or even to destroy its influence are categorized as illiberal recidivists engaged in an anti-Enlightenment project of historical regression. Their lack of understanding of, or faith in, the aggregate benevolence of the United States can result in American leaders characterizing anti-American sentiments as both irrational and morally repellent. The Manichean properties of this perspective were epitomized in America's total intransigence towards communism during the cold war. President Ronald Reagan felt that the United States had a moral right to categorize the Soviet Union as an 'evil empire'.[91] More recently, President George W. Bush summoned up the same nationalist fervour for dichotomy in describing Iraq, Iran, and North Korea as the 'axis of evil'[92] and in warning states that in the war against terrorism there could be no middle ground for compromise, neutrality, or ambiguity: '[N]ations are either with us or against us in the war on terror'.[93]

The distrust of those occupying political or moral space outside national parameters is not exclusive to the United States. However, American attitudes are unusual in this respect. The tradition in the United States is one of an open nationalism based upon a political creed that is notionally universal in character. Whether it is seen as corollary, or as a counterpart, to this tradition, American beliefs in the distinctiveness of the nation have fostered an enhanced view of its value and its need for special protection from outside forces. America's location, inception, and development as a nation have generated a strong identity of uniqueness and exclusive status in respect to other nations. When this theme of exceptionalism is combined with America's physical distance and cultural detachment from other nationalisms, it provides the foundation for a highly ambivalent view of the world. Even though its self-defined reputation as a global exemplar of liberal values remains central to American national identity, it is often these very values that are cited as the reason for exceptional measures to be taken to secure the United States against the threat of other values. The value-enriched conception

---

[89] For example, see Jenny Pearce, *Under the Eagle: U.S. Intervention in Central America and the Caribbean* (London: Latin America Bureau, 1981); Walter La Feber, *Inevitable Revolution: The United States in Central America* (New York: W. W. Norton, 1983); Robert Pastor, *Whirlpool: US Foreign Policy toward Latin America* (Princeton, NJ: Princeton University Press, 1992); Lars Schoultz, *Beneath the United States: A History of US Policy toward Latin America* (Cambridge, MA: Harvard University Press, 1998).

[90] Madeleine Albright comments made on NBC 'Today' show, 19 February 1998.

[91] President Ronald Reagan, speech to the Annual Convention of the National Association of Evangelicals (Orlando, Florida), 8 March 1983, http://www.ronaldreagan.com/sp_6.html.

[92] President George W. Bush, State of the Union Address, 29 January 2002, http://www.whitehouse.gov/news/releases/2002/01/20020129-11.html.

[93] President George W. Bush, 'President Bush Calls for New Palestinian Leadership', 24 June 2002, http://www.whitehouse.gov/news/releases/2002/06/20020624-3.html.

of American nationalism, therefore, is continually subjected to strain between open migration and closed borders; between assimilation and rejection; between isolationism and universalism; and between liberal tolerance and an overheated reaction against those who would abuse the privileges of liberty.

Louis Hartz's classic study of America's idiosyncrasies as an absolutist liberal nation led him to conclude that the United States did not, and probably could not, understand the world of ordinary nations. The alien remained synonymous with the unintelligible. Americans could only adjust to the world by not becoming part of it: 'An absolute national morality', Hartz records, 'is transpired either to withdraw from "alien" things or to transform them: it cannot live in comfort constantly by their side'.[94] Hartz's acute observations retain their pertinacity. American exceptionalism continues to be mediated through nationalism. It is extraordinary that the United States developed as a single nation. It is equally peculiar that a self-professed nation *for* the world should become not only one of the most nationalist countries *in* the world, but one with an outstanding incomprehension of, and repugnance for, the force of nationalism outside the United States. The irony is captured by Minxin Pei: '[D]espite the high level of nationalism in American society, US policymakers have a remarkably poor appreciation of the power of nationalism in other societies and have demonstrated neither skill nor sensitivity in dealing with its manifestations abroad'.[95]

[94] Hartz, *The Liberal Tradition in America*, p. 286.
[95] Pei, 'The Paradoxes of American Nationalism', p. 30.

Part IV

Overviews

16

Dealing with Ideas

INTRODUCTION

The point of departure for this journey was the apparent paradox between the advanced level of political stability in the United States and the simultaneous invocation of high principles and fundamental values in the normal processes of political conduct. At one level, the profusion of references to such elevated and uncompromising themes as liberty, equality, democracy, rights, and the rule of law can be construed as cultural generalizations, based upon a loose premise of basic consistency and presumptive incorporation. At another level, these ideas are habitually summoned up, and drawn upon, to define explicit points of difference between political positions. Moreover, their usage is often designed to polarize political distinctions and to question the legitimacy of opposing perspectives which in their own right depend upon the fundamentalism of American values for their counterarguments. Far from being relegated to the sphere of contextual background, ideas are conspicuously deployed in the very forefront of political argument.

The sweeping commitment to political principles and the adoption of uncompromising stances on values characterize the terms of engagement in American politics. 'When our politics are bereft of the rhetoric of large ideas', surmises George Will, 'our politics are strictly un-American'.[1] Enormous resources are expended in the competition to interpret and configure core values in the service of different political positions. Yet while the usage of key values as instruments of political conflict remains an integral feature of the political process, those self-same values are also relied upon to provide the basis for the conciliation and accommodation of divergent interests and persuasions. In effect, America's foundational principles appear to act as both the inducement to dissonance and the agency of cohesion. Ironically, the prevailing terms of political argument are the same terms in which negotiated settlements are framed and legitimized. The irony is further deepened by the way that the system's facility for mutual accommodation is cited as being indicative of a paucity of ideas and a lack of principled debate in American society.

Arguably, the most influential and most durable attempt to make sense of the apparent disjunction between the settled nature of American society and its

---

[1] George F. Will, 'The "Idea" of America', *Washington Post*, reprinted in *The Guardian Weekly*, 16 August 1992.

adherence to a value laden politics was provided by Louis Hartz in *The Liberal Tradition in America*.[2] As we noted in Chapter 10, Hartz advanced the proposition of a deeply rooted cultural attachment to liberal principles. Their emergence in American history was claimed to coincide with, and to be responsible for, the establishment of a dominant and popularly based capitalist order. In Hartz's view, this dynamic was combined with a national narrative of geographical expansion and social progress, to generate an all inclusive consensus upon the virtues of 'democratic capitalism'. Just as America's historical and social foundations were said to find their natural expression in the asserted continuity of liberal principles, so the asserted moral unanimity of American society was described by Hartz to be the manifestation of the United States's exceptional status as a spontaneous construction. In addition to offering a unified construction of American society, Hartz's thesis also represented an affirmation of a fundamental social unity based upon ideas and their relationship to the predominant systems of social formation in the New World. According to Hartz, America's attachment to liberal values, had in effect become a historical tradition. As such, liberal principles were so prevalent and authoritative that all mainline politics had become enfolded into an assimilative, self-perpetuating, and inescapable culture of liberal solidarity.

The reductive and deterministic properties of the Hartzian consensus had an overt appeal to cold war America but its resonance persisted long after the communist threat had subsided. Even now Hartz's paradigm of social progress, founded upon a static unity of ingrained attitudes and an inherent compulsion towards a liberal–capitalist norm, still acts as a coherent depiction of the American condition and of America's bequest to the rest of the world. In spite of its traditional leverage as a controlling explanation, Hartz's fusion of socio-economic forces, historical identity, and an intuitive ideology has not been immune to serious challenge. The strength of the Hartzian appeal has lain in its assertion of a direct causal relationship between the historical entrenchment of key ideas and the nature of the American polity. But it is precisely within its own terms of analytical reference that Hartz's synthesis of doctrinal norms and consensus conditions can be subjected to dispute.

For example, historical research into the origins and lineage of American capitalism have thrown doubts upon Hartz's claim that the entrepreneurial spirit had become so well established in seventeenth-century American settlements that market capitalism was a common point of identity for Americans emerging into political independence. Some social and economic historians have contested Hartz's proposition of a fundamental continuity of 'Lockian liberalism' and 'democratic capitalism'. These revisionist historians attempt to demonstrate that colonial settlements, especially in New England, did not reveal any distinguishable pattern of market formation, acquisitive behaviour, and profit maximization. On the contrary, they are shown as having been not only self-sufficient,

---

[2] Louis Hartz, *The Liberal Tradition in America: An Interpretation of American Political Thought Since the Revolution* (New York: Harcourt Brace Jovanovich, 1955).

stable, and disciplined entities, but community-based in their organization and outlook.[3]

It is asserted that individuals in these communities were not driven to produce surpluses for exchange on the basis of market forces and that whatever surpluses were achieved were distributed within the local communities on the basis of traditional forms of bartering, or of prices set by custom. Instead of emerging into a state of preformed capitalism as Hartz suggests, these historical analyses suggest that in the main most colonists had been pre-modern and pre-capitalist in their individual perspectives and social arrangements. Moreover, it is contended that the rise of activities that could be described as early capitalist in form (e.g. capital markets, asset transfers into liquid forms of wealth, interest rates, and borrowing practices linked to investment returns) first appeared *after* political independence had been secured. Far from constituting the hallmark of American continuity and the signature of America's inherent liberalism, capitalist values and behaviour can be interpreted as a development away from the prior condition of colonial existence.[4]

Hartz's theme of a one-to-one relationship between the historical and socio-logical basis of American life, and the presence of an ideational continuity, is also contested on other grounds. Even if the principle of a single tradition of liberal values is accepted as the basis of a social consensus, the extent to which such a principle is adhered to, or substantiated in practice, has remained a theme of continuing controversy. The intellectual and ideological continuity of American history posited by Hartz has been challenged by the advocates of the 'republican synthesis' (see Chapter 4) who point to an altogether different genealogy of culturally transmitted ideas. Those who give weight to republican themes rooted in the seventeenth-century Commonwealth rhetoric and classical history point to an early tradition of civic consciousness, public virtue, and other arguably pre-modern values during the formative period of the American polity. The debate with those who equate the same period with the propagation of property rights, economic freedoms, and individual interests has moderated in tone. Nevertheless, the claims of the neo-republicans have underlined the disputed nature of America's transformation into liberal modernity.

Other challenges to Hartz have concentrated upon alternative histories that seek to show different forms of continuity and different rates of social development for different segments of an ostensibly liberal order. It has generated an extensive

[3] See James A. Henretta, *The Origins of American Capitalism: Selected Essays* (Boston, MA: Northeastern University Press, 1991); Christopher Clark, *The Roots of Rural Capitalism: Western Massachusetts, 1780–1860* (Ithaca, NY: Cornell University Press, 1992); Michael Merrill, 'Putting "Capitalism" in Its Place: A Review of Recent Literature', *The William and Mary Quarterly*, 3rd series, vol. 52, no. 2 (April 1995), pp. 315–26.

[4] For a contrary view on what is a highly contentious debate in American historiography, see John F. Martin, *Profits in the Wilderness: Entrepreneurship and the Founding of New England Town in the Seventeenth Century* (Chapel Hill, NC: University of North Carolina Press/The Omohundro Institute of Early American History and Culture, 1991); William B. Rothenberg, *From Market-Places to a Market Economy: The Transformation of Rural Massachusetts, 1750–1850* (Chicago, IL: University of Chicago Press, 1992).

historiography on the missing or under-represented sectors and origins within the putative inclusiveness of the American consensus. Focused studies centring upon the categories of race, gender, and class in particular have fostered a profusion of separate histories related to discrete strands of historical experience, social development, and subcultural continuities.[5]

For example, in *Belated Feudalism* (1992),[6] Karen Orren disputes both the unilinear conception of American liberal development and the very basis of America's identity as a society historically devoid of feudal principles and perspectives. Her research concludes that the United States inherited from Britain a common law approach to labour relations that effectively insulated the area against state incursion. It did so to such an extent that it amounted to an active remnant of an ancient feudal order within the United States. Even though industrial capitalism provided the instrument of America's passage into modernity, it rested upon a set of judicially defended relationships in the workplace which originated in feudal law and custom: '[T]he law of master and servant remained a monument to order and authority... sealed off from deliberation and competition and other styles of liberal intercourse.'[7] Orren challenges the view that America's rise to industrialism in the late nineteenth century wrenched society away from a republican ideal of free labour. Her claim is that the 'belated feudalism' behind America's industrial organization continued unabated into the 1930s at which point there was a decisive break with the past, i.e. 'the final shift from the medieval system of government, centered in the judiciary, to the modern liberal state, centered in the national legislature'.[8] It was only then that America's liberal prospectus reached the level of fulfilment which Hartz assumed it had acquired by virtue of the republic's very existence.

The presumptive totality of America's liberal culture has been challenged on the basis of a prodigious array of postulated variations, deviations, and disjunctions. They pose a series of searching questions relating to the historical incidence, consistency, and uniformity of the liberal creed and its relationship to the existence or otherwise of a settled social order, and a continuous process of liberal development. This scepticism of a singular liberal base commanding near universal

---

[5] For example, see Rogers M. Smith, 'Beyond Tocqueville, Myrdal, and Hartz: The Multiple Traditions in America', *American Political Science Review*, vol. 87, no. 3 (September 1993), pp. 549–66; Rogers M. Smith, *Civic Ideals: Conflicting Visions of Citizenship in U.S. History* (New Haven, CT: Yale University Press, 1997), chs. 5–12; Gary Gerstle, 'The Protean Character of American Liberalism', *The American Historical Review*, vol. 99, no. 4 (October 1994), pp. 1043–73; Gary Gerstle, 'Liberty, Coercion and the Making of Americas', *Journal of American History* vol. 84, no. 2 (September 1997), pp. 524–58; Desmond King, *Making Americans: Immigration, Race, and the Origins of the Diverse Democracy* (Cambridge, MA: Harvard University Press, 2000); Gary Gerstle, *American Crucible: Race and Nation in the Twentieth Century* (Princeton, NJ: Princeton University Press, 2002); Desmond S. King, 'Racial Orders in American Political Development', *American Political Science Review*, vol. 99, no. 1 (February 2005), pp. 75–92.

[6] Karen Orren, *Belated Feudalism: Labor, the Law and Liberal Development in the United States* (Cambridge: Cambridge University Press, 1992).

[7] Ibid., p. 120.   [8] Ibid., p. 211.

assent from which all succeeding liberal arrangements have been derived is typified by David Greenstone and his work on the influences of President Abraham Lincoln.

Greenstone concurs with Hartz in asserting the existence of a liberal consensus at the inception of the republic. Nevertheless, in contrast to Hartz, Greenstone points out that an attachment to such fundamental liberal tenets as individual rights, private property, and political consent carried different meanings, attachments, and priorities within the context of late eighteenth- and early nineteenth-century America. Far from possessing a single liberal tradition, David Greenstone identifies the existence of two liberal traditions.[9] One dimension of this 'liberal bipolarity' emphasized the value of negative liberty and the need to resolve disputes by political accommodation without reference to any aspirational objectives. The other dimension projected moral questions and normative principles into the political realm. The concept of liberty associated with this tradition was positive in that its exponents believed that freedom needed to facilitate individuals into realising their potential for making moral choices.

While both these forms of liberalism resided in the singular foundations of America's normative and institutional republicanism, the two variants operated on different premises and carried divergent implications in respect to the purposes of political life. The issue of the 'place that autonomous individuals should have in a viable political community'[10] became the defining controversy within a liberal culture which was only nominally devoid of differentiation:

> For humanist liberals, the role of the political community is to provide collective goods and satisfy individual preferences equitably. For reform liberals, the role of the political community is to set standards of mastery and excellence ... whereas humanist liberals stress consent to institutions that resolve disputes over preferences, reform liberals emphasize consent to a culture's fundamental practices. These practices are adopted not as a matter of choice but simply because ... the individuals concerned participate in that culture.[11]

According to Greenstone, American exceptionalism is rooted not merely in the fact that 'Americans agree on certain liberal values but also because their most basic cultural opposition turns on classically liberal questions'.[12] As a consequence, 'a pervasively liberal culture need not be monolithically consensual'[13] in its effects.

Greenstone uses this concept of 'liberal bipolarity' to demonstrate how these two traditions had developed into an unsustainable duality over the question of slavery. The crisis culminated in the Civil War during which Greenstone claims that President Lincoln effectively combined the spheres of moral conscience and practical due process into a new synthesis upon the purpose and value of the union. While Hartz had largely dismissed the Civil War as an aberration, Greenstone asserts that it induced a fusion of the two liberal traditions into a

---

[9] J. David Greenstone, *The Lincoln Persuasion: Remaking American Liberalism* (Princeton, NJ: Princeton University Press, 1993).
[10] Ibid., p. 60.   [11] Ibid., pp. 59, 62.   [12] Ibid., p. 60.   [13] Ibid., p. 50.

durable and recognizable hybrid, which in essence amounted to a re-founding of the nation. Greenstone's own interpretation of Hartz is itself susceptible to critical review. To the extent that it effectively portrays the combination of two liberal traditions into one then it can be said that '[i]n some measure... Greenstone defends the thesis of American exceptionalism and seeks to give it a more convincing statement than Hartz's'.[14] However, in doing so, he necessarily underlines the existence of a deep fissure in the American liberal tradition. As a consequence, the revision can be interpreted as demonstrating the magnitude of a fault-line that neither President Lincoln nor any other agency has been able to rectify.

These kinds of challenges and reservations relating to the status of America's liberal past and the meaning attached to either its unitary history or its multiple narratives can generate serious doubts over the nature of American development and over the reach and leverage of its liberal principles.[15] These doubts are often compounded by allusions to forms of social behaviour such as intolerance, discrimination, exclusion, conformity, and even disorder that underline the contested nature of America's heritage in liberal principles. Judith Shklar points out that actual political conditions bear witness to the continuing flaws in American citizenship and in the representation of a unilinear conception of liberal progression. She asserts that 'America has not marched single file down a single straight liberal highway as both the lamenters and the celebrators of its political life have claimed'.[16] Instead there has been a continuity of 'conflicts arising from enduring anti-liberal dispositions'[17] set against the promises of equal rights. She continues:

It is because slavery, racism, nativism and sexism, often institutionalized in exclusionary and discriminatory laws and practices, have been and still are arrayed against the officially accepted claims of equal citizenship that there is a real pattern to be discerned in the tortuous development of American ideas of citizenship. If there is permanence here, it is one of lasting conflicting claims.[18]

Shklar's indictment exemplifies the problematic properties of such a culturally avowed liberal disposition set within a pluralistic matrix that can accommodate inequities and injustices.

A similar conclusion is drawn by Rogers Smith. As has already been noted above, Smith has sought to integrate illiberal hierarchies, institutions, and ideologies within the central corpus of American tradition. He refers not to one

---

[14] Lewis Parry, review of J. David Greenstone, *The Lincoln Persuasion: Remaking American Liberalism*, in *The William and Mary Quarterly*, 3rd series., vol. 51, no. 4 (October 1994), p. 841.

[15] See Smith, 'Beyond Tocqueville, Myrdal, and Hartz'; Louisa B. Green, 'The Liberal Tradition in American Politics: A Slow Boat to Democracy', in David F. Ericson and Louisa B. Green (eds.), *The Liberal Tradition in American Politics: Reassessing the Legacy of American Liberalism* (New York: Routledge, 1999), pp. 43–66.

[16] Judith Shklar, *American Citizenship: The Quest for Inclusion* (Cambridge, MA: Harvard University Press, 1991), p. 13.

[17] Ibid.   [18] Ibid., pp. 13–14.

overarching tradition but to three.[19] These are liberalism, republicanism, and what he terms the 'ascriptive tradition' of assigning selected sectors of the population to a marginalized and unequal status. The illiberal and undemocratic nature of such civic exclusion is often dismissed as anomalous when set against the grand narrative of a liberal hegemony. Smith's view is that the theme of inegalitarianism is far from being merely a temporary or insubstantial aberration but in fact amounts to an entrenched and even permanent tradition in its own right. Moreover, it is claimed that by recognizing the proportionate weight of this tradition in American history and social development, a more accurate understanding of the dynamics of ideas becomes possible.

In opening up to critical review the assumed premises of America's natural embodiment of liberal democracy, Smith's work has generated an entire genre of historiography relating to American political development and to the interconnectedness of political ideas, social conditions, and differential identities. He demonstrates the extraordinary ecology of racial, ethnic, and gendered inequalities supported by a prodigious range of discrimination based upon various legal, scientific, historical, nationalistic, intellectual, and custom-based criteria. In doing so, Smith establishes a serious claim that ascriptive hierarchies represent a profound conditioning agency upon the course of American history and one that continues to shape contemporary outlooks upon the nature of America's liberal order. In Smith's view, the compulsive nature of America's ascriptive attitudes and structures constitutes a tradition that is comparable to the liberal and republican traditions. Together these three mixed traditions are said to interact with one another and to engage in a mutually conditioning process of concurrence. The effect is that of a 'complex pattern of apparently inconsistent combinations'[20] of the three traditions underlined by the way in which it has been 'typical, not aberrational, for Americans to embody strikingly opposed beliefs in their institutions'.[21] In seeking to capitalize upon the mobilizing properties of ascriptive politics, leaders and their top-down strategies of identity formation are shown to transcend rather than explicitly to transgress the formal principles of American civil society. Thus, while exclusionary and inegalitarian practices would be tolerated and even institutionalized, they would at the same time be restrained by the need to avoid the appearance of directly violating liberal principles of civic equality or liberal legal requirements.

Extensive though these contradictory arrangements may have been, Smith struggles to establish a case for an autonomous tradition of liberal–republican denial. Although his mixed-tradition thesis is devoted to showing that the 'ascriptive tradition' is 'not merely the shadowy side of a hegemonic liberal republicanism',[22] it is evident that the meaning and substance of the tradition is closely dependent upon the gravitational force of a defining liberal norm. So much so in

---

[19] Smith, 'Beyond Tocqueville, Mrydal, and Hartz', pp. 549–66; see also Smith, *Civic Ideals*, chs. 5–12.

[20] Smith, 'Beyond Tocqueville, Mrydal, and Hartz', p. 558.

[21] Ibid.   [22] Ibid.

fact, that the 'ascriptive tradition' is largely conceived in the negative: namely in respect to what occurs when liberal principles are diminished or even conceivably switched off. Smith's insights into hybrid attitudes and conflicting affiliations are valuable not least in the way that they undermine the claims that the American polity has successively progressed towards an increasingly fuller realization of its founding ideals. The liberal presumption of a Whig conception of historical progression has been effectively challenged by Smith's demonstration that inequity and discrimination simply fluctuate throughout American history—dependent as they are upon political contingency rather than any consistent or inevitable dynamic of civic fulfilment. Because 'America has never been completely liberal', Smith points out that 'changes have come only through difficult struggles and then have often not been sustained'.[23] The call of ascriptive inegalitarianism has often proved to be more beguiling than appeals to liberal or republican idealism, or even to the principle of legal continuity.

[M]any examples, like the reductions in the rights of African-Americans from the Revolution to the 1850s, and from Reconstruction to the Progressive years, as well as the new restrictions imposed on married women in 1855, Asian-Americans in the late nineteenth century, and homosexuals in the twentieth, all indicate that neither the possession nor the fresh achievement of greater equality can guarantee against later losses of status due to renewed support for various types of ascriptive hierarchy.[24]

Notwithstanding the value of Smith's 'multiple traditions' approach in achieving a corrective re-evaluation of America's historical outlook towards communal identity and civil rights, it nevertheless has only a limited utility in explaining the usage and organization of America's core ideas, and offers little analysis on the relational linkages between these ideas and the three posited traditions.

It is evident that arguments continue to revolve around whether discriminatory and exclusionary practices can be construed as derivatives of traditional Lockian perspectives, or whether they constitute deviations or even departures from a guiding historical norm.[25] At the very best, these controversies underline the importance of genealogy and inheritance in the usage of American political ideas. In doing so, they illustrate both the dissonance between and within ideas, and the contested nature of the tradition, or traditions, that provide the medium within which ideas are related to contemporary contexts. In essence, the level of ideational and interpretive energy applied to these disputes represents a manifold indictment of the organizing logic of Hartz's original equation. The correlation of a core tradition and a clear historical continuity that together sustained a controlling liberal conformity used to possess both the explanatory force of an elegant simplicity and the leverage of a compelling orthodoxy. Even though its authority as a cultural synthesis has been in sharp decline for a considerable period, the Hartzian view

---

[23] Smith, 'Beyond Tocqueville, Mrydal, and Hartz', p. 550.   [24] Smith, *Civic Ideals*, p. 491.

[25] For a good overview of the disputed terrain, see Richard J. Ellis, *American Political Cultures* (New York: Oxford University Press, 1993) and James T. Kloppenberg, 'In Retrospect: Louis Hartz's *The Liberal Tradition in America*', *Reviews in American History*, vol. 29, no. 3 (September 2001), pp. 460–78.

retains a residual significance as a point of access to the examination of American political culture. What remains as significant as ever are the questions relating to the functioning ecology of American political ideas for which the Hartzian thesis sought to provide systemic answers.

ONE OR TWO AMERICAS

Many accounts of the role of ideas in American politics appear to gravitate to one or other of two alternative conceptions. They both possess properties that can offer an explanation of the relationship between diversity and cohesion. Moreover, they both purport to show how ideas are used to organize and sustain predominant patterns of social behaviour.

'Low Value Unity'

The first conception can be termed 'low value unity'. Here the primary character-istic of American society is deemed to be that of solidarity which is facilitated by, and expressed through, ideas that have a submerged and often subliminal currency. In its developed form, traditional American principles are simply taken as the presuppositions of civic membership and social intercourse. The accepted ubiquity of such a corpus of ideas can be so entrenched that the substance of the principles themselves becomes marginalized to the point of acting as the agency of an intuitive conformity. In this context, ideas are alluded to as depictions of an unarticulated corporate essence, rather than as precise expressions of distinct priorities.

Louis Hartz represents one brand of this conceptualization. A more developed version is provided by historians like Daniel Boorstin. The passage of American history to Boorstin deepens and replicates itself through the dynamics of America's idiosyncratic origins and experience. Values become simply a given feature of the society. They come preformed rather than being derivatives of Lockian individual-ism, English republicanism, or European liberalism: '"Givenness" is the belief that values in America are in some way or other automatically defined: given by certain facts of geography or history peculiar to us'.[26] Peculiarity in this sphere allows not just for ideational continuity but also for a measure of social self-assurance. An immigrant was 'not required to learn a philosophy so much as to rid his lungs of the air of Europe'.[27] American improvization, therefore, can supplant the need for structured rationales, or even for the conscious appreciation of embedded values. At its most severe, this outlook can tolerate and even endorse forms of political anti-intellectualism in which ideas are reduced either to simplistic clichés or to

[26] Daniel J. Boorstin, *The Genius of American Politics* (Chicago, IL: University of Chicago Press, 1953), p. 9.
[27] Ibid., p. 28.

crude constructions drawn from individual and social stereotypes. A perspective that places the usage of ideas in the service of a compulsive uniformity can also foster a climate of habitual 'unreason' which can occasionally take the form of intolerant nativism or irrational populism.

This theme of low value unity relates closely to the evidence drawn from surveys into the nature of belief systems in the United States. Despite the presence of a value-rich political discourse, it is contended that much of the American public is grossly deficient in its ability to understand political issues, and to structure its positions on different issues according to a coherent set of organizing principles. In his seminal study of the structure of beliefs within mass publics, Phillip Converse asserts that most American citizens do not appear to possess a clearly defined scheme of conceptual reference that would allow diverse issues to be sorted into consistent and logical alignments of response.[28] On the contrary, apart from an informed and intellectually engaged elite, the political thinking undertaken by the public reveals little evidence of an ordered set of overarching and integrated principles from which political evaluations, positions, and preferences are consciously formulated. As a consequence, most voters neither define nor use ideological terms to evaluate political parties and candidates. Their political preferences not only remain unrelated to one another, revealing a lack of ideological 'constraint'[29] in their political belief systems, but are also portrayed as being highly inconsistent and unstable. On this basis, it is suggested that political positions and the usage of ideas in America can lack the cognitive discipline, as well as the coherence and stability of ideological organization. The implication is that because the general public does not have the capacity to make coherent contributions to policy formulation, the processes of policy-making should be protected from the influence of a largely uninformed, disinterested, and overreactive citizenry.

Other analysts have reached broadly similar conclusions[30]—even to the extent of claiming that when individuals apparently adopt an ideologically based identification, or position themselves on an ideologically based continuum (e.g. liberal–conservative dimension), they mainly do so in a non-ideological and affective manner.[31] Converse's logic can be extended to take account of the reason for the

---

[28] Philip E. Converse, 'The Nature of Belief Systems in Mass Publics', in David E. Apter (ed.), *Ideology and Discontent* (New York: Free Press, 1964), pp. 206–61.

[29] 'Constraint' is Philip Converse's term for the level and agency of integration in attitude structure.

[30] For example, see Donald R. Kinder, 'Diversity and Complexity in American Public Opinion', in Ada W. Finifter (ed.), *Political Science: The State of the Discipline* (Washington, DC: The American Political Science Association, 1983), pp. 389–425; William G. Jacoby, 'Levels of Conceptualization and Reliance on the Liberal–Conservative Continuum', *Journal of Politics*, vol. 48, no. 2 (May 1986), pp. 423–32; W. Russell Neuman, *The Paradox of Mass Politics: Knowledge and Opinion in the American Electorate* (Cambridge, MA: Harvard University Press, 1986).

[31] Teresa E. Levitin and Warren E. Miller, 'Ideological Interpretations of Presidential Elections', *The American Political Science Review*, vol. 73, no. 3 (September 1979), pp. 751–71; Pamela Johnston Conover and Stanley Feldman, 'The Origins and Meaning of Liberal/Conservative Self-Identifications', *American Journal of Political Science*, vol. 25, no. 4 (November 1981), pp. 617–645; David O. Sears, 'Symbolic Politics: A Socio-Psychological Theory', in Shanto Iyengar and William J. McGuire (eds.), *Explorations in Political Psychology* (Durham, NC: Duke University Press, 1993), pp. 113–49.

high level of attitudinal imprecision. Arguably, it is precisely because America's core values are so adaptable to so diverse a set of interpretive perspectives, that it is possible to speculate that ideological disarray is symptomatic of the American condition.

The apparent disorganization in the articulation of beliefs, and the inconsistency in the way that values are asserted and applied, are often seen as inferring the existence of a basic unity that permits, and even facilitates, this level of unstructured particularism. The same sense of ideational licence and bounded dissonance is evident in the mainstream conception of American pluralism. A profusion of groups adopt different permutations of American ideals in support of their interests. In the political interplay of group demands, a multiplicity of ideational variants is also projected into the market dynamics of sublimated conflict. Interests and their sponsored ideas have necessarily to be compromised by one another through the channels of intermediation—otherwise know as the 'rules of the game'. The minimal unity that permits the existence of such rules is rooted in a common attachment to a corpus of basic values which are set at a sufficiently high level of generalization to allow for the process of mutual accommodation.

'High Value Disunity'

The other main device by which the relationship between ideas and politics is conceptualized in the United States pertains more to differentiation and disjunction rather than to generalized homogeneity. This type of conception can be termed 'high value disunity'. In the construction of 'low value unity' ideas are given a capacious property that allows differences to be minimized and understated. 'High value disunity' by contrast takes heterogeneity as its controlling theme. Deep-seated differences are not only accepted as a feature of social existence, they are portrayed as being rationalized and expressed through the medium of ideas. Within the terms of this perspective, ideas are used in a polarized and polarizing way. They facilitate the transition of differences into principled distinctions that by their very nature are not ordinarily susceptible to compromise and accommodation. While it may be the case that the ideas in question amount to different interpretations of universally acknowledged values, or else to differences in their priority and emphasis, the net effect remains the same. Ideas are constantly and habitually advanced as instruments and embodiments of differentiation. According to this conception, high principles and deep values are the defining characteristics of a form of politics that has to manage the conditions of ideational division on a continuous basis.

The usage of ideas to characterize and define a condition of concerted difference has come in a variety of forms. In the past, class-related themes have often served as organizing instruments of ideational distinction. However, these bases of differentiation have almost invariably been compounded by other sources of principled positioning. Race, gender, religion, sectional tradition, and ethnic identity all possess the reputation of being attributed agencies of conflict between and amongst American ideals. Whether it is a case of different values being given different priorities, or the same values being given differing contextual interpretations, one outcome remains constant: namely the projection of core values into the organization of American conflict.

'Two Nations'

The most recent addition to this idiom of a value-based dichotomy is afforded by the widely acknowledged phenomenon of America's 'culture wars'. This term has no precise definition but it is used to describe a profound divergence in social attitudes, outlooks, and norms that pivots upon distinctive polarities of moral and political principle. Instead of the cultural dimension acting as a focus of social cohesion, national identity, and political solidarity, the American creed becomes the object of fierce dispute. Issues relating explicitly to the sphere of cultural values not only inject divisive energies into political debate, but subsume policy discussion into the broader, more contentious, and far less negotiable medium of moralistic contention.

References have been made to a distinct bifurcation of values in which various principled positions are reduced to two deeply entrenched aggregates. These opposing outlooks are identified by different terms, yet in the main they are rooted in the distinction between traditionalism and progressivism. Traditionalists adhere to the conception of a dominant and historically sanctioned culture that evokes a sense of a natural moral order. Traditionalism also incorporates the conception of an idealized past against which contemporary society should be evaluated. Progressives on the other hand tend to give emphasis to the themes of emancipation, scepticism, and rational reflection. They are less constrained by tradition and custom, and are more likely to allow conditions to shape conceptions of freedom and morality in the light of evolutionary change. Traditionalists underline the significance of individual responsibility, family values, religious faith, and visceral patriotism. Progressives, by contrast, question the primacy and the meaning of family, religion, and nation in an effort to move beyond the established norms of belief and conduct.

The differences over the meaning ascribed to order, individual freedom, and moral consciousness find their expression in the embittered struggles generated in such 'wedge issue' areas as abortion, gay rights, school prayer, stem cell research, divorce law, pornography, gun control, and welfare provision. The controversies encountered in these fields suggest the presence of a measure of 'high value disunity' within contemporary American politics. On the one side are the varied claims of those who allude to the cultural value of equity, individual autonomy, and liberty from imposing constructions of social convention in favour of a multicultural expression of the American experience. Their opponents display an equally diverse set of propositions against the spread of what is characterized as secular humanism and moral relativism, and in favour of a greater emphasis upon the values of social cohesion, national unity, and moral order.

These disputes over what is termed the state of the nation, or even the condition of American civilization, generate a host of questions over the precise form of the conflict. Controversies surround the nature of the respective agendas, the roots of each side's intransigent postures, and the comparability of both adversaries as distinctive 'cultures'. Many of the responses to these controversies are discrete in nature and specific in application. They can lead to the direct penetration of deep-seated impulses into a political realm already marked by cross-cutting issues and disjointed opinion formation. Other conceptions of this phenomenon, however, suggest the existence of an underlying and more systemic structure to the apparent dissonance of value expression. What is not in doubt is that these conflicting positions create a mutual identity for one another. Each define themselves in relation to the threat posed by the other. Furthermore, they seek to maximize the legitimacy and leverage of their respective positions by appropriating American values to their cause and divesting their opponents of as many claims as possible to American authenticity. The resultant inflation in invective is strongly correlated with a deepening antagonism and with the onset of a structured impasse.

The theme of cultural contention has been adopted and developed in a number of ways. While some portrayals refer to a growing distinction in lifestyles and consumer choices, others give emphasis to the indications of a material and class basis to cultural differentiation. What is significant is that these differences are not merely translated into an important sub-theme of American politics but given the status of its central organizing principle. It is a common claim that the clash over culture amounts to an ideological cleavage that has been aided and supported by the recent polarization of liberal and conservative opinion between the Democratic and Republican parties. James Gimpel goes further and asserts that the ideological realignment of the parties has been guided by cultural attachments and that this is reflected in the spatial reconfiguration of the American population. The traditional mobility of American society is said to be having an adverse effect upon its customary diversity. Increasingly, people are choosing to live in neighbour-hoods that most closely correspond to their cultural and ideological dispositions. Gimpel's view is that this type of voluntary segregation is creating a 'patchwork nation' of self-contained ideological communities.[32] The spatial characteristics of this pattern of settlement can be said to amount to the tangible embodiment of deepening division over values.

The dynamics that suggest the existence of a 'patchwork nation' have been used to advance an even more sweeping depiction of the cultural divide. This relates to the asserted existence of two nations, each with its own dominant culture and its own territorial identity. While much of the support given to this notion owes more to rhetorical licence and popular discourse than to rigorous analysis, it nevertheless conveys the widespread perception of a nationwide duality. The 'two nations' proposition has received a further stimulus from the distribution of party strengths around the country. Following the presidential elections of

---

[32] James G. Gimpel and Jason E. Schuknecht, *Patchwork Nation: Sectionalism and Political Change in American Politics* (Ann Arbor, MI: University of Michigan Press, 2003).

2000 and 2004, states and even entire regions have become categorized as either blue (Democratic) or red (Republican) areas. The designation affords an apparent geographical solidity to the idea of two entities based upon an allegiance to two different sets of values. In January 2004, a Zogby International survey reported that the nation was 'deeply divided by party, ideology ... and values'. It summed up the division in terms of 'two different, yet parallel universes'.[33]

The persistence of high incumbency re-election rates in an increasingly polarized Congress, combined with the further consolidation of the 'red' and 'blue' states in the high turnout election of 2004, have given the notion of an entrenched values-divide further currency as a political phenomenon. In that year, Senator John Edwards attempted to appropriate the 'two nations' concept for the Democratic party. He used his position as vice-presidential candidate to reinvest the idea with the populist themes of economic inequality, class privilege, and social marginalization. Edwards claimed that President George W. Bush had an agenda to divide the country into 'two Americas—one privileged, the other burdened'.[34] Moreover, Edwards argued that in his first administration, President Bush had succeeded in achieving his objective:

Today, under George W. Bush, there are two Americas, not one: One America that does the work, another America that reaps the reward. One America that pays the taxes, another America that gets the tax breaks. One America that will do anything to leave its children a better life, another America that never has to do a thing because its children are already set for life. One America—middle-class America—whose needs Washington has long forgotten, another America—narrow-interest America—whose every wish is Washington's command. One America that is struggling to get by, another America that can buy anything it wants, even a Congress and a President.[35]

The strategy failed to achieve the desired effect because it was unable to calibrate into the established drives and agendas of cultural attachment. Attempts to utilize class lines ran up against the complex subtexts of social attitudes, manners, and prejudices.[36] More significantly, efforts to achieve social mobilization through the unifying clarity of populist economics were confounded by the challenge of a double dichotomy: (i) the perception of a pre-existing cultural divide; and (ii) a politics geared to the further exploitation of difference over American values and to an increased competition over the criteria of American authenticity.

---

[33] Zogby International, 'America Culturally Divided; Blue vs. Red States, Democrats vs. Republicans—Two Separate Nations, New O'Leary Report/Zogby Poll Reveals', 6 January 2004, http://www.zogby.com/news/ReadNews.dbm?ID=775; see also John K. White, *The Values Divide: American Politics and Culture in Transition* (New York: Chatham House, 2003); Stanley B. Greenberg, *The Two Americas: Our Current Political Deadlock and How to Break It* (New York: Thomas Dunne, 2004), chs. 3, 5–8; John Sperling, Suzanne Helburn, Samuel George, John Morris, and Carl Hunt, *The Great Divide: Retro vs. Metro America* (Sausalito, CA: PoliPoint Press, 2004).

[34] Senator John Edwards, 'Two Americas', speech text, 29 December 2003, http://www.johnedwards2004.com/page.asp?id=481.

[35] Ibid.

[36] See Thomas Frank, *What's the Matter with Kansas?: How Conservatives Won the Heart of America* (New York: Metropolitan/Henry Holt, 2004); Thomas Frank, 'What's the Matter with Liberals?', *New York Review of Books*, 12 May 2005.

'High value disunity' and 'low value unity' offer two signature approaches towards the relationship between ideas, society, and culture in the American context. Whatever their individual merits as analytical approaches, they raise the central difficulty of reaching an explanatory accommodation between such different conceptions of the ideational dimension in American politics. Given the stark clarity of America's core values and the palpable capacity for friction between them in a public discourse fixed upon high principle, the question turns to one of juxtaposition. On the one hand, it can be argued that the Hartzian consensus, or a comparable expression of assimilative unanimity, cannot give an adequate account of the ideational dynamics within American society. On the other hand, it can also be claimed that the portrayal of a society bifurcated on the grounds of polarized values also raises questions over the validity of such a depiction in a social context renowned for the cohesion of its value structure. The differences between these two pristine conceptions of ideas at work in American society create a need for different approaches to the problem of capturing the essence of the interaction of ideas and politics in the United States.

PRINCIPLES OF VARIABLE GEOMETRY

A significant method of addressing the place and usage of ideas in such a system is to focus not just upon the tensions between core values, but also on the gaps between stated ideals and the degree to which they are conveyed into social existence. The combination of entrenched, yet dissonant, ideas along with a social condition that is at variance with many of their implications is a widely recognized condition of American politics. It has fostered a number of different explanations that can account for the maintained attachment to the core values, even when they are palpably inconsistent with one another, or conspicuously misaligned with contemporary social priorities.

Fault-Line Shadows

The *first* analytical approach adopts a position of strategic ambiguity in the face of the usage of ideas that can accommodate the differences both between different core ideas and between their promise and reality. In doing so, it offers a form of understanding that takes the disjunctions in precisely the terms in which they commonly presents themselves. The tension between liberty and democracy, for example, is often compounded by an attitude structure that facilitates ambiguity. The expansion of guaranteed rights by government can at the same time both diminish some individuals' sphere of personal freedom, and curtail the government's own capacity to engage in schemes of social improvement. Moreover, demands for greater participation in government, and increased responsiveness from government, can occur in tandem with populist impulses against the state and against conventional channels of political behaviour. Most conspicuously, a strong civic, legal, and moral attachment to the principles of equality can coincide not only with a self-evidently unequal society, but also with an outlook that routinely overlooks the fault-line between a cultural ideal and its social reality.

In his classic text on the historical position of blacks in the New World, Gunnar Myrdal suggested that most Americans understood themselves to be believers in the principle of equality, irrespective of their actual treatment of the black minority.[37] In American society the doctrine of equality existed alongside an entrenched premise of white superiority. Myrdal argued that black equality would only ever be secured when whites became conscious of the discrepancy between their ideals and their actions. Implicit in his analysis, however, was the understanding that the value of equality and the conditions of inequality were both authentically American characteristics.

The disparity between an accepted governing principle on the one hand, and an evident deficiency in the application of such a principle to society's arrangements on the other, can be regarded as a form of cognitive dissonance. The unease at the discrepancy between the ingrained principle of equality, for example, and information relating to an evident condition of inequality is resolved by various strategies designed to close the gap between the spheres of belief and perception. Consciously or subconsciously, individuals in these circumstances tend both to marginalize the deviant information concerning actual conditions and to reinforce the belief system surrounding the original principle. Notwithstanding evidence to the contrary, cognitive dissonance refers to a compulsive need to manipulate beliefs and behavioural information, in order to make them consistent with one another.

A related source of explanation and management gives emphasis to the ability of individuals to hold divergent views at the same time. Instead of attempting to close the gap between different forms of cognition, an analysis pioneered by Lloyd Free and Hadley Cantril suggests that different positions are systematically compartmentalized in accordance with separate dimensions of response. Free and Cantril originated the proposition that American political attitudes are routinely split between the spheres of general principle and practical immediacy.[38] According to their survey of public attitudes, Americans do not differentiate between liberalism and conservatism by means of a single evaluative criterion. At the abstract ideological level, a majority of respondents emerged as possessing conservative beliefs in favour of a minimal state. However, when enquiries were shifted to the level of tangible and immediate government programmes, the study elicited just as strong a support for a practical liberalism. What Free and Cantril concluded was the existence of two simultaneous dimensions of meaning and attachment based upon ideological and operational frames of reference. They

[37] Gunnar Myrdal, *An American Dilemma: The Negro Problem and American Democracy* (New York: Harper, 1944); see also Stephen Brooks, *America through Foreign Eyes: Classical Interpretations of American Political Life* (Oxford: Oxford University Press, 2002), ch. 4.

[38] Lloyd A. Free and Hadley Cantril, *The Political Beliefs of Americans: A Study of Public Opinion* (New Brunswick, NJ: Rutgers University Press, 1967).

describe it as a 'schizoid combination of operational liberalism with ideological conservatism'.[39] This division between abstract values and their tangible repercussions carries weight. It corresponds to many patterns of American attitudes, where there is often a demonstrable distinction between positive responses to ideological statements and negative reactions to many of their policy consequences (e.g. simultaneous preferences for smaller government in general but for improved government services in particular).

The bifurcation between generic abstraction and contextual exemption can account for the persistence of disjunctions involving racial, gender, and ethnic equality, as well as those related to the positive and negative perceptions of the state, and to the ideals and self-interest of American foreign policy. The tolerance and equanimity that is shown towards such anomalies can lead to accusations of double standards and hypocrisy especially by non-Americans. By the same token, it can be claimed that American society is particularly aligned to the uninhibited articulation and veneration of a multiplicity of political principles. As a consequence, it has had to develop forms of equivocation that allows the strain over ideational priorities and practicalities to be reduced to mangeable proportions.

Material Differences

Reductionist organization offers a *second* device that can make sense of America's ideational variables. It relies on proposition that ideas can literally be split into physical compartments. This view asserts that different value priorities and different attitude structures can exist alongside one another but only on the basis of separate local or regional variations. Multiple attachments can, therefore, be rationalized in terms of territorial orientations and traditions. A substantial literature that addresses the issue of regional differences and subcultures in the United States exists. Many carry inferences of substantive variations in value priorities and traditions.[40] But attempts to refine these distinctions into precise patterns of ideational dispositions based upon subregions and subsets of principles pose exacting problems of defining criteria and assessing degrees of difference. A typology produced from such an exercise always risks creating a study guided by the pre-existing territorial units of analysis. In effect, spatial dimensions and even regional stereotypes can induce a tautological effect in which outcomes are heavily influenced by the initial categories of examination. More significantly, a typology of this kind is likely to be inherently

---

[39] Ibid., p. 37.
[40] For example, see Clyde A. Milner II, Patricia Nelson Limerick, and Charles E. Rankin (eds.), *Trails: Toward a New Western History* (Lawrence, KS: University Press of Kansas, 1991); Clyde A Milner II, Carol A. O'Connor, and Martha A. Sandweiss (eds.),*The Oxford History of the American West* (New York: Oxford University Press, 1994); Joseph F. Zimmerman, *The New England Town Meeting: Democracy in Action* (Westport, CT: Praeger, 1999); Joseph A. Conforti, *Imagining New England: Explorations of Regional Identity from the Pilgrims to the Mid-Twentieth Century* (Chapel Hill, NC: University of North Carolina Press, 2001); Michael Lind, *Made in Texas: George W. Bush and the Southern Takeover of American Politics* (New York: Basic Books, 2003).

predisposed towards thematic continuity. The importance of ideas in mobilizing challenge, justifying change, and organizing conflict is largely superseded by the analytical weight given to the theme of fixed and bounded spheres of ideational autonomy.

A derivative of this distributive strategy places the ideas themselves into different holding formations. An element of ordered regularity is usually provided by the reduction of ideas to two main spheres, or at least to variants of two clearly differentiated poles of political principle. This type of explanation not only favours the reduction of American values into a pairing of core values, but seeks to account for their collective existence through the presence of a single easily conceived division. The composition of these dualities varies in name and nature. For example, they can be rooted in the distinctions between the 'individual' and 'the community', between 'the private interest' and the 'public purpose', between 'reformism' and 'conservatism', between 'liberty' and 'equality', and between 'affirmative government' and 'anti-statism'. Three of the best known of these posited dualities relate to 'achievement' and 'equality'[41]; 'capitalism' and 'democracy'[42]; and 'freedom' and 'equality'.[43]

Reducing American values into two generic forms, however, raises more problems than it resolves. First, it does not avoid the persistent difficulty of determining which values rightfully belong to which camp, or which values or value divisions have priority over others in the reductive process towards two overarching principles. In *The American Ethos*, for example, Herbert McCloskey and John Zaller state at the outset that 'two major traditions of belief, capitalism, and democracy, have dominated the life of the American nation from its inception'.[44] They go on to point out that

[D]espite their central importance in American life, the values of the ethos are often in conflict. Some of the conflicts arise within the same strand of the ethos, for example, the conflict between the democratic values of majority rule and minority rights. Most, however, occur between the two major strands of the ethos—between the values of capitalism on the one side and democracy on the other. In our view, the tension that exists between capitalist and democratic values is a definitive feature of American life that has helped to shape the ideological divisions of the nation's politics.[45]

This might well be so, but there is considerable room for dispute over what is included in McCloskey and Zaller's notion of 'capitalism' and 'democracy'. In their scheme of analysis, liberty and equality, for example, are grouped together under democracy, while individual achievement and independence are located in the capitalism category.

A related problem with these sorts of dualities is more significant. It is that in having reduced the field to pairs of monolithic principles, the question of

---

[41] Seymour M. Lipset, *The First New Nation* (New York: W. W. Norton, 1979).

[42] Herbert McCloskey and John Zaller, *The American Ethos: Public Attitudes toward Capitalism and Democracy* (Cambridge, MA: Harvard University Press, 1984).

[43] Milton Rokeach, *The Nature of Human Values* (New York: Free Press, 1973).

[44] McCloskey and Zaller, *The American Ethos*, p. 1.   [45] Ibid.

their relationship to one another is largely overlooked. The chief difficulty here is that in classifying and even dramatizing the existence of a cultural duality of this depth, such studies tend to exacerbate, rather than to resolve, the problem of the evident coexistence of American values. In reformulating American values to two coalitions of principles centring, for example, upon liberty and equality, the position acquired is tantamount to a recognition of the formal irreducibility of liberty and equality to a single principle. An individual like Ronald Dworkin may go to great lengths to construct a finely grained philosophical treatise on the way in which liberty and equality might be reconciled by integrating freedom and personal responsibility into a condition of equal resources through a set of social incentives and individual calculations.[46] But for every occasion when such a closely reasoned conflation is attempted, there are innumerable instances when the ease of duality is preferred for the sake of organizational clarity. It is for this reason that Michael Novak's simple indictment of egalitarianism as 'egalityranny'[47] has such an immediate cachet. The term has a rhetorical impact because of the way it can imply and reaffirm the notion of a fundamental zero-sum relationship between these two core principles.

In giving prominence to the incompatibility of key principles, analytical dualisms often overlook the experiential concurrence and parallel status of purportedly divided values within American society. They can create a sense of artificiality in which two values, or two sets of values, are treated as independent entities rather than as constituent elements of a dynamic whole. In this respect, it is noticeable that when Allan Bloom characterizes American political culture as 'the majestic and triumphant march of two principles, the principles of freedom and equality, which give meaning to all that we have done or are doing',[48] he is prompted to add the following addendum: 'Everything that happens among us is a consequence of one or both of our principles—a triumph over some opposition to them, a discovery of a fresh meaning in them, a dispute about which of the two has primacy, and so forth.'[49] Reducing the ecology of ideational variables like this to two conglomerates generates a host of objections relating to ethical priority and cultural primacy. In essence, the analytical device of dualities tends both to oversimplify the matrix of animating principles, and to overlook the holistic dimension that allows for, and even stimulates, the eclectic use of values in an open-ended debate.

Turning Circles

The difficulties associated with dualities have fostered another source of explanatory symmetry. This *third* strategic instrument that is used to account for

---

[46] Ronald Dworkin, *Sovereign Virtue: The Theory and Practice of Equality* (Cambridge, MA: Harvard University Press, 2002).

[47] Michael Novak, 'The Closet Socialists', *The Christian Century*, 16 February 1977.

[48] Allan Bloom, 'Liberty, Equality and Sexuality', *Commentary*, April 1987.   [49] Ibid.

America's multiple allegiances to cross-cutting ideas and values is provided by the concept of recurrent cycles. Instead of having to determine which side of any duality takes precedence over the other, this strategy simply abandons the assessment in favour of a cycle of periodic supremacy, in which each side in turn alternates with the other for predominance. This form of explanation still relies upon the notion of a generalized bifurcation of segregated values but, with the cyclical device, their relationship to one another becomes simplified by reference to their alleged periodicity.

In this case, time is the answer to the problematic connections between, for example, individual achievement and equality. Rather than individualism following a linear form of progressive development, the assumption with this sort of cyclical device is that once the attachment to individualism has acquired a pre-eminent position, it stimulates a counter-reaction and with it a revival of interest in the egalitarian premises and principles of a democratic citizenship. One of the best known examples of this strategy is the cyclical model advanced by Arthur M. Schlesinger, Jr.[50] He explains the recurrent pattern of American history by reference to the public's rhythmic swings between a concern for the rights of the few and a concern for the wrongs of the many. The latter had produced movements to increase 'democracy' (i.e. 'public purpose'), while the former had generated demands to contain it (i.e. 'private interests'). A similar construct is provided by James Stimson whose use of public opinion analysis leads him to formulate the existence of cycles expressed as swings in public mood between conservatism and liberalism.[51]

James Morone discerns another type of recurrent cyclical pattern in his examination of America's history and social development. He draws attention to two derivatives of Puritanism that he believes alternate with one another on a regular basis. Periods of pronounced concern over social decay, combined with the censorious imposition of moral controls by government, come to be followed by periods when the primary impulse is oriented more to a Social Gospel outlook in which social ills are blamed less upon individual sin and personal culpability, and more upon the need for collective forms of communal revival through government programmes of public goods.[52]

Samuel P. Huntington offers an intriguing variation on the theme of cyclical change.[53] Instead of positing the alternation of different ideas, Huntington treats America's core values as a collective creed. He asserts that the political creed is a potent mix of liberty, equality, individualism, democracy, and the rule of law. For the most part these values coexist together in a loose package of distant ideals, but

[50] Arthur M. Schlesinger, Jr., 'The Cycles of American Politics', in Arthur M. Schlesinger, Jr., *The Cycles of American History* (Harmondsworth, UK: Penguin, 1989), pp. 23–48.

[51] James A. Stimson, *Public Opinion in America: Moods, Cycles, and Swings* (Boulder, CO: Westview, 1999), chs. 2, 9,

[52] James Morone, *Hellfire Nation: The Politics of Sin in American History* (New Haven, CT: Yale University Press, 2003).

[53] Samuel P. Huntington, *American Politics: The Promise of Disharmony* (Cambridge, MA: Belknap Press, 1981).

there always remains a discrepancy between these ideals and the reality of political conduct. Although Huntington endorses the Hartzian notion of a consensus of values, he asserts that such an underlying agreement generates tensions over the relationship between the high morality of American principles and the generally prosaic nature of political life. He claims that it is this disjunction which has fostered recurrent movements in American history to reassert the moral standing and collective force of the nation's ideals.

To Huntington, the gap between the reputation of American ideals and their actual status in American society produces a series of responses (i.e. cynicism; complacency; hypocrisy; moralism). Each response leads on from its predecessor to create a repetitive sequence, or cycle, of moral intensity and subsequent decline. It is the moralistic reaction to hypocrisy that produces convulsive surges of reform in an attempt to close the gap between America's ideals and its attainments. Huntington equates these movements with a form of psychological disorder on a mass scale which occur at critical points of maximum strain. According to Huntington, this cycle has produced four such outbursts of highly charged devotion to America's political creed (i.e. 'creedal passion'). The four periods in question coincided with the American Revolution, the Jacksonian era, the Progressive age, and the *angst* of the 1960s and early 1970s.[54] They were all motivated by the desire to revive the moral intensity of the American creed. Inevitably they have all ended in a reversion to complacency, cynicism, and hypocrisy, mostly because it has not been possible for any American government to fully live up to the ideals of the American creed. The duality envisaged by Huntington, therefore, is not based upon shifting priorities between different values so much as on changing social temperatures towards the moral content of America's aggregate value base.

Bruce Ackerman presents a different variant on the theme of collective shifts in outlook. Although he does not make explicit use of the device of cyclical change, he posits the existence of alternating periods of democratically informed activity. According to Ackerman's construct, long periods of 'normal politics', which are characterized by a disengaged citizenry, are punctuated by intense passages of 'constitutional politics'. During these periods, mobilized majorities reconfigure the public's conception of the fundamental principles inherent in the Constitution. The arousal of this kind of abnormal popular engagement and the long-term consequences that flow from it are said to amount to a transformation of the polity. Over the course of what is claimed to be a de facto revolution, the meanings attached to the constitutional principle of higher law are essentially revised in line with popularly conceived changes in ideational priorities. According to Ackerman, there have been three transforming periods in which exercises of public deliberation have led to profound constitutional modifications. The first occurred during the founding of the Constitution itself. The second transformation was marked by the passage of the Civil War Amendments, and third era coincided with the Supreme Court's ratification of the New Deal programme. All three were marked by a revival of acute interest in

---

[54] Ibid., ch. 5.

the animating ideas of the republic and in the need to arrive at a collective and lasting judgement on their configuration.[55]

The interpretative possibilities of alternating periods of ideational activity are far from being exhausted by Huntington and Ackerman. Political cycles come in a variety of shapes and sizes. According to Charles Forcey, for example, 'each wave of reform has run its course at intervals of twenty years or so since the founding of the republic'.[56] Arthur Schlesinger's cycles bring reform around in a thirty-year timescale, mostly because '[e]ach new generation, when it attains power, tends to repudiate the work of the generation it has displaced and to re-enact the ideals of its own formative days thirty years before'.[57] Samuel Huntington's recurrent pattern of responses, however, is longer, and therefore reform activity is confined to periods of maximum psychic disorder, which occur only once in every sixty to seventy years. But the chief weakness of all these cyclical patterns is not that they fail to coincide with one another, but that when ideas are used to imprint a pattern on American history, the ideas themselves ultimately become reduced to mere functions of the historical cycle. In other words, the normal collection of American values and their everyday relationship to one another become obscured, if not obliterated, by the overlay of historical epochs, which simply divide the ideas off from each other in separate time frames.

Whether the preferred pattern is that of a duality or a cycle, these strategic devices are normally less than satisfactory because of the way they tend to privilege elegant order at the expense of complex realism. Too often, these more structured frameworks of interpretation fail to take into account the analytical and political challenges of multiple core values. In particular, they do not convey a sufficient appreciation of the subtle traditions of usage and the sophisticated rules of the game that are associated with the iconic presence of a composite of principles within American society. It is precisely in this area of the linkage between general principles and their aggregated usages in political argument that offers a more sensitive, if often more elusive, alternative to the more conventional approaches and techniques of analysis in this area.

COMPOUNDS OF COEXISTENCE

This study has endeavoured to show that the ideas with currency and leverage within the framework of American politics are drawn from a common stock of governing principles, political ideals, and social traditions. The competitive struggle for ideational legitimacy is geared to optimizing the spread of claims to this multiple constituency of core values. It is the drive to create these linkages

---

[55] Bruce Ackerman, *We the People*, vol. 1: *Foundations* (Cambridge, MA: Harvard University Press, 1991); Bruce Ackerman, *We the People*, vol. 2: *Transformations* (Cambridge, MA: Belknap Press, 1998).

[56] Charles B. Forcey, *The Crossroads of Liberalism: Croly, Weyl, Lippmann and the Progressive Era, 1900–1925* (New York: Oxford University Press, 1961), pp. xv–xvi.

[57] Schlesinger, 'The Cycles of American Politics', p. 30.

that gives the conduct of American politics its distinctive character of principled promiscuity. Under its aegis, political utility becomes dependent upon a compulsive attentiveness to constructing aggregate rationales of ideas. It is this creative versatility with the basically fixed categories of American value that most closely approximates to a defining pattern, or organizing structure, that accounts for the way ideas and politics are practically aligned in the American context.

The energy and resources channelled into political argument are in large measure explained by the need to establish, maintain, refine, and deepen the various multiple connections to a segmented base of core ideas. The preceding chapters have demonstrated the pivotal significance of this historically and socially embedded matrix. Each political position not only has to engage with it, but also has to establish a plausible claim to embody a legitimate compound of those several properties that constitute the base. This is not to infer that the matrix is an ordered structure of values with settled meanings and priorities. Far from affording a calculus of precisely bounded properties, it is more akin to an evolving medium of adjacent values.

Likewise, the compounds derived from the segmented foundation of the matrix should not be conceived as genetically integrated thoroughbreds, but more as a set of constantly mutating hybrids. In fact, given the historical disjunctions between the core elements, as well as the problematic properties of their conceptual relationships to one another, the compounds should be viewed as continuous exercises in open-ended negotiation. Notwithstanding their structural deficiencies and their contingent properties, these compounds and the way they are formed from the foundational base remain highly significant. In drawing upon the plurality of ideas in the form of segmented traditions, principles, and impulses, and in cultivating persuasive melds of these differentiated strands, it is these compounds that shape and direct the organization of political argument and, thereby, the profile of policy agendas, debates, decisions, and outcomes. Accordingly, the cultivation of such compounds is central to an understanding of how ideas are woven into the fabric of American political conduct.

The significance of the compounds, however, is not confined to the mere state of their existence. The way they are formed and cultivated reveals a complex ecology that is dependent upon a set of understandings concerning the appropriate rules of engagement with the cluster of core ideas. These implicit expectations over working practices are integral to the effective functioning of such a disparate set of foundational reference points. Indeed, there can be little doubt that without the supportive conventions that facilitate the interaction between the ideational matrix and the construction of derivative compounds, the level of conflict within American society over its multiple values would be more severe in tone and more socially polarizing in effect. The normative requirements of working with such a set of primary colours not only underpins and protects the medium of exchange between them, but also affords another explanatory and political dimension to the mix.

It has been increasingly evident during the course of the analysis that ideas matter a very great deal in American politics. Political conflict is not only expressed forcibly in terms of ideas but is in many respects deeply rooted in the meaning and weight given to ideas. The compulsive usage of high principle and foundational precepts in political discourse is a defining characteristic of a society that remains highly self-conscious over the ethical idiom of its origins and purpose. Europeans tend to look quizzically upon the uninhibited use of moral absolutes in America's public sphere. Their perplexed response is compounded by the way issues are mined at depth with explorations that persistently address the most contested elements in the historical, republican, and liberal lexicons. Americans for their part often portray themselves as running the risk of being exploited by their preoccupations with deep principle. So much so in fact that they occasionally feel compelled to remind both themselves, and the world outside, of their need to adopt a more realistic outlook and to achieve a greater responsiveness to national self-interest in the formulation of policy decisions.

There is no question that America possesses a conspicuous disposition for raising both the temperature and the stakes in respect to their usage of political ideas. They routinely dismantle positions and policies, and subject them to intense value-based inspections. More often than not, this type of forensic examination pursues the logic of its own analysis to the point of unpacking even the most sophisticated constructions and reducing them to their elemental foundations. In other societies, this competitive unravelling of political positions would occasion serious polarization, or at least a form of reckless intransigence. And yet in the United States, dissection on this scale is not normally associated with any serious social costs, or risks to social cohesion. This is because ideational licence is tempered by social and attitudinal constraint. The fundamentalist character of compound formation and critique is matched by a pragmatic outlook that moderates the effects of the enriched ingredients of American political argument. In essence, Americans have developed ways of accommodating high principle and deep value within the parameters of negotiable differences, and of limiting discretion at the very same time as its range is affirmed.

This pattern of self-restraint possesses a number of characteristics and carries with it several implications. At its heart is an evident pre-requirement for any effective ideational compound in this context. A compound has to be a plausible and persuasive device for collating expressions and interpretations of the several baseline values. In one way or another, every compound needs to acknowledge and address each one of the individual components in the matrix of American principles. In effect, a compound has to establish an exchange relationship with each recognized strand of value; it has to respond to the need to create a broad appeal across different ideational bases. At the same time, it reaffirms and reinforces the segmented composition of the compound's constitutive elements and, as a consequence, the nature of the compound itself.

From the material presented in Chapters 10–15, it can be seen that compounds such as capitalism, liberalism, conservatism, and populism remain composites of multiple references to the core values. Each compound remains viable through its continuing engagement with these separate foundational bases. The proponents and advocates of a compound attempt to optimize the interpretative case for a fit between it and the plural nature of the republic's ideational traditions. Owing to the segmented composition of the base with its lack of ordered hierarchy or organic unity, and because of the competitive and contingent character of each compound's relationship with other compounds and the base, the net effect is that compounds remain thematically and structurally disjointed.

The coalitional format of these compounds means that they should be seen neither as fixed entities nor as points of fused meaning. Compounds are exactly that: composites that accommodate rather than synthesize the segmented plurality of core values. Because a successful compound has to possess a recognizable relationship with the full gamut of core values, the result is not a meld so much as a device by which the separate expressions of several values are effectively held in state of coexistence. Furthermore, because of the need of both to link each component element to a foundational theme of American value, and to ensure that all foundational themes receive appropriate representation, the advocacy of compounds is instrumental in preserving and deepening a tradition in the usage of ideas.

At one level, therefore, compounds reflect an expansive licence in the interpretation and application of ideas. At another level, however, compounds are not the result of a free range of selections and eclectic improvisations. Their construction and usage are guided by traditions of interpretation that draw upon, and are conditioned by, the cumulative experience of working with core elements that are taken to be separate yet concurrent phenomena. In essence, as the volume of interpretive appeals to foundational values increases in the quest to enhance the status of various compounds, so the source base of America's differentiated values is continually underscored. The matrix is habitually reaffirmed as conceptually segmented and only capable of being transposed into contemporary political discourse in the form of assemblages that are unmistakably evocative of that base.

Another aspect of this dynamic between the elemental matrix and the compounds derived from it is the way the latter always possess some generic basis of comparability. This may not always be apparent in the intense competition for political advantage. Nevertheless upon closer inspection, areas of shared strategic outlook become evident across different compounds. This common heritage of having to engage with the same set of high disparate values, in order to lay any claim to legitimacy, means that the interaction between compounds is not as negative and divisive as may ostensibly seem to be the case. On the contrary, political activity made through and on behalf of the compounds serves to underline their common purpose of assembling differing permutations of the same strands, and in doing so to give successive and reinforcing endorsements to the same strategic imperative.

While those affiliated to different compounds will oppose one another on a range of criteria, they will have very little incentive to allow their enmity to extend to the point of contesting, for example, the principle of liberty, the value of democracy, or the indispensability of the rule of law. On logical, prudential, normative, and even familial grounds, opposing positions have little to gain by seeking to differentiate themselves from one another by explicit reference to basic values.

This is not to deny that adversaries will seek to impugn each others' interpretation of such values, or to question the depth of their attachment to these common principles. What it does mean, however, is that political conflict is rarely pushed to the point where one party explicitly disparages, or distances itself, from a core value. It also means that a very vociferous and active culture of political dispute almost invariably stops short of allowing conflict to generate fundamentalist critiques— let alone any principled rejections—of any core value. Quite the reverse. Intense adversarial behaviour is marked by a conspicuous impulse to reiterate the inclusive presence of all the core values and to confirm them as a medium of political exchange and communication rather than as the object of contestation.

IDEAS AND NARRATIVES: THE ATTITUDINAL CREED

The conclusion that follows from a close examination of compounds and their dynamics is the underlying significance of the social disposition in maintaining the collegiate nature of America's core values. The forceful, and even flamboyant, interplay of principles is a conspicuous feature of American politics but it remains one that is predicated upon containment. For every example of a political argument, position, or movement seeking justification by reference to a single principle and to a purist logic flowing from it, there is a wealth of evidence indicating the presence of a more ecumenical outlook. It is the latter that qualifies and conditions narrow rationales into a broader engagement with the other key values in the American lexicon. Each case of an apparent preoccupation with a particular element has, therefore, to be set against the counterpoint of an advanced social impulse to accept that any one value can only coexist within the ecology of other central principles.

This impulse is at one and the same time both capacious and disciplined. It takes as a matter of deeply rooted experience that different ideas have a proximity to one another and that to feature one in particular is to offer a manifestly incomplete and ill-proportioned conception of a complex form of coexistence. As a consequence, political intercourse is marked by an organized facility that not only allows each core idea to be persistently qualified by the others, but ensures that political settlements are synonymous with securing a viable equilibrium between the variable logics of individual principles. What this amounts to is a less focused attachment to principle so much as a developed aptitude for the currency of ideas, and, in particular, a habituated understanding of how multiple ideas work in a social setting. Participants in American politics are usually highly adept at using indigenous constructions of values because they operate in an environment where this is expected as a sign of professional competence and cultural authenticity. In order to achieve leverage and remain effective, politicians need to be proficient in handling ideas and in relating issues to foundational principles.

The high status that is simultaneously afforded to different values is not simply a matter of individuals demonstrating a personal inclination to be fair minded, or to be consciously dedicated to achieving equitable, balanced, and holistic outcomes in which all values are given due expression. A strong social component relating to established custom, public trust, political utility, and normative prescription contributes towards maintaining the spread and coequal significance of America's core ideas. History, or at least America's conception of its past experience and the narratives that depict it, has been especially instrumental in generating the supportive attitudes required to allow a cluster of ideas to remain at the centre of social identity.

As this study has repeatedly conveyed, the course and meaning of American historical memory is fused with notions concerning the origins, authority, and continuity of those ideas that are considered to be both contemporary principles and governing bequests. In a host of different ways, the construction of historical consciousness is closely entwined with the cultural salience of ideas whose seminal significance rests upon their status as both foundational signatures and timeless agencies. The overall effect is one of a cultivated interdependency between the past and the present through the assigned imprimatur of ideas. In the United States, key ideas are consciously drawn from historical experiences. Their seminal status and their continuing pertinence are successively underlined by a compulsive recourse to the past and its avowed linkage to the present. By the same token, American history is shaped by the conception of ideas and by the need for them to have an organizing structure. In many respects, this has had the effect of history being mediated through the theme of ideational continuity. This equates not so much to a history *of* ideas, but to history *as* ideas.

America's core ideas, therefore, are habitually presented in the guise of history; a history which is in itself a construct of a social conviction in the indigenous force of ideas within the American republic. Just as the currency and authenticity of these seminal ideas are widely believed to have been formed in the past, so history is taken to be the chief instrument of both their transmission to, and their operation within, the present. Ideas have come to signify a continuing historical experience. Ideas and the compounds drawn from them are successively configured and reconfigured through the historical narratives that give meaning, shape, and direction to them. The constitutive narratives surrounding the core ideas provide not only a form of embedded continuity but also the licence and the means by which to engage in an open process of interpretive adaptation.

In this way, ideas are instrumental not only in eliciting an understanding of historical processes in the United States, but also in projecting the past into the present. As a consequence, historical references and frames of meaning feed seamlessly into public discourse. Sometimes this is depicted as a unilinear process of passively receiving an ideational inheritance and acknowledging its maturity and continuity as a fundamental influence. At other times, it is seen primarily as a reactive impulse born out of a sense of discontinuity with the past. Here the emphasis is one of restoration and the need to establish an authority by which contemporary attitudes and positions can be legitimized in relation to foundational ideals. Instead of the passive acceptance of an assumed tradition, this relationship to ideas is more akin to an active process of creating constructions of historical continuity. Both these dynamics have the effect of deepening and intensifying the symbiotic connection between America's core ideas and its conception of history. As history is increasingly used as a vehicle for ideas, so the discussion and exchange of ideas becomes increasingly permeated with interpretations of American history; leading in its turn to a further tightening of the circular process in which history is employed to explicate, elucidate, and reinforce the presence of an ideational fixture.

The interpenetration of American history and ideas is further deepened by the customary addition of a national narrative, as well as a sense of moral purpose, to the cumulative inference of an underlying unity. The idea of a national, and nationalizing, history has had great leverage in the United States primarily because it offers the prospect of making sense and affording order to the tumultuous speed and scale of America's settlement. This kind of epic history has also had to include those ideas that were either contemporaneously or retrospectively enshrined as foundational in status. As a result, each central idea is marked by its own national narrative, which by the nature of such an inclusive device, carries the strong implication of a historically embedded synthesis of values. In this light, the contribution of historical, national, and moral consciousness is often taken to be one of substantive integration based upon an ultimate yet necessary consistency of ideas.

This outlook is closely aligned to the common understanding of America as a society that it is defined by, and gives physical expression, to a creed. In this context, the United States is widely declared to be an exceptional nation with an exceptional allegiance to the principles of an exceptional creed. Accordingly, American society is often equated with a civil religion or a product of ideological exertion.[58] When President Bush wanted to mobilize the nation and restore belief in itself and its special status, he repeatedly resorted to making American identity synonymous with the embodiment and trusteeship of principles:

Americans of every party and background, Americans by choice and by birth, are bound to one another in the cause of freedom.... We felt the unity and fellowship of our nation when freedom came under attack, and our response came like a single hand over a single heart. And we can feel that same unity and pride whenever America acts for good, and the victims of disaster are given hope, and the unjust encounter justice, and the captives are set free.[59]

In the war on terror, the President persistently underlined his view that America was engaged in a conflict on the part 'of all who believe in progress and pluralism, tolerance and freedom...I ask you to uphold the values of America, and remember why so many have come here. We are in a fight for our principles'.[60] A national narrative of this order relies for its effect upon the theme of affirmation

[58] For example, see Anatol Lieven, *America: Right or Wrong* (London: HarperCollins, 2004), pp. 41–59.

[59] President George W. Bush, 'Inaugural Address', 20 January 2005, http://www.whitehouse.gov/news/releases/2005/01/20050120-1.html.

[60] President Bush, 'Address to a Joint Session of Congress and the American People', 20 September 2001', http://www.whitehouse.gov/news/releases/2001/09/20010920-8.html.

but another equally influential context of American values owes its leverage to the expression of loss and the need for renewal. Here the creative interplay of ideas and narrative takes the form of a 'jeremiad' in which an indictment of social corruption and spiritual dissolution is conjoined to an urgent appeal for repentance and restoration. The pattern is one of aroused contrition leading to a renewed covenant with primary values and, with it, the reclamation of a prior state of enhanced existence. The same set of ideas, therefore, can be configured into a vindication, or alternatively a critique, of the contemporary order and one that requires a continuous monitoring of its condition.[61]

Despite the habitual and official correlation of the United States with the force of collective principle, the linkage is a far more subtle and multilayered relationship than the standardized depiction of a nation unified by values. In fact, it is legitimate to claim that the chemistry of ideas in the United States is less significant for its inference of creedal integrity and clarity of substance, and more noteworthy for its contribution to those behavioural traits required to accommodate such a mix of principles within a self-consciously principled society. The skills, intuitions, and habits associated with working alongside different elemental ideas are themselves assisted by the various conceptualizations of a national history and of an organized narrative of American progression. It is reasonable to go further and to assert that the very notion of a set creed, as well as its embedded analogue of a teleological national history, are both products and representations of a medium for managing the consequences of a deep adherence to different values. Rather than the content or the logic of those ideas, it is the idiom within which they are located, and through which they are sustained in coexistent proximity, that constitutes the real creed, i.e. the political imagination and logistical acumen of working with a plurality of discrete values in a way that affords licence whilst at the same time cultivating restraint.

Whether this *attitudinal creed* is reducible to any precise pattern of causal factors or analytical characteristics is beyond the scope of this study. This advanced faculty might well be categorized as an intuitive tradition, rational calculation, attitudinal trait, or a prudential outlook. It might also be characterized as a conditioned reflex, a normative response, a cognitive arrangement, or an instrumental device. In all likelihood, the faculty of multiple engagement is probably derived from a combination of some or all of them. But what is more significant than its compositional properties, or its points of origin, is the central fact of its presence and the consequences that flow from it.

In focusing upon the attitudinal subtleties of ideational interplay, this analytical approach offers different insights not only into the nature of conflict in the United States but also into the society's capacity for moderating, suspending, and even resolving internal divisions. The attitudinal *creed* is a complex one that has been formed around the society's veneration for values, which are either implicitly or explicitly at variance with one another. The provenance afforded to such a

---

[61] See Sacvan Bercovitch, *The American Jeremiad* (Madison, WI: University of Wisconsin Press, 1978).

melange of ideas continues to pose a challenge not just to American society in the political management of its foundational ideas, but also to the observer looking for explanations of how an ideational mix of this magnitude operates in practice. The present study has sought to establish a base for examining the dynamics of coexistence between ideas within the American milieu. During the course of what has been an intensive analysis, this approach has opened up different vantage points and interpretive possibilities for examining issues in American politics. The utility of adopting a form of access commensurate with the multidimensionality of the subject matter has been reflected in the various cases featured in the previous chapters. But it would seem especially appropriate at this juncture to address three particular points of controversy that will further underline the importance of incorporating both the matrix of values and the customary rules of ideational engagement within any explanatory structure.

'CULTURE WARS'

Earlier in this chapter, the 'two cultures' argument was appraised in the terms in which the conflict is most commonly expressed: as a polarization of outlooks and positions leading to its characterization as a 'values divide'.[62] Along these lines, politics is cited as having increasingly become centred upon culture not just because so many points of contention feature an explicitly moral component, but because the scale and depth of the enmity generated by such issues are regarded as indicative of a lack of cultural cohesion. Many political divisions, therefore, are easily transmuted into being about culture and, thereupon, cited as further evidence of an explicit cleavage at the heart of American society.

The notion of a cultural schism is an elegant and popular portrayal of the type of political conflict that afflicts much of American politics. Nevertheless, it is also one that raises a host of analytical and interpretive questions. For example, it can be claimed that in a society distinguished by its veneration of foundational values, and their linkage to national identity, the assertion of a values-based bifurcation of society can amount to something of an overstatement. And yet, it is precisely on these grounds that the argument of division can seem at its most persuasive. In many respects, it is culturally justifiable to resort to the rhetorical force of the moral dimension in order to underline the severity of the conflict. In other words, it is precisely the United States' close association with an ethos of core values that makes the impulse to equate differences with moral dichotomies all the more appealing. In effect, it can be said that to substantiate the assertion of a deep division in American society, it is in fact necessary to characterize it as a values divide, i.e. the most significant way that the United States can be split and, therefore, the most effective method of conveying the presence of a deep disjunction.

[62] White, *The Values Divide.*

However, in examining ways to make the claim of a values divide plausible it would first be necessary to show how such a condition of moral conflict is qualitatively different from previous formations of political division. The usage of the term 'culture wars' implies a quantum shift not only in terms of the intensity of conflict, but also in respect to a change in the conventional style of political exchange. To demonstrate such a shift would require proof that American politics prior to the onset of 'culture wars' was notably less preoccupied, or driven, by values-based arguments. This would be as difficult to substantiate as the claim that there had come into existence two nations, or two Americas, existing in tandem with entirely different sets of values and priorities; and producing in their wake a syndrome of intransigence, intolerance, and dissolution.

Other forms of scepticism rely less on history, tradition, or logic and more upon empirical evidence of opinion configuration and voting behaviour. Morris Fiorina, for example, takes issue with those who claim that there is a cultural divide with each side possessing widely divergent views over principles, objectives, and the role of government in society. Fiorina's examination of attitudinal databases leads him to conclude that the debates over values in the public sphere have been exaggerated and distorted by the political class. While it is true that Republican, Democratic, and media elites have become polarized, the broad mass of the American citizenry are tolerant in manner and moderate, centrist, and even nuanced and ambivalent in their views. Political choices may have become more sharply divided but voter positions have not followed the same template of dogmatic bifurcation.[63] Others agree and point out, for instance, that it is difficult to substantiate the case for an agitatedly divided society when half the electorate regularly fails to vote, and where the public is both accustomed, and inclined, to compromise over difficult issues.[64] While the Pew Research Center acknowledged that there were indications of rising partisanship, its *Trends 2005* survey also 'confirmed that a number of consensus values endure' and that it 'remained the case that the points of public agreement on major subjects have been largely overshadowed by the partisan tenor of the times'.[65]

In spite of these reservations over the actual existence of a cultural schism or the presence of 'two nations', what cannot be denied is the ferocious intransigence and intemperate language that marks the conduct of those on both sides of a conflict that does exist over values. This may not amount to a de facto division running systematically throughout American society but it does constitute a severe strain upon the society's resource base for negotiated settlements and common action.

[63] Morris P. Fiorina, *Culture War? The Myth of a Polarized America* (Needham Heights, MA: Longman, 2004).

[64] See Alan Wolfe, *One Nation, after All: What Middle-Class Americans Really Think about God, Country, Family, Racism, Welfare, Immigration, Homosexuality, Work, The Right, The Left and Each Other* (New York: Penguin, 1999); Jay Tolson, 'How Deep the Divide? Scholars and Pundits Don't Agree on the Meaning of Red and Blue—or Whether the Nation is Deeply Split', *U.S News & World Report*, 25 October 2004.

[65] PewResearch Center, *Trends 2005* (Washington, DC: Pew Research Center, 2005), p. 13, http://pewresearch.org/publications/trends/trends2005.pdf.

The mutual disrespect can be gauged by the following examples of the genre. The acrimonious nature of the highly voluble schism can be gauged by the titles adopted for the works of polemicists on both sides of the argument in the Bush era. They include on the liberal side *Lies and the Lying Liars Who Tell Them: A Fair and Balanced Look at the Right*; *The I Hate Republicans Reader: Why the GOP is Totally Wrong about Everything*; *Crimes against Nature: How George W. Bush and His Corporate Pals Are Plundering the Country and Hijacking Our Democracy*; and *Banana Republicans: How the Right Wing Is Turning America into a One-Party State.*[66] The conservative ripostes have been equally pungent in tone: *Liberalism Is a Mental Disorder: Savage Solutions*; *The Vast Left Wing Conspiracy: The Untold Story of How Democratic Operatives, Eccentric Billionaires, Liberal Activists, and Assorted Celebrities Tried to Bring Down a President—and Why They'll Try Even Harder Next Time*; and *Unhinged: Exposing Liberals Gone Wild.*[67]

This kind of animus has often been attributed to a high level of frustration generated by agendas remaining unfulfilled, by the high incidence of institutional gridlock, and by the conviction on the part of each side that its opponents occupy an establishment position with influence that is disproportionate to their numbers. Implicit in this antagonism, however, is another conditioning influence that relates much more closely to the theme of this study. This is the belief shared on both sides that their respective adversaries have infringed both the aggregative conventions of compound construction and the spirit of working with the matrix of America's core values. In this respect, the antagonism is fuelled not merely by the content of positions and proposals, but by what these substantive agendas signify in the way they have been arrived at and subsequently defended. In effect, each side in the 'culture war' is motivated as much by what is perceived to be their opponents' attitude or approach to politics as it is by their material positions on issues.

When an adversary is seen to be deliberately misreading or misinterpreting a core value, or else exploiting an ambiguity or mixed tradition with a determination to maximize an advantage to the detriment of any collective notion of proper conduct, the outcome will be one of increased suspicion and decreased cooperation. A matrix of coexistent ideas is a delicate and subtle phenomenon. It is dependent upon an attitude structure that allows for the social mediation of

[66] Al Franken, *Lies and the Lying Liars Who Tell Them: A Fair and Balanced Look at the Right* (New York: Penguin, 2003); Clint Willis, *The I Hate Republicans Reader: Why the GOP is Totally Wrong about Everything* (New York: Thunder's Mouth Press, 1 September 2003); Robert F. Kennedy, Jr., *Crimes against Nature: How George W. Bush and His Corporate Pals Are Plundering the Country and Hijacking Our Democracy* (New York: HarperCollins, 2004); Sheldon Rampton and John Stauber, *Banana Republicans: How the Right Wing Is Turning America into a One-Party State* (New York: Jeremy P. Tarcher/Penguin, 2004).

[67] Ann Coulter, *Treason: Liberal Treachery from the Cold War to the War on Terrorism* (New York: Crown Forum, 2003); Michael Savage, *Liberalism Is a Mental Disorder: Savage Solutions* (Nashville, TN: Nelson Current, 2005); Byron York, *The Vast Left Wing Conspiracy: The Untold Story of How Democratic Operatives, Eccentric Billionaires, Liberal Activists, and Assorted Celebrities Tried to Bring Down a President—and Why They'll Try Even Harder Next Time* (New York: Crown Forum, 2005); Michelle Malkin, *Unhinged: Exposing Liberals Gone Wild* (Washington, DC: Regnery Publishing, 2005).

the plural values. As a consequence, those political participants who see their own interpretations of these values as exclusively authentic, and who zealously try to force issues to a conclusion, do so at the risk of undermining the source of their own claims to legitimacy.

The terms and conditions of America's reputed 'culture wars' possess strong resonances with this type of deterioration. Adversaries do not merely denounce the substance of each other's policy positions. More significantly, they object to the motives, style, and behaviour that are assumed to underlay the adoption of such robust and aggressive postures. Each perceives the other as engaging in a wilful misuse of American values and a dangerous misunderstanding of what is required for this panoply of ideas to be managed in a social setting. In accusing each other of reckless excess, bad faith, and defiant betrayal, adversaries not only create a deepening dynamic of distrust but also exert severe strain upon the channels and protocols of ideational accommodation. As a consequence of this dynamic, it becomes evident that the widely acclaimed phenomenon of cultural politics is less about the clarity of palpable positions and more about a substratum of political life that becomes increasingly evident as the claims of infringement rise in volume and intensity.

TRADITION OF PROGRESS

Although American society assigns a high status and value to progress, it also possesses a strong adherence to the forces and presumptions of tradition. Like progress, the appeal of tradition is manifold and has the capacity to reduce a broad range of phenomena to its own criteria. But while progress has an evident orientation towards inner-directed and future-oriented change through liberated reason, critical intelligence, and freedom of action, tradition is associated with the forces of intuition, instinct, and caution. Traditionalism is concerned with the uncertainty of gain but more specifically with the expense of loss. Traditionalists place their energy and trust in the service of what already exists rather than risking the present for an unknown and possibly dangerous future. American society and politics have been strongly influenced by the compulsion to temper the iconoclasm of progress with a measured appreciation of historical inheritance and established custom. This respect for the past is reflected in a variety of social forms and practices. They range from America's high incidence of religious observance to its attachment to numerous institutional checks and balances; and from the continuity of social hierarchies through inherited wealth, educational privilege, and other forms of exclusiveness to its veneration of those foundational values embedded in the Founding Fathers' eighteenth-century Constitution.

Notwithstanding the individual significance of these strands of traditionalism, it is America's historical consciousness that is probably the most notable element in the republic's capacity for retrospection. In *Mystic Chords of Memory*,[68] Michael Kammen examines the emergence of an American tradition of tradition. He finds that in large measure it was the result of a concerted response to a perceived lack of appreciation of what was being lost in an increasingly protean social order. Kammen poses the question of when and how the United States became 'a land of the past [and] a culture with a discernible memory'.[69] His answer is that there was a conscious drive to establish an American history, and to secure the past and, with it, the future. Kammen surveys the social construction of historical tradition and the way that it developed into a profusion of forms, commemorations, and symbols. The emergence of a national narrative and of a cultivated attachment to the past in turn reflected the needs and anxieties of a society which had become concerned over its lack of anchorage. In the middle of the nineteenth century, for example, America was widely seen to be a standing repudiation of the past and to be a society united by a conception of the future rather than by any ties to history. Accordingly, for most of the nineteenth century, American history was rarely included in the standard school curriculum. This outlook changed dramatically in the late nineteenth century and early twentieth century when indifference towards tradition and historical memory was transformed into a passionate interest in the past and in the value of recollection, preservation, and revival.

Several factors are thought to have been pertinent to this shift. They include the claim that history and tradition had become surrogates for religion and faith in an era increasingly dominated by science, technology, and social Darwinism. Another factor is said to be the onset of mass immigration, which had generated severe challenges over American identity. Kammen also points to the significance of a postulated dynamic of historical interest that is activated by a prior condition of disinterest. In effect, the sheer rootlessness of a society geared towards a condition of flux in the service of an indeterminate future ultimately produced a corrective and proportionately accelerated attachment to a national memory and with it a comprehending frame of reference for meaning and judgement. It is acknowledged that the history produced during such periods of renaissance can be manufactured to serve various contemporary needs and, as a consequence, will often be selective in construction and biased in tone. Nevertheless, the drive for historical consciousness—however flawed in precision and purpose—indicates the presence of a cultural disposition towards eliciting continuity and valuing tradition. Equally, it underlines a susceptibility towards assessing the present against criteria drawn from the past.

The attachment to, and usage of, the past is particularly conspicuous when anxiety over the present is transmuted into a perception of a break with history, which in its turn arouses a heightened desire to recapture the essence of a previous era. This sense of history is oriented not so much to continuity as

---

[68] Michael Kammen, *Mystic Chords of Memory: The Transformation of Tradition in American Culture* (New York: Knopf, 1991).

[69] Ibid., p. 7.

to loss. Kammen regards the period following the Second World War as one which evoked a 'pronounced sense of discontinuity between past and present'.[70] Michael Elliot takes a different view.[71] In looking back from the late 1990s, Elliot observes how the 1950s had become the defining expression of social harmony, economic prosperity, and national purpose to all those who were troubled by the contemporary strains and accelerated changes of post-cold war America. In this light, the 1950s not only seemed like a lost 'golden age', but was one that could be recovered and reinstated. Although Elliot is clear that both elements of the equation were created myths, he, like Kammen, recognizes the power of historical memory in the United States.

The conscious evocation of memory was a central component in the appeal of President Ronald Reagan in the late 1970s and 1980s. During his presidency, President Reagan openly sought to lead the country by fashioning a symbolic and nostalgic resonance with the 1950s. In this campaign, he was following a well-worn American tradition in which history is used to substantiate policy positions at the same time that ideas are presented in the form of history. Like many successful leaders, movements, and campaigns before and since, he knew how to combine a radical critique of the present with the construction of a renewable past.[72] In other words, in America, the call of tradition can and has been used to support reform, mobilize transformative change, and even secure progress.

The relationship between tradition and progress in American society is generally depicted as one of polar opposites. They are often used to define and substantiate opposing forces in American political argument. For example, while reform liberalism is generally equated with rational inquiry and informed critique in the service of individual emancipation and social improvement, conservatives are reputed to give a higher priority to the need to preserve the social fabric and the inheritance of history from the disruptive intervention of 'progressives'. When President Bush won re-election to the presidency in 2004, both his programme and his assiduous cultivation of the evangelical constituency prompted commentators to characterize the result as a triumph of faith and unreason over intelligence reason. Garry Wills, for example, speculated over whether America 'could still be called an Enlightened nation'.[73] Although it had been a celebrated 'product of Enlightenment values'[74] in the past, Wills claimed that the United States had come to resemble its enemies:

---

[70] Ibid., p. 533.

[71] Michael Elliot, *The Day before Yesterday: Reconsidering America's Past, Rediscovering the Present* (New York: Simon & Schuster, 1996).

[72] William K. Muir, Jr., 'Ronald Reagan: The Primacy of Rhetoric', in Fred I Greenstein (ed.), *Leadership in the Modern Presidency* (Cambridge, MA: Harvard University Press, 1988), pp. 260–95; Robert Dallek, *Ronald Reagan: The Politics of Symbolism* (Cambridge, MA: Harvard University Press, 1999), chs. 2, 3, 5; Gil Troy, *Morning in America: How Ronald Reagan Invented the 1980's* (Princeton, NJ: Princeton University Press, 2005).

[73] Garry Wills, 'The Day the Enlightenment Went Out', *New York Times*, 7 November 2004.

[74] Ibid.

The secular states of modern Europe do not understand the fundamentalism of the American electorate. It is not what they had experienced from this country in the past. In fact, we now resemble those nations less than we do our putative enemies. Where else do we find fundamentalist zeal, a rage at secularity, religious intolerance, fear of and hatred for modernity? ... It is not too early to start yearning back toward the Enlightenment.[75]

Even though the presentation of such forcible opinions attempt to draw on the apparent schism between progress and tradition, the actual relationship between these two working characterizations of American life is much more ambiguous and much less dichotomous than it is commonly reputed to be.

In general terms, the allusions to both progress and tradition are used as a critique of the present and a reaction against the status quo. Moreover they are both employed in a holistic manner to provide a collective centre of meaning and a point of departure for normative assessment. In a more specific sense, the references to progress and tradition in American political discourse not only reflect the existence of comparable attitude structures in relation to values and ideas, but suggest a close and substantive relationship between the two categories themselves. In the course of American development and in respect to contemporary outlooks, the theme of progress has taken on many of the attributes more commonly associated with tradition. The necessity of, and the assumptions surrounding, progress have become an intuitive part of the American experience and the outlook emanating from it. By the same token, American tradition is strongly conditioned by the notion of progress and by its continuity within American identity. In the same way that tradition is seen as supporting progress, so successive change is commonly constructed as a tradition. In sum, progress by tradition becomes conflated with a tradition of progress. As a consequence, it is plausible to argue that there exists 'a relentlessly dialogical relationship between the values of tradition and progress (or modernism) in American culture'.[76]

The wider significance of the way progress and tradition can transcend one another in American political discussion is that the mass of mainstream opinion in the centre of the political spectrum will experience comparable resonances with the claims of both progress and tradition. Even though they may be employed in a polarized way, the historical, explanatory, and prescriptive properties associated with progress and tradition evoke a complex arrangement of related alignments. The significance of this mixture of idioms is that it underlines the dynamic properties of American commonality and the way that ostensibly discordant themes run concurrently within an attitude structure that is conditioned by central principles infused with different historical narratives, social impulses, and political memories.

The intricate juxtaposition of tradition and progress within the American condition is well represented in the *World Value Surveys* conducted by the University of Michigan. The Surveys plot individual national cultures according to two broad categories. The first relates to the degree of attachment to traditional values.

[75] Wills, 'The Day the Enlightenment Went Out'.
[76] Kammen, *Mystic Chords of Memory*, p. 13.

These are identified as those values that give priority to family cohesion, religious doctrine, and patriotic instinct. Traditionalist societies are distinguished by a deference to authority and by a belief in absolute moral standards, which together lead to the rejection of abortion, euthanasia, suicide, and divorce. The second category is defined by the 'quality of life'. This theme addresses how values can be influenced by the level of insecurity experienced in a society, and by the need for individuals to concern themselves with the imperative to maintain their own survival. People with a low quality of life dwell upon the needs for survival and, accordingly, tend to be fearful of what is seen to be new, different, or challenging to a settled order of marginal existence. Those who have little pattern of security, or even of a supply of food, tend to have a heightened intolerance towards anything, or anyone, that might threaten the tenuous sources of subsistence (e.g. outgroups such as foreigners, gays and lesbians, AIDS victims, the mentally handicapped). As societies develop, it is thought that they improve their quality of life and become more open-textured, pluralist, and tolerant. Once survival can be taken for granted, the priorities shift 'from an overwhelming emphasis on economic and physical security toward an increasing emphasis on subjective well-being, self-expression, and quality of life'.[77] Individuals are permitted and even encouraged to cultivate the values of personal emancipation and development within a context of social trust and political moderation.

Strongly associated with this movement away from survival values is the erosion of traditional attachments and a progressive shift towards a more secular and rational outlook. When these two sets of values are assigned to two axes, then the predominant pattern of social development and cultural change is shown to follow a trend in which traditionalism is increasingly replaced by more secularism, whilst survival values progressively give way to a 'post-industrial' perspective (see Fig. 16.1).

This developmental template is epitomized by a clustering of western industrialized societies in the quadrant representing non-traditionalism and non-survivalism. However, a handful of these societies do not conform to this course of parallel development. Of these, the United States is arguably the most significant exception to the norm. Its rating on the quality of life dimension is typical of an advanced modern society. Nevertheless, its position on the tradition–secular axis is conspicuously atypical; especially for a society that is widely reputed to be the most dynamic, developed, and progressive expression of modernity. Far from being marginally more traditionalist than other comparable societies, the *World Value Surveys* indicate that the United States has a stronger attachment to traditional values than any European country except Ireland—and even Ireland shows signs of being in a transitionary process towards greater secularism. The level of traditionalism in the United States by contrast appears to be entrenched and static. In sum, the survey evidence suggests that American society possesses a stark and rare disjunction between two commonly accepted aspects of social

---

[77] Quoted from World Value Surveys, 'Introduction to World Vales Surveys', World Value Surveys, http://www.worldvaluessurvey.org/.

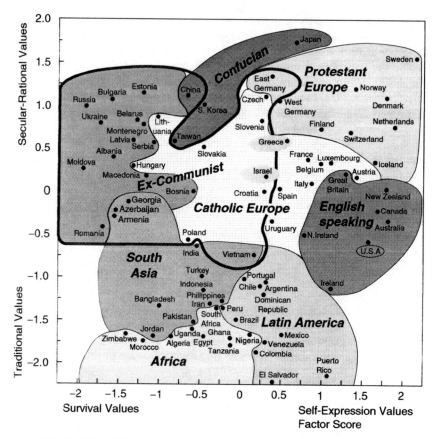

Figure 16.1. Inglehart Values Map. A cross-cultural survey of major human concern relating to two sectors: (i) traditional–secular/rational; and (ii) survival–self-expression

Source: World Values Survey (2000) (http://www.worldvaluessurvey.org/statistics/some_findings.html)

development. Even though the United States has helped to popularize the notion that these two dimensions are conjoined phenomena, America's own social matrix reveals them to be idiosyncratically disconnected.

The outlooks associated with progress and tradition run concurrently in American society and possess a complex set of dual properties. This is not to say that progress and tradition cannot become the organizing basis for social conflict. Much of the rhetoric in the 'two cultures' or 'two nations' debates is directly derived from attempts to define developments purely in terms of the relationship to either progress or tradition. The implication of these charges and counter-charges is that the properties associated with progress and tradition are in essence mutually exclusive and, as a consequence, their presence in society will invariably be marked by tension and conflict. While acknowledging the potential for differentiation, it is also important to underline the consequences that flow from the way that progress and tradition are commonly enfolded into one another within the context of American political argument. Ironically, this intermixture is particularly conspicuous in the very debate that is so often cited as demonstrating the segregation of progress and tradition.

Much of the polemic surrounding the 'culture wars' conflict is fuelled by the accusation that America's historical continuity has been needlessly and recklessly disrupted. Traditionalists claim that the agendas and achievements of reform liberalism have created a dysfunctional society and that this amounts to a break in the historical development of the United States. The liberal ethos of a pluralist and rights-based multicultural society is viewed by traditionalists both as a ruthless assault upon American identity and as a form of cultural disinheritance. However well-intentioned liberal reform may be, it is regarded as dangerously one-dimensional in character and too dismissive of the need to protect and cultivate the customs, conventions, and mutual understandings that inhabit a successful social order. This concern over rootlessness and social disintegration prompts calls to return to an earlier state of existence, or at least to a conception of the past that is considered to be recoverable.

Progressives make equally pungent assessments of traditionalism but, paradoxically, these rely in the main upon precisely the same format of an asserted historical disjunction for their critical leverage. The indictment here is that the settled order of evolutionary change in society is threatened by the disarray that will ensue from attempts to reverse the policies and practices that are alleged to have become integrated over time into the social fabric. Because their avowed aim is to return America to an idealized past, conservatives on the radical right or those aligned with the religious right, for example, are accused of possessing an ahistorical outlook, or even an anti-historical attitude, towards the processes of social adaptation. Under the guise of reunifying the country, these traditionalists stand accused of having a deluded sense of nostalgia that is divisive and iconoclastic in its effect.

In underlining the significance of habits and attitudes related to the conjunction of ideas and history in American politics, it may be thought that this is tantamount to reintroducing a Hartzian consensus back into the centre of the explanatory matrix. Hartz's celebrated reductionist account of American history and politics featured an attempt to fuse Lockian liberalism with Burkean conservatism. The intention was to demonstrate the presence of rational principle conjoined with irrational attachment. In essence, it was alleged that liberalism had irreversibly converged with conservatism within the unique conditions of the American republic. To Hartz, the very nature of America's social development meant that 'the "prejudice" of Burke in America was liberal'.[78] Because of a 'capacity to combine rock-ribbed traditionalism with high inventiveness [and] ancestor worship with ardent optimism',[79] America's moral unanimity could be accounted for as an irrational attachment to liberal principles. As a consequence of facilitating this conflation, American society can be said to have formed a unified and unvarying allegiance to a clear configuration of values.

---

[78] Hartz, *The Liberal Tradition in America*, p. 62.   [79] Ibid., p. 50.

The organizing rationale of this current study does not share the Hartzian conception of an ideationally homogenized society. While Hartz's holistic conception of America's foundational ideas is an attractive proposition, the argument in this analysis is that the Hartzian presumption is ill-founded at the conceptual, cognitive, and practical levels. The present analysis does not conclude that the advanced level of social integration and the high incidence of ideational reference can be equated with the direct expression of an explicit consensus based upon a narrow base of undifferentiated value. While this study has focussed upon the definition, usage, and implications of a set of core ideas, it has been evident throughout the course of this analysis that these ideas remain differentiated from each other. They are not part of a seamless generalized whole. Instead, they provide the elemental basis for the inventiveness of derivative compounds. The core ideas do not represent a fixed basis for political argument and action. They afford a medium and a language of political exchange within which the meaning and authenticity of the ideas themselves become compounded into the immediate objects of contested positions. For the plurality of key ideas to remain politically workable as concurrent sources of legitimacy, a complex and supple infrastructure of practical usage has evolved that both acknowledges their substantive difference, but also recognizes the historical and social cross-references that exist between them. Attempts to reduce this conceptual and attitudinal ecology to a single unified summation, or even to two generic constructs like progress and tradition, invariably fail to grasp either the fissiparous properties of American ideas, or the patterns of usage that allow them to coexist as separate centres of value.

UNIQUENESS AND UNIVERSALITY

Another example of an apparent duality obscuring an altogether more nuanced interpretive mix of core ideas is that provided by the issue of whether American identity is characterized by its sense of uniqueness or by its position as a source of universal value. These two conceptions relating to the essence, meaning, and role of the United States have often generated deep strains both within American society and in the relationships between the republic and the external world. The conceptual and political tensions between these two self-images are widely cited as major determinants of America's political position and historic purpose within the international sphere. Far from evoking a coherent and stable theme of itself, these two outlooks ostensibly suggest a schizoid condition that fosters a volatile approach to foreign policy-making with disruptive and even damaging consequences.

One dimension of American identity is firmly rooted in the conviction that it is a wholly exceptional society not just because of its position in the new world, but because its unique social chemistry allowed it to become synonymous with the sort of advanced social principles, which in most countries remain only aspirations. In the United States, liberty, equality, and democracy can be taken as merely traditional and self-evident features of America's indigenous experience. They are not regarded as a set of values to be striven for, so much as a set of pre-existing conditions to be protected and embellished. As a consequence, they are widely assumed to embody the essence of America, i.e. that which makes America different and renders it a new world.

The generic term 'American democracy', therefore, means far more than a condition of democracy existing in the United States. American democracy is seen as a qualitatively exceptional form of democracy whose idiosyncratic nature is derived from the peculiarities of America itself. According to this perspective, American democracy is not strictly comparable to other democracies. More precisely, the United States is not comparable to other nations because it is no ordinary democracy. It is taken to be the definitive democracy which other countries may seek to emulate but which never succeed in doing so because they lack the social chemistry of the New World. Democracy in this iteration is the climactic end product of America's naturalistic experience and, therefore, the supreme expression of America's inherent nature. It serves to define American identity in relation to outsiders, to explain and vindicate America's unequalled economic and social expansion, and to provide a reassuring defence against the degenerate corruption of the Old World. In short, American democracy conveys the idea that America is unique and that its democracy is not transferable.

This perspective is qualified by another, and equally traditional, interpretation of the American condition. It is the belief that American democracy is different in scope but not essentially in kind, and that, as a consequence, it should be seen more as a model democracy capable of being copied elsewhere. This conception of America as a vanguard of social progress has its roots in the early republic and especially in the combination of Enlightenment principles and the notion of a naturalized society. In the light of this perspective, human and social possibilities had been released in the emancipatory conditions of the New World. In Peter Gay's words, 'the American Revolution converted America from an importer of ideas into an exporter. What it exported was, of course, mainly itself, but that was a formidable commodity—the program of Enlightenment in practice'.[80]

While the Old World could only imagine and formulate sets of enlightened social proposals, the United States could be said to have enacted them. America, liberated from imperial rule and British orthodoxy, served to enhance an intellectual emancipation that in its turn led to a more secular and practical application of intelligence to human affairs. The belief in the systematic examination and appraisal of human nature and in the construction of political institutions on the basis of autonomous and collective experience was central to America's reputation for humane progress. Accordingly, America's professed contempt for history and established authority, together with its attachment to science and technology,

---

[80] Peter Gay, *The Enlightenment: an Interpretation*, vol. II: *The Science of Freedom* (London: Weidenfeld & Nicolson, 1970), p. 21. For a more measured exposition of the Enlightenment in the American context, see Robert A. Ferguson, *The American Enlightenment, 1750–1820* (Cambridge, MA: Harvard University Press, 1997).

practical utility, social progress, and personal liberty came to stand not only as a general inspiration to the rest of the world but as a realizable objective for other countries. America's status as a democracy may have been idiosyncratic and unusual, but not unique. In the spirit of the Enlightenment, American democracy can and has been seen as possessing a universal property. It suggests the possibility that America could act as an international example whose reputation as a model of democracy is equated with its applicability to other nations and cultures.

The implications of these two perspectives can be starkly different from one another. On many occasions, they are seen as constituting two sides of a deep dichotomy in American identity. On the basis of logic or instinct, the conceptions of America as either a unique entity, or a universal phenomenon, can be viewed not merely as alternatives but as two interpretative syndromes existing in a zero-sum relationship to one another. The circumstances and effects of America's historical idiosyncrasy have been strongly associated with international disengagement, isolationism, and cultural introspection. Conversely, the universalist depiction brings with it an emphasis upon outward engagement, expansive purpose, and the active propagation of the American model. In a more pronounced portrayal, universalism is viewed as being linked to American ideals and to the moral responsibility of acceding to them both at home and abroad. Uniqueness on the other hand can become synonymous with self-interest, unreflective nativism, and the view that the national interest rarely coincides with the international interest.

And yet despite the appearance of being mutually exclusive categories, the meanings ascribed to, and the usages associated, with uniqueness and universality reveal a close interdependency. Both concepts draw upon, and derive moral weight from, the same resource of American ideas. Both are grounded in the need to explicate those ideas. And both reflect the significance of these core ideas in arriving at an understanding both of America's existence and of the ramifications that flow from its prominence in a world which is traditionally regarded as being external to the United States. In the fluid and competitive medium of ideational constructions, the attributions of uniqueness and universality move in and out of fields of description, areas of normative prescription, and levels of analytical exposition. In the course of such a process, the characteristics in question become less differentiated from one another and can even reach a point where they can become interdependent upon one another. For example, just as a sense of uniqueness can be said to provide the necessary precondition for a commitment to transform the world according to American principles, so it can be argued that the conviction in the universal message of American democracy can only be founded upon an interior certainty in the status of its superlative uniqueness.

Arguments abound between 'universalists' on the one hand who assert that the United States constitutes a guiding exemplar for others on the basis of a common applicability of ideas and principles, and 'cultural essentialists' on the other who maintain that America is different in the same way that all nations are unique because of the idiosyncrasies social tradition, population mix, and historical experience. However, on closer inspection the premises of these arguments tend to fold into one another as exemplars are required to be outstanding, while the affirmation of great difference generally infers a wider purpose. From the patterns of usage in such a context, it becomes increasingly evident that both uniqueness and universality are based upon America's sense of moral distinction and political exceptionalism, which carries with it an intense interest in how America's heritage of principle is juxtaposed with a world of uncertain ethical status. This in turn reflects a deep concern over how various national narratives can relate to the theme of a select society and to its moral correlation with the existence of a singular covenant that allows for self-conscious distinction but also for exhortation in the midst of adversity as well as for expansive propagation and righteous conversion.

The United States posture during the cold war epitomizes how the crosscurrents of uniqueness and universality can be simultaneously significant in America's outlook upon global politics. America's belief in the spontaneity and universalism of the social dynamics supporting liberal democracy was affronted by the Soviet Union's rejection of the natural authenticity of the American way. To successive US administrations, communism represented a denial of America's own experience of nature. In effect, it amounted to a perversion of nature itself. American freedom was simply taken to mean genuine freedom. The defining cold war position adopted by the United States was set out in *NSC 68: Objectives and Programs for National Security* (1950).[81] In it, the conflict between communism and the United States was defined as 'momentous, involving the fulfilment or destruction not only of the Republic but of civilization itself'.[82] Given that the assault on free institutions was worldwide and that liberty was now conceived to be internationally indivisible, the confrontation with the Soviet Union 'impose(d) on us, in our own interests, the responsibility of world leadership'.[83]

The cold war drew the United States decisively onto the world stage and into a host of alliances that would ensure its active engagement in international politics on a permanent basis. It was no longer enough that American democratic values were transferable to other countries. It was now strategically and ideologically imperative that they were actually transferred to, and established in, as many nations as possible. The validity of America's democratic principles, and the sense of national purpose activated by these principles, had been given an international dimension. The text of the *NSC 68* made it clear that '[T]he assault on free institutions is world-wide now, and in the context of the present polarization of power a defeat of free institutions anywhere is a defeat everywhere'.[84] As a consequence, it was necessary for the United States to take

---

[81] *NSC 68: Objectives and Programs for National Security* (1950), http://www.fas.org/irp/offdocs/nsc-hst/nsc-68.htm.

[82] 'Background to the Present Crisis', *NSC 68: Objectives and Programs for National Security*.

[83] 'Conclusions and Recommendations', *NSC 68: Objectives and Programs for National Security*, http://www.fas.org/irp/offdocs/nsc-hst/nsc-68-cr.htm.

[84] 'The Underlying Conflict in the Realm of ideas and Values between the U.S. Purpose and the Kremlin Design', *NSC 68: Objectives and Programs for National Security*, http://www.fas.org/irp/offdocs/nsc-hst/nsc-68-4.htm.

the lead in building 'a successfully functioning political and economic system in the free world'.[85] According to this logic, it was 'only by practical affirmation, abroad as well as at home, of our essential values, that we [could] preserve our own integrity'.[86]

The cold war succeeded in polarizing world politics and in creating an ideological dichotomy in which coexistence was interpreted as illegitimate and where critical dissent was circumscribed for the greater good of America's war effort in the battle of ideas. The American disposition to regard 'truths to be self-evident'[87] was extended to American behaviour abroad to defend such truths. Democracy was equated not only with American democracy but with whatever American leaders and forces ascertained to be necessary to the American defence of the free world.

As a consequence, American foreign policy decisions and actions overseas came to be explained and defended according to a set of permanent first principles of cold war intentions and objectives. The prosecution of the cold war became a distinctly American responsibility and one characterized by American notions of virtue and vice. It was also an extrapolation of America's past development, and of the moral purpose and benign mission served by the nature of its unprecedented growth. The international confrontation with communism, therefore, was not merely a test of American democracy's universality; it was also a means by which America might revive itself through an enhanced self-awareness of its extraordinary democratic credentials.

Even sixty years after the Second World War and even with the conclusion of the cold war, America remains concerned over its precise relationship with the rest of the world and, in particular, with the integrity of its uniqueness in possessing a universal significance. American presidents have continued to articulate an inner sense of national identity and to mobilize public opinion over foreign policy objectives by reference to the narrative traditions and rhetorical instruments of exceptionalism.[88] The world continues to reflect America's own sense of itself and to facilitate a process of successive reaffirmation of America's peculiar democratic virtue. By the same token, America's self-professed role as the 'redeemer nation'[89] remains integral to its sense of historic purpose.

When the end of cold war era brought about the decline of communism, the collapse of the Soviet Union, and the emergence of the United States as the sole superpower, President Bush described it as 'a victory for all humanity'.[90] He

---

[85] 'Possible Courses of Action', *NSC 68: Objectives and Programs for National Security*, http://www.fas.org/irp/offdocs/nsc-hst/nsc-68-9.htm.

[86] 'The Underlying Conflict in the Realm of Ideas and Values between the U.S. Purpose and the Kremlin Design', *NSC 68: Objectives and Programs for National Security*.

[87] Declaration of Independence (1776).

[88] Trevor B. McCrisken, *American Exceptionalism and the Legacy of Vietnam: US Foreign Policy Since 1974* (Basingstoke, UK: Palgrave Macmillan, 2004).

[89] See Ernest L. Tuveson, *Redeemer Nation: The Idea of America's Millennial Role* (Chicago, IL: University of Chicago Press, 1968).

[90] President George H. W. Bush, 'Address before a Joint Session of the Congress on the State of the Union', 29 January 1991, http://www.presidency.ucsb.edu/ws/index.php?pid=19253.

continued: 'America's leadership is indispensable. Americans know that leadership brings burdens and sacrifices. But we also [know] why the hopes of humanity turn to us. We are Americans. We have a unique responsibility to do the hard word of freedom'.[91] President Bill Clinton, the first post-cold war chief executive, showed little sign of deviating from the established hybrid. In President Clinton's view, American democracy remained 'the envy of the world'.[92] Given that 'our mission is timeless',[93] it was necessary to retain American prominence: 'America must continue to lead the world we did so much to make.'[94] According to this perspective, the Old World might pose dangers to the United States, but it still provided a defining factor in America's democratic consciousness, and the chief reason behind the society's self-assurance in seeking to enlighten and redeem the remainder of humanity without compromising its own principles.

Since the end of the cold war, considerable speculation has arisen surrounding the question of whether the United States, by the very process of its pre-eminence, has paradoxically resulted in becoming indistinguishable from the rest of the world. According to the logic of Francis Fukuyama, the collapse of communism finally clarified America's international position. With the unqualified dominance of liberal democracy and with the culture of the free market assured, the United States and its values could be regarded as marking an 'end of history'. Despite its flaws, no other system of thought had survived the twentieth century. As a consequence, the United States not only stood as the predominant single superpower but as the archetype of a society that could be represented as the culminating point of social and political evolution.

The sentiments echoed by Fukuyama and others suggested that the United States might adopt a more consistent posture towards the rest of the world. In the terms of Louis Hartz's classic maxim, America possessed the kind of moral absolutism that impelled it either to withdraw from a recidivist world, or alternatively to transform it in line with America's own dispositions.[95] It could be said that Fukuyama's view had now neutralized Hartz's duality. With America's democratic supremacy and cultural hegemony assured, the world was now no longer qualitatively different to the United States. There was no reason for America to retreat into its own democracy because it would now only be withdrawing from its own mirror image.

On closer inspection, this level of universalism on the part of the United States remains more apparent than real. America still finds it objectionable to be cast as a country like the rest—even if the rest have been, or are in the process of becoming, Americanized. The United States remains instinctively insistent that it is, and must continue to be, a wholly extraordinary country. It is still predisposed towards Woodrow Wilson's axiom that the United States is the 'only idealistic nation in

---

[91] Ibid.
[92] President William J. Clinton, 'Inaugural Address', 20 January 1993, http://www.presidency.ucsb.edu/ws/index.php?pid=46366.
[93] Ibid.   [94] Ibid.   [95] Hartz, *The Liberal Tradition in America*, p. 286.

existence'.[96] Uniqueness remains an axiomatic element of American identity. It is integral to America's exceptionally demonstrative nationalism and its fervent patriotism. The United States can only ever feel different through what it considers to be its exceptionally democratic society, i.e. its only serious historical claim to uniqueness. The circularity of this view is far less important than its effect, which is to satisfy America's need to be different from the world and to fulfil its *raison d'être* of having something to offer the world. In essence, America needs to be unique in order to be universal in an active, originating, and controlled way.

AN AMERICAN SOPHISTICATION

The point of departure for this excursion into the nature of American political ideas was the apparent disjunction between the fixity of an embedded set of central principles within society, and the fluid and even volatile manner of their usage as a medium of political exchange. In examining the dynamics between political thought and practice in the United States, it has become necessary to take two defining perspectives into account.

The first is that outlook which takes American political values to be essentially a conflation of signature themes. In the same way that these ideas have been and remain instrumental in the political development of the United States, so the substance, meaning, and clarity of American identity becomes integrally related to a cluster of values that are taken to be grounded in a conception of their generic commonality. In effect, the evident stability and unity of the United States underwrites the presumption of a historically and socially sanctioned order of interlocking ideas. The second distinguishing conception of American political values is one in which they are not taken to be an intrinsic part of a historically based and imperturbable structure of undifferentiated ideas. On the contrary, they are seen and used as separate strands of value, each with different sources, properties, and implications. Far from history and tradition providing a presumption of unity, they afford a licence for dispute and a means by which the conceptual and political inconsistencies between different key ideas can be subjected to sustained and critical examination.

Both these perspectives carry familiar yet different associations. The corporatist view in which multiple ideas are presumed to possess both an interior logic and a collective coherence is closely related to notions of a consensus-based society and of a single encompassing tradition. This unidimensional conception of the relationship between ideas and culture provides the main foundation to the popular claims that American society is characterized by (i) a narrow spectrum of political difference; (ii) a myopic pluralism driven by pragmatic accommodation

---

[96] President Woodrow Wilson, 'Address Supporting the League of Nations' (8 September 1919), in Albert Shaw (ed.), *The Messages and Papers of Woodrow Wilson*, vol. 2 (New York: Review of Reviews Corporation, 1924), p. 822.

and incremental adjustment; and (iii) a static style of politics which allows for institutional gridlock and minimal innovation. Moreover, it is the presumption of a set of 'core ideas' that infers the existence of an irreducible and recognizable baseline of American authenticity—one which is exemplified in the form of a de facto 'creed' and, with it, an instrument of single-minded conformity.

The alternative conception of American political ideas is one in which conflict is fuelled and structured by reference to different individual components of the creed. In this context, the creed does not merely lend itself to selective emphasis; it encourages ideational dispute by giving emphasis to a series of primary values, each one of which can afford a purist and even absolutist approach to the requirements and priorities of social organization. In American culture, ideas such as freedom, rights, democracy, and equality are assigned a fundamental and, thereby, comparable status within the identity of the republic. As a consequence, differing constructions of each individual value are continually being formulated and reformulated. At the same time, the horizontal dimension of multiple differentiated values fosters a host of interpretive possibilities over the nature of their respective relationships. In effect, American politics can be viewed as a profusion of primal conflicts over the meaning and significance of elemental principles, and over the dynamics and consequences of the interplay between them. The licence afforded in an open society to pursue these analytical questions and to draw them tightly into the political realm of policy disputes and contested resources means that American society can be viewed as an ongoing and fractious battle of foundational ideas.

Far from being distinguished by a paucity of ideological dispute derived from a creed of mutually inclusive principles, it can be claimed that American politics is governed more by elemental arguments, fundamentalist positions, first principles, and philosophically loaded wedge issues. In contrast to the picture of a self-regulating equilibrium of pluralist politics suggested by the emollient inclusiveness of the creed, this more combative perspective does not find negotiated compromise to be a plausible signature of conventional political conduct within American society. On the contrary, political interaction through this lens is seen as being far removed from the quiescence of mutual adjustment. It is defined more by reference to a public discourse pervaded by (i) numerous references to virtue and corruption, liberty and tyranny, and to good and evil; (ii) a developed preoccupation with the forms and essences of political principle set within a social order; (iii) the continuous claims made on behalf of different core values, and the ramifications that ensue from the full extension of argued positions from primary categories of principle; (iv) the persistent reference to historical themes, figures, and events to provide explicit guidance and moral force in the application of principle to contemporary political issues; and (v) a compulsive engagement with elemental criteria of legitimacy as the basis of political exchange leading to epic encounters of principle and even to claims that there exist two cultures or two nations.

At first, it would appear that the integrationist and differentiated perspectives of American ideas have nothing in common with one another. The present study challenges this assumption by suggesting that the two conceptualizations have an underlying connection. In effect, they are both constituent features of a complex and variable phenomenon in which American society works with and through an ideationally loaded medium that simultaneously projects different ideas into high relief, while fostering an attitude structure capable of maintaining them in a state of manageable coexistence. As this study has attempted to convey, the United States possesses a highly pronounced ideational dimension within its politics. It is a dimension that draws explicitly upon American history and tradition. It is also a dimension that infuses almost every issue with a self-conscious set of high principles and unequivocal values. The struggle for leverage and legitimacy within such an intense context leads to a succession of bidding wars centring upon competitive claims of ideational authenticity. This normally entails the aggregation of core ideas into compounds capable of commanding respect and exerting persuasion through their claims to embody the combined spirit, or optimal mix, of American values. Accordingly, political conduct in the United States is distinguished by its profusion of disputes over the meaning and applicability of primary values and over the respective alignments of political positions in respect to those values.

Despite the existence of what is an ingrained tradition of familiarly intensive dispute, the political usage of these ideas is fundamentally conditioned by the very plurality of their existence. It is this notion of having to work with, and to deal with, multiple and competing priorities of public value that gives American politics its characteristic signature. American society offers an extensive licence to engage in the interpretive explorations of individual ideas under the aegis of republican virtue or liberal inquiry. But American society also provides a way for these ideas and their varied sponsors to coexist effectively within a bounded space of tolerable intensity. The controlling premise that all the core values have a comparable ancestry and, thereby, a 'family resemblance' means that even in the midst of serious contention there exists a generic medium of interpretive enterprise and cross-referencing legitimation.

Because of the segmented character of the value base, it is rare in American discourse to have a direct and explicit clash of ideas. Fundamentalist assertions abound over the centrality of individual ideas but there is little direct engagement between ideas by opposing parties in political disputes. Core ideas are not really contested on a one-to-one basis. The operational assumption that there exists a natural association of values means that it is very unusual for claims to be made in which one idea is given a marked priority over others, or where one value is underlined to the point of clearly excluding or marginalizing all the others. Effective leadership in the United States—whether it is designed to be transformative or consolidationist—may feature a particular value, or subset of values, but not to the extent of discounting or dismissing other core values. On the contrary, it is customary for leaders to substantiate their claims to leadership on the grounds of their explicit or implicit allegiance to the full panoply of American ideas. The points on which leaders differentiate themselves from one another is in their narrative constructions of this corpus of ideas, through which the constituent elements are variously assembled, organized, and prioritized into distinguishable signatures.

In the same mould, the conventional style of political complaint is to accuse an opponent of not appreciating or not conforming to the traditional quota of core values. More often than not, political opposition is pushed to the point of claiming that the views or positions of an adversary amount to an actual breach of American values. Rather than seeking to polarize positions around different subsets of ideas, the standard form of critique is almost invariably one that is designed to reaffirm the full adherence on the part of the complainant to all the mainstream ideas associated with American identity. At the same time, such a complaint casts doubt upon an opponent's affiliation to one or more core values. Accusations like these may carry the implication of a lack of understanding or a misapprehension by outsiders or others similarly charged with being uninitiated in the rules of the ideational game. On other occasions, these alleged breaches of value may infer an altogether more pernicious type of nonconformism that is couched as being deliberately insidious and even disruptive in its purpose. Whether these critiques are rooted in charges of negligence or malice, they both tend to have the same effect upon those subjected to criticism: a reactive surge to rebut the accusations and to engage in a competitive process of conformity to all the core values in whichever permutations they are conjoined for political effect.

The protocols of critique and rebuttal are symptomatic of a generalized dynamic of ideational engagement in the United States. Ostensibly, there is extensive discretion in the selection, interpretation, and application of ideas in political discourse. Indeed the scale of ideational licence is so open-ended that it is very difficult to elicit, or to impose, any precise system of explanation in respect to the usage of ideas. Attempts to demonstrate the existence of a single all-encompassing tradition based upon a fixed notion of liberalism break down under the weight of dispute not only over the meaning of liberalism, but also over the consistency of its social presence. As we have already noted, other efforts to create patterns of ideational behaviour often seek to incorporate and systematize diversity by invoking the device of cyclical models in which two or more ideational themes are shown to form sequences of periodic dominance. But these constructs are vulnerable to the charge of being formulaic and distortive. All of them tend to underestimate the intense and volatile nature of the ideational energies within American politics.

The study and usage of ideas is strongly associated with the properties of rigour, consistency, and coherence. The treatment of ideas in American society is often portrayed as being deficient in precisely these qualities. Consensus historians, for example, have been very influential in inferring the existence of a ubiquitous unity in the American experience. Because tradition is said to have conferred an indigenous hierarchy of values upon America, then it is commonly concluded that 'no nation has ever been less interested in political philosophy or produced less in the way of theory'.[97] Such a conception of American history lends strong support to the traditional notion that America's social consensus is both a contributory cause and a direct expression of the country's lack of ideological orientation.

---

[97] Boorstin, *The Genius of American Politics*, p. 8.

It has been noted above (pp. 401–3) that electoral studies and survey evidence can offer substance to the suggestion that American voters appear not to require a high level of ideological sophistication in reaching their decisions or justifying their choices. Other studies have produced similar findings on the apparently tenuous relationship between the issue positions of the American public, and the existence of larger and overarching points of reference that might shape and organize such attitudes. The conclusions are often couched in terms of hard realism. The genre is typified by the authors of *The American Voter* who conclude that the 'failure to locate more than a trace of "ideological" thinking in the protocols of our surveys, emphasizes the general impoverishment of political thought in a large proportion of the electorate'.[98]

This remains a commonly held conclusion but it is too harsh a judgement. It leaves the impression that American politics is guided either by a monolithic tradition of unreflective conformity, or by a superficial eclecticism combining rootlessness with randomness. Neither captures the essence of what is a far more complex and subtle set of processes. The usage of ideas is distinguished by licence and ingenuity, but also by a sense of constraint rooted in a common basis of social principle that is expressed through the invocation of core values. The social attachment to the language and leverage of these ideas means that they act as a medium of exchange so that even when they are simultaneously employed by diametrically opposed positions, the constituent ideas provide a transcendent form of mutual conditioning. Enormous interpretive discretion is afforded to the treatment and understanding of ideas such as freedom, democracy, equality, and individualism, but this does not mean that their usage is arbitrary, vicarious, or even unstructured. Protocols and conventions inherent in the multiple nature of the ideational base, and intrinsic in the extensive social experience of their simultaneous usage, contribute towards a sense of collective constraint.

The sweeping and elemental timbre of the individual ideas is bounded not only by a cultural intuition over the permissible usage of the ideas in the American context, but also by the necessity of aggregating the core ideas together into persuasive compounds. More often than not, such aggregations take the form of suggestive narratives imputing triumphant legitimacy and prospective beneficence in the furtherance of a cause, whilst inferring a breach of faith and even betrayal and corruption on the part of those opposed to it. Contending forces indict one another for their alleged partiality and ideational unevenness. All successful compounds contain credible and, therefore, defensible representations of all the core ideas. Considerable room for interpretive manoeuvre exists within the matrix of ideas but, as has been noted, this is not synonymous with a completely open system of 'pick and mix' choices. The American way with ideas is grounded, both implicitly and explicitly, in a traditional impulse to view them as being contiguous to one another. This affords extended latitude in creating various ideational permutations because they are all set against, and conditioned by, the

---

[98] Angus Campbell, Philip E. Converse, Warren E. Miller, and Donald L. Stokes, *The American Voter* (New York: Wiley, 1960), p. 543.

working presumption that the core ideas possess the basic property of mutual adhesion. It is this outlook which not only assists the social management of the cluster of key ideas, but which is instrumental in conditioning the composition and shape of those derivative compounds that are deemed to be legitimate.

The defining feature of American political discourse, therefore, is that it is a bounded yet highly creative interplay of several ideas. The net effect is far removed from being a standardized meld of principles, or a fixed conception of a consensual order, or a patterned bifurcation of values. On the contrary, it is evident that American political life is informed and energized by a dynamic of stable instability based upon the cultural coexistence of ideas that are separate and distinct from one another but which are also collectively integral to American identity. The significance of these several core ideas, therefore, lies not just in their individual meaning and status, but with the social attitudes required to develop a sophisticated and adaptable modus operandi for engaging with so many conceptual attachments at the same time.

17

Present and Future Challenges

INTRODUCTION

The social conflation of ideas in American society does not infer a condition of stasis or a self-regulating equilibrium. On the contrary, it is highly dynamic, always in a process of reconfiguration, and is continually being confronted by challenges. Any claims of a conclusive victory in the battle of ideas, or more accurately in the battle over the usage of pre-selected ideas, have to be treated with scepticism. The most notable recent example of such a presumption of settled finality has been the reputed pre-eminence of conservatism in political debate over the past twenty-five years. Conservatism has been widely referred to as the contemporary foundation of a newly emerged American consensus in which core values have been reconfigured in such a way as to suggest the existence of a conservative hegemony.[1] However, when such propositions are examined more closely, the notion of even a temporary settlement of ideas increasingly assumes the appearance of a chimera. So many caveats, qualifications, and exceptions have to be incorporated within the rubric of this order of hegemony that it throws doubt over its level of thematic and political integrity. Moreover, as this study has already noted, the meaning and substance of contemporary conservatism remains a highly contested sphere of interpretation.

Noteworthy though these objections may be, the main argument against the presence of a clearly defined hegemony is its inference of a settled state of final fulfilment. Nothing could be less likely in the ecosystem of American ideas where the weight and positioning of primary values experience a permanent condition of mutual readjustment. Continual challenge is the defining characteristic of a system that affords such prominence to so many core ideas and foundational principles. Actions and reactions on behalf of, and in opposition to, varied calibrations of multiple ideas are the stock in trade of American politics. They are also the reason for the establishment of such a deeply embedded set of understandings over the way that political engagement can be conducted in a culture so richly endowed with principles of comparable worth and tradition. The serious challenges to such a system of orchestrated ideational dispute, therefore, are those which will disrupt, or have the potential to disturb, the customary processes of exchange as well as the understandings that connect America's core ideas to the society's sense of its

---

[1] For example, see John Micklethwait and Adrian Wooldridge, *The Right Nation: Conservative Power in America* (New York: Penguin, 2004).

own identity. It is these more fundamental challenges that are likely to subject the attitudinal creed and the matrix of principles to the severest examination.

CULTURAL FEARS

The normal course of ideational dispute and competitive compound construction can be undermined by phenomena that disorientate the processes by which core ideas are mixed into competitive hybrids. An example of a particular condition that can be taken to constitute just such a systemic problem for America's ideational ecology is the growing scale of income inequality in a notionally egalitarian society. When this is taken in conjunction with the indicators of decline in 'social capital', political participation, civic trust, and community cohesion, then the risk is that sectors of the population will be too marginalized and alienated to have anything other than a distrustful, and even cynical, outlook towards the standard medium of ideational exchange. Efforts can be made to remind the disaffected of the possible political leverage that can be derived from the interpretive licence implicit in the matrix of core values. Others, however, are less sanguine and point to what are arguably deeper and more intractable sources of dysfunction.

At a fundamental level, the United States has always attracted critical attention because of its position as a society that epitomizes the character of the liberal ethos. Critiques of liberalism in this generic sense tend to be drawn towards the gravitational force of America's own proclaimed identity as the exemplar of a liberal polity. As a consequence, many of the problematic elements within liberalism are alleged to be revealed with particular clarity in the United States. This is especially so in respect to several structural indictments of the liberal perspective. These include (i) the conceptual and logical problems associated with the liberal ideal of the neutral state; (ii) the presumption of a largely self-regulating form of social justice based upon individual opportunity and mobility set within a context of the free interplay of interests; and (iii) the issue of the limits and conditions of liberal tolerance, and the question of whether social licence is conditioned by a state whose neutrality emanates from an underlying belief in the superiority of the liberal conception.

Perhaps the most serious allegation is that liberal society in general, and American society in particular, generates its own form of disintegration. In essence, the charge here is that modern liberal society simply takes for granted the social cohesion and moral solidity that allows a society to foster a sense of identity through common experience and historical continuity. It can be claimed that liberal nationalism confuses inclusion with solidarity, and that liberal society not only permits but actively promotes alternative associations and loyalties that inevitably weakens the nation as a central force of associative identity.[2]

---

[2] For example, see Peter J. Spiro, 'The Citizenship Dilemma', *Stanford Law Review*, vol. 51, no. 3 (February 1999), pp. 507–639.

Owing to the liberal sponsorship of a morally neutral society and the subsequent failure to invest serious meaning into public life, it can be argued that a liberal polity is inherently unable to sustain its own social and moral preconditions. Despite the benefits of modernity's material progress, it is alleged that a liberal society has neither the means to identify the presence of cultural decline, nor the capacity to reverse it. Theorists like Michael Sandel, for example, complain that over the past sixty years the American government has become a system of 'procedural liberalism' in which the state performs the role of merely acting as a neutral arbiter between competing interests. The result is that no centre is developed through which the public good can be expressed and refined as a normative standard of conduct and aspiration. In effect, the civic substance of the republic has been displaced by an inert neutrality of competing rights.[3] Sandel's views coincide with the sentiments that animate various political voices and movements in the United States (e.g. the religious right, communitarian movement). These register a deep anxiety over what is declared to be the eroded levels of civic consciousness and social cohesion set against a larger context of what is seen to be a pathology of cultural relativism and moral impoverishment.

This kind of cultural pessimism is typified by Samuel Huntington in his study into another feature of society which he claims is affecting the contemporary state of American identity. In *Who Are We: America's Great Debate* (2004),[4] Huntington alludes not just to the central importance of a set of creedal values which he acknowledges are universal in nature, but to the structural significance of a correlated creedal culture that supports and nurtures the core values in society. Throughout the course of American history, Huntington claims that the social development of the United States has been based on a distinctively 'Anglo-Protestant' system of values and culture. Although this originated in the seventeenth and eighteenth centuries, it had guided the experiment in self-government since the inception of the republic. Becoming American, therefore, entailed a double assimilation: the adoption of its creedal values and the absorption of an Anglo-Protestant ethos by which those values were propagated and ingrained in social life. This dynamic of assimilation had not only successfully incorporated successive waves of mass immigration into American society but has secured the historical continuity and dominance of an Anglo-Protestant culture.

It is against such a background that Huntington draws attention to the Hispanic challenge to what he regards as the cultural foundations of American republicanism and its values. Due to a series of factors, the scale and concentration of Hispanic immigration have set in motion a transformative process that Huntington claims have explicit and implicit trajectories. These are considered to be not only disruptive but also dangerous to the cohesion and identity of American society. From the de facto sanctioning of illegal immigration to the rise of official bilingualism, and from the differences in religious traditions to the emergence of

---

[3] Michael J. Sandel, *Democracy's Discontent: America in Search of a Public Philosophy* (Cambridge, MA: Belknap Press, 1996), ch. 9.

[4] Samuel P. Huntington, *Who Are We? America's Great Debate* (London: Simon & Schuster, 2004).

dual citizenship and the progressive 'denationalization' of American elites, the net effect is said to be one of cultural erosion. Far from being assimilated, it is alleged that Latinos are in effect recreating America in their own terms and, therefore, in accordance with their own cultural priorities which are intrinsically different from the Anglo-Protestant tradition. According to Huntington, the trend is set to become a 'cultural division...that will replace the racial division between blacks and whites as the most serious cleavage in American society'.[5]

Huntington asserts that the United States is culturally adrift and is threatened with a process of 'national deconstruction'. According to this view, multicultural-ism means that a society that has become accustomed to, and dependent upon, a dominant ethos is in jeopardy of serious disintegration. The issue facing America, therefore, is whether it will 'continue to be a country with a single national language and a common Anglo-Protestant mainstream culture', or whether it will descend into 'two peoples with two languages and two cultures'.[6] The conse-quences for the fabric of civic trust and social convention would be compounded by a declining sense of cultural consciousness over what is being lost. Huntington's sense alarm prompts the following injunction:

[S]ome societies...are also capable of postponing their demise by halting and reversing the processes of decline and renewing their vitality and identity. I believe that America can do that and that Americans should recommit themselves to the Anglo-Protestant culture, traditions, and values that for three and a half centuries have been embraced by Americans of all races, ethnicities, and religions and that have been the source of their liberty, unity, power, prosperity, and moral leadership for good in the world.[7]

Understandably, Huntington's thesis has been contested on a number of grounds. Not the least of them has been the criticism that it is informed by a nativist outlook that paradoxically calls into question the very values of the 'Anglo-Protestant tradition' which Huntington is so intent upon preserving.[8] But what is not in question is the specification and logic of the stated anxiety. In defining the danger as that which is seen to be eroding the cultural foundations of American ideas and their usage in social organization and political exchange, Huntington's jeremiad is thoroughly representative of a well-established and influential genre.

Another type of challenge is posed by a more generalized force of malaise and anxiety that allegedly can disorientate customary patterns of ideational coexis-tence. The condition of fear is increasingly cited as both a political resource that is fostered by government as well as a social phenomenon that is suggestive of power-lessness, vulnerability, and a reduced sense of agency on the part of the individual

---

[5] Ibid., p. 324.

[6] Ibid., p. 318; see also Patrick J. Buchanan, *The Death of the West: How Dying Populations and Immigrant Invasions Imperil Our Country and Civilization* (New York: Thomas Dunne, 2002), chs. 6–8.

[7] Huntington, *Who Are We?*, p. xvii.

[8] For example, see Alan Wolfe, 'Native Son: Samuel Huntington Defends the Homeland', *Foreign Affairs* (May/June 2004), pp. 120–25; Andrew Hacker, 'Patriot Games', *The New York Review of Books*, 24 June 2004.

citizen.[9] The sources of fear are many and varied. They find outlets in such issues as environmental degradation, climate change, energy supply, economic stability, immigration, drug abuse, crime, disease control, food safety, globalization, and terrorism. By giving credence to fears engendered in such areas, governments have been able to mobilize resources and to accumulate powers on a scale that would be inconceivable without the stimulus of concerted public anxiety. This dynamic was demonstrated to dramatic effect during the prolonged aftermath of the terrorist attacks of 11 September 2001, when the Bush administration was able to secure a radical and accelerated transformation of both the federal government's structure of internal security and the United States planning for force projection overseas.

The repeated evocation of fear by the Bush administration in general, and the President in particular, has prompted commentators to speculate upon the damage such an outlook can create within a liberal democracy. In addition to the claims that dissent has increasingly been criminalized and civil liberties diminished are the references to a 'politics of fear [that] is everywhere',[10] to a 'national identity of victimhood',[11] and even to a 'republic of fear'.[12] These appellations are all associated with an anxiety that fear is not only leading individuals to disengage from the public sphere but also allowing political power to become concentrated at the centre. The net effect is one of permitting both the government and the citizenry to undermine the very values that are feared to be under assault by external agencies.

Fear is not only a political resource enabling governments to increase their authority. It is in a more immediate sense an impulse of unqualified urgency that introduces strong emotive and affective dimensions into the fabric of social processes. A fear can relate to a specific grievance or source complaint. But a fear can also give expression to a more amorphous anxiety over a perceived threat, or else over a concealed or unintelligible force, that is intent upon inflicting some form of harm—a danger often made all the more threatening because of its lack of political recognition. The propagation of fear in contemporary society, and particularly in American society, has been said to reflect a chronic paucity of positive conceptions of human ends. To this extent, social fear can be equated with an anti-Enlightenment reaction against the premise of sustainable progress. Frank Furedi notes that the cumulative effect of fears 'is to transform fear into a cultural perspective through which society makes sense of itself'. In this respect, fear is 'rarely about anything specific—it is about everything'.[13] Such a negative

---

[9] See Frank Furedi, *Culture of Fear: Risk Taking and the Morality of Low Expectation* (New York: Continuum International Publishing Group–Academi, 2002); see also Corey Robin, *Fear: The History of a Political Idea* (New York: Oxford University Press, 2004).

[10] Elaine Kitchel, 'CheneySpeak: Scaring Us', *Intervention Magazine*, 11 September 2004, http://www.interventiomag.com/Secondary/modules.php?file=article&name=News&op=modload&sid=877.

[11] Joanna Bourke, 'The Politics of Fear Are Blinding Us to the Humanity of Others', *The Guardian*, 1 October 2005.

[12] Sidney Blumenthal, 'Bush's Bunker Strategy', *Salon.com*, http://www.salon.com/opinion/blumenthal/2005/11/03/vanguard/index_np.html.

[13] Frank Furedi, 'The Politics of Fear', http://www.spiked-online.com/Articles/0000000CA760.htm.

foundation has become more prominent as a generic condition in American society since the end of the cold war. Whether it is the onset of terrorist threats and asymmetric warfare, or the concern over the moral condition of American culture, or the prospect of a purported 'clash of civilizations', the level of fear as a conditioning agency of social action is thought to have undergone a marked increase.

As a consequence of this level of personal and social insecurity, it is claimed that American society has become 'dumbed down'[14] in terms of cultural standards. Alternatively, it is asserted that the United States has not only been aroused into accepting the need for illiberal measures and aggressive military action, but has also been desensitized in respect to mounting evidence of economic inequities and social injustice. Within the parameters of such a context, it is possible to argue that the United States has been unreflective in its actions and has allowed some of its core ideas to be compromised, reformulated, or even suspended under the pressure of political unreason. Accordingly, the challenge to America's processes of ideational exchange is that of a displacement of reason into a condition that John Lukacs describes as a degenerate and corrupting form of popular sovereignty that organizes fear and resentment into an impulsive, vulgar, belligerent, brutalizing, and intolerant regime.[15]

THE INTERNATIONAL CHALLENGE

Arguably, the most searching challenge to the customary parameters of America's ideational intercourse, and the one most likely to disrupt them on a long-term basis, is that posed by the prominence of the United States and its values in the contemporary world. The historical strains incurred by the progressive enlargement of the United States' global reach, together with their implications for America's liberal and republican identity, have been noted earlier. The current challenge is founded upon the well-established cultural anxieties relating to power, autonomy, purpose, and principle. However, in the context of the twenty-first century and in the light of recent events, these familiar concerns have been transformed into a more serious disruption to America's self-assurance in the command and control of its own ideational credentials.

At the outset of the post-cold war period, the United States had acquired a position of unqualified international pre-eminence. Ostensibly, it appeared that the United States was not only the victor in the cold war but the defining model for the future development of the global order. It was now the undisputed epicentre

---

[14] See Katharine Washburn and John F. Thornton (eds.), *Dumbing Down: Essays on the Strip-Mining of American Culture* (New York: W. W. Norton, 1996); Morris Berman, *The Twilight of American Culture* (New York: W. W. Norton, 2001), pp. 1–70, 103–31; David G. Myers, *The American Paradox: Spiritual Hunger in an Age of Plenty* (New Haven, CT: Yale University Press, 2000).

[15] John Lukacs, *Democracy and Populism: Fear and Hatred* (New Haven, CT: Yale University Press, 2005).

of liberal democracy and, therefore, was in a position to define the nature of the victory. In many respects, the Enlightenment project of material progress and human development was stripped down to a one-to-one symmetry with American experience, guidance, and know-how. During the 1990s, the United States was largely responsible for the contraction of the world in its own image. Integration proceeded exponentially through financial investments, overseas acquisitions, communications networks, and knowledge-based industries that were all centred upon America in origin and application. The surge towards democratization, trade liberalization, privatization, and structural adjustment programmes bore the imprint of the United States. The 'Washington consensus' itself was made synonymous with the presumption of a global consensus upon the American ethos of the free market and upon America's centrality in the processes of globalization.[16]

In this context, the uniqueness of American democracy could be construed as the original patent for an international system evolved by democratic progression into a form of liberated fusion. The United States had become the reference point of emulation. It was now able to define democracy exclusively in terms of itself. Flexible markets, freedom of choice, and self-determination would allow others to engage with the United States as full participants in the international economy. The operating assumption was that emancipated reason and self-interest would release societies into a natural harmonization with western democracies in general and the United States in particular. This was an era when the sheer scale of America's global force became fully evident. In terms of 'hard power', the US military acquired a position in which it surpassed the size of the next ten national forces combined. It was also a period when analysts could refer categorically to the 'soft power' of America's cultural prestige, normative presence, and international reputation.[17] 'Soft power' was as far reaching as 'hard power' and, arguably, more rooted in the real nature of America's global leverage. If an empire could be said to exist, then it was not merely an 'empire by invitation',[18] but an intrinsic empire of the mind.

In 1997, Charles Krauthammer evoked the spirit of American benevolence and global emancipation which accompanied the US achievement in having 'stood down the Soviet Empire and destroyed the very idea of communism'.[19] American hegemony was 'good for the world'[20] because it provided peace, stability, and

---

[16] See John Williamson, 'What Should the World Bank Think about the Washington Consensus?', *The World Bank Research Observer*, vol. 15, no. 2 (August 2000), pp. 251–64; William Finnegan, 'The Economics of Empire: Notes on the Washington Consensus', *Harper's Magazine*, May 2003.

[17] See Joseph S. Nye, *Bound to Lead: The Changing Nature of American Power* (New York: Basic Books, 1990); Joseph S. Nye, *Soft Power: The Means to Success in World Politics* (New York: Public Affairs, 2004).

[18] Geir Lundestad, *The American 'Empire' and Other Studies of US Foreign Policy in Comparative Perspective* (Oxford: Oxford University Press, 1990), p. 55.

[19] Charles Krauthammer, 'America Rules: Thank God', *Time*, 4 August, 1997.   [20] Ibid.

security on an unprecedented scale. Krauthammer continued his celebration in a form that combined external outreach with traditional inwardness:

[T]he world does not live by safety alone. American dominance brings something more: the American creed. We are a uniquely ideological nation. We do not define ourselves by race of blood but by adherence to a proposition—a proposition so humane and attractive that it has, independently of American power, won near universal adherence.... Individual rights, government by consent, protection from arbitrary power, the free exchange of goods and ideas. We inherited them. We codified them. And now we propagate them. The world could do worse than be dominated by a country so committed to these ideas that it cannot help trying to foist them on everyone else.[21]

Ironically, the expansion of America's global reach in the 1990s brought in its wake an increase in global interdependency. The United States could successfully exert pressure upon other societies to comply with international agreements on trade, transport, finance, investment, labour practices, and intellectual property rights. By the same token, the United States found that integration and cooperation cut both ways. America became increasingly dependent upon other states for regulating capital transfers, monitoring the drugs trade, gathering intelligence on security threats, controlling the proliferation of nuclear weapons, and promoting social and economic development. Moreover, the global economy and information revolution gave greater influence to non-state organizations, thereby, requiring further efforts by the United States in developing structures of cooperation.

The state of American pre-eminence, therefore, was tightly bound to and conditioned by a multilateral international order. 'Hyperpower' now appeared to run concurrently with global governance; and 'unipolarity' with the ganglia of the international community. These cross-cutting ambiguities generated points of confusion and even serious concerns over whether the United States was making the most of what was widely recognized to be a historic opportunity. The Clinton era was marked by the disarray evoked by the need to determine the character and limits of America's role in the post-cold war world. The Clinton presidency, in particular, was widely criticized for its apparent lack of strategic vision at a time of dislodged certainties and porous borders. The old anchorage points of the cold war had given America social cohesion and international purpose. Now, greater autonomy and choice for the United States increased the likelihood of inconsistency and even eclecticism. President Bill Clinton's temporizing style served to compound the impression of an administration with an episodic approach to international problems.

The Clinton administration became associated with the exertion of America's economic power and the build-up of the country's military capacity. It also developed a conspicuous attachment to racial and gender equality, and to the defence of human rights.[22] Nevertheless, President Clinton's record on UN peacekeeping and

---

[21] Ibid.
[22] See Martin Walker, *Clinton: The President They Deserve* (London: Vintage, 1997), chs. 10, 12, 13; Sidney Blumenthal, *The Clinton Wars* (New York: Farrar, Straus & Giroux, 2003), chs. 4, 9, 14; Virginia Sapiro and David T. Canon, 'Race, Gender and the Clinton Presidency', in Colin Campbell and Bert A.

humanitarian military intervention was often marked by confusion, indecision, and delay. The disasters of omission in Rwanda and Bosnia were interleaved with the conflated ambiguities of American actions in Kosovo and the Middle East. Within such a matrix of new issues, themes, and theatres, the administration often appeared to suffer from a lack of overall direction. It was criticized for being excessively circumscribed by international networks, treaties, and pacts. Whether it was the high expectations of the peace dividend, or the genuinely complex nature of the emergent post-cold war order, the Clinton White House came under increasing assault for what was seen to be an opaque foreign policy that made America's position ambivalent within an increasingly melded world. Many complaints centred upon the loss of American identity and autonomy inside the multilateral architecture of collective security. The apparent diffusion of America's distinctiveness was equated in some quarters with a sense of diminishing moral capital and, thereby, a decline in moral direction.[23]

While the promotion of democracy and free markets was generally acknowledged to be a worthy prospectus in the abstract, concerns were increasingly raised over the practicalities of social change and, in particular, over those societies that opted for a course at variance with American ideals. Other concerns were raised (i) by the issue of whether the Clinton administration was able consistently to distinguish between what was considered to be vital from that which was merely desirable in policy objectives; and (ii) by the question of whether Washington was needlessly diverted into expensive social experiments in 'nation building'. These concerns were exemplified in the 'Statement of Principles (1997)' establishing the formation of the Project for the New American Century (PNAC). The neoconservative-based organization drew attention to the need to combine the active promotion of American interests with the projection of American principles under the aegis of a revitalized 'national leadership that accepts the United States' global responsibilities'.[24] To PNAC supporters, a renewed combination of 'military strength and moral clarity' would allow the United States not only to attend to its 'unique role in preserving and extending an international order friendly to our security, our prosperity, and our principles' but also to 'challenge regimes hostile to our interests and values'.[25]

It was against such a background of radical dissent over traditional diplomacy and multilateral processes that the presidency of George W. Bush was formed. The

Rockman (eds.), *The George W. Bush Presidency: Appraisals and Prospects* (Washington, DC: CQ Press, 2004), pp. 169–99; Emily O. Goldman and Larry Berman, 'Engaging the World: First Impressions of the Clinton Foreign Policy Legacy', in Campbell and Rockman (eds.), *The George W. Bush Presidency*, pp. 226–53.

[23] See Michael A. Ledeen, *Freedom Betrayed: How America Led a Global Democratic Revolution, Won the Cold War, and Walked Away* (Washington, DC: American Enterprise Institute Press, 1996), pp. 75–87; Stefan Halper and Jonathan Clarke, *America Unbound: The Neoconservatives and the Global Order* (Cambridge: Cambridge University Press, 2004), pp. 83–90; Andrew Bacevich, *The New American Militarism: How Americans Are Seduced by War* (New York: Oxford University Press, 2005), ch. 3.

[24] Project for the New American Century, 'Statement of Principles', 3 June 1997, http://www.newamericancentury.org/statementofprinciples.htm. [25] Ibid.

new administration's negative outlook on such issues as the Kyoto Protocol, the International Criminal Court, and the retention of the Anti-Ballistic Missile Treaty bore the hallmarks of this schismatic outlook, which combined American emancipation with the notion of visionary leadership and global obligation. These predispositions were dramatically deepened by the terrorist attacks of 11 September 2001, which inflated the status of the Bush presidency and mobilized the American public behind the need for urgent and concerted action. The identification, the threat, and the ramifications of American action were guided by a strategic and polemical thrust that was intent upon enhancing legitimacy through the fusion of power and principle. Ideational mobilization went hand in hand with military deployment. As a result, American security became increasingly defined by reference to the need for strategic action in the defence of American democracy and, therefore, in the name of global democracy.

The aftermath of 9/11 has been one of declared Manichean polarities fuelled by claims to moral certainties, moral imperatives, and moral leadership. The established state-based order of collective security has been challenged by new doctrines of pre-emptive war, regime change, and a free market for 'coalitions of the willing'.[26] To the Bush administration, the organic mix of terrorist organizations, rogue states, and biological, chemical, and nuclear technologies formed a threat that could neither be contained nor deterred by conventional means.

[N]ew threats...require new thinking. Deterrence—the promise of massive retaliation against nations—means nothing against shadowy terrorist networks with no nation or citizens to defend. Containment is not possible when unbalanced dictators with weapons of mass destruction can deliver those weapons on missiles or secretly provide them to terrorist allies....If we wait for threats to fully materialize, we will have waited too long.[27]

Because of this need 'to be ready for preemptive action when necessary to defend our liberty',[28] the cold war apparatus of the national security state has been deepened and combined with a homeland security society reaching deep into areas previously protected by civil liberties and constitutional constraints. President Bush declared a long war on terror in which 9/11 served to alert the American nation and to mobilize its resources against an elusive and amorphous threat. The war has generated a profusion of high-impact measures from the invasions of Afghanistan and Iraq to aggressive diplomatic postures and raw challenges to the utility of international organizations in general and the United Nations in particular. It has also fostered a state of myopia over the drive to maximize security through the free propagation of surveillance measures and cross-referenced

---

[26] President George W. Bush, 'President Bush, President Havel Discuss Iraq, NATO', Press Conference by President Bush and President Havel of Czech Republic, 20 November 2002, http://www.whitehouse.gov/news/releases/2002/11/20021120-1.html.

[27] President George W. Bush, 'Speech at the Graduation Ceremony at the United States Military Academy at West Point', New York, 1 June, 2002, http://www.whitehouse.gov/news/releases/2002/06/print/20020601-3.html.

[28] Ibid.

databases. In effect, soft societal pre-emption has been coupled with its hard military equivalent.

The asymmetrical attack on the United States has brought in its wake an asymmetrical response that has exposed once again the ambiguities between uniqueness and universalism within American identity and the nation's posture towards the world. Democracy has been repeatedly invoked by President Bush as the method, the motive, and the objective of American action during the emergency. Liberation is stated as a self-evident process of emancipation into democracy. Enemies are defined as rogue states which are necessarily undemocratic and, therefore, open to terrorist networks and to the trade in weapons of mass destruction. Just as the moral undertow follows the tidal forces of American democratic experience, so the Bush administration has had no inhibitions in summoning up the universal theme of America's historical destiny to release oppression into freedom and democracy. The president has sought to be reassuring in that the liberty which America prized should be seen not as 'America's gift to the world' but as 'God's gift to humanity'.[29] America's role, therefore, is one of abiding by the ministrations of history and making 'sacrifice for the liberty of strangers'.[30] The publicly stated challenge has remained one of exceptional obligation: '[I]t is both our responsibility and our privilege to fight freedom's fight.... In a single instant, we realized that this will be the decisive decade in the history of liberty, that we've been called to a unique role in human events'.[31]

The violent and complex circumstances surrounding the Iraq war has raised, or revived, the issue of whether the United States constitutes a de facto empire in the contemporary global order. The explicit or implicit pretensions of the United States as an expansionist imperial force have had a long history stretching back to the early nineteenth century when westward expansion laid the foundation for the historical and moral rationale of 'manifest destiny'. From a critical viewpoint, the United States is cited as being congenitally imperial in its appetites and designs. During the nineteenth century, the momentum to acquire land and to settle the interior of the continent led to the indigenous native populations being forcibly dispossessed and in many cases treated so badly that it amounted to a campaign of genocide.[32] It is possible to assert that America has always been an expansionary and imperialist power. Just as the pattern of its interior settlement was tantamount to a de facto internal imperialism, so its later pattern of influence over other countries (i.e. de facto external empire) could be seen as merely an extension of the same pre-existing set of dynamics. To William Appleman Williams, for example,

[29] President George W. Bush, 'State of the Union Address', 28 January 2003, http://www.whitehouse.gov/news/releases/2003/01/20030128-19.html.

[30] Ibid.

[31] President George W. Bush, 'State of the Union Address', 29 January 2002, http://www.whitehouse.gov/news/releases/2002/01/20020129-11.html.

[32] David E. Stannard, *American Holocaust: The Conquest of the New World* (New York: Oxford University Press, 1992), chs. 4, 6; Gloria Jahoda, *Trail of Tears* (New York: Wings Books/Random House, 1995); Dee Brown, *Bury My Heart at Wounded Knee: An Indian History of the American West* (New York: Henry Holt, 2001).

both patterns of United States history reveal the same controlling impulse towards empire, which ranks as the defining characteristic of the American experience.[33]

For much of the twentieth century, the United States was engaged in what it regarded as a crusade against communism, which was conceived as a centralized, expansionist, and imperial phenomenon. In the process, the United States was widely interpreted as having acquired imperial characteristics itself, especially in relation to its own spheres of influence. During this period, the record of US foreign policy shows that in many areas the furtherance of American welfare and security had a far higher priority than the rights of other nations to self-determination. Moreover, the United States actively intervened abroad to ensure that the shape and policy of overseas governments conformed to the overriding interests of what Henry Kissinger termed the 'master democracy'.[34]

Contrary to its own revolutionary origins and the implicitly evolutionary principles of its declared national ethos, the United States has been a potent force for counter-revolution in the twentieth century. To Michael H. Hunt, America's record in this respect is clear and consistent. Since its inception, a single ideology has informed and motivated foreign policy. This ideology, which has been conspicuously prominent since the Second World War, is composed of three elements: a conception of national mission, the classification of other peoples according to a racial hierarchy, and an overt hostility towards social revolutions.[35] This outlook had legitimated over forty military and covert interventions in the United States' 'sister republics' in Latin America since 1900.[36] Very often they have been made on behalf of palpably undemocratic governments and forces. But to a critic like Noam Chomsky, American behaviour in Latin America is only part of a much larger pattern of malignant American policy around the world.

[W]e invaded South Vietnam, overthrew the democratic capitalist government of Guatemala in 1954 and have maintained the rule of murderous gangsters ever since, ran by far the most extensive international terror operations in history against Cuba from the early 1960s and Nicaragua through the 1980s, sought to assassinate Lumumba and installed and maintained the brutal and corrupt Mobutu dictatorship, backed Trujillo, Somoza, Marcos, Duvalier, the generals of the southern cone, Suharto, the racist rulers of southern Africa, and a whole host of other major criminals; and on, and on.[37]

In the twenty-first century, the allusions to American imperialism have been generated by the global pre-eminence of the US economy, the liberalization of markets

---

[33] William Appleman Williams, *The Roots of the Modern American Empire: A Study of the Growth and Shaping of Social Consciousness in a Marketplace Society* (London: Blond, 1970); William Appleman Williams, *The Tragedy of American Diplomacy* (New York: W. W. Norton, 1988).

[34] Henry Kissinger, *White House Years* (Boston, MA: Little, Brown, 1979), pp. 657–9.

[35] Michael H. Hunt, *Ideology and U.S. Foreign Policy* (New Haven, CT: Yale University Press, 1987); see also David F. Schmitz, *The United States and Right-Wing Dictatorships 1965–1989* (Cambridge: Cambridge University Press, 2006).

[36] See Jenny Pearce, *Under the Eagle: U.S. Intervention in Central America and the Caribbean* (London: Latin America Bureau, 1981); Lars Schoultz, *Beneath the United States: A History of US Policy toward Latin America* (Cambridge, MA: Harvard University Press, 1998).

[37] Noam Chomsky, *Deterring Democracy* (London: Vintage, 1992), pp. 13–14.

and capital transfers, the technological supremacy of the American military, the cultural hegemony of America's 'soft power', and the emergence of a dominant norm rooted in American identity. Out of this matrix has emerged a profusion of analyses that employ imperial reference points in relation to the nature and scale of American outreach, as well as to the increased indications of American unilateralism and forceful leadership. To a Marxist or neo-Marxist perspective, American behaviour in respect to international law and multilateral processes, and American action in relation to 'rogue states' and the 'war on terror', serve merely to reaffirm what is claimed always to have been an underlying dynamic in the US conception of peace and security. This refers to the United States' need to defend and advance its economic and strategic interests even at the expense of compromising its own emancipatory rationale. The view is one in which America is continually having to contend with the inherent contradictions of its economy, which in turn leads to an increasing need to project military power in order to achieve greater access and control over diminishing resources.

The structural dynamics of this alleged 'new imperialism'[38] generates a panoply of claims ranging from the existence of a state of perpetual war to the destabilizing dynamics of the American economy; from the incidence of human rights violations within client states to the undermining of national sovereignty even to the point where it can be said that 'American hyperpower marks the end of the post-colonial era'.[39] In his study of US intervention in Columbia, Doug Stokes points out that far from any disjunction in policy objectives between the cold war and the post-cold war periods, there is evidence of a clear continuity of coercive purpose in Washington's security assistance. Notwithstanding the professed shift from containing communist insurgency to one of counter-terrorist and counter-narcotic operations, Stokes asserts that the rationale has remained the same as it has done throughout much of the preceding century.

The USA is neither targeting the primary drug traffickers nor fighting a war on international terrorism in Columbia. Instead the USA has continued to fund and train the Columbian military for a CI [i.e. counter-insurgency] war against both the Columbian insurgents and progressive sections of Columbian civil society throughout the post-Cold War era. As such ... the US post-Cold War objectives form an overarching continuity with their earlier Cold War policy and objectives. This continuity is due to the fact that US economic and strategic interests in Columbia have remained the same.[40]

Whether the analysis is one of revised continuity or reversed discontinuity, the outcome is one in which the United States is portrayed as an aggressive imperial force following its own economic and strategic imperatives with the objective of dominating the global order.

The inferences and indictments of imperialism surrounding the United States have received a further stimulus with the American-led invasions, and subsequent

---

[38] See David Harvey, *The New Imperialism* (Oxford: Oxford University Press, 2005); see also Leo Panitch and Colin Leys (eds.), *The Socialist Register 2004: The New Imperial Challenge* (New York: Monthly Review Press, 2003).

[39] Martin Jacques, 'The Power of One', *The Guardian*, 26, May 2003.

[40] Doug Stokes, *America's Other War: Terrorizing Columbia* (London: Zed Books, 2005), p. 2.

occupations, of Afghanistan and Iraq.[41] In the case of Iraq in particular, the projection of military force in the support of coercive regime change and imposed social transformation aroused renewed accusations of empire building on the part of the United States. There were widespread denunciations that the Bush administration had breached international law and marginalized the institutional structures of peace and collective security, in order to pursue its own geostrategic interests in the name of a global war on terror. In what was portrayed by the US government as a preventative strategy of counter-terrorism and a justified form of liberal interventionism was just as easily transfigured into a prelude to a new imperial moment. Even the projected plan of introducing democracy into Iraq and establishing the country as a regional model for the Middle East was interpreted in many quarters as a form of exerting sustained US influence and establishing a deeper hegemonic presence in an area of vital significance to America's continued global dominance. With the deepening crisis over the subsequent insurgency in Iraq and the threat of disorder degenerating into civil war, American coalition forces were increasingly placed in a position where they could be depicted as an occupying power intent upon subjugating local resistance in an effort to refashion a rogue or failing state in its own image and in accordance with its own long-term security priorities.[42]

Another perspective adopts a quite different approach to the issue of empire. This view tolerates the notion of empire both in terms of historical nostalgia for a time-tested form of governance, and in relation to the need to respond to the new challenges of the post-cold war world. Niall Ferguson, for example, is unrestrained in his prescription for America to act as a 'liberal empire'. An empire can, in Ferguson's view, be a source of progress, peace, order, and justice in which minorities can be protected and security maintained. While the United States has the power to run such a liberal empire, Ferguson declares that at present it has neither the will nor the professional competence to realize its potential for exerting formal rule and for providing the kind of progressive and humanitarian intervention that the United Nations has signally failed to produce. The net effect is that 'officially... the United States remains an empire in denial'.[43] Michael Ignatieff is more circumspect but he too sees merit in 'an empire lite'.[44] Unlike previous empires based upon conquest, occupation, and colonization, the American empire is 'a new invention in the annals of political science'.[45] It is an entity dedicated to

---

[41] Roger Burbach and Jim Tarbell, *Imperial Overstretch: George W. Bush and the Hubris of Empire* (London: Zed Books, 2004); Rodrigue Tremblay, *The New American Empire* (Haverford, PA: Infinity, 2004).

[42] Alejandro Colás and Richard Saull, 'Introduction: The War on Terror and American Empire after the Cold War', in Alejandro Colás and Richard Saull (eds.), *The War on Terrorism and the American 'Empire' after the Cold War* (London: Rouledge, 2006), pp. 1–35; Michael Cox, 'The Imperial Republic Revisited: The United States in the Era of Bush', in Colás and Saull (eds.), *The War on Terrorism and the American 'Empire' after the Cold War*, pp. 175–201.

[43] Niall Ferguson, *Colossus: The Rise and Fall of the American Empire* (London: Penguin, 2005), p. 6.

[44] Michael Ignatieff, 'The Burden', *New York Times Magazine*, 5 January 2003.

[45] Ibid.

human rights and liberal democracy and devised by a people who 'like to think of themselves as the friend of freedom everywhere'.[46] To Ignatieff, even though it is 'an empire without consciousness of itself' it is expected to carry out 'imperial functions in places that America has inherited from the failed empires of the 20th century'.[47]

Imperial critics and imperial apologists, however, are not the norm in rationalizing the present and future status of America as a superpower. The mainstream American outlook on the subject remains very wary over any association with the terminology of empire. In the republican lexicon, empire still denotes a sense of lost virtue, corruption, and ultimately collapse. America's political identity was formed in opposition to, and in reaction against, the presumption of empire. Its core ideas remain so strongly rooted in anti-imperial derivatives that any suggestion of an attribution of empire to American action or policy is likely to be taken as a cultural affront. Given that the essence of imperialism is rule without consent over different peoples, America's defining ethos of liberty, popular sovereignty, equality, self-determination, democratic nationalism, and the rule of law seem to offer the comfort of a contradiction in terms.

Those who dispute the attribution of empire do so through the logic of ideas and by recourse to American history through the medium of ideas. Lewis Lapham, for example, insists that the American people have never been 'infected with the virus of imperial ambition; nor have we acquired an exalted theory of the state that might allow us to govern subject peoples with a firm hand and an easy conscience'.[48] As an 'authentically civilian nation', there is an 'absence of a citizen army prepared to fight for what it believes to be the glory of both its public and private self'.[49] When US forces are deployed, the impression given is that they are sent abroad reluctantly and that they are motivated by a spirit of emancipation. Even when summoning the national will to confront terrorism, President Bush took great pains to disavow any hint of imperial ambition in the 'war on terror'. The campaign was enfolded into a liberal ethos of national disinterestedness in any material or strategic gains that might ensue from the operation:

America has no empire to extend or utopia to establish. We wish for others only what we wish for ourselves—safety from violence, the rewards of liberty, and the hope for a better life.[50]

America is a nation with a mission, and that mission comes from our most basic beliefs. We have no desire to dominate, no ambitions of empire. Our aim is a democratic peace—a peace founded upon the dignity and rights of every man and woman. America acts in this

---

[46] Ignatieff, 'The Burden'.   [47] Ibid.

[48] Lewis H. Lapham, 'The American Rome: On the Theory of Virtuous Empire', *Harpers*, August 2001.

[49] Ibid.

[50] President Bush, 'Speech at the Graduation Ceremony at the United States Military Academy at West Point'.

cause with friends and allies at our side, yet we understand our special calling: This great republic will lead the cause of freedom.[51]

Notwithstanding the historical, ideational, and terminological traditions relating to America's contradistinction to the principles of empire, the prospect that the United States may be evolving into a reconfiguration of empire continues to arouse anxiety. Various disclaimers are offered in mitigation. The most common is the assertion that if America is an empire, then it is not like any other empire. The phenomenon can be interpreted as a voluntary association or an 'inadvertent empire'[52] based upon ideological commonality and mutual economic advantage, rather than upon territorial control and social division. Others are not so sanguine and are alarmed that, irrespective of intentions or design, the United States is being drawn into a process of 'imperial overstretch' and drawn into grand-scale interventions into intractable problem areas.[53]

Whether it is through drift, or misadventure, the concern is that the United States is undermining its own republican integrity though international exertions that are not only dangerous in their own right but are likely to be self-defeating in their long-term effects. In essence, the criticism is that national self-belief can be, and has been, superseded by doctrinaire and even arrogant cultural presumption which over time has led to almost every region in the world having a justifiable grievance against the United States.[54] American outreach is said to entail a dynamic of diminishing returns as reactive alienation progressively displaces recipient acquiescence in an Americanized future. According to this perspective, the risks attendant upon the United States' global position and ambition are for the most part concealed through America's own historical and ideational bias. Andrew Bacevich, for one, believes that the United States needs to be far more alert to the condition of empire denial:

[T]he conceit that America is by its very nature innocent of imperial pretensions has become not only untenable but also counterproductive: it impedes efforts to gauge realistically the challenges facing the United States as a liberal democracy intent upon presiding over a global order in which American values and American power enjoy pride of place.[55]

In effect, for America to act in the role of a benevolent sponsor of liberal democratic values, it is first necessary for it to be sensitized to the condition of its own liberal democracy and, thereby, to its credentials as a functioning global norm.

America's foundational ideas and organizing principles represent the cornerstone of its claims to being a source of global legitimacy and an inspirational

---

[51] President George W. Bush, 'State of the Union Address', 20 January 2004, http://www. whitehouse.gov/ news/releases/2004/01/20040120-7.html.

[52] William E. Odom and Robert Dujarric, *America's Inadvertent Empire* (New Haven, CT: Yale University Press, 2004)

[53] The term 'imperial overstretch' was originally popularized by Paul Kennedy. See Paul M. Kennedy, *The Rise and Fall of the Great Powers: Economic Change and Military Conflict from 1500 to 2000* (London: Fontana, 1988), pp. 666–74.

[54] See Chalmers Johnson, *The Sorrows of Empire* (London: Verso, 2004).

[55] Andrew Bacevich, *American Empire: The Realities and Consequences of US Diplomacy*, p. 243.

exemplar of modernity. And yet, it is precisely this dimension which is currently placed under enormous challenge in the international sphere.

CHALLENGE OF DEMOCRACY

Democracy promotion has been the centrepiece of the United States' post-cold war project. It summons up the universalism and professed benevolence of America's conception of itself, as well as the realization of a historic opportunity when the pre-eminence of the United States could provide the security and inspiration for a genuine transformation of societies into a collective existence of democratic peace. Within this framework, tyrannies were initially expected to dissolve through the agency of a global consensus. According to the neo-liberal perspective, progress would be ensured through multiple peace dividends, whilst globalization would release the potential for free markets and wealth creation on an unprecedented scale. The neoconservatives have been distinguished by a more measured optimism. It recognizes the permanent existence of evil in the world and the need to confront it with both a sense of moral clarity and a willingness to use force, instead of relying upon the self-regulating dynamics of economic activity. Whether the active impulse is one of redeeming failing economies and failing states through economic liberalization, or seizing the security initiative from rogue states through emancipatory intervention, the rationale has been the same: that different societies can be released into a state of liberal democracy either by processes directly sponsored by the United States, or by international agencies reflecting American conceptions of development. And yet, in spite of the emancipatory discourse surrounding these positions, they have both succeeded in arousing a profusion of critiques that taken in total now constitute one of the most difficult and potentially most serious challenges confronting the United States.

The indictment can be subdivided into three main components. *First*, is the reaction against the American presumption that its own traditions and perspectives not only define the necessary end point of human aspiration and emancipation, but also determine the means and methods by which this culminating model is to be brought into existence on a global basis. Indigenous suppositions on such a scale provoke cultural resistance in many societies which dispute the priority assigned to American values, and which contest America's right to invoke one conception of societal integrity as the controlling standard in all contexts. As American cultural hegemony has deepened, so it has brought in its wake an intensifying backlash not only against the perceived excesses and moral corruption of the West but also against the attempts to transpose this syndrome elsewhere under the auspices of a settled norm of democratic life. The insistent ethical objections both to the generic culture of the United States and to the perceived consequences of its central values can create or at least rationalize those divisions in the world which some analysts have described as a 'clash of civilizations,'[56] or a 'clash of fundamentalisms'[57] or even a 'third world war'.[58]

A *second* theme in the critique of Americanized democracy relates to the alleged partiality of a system that is purportedly balanced and neutral in theory but which in many areas of the world is seen to be biased in favour of America's economic and strategic interests. Notwithstanding the question of the inherent value or theoretical legitimacy of America's democratic principles, its de facto operation is one that is seen to consolidate and extend the reach of American power. To this extent, the promotion of democracy is taken as having an instrumental character-istic. It is seen as being irrevocably tied to that mix of property rights, corporate power, market dynamics, capital accumulation, and political pluralism with which America's international reputation is most closely identified. In another context, the desire to spread democracy can also be associated with the realist need to use both the hard and soft dimensions of US power, in order to project American spheres of influence and to maintain peace and security in the international order. In this critical respect, democracy can serve as a pretext or rationale not so much for emancipatory transformation as for maintaining the equilibrium of America's corporate power and strategic dominance.[59]

The *third* strand that is discernible in the reaction against America's spon-sorship of democracy is represented by the proposition that the processes of American democracy are flawed and operate to the disadvantage of most of the citizenry. The claim here is one of a disjunction between ideals and reality, and between form and essence, in the United States' own record of democratic gov-ernance. In seeking to impart the virtues of democracy to the outside world, the United States has increasingly placed itself in a position where the problems with its own democratic credentials are projected into high relief through the lens of critical international attention.

To an extent, the discrepancies between American democratic principles and their application are simply representative of the deep and problematic relation-ship between government and consent that lies at the heart of any democratic structure. Nevertheless, when such tensions are portrayed as afflicting a demo-cratic superpower engaged in an international campaign to democratize other societies, the effect can be one of embarrassment and damage to the moral and political authority of democratization's chief sponsor. Overseas observers can point to the inconsistencies in American actions abroad. Because the United

---

[56] Samuel P. Huntington, *The Clash of Civilizations and the Remaking of World Order* (New York: Simon & Schuster, 1996).

[57] Tariq Ali, *The Clash of Fundamentalisms: Crusades, Jihads and Modernity* (London: Verso, 2002).

[58] Norman Podhoretz, 'World War IV: How It Started, What It Means, and Why We Have to Win', *Commentary*, September 2004.

[59] See William Robinson, 'Promoting Capitalist Polyarchy: The Case of Latin America', in Michael Cox, G. John Ikenberry, and Takashi Inoguchi (eds.), *American Democracy Promotion: Impulses, Strategies, and Impacts* (New York: Oxford University Press, 2000), pp. 308–25; Barry Gills, 'American Power, Neo-Liberal Economic Globalization, and Low Intensity Democracy: An Unstable Trinity', in Cox, Ikenberry, and Inoguchi (eds.), *American Democracy Promotion*, pp. 326–44; Harvey, *The New Imperialism*, ch. 5.

States acts as the chief advocate for the merits of democracy as well as the self-defined exemplar of democratic virtues, it places itself in a highly exposed position when it acts upon its core ideas in an international setting. Critics are quick to apply democratic criteria to the actions undertaken by the United States in the name of democracy. Whether it is the political usage of intelligence agencies and sources in the prosecution of war, or the deployment of the US military as an occupying force in Iraq, or the treatment of detainees and the use of torture in the interrogation of terrorist suspects, or its resort to opt-outs to selected international agreements,[60] the United States finds itself judged on the basis of its own claims to the universalizing properties of democracy.

More disconcerting for the United States is when the focus of international criticism shifts to the nature of American society itself. No longer inhibited by cold war imperatives and loyalties, other western democracies have been increasingly inclined to take a more measured view of the United States model. Such scepticism comes in a variety of forms. Some question the role of money and particularly corporate finance in the conduct of elections and the construction of political agendas.[61] Others look critically at the self-negating properties of America's complex system of checks and balances that is alleged to prevent the formation of a majority-based governance.[62] Human rights and democratic accountability represent another source of concern in a society that allows policy in such controversial areas as abortion and capital punishment to be determined by courts rather than by elected politicians.[63]

The issue of social justice offers an alternative ground of complaint for outside observers who find it difficult to reconcile American wealth with the level of social

---

[60] See Mark Danner, *Torture and Truth: America, Abu Ghraib, and the War on Terror* (New York: New York Review Books, 2004); Karen J. Greenberg and Joshua L. Dratel (eds.), *The Torture Papers: The Road to Abu Ghraib* (New York: Cambridge University Press, 2005); Jane Meyer, 'Outsourcing Torture: The Secret History of America's "Extraordinary Rendition" Program', *The New Yorker*, 14 February 2005.

[61] Greg Palast, *The Best Democracy Money Can Buy: An Investigative Reporter Exposes the Truth about Globalization, Corporate Cons, and High Finance Fraudsters* (London: Robinson, 2002), ch. 2; Arianna Huffington, *Pigs at the Trough: How Corporate Greed and Political Corruption Are Undermining America* (New York: Three Rivers, 2003), pp. 77–151; The Center for Responsive Politics, 'Industry Profiles: Who Gives', http://www.opensecrets.org/industries/index.asp; Bill Mesler, 'Financing the Election: Soft Money Out, Bundling in: Corporate Backers Spend More, Get More', *CorpWatch*, 22 July 2004, http://www.corpwatch.org/article.php?id=11460.

[62] John J. Coleman, 'Unified Government, Divided Government, and Party Responsiveness', *The American Political Science Review*, vol. 93, no. 4 (December 1999), pp. 821–35; Jonathan Rauch, *Government's End* (New York: Public Affairs, 1999), chs. 6–8; Morris P. Fiorina, *Divided Government*, 2nd edn (Needham Heights, MA: Longman, 2003), chs. 6, 11; David S. Broder, 'Polar Politics', *Washington Post*, 6 May 2004; Paul Glastris, 'Perverse Polarity', *Washington Monthly*, June 2004.

[63] Jamin B Raskin, *Overruling Democracy; The Supreme Court versus The American People* (New York: Routledge, 2003); Anthony Lewis, *The Myth of the Imperial Judiciary: Why the Right Is Wrong about the Courts* (New York: New York University Press, 2003); Phyllis Schlafly, *The Supremacists: The Tyranny of Judges and How to Stop It* (Dallas, TX: Spence Publishing, 2004); Robert H. Bork, *A Country I Do Not Recognize: The Legal Assault on American Values* (Stanford, CA: Hoover Institution Press, 2005); Mark R. Levin, *Men in Black: How the Supreme Court Is Destroying America* (Chicago, IL: Regnery, 2005).

inequality and the close correlation of poverty with racial and ethnic minorities.[64] Godfrey Hodgson's lament typifies the disquiet arising from the marked persistence of the regressive and inequitable elements in American society over the past twenty-five years.

Great and growing inequality has been the most salient social fact about the America of the conservative ascendancy....Resentments were calmed by the idea that, if Americans were substantively more and more unequal, they had greater opportunities than ever to acquire status and possessions. The reality has been that gross and growing inequality, in a society where the rich were increasingly segregated by...geography, education, culture, and politics, amounted to nothing less than a reemergence of the class divisions that most Americans were proud to have put behind them decades before.[65]

Hodgson's concerns have recently found resonance in Americans' own disquiet over the widening gulf between the rich and poor which was graphically illustrated in the civic turmoil surrounding the impact of Hurricane Katrina upon New Orleans in 2005.[66] When such incidents are combined with research indicating a marked disjunction between rising corporate profits over the period 2001–2006 (+72%) and reduced median household income (i.e −0.5%) over the same period, and with numerous studies on the enduring nature of poverty and the widening disparities in income particularly in respect to the top 1 per cent of earners,[67] an impression that equal opportunity and social mobility are locked into a process of contraction can be generated.

An additional example of where America's democratic credentials can provoke overseas scepticism is in the field of civil liberties. In the wake of 9/11 and with the need to increase security, the federal government has been invested with sweeping powers of surveillance, arrest, detention, and deportation. At the

---

[64] Gary Burtless, 'Growing American Inequality: Sources and Remedies', in Henry J. Aaron and Robert D. Reischauer (eds.), *Setting National Priorities: The 2000 Election and Beyond* (Washington, DC: Brookings Institution, 1999), pp. 137–66; Godfrey Hodgson, *More Equal Than Others: America from Nixon to the New Century* (Princeton, NJ: Princeton University Press, 2004); Lee A. Daniels (ed.), *The State of Black America 2005: Prescriptions for Change* (New York: National Urban League Publications, 2005).

[65] Hodgson, *More Equal Than Others*, pp. xvii–xviii.

[66] American Political Science Association, Task Force on Inequality and American Democracy, 'American Democracy in an Age of Rising Inequality' (Washington, DC: American Political Science Association, 2004), http://www.apsanet.org/section_256.cfm; Jonathan Alter, 'The Other America: An Enduring Shame', *Newsweek*, 19 September 2005; Larry M. Bartels, 'Is the Water Rising? Reflections on Inequality and American Democracy', *PS: Political Science and Politics*, vol. 39, no. 1 (January 2006), pp. 39–42.

[67] See Thomas Piketty and Emmanuel Saez, 'Income Inequality in the United States 1913–2002' (Berkeley, CA: Econometrics Software Laboratory Archive, 2004), http://elsa.berkeley.edu/~saez/piketty-saezOUP04US.pdf; David H. Autor, Lawrence F. Katz, and Melissa S. Kearney, 'The Polarization of the U.S. Labour Market', *National Bureau of Economic Research Working Paper No 11986*, January 2006; 'The Rich, the Poor and the Growing Gap between Them', *The Economist*, 17 June 2006; Krishna Guha, Edward Luce, and Andrew Ward, 'Anxious Middle: Why Ordinary Americans Have Missed Out on the Benefits of Growth', *Financial Times*, 2 November 2006; Aviva Aron-Dine and Isaac Shapiro, 'New Data Show Extraordinary Jump in Income Concentration in 2004' (Washington, DC: Center on Budgetary and Policy Priorities, 2006), http://www.cbpp. org/7-10-06inc.htm.

same time, American society itself is alleged to have become increasingly militarized even to the extent of adopting a warrior culture. This is reflected in the prerogative powers ceded to a presidency which is seen to be dedicated to the imperatives of US security through international dominance and domestic vigilance.[68]

It is possible to attribute some of these critiques to compulsive anti-Americanism which fails to recognize either the unique predicament of the United States, or the global responsibilities of a superpower that will inevitably generate strains between its animating principles and the exigencies of world politics. But such a view risks overlooking a deeper set of developments and the real nature of the challenge to the United States. When the American message of universalism is combined with the forces of globalization and the penetrative properties of American popular culture, the net effect is that of a liberalization of the cultural trade. Overseas observers and analysts now proceed on the basis that they are part of a universalist community that has the right of reply to the United States through a common medium. Integral to this development is a belief in the interpretative licence to challenge and contest the United States on its home ground of the meaning and values of liberal democracy. This critical medium is complemented by the profusion of complaints and grievances levelled by Americans at the political, strategic, and personal competence of the Bush administration. The effect is to give a further stimulus to those non-Americans who engage with the United States on the basis of its own appropriated discourse.

The overall trend in this medium of exchange is for the United States to become increasingly marginalized in its own epic of democratization. Americans may claim credit for the highest ever incidence of democracies in the world, 'yet freedom's global dispersion owes less to America and more to a contagion of local civic courage'.[69] America's direct role in the democratic revolutions in the post-cold war era has been minimal. Moreover, the recent emphasis upon democracy in American foreign policy priorities is seen to be highly selective. It is seen to be geared towards stabilizing allies on the one hand (e.g. Egypt, Saudi Arabia) while securing regime change through popular uprisings in states deemed to be hostile to the United States (e.g. Iran, Syria). Outside observers remain suspicious of the motives underlying America's conception of liberal democracy and its commitment to the enlargement of democracy on a global scale.

Voices from within the United States now increasingly express concerns over the prospect of negative consequences flowing from the accelerated promotion of democracy in areas that are deficient in structures of civil society or traditions of constitutional rule. Far from optimizing the possibilities of liberal democratic

---

[68] *Civil Liberties after 9-11: The ACLU Defends Freedom* (New York: American Civil Liberties Union Foundation, 2002); Matthew Brzezinski, *Fortress America: On the Front Lines of Homeland Security* (New York: Bantam, 2005); Robert O'Harrow, *No Place to Hide: Behind the Scenes of Our Emerging Surveillance Society* (New York: Free Press, 2005); Amnesty International, 'War on Terror', http://www.amnestyusa.org/waronterror/index.do.

[69] Michael Ignatieff, 'Who Are Americans to Think That Freedom Is Theirs to Spread?', *New York Times*, 26 June 2005.

order within societies, or democratic peace between them, the impulse towards sponsoring democratization is seen in some quarters as posing a direct threat to the levels of freedom existing inside regimes in the process of democratic transition. With neither the cultural fabric of liberal norms nor the intermediary layers and conditioning agencies of a deeply rooted pluralist society, electoral democracy can be used to serve the interests of unrepresentative and aggressively defensive elites. Repressive governments can use elections or populist causes to reconfigure their legitimacy and to add democratic authority to the pursuit of illiberal ends. By the same token, democratization can lead to volatile regimes whose conception of the democratic process may be far removed from western norms and whose transformative agendas may turn them into 'dangerous democracies' in respect to international peace and security.[70] Even an ostensible proponent of robust democratization like Francis Fukuyama felt that by the end of 2005, the Bush administration's doctrine of democratic promotion through coercive regime change had been shown to be flawed on practical grounds. To Fukuyama, a benevolent hegemon has to show a basic level of competence and a capacity to think beyond the superficial categories of political rhetoric.

The Iraq war seems to have been planned on the assumption that democracy was a kind of default condition to which societies reverted once tyrants were removed, rather than a collection of complex institutions that needed to be painstakingly built over years. The administration grossly underestimated the costs and capabilities required to stabilize Iraq.[71]

Simplistic assumptions over the dynamics of social change risk creating an unstable mix of high expectations combined with minimal outcomes and a desire to establish accelerated exit strategies for US forces.

As has been noted, international concern has grown over the state of civil liberties in the United States and over the reputed militarization of American society. At the same time, there has been increasing interest in the possibility of alternative models of democracy (e.g. European Union) and of different pathways, or points of access, to more indigenously conditioned forms of democratic existence (e.g. Islamic variants). These are reasons that lead Michael Ignatieff to note regretfully that while there are more democracies than ever before, '[n]ever has America been more alone in spreading democracy's promise'.[72] Emmanuel Todd goes further and claims that while democracy will spread around the world, it is very unlikely that the United States will be instrumental in its expansion. On the contrary, the United States is seen as a model of aversion for aspiring democracies. America's financial weaknesses, social divisions, and international actions together with its psychic need to identify an adversarial 'other' (i.e. the Arab and Muslim

---

[70] Fareed Zakaria, *The Future of Freedom: Illiberal Democracy at Home and Abroad* (New York: W. W. Norton, 2003), pp. 59–118, 239–56; Edward D. Mansfield and Jack Snyder, *Electing to Fight: Emerging Democracies Go to War* (Cambridge, MA: MIT Press, 2005).

[71] Francis Fukuyama, 'The Bush Doctrine, Before and After', *Financial Times*, 11 October 2005.

[72] Ignatieff, 'Who Are Americans to Think That Freedom Is Theirs to Spread?'

world) mean that it cannot and should not be considered as a universal point of democratic reference.[73]

It may be because of the brutality of the Iraq War or the iconic significance of the US military practices of detention and interrogation. It may be attributable to the sweeping rationales of the war on terror, or the common associations of America with arrogance, hypocrisy, and double standards. Whatever the causal agencies may have been, it is widely suggested that the international brand name of the United States has suffered a significant decline since 2001. The style of Bush's presidency has been a particular focal point of international complaint. Surveys of global opinion on the preferred outcome of the 2004 presidential election revealed almost without exception a cross-national preference for the President Bush's Democratic opponent, John Kerry.[74] On a deeper and more systemic level, the Pew Global Attitudes Survey reported in 2005[75] that the United States had fallen dramatically in the poll on favourable attitudes towards different countries. When respondents from sixteen countries were asked to rank order five nations (United States, France, Germany, Japan, China) in terms of favourable perceptions, the United States came last in every case except three (India, Poland, and China). Across Europe, for example, China proved to be more popular than the United States.

The Pew Survey also reported that America's reputation as the land of opportunity was experiencing a significant decline with India as the only one in the pool of respondents naming the United States as the recommended destination for a good life. The Pew Survey concluded that the integrity of America's brand name as a cultural identity faced the prospect of becoming seriously compromised: 'In the eyes of others, the US is a worrisome colossus, too quick to act unilaterally, too slow to solve the world's problems, too prone to widening the global gulf between rich and poor'.[76] It used to be the case that negative survey responses towards America could be attributed to policy disputes or to personal animosity towards a leader, rather than to the country, its people, and its values. The Pew Survey disputes this interpretation and suggests that overseas attitudes have shifted to a more systemic level of scepticism and distrust towards American society in general.

In sum, because of the United States' actions abroad and because of the observed inequities within American society, increasing concerns have arisen over the virtues, and even the legitimacy, of American democracy as a defining model

[73] Emmanuel Todd, *After the Empire: The Breakdown of the American Order* (New York: Columbia University Press, 2003).

[74] For example in a survey conducted by Globescan covering al the regions of the world, the only countries where President Bush was clearly preferred were the Philippines, Nigeria, and Poland. India and Thailand were divided. On average, Kerry was favoured by more than a two to one margin. See Globescan, 'Poll of 35 Countries Finds 30 Prefer Kerry', http://www.globescan.com/news_archives/GlobeScan-PIPA_Release.pdf.

[75] PewResearch Center, 'Pew Global Attitudes Project: U.S. Image Up Slightly, But Still Negative—American Character Gets Mixed Reviews', 23 June 2005, http://pewglobal.org/reports/display.php?ReportID=247.

[76] Pew Research Center, *Trends 2005* (Washington, DC: Pew Research Center, 2005), p. 106.

of a democratic polity. As America's global position becomes more consolidated, its self-declared role as an exemplar of democratic potential becomes increasingly exposed to critical assessment. In many respects, the ethical and cultural assault upon American democracy becomes the natural countervailing agency to the economic and military pre-eminence of the United States. It would not be an overstatement to suggest that, in the international sphere, the United States is in danger of losing its hegemonic position in relation to a discourse on contemporary democracy that it has traditionally assumed to be its own. In the eighteenth century, the American colonists used the principles, traditions, and logic of the contemporary British constitution to contest the actions of the imperial authority. It is now possible to discern a similar pattern of ideational influence in reverse. This relates to American conceptions of democracy being deployed against the prevailing conditions of democracy in American society itself and against the actions taken in its name by the United States. This dynamic is perhaps best represented by the global justice movement which, far from seeing the United States as a source of inspiration and model of emulation, regards it instead as the antithesis of the democratic ideal. This viewpoint sees the United States as marked out by inequality, polarization, and unaccountability. According to a leading advocate of the movement, the requirement must be to deploy democracy against its traditional patron in 'what will surely be the big fight of the early 21st century: global democracy versus American empire'.[77]

FIXTURES AND FITTINGS

The working premise of this study has been that political ideas are the measure of American society. At every level of social intercourse, the meaning, ancestry, and presence of core ideas act not only as reference points in discussion but as forceful vehicles of argument and legitimacy. As a consequence, American debates are characteristically fundamentalist in tone as disputes are almost invariably translated into different conceptions, interpretations, and iterations of those central values with which the United States is most closely associated. Turning points in American history, therefore, are usually seen as having been animated and defined by shifts in the balance between and amongst its indigenous values. In the same manner, threats to American society are equated with ideas that are deemed to be alien in their nature, in their origin, or in the means of their advocacy. Accordingly, the ideational dimension is instrumental in the identification of crises in American politics. A crisis is defined in relation to a perceived assault upon, or a subversion of, one or more American values. Because of the way ideas are conjoined to national identity, a crisis in one place is synonymous with a crisis in the other. A national crisis, therefore, is construed as a crisis of democracy, of freedom, of rights, or of the rule of law.

[77] George Monbiot, 'An Empire of Denial', *The Guardian*, 1 June 2004.

A good deal of American political comment dwells upon the frustration derived from a complex system of fragmented government in which a profusion of competing interests generate a form of structured immobilism. However, a far greater deal of discussion centres upon the expansive qualities of America's core ideas. It is clear from this study that American political discourse is suffused with references to fundamental principles—to their meanings, traditions, and implications. Political debate is redolent with explicit and implicit propositions relating to the way that foundational ideas can be persuasively combined for maximum effect. Just as political grievances and complaints are refracted through the lens of key ideas, so solutions are necessarily presented through recourse to the primary colours of deep principle.

Such a manner of political intercourse is far from being an option of least resistance or of social ease. It is a demanding and arduous compulsion. But it is also a necessary one because the claims to legitimacy are under constant review from competing interpretations and aggregations of American value. As a consequence, Americans have developed a remarkable facility not only for injecting multiple principles into political discussion but also for identifying and underlining the tensions that can exist between them. The inherent strains between, for example, the rule of law and majority rule, the individual and democracy, and freedom and equality are persistently reduced to their starkest terms in the battle for ideational position. Likewise extensive political and intellectual energies are expended in the cause of closing divisions and recombining ideas into a viable coherence. John Hexter once claimed that his fellow historians could be broken down into 'splitters' and 'lumpers'.[78] Using the same terminology in respect to ideational dispute, it is evident that in American political exchange, there are not only as many splitters as lumpers, but in most circumstances individuals are engaging both activities at the same time. It is the compulsive usage of iconic ideas and the incessant examination of their meaning and application that animates political exchange in the United States. At the same time that those ideas can give visceral expression to difference, it is also evident that they constitute the collective basis upon which the social licence is afforded to highly principled argument.

Contrary to its reputation for pragmatism and political equilibrium, therefore, American politics has a highly developed attachment to ideational struggle. Policy debates are not easily resolved because of the way they arouse elemental disputes over core values and, in particular, over how they are compounded together. In strong contrast to most western democracies, American policy debates are distinguished by their lack of finality. Adversaries continually seek to reopen decisions on the basis of recalibrating a particular aggregate of core ideas, rediscovering a historical theme, reviving interest in the original intent of the republic's founding ideals, or locating fresh meaning in recontextualized ideas. Ideas are not marginalized in this style of social intercourse. On the contrary, they constitute an enriched source of political raw materials that are central to the conduct, style, and technique of political exchange in American society.

[78] John H. Hexter, *On Historians* (Cambridge, MA: Harvard University Press, 1979), pp. 1–10.

It is inaccurate, therefore, to dismiss the common modes of political thinking in American society as being simplistic, reflexive, and unstructured in nature. The practice of political thought may not satisfy the criteria of ideological organization and consistency but this does not mean that the usage of political ideas and principles is devoid of complexity, invention, and even subtlety. Quite the opposite. Political argument in the United States is habitually embedded in the cognitive and evaluative demands of working with multiple values, each one of which carries strong historical and cultural attachments. In this crowded conceptual field of first principles, 'conflict and ambivalence is interpreted not as confusion, inconsistency, or lack of sophistication but as a problem of reconciling the multiple values, beliefs, and principles simultaneously present in the political culture'.[79] It may well be that some values will be given a marginally greater weight than others by some sectors of the population, or that selected values will have a slightly greater degree of leverage at different times or between different issue areas.[80] But these variations should neither distract attention from the overall ecology of a highly dynamic cluster of readily usable ideas, nor undermine the visceral appeal of manoeuvring between and amongst them in the language of political contention.

In the United States, it is not simply that big ideas are always lying beneath the surface; it is more that their presence constantly animates and shapes the entire process of politics as their respective advocates maintain a complex ecology of contested compounds. It can even be claimed that it is the very intensity of this ideational outlet that acts as a corrective counterweight to the technicalities of negotiated accommodation required for coalition-building in a fragmented political system. At the same time that this dimension might be said to facilitate the mundane give-and-take of political compromise, it can also offer a reasoned antidote to, and an emotional release from, the inertial properties of political incrementalism and institutional gridlock.

In attempting to give an overview of the aggregative dynamics and extraordinary virtuosity of America's usage of key political ideas, the study has inevitably raised more questions than it has addressed. The issue of whether the currency of core ideas represents a deep level of settlement in American society, or whether their provenance in debate reflects a lack of settlement, remains a highly problematic subject of inquiry. It is closely related to the question of whether the ideationally based traditions and energies of American society can be reduced to a single core identity or core tradition. If this is a sustainable proposition, it raises the further conundrum of the extent to which such a core identity, or core tradition, is itself reducible in turn to a precise set of core ideas, or at least to the notion of an established social understanding of the core ideas. Even if this connection is assumed to exist, it still poses the problem of whether separate ideas

---

[79] Stanley Feldman and John Zaller, 'The Political Culture of Ambivalence: Ideological Responses to the Welfare State', *Journal of Political Science*, vol. 36, no. 1 (February 1992), p. 270.

[80] For example, see Stanley Feldman, 'Structure and Consistency in Public Opinion: The Role of Core Beliefs and Values', *Journal of Political Science*, vol. 32, no. 2 (May 1988), pp. 416–40; Feldman and Zaller, 'The Political Culture of Ambivalence: Ideological Responses to the Welfare State', pp. 268–307.

have an intrinsic or inherent relationship to one another, or whether a unity is imposed upon them through the cultivation of a holistic outlook towards such ideas in American society.

Given that the United States is often characterized as traditionalist in its attitudes, then its set of core ideas can be interpreted as providing the operational premise of a stable social order. Arguably, such a community would always endeavour to maintain the impression of ideational unity for the sake of its own security. The possible nature of such a posited imposition opens up a further problematic dimension, i.e. the extent to which different ideas possess a distinctive essence which, while not immune to contextual influences, allows them to be substantially more than the mere epiphenomena of economic and social structures. Although American ideas have an evident association with the exigencies of social cohesion and continuity, it is equally the case that they can also be deployed as conspicuous instruments of political contention and social change. Assigning proportionate weight to the inherent contribution of core ideas to society's continuity on the one hand, and to the cause of radical change on the other, remains as elusive as attempting to elicit any conclusive order of cultural priority from the cluster of foundational ideas.

These types of questions are neither insignificant nor unrelated to the subject matter of this study. However, they are not central to the purpose or design of the selected area of exposition. The objective has been to allow that which is commonly been taken as read to be revealed in all its manifold complexity and extravagant diversity. The presumption of a set of core ideas in American society is usually taken at face value: as a formal and even prosaic reference to a set of socially embedded and interconnected ideas whose exact relationship to one another is deemed to be less significant than the consolidated effect of their reputed proximity or their purportedly organic linkage to America's sense of itself. But as this study has tried to convey, it is the conception, or invocation, of a singular composite of key ideas that belies an immense, intricate, and dynamic set of ideational relationships and political contingencies.

Being an American in this context, therefore, is not so much about a precise affiliation to a fixed tradition, or 'creed', of amalgamated values. Instead, it is more about an acquired facility for negotiating passageways between concurrent centres of value and for creating ideational hybrids that will attract political support whilst reaffirming the full expanse of the foundational base of core ideas. While much of the enclosed analysis will have a bearing on the types of general issue mentioned above, it is important to underline that the consistent focus of the study has been to explore and reveal the normative parameters, the inventive opportunities, and the substantive consequences that are inherent within such an extraordinary medium of ideational construction and reconstruction.

Many analyses touch upon this rich matrix of mutually conditioned points of value but they tend to do so only partially or obliquely. This is because their focus or perspective is more closely connected to other forms of objects of inquiry. As a consequence, the cultural and historical, as well as the psychological and affective properties of the mix are largely lost in the gaps that exist (i) between political theory and the study of policies, issues, and institutions; (ii) between the retrospective impulses to the past and the contemporary dimensions of the present; (iii) between the broad scale aspects of mass behaviour and the particularities of individuals, groups, and elites; and (iv) between the generic claims of unsystematized beliefs and random non-attitudes on the one hand, and the dense methodological debates surrounding whether individual ideas can be disaggregated from the pack and subjected to comparative measurement on the other. This study has deliberately sought to immerse itself in such gaps and, in doing so, to bring the multifaceted effects of the ideational admixture nearer to the surface. In doing so, it has illustrated something of the depth and interconnectedness not only between political ideas, actions, and processes in the United States, but between the central priority given to a set of core values and the attitudinal traditions, social conventions, and layers of historical consciousness that govern the American way of discussing and doing politics.

Index